Lecture Notes in Computer Science 8049

Commenced Publication in 1973
Founding and Former Series Editors:
Gerhard Goos, Juris Hartmanis, and Jan van Leeuwen

Zhiming Liu Jim Woodcock Huibiao Zhu (Eds.)

Theoretical Aspects of Computing – ICTAC 2013

10th International Colloquium
Shanghai, China, September 4-6, 2013
Proceedings

Springer

Volume Editors

Zhiming Liu
United Nations University
International Institute for Software Technology
P.O. Box 3058, Macau, China
E-mail: z.liu@iist.unu.edu

Jim Woodcock
University of York
Department of Computer Science
Deramore Lane, York YO10 5GH, UK
E-mail: jim@cs.york.ac.uk

Huibiao Zhu
East China Normal University
Software Engineering Institute
3663 Zhongshan Road (North), Shanghai 200062, China
E-mail: hbzhu@sei.ecnu.edu.cn

ISSN 0302-9743 e-ISSN 1611-3349
ISBN 978-3-642-39717-2 e-ISBN 978-3-642-39718-9
DOI 10.1007/978-3-642-39718-9
Springer Heidelberg Dordrecht London New York

Library of Congress Control Number: 2013943263

CR Subject Classification (1998): F.3, D.2.4, F.1, I.2.2-3, F.4, D.3, G.2

LNCS Sublibrary: SL 1 – Theoretical Computer Science and General Issues

Typesetting: Camera-ready by author, data conversion by Scientific Publishing Services, Chennai, India

Printed on acid-free paper

Springer is part of Springer Science+Business Media (www.springer.com)

Preface

This volume contains the papers presented at ICTAC 2013: The 10th International Colloquium on Theoretical Aspects of Computing held during September 4–6, 2013, in Shanghai. There were 64 submissions and each was reviewed by at least three Program Committee members; the committee decided to accept 22 papers after thorough online discussions. The program also included three invited talks by Luca Cardelli, He Jifeng, and Marta Kwiatkowska. The conference was managed using the online system EasyChair.

The International Colloquia on Theoretical Aspects of Computing (ICTAC) is a series of annual events funded in 2003 by the United Nations University International Institute for Software Technology (UNU-IIST). Its purpose is to bring together practitioners and researchers from academia, industry, and government to present research results and exchange experience and ideas. Beyond these scholarly goals, another main purpose is, as a mandate of the United Nations University, to promote cooperation in research and education between participants and their institutions from developing and industrial regions.

This year's *ICTAC* was specially dedicated to He Jifeng as part of the celebrations of his 70th birthday. It was also associated with two other events.

- *The ICTAC Software Engineering School on Unifying Theories and Formal Engineering Methods*, held in Shanghai during August 26–30, 2013. LNCS volume 8050, Springer 2013.
- *The Festschrift Symposium* held in Shanghai during September 1–3, 2013. Essays in Honor of He Jifeng on the Occasion of his 70th Birthday. LNCS volume 8051, Springer 2013.

The colloquium was supported and organized by East China Normal University, UNU-IIST and University of York. We are happy to thank these organizations and the colleagues there who contributed to the organization. We are grateful to the invited speakers for their talks. We would like to acknowledge the authors for submitting their work to the conference, and the PC members and their subreviewers for their hard and professional work in the review and selection process. Last, but not least, we thank Springer for their cooperation in publishing the proceedings of ICTAC 2013.

June 2013

Zhiming Liu
Jim Woodcock
Huibiao Zhu

Organization

Steering Committee

Ana Cavalcanti, UK
John Fitzgerald, UK
Martin Leucker, Germany
Zhiming Liu, Macau SAR, China
Tobias Nipkow, Germany
Augusto Sampaio, Brazil
Natarajan Shankar, USA

Conference Chairs

Zhou Chaochen	Chinese Academy of Sciences, China
Peter Haddawy	UNU-IIST, Macau SAR, China
Bill Roscoe	University of Oxford, UK

Program Chairs

Zhiming Liu	UNU-IIST, Macau SAR, China
Jim Woodcock	University of York, UK
Huibiao Zhu	East China Normal University, China

Program Committee

Farhad Arbab	CWI and Leiden University, The Netherlands
Michael Butler	University of Southampton, UK
Ana Cavalcanti	University of York, UK
Zhenbang Chen	National University of Defense Technology, China
Meenakshi D'Souza	IIIT Bangalore, India
Thao Dang	VERIMAG, France
Van Hung Dang	University of Engineering and Technology, Vietnam
David Deharbe	Universidade Federal do Rio Grande do Norte, Brazil
Jinsong Dong	National University of Singapore, Singapore
Zhenhua Duan	Xidian University, China
John Fitzgerald	Newcastle University, UK
Marcelo Frias	Instituto Tecnologico Buenos Aires, Argentina

Martin Fränzle	Carl von Ossietzky Universität Oldenburg, Germany
Lindsay Groves	Victoria University of Wellington, New Zealand
Kim Guldstrand Larsen	Aalborg University, Denmark
Ian J. Hayes	University of Queensland, Australia
Zhenjiang Hu	NII, Japan
Lei Ju	Shandong University, China
Daniel Kroening	Oxford University, UK
Martin Leucker	University of Lübeck, Germany
Zhiming Liu	UNU-IIST, Macau SAR, China
Annabelle Mciver	Macquarie University, Australia
Dominique Mery	Université de Lorraine, France
Tobias Nipkow	Technische Universität München, Germany
Paritosh Pandya	TIFR, India
Jun Pang	University of Luxembourg, Luxembourg
Geguang Pu	East China Normal University, China
Shengchao Qin	Teesside University, UK
Zongyan Qiu	Peking University, China
Abhik Roychoudhury	National University of Singapore, Singapore
Augusto Sampaio	Federal University of Pernambuco, Brazil
Ondrej Sery	University of Lugano, Switzerland
Natarajan Shankar	SRI, US
Marjan Sirjani	Reykjavik University, Iceland
Andrzej Tarlecki	Warsaw University, Poland
Mark Utting	The University of Waikato, New Zealand
Tarmo Uustalu	Tallinn University of Technology, Estonia
Farn Wang	National Taiwan University, Taiwan
Burkhart Wolff	University Paris-Sud, France
Jim Woodcock	University of York, UK
Wang Yi	Uppsala University, Sweden
Naijun Zhan	Chinese Academy of Sciences, China
Jianhua Zhao	Nanjing University, China
Jianjun Zhao	Shanghai Jiao Tong University, China
Huibiao Zhu	East China Normal University, China

Local Organization

Mingsong Chen, Jian Guo, Xiao Liu, Geguang Pu, Fu Song, Min Zhang
East China Normal University

Webmaster

Huixing Fang, East China Normal University

Additional Reviewers

Akbari, Saieed
Alviano, Mario
Andriamiarina, Manamiary Bruno
Arlt, Stephan
Banerjee, Abhijeet
Benke, Marcin
Brain, Martin
Bucheli, Samuel
Chen, Xin
Colvin, Robert
Craciun, Florin
D'Souza, Deepak
David, Alexandre
Decker, Normann
Edmunds, Andrew
Faber, Johannes
Fantechi, Alessandro
Gurfinkel, Arie
He, Guanhua
Herde, Christian
Huang, Yanhong
Khakpour, Narges
Khanh, Nguyen Truong
Kim, Jin Hyun
Krishnaswami, Neelakantan
Kumar, Sandeep
Laursen, Simon
Li, Jianwen
Liu, Wanwei
Long, Quan
Luckcuck, Matthew
Martins Moreira, Anamaria
Merz, Stephan
Mohan M., Raj
Mu, Chunyan
Narayanaswamy, Ganesh
Nogueira, Sidney
Oliveira, Marcel Vinicius Medeiros
Pierce, Ken
Qi, Dawei
Sabouri, Hamideh
Salehi Fathabadi, Asieh
Schubert, Aleksy
Schäf, Martin
Sharma, Subodh
Shi, Ling
Singh, Neeraj
Srba, Jiri
Stümpel, Annette
Su, Ting
Swaminathan, Mani
Truong, Hoang
Vojdani, Vesal
Wang, Shuling
Wijs, Anton
Winter, Kirsten
Wu, Xi
Wu, Xiaofeng
Yang, Shaofa
Zhang, Chenyi
Zhang, Shaojie
Zhao, Hengjun
Zhao, Yongxin
Zheng, Manchuan
Zhu, Jiaqi
Zou, Liang

Sponsoring Institutions

- East China Normal University (Shanghai, China)
- United Nations University - International Institute for Software Technology (Macau SAR, China)
- The University of York (UK)

Table of Contents

Stochastic Pi-calculus Revisited

Luca Cardelli[1] and Radu Mardare[2,*]

[1] Microsoft Research, Cambridge, UK
[2] Aalborg University, Denmark

Abstract. We develop a version of stochastic Pi-calculus with a semantics based on measure theory. We define the behaviour of a process in a rate environment using measures over the measurable space of processes induced by structural congruence. We extend the stochastic bisimulation to include the concept of rate environment and prove that this equivalence is a congruence which extends the structural congruence.

1 Introduction

The problem of specifying and analyzing nondeterministic concurrent systems has found a successful solution in the class of *Process Algebras* (PAs) [2]. The compositionality of the processes is reflected by the construction principles of PAs, while their behaviours are transition systems. As a result, one obtains a class of processes with an elegant algebraic-coalgebraic structure, supported by appealing theories and easy to adapt to various modelling requirements.

The same approach has been taken for probabilistic and stochastic concurrent systems. *Probabilistic process algebras* [2], *interactive Markov chain algebra* [16,4] and *stochastic process algebras* (SPA) such as TIPP [13], PEPA [14,15], EMPA [3] and *stochastic Pi-calculus* [22] are extensions of classic PAs. The nondeterminism is replaced by a race policy and this requires important modifications in the semantic format. Stressed to mimic the pointwise structural operational semantics (SOS) of nondeterministic PAs, SPAs find *ad hoc* solutions to the problems introduced by stochasticity, such as the *multi-transition system* approach of PEPA or the *proved SOS* approach of stochastic Pi-calculus. These result in complex constructs that are difficult to extend to a general format for well-behaved stochastic specifications and problematic when recursion or fresh name quantification are considered. As emphasized by Klin and sassone in [17], for stochastic Pi-calculus of Priami [22] the parallel composition fails to be associative up to bisimulation, while for PEPA, if arbitrary relations between the rates of processes and subprocesses are allowed, stochastic bisimulation ceases to be a congruence. An explanation for these situations is given in [17]: the information carried by the aforementioned SOS frameworks is excessive, while a well-behaved framework should only carry the exact amount of data required for the derivation of the intended semantics.

* Research supported by the VKR Center of Excellence MT- LAB and by the Sino-Danish Basic Research Center IDEA4CPS.

Z. Liu, J. Woodcock, and H. Zhu (Eds.): ICTAC 2013, LNCS 8049, pp. 1–21, 2013.

These problems motivate our research, initiated with [7], that aims to reconsider the semantics of SPAs from a perspective faithful to the algebraic-coalgebraic structure of stochastic processes. The key observation is that *structural congruence* induces a σ-algebra on processes and organizes a measurable space of stochastic processes. We propose a semantics that assign to each process a set of measures indexed by observable actions. Thus, difficult instance-counting problems that otherwise require complicated versions of SOS can be solved by exploiting the properties of measures (e.g. additivity). Our previous work showed that along this line one obtains an elegant semantics that resembles the one of nondeterministic PAs and provides a well-behaved notion of bisimulation. In previous work [7] we proved this concept for a fragment of stochastic CCS. In this paper we extend the work to stochastic Pi-calculus with channel-based communication, mobility, fresh name quantification and replication. This calculus is designed to satisfy the specific requirements of Systems Biology.

There are several novel ideas in our approach. The processes are interpreted in *stochastic environments* that associate *basic rates* to channels. In a rate environment E, a process P has associated a class of measures μ, written $E \vdash P \to \mu$. For each action α, $\mu(\alpha)$ is a measure over the space of processes; $\mu(\alpha)(S) \in \mathbb{Q}^+$ is the rate of an exponentially distributed random variable that characterizes the α-transitions from P to (elements of) a measurable set S. Only the structural congruence-closed sets are measurable. This is essential for modelling in systems biology, where such sets represent chemical soups[1]. This choice provides simple solutions to the problems of replications and bound outputs which otherwise, as with Milner's Abstraction-Concretion method [20], require complicated high-order reasoning. Also novel is our *stochastic bisimulation* that extends other similar ones [19,17,7,21,8] by making explicit the role of the rate environments. We show that bisimulation is a congruence that extends structural congruence.

Related Works. The idea of transitions from states to measures has been advocated in the context of probabilistic automata [18,24] and Markov processes [21]. The *transition-systems-as-coalgebras* paradigm [10,23] exploits it providing a uniform characterisation of transition systems that covers the sequence nondeterministic, probabilistic and stochastic systems. A general SOS format for SPAs without new name operators or recursion is proposed in [17]. In [8,9] these ideas are applied to particular SPAs with pointwise semantics. With respect to these works, in our paper we consider a different measurable space that not only answers to practical modelling requirements, but also simplifies the semantics and gives us smooth solutions for the fresh name quantification and replication without requiring additional constructs. Formally, while the other frameworks focus on the monads freely generated by the algebraic signature of the calculus, we have considered the equational monad defined by the structural congruence. The use of name environments has been considered in [11,12] where it involves the machinery of nominal sets. We have tried to avoid this together with any coalgebraic description of the lifting from processes to measures, as our intention

[1] Structural congruence has been introduced in [1] as a chemical analogy.

is to make these ideas accessible also for the readers less familiar with the jargon of Category Theory.

Relation to Nondeterministic Pi-calculus. There is no trivial relation between nondeterministic Pi-calculus and our stochastic Pi-calculus, in the sense that one cannot simply recover the semantics of the other by simple mathematical transformations. This is because the measure-based semantics of stochastic-Pi calculus require important modification of the SOS rules. One example regards the replication: while in classic Pi-calculus $!a(b) \equiv a(b)|!a(b)$, in stochastic Pi this is illegal since the rate of the input on channel a in the process $a(b)|!a(b)$ is strictly bigger than the rate of the same input in the process $!a(b)$. For this reason in stochastic Pi there exist no structural congruence rules of type $!P \equiv P|!P$ or $!!P \equiv !P$ since such rules would generate processes with infinite rates; instead, there are dedicated SOS rules that establish the correct behaviours.

2 Preliminaries

In this section we introduce the terminology and the notations used in the paper.

For the sets A and B, 2^A denotes the powerset of A and B^A the class of functions from A to B. For an equivalence relation $\sim$ on A, $A^\sim$ is the set of equivalence classes and $a^\sim$ the equivalence class of $a \in A$.

Given a set M, $\Sigma \subseteq 2^M$ that contains the element M and is closed under complement and countable union is a *σ-algebra* over M; (M, Σ) is a *measurable space* and the elements of Σ are *measurable sets.*

A *measure* on (M, Σ) is a countably additive set function $\mu : \Sigma \to \mathbb{R}^+$ such that $\mu(\emptyset) = 0$. The *null measure* $\mathbb{0}$ is such that $\mathbb{0}(M) = 0$. For $N \in \Sigma$, the *N-Dirac measure* D_N is defined by $D_N(N') = 1$, if $N \subseteq N'$ and $D_N(N') = 0$ otherwise. $\Delta(M, \Sigma)$ denotes the set of measures on (M, Σ).

If $\mathfrak{R} \subseteq M \times M$, $N \subseteq M$ is $\mathfrak{R}$-closed iff $\{m \in M \mid \exists n \in N, (n, m) \in \mathfrak{R}\} \subseteq N$. If (M, Σ) is a measurable space, $\Sigma(\mathfrak{R})$ is the set of measurable $\mathfrak{R}$-closed sets.

3 Stochastic Pi-calculus

In this section we introduce a version of stochastic Pi-calculus equipped with an *early semantics* [2] expressed in terms of measure theory. Being developed mainly for applications in Systems Biology, this calculus is designed to respect the *chemical kinetics* (the *Chemical Master Equation*) [5] which provides the mathematical principles for calculating the rates of the channel-based communications. The class $\mathbb{P}$ of processes is endowed with structural congruence which generates a σ-algebra Π on $\mathbb{P}$. In addition, rate environments assign base rates to channel names. The behaviour of a process P in a rate environment E is defined by an indexed set of measures $\mu : \mathbb{A}^+ \to \Delta(\mathbb{P}, \Pi)$, where $\mathbb{A}^+$ is the set of actions.

3.1 Syntax

Definition 1 (Processes). *Let $\mathcal{N}$ be a countable set. The* stochastic processes *are defined, on top of* 0, *for arbitrary* $r \in \mathbb{Q}^+$ *and* $a, b, c \in \mathcal{N}$, *as follows.*

$$P := 0 \,\vdots\, x.P \,\vdots\, (a@r)P \,\vdots\, P|P \,\vdots\, P+P \,\vdots\, !P, \qquad x := a(b) \,\vdots\, a[b].$$

Let $\mathbb{P}$ be the set of stochastic processes. 0 stands for the inactive process. An *input* "$a(b)$" is the capability of the process $a(b).P$ to receive a name on channel a that replaces b in all its occurrences inside P. An *output* prefix "$a[b]$" represents the action of sending a name b on channel a. "$(a@r)$" is the *fresh name operator* that, unlike in nondeterministic PAs, also specifies the rate r of the fresh name. As usual in Pi-calculus, we have the *parallel composition* "|", the *choice operator* "+" and the *replication operator* "!".

For arbitrary $P \in \mathbb{P}$, we define the set $fn(P)$ of the *free names* of P inductively by $fn(0) = \emptyset$, $fn(a(b).P) = (fn(P) \setminus \{b\}) \cup \{a\}$, $fn(a[b].P) = fn(P) \cup \{a, b\}$, $fn(P|Q) = fn(P+Q) = fn(P) \cup fn(Q)$, $fn((a@r)P) = fn(P) \setminus \{a\}$ and $fn(!P) = fn(P)$. As usual in process algebras, for arbitrary $a, b \in \mathcal{N}$, we write $P_{\{a/b\}}$ for the process term obtained from P by substituting all the free occurrences of b with a, renaming as necessary to avoid capture.

Definition 2 (Structural congruence). *Structural congruence is the smallest equivalence relation* $\equiv \subseteq \mathbb{P} \times \mathbb{P}$ *satisfying the following conditions.*
I. $(\mathbb{P}, |, 0)$ *is a commutative monoid for* $\equiv$, *i.e.,*
1. $P|Q \equiv Q|P$; 2. $(P|Q)|R \equiv P|(Q|R)$; 3. $P|0 \equiv P$.

II. $(\mathbb{P}, +, 0)$ *is a commutative monoid for* $\equiv$, *i.e.,*
1. $P+Q \equiv Q+P$; 2. $(P+Q)+R \equiv P+(Q+R)$; 3. $P+0 \equiv P$.

III. $\equiv$ *is a congruence for the algebraic structure of* $\mathbb{P}$, *i.e., if* $P \equiv Q$, *then*
1. $P|R \equiv Q|R$; 2. $P+R \equiv Q+R$; 3. $!P \equiv !Q$;
4. $a[b].P \equiv a[b].Q$ 5. $(a@r)P \equiv (a@r)Q$; 6. $a(b).P \equiv a(b).Q$.

IV. *the fresh name quantifiers satisfy the following conditions*
1. *if* $a \neq b$, *then* $(a@r)(b@s)P \equiv (b@s)(a@r)P$; 2. $(a@r)0 \equiv 0$;
3. *if* $a \notin fn(P)$, *then* $(a@r)(P|Q) \equiv P|(a@r)Q$ *and* $(a@r)(P+Q) \equiv P+(a@r)Q$.

V. *the replication satisfies the following conditions*
1. $!0 \equiv 0$; 2. $!(P|Q) \equiv !P|!Q$.

VI. $\equiv$ *satisfies the alpha-conversion rules*
1. $(a@r)P \equiv (b@r)P_{\{b/a\}}$; 2. $a(b)P \equiv a(c)P_{\{c/b\}}$.

If Q is obtained from P by alpha-conversion (VI) 1-2, we write $P \equiv^* Q$. Let Π be the set of the $\equiv$-closed subsets of $\mathbb{P}$. Note that $\mathbb{P}^{\equiv}$ is a countable partition of $\mathbb{P}$ and Π is the σ-algebra generated by $\mathbb{P}^{\equiv}$.

Notice that, unlike in the nondeterministic case, we do not have $!!P \equiv !P$ nor $!P \equiv P|!P$. These are not sound due to the rate competition which else will generate processes with infinite rates.

Theorem 1 (Measurable space). $(\mathbb{P}, \Pi)$ *is a measurable space of processes.*

The measurable sets of $\mathbb{P}$ are the unions of $\equiv$-equivalence classes on $\mathbb{P}$. In what follows $\mathcal{P}, \mathcal{R}, \mathcal{Q}$ range over Π. We lift some functions and algebraic operations from processes to measurable sets, for arbitrary $a, b \in \mathcal{N}$ and $r \in \mathbb{Q}^+$, as follows.

$$fn(\mathcal{P}) = \bigcup_{P \in \mathcal{P}} fn(P), \qquad \mathcal{P}_{\{a/b\}} = \bigcup_{P \in \mathcal{P}} P_{\{a/b\}}, \qquad \mathcal{P}|\mathcal{Q} = \bigcup_{P \in \mathcal{P}}^{Q \in \mathcal{Q}} (P|Q)^{\equiv},$$

$$\mathcal{P}_{\mathcal{Q}} = \bigcup_{R|Q \in \mathcal{P}}^{Q \in \mathcal{Q}} R^{\equiv}, \qquad (a@r)\mathcal{P} = \bigcup_{P \in \mathcal{P}} (a@r)P^{\equiv}.$$

It is not difficult to see that these operations are internal operations on Π.

3.2 Rate Environments

Now we introduce *rate environments* used to interpret stochastic processes. They are partial functions on $\mathcal{N}$ assigning rates to channels. We chose to introduce them in the "process algebra style" instead of defining a type systems for environment correctness, which would complicate the semantics.

Definition 3 (Rate Environment). *The* rate environments *associated to* $\mathcal{N}$ *are defined, on top of a constant* ε*, for arbitrary* $a \in \mathcal{N}$ *and* $r \in \mathbb{Q}^+$*, by*

$$E := \varepsilon \ \vdots \ E, a@r.$$

Let $\mathbb{E}$ be the set of rate environments. A suffix $a@r$ is called *rate declaration.* If $a@r$ appears in E, we write $a@r \in E$. ε stands for the *empty environment.* We treat "," as concatenation symbol for rate environments and use "E, E'" to denote the concatenation of E and E'; ε is the empty symbol for concatenation.

For $E = E_1, ..., E_n \in \mathbb{E}$ and $\{1, .., n\} = \{i_1, .., i_k\} \cup \{j_1, .., j_{n-k}\}$ with $i_1 < .. < i_k$, $j_1 < ... < j_{n-k}$, if $E' = E_{i_1}, .., E_{i_k}$ and $E'' = E_{j_1}, .., E_{j_{n-k}}$, we write $E' \subset E$ and $E'' = E \setminus E'$. Notice that $\varepsilon \subset E$, $E \subset E$, $E = E \setminus \varepsilon$ and $\varepsilon = E \setminus E$.
The *domain of a rate environment* is the partial function on $\mathbb{E}$ defined as follows.

1. $dom(\varepsilon) = \emptyset$;
2. if $dom(E)$ is defined and $a \notin dom(E)$, then $dom(E, a@r) = dom(E) \cup \{a\}$;
3. undefined otherwise.

In what follows, whenever we use $dom(E)$ we implicitly assume that dom is defined in E. Observe that, if $a \in dom(E)$, then there exists a rate declaration $a@r \in E$ and for no $s \neq r$, $a@s \in E$; for this reason we also write $r = E(a)$. When $dom(E)$ is defined, let $dom(E)^* = \{a \in dom(E) \text{ s.t. } E(a) \neq 0\}$.

3.3 The Class of Indexed Measures

The semantics will involve terms of type $E \vdash P \to \mu$, where E is a rate environment, P is a process and $\mu : \mathbb{A}^+ \to \Delta(\mathbb{P}, \Pi)$ is a mapping that defines a set of labeled measures. The labels are the observable actions collected in the set $\mathbb{A}^+$ defined below.

$$\mathbb{A} = \{a[b], a[@r], ab, \text{ for } a, b \in \mathcal{N}, r \in \mathbb{Q}^+\} \text{ and } \mathbb{A}^+ = \mathbb{A} \cup \{\tau\}.$$

We denote by $\mathfrak{M}$ the set $\Delta(\mathbb{P}, \Pi)^{\mathbb{A}^+}$ of labeled measures.

The observable actions consist of four classes: (i) *free outputs* of type $a[b]$ denoting the action of sending a free name b over the channel a, (ii) *bound outputs* of type $a[@r]$ denoting the action of sending a fresh unspecified name, with base-rate r, on channel a, (iii) *input actions* of type ab representing the fact that channel a has received a name b (as the result of an output action on a), (iv) *internal action* τ – communications. In what follows we use α, α_i to represent arbitrary elements of $\mathbb{A}^+$.

Notice the relation between the syntactic prefixes of the calculus and the observable actions. The output prefixes, as in Pi-calculus, represent observable output actions. The input prefix of the calculus, such as $a(b)$ in the process $a(b).P$, does not represent an authentic action, but the capability of P to receive a name on channel a; consequently we adopt an *early semantics* [2]: if a name c is sent on a, the input action is ac and it labels the transitions to $P_{\{c/b\}}$. In this way, to a single prefix $a(b)$ correspond as many input actions ac as names c can be sent on a in the given rate-environment. Unlike the nondeterministic case, for stochastic Pi-calculus we cannot define a *late semantics* [2] because only the input actions of type ac correspond to a measure on the space of processes, while $a(b)$ represents a set of measures, one for each name received. Because our semantics aims to associate a measure to each process and action label, we need to refuse the inputs of type $a(b)$ in the set of labels and chose an early semantics.

The bound output $a[@r]$ in the form that ignores the argument of communication is novel. It labels a bound output of type $(b@r)a[b].P$. The example below explains its action; anticipating the semantics, $E \vdash P \xrightarrow{\alpha,r} Q^{\equiv}$ means that in the environment E, P can do an α-transition with rate r to the elements of $Q^{\equiv}$.

Example 1. The processes $Q = (b@r)a[b].P$ and $R = (c@r)a[c].P_{\{c/b\}}$ are structural congruent and we want them bisimilar in our semantics. If we consider that the (only) observable transition in which Q can be involved is $a[b@r]$, as it is done in other PAs, then the transition is $E \vdash (b@r)a[b].P \xrightarrow{a[b@r],E(a)} (b@r)P^{\equiv}$, while for R the transition is $E \vdash (c@r)a[c].P_{\{c/b\}} \xrightarrow{a[c@r],E(a)} (c@r)P^{\equiv}_{\{c/b\}}$. Obviously, $(b@r)P^{\equiv} = (c@r)P^{\equiv}_{\{c/b\}}$, but if $b \neq c$, then $a[b@r] \neq a[c@r]$ and in effect, Q and R are not bisimilar in this interpretation.

For obtaining the expected bisimulations, for any $b, c \in \mathcal{N}$, $a[b@r] = a[c@r]$; and this is equivalent with accepting that an external observer can only see that a private name with the base rate r has been sent on channel a without seeing the name. Hence, the real observable action has to be $a[@r]$.

Our solution is similar to the *Abstraction-Concretion method* proposed in [20] for nondeterministic Pi-calculus. $a[@r]$ does the job of Abstraction, as our measurable sets of processes are Milner's *abstracted processes.* Only that in our case, because the transitions are not between processes but from processes to structural-congruence classes, we need no Concretions. So, the main advantage of our approach is that it solves the problem of bound outputs without using higher order syntax as in the classic Pi-calculus.

Before proceeding with the operational semantics, we need to define a set of operations on $\mathfrak{M}$ that lift the process constructors of stochastic Pi-calculus to the level of the labeled distributions over the space of processes. These operations reflect the complexity of the normal forms of the τ-reductions for stochastic Pi and for this reason the reader is invited to study Definition 4 in the context of the operational semantics presented in the next section. The SOS rules clarify and prove the correctness of these operations.

Let $\mathbb{A}_@$ denote the set $\{a[@r],\ \text{for } a \in \mathcal{N}, r \in \mathbb{Q}^+\}$ of bound output actions and $\mathbb{A}_a$ denotes the set $\{a[b], ab, a[@r],\ \text{for } b \in \mathcal{N}, r \in \mathbb{Q}^+\}$ of actions on channel a. A labeled measure $\mu \in \mathfrak{M}$ has *finite support* if the set of output actions $\alpha \in \mathbb{A}^+$ with $\mu(\alpha) \neq \mathbb{0}$ is finite or empty. Recall that $\mathbb{0}$ denotes the null measure and $D_{P^\equiv}$ the $P^\equiv$-Dirac measure.

Definition 4. *Consider the following operations on $\mathfrak{M}$ defined for arbitrary $\mu, \eta \in \mathfrak{M}$, $E \in \mathbb{E}$, $\alpha \in \mathbb{A}^+$, $a, b, c \in \mathcal{N}$, $P \in \mathbb{P}$ and $\mathcal{P}, \mathcal{Q}, \mathcal{R} \in \Pi$.*
1. Operations of arity 0.
(i) Let $\overline{\mathbb{0}} \in \mathfrak{M}$ defined by $\overline{\mathbb{0}}(\alpha) = \mathbb{0}$ for any $\alpha \in \mathbb{A}^+$;
(ii) Let $E^{a[b]}_{P^\equiv}, E^{a(b)}_{P^\equiv} \in \mathfrak{M}$ defined whenever $fn(P) \subseteq dom(E)$, by
$E^{a[b]}_{P^\equiv}(a[b]) = E(a)D_{P^\equiv}$ *and* $E^{a[b]}_{P^\equiv}(\alpha) = \mathbb{0}$, *for* $\alpha \neq a[b]$;
$E^{a(b)}_{P^\equiv}(ac) = E(a)D_{P^\equiv_{\{c/b\}}}$ *and* $E^{a(b)}_{P^\equiv}(\alpha) = \mathbb{0}$, *for* $\alpha \neq ac$.
2. Operations of arity 1.
(i) Let $\mu_{\mathcal{P}} \in \mathcal{M}$ defined by $\mu_{\mathcal{P}}(\alpha)(\mathcal{R}) = \mu(\alpha)(\mathcal{R}_{\mathcal{P}})$.
(ii) Let $(a@r)\mu \in \mathcal{M}$ defined by

$$(a@r)\mu(\alpha)(\mathcal{R}) = \begin{cases} \mu(\alpha)(\mathcal{P}), & \text{if } \alpha \notin \mathbb{A}_a \cup \mathbb{A}_@, \mathcal{R} = (a@r)\mathcal{P} \\ \mu(b[a])(\mathcal{P}) + \mu(b[@r])(\mathcal{P}), & \text{if } \alpha = b[@r], \mathcal{R} = (a@r)\mathcal{P} \\ 0, & \text{otherwise.} \end{cases}$$

3. Operations of arity 2.
(i) Let $\mu \oplus \eta \in \mathcal{M}$, defined by $(\mu \oplus \eta)(\alpha) = \mu(\alpha) + \eta(\alpha)$.
(ii) For $\mu, \eta \in \mathfrak{M}$ with finite support, let $\mu\ {}_{\mathcal{P}}\!\otimes^E_{\mathcal{Q}}\ \eta \in \mathcal{M}$ defined by
- for $\alpha \in \mathbb{A}$, $\quad (\mu\ {}_{\mathcal{P}}\!\otimes^E_{\mathcal{Q}}\ \eta)(\alpha)(\mathcal{R}) = \mu_{\mathcal{Q}}(\alpha)(\mathcal{R}) + \eta_{\mathcal{P}}(\alpha)(\mathcal{R})$;

- for τ, $\quad (\mu\ {}_{\mathcal{P}}\!\otimes^E_{\mathcal{Q}}\ \eta)(\tau)(\mathcal{R}) = \mu_{\mathcal{Q}}(\tau)(\mathcal{R}) + \eta_{\mathcal{P}}(\tau)(\mathcal{R}) +$

$$\sum_{\substack{a \in dom(E)^* \\ b \in \mathcal{N} \\ \mathcal{P}_1|\mathcal{P}_2 \subseteq \mathcal{R}}} \frac{\mu(a[b])(\mathcal{P}_1) \cdot \eta(ab)(\mathcal{P}_2) + \eta(a[b])(\mathcal{P}_1) \cdot \mu(ab)(\mathcal{P}_2)}{E(a)} +$$

$$\sum_{\substack{((x@r)y[x].P'|P'') + P'''^\equiv \subseteq \mathcal{P} \\ (y(z).Q'|Q'') + Q'''^\equiv \subseteq \mathcal{Q} \\ (x@r)(P'|Q'_{\{x/z\}})|P''|Q''^\equiv \subseteq \mathcal{R}}} \frac{\mu(y[@r])((x@r)P'|P''^\equiv) \cdot \eta(yx)(Q'_{\{x/z\}}|Q''^\equiv)}{E(a)} +$$

$$\sum_{\substack{(y(z).P'|P'') + P'''^\equiv \subseteq \mathcal{P} \\ ((x@r)y[x].Q'|Q'') + Q'''^\equiv \subseteq \mathcal{Q} \\ (x@r)(P'_{\{x/z\}}|Q')|P''|Q''^\equiv \subseteq \mathcal{R}}} \frac{\mu(yx)(P'_{\{x/z\}}|P''^\equiv) \cdot \eta(y[@r])((x@r)Q'|Q''^\equiv)}{E(a)}$$

Observe that because we work with functions with finite support and because $dom(E)$ is defined and finite, the sums involved in the definition of $\mu\ {}_{\mathcal{P}}\!\otimes^E_{\mathcal{Q}}\ \eta$ have finite numbers of non-zero summands. These operations are the building blocks for the lifting of the algebraic structure of processes to the level of functions: operations of arity 0 encode process 0 and prefixing, operations of arity 1 encode the quotient and fresh name quantification and operations of arity 2 correspond to choice and parallel composition. For understanding their role, the reader is referred to the semantic rules introduce in the next section.

Lemma 1. *1. For $\mu, \eta, \rho \in \mathfrak{M}$ it holds that $\mu \oplus \eta \in \mathfrak{M}$ and*
(a). $\mu \oplus \eta = \eta \oplus \mu$, (b). $(\mu \oplus \eta) \oplus \rho = \mu \oplus (\eta \oplus \rho)$, (c). $\mu = \mu \oplus \overline{\mathbb{0}}$.
2. For $\mu, \eta, \rho \in \mathfrak{M}$ with finite support, $\mu\ {}_{\mathcal{P}}\!\otimes^E_{\mathcal{Q}}\ \eta \in \mathfrak{M}$ and
(a). $\mu\ {}_{\mathcal{P}}\!\otimes^E_{\mathcal{Q}}\ \eta = \eta\ {}_{\mathcal{Q}}\!\otimes^E_{\mathcal{P}}\ \mu$, (b). $(\mu\ {}_{\mathcal{P}}\!\otimes^E_{\mathcal{Q}}\ \eta)\ {}_{\mathcal{P}|\mathcal{Q}}\!\otimes^E_{\mathcal{R}}\ \rho = \mu\ {}_{\mathcal{P}}\!\otimes^E_{\mathcal{Q}|\mathcal{R}}\ (\eta\ {}_{\mathcal{Q}}\!\otimes^E_{\mathcal{R}}\ \rho)$,
(c). $\mu\ {}_{\mathcal{P}}\!\otimes^E_{0\equiv}\ \overline{\mathbb{0}} = \mu$.

3.4 Semantics

The *stochastic transition relation* is the smallest relation $\mathfrak{T} \subseteq \mathbb{E} \times \mathbb{P} \times \mathfrak{M}$ satisfying the semantics rules listed below, where $E \vdash P \to \mu$ denotes $(E, P, \mu) \in \mathfrak{T}$; it states that the behaviour of P in the environment E is defined by the mapping $\mu \in \mathfrak{M}$. For each $\equiv$-closed set of processes $\mathcal{P} \in \Pi$ and each $\alpha \in \mathbb{A}^+$, $\mu(\alpha)(\mathcal{P}) \in \mathbb{Q}^+$ represents the total rate of the α-reductions of P to the elements of $\mathcal{P}$. The rules involve also predicates of type $E \vdash ok$ that encode the correctness of E, i.e. that the environment associates base rates to a finite number of channels only, and that no channel appears in more than one rate declaration in that environment. Recall that $\equiv^*$ denotes alpha-conversion.

$$(Env\varepsilon).\ \frac{}{\varepsilon \vdash ok} \qquad (Env@).\ \frac{E \vdash ok \quad a \notin dom(E)}{E, a@r \vdash ok}$$

$$(Null).\ \frac{E \vdash ok}{E \vdash 0 \to \overline{\mathbb{0}}} \qquad (Out).\ \frac{E \vdash ok \quad fn(a[b].P) \subseteq dom(E)}{E \vdash a[b].P \to E^{a[b]}_{P\equiv}}$$

$$(Sum).\ \frac{E \vdash P \to \mu \quad E \vdash Q \to \eta}{E \vdash P + Q \to \mu \oplus \eta} \qquad (Imp).\ \frac{E \vdash ok \quad fn(a(b).P) \subseteq dom(E)}{E \vdash a(b).P \to E^{a(b)}_{P\equiv}}$$

$$(New).\ \frac{E, a@r \vdash P \to \mu}{E \vdash (a@r)P \to (a@r)\mu} \qquad (Par).\ \frac{E \vdash P \to \mu \quad E \vdash Q \to \eta}{E \vdash P|Q \to \mu\ {}_{P\equiv}\!\otimes^E_{Q\equiv}\ \eta}$$

$$(Alpha).\ \frac{E \vdash P \to \mu \quad P \equiv^* Q}{E \vdash Q \to \mu} \qquad (Rep).\ \frac{E \vdash P \to \mu}{E \vdash !P \to \mu_{!P\equiv}}$$

$(Null)$ guarantees that in any correct environment the behaviour of process 0 is described by $\overline{\mathbb{0}}$, which associates the rate 0 to any transition.

(Out) and (Imp) have similar actions. They associates to any prefixed process $x.P$, where $x \in \{a(b), a[b] \mid a, b \in \mathcal{N}\}$, the mapping $E^{x}_{P^{\equiv}}$ which, as described in Definition 4, associates the base-rate of the channel of x to the x-transitions from $x.P$ to $P^{\equiv}$ and rate 0 to the other transitions.

(Sum) computes the rate of the α-transitions from $P + Q$ to $\mathcal{R} \in \Pi$, as the sum of the rates of the α-transitions from P and Q to $\mathcal{R}$ respectively.

(Par) describes the possible interactions between the processes. If $\rho = \mu\ {}_{P^{\equiv}}\!\otimes^{E}_{Q^{\equiv}}\ \eta$, the rate $\rho(\alpha)(\mathcal{R})$ of the α-transitions from $P|Q$ to $\mathcal{R}$ for $\alpha \neq \tau$, is the sum of the rates $\mu(\alpha)(\mathcal{R}_{Q^{\equiv}})$ and $\eta(\alpha)(\mathcal{R}_{P^{\equiv}})$ of the α-transitions from P to $\mathcal{R}_Q$ and from Q to $\mathcal{R}_P$ respectively; the rate of the τ-transitions from $P|Q$ to $\mathcal{R}$ is the sum of the rates of the τ-transitions that P or Q can do independently plus the rate of all communications between P and Q (bound represented by the first sum in Definition 4 3.(ii) and unbound represented by the last two sums). Because we use the base rate of the channel a when we calculate the rates of both inputs and outputs on a, the sums in Definition 4 3.(ii) are normalised by $E(a)$.

(New) establishes that the rate of the transitions from $(a@r)P$ to $(a@r)\mathcal{R} \in \Pi$ in the environment E is the rate of the corresponding transitions from P to $\mathcal{R}$ in the environment $E, a@r$. The only thing one needs to take care of (see Definition 4) is when an output becomes bound while (New) is used. Consider, for instance, the process $Q = b[a].P + (c@r)b[c].P_{\{c/a\}}$.

$E, a@r \vdash Q \overset{b[a],E(b)}{\longrightarrow} P^{\equiv}$ and $E, a@r \vdash Q \overset{b[@r],E(b)}{\longrightarrow} (c@r)P^{\equiv}_{\{c/a\}}$.
Now, if we consider $(a@r)Q \equiv (a@r)b[a].P + (c@r)b[c].P_{\{c/a\}}$, because $(a@r)P \equiv (c@r)P_{\{c/a\}}$, the rates of the transitions in the environment E should be

$E \vdash (a@r)Q \overset{b[a],0}{\longrightarrow} (a@r)P^{\equiv}$ and $E \vdash (a@r)Q \overset{b[@r],2E(b)}{\longrightarrow} (a@r)P^{\equiv}$.
Notice that the rate of $b[a]$-transition of Q contributes to the rate of $b[@r]$-transition of $(a@r)Q$ and this is how Definition 4 introduces $(a@r)\mu$.

(Rep) encodes the intuition that in the case of stochastic systems, if $E \vdash P \overset{\alpha,r}{\longrightarrow} Q^{\equiv}$, then $E \vdash\, !P \overset{\alpha,r}{\longrightarrow}\, !P|Q^{\equiv}$.

$(Alpha)$ proves properties by alpha-conversion: it guarantees that the behaviour of a process does not change if the bound variables are renamed. The standard presentations of PAs with unlabeled reduction mix structural congruence with reductions by rules of type (Struct). Because our reductions are labeled (the labels are hidden into the mappings), alpha conversion needs to be separately incorporated both in the algebra and coalgebra.

The next example illustrates some transitions in our framework.

Example 2. $E \vdash (b@r)(a[b].P)|a(c).Q \overset{\tau,E(a)}{\longrightarrow} (b@r)(P|Q_{\{b/c\}})^{\equiv}$.

From (Out) or (Imp) we derive $E, b@r \vdash a[b].P \overset{a[b],E(a)}{\longrightarrow} P^{\equiv}$. (New) gives us further that $E \vdash (b@r)a[b].P \overset{a[@r],E(a)}{\longrightarrow} (b@r)P^{\equiv}$ and this is the only transition with non-zero rate. Observe that the definition of $E^{a(c)}_{Q^{\equiv}}$ implies $E \vdash a(c).Q \overset{ab,E(a)}{\longrightarrow} Q^{\equiv}_{\{b/c\}}$.

Applying the definition of $_{(b@r)(a[b].P)^{\equiv}\otimes^{E}_{a(c).Q^{\equiv}}}$, we obtain $E \vdash (b@r)(a[b].P)|a(c).Q \xrightarrow{\tau,s} (b@r)(P|Q_{\{b/c\}})^{\equiv}$ for $s = E(a)$ if $E(a) \neq 0$ and $s = 0$ if $E(a) = 0$.

A consequence of this result is the well known case of communication of a private name used for a private communication.

$$E \vdash (b@r)(a[b].b(e).P)|a(c).c[d].0 \xrightarrow{\tau,E(a)} (b@r)(b(e).P|b[d].0)^{\equiv} \xrightarrow{\tau,r} (b@r)P^{\equiv}_{\{d/e\}}.$$

The first transition is a particular case of the example. For the second transition we apply the case 3 (ii) of Definition 4.

Remark 1. In stochastic Pi calculus it is not possible to define a binary operator on $\mathfrak{M}$ that reflects, for a fixed environment E, the parallel composition of processes. Assume that there exists an operator $\otimes^E$ such that if $E \vdash P \to \mu$ and $E \vdash Q \to \eta$, then $E \vdash P|Q \to \mu \otimes^E \eta$. The processes $P = a[b].0|c[d].0$ and $Q = a[b].c[d].0 + c[d].a[b].0$ have associated, in any correct environment E, the same mapping $\mu \in \mathfrak{M}$. Suppose that $E \vdash R \to \eta$, where $R = e[f].0$. If, indeed, the operator $\otimes^E$ is well defined, then $E \vdash P|R \to \mu\otimes^E\eta$ and $E \vdash Q|R \to \mu\otimes^E\eta$, i.e. $P|R$ and $Q|R$ have associated the same mapping. But this is not the case, because $P^{\equiv} \neq Q^{\equiv}$ and

$E \vdash P|R \xrightarrow{e[f],E(e)} P^{\equiv}$ and $E \vdash P|R \xrightarrow{e[f],0} Q^{\equiv}$, while

$E \vdash Q|R \xrightarrow{e[f],0} P^{\equiv}$ and $E \vdash Q|R \xrightarrow{e[f],E(e)} Q^{\equiv}$.

This explains why we need to index $\otimes^E$ with $P^{\equiv}$ and $Q^{\equiv}$ and why the algebraic signature is changed when the structure of processes is lifted to indexed measures.

The next theorem states that $\mathfrak{T}$ is well defined and characterizes the correctness of an environment.

Theorem 2. *(i) If $E \vdash ok$ and $fn(P) \subseteq dom(E)$, then there exists a unique $\mu \in \mathfrak{M}$ such that $E \vdash P \to \mu$.*
(ii) If $E \vdash P \to \mu$, then $E \vdash ok$. Moreover, $E \vdash ok$ iff $E \vdash 0 \to \overline{\mathbb{0}}$.

Unlike in other process algebras, our semantics does not contain a (Struct) rule stating that structural congruent processes behave identicaly. However, such a result can be proved.

Theorem 3. *If $E \vdash P' \to \mu$ and $P' \equiv P''$, then $E \vdash P'' \to \mu$.*

The next lemma describes how the environments can vary without influencing the mapping associated to a process.

Lemma 2. *1. If for any $a \in \mathcal{N}$ and $r \in \mathbb{Q}$, $[a@r \in E$ iff $a@r \in E']$, then $E \vdash P \to \mu$ iff $E' \vdash P \to \mu$.*
2. If $E' \vdash ok$, $E \subset E'$ and $E \vdash P \to \mu$, then $E' \vdash P \to \mu$.
3. If $E \subset E'$, $E \vdash P \to \mu$ and $dom(E' \setminus E) \cap fn(P) = \emptyset$, then $E' \vdash P \to \mu$.

4 Stochastic Bisimulation

In this section we focus on stochastic bisimulation that reproduces, at the stochastic level, Larsen-Skou probabilistic bisimulation [19]. We have introduced a similar concept in [7] for the case of stochastic CCS. The novelty with the present definition consists in the role of the rate environments: two processes are stochastic bisimilar if they have similar stochastic behaviours in any rate environment.

Definition 5 (Stochastic Bisimulation). *A* rate-bisimulation *on $\mathbb{P}$ is an equivalence relation $\mathfrak{R} \subseteq \mathbb{P} \times \mathbb{P}$ such that $(P, Q) \in \mathfrak{R}$ iff for any $E \in \mathbb{E}$,*
– if $E \vdash P \to \mu$, then there exists $\eta \in \mathfrak{M}$ such that $E \vdash Q \to \eta$ and for any $C \in \Pi(\mathfrak{R})$ and $\alpha \in \mathbb{A}^+$, $\mu(\alpha)(C) = \eta(\alpha)(C)$.
– if $E \vdash Q \to \eta$, then there exists $\mu \in \mathfrak{M}$ such that $E \vdash P \to \mu$ and for any $C \in \Pi(\mathfrak{R})$ and $\alpha \in \mathbb{A}^+$, $\eta(\alpha)(C) = \mu(\alpha)(C)$.

Two processes $P, Q \in \mathbb{P}$ are stochastic bisimilar, denoted $P \sim Q$, if there exists a rate-bisimulation connecting them.

Observe that stochastic bisimulation is the largest rate-bisimulation on $\mathbb{P}$.

Example 3. If $a, b, x, y \in \mathcal{N}$, $a \neq b$ and $x \notin fn(b[y].Q)$, then

$$a(x).P|b[y].Q \sim a(x).(P|b[y].Q) + b[y].(a(x).P|Q).$$

Indeed, for any compatible rate environment E,

$$E \vdash a(x).P|b[y].Q \to E_P^{a(x)} \ {}_{a(x).P}\!\otimes_{b[y].Q} E_Q^{b[y]},$$

$$E \vdash a(x).(P|b[y].Q) + b[y].(a(x).P|Q) \to E^{a(x)}_{P|b[y].Q} \oplus E^{b[y]}_{a(x).P|Q}$$

and for arbitrary $C \in \Pi(\sim)$,

$$E_P^{a(x)} \ {}_{a(x).P}\!\otimes_{b[y].Q} E_Q^{b[y]}(\alpha)(C) = E^{a(x)}_{P|b.Q} \oplus E^{b[y]}_{a(x).P|Q}(\alpha)(C) =$$

The previous example shows bisimilar processes which are not structurally congruent. The reverse affirmation is not true.

Theorem 4. *If $P \equiv Q$, then $P \sim Q$.*

The next theorem, stating that stochastic bisimulation is a congruence, proves that we have identified a well-behaved semantics.

Theorem 5 (Congruence). *If $P \sim Q$, then*
1. *for any $a, b \in \mathcal{N}$, $a(b).P \sim a(b).Q$ and $a[b].P \sim a[b].Q$;*
2. *for any $R \in \mathbb{P}$, $P + R \sim Q + R$,*
3. *for any $a \in \mathcal{N}$ and $r \in \mathbb{Q}^+$, $(a@r)P \sim (a@r)Q$;*
4. *for any $R \in \mathbb{P}$, $P|R \sim Q|R$.*
5. *$!P \sim !Q$.*

5 Conclusions and Future Work

In this paper we have proposed a way of introducing stochastic process algebras that is faithful to the algebraic-coalgebraic structures of the concurrent Markovian processes. The semantics is given in terms of measure theory and describes the lifting of the algebraic structure of processes to the level of measures on the measurable space of processes. The paper treats the case of the complete stochastic Pi-calculus. Instead of the discrete measurable space of processes, we consider the measurable space induced by structural congruence and this idea has important advantages. Firstly, it matches practical modelling requirements: the identity of a system is not given by the stochastic process used to model it, but by its structural-congruence class (for systems biology this represents a chemical soup). Secondly, by working with measures on this space, we get important advantages on the level of the underlying theory such as a simple and elegant semantics, simple solutions for the problems related to bound output and replication (that otherwise require complicate transition labeling and higher order reasoning) and a well-behaved notion of stochastic bisimulation including associativity. Other advantages derive from the use of the rate environments that guarantees a certain robustness in modelling: a model cab be easily refined by modifying its rate environment.

Our approach opens some future research directions. One is the study of the GSOS format where the main challenges are to understand the underlying category and the equational monad induced by structural congruence. Another is the definition of a pseudometric, similar with the one we introduce in [7], to measure the distance between processes in terms of similar behaviours. Our semantics is particularly appropriate for introducing such metrics via the metrics on measures such as the Kantorovich metrics on distributions used, for instance, in [21]. This SPA is also particularly appropriate for logical analysis using an equational-coequational logic as the one we propose in [6], which will allow a canonic characterization of the measurable space of processes.

References

1. Berry, G., Boudol, G.: The Chemical Abstract Machine. In: Proc. POPL, pp. 81–94 (1990)
2. Bergstra, J.A., et al. (eds.): Handbook of Process Algebra. Elsevier (2001)
3. Bernardo, M., Gorrieri, R.: A tutorial on EMPA: A theory of concurrent processes with nondeterminism, priorities, probabilities and time. TCS 202(1-2) (1998)
4. Bravetti, M., Hermanns, H., Katoen, J.-P.: YMCA: Why Markov Chain Algebra? ENTCS 162 (2006)
5. Cardelli, L.: A Process Algebra Master Equation. In: Proc. QEST 2007 (2007)
6. Cardelli, L., Larsen, K.G., Mardare, R.: Modular Markovian Logic. To appear in Proc. ICALP 2011 (2011)
7. Cardelli, L., Mardare, R.: The Measurable Space of Stochastic Processes. In: QEST 2010. IEEE Press (2010)
8. De Nicola, R., Latella, D., Loreti, M., Massink, M.: Rate-Based Transition Systems for Stochastic Process Calculi. In: Albers, S., Marchetti-Spaccamela, A., Matias, Y., Nikoletseas, S., Thomas, W. (eds.) ICALP 2009, Part II. LNCS, vol. 5556, pp. 435–446. Springer, Heidelberg (2009)
9. de Nicola, R., Latella, D., Loreti, M., Massink, M.: On a uniform framework for the definition of stochastic process languages. In: Alpuente, M., Cook, B., Joubert, C. (eds.) FMICS 2009. LNCS, vol. 5825, pp. 9–25. Springer, Heidelberg (2009)

10. de Vink, E.P., Rutten, J.: Bisimulation for probabilistic transition systems: A coalgebaic approach. TCS 221(1-2) (1999)
11. Fiore, M.P., Turi, D.: Semantics of name and value passing. In: LICS 2001. IEEE Press (2001)
12. Fiore, M.P., Staton, S.: A congruence rule format for name-passing process calculi. Inf. and Comp. 207(2) (2009)
13. Gotz, N., Herzog, U., Rettelbach, M.: TIPP - A language for timed processes and performance evaluation. Tech.Rep. 4/92 IMMD VII, University of Erlangen-Nurnberg
14. Hillston, J.: A compositional approach to performance modelling. Distinguished dissertation in Computer Science. Cambridge University Press (1996)
15. Hillston, J.: Process algebras for quantitative analysis. In: LICS 2005. IEEE Press (2005)
16. Hermanns, H.: Interactive Markov Chains. In: Hermanns, H. (ed.) Interactive Markov Chains. LNCS, vol. 2428, pp. 57–88. Springer, Heidelberg (2002)
17. Klin, B., Sassone, V.: Structural Operational Semantics for Stochastic Process Calculi. In: Amadio, R.M. (ed.) FOSSACS 2008. LNCS, vol. 4962, pp. 428–442. Springer, Heidelberg (2008)
18. Kwiatkowska, M., Norman, G., Segala, R., Sproston, J.: Automatic Verification of Real-Time Systems With Discrete Probability Distributions. In: Katoen, J.-P. (ed.) ARTS 1999. LNCS, vol. 1601, pp. 75–95. Springer, Heidelberg (1999)
19. Larsen, K.G., Skou, A.: Bisimulation through probabilistic testing. Inf. and Comp. 94 (1991)
20. Milner, R.: Communicating and Mobile Systems: The Pi-Calculus. Cambridge Univ. Press (1999)
21. Panangaden, P.: Labelled Markov Processes. Imperial College Press (2009)
22. Priami, C.: Stochastic π-Calculus. Computer Journal 38(7) (1995)
23. Rutten, J.: Universal coalgebra: a theory of systems. TCS 249 (2000)
24. Segala, R., Lynch, N.: Probabilistic Simulations for Probabilistic Processes. Nordic J. of Comp. 2(2) (1995)
25. Turi, D., Plotkin, G.D.: Towards a mathematical operational semantics. In: LICS 1997. IEEE Press (1997)

Appendix

In this appendix we have collected some of the proofs of the main results presented in the paper.

Proof (Theorem 2). (i) Firstly, we prove the existential part by induction on the structure of P.

For $P = 0$, $P = a[b].Q$ and $P = a(b).Q$, (Null), (Out) and (Imp) respectively guarantee the existence of μ.

For $P = Q + R$: the inductive hypothesis proves that there exist two functions η, ρ such that $E \vdash Q \to \eta$ and $E \vdash R \to \rho$. From (Sum) we obtain that there exists $\mu = \eta \oplus \rho$ such that $E \vdash P \to \mu$.

For $P = Q|R$: the inductive hypothesis guarantees that there exist two functions η, ρ such that $E \vdash Q \to \eta$ and $E \vdash R \to \rho$. From (Par) we obtain that exists $\mu = \eta\langle_{Q\equiv} E_{R\equiv}\rangle\rho$ such that $E \vdash P \to \mu$.

For $P = (a@r)Q$: if $a \notin dom(E)$, then $E, a@r \vdash ok$ and the inductive hypothesis guarantees the existence of η such that $E, a@r \vdash Q \to \eta$. Further, applying (New), we get $E \vdash P \to (a@r)\eta$. If $a \in dom(E)$, let $b \in \mathcal{N} \setminus dom(E)$. Then $E, b@r \vdash ok$ and the inductive hypothesis guarantees the existence of η such that $E, b@r \vdash Q_{\{b/a\}} \to \eta$. Further, applying (New), we get $E \vdash (b@r)Q_{\{b/a\}} \to (b@r)\eta$ and (Alpha) gives $E \vdash (a@r)Q \to (b@r)\eta$.

For $P =!Q$: the inductive hypothesis guarantees the existence of a unique η such that $E \vdash Q \to \eta$, and using (Rep), $E \vdash P \to \eta_{!Q}$.

The uniqueness part is done by induction on derivations.

The rules (Envε) and (Env@) are only proving the correctness of environments and consequently will not interfere with our proof.

Observe that all the derivations involving only the rules (Sum), (Par), (New) and (Rep), called in what follows *basic proofs*, demonstrate properties about processes with a more complex syntax than the processes involved in the hypotheses. Consequently, taking (Null), (Out) and (Imp) as basic cases, an induction on the structures of the processes involved in the derivations shows the uniqueness of μ for the situation of the basic proofs. Notice, however, that due to (New) a basic proof proves properties of type $E \vdash P \to \mu$ only for cases when $new(P) \cap dom(E) = \emptyset$, where $new(P)$ is the set of names of P bound by fresh name quantifiers. To conclude the proof we need to show that if $Q = P_{\{a/b\}}$ with $a, b \notin fn(P)$ and if $E \vdash P \to \mu$ and $E \vdash Q \to \eta$ can be proved with basic proofs, then $\mu = \eta$.We do this by induction on P.
If $P = 0$, then $Q = 0$ and $\eta = \mu = \overline{\mathbb{0}}$.
If $P = c[d].R$, then $Q = c[d].R_{\{a/b\}}$ and $a, b \notin fn(R)$. Moreover, $\mu = E^{c[d]}_{R^{\equiv}}$ and $\eta = E^{c[d]}_{R^{\equiv}_{\{a/b\}}}$. But because $a, b \notin fn(R)$, $R \equiv R_{\{a/b\}}$ implying further $\mu = \eta$.
If $P = c(d).R$, then if $d \neq b$ the proof goes as in the previous case. If $P = c(b).R$, then $Q = c(a).R_{\{a/b\}}$, $\mu = E^{c(b)}_{R}$ and $\eta = E^{c(a)}_{R_{\{a/b\}}}$ and $\mu = \eta$.
If $P = S + T$, then $Q = S_{\{a/b\}} + T_{\{a/b\}}$. Let $E \vdash S \to \rho$ and $E \vdash T \to \nu$, then $E \vdash S_{\{a/b\}} \to \rho$ and $E \vdash T_{\{a/b\}} \to \nu$. Hence, $\mu = \eta = \rho \oplus \nu$.
If $P = S|T$ the proof goes as in the previous case.
If $P =!R$, $Q =!R_{\{a/b\}}$. Suppose that $E \vdash R \to \rho$. From the inductive hypothesis we also obtain that $E \vdash R_{\{a/b\}} \to \rho$. Because $a, b \notin fn(R)$, $!R \equiv !R_{\{a/b\}}$.
If $P = (c@r)R$ with $c \neq b$, then $Q = (c@r)R_{\{a/b\}}$. Because we are in the case of a basic proof, $c \notin dom(E)$. Suppose that $E, c@r \vdash R \to \rho$. This is the unique hypothesis that proves $E \vdash P \to \mu$. Then, $\mu = (c@r)\rho$ and the inductive hypothesis implies that $E, c@r \vdash R_{\{a/b\}} \to \rho$ is the unique hypothesis that proves $E \vdash Q \to \eta$. Further, $E \vdash (c@r)R_{\{a/b\}} \to (c@r)\rho$ and $\mu = \eta$.
If $P = (b@r)R$, then $Q = (a@r)R_{\{a/b\}}$. Because we work with basic proofs, we have $a, b \notin dom(E)$. A simple induction proves that if $E, b@r \vdash R \to \rho$, then $E, a@r \vdash R_{\{a/b\}} \to \rho'$, where for any $\alpha \in \mathbb{A}^+$ and any $\mathcal{R} \in \Pi$, $\rho(\alpha)(\mathcal{R}) = \rho'(\alpha_{\{a/b\}})(\mathcal{R}_{\{a/b\}})$. From here we get $(b@r)\rho = (a@r)\rho'$. Observe that $E, b@r \vdash R \to \rho$ is the unique hypothesis that can be used in a basic proof to derive $E \vdash (b@r)R \to \mu$ and $\mu = (b@r)\rho$. Similarly, $E, a@r \vdash R_{\{a/b\}} \to \rho'$ is

the unique hypothesis to prove $E \vdash (a@r)R_{\{a/b\}} \to \eta$ and $\eta = (a@r)\rho'$. Hence, also in this case, $\mu = \eta$.

In this way we have proved that any couple of alpha-converted processes have associated the same mapping by basic proofs. In addition, (Alpha) guarantees that any kind of proof associates to alpha-converted processes the same mapping and this concludes our proof.

(ii) We prove the first part by induction on derivations. The second part is a consequence of the first part and (Null).
If $E \vdash P \to \mu$ is proved by (Null), (Out) or (Imp), $E \vdash ok$ is required.
If $E \vdash P \to \mu$ is proved by (Sum), $P = Q + R$, $\mu = \eta \oplus \rho$ and $E \vdash Q \to \eta$ and $E \vdash R \to \rho$ are the hypothesis and we can use the inductive hypothesis.
If $E \vdash P \to \mu$ is proved by (Par), the argument goes as in the previous case.
If $E \vdash P \to \mu$ is proved by (New), then $P = (a@r)Q$ and the hypothesis is of type $E, a@r \vdash Q \to \eta$. The inductive hypothesis gives $E, a@r \vdash ok$ and this can only be proved by (Env@) from $E \vdash ok$.
If $E \vdash P \to \mu$ is proved by (Rep), then $P = !Q$ and $E \vdash Q$ is the hypothesis and we can apply the inductive step.
If $E \vdash P \to \mu$ is proved by (Alpha), we can use the inductive hypothesis again.

Proof (Lemma 2). **1.** A simple induction on derivations that involve only (Envε) and (Env@) proves that $E \vdash ok$ iff $E' \vdash ok$. For proving our lemma we will proceed with an induction on the derivation of $E \vdash P \to \mu$.

If $E \vdash P \to \mu$ is proved by (Null), we have that $P = 0$ and due to Theorem 2, $\mu = \overline{\mathbb{0}}$. Applying (Null) we obtain $E' \vdash P \to \mu$.

If $E \vdash P \to \mu$ is proved by (Out) or (Imp), we have that $P = x.Q$ and $\mu = E^x_Q$. Because $E^x_Q = E'^x_Q$ and $dom(E) = dom(E')$, we obtain $E' \vdash P \to \mu$.

If $E \vdash P \to \mu$ is proved by (Sum), we have that $P = Q + R$, $\mu = \eta \oplus \rho$ and the hypothesis are $E \vdash Q \to \eta$ and $E \vdash R \to \rho$. From the inductive hypothesis we obtain $E' \vdash Q \to \eta$ and $E' \vdash R \to \rho$. Applying (Sum), $E' \vdash P \to \mu$.

If $E \vdash P \to \mu$ is proved by (Par) we have that $P = Q|R$, $\mu = \eta \;{}_Q\!\otimes^E_R\; \rho$ and the hypothesis are $E \vdash Q \to \eta$ and $E \vdash R \to \rho$. From the inductive hypothesis we obtain $E' \vdash Q \to \eta$ and $E' \vdash R \to \rho$. Further, applying (Par) we get $E' \vdash P \to \eta \;{}_Q\!\otimes^{E'}_R\; \rho$. But $\eta \;{}_Q\!\otimes^E_R\; \rho = \eta \;{}_Q\!\otimes^{E'}_R\; \rho$.

If $E \vdash P \to \mu$ is proved by (Rep), we have that $P = !Q$, $\mu = \eta_{!Q}$ and the hypothesis is $E \vdash Q \to \eta$. Applying the inductive step we get $E' \vdash Q \to \eta$ and (Rep) guarantees that $E' \vdash P \to \mu$.

If $E \vdash P \to \mu$ is proved by (New), we have that $P = (a@r)Q$, $\mu = (a@r)\eta$ and the hypothesis is $E, a@r \vdash Q \to \eta$. Hence, $a \notin dom(E) = dom(E')$ and we can apply the inductive hypothesis because $b@s \in E, a@r$ iff $b@s \in E', a@r$ and obtain $E', a@r \vdash Q \to \eta$ where from we get $E' \vdash P \to \mu$.

If $E \vdash P \to \mu$ is proved by (Alpha), we have that $P = Q_{\{a/b\}}$ with $a, b \notin fn(P) = fn(Q)$ and the hypothesis is $E \vdash Q \to \mu$. The inductive hypothesis gives $E' \vdash Q \to \mu$ and because $a, b \notin fn(Q)$, (Alpha) proves $E' \vdash P \to \mu$.

2. Induction on the derivation of $E \vdash P \to \mu$.

If $E \vdash P \to \mu$ is proved by (Null), we have that $P = 0$ and due to Theorem 2, $\mu = \overline{\mathbb{0}}$. Applying (Null) we obtain $E' \vdash P \to \mu$.

If $E \vdash P \to \mu$ is proved by (Out) or (Imp), we have that $P = x.Q$ and due to Theorem 2, $\mu = E^x_Q$. Because $fn(P) \subseteq dom(E) \subseteq dom(E')$ and $E^x_Q = E'^x_Q$, we obtain $E' \vdash P \to \mu$.

If $E \vdash P \to \mu$ is proved by (Sum), we have that $P = Q + R$, $\mu = \eta \oplus \rho$ and the hypothesis are $E \vdash Q \to \eta$ and $E \vdash R \to \rho$. From the inductive hypothesis we obtain $E' \vdash Q \to \eta$ and $E' \vdash R \to \rho$. Further, applying (Sum) we get $E' \vdash P \to \mu$.

If $E \vdash P \to \mu$ is proved by (Par) we have that $P = Q|R$, $\mu = \eta \;{}_Q\!\otimes^E_R \rho$ and the hypothesis are $E \vdash Q \to \eta$ and $E \vdash R \to \rho$. From the inductive hypothesis we obtain $E' \vdash Q \to \eta$ and $E' \vdash R \to \rho$. Further, applying (Par) we get $E' \vdash P \to \eta \;{}_Q\!\otimes^{E'}_R \rho$. But $\eta \;{}_Q\!\otimes^E_R \rho = \eta \;{}_Q\!\otimes^{E'}_R \rho$.

If $E \vdash P \to \mu$ is proved by (Rep), we have that $P = !Q$, $\mu = \eta_{!Q}$ and the hypothesis is $E \vdash Q \to \eta$. Applying the inductive step we get $E' \vdash Q \to \eta$ and (Rep) guarantees that $E' \vdash P \to \mu$.

If $E \vdash P \to \mu$ is proved by (Alpha), we have that $P = Q_{\{a/b\}}$ with $a, b \notin fn(P) = fn(Q)$ and the hypothesis is $E \vdash Q \to \mu$. As before, the inductive hypothesis guarantees that $E' \vdash Q \to \mu$ and because $a, b \notin fn(Q)$, (Alpha) proves that $E' \vdash P \to \mu$.

If $E \vdash P \to \mu$ is proved by (New), we have that $P = (a@r)Q$, $\mu = (a@r)\eta$ and the hypothesis is $E, a@r \vdash Q \to \eta$. Hence, $a \notin dom(E)$. If $a \notin dom(E')$, the inductive hypothesis guarantees that $E', a@r \vdash Q \to \eta$ where from we get $E' \vdash P \to \mu$. If $a \in dom(E')$, let $b \notin dom(E') \cup fn(P)$. Because $E, a@r \vdash Q \to \eta$ is provable, also $E, b@r \vdash Q_{\{b/a\}} \to \eta_{\{b/a\}}$ is provable, where $\eta_{\{b/a\}}$ is the mapping obtained from η replacing all the occurrences of a in the definition of η (in processes and labels) with b. Moreover, to each proof of $E, a@r \vdash Q \to \eta$ corresponds a proof of $E, b@r \vdash Q_{\{b/a\}} \to \eta_{\{b/a\}}$ that is, from the point of view of our induction, at the same level with the proof of $E, a@r \vdash Q \to \eta$. Consequently, we can apply the inductive hypothesis to $E, b@r \vdash Q_{\{b/a\}} \to \eta_{\{b/a\}}$ and obtain $E', b@r \vdash Q_{\{b/a\}} \to \eta_{\{b/a\}}$. (New) implies $E' \vdash (b@r)Q_{\{b/a\}} \to (b@r)\eta_{\{b/a\}}$ and (Alpha) $E' \vdash (a@r)Q \to (b@r)\eta_{\{b/a\}}$. To conclude, it is sufficient to verify that $(a@r)\eta = (b@r)\eta_{\{b/a\}}$.

3. The proof goes similarly with the proof of the previous case. We use an induction on the derivation of $E \vdash P \to \mu$.

If $E \vdash P \to \mu$ is proved by (Null), we have that $P = 0$ and $\mu = \overline{\mathbb{0}}$. Applying (Null) we obtain $E' \vdash P \to \mu$.

If $E \vdash P \to \mu$ is proved by (Out) or (Imp), we have that $P = x.Q$ and $\mu = G'^x_Q$. Because $fn(P) \subseteq dom(E)$, $fn(P) \cap dom(E \setminus E') = \emptyset$ and $E^x_Q = E'^x_Q$, we obtain $E' \vdash P \to \mu$.

If $E \vdash P \to \mu$ is proved by (Sum), we have that $P = Q + R$, $\mu = \eta \oplus \rho$ and the hypothesis are $E \vdash Q \to \eta$ and $E \vdash R \to \rho$. From the inductive hypothesis we obtain $E' \vdash Q \to \eta$ and $E' \vdash R \to \rho$. Further, applying (Sum) we get $E' \vdash P \to \mu$.

If $E \vdash P \to \mu$ is proved by (Par) we have that $P = Q|R$, $\mu = \eta \;{}_Q\!\otimes^E_R \rho$ and the hypothesis are $E \vdash Q \to \eta$ and $E \vdash R \to \rho$. From the inductive hypothesis we obtain $E' \vdash Q \to \eta$ and $E' \vdash R \to \rho$. Further, applying (Par) we get $E' \vdash P \to \eta\ {}_Q\!\otimes_R^{E'} \rho$. But $\eta\ {}_Q\!\otimes_R^{E} \rho = \eta\ {}_Q\!\otimes_R^{E'} \rho$.

If $E \vdash P \to \mu$ is proved by (Rep), we have that $P = !Q$, $\mu = \eta_{!Q}$ and the hypothesis is $E \vdash Q \to \eta$. Applying the inductive step we get $E' \vdash Q \to \eta$ and (Rep) guarantees that $E' \vdash P \to \mu$.

If $E \vdash P \to \mu$ is proved by (Alpha), we have that $P = Q_{\{a/b\}}$ with $a, b \notin fn(P) = fn(Q)$ and the hypothesis is $E \vdash Q \to \mu$. As before, the inductive hypothesis guarantees that $E' \vdash Q \to \mu$ and because $a, b \notin fn(Q)$, (Alpha) proves that $E' \vdash P \to \mu$.

If $E \vdash P \to \mu$ is proved by (New), we have that $P = (a@r)Q$, $\mu = (a@r)\eta$ and the hypothesis is $E, a@r \vdash Q \to \eta$. Hence, $a \notin dom(E)$ and because $dom(E') \subseteq dom(E)$, we obtain that $a \notin dom(E')$. Because $E, a@r \subset E', a@r$ and $dom((E', a@r) \setminus (E, a@r)) = dom(E' \setminus E)$, we can apply the inductive hypothesis and from $E, a@r \vdash Q \to \eta$ we obtain $E', a@r \vdash Q \to \eta$ where from we get $E' \vdash P \to \mu$.

Proof (Theorem 5). From $P' \equiv P''$ we obtain that $fn(P') = fn(P'')$ and Theorem 2 ensures that $E \vdash P' \to \mu$ implies that there exists a unique μ' such that $E \vdash P'' \to \mu'$.

We prove now that $E \vdash P' \to \mu$ implies $E \vdash P'' \to \mu$. The proof is an induction following the rules of structural congruence presented in Definition 2.

Rule I.1: if $P' = P|Q$ and $P'' = Q|P$. Suppose that $E \vdash P \to \eta$ and $E \vdash Q \to \rho$. Then $\mu = \eta\ {}_P\!\otimes_Q^{E} \rho$ and Lemma 1 guarantees that $E \vdash P'' \to \mu$.

Similarly we can treat all the rules of group I.

Rules of group II: As previously, the results derive from the properties of $\oplus$ stated in Lemma 1.

Rules of group III: If ($P' = P|R$ and $P'' = Q|R$), or ($P' = P + R$ and $P'' = Q + R$), or ($P' = x.P$ and $P'' = x.Q$), or ($P' = !P$ and $P'' = !Q$) for $P \equiv Q$, we can apply the inductive hypothesis that guarantees that $E \vdash P \to \eta$ iff $E \vdash Q \to \eta$. Further, if $E \vdash R \to \rho$, we obtain the desired results because $\eta\ {}_P\!\otimes_R^{E} \rho = \eta\ {}_Q\!\otimes_R^{E} \rho$, $\eta \oplus \rho = \eta \oplus \rho$, $E_P^x = E_Q^x$ and $\mu_{!P} = \mu_{!Q}$.
If $P' = (a@r)P$ and $P'' = (a@r)Q$, we have two subcases.

Subcase 1: $a \notin dom(E)$. Suppose that $E, a@r \vdash P \to \eta$. From the inductive hypothesis we obtain that $E, a@r \vdash Q \to \eta$. Further, rule (New) proves that $\mu = (a@r)\eta$ and $E \vdash (a@r)Q \to \mu$.

Subcase 2: $a \in dom(E)$. Let $b \in \mathcal{N} \setminus dom(E)$. Suppose that $E, b@r \vdash P_{\{b/a\}} \to \eta$. Then, (New) implies $E \vdash (b@r)P_{\{b/a\}} \to (b@r)\eta$ and (Alpha) proves $E \vdash (a@r)P \to (b@r)\eta$. Hence, $\mu = (b@r)\eta$. On the other hand, the inductive hypothesis implies $E, b@r \vdash Q_{\{b/a\}} \to \eta$, (New) proves $E \vdash (b@r)Q_{\{b/a\}} \to (b@r)\eta$ and (Alpha) implies $E \vdash (a@r)Q \to (b@r)\eta$.

Rule IV.1: If $P' = (a@r)(b@s)P$ and $P'' = (b@s)(a@r)P$. Let $c, d \in \mathcal{N} \setminus dom(E)$. Suppose that $E; c@r; d@s \vdash P_{\{c/a, d/b\}} \to \eta$. Applying twice (New) we obtain $E \vdash (c@r)(d@s)P_{\{c/a,d/b\}} \to (c@r)(d@s)\eta$ and applying twice (Alpha) we get $E \vdash (a@r)(b@s)P \to (c@r)(d@s)\eta$. Hence, $\mu = (c@r)(d@s)\eta$. On the other hand, Lemma 2.1 guarantees that $E; c@r; d@s \vdash P_{\{c/a,d/b\}} \to \eta$ implies $E; d@s; c@r \vdash P_{\{c/a,d/b\}} \to \eta$ and, as before, we eventually obtain $E \vdash (b@s)(a@r)P \to (d@s)(c@r)\eta$. Now it is suficient to verify that $(d@s)(c@r)\eta = (c@r)(d@s)\eta$.

Rule IV.2: If $P' = (a@r)0$ and $P'' = 0$. In this case it is sufficient to notice that $(a@r)\overline{\mathbb{0}} = \overline{\mathbb{0}}$.

Rule IV.3: If $P' = (a@r)(P|Q)$ and $P'' = P|(a@r)Q$, where $a \notin fn(P)$. Let $b \in \mathcal{N} \setminus (dom(E) \cup fn(P))$. Suppose that $E, b@r \vdash P \to \eta$ and $E, b@r \vdash Q_{\{b/a\}} \to \rho$. Observe that because $a \notin fn(P)$, we also have $E, b@r \vdash P_{\{b/a\}} \to \eta$. Further we obtain

$$E, b@r \vdash (P|Q)_{\{b/a\}} \to \eta \ {}_{P_{\{b/a\}}}\!\otimes^{E,b@r}_{Q_{\{b/a\}}} \rho \text{ and}$$

$$E \vdash (b@r)((P|Q)_{\{b/a\}}) \to (b@r)(\eta \ {}_{P_{\{b/a\}}}\!\otimes^{E,b@r}_{Q_{\{b/a\}}} \rho).$$

Now we apply (Alpha) and obtain

$$E \vdash (a@r)(P|Q) \to (b@r)(\eta \ {}_{P}\!\otimes^{E,b@r}_{Q_{\{b/a\}}} \rho).$$

On the other hand, because $b \notin fn(P)$, from $E, b@r \vdash P \to \eta$ Lemma 2.2 proves $E \vdash P \to \eta$ and from $E, b@r \vdash Q_{\{b/a\}} \to \rho$ we obtain, applying (New), $E \vdash (b@r)Q_{\{b/a\}} \to (b@r)\rho$. And further,

$$E \vdash P|(b@r)Q_{\{b/a\}} \to \eta \ {}_{P}\!\otimes^{E}_{(b@r)Q_{\{b/a\}}} (b@r)\rho.$$

Applying (alpha) we obtain

$$E \vdash P|(a@r)Q \to \eta \ {}_{P}\!\otimes^{E}_{(b@r)Q_{\{b/a\}}} (b@r)\rho.$$

A simple verification based on the observation that (if for all $R \in \mathcal{R}$, $b \notin fn(R)$, then $(b@r)\mathcal{R} = \mathcal{R}$) proves that

$$(b@r)(\eta \ {}_{P}\!\otimes^{E,b@r}_{Q_{\{b/a\}}} \rho) = \eta \ {}_{P}\!\otimes^{E}_{(b@r)Q_{\{b/a\}}} (b@r)\rho.$$

Similarly can be proved that case $P' = (a@r)(P + Q)$ and $P'' = P + (a@r)Q$, where $a \notin fn(P)$.

Rules of group V: By a simple verification one can prove that $\overline{\mathbb{0}}_{!0} = \overline{\mathbb{0}}$. For the second rule, observe that if $E \vdash P \to \eta$ and $E \vdash Q \to \rho$, then $E \vdash !(P|Q) \to (\eta \ {}_{P}\!\otimes^{E}_{Q} \rho)_{!(P|Q)}$ and $E \vdash !P|!Q \to \eta \ {}_{!Q|P}\!\otimes^{E}_{!P|Q} \rho$. And a simple verification proves that

$$(\eta \ {}_{P}\!\otimes^{E}_{Q} \rho)_{!(P|Q)} = \eta \ {}_{!Q|P}\!\otimes^{E}_{!P|Q} \rho.$$

Rules of group VI: These rules are a direct consequence of (Alpha).

Proof (Theorem 5). **1. Prefix:** For any $C \in \Pi(\sim)$, $P \in C$ iff $Q \in C$. This entails that for any $E \in \mathbb{E}$ with $fn(x.P) \cup fn(x.Q) \subseteq dom(E)$ and any $\alpha \in \mathbb{A}^+$, $E^x_P(\alpha)(C) = E^x_Q(\alpha)(C)$.

2. Choice: We can suppose, without loosing generality, that $E \vdash P \to \mu$, $E \vdash Q \to \eta$ and $E \vdash R \to \rho$ (the other cases are trivially true). Then, $E \vdash P + R \to \mu \oplus \rho$ and $E \vdash Q + R \to \eta \oplus \rho$. Let $C \in \Pi(\sim)$ and $\alpha \in \mathbb{A}^+$. Because $P \sim Q$, $\mu(\alpha)(C) = \eta(\alpha)(C)$ implying $\mu(\alpha)(C) + \rho(\alpha)(C) = \eta(\alpha)(C) + \rho(\alpha)(C)$. This means that $(\mu \oplus \rho)(\alpha)(C) = (\eta \oplus \rho)(\alpha)(C)$.

3. Fresh name quantification: Let $E \in \mathbb{E}$ and $b \notin dom(E) \cup fn(P) \cup fn(Q)$. Observe that from $P \sim Q$, following an observation that we used also in the proof of Lemma 2 concerning the relation between a mapping η its correspondent $\eta_{\{b/a\}}$, we derive $P_{\{b/a\}} \sim Q_{\{b/a\}}$. Suppose that $E, b@r \vdash P_{\{b/a\}} \to \mu$ and $E, b@r \vdash Q_{\{b/a\}} \to \eta$. Applying (New) we obtain $E \vdash (b@r)P_{\{b/a\}} \to (b@r)\mu$ and $E \vdash (b@r)Q_{\{b/a\}} \to (b@r)\eta$. (Alpha) implies $E \vdash (a@r)P \to (b@r)\mu$ and $E \vdash (a@r)Q \to (b@r)\eta$. From $P_{\{b/a\}} \sim Q_{\{b/a\}}$ we obtain that for any $\alpha \in \mathbb{A}^+$ and any $C \in \Pi(\sim)$, $\mu(\alpha)(C) = \eta(\alpha)(C)$. to conclude the proof it is sufficient to verify that $(b@r)\mu(\alpha)(C) = (b@r)\eta(\alpha)(C)$.

4. Parallel composition: For the beginning we consider the processes that, to all syntactic levels, contain no subprocess form the class $0^{\equiv}$ in a parallel composition. Let's call them *processes with non-trivial forms.* We will first prove the lemma for processes with non-trivial forms.

For arbitrary $n \in \mathbb{N}$, let $\mathbb{S}^n$ be the set of process terms with non-trivial forms and no more than n occurrences of the operator "$|$". Let $\sim^n \subseteq \mathbb{S}^n \times \mathbb{S}^n$ be the largest rate-bisimulation defined on $\mathbb{S}^n$. We define $\approx^n \in \mathbb{S}^n \times \mathbb{S}^n$ by

$$\approx^n = \sim^{n-1} \cup$$

$$\{(P_1|...|P_k, Q_1|...|Q_k), (P_1 + ...P_k, Q_1 + ...Q_k) \text{ for } P_i \sim^{n-1} Q_i, i = 1..k, k \leq n\}.$$

We show, by induction on n, that $\approx^n$ is a rate-bisimulation, i.e. that $\approx^n \subseteq \sim^n$.

Suppose that $P \approx^n Q$. We need to prove that if $E \vdash P \to \mu$ and $E \vdash Q \to \eta$, then for any $\alpha \in \mathbb{A}^+$ and any $C \in \Pi(\approx^n)$, $\mu(\alpha)(C) = \eta(\alpha)(C)$.

Observe that, from the way we construct $\approx^n$, there are three possibilities: either $P \sim^{n-1} Q$, or $P = P_1 + ...P_k$ and $Q = Q_1 + ...Q_k$, or $P = P_1|...|P_k$ and $Q = Q_1|...|Q_k$, for $k \leq n$, with $P_i \sim^{n-1} Q_i$ for each $i = 1..k$. In the first two cases, using also the case of choice operator that we have already proved, it is trivial to verify that $\mu(\alpha)(C) = \eta(\alpha)(C)$.

To prove the last case observe for the beginning that because $\sim^{n-1} \subseteq \sim^n$, the inductive hypothesis guarantees that for each $i = 1..k$,
$P_1|...|P_{i-1}|P_{i+1}|...|P_k \approx^{n-1} Q_1|...|Q_{i-1}|Q_{i+1}|...|Q_k$ and consequently that
$P_1|...|P_{i-1}|P_{i+1}|...|P_k \sim^{n-1} Q_1|...|Q_{i-1}|Q_{i+1}|...|Q_k$.

Suppose that $E \vdash P_i \to \mu_i$ and $E \vdash Q_i \to \eta_i$ for all $i = 1..k$. Then,

$$\mu = \mu_1 \;{}_{P_1}\!\otimes^E_{P_2|...|P_k} (\mu_2 \;{}_{P_2}\!\otimes^E_{P_3|...|P_k} (...(\mu_{k-1} \;{}_{P_{k-1}}\!\otimes^E_{P_k} \mu_k)...),$$

$$\eta = \eta_1 \;{}_{Q_1}\!\otimes^E_{Q_2|...|Q_k} (\eta_2 \;{}_{Q_2}\!\otimes^E_{Q_3|...|Q_k} (...(\eta_{k-1} \;{}_{Q_{k-1}}\!\otimes^E_{Q_k} \eta_k)...),$$

Consider an arbitrary $\alpha \in \mathbb{A}$. Then,

$$\mu(\alpha)(C) = \sum_{i=1..k} \mu_i(\alpha)(C_{P_1|...|P_{i-1}|P_{i+1}|...|P_k}),$$

$$\eta(\alpha)(C) = \sum_{i=1..k} \eta_i(\alpha)(C_{Q_1|...|Q_{i-1}|Q_{i+1}|...|Q_k}).$$

Because $C \in \Pi(\approx^n)$, $C_{P_1|...|P_{i-1}|P_{i+1}|...|P_k}$ and $C_{Q_1|...|Q_{i-1}|Q_{i+1}|...|Q_k}$ contain only processes with at most $n-1$ occurrences of $|$, for any i. And because $P_1|...|P_{i-1}|P_{i+1}|...|P_k \sim^{n-1} Q_1|...|Q_{i-1}|Q_{i+1}|...|Q_k$, we obtain

$$C_{P_1|...|P_{i-1}|P_{i+1}|...|P_k} = C_{Q_1|...|Q_{i-1}|Q_{i+1}|...|Q_k} \in \Pi(\sim^{n-1}).$$

Further, using the fact that $\sim^{n-1}$ is a rate bisimulation, we obtain

$$\mu(\alpha)(C_{P_1|...|P_{i-1}|P_{i+1}|...|P_k}) = \eta(\alpha)(C_{Q_1|...|Q_{i-1}|Q_{i+1}|...|Q_k})$$

that implies $\mu(\alpha)(C) = \eta(\alpha)(C)$.

A similar argument proves the case $\alpha = \tau$. Consequently, $\approx^n$ is a rate-bisimulation.

Returning to our lemma, suppose that P and Q are two processes with non-trivial forms such that $P \sim Q$. Then, there exists $n \in \mathbb{N}$ such that $P \sim^n Q$. Suppose that $R \in \mathbb{S}^m$ for some $m \in \mathbb{N}$. Then $P \sim^{m+n-1} Q$ and $R \sim^{m+n-1} R$ implying $P|R \approx^{m+n} Q|R$. Because $\approx^{m+n}$ is a rate-bisimulation, we obtain that $P|R \sim Q|R$.

If P, Q or R (or some of them) have "trivial forms", then there exist $P' \equiv P$, $Q' \equiv Q$ and $R' \equiv R$ with non-trivial forms. And because the bisimulation is an equivalence that extends the structural congruence, we obtain the desired result also for the general case.

5. Replication: We use the same proof strategy as for the parallel composition. We say that a process is in canonic form if it contains no parallel composition of replicated subprocesses and no replicated process from the class $0^{\equiv}$. In other words, $!(P|Q)$ is in canonic form while $!P|!Q$ and $!(P|Q)|!!0$ are not; using the structural congruence rules, we can associate to each process P a structural congruent process with a canonic form called a canonic representative for P. Notice also that all the canonic representatives of a given process have the same number of occurrences of the operator "!". Let $\mathbb{S}_*$ be the set of process terms with canonic form. Observe that because structural congruence is a subset of bisimulation, it is sufficient to prove our lemma only for processes in $\mathbb{S}_*$.

As before, let $\mathbb{S}_*^n$ be the set of processes (in canonic form) with no more than n occurrences of the operator "!". Let $\sim^n$ be the stochastic bisimulation on $\mathbb{S}_*^n$ and $\approx^n \subseteq \mathbb{S}_*^n \times \mathbb{S}_*^n$ defined by

$$\approx^n = \sim^{n-1} \cup \{(!P, !Q) \mid P \sim^{n-1} Q\}.$$

We firstly show, inductively on n, that $\approx^n$ is a rate-bisimulation. Consider two arbitrary processes P and Q such that $P \approx^n Q$. We prove that if $E \vdash P \to \mu$ and $E \vdash Q \to \eta$, then for arbitrary $\alpha \in \mathbb{A}^+$ and $C \in \Pi(\approx^n)$, $\mu(\alpha)(C) = \eta(\alpha)(C)$.

Observe that if $P \approx^n Q$, then either $P \sim^{n-1} Q$, or $P \equiv !R$ and $Q \equiv !S$ with $R \sim^{n-1} S$. In the first case the equality is trivially true. In the other case, suppose that $E \vdash R \to \mu'$ and $E \vdash S \to \eta'$. Then, $\mu = \mu'_{!R}$ and $\eta = \eta'_{!S}$. We have

$$\mu(\alpha)(C) = \mu'(\alpha)(C_{!R}), \qquad \eta(\alpha)(C) = \eta'(\alpha)(C_{!S}).$$

We prove that $C_{!R} = C_{!S}$. Let $U \in C_{!R}$. Then, $U|!R \in C$ and from the construction of $C \in \Pi(\approx^n)$, we obtain that there exists $T \in \mathbb{S}_*^{n-1}$ such that $U = !T$. Because $!R|!T \in C$, $!(R|T) \in C$. Now, from $R \sim^{n-1} S$ we obtain $R \sim S$ and because $T \sim T$, the case of parallel operator that we have proved guarantees that $R|T \sim S|T$. But the canonic representatives V, W of $R|T$ and $S|T$ respectively are in $\mathbb{S}_*^{n-1}$ meaning that $V \sim^{n-1} W$. The construction of $\approx^n$ guarantees further that $!V \approx^n !W$ and because $W \equiv S|T$ we obtain $!(S|T) \in C$ and $U \equiv !T \in C_{!S}$.

Because $C_{!R} = C_{!S}$ and $\mu'(\alpha)(C_{!R}) = \eta'(\alpha)(C_{!S})$ (this is implied by $R \sim^{n-1} S$), then $\mu(\alpha)(C) = \eta(\alpha)(C)$.

A Clock-Based Framework for Construction of Hybrid Systems

He Jifeng

Shanghai Key Laboratory of Trustworthy Computing
East China Normal University, China

Abstract. Hybrid systems are composed by continuous physical component and discrete control component where the system state evolves over time according to interacting law of discrete and continuous dynamics. Combinations of computation and control can lead to very complicated system designs. Rather than address the formal verification of hybrid systems, this paper forcuses on general modelers, aimed at modelling hybrid dynamics in such a way one can extract the specification of the control component from the specification of the total system and the desire behaviour of the physical component. We treat more explicit hybrid models by providing a mathematical framework based on clock and synchronous signal. This paper presents an abstract concept of *clock* with two suitable metric spaces for description of temporal order and time latency, and links clocks with synchronous events by showing how to represent the occurrences of an event by a clock. We tackle discrete variables by giving them a clock-based representation, and show how to capture dynamical behaviours of continuous components by recording the time instants when a specific type of changes take place. This paper introduces a clock-based hybrid language for description and reasoning of both discrete and continuous dynamics, and applies it to a family of physical devices, and demonstrates how to specify a water tanker and construct and verify its controller based on clocks.

1 Introduction

Hybrid systems is an emergent area of growing importance, emphasising a systematic understanding of dynamic systems that combine digital and physical effects. Combinations of computation and control can lead to very complicated system designs. They occur frequently in automotive industries, aviation, factory automation and mixed analog-digital chip design.

Hybrid systems are composed by continuous physical component and discrete control component where the system state evolves over time according to interacting law of discrete and continuous dynamics. For discrete dynamics, the hybrid system changes state instantaneously and discontinuously. During continuous transitions, the system state is a continuous function of continuous time and varies according to a differential equation. Hybrid system modelers mix discrete time reactive systems with continuous time ones. Systems like Simulink

Z. Liu, J. Woodcock, and H. Zhu (Eds.): ICTAC 2013, LNCS 8049, pp. 22–41, 2013.

treat explicit models made of Ordinary Differential Equations, while others, like Modelica provide more general implicit models defined by Differential Algebraic Equations. For hybrid systems a variety of models have been developed, among them , hybrid automata [2,13,29], phase transition system [19], declarative control [16], extended state-transition system [30], and hybrid action systems [25]. We refer the reader to [8] for an overview of languages and tools related to hybrid systems modeling and analysis.

Hybrid systems are notoriously hard to analyse and verify. As a standard verification technique, model checking [9,24] has been used successfully for verifying temporal logic properties of finite-state abstraction of automata transition systems by exhaustive state space exploration. Because the continuous state space of hybrid systems does not admit equivalent finite-state abstraction, model checkers for hybrid automata use various approximations. However, the standard model checking approaches cannot be used to treat nonlinear dynamics in the discrete transitions and the approximations in the continuous dynamics. An alternative is to use a combination of decision procedures for real arithmetic and interactive theorem proving. [21] proposes a logic called Differential Dynamic Logic for specifying properties of hybrid systems, and develops a powerful verification tool for reasoning about complex hybrid systems.

Rather than address the formal verification of hybrid systems, this paper forcuses on general modelers, aimed at modelling hybrid dynamics in such a way one can extract the specification of the control component from the specification of the total system and the desire behaviour of the physical component. We treat more explicit hybrid models by providing a mathematical framework based on clock and synchronous signal [6], and organise this paper in the following way:

- In Section 2, we present an abstract concept of *clock* with two suitable metric spaces for description of temporal order and time latency, and link clocks with synchronous events by showing how to represent the occurrences of an event by a clock.
- Section 3 provides a set of operations on clocks used for description of discrete dynamics, and explores their algebraic properties.
- Section 4 discusses the notion of *location*, and treat a *local clock* as the combination of a clock with its residence. It also introduces temporal order and time latency, based on the metrics defined on clocks, to local clocks residing in different locations, and illustrates how to specify time delay in the distributed systems using local clocks. We close Section 4 by formalising *global clock* as the equivalent class of local clocks.
- In Section 5, we tackle discrete variables by giving them a clock-based representation, and show how to capture dynamical behaviours of continuous components by recording the time instants when a specific type of changes take place.
- Section 6 introduces a clock-based hybrid language for description and reasoning of both discrete and continuous dynamics.
- Section 7 applies the specification mechanism introduced in Section 6 to a family of physical devices, and demonstrates how to specify a water tanker and construct and verify its controller based on clocks.

2 Clock

A clock c is an increasing sequence of non-negative reals. We use the notation $\mathbf{Set}(c)$ to denote the set of all elements of c, and its low and high rates $\triangle(c)$ and $\nabla(c)$ by

$$\triangle(c) =_{df} \mathbf{inf}\{(c[i+1] - c[i]) \mid i \in Nat\}$$

$$\nabla(c) =_{df} \mathbf{sup}\{(c[i+1] - c[i]) \mid i \in Nat\}$$

c is called a periodic clock when $\triangle(c) = \nabla(c)$.

Definition 2.1 (Healthy clock)

c is a *healthy clock* if it does not speed up infinitely, i.e.,

$$\triangle(c) > 0$$

Lemma 2.2 If c is infinite and healthy then $\mathbf{lim}_{i \leftarrow \infty} c[i] \ = \infty$.

Definition 2.3 (Partial order on clocks)

Clock c is *finer* than clock d if d is a *sub-sequence* of c

$$\mathbf{Set}(d) \subseteq \mathbf{Set}(c)$$

We record this fact by $c \sqsupseteq d$.

Lemma 2.4
$\sqsupseteq$ is a partial order on clocks.

Definition 2.5 (Least upper bounds)

Let c and d be clocks. We define $c \parallel d$ as the least bound of c and d with respect the partial order $\sqsupseteq$.

Lemma 2.6 $\mathbf{Set}(c \parallel d) \ = \ \mathbf{Set}(c) \cup \mathbf{Set}(d)$

Definition 2.7

c runs faster than d if for all $i \in Nat$

$$c[i] \leq d[i]$$

We denote this by $c \preceq d$.

Lemma 2.8 $\preceq$ is a partial order on clocks.

Definition 2.9 (Metric Space of Clocks)

Let c and d be clocks. Define

$$\rho(c, d) \ =_{df} \ \mathbf{sup}\,\{\|c[i] - d[i]\| \mid i \in Nat\}$$

ρ is a metric on the set of clocks.

Theorem 2.10

(1) $\rho(c, d) \geq 0$
(2) $\rho(c, d) = 0$ iff $c = d$
(3) $\rho(c, d) = \rho(d, c)$
(4) $\rho(c, e) \leq \rho(c, d) + \rho(d, e)$

Example 2.11 (Time properties of a buffer)

Let c and d be clocks recording time instants when the input and output of a buffer occur respectively. Because the output is always preceded by the corresponding input, the buffer is subject to the following law.

$$c \preceq d$$

Furthermore, its transmission latency can be specified by $\rho(c, d)$.

Example 2.12 (Event vs Clock)

Let e be an event. We will use the notation **clock**(e) to denote the clock that records the time instants when the event e occurs.

Let c be a clock. We will use the notation **event**(c) to denote the event whose occurrence are recorded by clock c, where we neglect the name of the corresponding event for convenience. Clearly we have

$$\mathbf{clock}(\mathbf{event}(c)) = c$$

3 Clock Operations

Definition 3.1 (Projection)

Let c be a clock, and $P(i)$ a predicate with the integer variable i. The notation $P \lhd c$ denotes the clock defined by

$$\mathbf{Set}(P \lhd c) =_{df} \{c[i] \mid i \in Nat \wedge P(i)\}$$

Example 3.2

(1) $Hour = \mathbf{dividable}(i, 60) \lhd Minute$

where $\mathbf{dividable}(i, 60) =_{df} \exists n : Nat \bullet (i = 60 \times n)$

and $Minute =_{df} Nat$.

(2) Clock $c' = < c[1], .., c[n], .. >$ can be rewritten as $(i > 0) \lhd c$

Lemma 3.3 The projection operator preserves the clock healthiness property.

Proof. Direct from $\Delta(c) \leq \Delta(P \lhd c)$.

The projection operator satisfies the following properties

Theorem 3.4

(1) $true \lhd c = c$

(2) $(P \vee Q) \lhd c \;=\; (P \lhd c \parallel Q \lhd c)$

(3) $c \preceq d$ implies $P \lhd c \;\preceq\; P \preceq d$

(4) $P \lhd c \;\sqsupseteq\; (P \vee Q) \lhd c$

Definition 3.5 (Filter)

Let c be a clock, and $R(x)$ a predicate where variable x ranges over non-negative reals. The notation $c \rhd R$ denotes the clock, defined by

$$\mathbf{Set}(c \rhd R) \;=_{df}\; \{c[i] \mid i \in Nat \wedge R(c[i])\}$$

From the above definition it follows that the filter operator can be redefined by the projection operator:

Theorem 3.6 (Filer vs Projection)

$(c \rhd R) \;=\; (R \circ c) \lhd c$

Lemma 3.7. The filter operator preserves the clock healthiness property.

Proof. From Lemma 3.3 and Theorem 3.6.

The filter operator $\rhd$ satisfies the following properties.

Theorem 3.8

(1) $c \rhd true \;=\; c$

(2) $(c \rhd R) \rhd S \;=\; c \rhd (R \wedge S)$

(3) $c \to (R \vee S) \;=\; (c \to R) \parallel (c \rhd S)$

(4) $(c \parallel d) \rhd R \;=\; (c \rhd R) \parallel (d \rhd R)$

(5) $c \sqsupseteq d$ implies $(c \rhd R) \sqsupseteq (d \rhd R)$

(6) $c \rhd R \;\sqsupseteq\; c \rhd (R \vee S)$

Definition 3.9 (Shift)

Let c be a clock and r a non-negative real number. The notation $r >> c$ represents the clock defined by

$$\mathbf{Set}(r >> c) \;=_{df}\; \{c[i] + r \mid i \in Nat\}$$

Lemma 3.10. The shift operator preserves the clock healthiness property.

Proof. From the fact that $\triangle(r >> c) = \triangle(c)$

The shift operator satisfies the following properties

Theorem 3.11

(1) $0 >> c \;=\; c$

(2) $r1 >> (r2 >> c) \;=\; (r1 + r2) >> c$

(3) $r >> (c \parallel d) \;=\; (r >> c) \parallel (r >> d)$

(4) $P \lhd (r >> c) \;=\; r >> (P \lhd c)$

(5) $(r >> c) \rhd R(x)) \;=\; r >> (c \rhd R(x + r))$

(6) $c \sqsupseteq d$ implies $r >> c \sqsupseteq r >> d$

(7) $c \preceq d$ implies $r >> c \preceq r >> d$

Definition 3.12 (Intersect)

Let c and d be clocks, and $P(i)$ a predicate on integer variable i. The notation $c \overset{P}{\hookleftarrow} d$ denotes the clock defined by

$$c \overset{P}{\hookleftarrow} d \;=_{df}\; ((i < k) \lhd c) \parallel (c[k-1] >> d)$$

where $k \;=_{df}\; \mathbf{Min}\{i \mid i \in Nat \wedge \neg P(i)\}$, and $c[-1] \;=_{df}\; 0$.

Lemma 3.13
If both c and d are healthy, then $c \overset{P}{\hookleftarrow} d$ is also healthy.

Proof. From the fact that $\triangle(c \overset{P}{\hookleftarrow} d \geq \mathbf{min}(\triangle(c), \triangle(d))$

Theorem 3.14

(1) $c \overset{true}{\hookleftarrow} d \;=\; c$

(2) $c \overset{false}{\hookleftarrow} d \;=\; d$

(3) $c \overset{i \leq n}{\hookleftarrow} d \;=\; (\{i \leq n\} \lhd c) \cdot (c[n] >> d)$

(4) $c \overset{P}{\hookleftarrow} (d \parallel e) \;=\; (c \overset{P}{\hookleftarrow} d) \parallel (c \overset{P}{\hookleftarrow} e)$

(5) $r >> (c \overset{P}{\hookleftarrow} d) \;=\; (r >> c) \overset{P}{\hookleftarrow} d$

Definition 3.15 (Interrupt)

Let c and d be clocks, and $R(x)$ a predicate on real-value variable x. The notation $c \overset{R}{\hookrightarrow} d$ represents the clock defined by

$$c \overset{R}{\hookrightarrow} d =_{df} (i < k) \lhd c \parallel (c[k-1] >> d)$$

where $k \;=_{df}\; \mathbf{Min}\{i \mid i \in Nat \wedge \neg R(c[i])\}$.

Theorem 3.16 (Link between Intersect and Interrupt)

$c \overset{R}{\hookrightarrow} d \;=\; c \overset{R(c[i])}{\hookleftarrow} d$

Lemma 3.17. If both c and d are healthy, then $c \overset{R}{\hookrightarrow} d$ is also healthy.

The interrupt operator satisfies the following properties

Theorem 3.18

(1) $c \overset{true}{\hookrightarrow} d \;=\; c$

(2) $c \overset{false}{\hookrightarrow} d \;=\; d$

(3) $c \overset{x \leq c[n]}{\hookrightarrow} d \;=\; c \rhd \{x \leq c[n]\} \cdot (c[n+1] >> d)$

(4) $c \overset{R}{\hookrightarrow} (d \parallel e) \;=\; (c \overset{R}{\hookrightarrow} d) \parallel (c \overset{R}{\hookrightarrow} e)$

(5) $r >> (c \overset{R}{\hookrightarrow} d) \;=\; (r >> c) \overset{R}{\hookrightarrow} d$

4 Local Clock and Global Clock

Definition 4.1 (Local Clock)

Let l be a label denoting a *location*, and c a clock. The notation

$$l : c$$

represents the clock c that locates at location l.

We are going to extend the definitions of $\sqsupseteq$, $\preceq$ and ρ to local clocks at the same location as follows:

$$l : c \sqsupseteq l : d =_{df} (c \sqsupseteq d)$$
$$l : c \preceq l : d =_{df} (c \preceq d)$$
$$\rho(l : c,\ l : d) =_{df} \rho(c,\ d)$$

Definition 4.2 (Time Lag)

For locations l_1 and l_2, we use

$$\delta_t(l_1,\ l_2)$$

to denote the *time lag* between l_1 and l_2, which is solely captured by the following law:

Law $\delta_t(l_1,\ l_3) \;=\; \delta_t(l_1,\ l_2) \;+\; \delta_t(l_2,\ l_3)$

Corollary 4.3 (1) $\delta_t(l,\ l) \;=\; 0$

(2) $\delta_t(l_1,\ l_2) \;=\; -\delta_t(l_2,\ l_1)$

Proof. By setting $l_1 \;=\; l_2 \;=\; l_3 \;=\; l$ we obtain (1) from the above law. The conclusion (2) follows from the fact

$$\delta_t(l_1,\ l_2) + \delta_t(l_2,\ l_1) \;=\; \delta_t(l_1,\ l_1) \;=\; 0$$

Definition 4.4 (Counterpart)

Let $l : c$ be a clock, and $\hat{l}$ a location. The notation $\hat{l} : (l : c)$ stands for the *counterpart* of the local clock $l : c$ at the location $\hat{l}$:

$$\hat{l} : (l : c) \;=_{df}\; \hat{l} : (\delta_t(l,\ \hat{l}) >> c)$$

Theorem 4.5

(1) $l : (l : c) \;=\; l : c$

(2) $l_1 : (l_2 : (l_3 : c)) \;=\; l_1 : (l_3 : c)$

Proof (1) comes from Theorem 3.11(1) and Corollary 4.3. (2) follows from **Law** of the time lag function.

Definition 4.6 (Metric Space of Local Clocks)

Define $\rho(l_1 : c_1,\ l_2 : c_2) \;=_{df}\; \rho(l_2 : (l_1 : c_1),\ l_2 : c_2)$. We are going to show that ρ is a metric function on local clocks.

Theorem 4.7

(1) $\rho(l_1 : c_1,\ l_2 : c_2) \;=\; \rho(l_2 : c_2,\ l_1 : c_1)$

(2) $\rho(l_1 : c_1,\ l_3 : c_3) \le \rho(l_1 : c_1,\ l_2 : c_2) + \rho(l_2 : c_2,\ l_3 : c_3)$

(3) $\rho(l : c,\ \hat{l} : (l : c)) \;=\; 0$

Proof of (1) LHS {Def 4.6}

$= \rho(l_2 : (\delta_t(l_1, l_2) >> c_1),\ l_2 : c_2)$ {Def 4.1}

$= \rho(\delta_t(l_1, l_2) >> c_1,\ c_2)$ {Def of 2.9}

$= \rho(c_1,\ -\delta_t(l_1, l_2) >> c_2)$ {Theorem 2.10(3)}

$= \rho(-\delta_t(l_1, l_2) >> c_2,\ c_1)$ {Corollary 4.3(1)}

$= \rho(\delta_t(l_2, l_1) >> c_2,\ c_1)$ {Def 4.6}

$= RHS$

Proof of (2) LHS {Def 4.6}

$= \rho(\delta_t(l_1, l_3) >> c_1,\ c_3)$ {Law of Def 4.2}

$= \rho((\delta_t(l_1, l_2) + \delta_t(l_2, l_3)) >> c_1,\ c_3)$ {Def 2.9}

$= \rho(\delta_t(l_1, l_2) >> c_1,\ -\delta_t(l_2, l_3) >> c_3)$ {*Theorem* 2.10(4)}

$\le \rho(\delta_t(l_1, l_2) >> c_1,\ c_2) + \rho(c_2,\ -\delta_t(l_2, l_3) >> c_3)$ {Def 3.9}

$= \rho(\delta_t(l_1, l_2) >> c_1,\ c_2) + \rho(\delta_t(l_2, l_3) >> c_2,\ c_3)$ {Def 4.6}

$= RHS$

Proof of (3) LHS {Def 4.4}

$= \rho(l : c,\ \hat{l} : (\delta_t(l, \hat{l}) >> c))$ {Def 4.6}

$= \rho(\hat{l} : (l : c),\ \hat{l} : (\delta_t(l, \hat{l}) >> c))$ {Def 4.4}

$= \rho(\hat{l} : (\delta_t(l, \hat{l}) >> c),\ \hat{l} : (\delta_t(l, \hat{l}) >> c))$ {Def 4.1}

$= \rho((\delta_t(l, \hat{l}) >> c),\ (\delta_t(l, \hat{l}) >> c))$ {Theorem 2.10(2)}

$= RHS$

Definition 4.8 (Partial order on local clocks)
Define

$$l_1 : c_1 \sqsupseteq l_2 : c_2 =_{df} l_2 : (l_1 : c_1) \sqsupseteq l_2 : c_2$$
$$l_1 : c_1 \preceq l_2 : c_2 =_{df} l_2 : (l_1 : c_1) \preceq l_2 : c_2$$

Theorem 4.9

(1) $l_2 : (l_1 : c_1) \sqsupseteq l_2 : c_2$ iff $l_1 : c_1 \sqsupseteq l_1 : (l_2 : c_2)$

(2) $l_2 : (l_1 : c_1) \preceq l_2 : c_2$ iff $l_1 : c_1 \preceq l_1 : (l_2 : c_2)$

Proof of (1) LHS {Def 4.8}

$\equiv \quad l_2 : (l_1 : c_1) \sqsupseteq l_2 : c_2$ {Def 4.4}

$\equiv \quad l_2 : (\delta(l_1, l_2) >> c_1) \sqsupseteq l_2 : c_2$ {Def 4.1}

$\equiv \quad \delta(l_1, l_2) >> c_1 \sqsupseteq c_2$ {Def 2.7}

$\equiv \quad c_1 \sqsupseteq -\delta(l_1, l_2) >> c_2$ {Corollary 4.3(1)}

$\equiv \quad c_1 \sqsupseteq \delta(l_2, l_1) >> c_2$ {Def 4.1}

$\equiv \quad l_1 : c_1 \sqsupseteq l_1 : (\delta(l_2, l_1) >> c_2)$ {Def 4.4}

$\equiv \quad RHS$

Example 4.10

Assume that *ch* is a channel used to link locations l_1 and l_2. Suppose that $l_1 : c_1$ and $l_2 : c_2$ are local clocks that record the input events at location l_1 and the corresponding output events at location l_2. Clearly

$$(l_1 : c_1) \preceq (l_2 : c_2)$$

The latency of the channel *ch* is defined by

$$\rho(l_1 : c_1,\ l_2 : c_2)$$

Definition 4.11 (Equivalence)

We introduce the binary relation $\sim$ between local clocks as follows:

$$(l_1 : c_1) \sim (l_2 : c_2) =_{df} \rho(l_1 : c_1,\ l_2 : c_2) = 0$$

Lemma 4.12

$l_1 : c_1 \sim l_2 : c_2$ iff $c_2 = \delta_t(l_1, l_2) >> c_1$

Proof. From Definition 4.4 and 4.6.

Theorem 4.13

$\sim$ is an equivalent relation on local clocks.

Proof

$l_1 : c_1 \sim l_2 : c_2$ {Lemma 4.12}

$\equiv c_2 = \delta_t(l_1, l_2) >> c_1$ {Corollary 4.3(1)}

$\equiv c_2 = -\delta_t(l_2, l_1) >> c_1$ {Def 3.9}

$\equiv c_1 = \delta(l_2, l_1) >> c_2$ {Lemma 4.12}

$\equiv l_2 : c_2 \sim l_1 : c_1$

$(l_1 : c_1 \sim l_2 : c_2) \wedge (l_2 : c_2 \sim l_3 : c_3)$ {Lemma 4.12}

$\equiv c_2 = \delta_t(l_1, l_2) >> c_1 \wedge c_3 = \delta_t(l_2, l_3) >> c_2$ {Theorem 3.11(2)}

$\Rightarrow c_3 = (\delta_t(l_1, l_2) + \delta_t(l_2, l_3)) >> c_1$ {Law of Def 4.2}

$\equiv c_3 = \delta_t(l_1, l_3) >> c_1$ {Lemma 4.12}

$\equiv l_1 : c_1 \sim l_3 : c_3$

Theorem 4.14

(1) $\sim; \sqsupseteq \ = \ \sqsupseteq \ = \ \sqsupseteq; \sim$

(2) $\sim; \preceq \ = \ \preceq \ = \ \preceq; \sim$

Definition 4.15 (Global Clock)

A global clock $[l : c]$ is defined as an equivalent class of local clocks:

$$[l : c] =_{df} \{\hat{l} : d \mid (l : c) \sim (\hat{l} : d)\}$$

Define

$$[l_1 : c_1] \sqsupseteq [l_2 : c_2] =_{df} l_1 : c_1 \sqsupseteq l_2 : c_2$$

$$[l_1 : c_1] \preceq [l_2 : c_2] =_{df} l_1 : c_1 \preceq l_2 : c_2$$

From Theorem 3.14 it follows that both $\sqsupseteq$ and $\preceq$ are well-defined.

Definition 4.16 (Metric space of global clocks)

We define

$$\rho([l_1 : c_1], [l_2 : c_2]) =_{df} \rho(l_1 : c_1, l_2 : c_2)$$

Lemma 4.17 ρ is well-defined.

Proof. Assume that $l_1 : c_1 \sim \hat{l} : d$.

$\rho([\hat{l} : d], [l_2 : c_2])$ {Def 4.16}

$= \rho(\hat{l} : d, l_2 : c_2)$ {Theorem 4.7(2)}

$\leq \rho(\hat{l} : d, l_1 : c_1) + \rho(l_1 : c_1, l_2 : c_2)$ {Def 4.11}

$= \rho(l_1 : c_1, l_2 : c_2)$ {Def 4.16}

$= \rho([l_1 : c_1], [l_2 : c_2]$

From the symmetry of $\sim$ we can show

$$\rho([l_1 : c_1], [l_2 : c_2]) \leq \rho([\hat{l} : d], [l_2 : c_2])$$

as required.

Theorem 4.18

ρ is a metric function on global clocks.

Proof. From Definition 4.16 and Theorem 4.7.

5 Discrete Variable

Definition 5.1 (Discrete Variable)

x is a *discrete variable* if there exists a *healthy* clock c with $c[0] = 0$ such that x keeps constant over every interval $[c[i],\ c[i+1]]$.

We introduce the clock **change**(x) to record the time instants when the value of x changes

$$\mathbf{change}(x) \;=\; \{t \mid t = 0 \vee (x(t-0) \neq x(t))\}$$

where $x(t-0)$ is defined as the left limit of x at the time instant t

$$x(t-0) \;=_{df}\; \mathbf{lim}_{\delta \to 0} x(t-\delta)$$

Example 5.2

Let b be a Boolean expression. We introduce two clocks to describe its rising edge and falling edge respectively

$$\mathbf{rising}(b) =_{df} \{t \mid \neg b(t-0) \wedge b(t)\}$$

$$\mathbf{falling}(b) =_{df} \mathbf{rising}(\neg b)$$

For simplicity we set $b(0-0) \;=_{df}\; \neg b(0)$.

Clock **rising** and **falling** can be used to describe the dynamic feature of continuous functions.

Example 5.3

Consider a continuous function f and set

$$\mathbf{climb}(f,\ r) =_{df} \mathbf{rising}(f \geq r)$$

$$\mathbf{drop}(f,\ r) =_{df} \mathbf{falling}(f \leq r)$$

$$\mathbf{cross}(f,\ r) =_{df} (\mathbf{climb}(f,\ r) \;\|\; \mathbf{drop}(f,\ r))$$

Definition 5.4 (Specification of Discrete Variables)

Let c be a clock, and s a sequence of reals with the same length as c. The pair $(c,\ s)$ defines a discrete variable x where for all $n \in Nat$

$$x(t) \;=\; s[n] \qquad\qquad \text{whenever } t \in [c[n],\ c[n+1])$$

Specially, $(c,\ s)$ is a canonical form if $s[n] \neq s[n+1]$ for all $n \in Nat$.

Example 5.5 (Deriving canonical specification)

Let x be a discrete variable, and set

$$c_x =_{df} \mathbf{change}(x)$$

$$s_x =_{df} x \circ c_x$$

Clearly (c_x, s_x) is a canonical specification of x.

A specification (c, s) can be converted to a canonical form in the following way. Set

$$P(i) =_{df} i = 0 \vee (s[i-1] \neq s[i])$$

and define

$$c' =_{df} P \lhd c$$
$$s' =_{df} P \lhd s$$

It is easy to show that (c', s') is a canonical form. We use the notation $\textbf{cano}(c, s)$ to represent the above canonical specification (c', s').

Example 5.6 (Sampling a continuous function)

Let c be a clock with $c[0] = 0$ and f a continuous function. The notation $f(c)$ represents the discrete variable specification $(c, f \circ c)$.

Example 5.7 (Time shifting)

Let x be a discrete variable, and r a non-negative real. The notation $r >> x$ represents the discrete variable that has the behaviour as x except that its clock is the shift of c_x:

$$(r >> x) =_{df} (< 0 > \cdot (r >> c_x), s_x)$$

Example 5.8 (Lift of operators of reals)

Let op be a binary operator of reals. Define its lift on discrete variables x and y by

$$x \, op \, y =_{df} \textbf{cano}(c, s)$$

where $c =_{df} c_x \| c_y$, and

$$s[n] =_{df} \begin{cases} s_x[i] \, op \, s_y[j] & if \; c[n] = c_x[i] \wedge \\ & \quad c_y[j] \leq c[n] < c_y[j+1] \\ s_x[j] \, op \, s_y[i] & if \; c[n] = c_y[i] \wedge \\ & \quad c_x[j] \leq c[n] < c_x[j+1] \end{cases}$$

6 Modeling Mechanism

Definition 6.1 (Assign Discrete Expressions to Discrete Variables)

Let x be a discrete variable, and e a discrete expression. The equation

$$x = e$$

generates the canonical specification (c_e, s_e) for x.

Example 6.2

Let x be a discrete variable, and u a continuous variable. Assume that c is a clock with $c[0] = 0$. The equation

$$x = u(c)$$

samples the value of u at every time instant of clock c, and generates the following canonical specification for x

$$\mathbf{cano}(c,\ u \circ c)$$

Definition 6.3 (Ordinary Differential Equations)

Let u be a continuous variable, and f a continuous function. The equation

$$\dot{u} = f\ \mathbf{init}\, a$$

specifies the following relation between u and f

$$\forall t \bullet (\dot{u} = f) \wedge (u(0) = a)$$

Definition 6.4 (Update the Boundary Values)

Let y be a discrete variable. The equation

$$\dot{u} = f\ \mathbf{reset}\ y$$

enables us to modify the boundary value of continuous variable u by assigning $s_y[n]$ to u at the time instant $c_y[n]$. The equation specifies the following relation between u and y:

$$\bigwedge_n (\dot{u} =_{I_n} f) \wedge u(c_y) = s_y$$

where $I_n =_{df} [c_y[n],\ c_y[n+1])$ and

$$(u =_I v) =_{df} \forall t \in I \bullet (u(t) = v(t))$$

7 Examples

7.1 Buffer

Let *in* and *out* represent the input and output events of a buffer. A timing specification of the buffer is

$$\mathbf{clock}(in) \preceq \mathbf{clock}(out)$$

We can add the following constraint to specify the transmission latency

$$\rho(\mathbf{clock}(in),\ \mathbf{clock}(out)) \leq l$$

Another specification is deterministic which treats *in* and *out* as discrete variables, and uses the following assignment to link *out* with *in*:

$$out = (l >> in)$$

7.2 Sensor

An *active* sensor reads the state of its environment periodically. Its behaviour can be specified by the assignment

$$out = r >> u(c) \qquad \text{where}$$

1. out a discrete variable denoting the output of the sensor
2. u a continuous variable representing the environment
3. c a *prior fixed* periodical clock specifying the sampling rate of the sensor
4. r a positive real denoting the sampling delay.

A *passive* sensor is used to monitor the *change* of its environment, where we assume that the state of the environment can be modelled by a discrete variable. In this case, the sensor is ignited only when the discrete variable changes its value.

$$out = r >> in$$

where in is a discrete variable representing its environment.

Another type of *passive* sensors can be specified by the following assignment

$$out = r >> in(c)$$

where in is a continuous variable representing the environment, and c is a clock describing some *dynamic feature* of in such as $\mathbf{climb}(in, 40)$ and $\mathbf{falling}(in, -10)$.

7.3 Actuator

An actuator with in and out as its ports can be specified by

$$out = r >> f(in)$$

where

1. both in and out are discrete variables, and
2. r represents the transmission delay satisfying
$$r < \Delta(c_{in})$$
3. f is a function which maps input received from the port in to output delivered to the port out

If we model in and out as events, then the specification of an actuator can be

$$\begin{aligned}\mathbf{clock}(in) \preceq \mathbf{clock}(out) \preceq \mathbf{clock}(in)' \wedge \\ \rho(\mathbf{clock}(in), \mathbf{clock}(out)) \leq r \wedge \\ \mathbf{message}(out) = f(\mathbf{message}(in))\end{aligned}$$

7.4 Water Tank Controller

The system is used to control the water level h in a tank by switching a control valve. The goal is to keep the water level between L and H units.

(Req_1) $L \leq h \leq H$

Suppose that the valve is *open* initially, and the water level is h_{init} unit, and rising at constant speed a. Once the valve is *closed*, the water level will drop at speed b until the valve is reopened. In this case, the status of the control valve can simply be captured by the Boolean expression $valve = open$ because it only takes either *open* or *closed* as its value. Define

$$\mathbf{clock}(on) =_{df} \mathbf{rising}(valve = open)$$

$$\mathbf{clock}(off) =_{df} \mathbf{falling}(valve = open)$$

Clearly $\mathbf{clock}(on)$ and $\mathbf{clock}(off)$ are required to meet the following conditions:

(Req_2) $\mathbf{clock}(on) \preceq \mathbf{clock}(off) \preceq \mathbf{clock}(on)'$

(Req_3) $\mathbf{clock}(off) \cap \mathbf{clock}(on) = \emptyset$

We introduce a discrete variable x to model the current speed at which the water level changes, which has a as its initial value, and then changes its value from a to $-b$ once the valve is closed, and switches back to a when the valve is reopened:

$$x =_{df} (\mathbf{clock}(on) \| \mathbf{clock}(off), (< a >< -b >)^*)$$

The behaviour of the water tank is described by the following equation

(Eq_1) $\dot{h} = x$ **init** h_{init}

Now we are asked to design $\mathbf{clock}(on)$ and $\mathbf{clock}(off)$ to meet three requirements listed before.

Design 1

Let $\epsilon < \mathbf{min}(H - h_{init}, h_{init} - L)$.

Lemma 7.1. $H - \epsilon > h_{init} > L + \epsilon$

Proof. From the assumption $\epsilon < \mathbf{min}(H - h_{init}, h_{init} - L)$

We choose $\mathbf{clock}(on)$ and $\mathbf{clock}(off)$ to satisfy the following conditions:

(1) $\mathbf{climb}(h, H - \epsilon) \preceq \mathbf{clock}(off)$

(2) $\mathbf{clock}(off) \preceq (\epsilon/a >> \mathbf{climb}(h, H - \epsilon))$

(3) $\mathbf{drop}(h, L + \epsilon) \preceq \mathbf{clock}(on)'$

(4) $\mathbf{clock}(on)' \preceq (\epsilon/b >> \mathbf{drop}(h, L + \epsilon))$

where the first two conditions ensure that the valve will be closed soon after the water level is higher than $H - \epsilon$, while the final two conditions indicate that the valve will be reopen if the water level is lower than $L + \epsilon$.

We are going to verify that the above design satisfies the requirements Req_1, Req_2 and Req_3.

Lemma 7.2. Over the interval $I =_{df} (\mathbf{clock}(on)[0], \mathbf{clock}(off)[0])$, $\dot{h} =_I a$, and

$$(H - \epsilon) \leq h(\mathbf{clock}(off)[0]) \leq H$$

Proof. Let $l = \mathbf{climb}(h, H-\epsilon)[0]$ and $r = \mathbf{clock}(off)[0]$. From the conditions (1) and (2) of $\mathbf{clock}(off)$ it follows that

$$l \leq r \leq l + (\epsilon/a) \qquad (*)$$

We have

$$\begin{array}{lll} & H - \epsilon & \{\text{Def of } \mathbf{climb}\} \\ = & h(l) & \{h \text{ is increasing on}[l, r]\} \\ \leq & h(r) & \{\text{Calculation}\} \\ = & h(c + (d - c)) & \{\text{Equation } (Eq_1)\} \\ = & h(l) + \int_l^r \dot{h}\, dt & \{\text{Def of } x\} \\ = & (H - \epsilon) + a \times (r - l) & \{\text{Conclusion } (*)\} \\ \leq & H & \end{array}$$

Lemma 7.3. $\dot{u} =_{I_n} -b$ over every interval $I_n =_{df} (\mathbf{clock}(off)[n], \mathbf{clock}(on)[n+1])$, and

$$(L + \epsilon) \geq h(\mathbf{clock}(on)[n+1]) \geq L$$

Proof. Let $l = \mathbf{drop}(h, H - \epsilon)[n]$ and $r = \mathbf{clock}(on)[n+1]$. We have

$$l \leq r \leq l + (\epsilon/b) \qquad (*)$$

from the conditions (3) and (4) of $\mathbf{clock}(on)$, and

$$\begin{array}{lll} & L + \epsilon & \{\text{Def of } \mathbf{drop}\} \\ = & h(l) & \{h \text{ is decreasing on } [l, r]\} \\ \geq & h(r) & \{\text{Calculation}\} \\ = & h(c + (d - c)) & \{\text{Equation } (Eq_1)\} \\ = & h(l) + \int_l^r \dot{h}\, dt & \{\text{Def of } x\} \\ = & (L + \epsilon) + -b \times (r - l) & \{\text{Conclusion } (ast)\} \\ \geq & L & \end{array}$$

Lemma 7.4. Over every interval $J_n =_{df} (\mathbf{clock}(on)[n], \mathbf{clock}(off)[n])$, $\dot{h} =_J a$, and

$$(H - \epsilon) \leq h(\mathbf{clock}(off)[n]) \leq H$$

Proof. Similar to **Lemma 7.3.**

Lemma 7.5. Clock $\mathbf{clock}(off) \| \mathbf{clock}(on)$ is healthy.

Proof. From the conditions (1)-(4) of **Design 1** and Lemma 7.2–7.4 it follows that for all $n \geq 1$

$$\begin{array}{lll} & (\mathbf{clock}(on)[n] - \mathbf{clock}(off)[n-1]) & \{\text{Condition } (1)-(4)\} \\ \geq & (\mathbf{drop}(h,\, L+\epsilon)[n-1] - \mathbf{climb}(h,\, H)[n]) & \{\text{Lemma 7.3}\} \\ \geq & (H-L-\epsilon)/b & \end{array}$$

and

$$\begin{array}{lll} & (\mathbf{clock}(off)[n] - \mathbf{clock}(on)[n]) & \{\text{Condition } (1)-(4)\} \\ \geq & (\mathbf{climb}(h,\, H-\epsilon)[n] - \mathbf{drop}(h,\, L)[n] & \{\text{Lemma 7.4}\} \\ \geq & (H-L-\epsilon)/a & \end{array}$$

Theorem 7.6 $\forall t \bullet (L \leq h(t) \leq H$

Proof. From **Lemma 7.2** we conclude that over $[\mathbf{clock}[0],\, \mathbf{clock}(off)[0])$

$$L \leq h(t) \leq M$$

holds. **Lemma 7.3** implies that

$$H \geq u(\mathbf{clock}(off)[n]) \geq h(t) \geq h(\mathbf{clock}(on)[n+1]) \geq L$$

holds over every interval $(\mathbf{clock}(off)[n],\, \mathbf{clock}(on)[n+1])$.
From Lemma **Lemma 7.4** we conclude that

$$L \leq u(\mathbf{clock}(on)[n]) \leq h(t) \leq h(\mathbf{clock}(off)[n]) \leq H$$

holds over every interval $(\mathbf{clock}(on)[n],\, \mathbf{clock}(off)[n])$.

The conclusion follows from **Lemma 7.1** and **Lemma 2.2**.

Design 2

We decide to divide the controller into a control unit with a sensor where the latter monitors the water level and sends the events *high* and *low* to the former.

We require that the sensor satisfies

$$\begin{array}{c} \mathbf{climb}(u,\, H-\epsilon) \preceq \mathbf{clock}(high) \wedge \\ \mathbf{clock}(high) \preceq \epsilon/(2a) >> \mathbf{climb}(u,\, H-\epsilon) \wedge \\ \mathbf{drop}(u,\, L+\epsilon) \preceq \mathbf{clock}(low) \wedge \\ \mathbf{clock}(low) \preceq \epsilon/(2b) >> \mathbf{drop}(u,\, L+\epsilon) \end{array}$$

The control unit sends the control command to the valve at the receipt of *high* and *low* from the sensor. It is required to satisfy

$$\begin{array}{c} \mathbf{clock}(high) \preceq \mathbf{clock}(off) \wedge \\ \mathbf{clock}(off)) \preceq (\epsilon/2a) >> \mathbf{clock}(high) \wedge \\ \mathbf{clock}(low) \preceq \mathbf{clock}(on) \wedge \\ \mathbf{clock}(on) \preceq (\epsilon/2b) >> \mathbf{clock}(low) \end{array}$$

Theorem 7.7
If $l1$, $r1 \leq \epsilon/2a$ and $l2$, $r2 \leq \epsilon/2b$, then

$$\begin{aligned}\mathbf{clock}(high) &= r1 >> \mathbf{climb}(u,\ H - \epsilon)\\ \mathbf{clock}(low) &= r2 >> \mathbf{drop}(u,\ L + \epsilon)\end{aligned}$$

and

$$\begin{aligned}\mathbf{clock}(off) &= l1 >> \mathbf{clock}(high)\\ \mathbf{clock}(on) &= l2 >> \mathbf{clock}(low)\end{aligned}$$

are correct designs of the sensor and the control unit.

8 Discussion

Hybrid systems is an emerging area of growing importance, where the system state evolves over time according to interacting laws of discrete and continuous dynamics. Combinations of computation and control can lead to very complicated system design. This paper proposes a clock-based framework in support of specification and design of hybrid systems:

- The behaviour of our system is described in terms of system state and interaction.
- The discrete variables of our system can be identified with a clock which records the time instants when the discrete jump takes place.
- The continuous transitions can be captured by differential equations where some of continuous dynamics are identified with a clock.
- Interacting events can also be specified by clock. As a result, clock variables become the first-class ingredients in our specification stage.
- The timing features of our system such as time latency and scheduling policy can also be described by the temporal orders introduced in our mechanism.

In summary, first order logic annotated with clock can easily be used for verifying the safety properties of hybrid system models. It handles actual operational models of hybrid systems such as discrete interactions and continuous transitions. Its strength also lies in tackling various timing feature of hybrid systems.

In future, we will deliver a hybrid parallel programming language with clock as a uniform compositional models for hybrid systems, and establish its link with the existing modelling languages [11,18,26,28].

Acknowledgement. This work was supported by National Science Foundation of China (No. 61021004 and No. 61061130541), National High Technology Research and Development Program of Ministry of Science and Technology of China (No. 2011AA010101), National Basic Research Program of Ministry of Science and Technology of China (No. 2011CB302904), Shanghai Knowledge Service Platform Project (No. ZF1213) and Doctoral Fund of Ministry of Education of China (No. 20120076130003).

References

1. Alur, R., Dill, D.: A theory of timed automata. Theoretical Computer Science 126(2), 183–235 (1994)
2. Alur, R., Courcoubetics, C., Henzinger, T.A., Ho, P.H.: Hybrid automata: An algorithmic approach to the specification and verification of hybrid systems. In: Grossman, R.L., Ravn, A.P., Rischel, H., Nerode, A. (eds.) HS 1991 and HS 1992. LNCS, vol. 736, pp. 209–229. Springer, Heidelberg (1993)
3. Alur, R., Courcoubetics, C., Halbwachs, N., Henzinger, T.A., Ho, P.-H., Nicolin, X., Olivero, A., Sifakis, J., Yovine, S.: The algorithmic analysis of hybrid systems. Theoretical Computer Science 138(1), 3–34 (1995)
4. Benveniste, A.: Compositional and uniform modelling of hybrid systems. IEEE Trans. on Automatic Control 43(4), 579–584 (1998)
5. Benveniste, A., Cailland, B., Pouzet, M.: The fundamentals of hybrid system modelers. In: CDC, pp. 4180–4185. IEEE (2010)
6. Berry, G., Gonthier, G.: The Esterel synchronous programming language: design, semantics and implementation. Science of Computer Programming 19(2), 87–152 (1992)
7. Berry, G.: Constructive Semantics of Esterel: From Theory to Practice. In: Nivat, M., Wirsing, M. (eds.) AMAST 1996. LNCS, vol. 1101, p. 225. Springer, Heidelberg (1996)
8. Carloni, L.P., Passerone, R., Pinto, A., Sangiovanni-Vincentelli, A.L.: Languages and tools for hybrid system design. Foundations and Trends in Electronic Design Automation 1(1/2) (2006)
9. Clarke, E.M., Emerson, E.A.: Design and synthesis of synchronisation skeletons using branching-time temporal logic. In: Kozen, D. (ed.) Logic of Programs 1981. LNCS, vol. 131, pp. 52–71. Springer, Heidelberg (1982)
10. Harel, D.: Statecharts: a visual formalism for complex systems. Science of Computer Programming 8(3), 231–274 (1987)
11. He, J.: From CSP to hybrid systems. In: Roscoe, A.W. (ed.) A Classical Mind: Essays in Honour of C.A.R. Hoare, pp. 171–189 (1994)
12. Henzinger, T.A., Horowitz, B., Kirsch, C.K.: Giotto: A time-triggered language for embedded programming. Technical report, Department of Electronic Engineering and Computer Science, University of California, Berkeley (2001)
13. Henzinger, T.A.: The theory of hybrid automata. In: LICS, pp. 278–292. IEEE Computer Society (1996)
14. Iwasaki, Y., Farquhar, A., Saraswat, V.A., Bobrow, D.G., Gupta, V.: Modeling time in hybrid systems: How fast is "instantaneous"? In: IJCAI, pp. 1773–1781 (1995)
15. Katok, A., Hasselblatt, B.: Introduction to the Modern Theory of Dynamic Systems. Cambridge University Press (1996)
16. Kohn, W.: A Declarative Theory for Rational Controllers. In: Proceedings of 27th CDC, pp. 130–136 (1988)
17. Lee, E.A., Zheng, H.: Leveraging synchronous language principles for heterogeneous modeling and design of embedded systems. In: EMSOFT, pp. 114–123 (2007)
18. Jing, L., Ziwei, L., Mallet, H.J.F., Zuohua, D.: Hybrid MARTR Statechart. Frontiers of Computer Science 7(1), 95–108 (2013)
19. Maler, O., Manna, Z., Pnueli, A.: From timed to hybrid systems. In: Huizing, C., de Bakker, J.W., Rozenberg, G., de Roever, W.-P. (eds.) REX 1991. LNCS, vol. 600, pp. 447–484. Springer, Heidelberg (1992)

20. Nikoukhah, R.: Hybrid dynamics in Modelica: Should all events be considered synchronous? In: EOOST 2007, pp. 37–48 (2007)
21. Platzer, A.: Differential dynamic logic: Automated theorem proving for hybrid systems. Ph.D. thesis, Department of Computing Science, University of Oldenburg (2008)
22. Perko, L.: Differential equations and dynamic systems. Springer (2006)
23. Mosterman, P.J., Zander, J., Hamon, G., Denckla, B.: Towards Computational Hybrid System Semantics for Time-Based Block Diagrams. In: ADHS 2009, pp. 376–385 (2009)
24. Queille, J.P., Sifakis, J.: Specification and verification of concurrent systems in CESAR. In: Dezani-Ciancaglini, M., Montanari, U. (eds.) Programming 1982. LNCS, vol. 137, pp. 337–351. Springer, Heidelberg (1982)
25. Ronkko, M., Ravn, A.P., Sere, K.: Hybrid action systems. Theoretical Computer Science 290(1), 937–973 (2003)
26. Society of Automotive Engineers. SAE Standards: Architecture Analysis and Design Language (AADL). AS5506 (2004)
27. Sikora, E., Tenbergen, B., Pohl, K.: Requirements engineering for embedded systems: An investigation of industry needs. In: Berry, D. (ed.) REFSQ 2011. LNCS, vol. 6606, pp. 151–165. Springer, Heidelberg (2011)
28. Simulink, `http://www.mathworks.com/products/simulink/`
29. Tavermini, L.: Differential automata and their discrete simulations. Non-Linear Analysis 11(6), 665–683 (1987)
30. Chen, Z.C., Ji, W., Ravn, A.P.: A formal description of hybrid systems. In: Alur, R., Sontag, E.D., Henzinger, T.A. (eds.) HS 1995. LNCS, vol. 1066, pp. 511–530. Springer, Heidelberg (1996)

Advances in Quantitative Verification for Ubiquitous Computing

Marta Kwiatkowska

Department of Computer Science, University of Oxford, Oxford, OX1 3QD

Abstract. Ubiquitous computing, where computers 'disappear' and instead sensor-enabled and software-controlled devices assist us in everyday tasks, has become an established trend. To ensure the safety and reliability of software embedded in these devices, rigorous model-based design methodologies are called for. Quantitative verification, a powerful technique for analysing system models against quantitative properties such as "the probability of a data packet being delivered within 1ms to a nearby Bluetooth device is at least 0.98", has proved useful by detecting and correcting flaws in a number of ubiquitous computing applications. In this paper, we focus on three key aspects of ubiquitous computing: autonomous behaviour, constrained resources and adaptiveness. We summarise recent advances of quantitative verification in relation to these aspects, illustrating each with a case study analysed using the probabilistic model checker PRISM. The paper concludes with an outline of future challenges that remain in this area.

1 Introduction

Ubiquitous computing, also known as pervasive computing, was envisaged by Mark Weiser in [49], where he predicted that computers will "weave themselves into the fabric of everyday life until they are indistinguishable from it". Today, powered by advances in microelectronics, mobile phone technology and cloud computing, we are witnessing a tremendous growth in device technologies for software-controlled 'smart' devices that support our daily activities and autonomously make decisions on our behalf. They can sense what is around them, remember the context and adapt to new situations. They can communicate wirelessly with other devices and humans, and are Internet-enabled. Applications are endless, from environmental and health monitoring, through home appliance networks, to self-driving cars. A related vision is the 'Internet of Things', where everyday objects (called 'everyware' by Adam Greenfield) are enhanced with information processing capabilities.

The growing dependence of society on ubiquitous computing calls for rigorous device design methodologies, which is particularly important for their embedded software that controls the device actions and whose failure can lead to costly recalls. Model-based design methodologies have the potential to improve the reliability of devices and reduce the development effort through code generation and software reuse via product lines. In particular, automated verification via

Z. Liu, J. Woodcock, and H. Zhu (Eds.): ICTAC 2013, LNCS 8049, pp. 42–58, 2013.

model checking provides the means to systematically verify software against correctness requirements such as "the smartphone will never reveal private data to unauthorised contacts". These techniques have been successfully applied to TinyOS sensor network software [5] with respect to safety assertions. However, when modelling ubiquitous computing devices we often need to include quantitative aspects such as probability, time delays and resource usage in the models. Probability is needed because of inherent unreliability of wireless communication technologies such as Bluetooth and ZigBee, which use randomised back off schemes to minimise collisions; also, embedded devices are frequently powered by battery and components may be prone to failure. *Quantitative verification* [33] techniques are well suited to this case, where systems are modelled as variants of Markov chains, annotated with real-time and quantitative costs/rewards. The aim is to automatically establish quantitative properties, such as "the probability of a monitoring device failing to issue alarm when a dangerous rise in pollutant level is detected", "the worst-case expected time for a Bluetooth device to discover another device in vicinity", or "the minimum expected power consumption of the smartphone while looking up directions with GPS". Quantitative, probabilistic verification has been implemented in the probabilistic model checker PRISM [36], which has been applied to a wide range of case studies from the ubiquitous computing domain, resulting in automatic detection and diagnosis of software flaws and unexpected trends.

In this paper, we provide a brief overview of quantitative verification techniques, including typical features of the models and property specification notations. We then describe a selection of recent advances, highlighting the following three key aspects of ubiquitous computing devices:

1. *autonomous behaviour*: increasingly, we are relying on ubiquitous computing devices to act autonomously on our behalf, including *safety-critical* applications such as self-driving cars, or robotic search and rescue missions;
2. *constrained resources*: the embedded processors have limited memory and CPU speed, are often battery powered, and employ unreliable communication technologies, and yet they are expected to *reliably and timely* perform critical functions such as financial transactions;
3. *adaptiveness*: ubiquitous computing devices are typically enabled and managed by cloud services, which dynamically adapt behaviours to changing requirements and environmental context, necessitating continuous monitoring and runtime verification to provide *dependability* assurance.

We illustrate each of the above with a typical case study drawn from the ubiquitous computing domain, describing the modelling approach taken and lessons learnt. The case studies involve PRISM and pertain to sensor-enabled mobile devices such as autonomous robots and smartphones. The requirements that we wish to ensure include: "the robot will successfully arrive at the exit with probability greater than 0.99, without hitting any obstacles" (autonomous behaviour); "the email protocol will ensure that the total energy cost of sending a message does not exceed a specified bound, even if the bit error rate is high (constrained resources); and "the device will maintain 0.97 minimum probability of delivering sensor readings to the beacon within 5ms, even if the bandwidth drops from time to time" (adaptiveness). We conclude by outlining future research challenges in quantitative verification for ubiquitous computing.

The paper is organised as follows. In Section 2 we give an overview of quantitative verification techniques, focusing on Markov chain and Markov decision process models, and the corresponding temporal logics, PCTL and CSL. Section 3 demonstrates recent advances of quantitative verification by highlighting a number of case studies from ubiquitous computing, all analysed with the PRISM model checker [36]. Section 4 concludes the paper by summarising future research challenges.

2 Quantitative Verification Basics

We give a brief overview of a selection of probabilistic models and specification formalisms used in automated quantitative verification. The models have been chosen according to case studies presented in the next section. We note that all models and specification notations discussed here are supported by PRISM [36].

2.1 Markov Decision Processes

In ubiquitous computing devices probabilistic behaviour typically coexists with nondeterminism. Probability is the result of a random event, for example an electronic coin toss, sensor failure or stochastic delay, and nondeterminism is used to model concurrent execution or action-based control. Both nondeterminism and (discrete) probability are present in the classical model of *Markov decision processes (MDPs)*.

Let S be a finite set; we denote the set of probability distributions over S by $Dist(S)$.

Definition 1 (MDP). *A* Markov decision process (MDP) *is a tuple* $\mathcal{M} = (S, \bar{s}, Act, \mathbf{P}, AP, L)$, *where*

- S *is a finite set of states and* $\bar{s} \in S$ *is the initial state;*
- Act *is a finite set of actions;*
- $\mathbf{P} : S \times Act \times S \in [0,1]$ *is a transition probability matrix where* $\sum_{s' \in S} \mathbf{P}(s, a, s') \in \{0,1\}$ *for any* $s \in S$ *and* $a \in Act$*;*
- AP *is a set of atomic propositions;*
- $L : S \to 2^{AP}$ *is a labelling of states with atomic propositions.*

We let $\delta(s) \subseteq Act$ denote the set of actions enabled in s, i.e. $a \in \delta(s)$ if $\sum_{s' \in S} \mathbf{P}(s, a, s') = 1$. The MDP executes as follows: in each state s the successor state is chosen by, first, nondeterministically selecting an enabled action $a \in \delta(s)$, and, second, choosing the successor according to the probability distribution $\mathbf{P}(s, a)$. A *path* of $\mathcal{M}$ is of the form $\pi = s_0 a_0 s_1 a_1 s_2 \cdots$ where $a_i \in \delta(s_i)$ and $\mathbf{P}(s_i, a_i, s_{i+1}) > 0$ for each $i \geq 0$.

To reason formally about the behaviour of MDPs, we use the notion of *strategies* (also called *adversaries* or *policies*), which resolve all the nondeterministic choices in a model. Formally, a strategy is a function σ that maps a finite path ending in s to an action in $\delta(s)$ based on the history of choices made so far. Under a particular strategy, the behaviour of an MDP is fully probabilistic and we can define a probability space over the possible paths through the model using standard construction [31].

A *discrete-time Markov chain (DTMC)* is an MDP $\mathcal{D} = (S, \bar{s}, Act, \mathbf{P}, AP, L)$ with $|Act| = 1$, where $\sum_{s' \in S} \mathbf{P}(s, a, s') = 1$ for all $s \in S$. Thus, a DTMC can be viewed as a single transition probability matrix $\mathbf{P} : S \times S \in [0, 1]$, with all rows summing up to 1. We omit *Act* from the tuple when referring to DTMCs.

MDP properties are typically expressed in temporal logics. The logic PCTL (Probabilistic Computation Tree Logic) [30], a probabilistic extension of the temporal logic CTL is defined below.

Definition 2. *The syntax of PCTL is given by:*

$$\Phi ::= true \mid a \mid \neg\Phi \mid \Phi \wedge \Phi \mid \Phi \vee \Phi \mid \mathrm{P}_{\sim p}[\psi]$$
$$\psi ::= \mathrm{X}\,\Phi \mid \Phi\,\mathrm{U}^{\leq k}\,\Phi \mid \Phi\,\mathrm{U}\,\Phi$$

where a is an atomic proposition, $\sim \in \{<, \leq, \geq, >\}$, $p \in [0, 1]$ and $k \in \mathbb{N}$.

PCTL formulae Φ are interpreted over the states of an MDP. As path formulae we allow $\mathrm{X}\,\Phi$ ("Φ is satisfied in the *next* step"), $\Phi_1\,\mathrm{U}^{\leq k}\,\Phi_2$ ("Φ_2 is satisfied within k steps and Φ_1 is true *until* that point") and $\Phi_1\,\mathrm{U}\,\Phi_2$ ("Φ_2 is eventually satisfied and Φ_1 is true *until* then"). The usual derived variants $\mathrm{F}\,\Phi$, $\mathrm{G}\,\Phi$ are also permitted. We say that a state $s \in S$ *satisfies* a PCTL formula Φ, denoted $s \models \Phi$, if the probability of a path formula ψ being true in s satisfies the bound $\sim p$ *for all strategies*. We can also use PCTL in *quantitative* form, e.g. $\mathrm{P}_{min=?}[\ \psi\ ]$, which returns the *minimum/maximum* probability of satisfying ψ. Examples of PCTL properties are:

- $\mathrm{P}_{\max=?}[\,\mathrm{F}\ lost\,]$ - "the maximum probability, over all possible strategies, of the protocol losing a message";
- $\mathrm{P}_{\min=?}[\,\mathrm{F}^{\leq 10}\ deliver\,]$ - "the minimum probability, over all possible strategies, of the protocol delivering a message within 10 time steps";
- $\mathrm{P}_{\geq 1}[\,near\_supplies\ \mathrm{U}\ exit\,]$ - "under all possible strategies, with probability 1, the robot always remains near supplies until exiting".

Model checking PCTL over MDPs requires a combination of graph-based algorithms and numerical solution techniques. Typically, we are interested in the best- or worst-case behaviour and compute the minimum or maximum probability that some event occurs, quantifying over all possible strategies. The minimum and maximum probabilities can be computed by solving linear optimisation problems, which can be implemented using dynamic programming or LP solvers.We can also *synthesise* the strategy that achieves the minimum/maximum probability. For the case of DTMCs, it suffices to solve linear equation systems. More expressive logics such as LTL or PCTL* can also be defined, albeit their model checking becomes more expensive. The usual approach is to convert the LTL formula to a deterministic Rabin automaton and perform verification on the *product* of this automaton and the original MDP; see e.g. [2,23].

2.2 Continuous-Time Markov Chains

In MDPs, the progress of time is modelled by discrete time steps, one for each transition of the model. For many applications, it is preferable to use a *continuous* model of time, where the delays between transitions can be arbitrary real values. A natural extension of MDPs with real-time (not discussed here) is probabilistic timed automata [39]. We focus on the simpler, classical model of *continuous-time Markov chains (CTMCs)*, which have no nondeterminism, and extend DTMCs with real-time by modelling transition delays with exponential distributions.

Definition 3. *A continuous-time Markov chain (CTMC) is* $\mathcal{C} = (S, \bar{s}, \mathbf{P}, E, AP, L)$ *where:*

- $(S, \bar{s}, \mathbf{P}, AP, L)$ *is a DTMC;*
- $E : S \to \mathbb{R}_{\geq 0}$ *is the* exit rate.

In a CTMC $\mathcal{C}$, the residence time of a state $s \in S$ is a random variable governed by an exponential distribution with parameter $E(s)$. Therefore, the probability to exit state s in t time units is given by $\int_0^t E(s) \cdot e^{-E(s)\tau} d\tau$. To take the transition from s to another state s' in t time units, the probability equals $\mathbf{P}(s, s') \cdot \int_0^t E(s) \cdot e^{-E(s)\tau} d\tau$.

Intuitively, the CTMC executes as follows: in each state s, it stays in this state for time t, drawn from exponential distribution with parameter $E(s)$, and then moves to state s' with probability $\mathbf{P}(s, s')$. A *timed path* of $\mathcal{C}$ is a finite or infinite sequence $s_0 t_0 s_1 t_1 s_2 \cdots t_{n-1} s_n \ldots$, where $t_i \in \mathbb{R}_{>0}$ for each $i \geq 0$. As for DTMCs, a probability space over the paths through a CTMC can be defined [3], where events correspond to certain sets of paths.

To specify quantitative properties of CTMCs, the logic CSL [3] has been proposed, which is syntactically similar to PCTL, except that it now includes continuous versions of the step-bounded path operators.

Definition 4. *The syntax of CSL is given by:*

$$\Phi ::= true \mid a \mid \neg\Phi \mid \Phi \wedge \Phi \mid \Phi \vee \Phi \mid \mathrm{P}_{\sim p}[\psi] \mid \mathrm{S}_{\sim p}[\Phi]$$
$$\psi ::= \mathrm{X}\,\Phi \mid \Phi\,\mathrm{U}^{[t,t']}\,\Phi \mid \Phi\,\mathrm{U}\,\Phi$$

where a is an atomic proposition, $\sim \in \{<, \leq, \geq, >\}$, $p \in [0,1]$ *and* $t, t' \in \mathbb{R}_{\geq 0}$.

The path formula $\Phi_1\,\mathrm{U}^{[t,t']}\,\Phi_2$, where $t, t' \in \mathbb{R}_{\geq 0}$ is true for a path if Φ_1 is satisfied at all time points until Φ_2 becomes true at a time point belonging to the interval $[t, t']$. The usual unbounded until $\Phi_1\,\mathrm{U}\,\Phi_2$ corresponds to the interval $[0, \infty)$. As for PCTL, we can define the derived variants, e.g. $\mathrm{F}\ \Phi$. The probabilistic operator formula $\mathrm{P}_{\sim p}[\psi]$ is true in state s if the probability of paths from s

that satisfy ψ meets the probability bound $\sim p$. The formula $S_{\sim p}[\Phi]$ denotes steady-state, and is true in state s if the long-run probability residing in state satisfying Φ meets the probability bound $\sim p$. Examples of CSL properties are:

- $P_{=?}[\,F^{[5,5]}\,\neg empty\,]$ - "the probability of the robot's battery not being depleted at time 5 mins";
- $P_{=?}[\,near\_supplies\ U^{[0,5.5]}\ exit\,]$ - "the probability of the robot remaining near supplies before exiting safely within 5.5 mins";
- $S_{\geq 0.99}[\,\neg fail\,]$ - "the long-run probability of the robot being operational is at least 0.99".

Model checking for CSL over CTMCs proceeds by discretisation into a DTMC. The steady-state operator is computed by solving a linear equation system, whereas the probabilistic operator reduces to transient probability calculation, and is typically implemented using *uniformisation*, an efficient iterative numerical method. For more information see e.g. [34]. More expressive, durational properties for CTMCs can also be defined and automatically verified [15].

2.3 Adding Costs and Rewards

The above probabilistic models can be augmented with *reward* information (also referred to as *cost*), which enables the computation of expected reward values. For simplicity, we only show the extension for DTMCs. For $\mathcal{D} = (S, \bar{s}, \mathbf{P}, AP, L)$, we define a *reward structure* $(\underline{\rho}, \iota)$, where: $\underline{\rho} : S \to \mathbb{R}_{\geq 0}$ assigns rewards to states, and $\iota : S \times S \to \mathbb{R}_{\geq 0}$ assigns rewards to transitions. The state reward vector $\underline{\rho}(s)$ is the reward acquired in state s per time step, and the transition reward $\iota(s, s')$ is acquired each time a transition between states s and s' occurs.

Reward structures can be used to represent a variety of different aspects of a system model, for example "number of sensors that have reached consensus" or "the expected energy consumed in the start-up phase". To express reward-based properties for DTMCs, the logic PCTL can be extended [34] with additional operators:

$$R_{\sim r}[\,C^{\leq k}\,] \mid R_{\sim r}[\,I^{=k}\,] \mid R_{\sim r}[\,F\,\Phi\,]$$

where $\sim\in\{<, \leq, \geq, >\}$, $r \in \mathbb{R}_{\geq 0}$, $k \in \mathbb{N}$ and Φ is a PCTL formula. The formula $R_{\sim r}[\,\psi\,]$ is satisfied in a state s if, from s, the *expected* value of reward ψ meets the bound $\sim r$. The formula ψ can take the form: $C^{\leq k}$, which refers to the reward *cumulated* over k time steps; $I^{=k}$, the state reward after exactly k time steps (*instantaneous*); and $F\,\Phi$, the reward cumulated before a state satisfying Φ is *reached*. Similarly to the P operator, we also use the *quantitative* form $R_{=?}[\,\psi\,]$, meaning the value of the expected reward. The following are examples of reward properties assuming appropriate reward structures have been defined:

- $R_{=?}[C^{\leq 10}]$ - "the expected power consumption within the first 10 time steps of operation";
- $R_{=?}[I^{=100}]$ - "the expected number of regions visited by the robot after 100 time steps have passed";

– $R_{\geq 5}[F\ exit]$ - "the expected number of regions visited by the robot until exiting is at least 5".

Model checking for the reward operators for DTMCs reduces to a combination of graph algorithms and solution of linear equations; see e.g. [34] for more information. An extension of CSL with the reward operator was formulated in [34]. Cumulative and instantaneous reward operators can also be added to PCTL for MDPs [23], where minimum/maximum expected rewards, denoted by $R_{max=?}[\cdot]$ in quantitative form, are computed over all strategies. Steady-state rewards, respectively long-run average in the case of MDPs, can also be defined [34,23].

2.4 Quantitative Verification with PRISM

Quantitative verification techniques have been implemented within PRISM [36,1], a probabilistic model checker developed at the Universities of Birmingham and Oxford. PRISM provides direct support for DTMCs, MDPs and CTMCs, as well as two additional models not discussed here, probabilistic timed automata (PTAs) and stochastic multi-player games (SMGs), the latter via the tool PRISM-games [11]. The models are specified using a high-level modelling language based on guarded command notation. Quantitative properties can be specified in the temporal logics PCTL, LTL, PCTL* and CSL, which include both probabilistic and reward operators.

PRISM is primarily a *symbolic* model checker based on variants of Binary Decision Diagrams (BDDs), but it also makes extensive use of *explicit* storage schemes such as sparse matrices and arrays, and implements multiple engines for efficiency and scalability. The verification algorithms can provide either *exact*, numerical solutions to the induced linear equation systems or linear programming problems, typically computed iteratively, or *approximate* the probability/expectation by sampling executions using Monte Carlo techniques and performing statistical inference to estimate the probability of satisfying the property (also known as *statistical model checking*). Parametric models are now supported [16]. It is also possible to *simulate* the model and *synthesise* the strategy that minimises/maximises the probability or reward [1].

PRISM's graphical user interface, shown in Figure 1, provides a model editor, a simulator for model debugging and strategy exploration, and graph-plotting functionality. Models and properties can be specified using parameters, and *experiments* facilitate the search for flaws or unusual trends, by plotting the values of quantitative queries as the parameters in the model or property are varied.

PRISM is free and open-source (released under the GPL license), runs on most major operating systems, and has been applied to several application domains, including distributed algorithms, security protocols, dependability, planning, workflows, and biology; see [1] for more information.

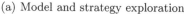

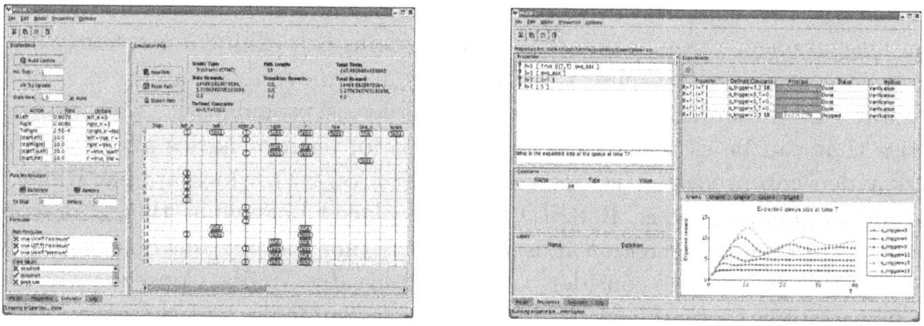

(a) Model and strategy exploration

(b) Experiments and graph plotting

Fig. 1. Screenshots of the PRISM graphical user interface

3 Quantitative Verification for Ubiquitous Computing

Quantitative verification is a powerful and widely applicable method, which has been successfully applied in the context of ubiquitous computing. We mention, for example, the modelling and analysis of performance and energy consumption of the Bluetooth device discovery protocol [17], which established for the first time that the worst-case time to hear one message is unusually long, about 2.5s. Similar analyses have been performed for the IEEE 802.11 WiFi [40] and 802.15.4 ZigBee sensor network protocols [27]. Further studies concerning mobile devices include performability of several dynamic power management schemes [45].

The ultimate challenge is to apply these techniques to real-world ubiquitous computing scenarios, which are expanding rapidly. In this paper, we survey some of the recent advances by focusing on three key aspects of ubiquitous computing devices: *autonomous behaviour*, *constrained resources* and *adaptivity*. Each aspect will be illustrated by means of case studies that use PRISM.

3.1 Autonomous Behaviour

A growing number of ubiquitous computing applications involves designing autonomous robotic missions, such as those used in planetary exploration, for example Mars Rover, or disaster search and rescue. A key challenge for the designers is to construct a mission so that it satisfies some high-level goals, and executes in a timely manner and without fault. In addition, technological progress towards self-parking and self-driving cars calls for software tools to support the design of safe autonomous vehicle control.

In this section, we highlight the research aimed at automated generation of control strategies for robotic vehicles in dynamic environments as reported in [43]. The approach is based on the observation that temporal logic such as CTL can be used to specify the mission goals, for example, "the robot will remain in safe regions until exiting successfully". Under the assumption that the environment is static and can be partitioned into a finite-state transition system, conventional model checking tools can be applied to analyse and generate strategies in this case. However, one has to consider *noise* on sensors induced from measurement errors; similarly, control actions can exhibit *uncertainty* due to actuator error, in the sense that the robot can move to an adjacent region or remain in the current region, and this choice is probabilistic, with probabilities that can be estimated. Natural models for such scenarios are therefore Markov decision processes (as overviewed in Section 2.1), which are partitioned into finitely many regions. If RFID tags are placed in regions, the robot can uniquely determine the region it is in; we can thus assume full observability, thus avoiding the need to consider partially-observable MDPs. Consequently, we can now employ temporal PCTL to specify mission goals, and the above goal now becomes: "what is the probability that the robot will remain in safe regions until exiting successfully?".

The problem can be stated as follows. Consider a robot moving in a partitioned environment with static obstacles modelled as a Markov decision process $\mathcal{M}$. Given a PCTL formula Φ that specifies the mission goal, determine a control strategy that *optimises* the probability of satisfying Φ. Clearly, this problem can be solved by applying quantitative verification as described in Section 2.1, namely, computing the minimum/maximum probability or expectation, and then *synthesising* the optimal strategy.

In previous work, the authors considered *safe vehicle control* in city environments, and developed a tool for synthesising control strategies from PCTL based on PRISM. Later, they extended the synthesis algorithms to include expected reward specifications to incorporate aspects such as time and energy cost, as well as Boolean combinations of PCTL formulae [43]. They also validated their approach using an experimental testbed that employs iRobot Create[1], the popular programmable robot. The following are examples of actual mission goal specifications from [43]:

- $\mathrm{P}_{max=?}[\,(\mathbf{S} \vee (\mathbf{R} \wedge \mathbf{M_1}))\,\mathrm{U}\,\mathbf{D_1}\,]$ - "reach *Destination 1* by driving through either only *Safe* regions or through *Relatively Safe* regions only if *Medical Supply 1* is available at such regions";
- $\mathrm{P}_{max=?}[(\,\mathrm{P}_{\leq 0.5}[\mathrm{X}\mathbf{R}] \wedge \neg\mathbf{U})\mathrm{U}\mathbf{D_1}\,]$ - "reach *Destination 1* by going through the regions from which the probability of converging to a *Relatively safe* region is less than 0.5 and always avoiding *Unsafe* regions".

The results reported are encouraging, with the tool able to synthesise control strategies for MDPs with 1000 states, though the construction of the MDP using Monte Carlo simulation can be expensive.

Strategy synthesis from LTL specifications has been formulated, e.g., in [32,50]. Probabilistic verification of coordinated foraging-and-reacting multi-robotic missions is considered in [8], where compositionality is employed to improve scalability. We remark that more complex mission goals may require *multi-objective* specifications, where the simultaneous satisfaction of more than one property, e.g. maximise the probability of reaching target and minimise expected travelling time, is needed. Automated verification and synthesis for multi-objective

[1] `http://verifiablerobotics.com/CreateMATLABsimulator/createsimulator.html`

specifications for MDPs have been developed [25], allowing for the exploration of trade-offs between the component properties, and applied to synthesis of strategies for the team formation protocol. In recent work, we have developed synthesis algorithms for autonomous driving for conjunctive multi-objective specifications for stochastic game models, based on actual map data [13].

3.2 Constrained Resources

Ubiquitous computing devices are frequently wearable, for example, low-cost RFID tags and wireless body sensors, and consequently have limited memory and computational capacity. At the same time, they may need to execute computationally intensive tasks, such as authentication and communication in unreliable wireless media. Typically battery-powered, where it is either difficult or inconvenient to access energy renewal sources, the need for high-quality resource management protocols for such devices is paramount. Quantitative verification has previously been applied to analyse dynamic power management schemes for mobile devices [45] and energy harvesters [48]. Here, we highlight a recent case study that applied quantitative verification with PRISM to analyse the computational and transmission cost of an electronic email protocol [4], with the view to provide tool-assisted systematic analysis of the protocol for a variety of mobile environments.

The Certified E-mail Message Delivery (CEMD) protocol studied in [4] is used on mobile devices such as smartphones and PDAs, including low-cost hardware, frequently operating in noisy environments with high bit error rate. The CEMD protocol provides a number of security features, such as fairness (neither sender nor recipient should gain advantage upon interruption), timeliness (all participants should be able to exit the protocol in a given finite time), and confidentiality (only the intended participant should learn the contents of an email message, implemented using RSA encryption). In view of the computational cost of RSA operations, it is important for the designers to understand the impact of executing the email service on CPU performance and energy consumption. To this end, a CTMC model of the protocol is developed in PRISM, and parameterised based on the popular Texas Instruments TMS320C55x processor which performs at the low frequency end of 200MHz, hence maintaning the ability to provide services in low power modes. Then a detailed analysis is performed using the derived parameters, also taking into account the number of parallel sessions and realistic bit error rates of typical mobile communication technologies, both of which affect the performance.

The quantitative analysis is focused on *computational* and *transmission* costs of the CEMD protocol, respectively defined as a function of the CPU cycles needed to perform RSA operations, and a function of the negative acknowledgement rate and bit error rate of the wireless medium. The properties are expressed as CSL formulae, and analysed for different values of the parameters, assuming suitable reward structures:

- $\mathrm{P}_{=?}[\mathrm{F}^{[0,T]}\,\mathit{finish}]$ - "the probability of completing all protocol's sessions in finite time T";

- $R_{=?}[C^{\leq T}]$ - "the expected computational cost of completing all protocol's sessions in finite time T".

The analysis has revealed that the CEMD protocol is highly dependent on the specific characteristics of the environment that it runs on, with widely different behaviour, and may lead to instabilities. The derived model of the protocol provides a sound foundation for a methodology to analyse further quantitative aspects of the protocol, for example energy consumption.

Resource efficiency, particularly in relation to energy, is a major design issue for ubiquitous computing devices. Quantitative analysis of low-cost RFID authentication protocol was performed in [47]. The effect of mobility and transmission range on energy consumption was considered for mobile process calculi frameworks in [28]. The quantitative analysis of a smartgrid protocol using PRISM-games [10,11] revealed a flaw, which was fixed by introducing incentives to prevent selfishness.

3.3 Adaptiveness

Many ubiquitous computing applications continuously monitor the environment by means of sensors and must adapt to new scenarios. Ubiquitous computing systems such as home networks are enabled by service-based systems, typically based on cloud computing [18], which dynamically adapt behaviours to the changing requirements and contexts. It has been argued [6] that the need to continuously provide reliability, dependability and performance guarantees for adaptive systems calls for *quantitative runtime verification*. This is different from offline quantitative verification performed at the design stage, as described in Section 2, where a model is developed and analysed pre-deployment in order to improve the design. Runtime verification, in contrast, is invoked as the system is being executed, intercepting and steering its execution to ensure that given requirements are continuously satisfied in spite of adaptation.

In [7], we have developed an extensive framework called QoSMOS which can be used to dynamically manage and optimise the performance of service-based systems. The framework has been demonstrated on a typical ubiquitous computing healthcare scenario, called TeleAssistance, where patients are remotely monitored, with data being sent to a medical lab for analysis, and there is a requirement to guarantee a certain QoS level of delivering a specific service, for example to change the dosage of a drug. The system is built as a workflow of web services, and may suffer from component failures. The framework proceeds autonomically, repeatedly invoking the monitoring, analysis, planning and execution stages (so called MAPE loop) as follows:

- *monitor* the reliability, workload and response time of services, to derive an operational model;
- *analyse* performance and QoS requirements, utilising the values of parameters obtained from the monitoring phase;

- *plan* adaptation of the system based on the results of analysis, which may involve changing the resource allocation or selection of optimal service;
- *execute* the adaptation of the system.

The models used for the TeleAssistance application are DTMCs and CTMCs, and the following are example requirements:

- $\mathrm{P}_{\leq 0.13}[\,\mathrm{F}\, \mathit{failedAlarm}\,]$ - "the probability that at an alarm failure ever occurs during the lifetime of the system is less than 0.13" (PCTL property);
- $\mathrm{R}_{\leq 0.05}[\,\mathrm{F}^{[0,86400]}\, \mathit{dropped}\,]$ - "the probability of a *changeDrug* request being dropped due to the request queue being full during a day of operation is less than 0.05" (CSL property).

The QoSMOS framework implements the analysis stage using quantitative verification with PRISM. This involves executing PRISM verification tasks at runtime, which works well when the number of services is small, but may become impractical when the size of the model or the number of tasks increases. To improve efficiency, one can employ *parametric* approaches, e.g. [22], and specifically *parameter synthesis* [29]. We consider parametric probabilistic models, where probabilities are specified in terms of expressions over parameters, rather than concrete values. Then, the parameter synthesis problem aims to determine the valuations for parameters which guarantee the satisfaction of a given property, and can be solved by means of constraint solving. In recent work, we have applied sampling-based and swarm intelligence techniques to heuristically search for a good valuation of parameters for parametric models [16] (parametric MDPs and DTMCs/CTMCs). We note that this approach only finds one such valuation, rather than all the valuations for parameters. However, it may result in performance improvement by orders of magnitude, and is therefore particularly well suited to runtime verification scenarios.

The parameter synthesis methods, both those based on constraint solving as well as heuristic search, have recently been implemented within PRISM [16]. Alternative approaches to improve efficiency of quantitative runtime verification include incremental model construction and incremental verification [26], which avoid the need to rerun a verification task by reusing results from previous verifications.

3.4 Further Advances

We briefly summarise further developments in quantitative verification that have shown promise.

Compositional Probabilistic Verification. The complexity of ubiquitous computing scenarios demands improvements in the capacity of quantitative verification tools. Compositional assume-guarantee techniques have the potential to improve the scalability of model checking by subdividing the verification into separate tasks for each component of the system being analysed. For example, to verify property G on a two-component system $M_1 \| M_2$ we (i) check that, under the assumption that some property A holds, M_2 is guaranteed to satisfy G;

and (ii) check that M_1 always satisfies the assumption A under any context. In recent work [37,24], *compositional assume-guarantee* techniques have been developed for MDPs, for both quantitative safety and liveness properties. Several proof rules have been developed to support compositional probabilistic model checking of MDPs, and implementation in terms of multi-objective probabilistic model checking [19] has been provided as an extension of PRISM, which yields substantial improvement over monolithic methods. The process can be fully automated for safety properties by applying automata learning techniques [20,21] to generate assumptions.

Cooperative and Competitive Behaviour. Ubiquitous computing involves communities of self-interested agents, who may need to cooperate to achieve certain goals. Traditionally, cooperative behaviour has been analysed using game theory. Building upon this, we develop quantitative verification methods for *multi-player stochastic games*, which model communities of agents that can exhibit probabilistic behaviour, for example as a result of random choices. Property specifications are stated in terms of a probabilistic and reward extension of the well-known logic ATL, called rPATL [10], which can express properties such as: "does the coalition have a strategy to ensure that consensus is reached with probability at least 0.8, irrespective of the strategies of the other players?". The framework has been applied to the analysis of a smartgrid protocol, collective decision making for sensor networks and user-centric networks, where we discovered and corrected flaws in existing protocols [10,41]. The techniques have been implemented as an extension of PRISM [11], and include both verification, as well as strategy synthesis. Recently, an extension with multi-objective properties was formulated [12].

Probabilistic Real-Time Protocols. Many ubiquitous computing applications require consideration of probability and continuous real-time, in conjunction with nondeterminism that is used to model distributed computation. The model of *probabilistic timed automata* (PTAs) [39] can be viewed as a Markov decision process extended with real-valued clocks or, alternatively, an extension of the well-known timed automata formalism with discrete probabilistic choice. PTAs naturally model distributed randomised algorithms with timing, for example the ZeroConf protocol, as well as the medium access protocols for wireless networks, including WiFi, Bluetooth and ZigBee; all have been analysed with PRISM [1]. A number of techniques have been developed for quantitative verification of PTAs, including the *digital clocks* [38] approach; forwards [39] and backwards reachability [40] based on *zones*; and *game-based quantitative abstraction-refinement* [35]. Strategy synthesis is also possible [46]. PRISM provides native support for PTAs, via the techniques of [35] and [38].

Medical Devices. Embedded software is increasingly often used in medical devices, which monitor and control physical processes such as electrical signal in the heart or dosage of insulin. For example, an implantable cardiac pacemaker device reads electrical signals from sensors placed on the heart muscle, monitors the timing between heart beats, and, if any are missed, generates signals to stimulate the heart, maintaining the rate of 60-100 beats per minute. Quantitative verification can provide automated means to verify safety properties of the pacemaker, but the models must incorporate *continuous dynamics*, necessary to model the electrical signal in the heart, in addition to timing and probabilities. A further difficulty is the need to verify the properties against realistic heart models. Recently, we developed two physiologically relevant heart models, one based on ECG signals [9] and the other on a network of cardiac cells [14]. We have composed the heart models with timed automata models of pacemaker software, and subjected the composed system to quantitative verification. We are able to verify basic safety properties, for example whether the pacemaker corrects the slow beat of the heart, as well as more complex properties, such as providing a detailed analysis of energy consumption.

A specific challenge of medical devices is that they need to interface to biological systems. Quantitative modelling and verification technology has already been applied to DNA computing devices [44], where it was able to automatically discover and diagnose a design error. These methods are applicable to molecular sensing devices at the nanoscale.

4 Challenges and Future Directions

Ubiquitous computing was conceived over 20 years ago by Marc Weiser [49] and has been unstoppable since. Mobile devices have far outstripped the sales of desktop PCs. Enhanced with a multitude of sensors, smartphones and tablets are being used for a variety of tasks, from email, through looking up restaurants nearby, to monitoring of the heart rate and air pollution.

The emergence of ubiquitous computing has posed new challenges for software and device designers. Ubiquitous computing was recognised in the UK as a Grand Challenge [42], subdivided into: the engineering of ubiquitous computing devices, their scientific understanding, and human interaction mechanisms. The research on quantitative verification reported in this paper contributes to the scientific understanding of ubiquitous computing led by Robin Milner, and is related to the Verified Software initiative of Tony Hoare. Quantitative verification research is very much inspired by their vision. It naturally complements the core activities of the two initiatives, focusing on practical, algorithmic solutions, that have the potential to drive the development of industrially-relevant methodologies and software tools to support the design of ubiquitous computing devices.

Much progress has been made in quantitative verification for ubiquitous computing, as reported here and elsewhere, and supported by effective software tools. Successes include synthesising safe strategies for autonomous vehicles; analysing quantitative trends of low-level network protocols; finding and correcting flaws in smartgrid energy distribution protocols; development of methodologies for the verification of medical devices; and adaptive service-based frameworks which can continuously guarantee the satisfaction of given QoS properties. Key limitations of current techniques are poor scalability of quantitative verification; lack of effective methods for integrating discrete, continuous and stochastic dynamics;

and poor efficiency of quantitative runtime verification. The scale and complexity of the ubiquitous computing scenarios are so great that the challenges that remain seem prohibitive. We anticipate that following topics will be particularly difficult: scalability of quantitative verification; compositional quantitative frameworks; effective runtime steering; quality assurance for embedded software; efficiency of strategy synthesis for autonomous control in dynamic scenarios; and quantitative verification for stochastic hybrid systems.

Acknowledgements. This research is supported in part by ERC Advanced Grant VERIWARE and the Institute for the Future of Computing, Oxford Martin School.

References

1. PRISM, `http://www.prismmodelchecker.org`
2. Baier, C., Katoen, J.P.: Principles of Model Checking. MIT Press (2008)
3. Baier, C., Haverkort, B., Hermanns, H., Katoen, J.P.: Model-checking algorithms for continuous-time Markov chains. IEEE Transactions on Software Engineering 29, 524–541 (2003)
4. Basagiannis, S., Petridou, S.G., Alexiou, N., Papadimitriou, G.I., Katsaros, P.: Quantitative analysis of a certified e-mail protocol in mobile environments: A probabilistic model checking approach. Computers & Security 30(4), 257–272 (2011)
5. Bucur, D., Kwiatkowska, M.: On software verification for TinyOS. Journal of Software and Systems 84(10), 1693–1707 (2011)
6. Calinescu, R., Ghezzi, C., Kwiatkowska, M., Mirandola, R.: Self-adaptive software needs quantitative verification at runtime. Communications of the ACM 55(9), 69–77 (2012)
7. Calinescu, R., Grunske, L., Kwiatkowska, M., Mirandola, R., Tamburrelli, G.: Dynamic QoS management and optimisation in service-based systems. IEEE Transactions on Software Engineering 37(3), 387–409 (2011)
8. Chaki, S., Giampapa, J.A.: Probabilistic verification of coordinated multi-robot missions. In: Bartocci, E., Ramakrishnan, C.R. (eds.) SPIN 2013. LNCS, vol. 7976, pp. 135–153. Springer, Heidelberg (2013)
9. Chen, T., Diciolla, M., Kwiatkowska, M., Mereacre, A.: Quantitative verification of implantable cardiac pacemakers. In: Proc. 33rd Real-Time Systems Symposium (RTSS). IEEE Computer Society (2012)
10. Chen, T., Forejt, V., Kwiatkowska, M., Parker, D., Simaitis, A.: Automatic verification of competitive stochastic systems. In: Formal Methods in System Design (to appear, 2013)
11. Chen, T., Forejt, V., Kwiatkowska, M., Parker, D., Simaitis, A.: PRISM-games: A model checker for stochastic multi-player games. In: Piterman, N., Smolka, S.A. (eds.) TACAS 2013 (ETAPS 2013). LNCS, vol. 7795, pp. 185–191. Springer, Heidelberg (2013)
12. Chen, T., Forejt, V., Kwiatkowska, M., Simaitis, A., Wiltsche, C.: On stochastic games with multiple objectives. In: Proc. MFCS 2013. LNCS, Springer (2013)
13. Chen, T., Kwiatkowska, M., Simaitis, A., Wiltsche, C.: Synthesis for multi-objective stochastic games: An application to autonomous urban driving. In: Proc. QEST 2013 (to appear, 2013)

14. Chen, T., Diciolla, M., Kwiatkowska, M.Z., Mereacre, A.: A Simulink hybrid heart model for quantitative verification of cardiac pacemakers. In: Proc. HSCC 2013, pp. 131–136. ACM (2013)
15. Chen, T., Diciolla, M., Kwiatkowska, M.Z., Mereacre, A.: Symbolic model checking for probabilistic timed automata. In: ACM Transactions on Computational Logic (to appear, 2013)
16. Chen, T., Hahn, E.M., Han, T., Kwiatkowska, M., Qu, H., Zhang, L.: Model repair for Markov decision processes. In: Proc. TASE 2013. IEEE (to appear, 2013)
17. Duflot, M., Kwiatkowska, M., Norman, G., Parker, D.: A formal analysis of Bluetooth device discovery. Int. Journal on Software Tools for Technology Transfer 8(6), 621–632 (2006)
18. Egami, K., Matsumoto, S., Nakamura, M.: Ubiquitous cloud: Managing service resources for adaptive ubiquitous computing. In: PerCom Workshops, pp. 123–128 (2011)
19. Etessami, K., Kwiatkowska, M., Vardi, M., Yannakakis, M.: Multi-objective model checking of Markov decision processes. Logical Methods in Computer Science 4(4), 1–21 (2008)
20. Feng, L., Kwiatkowska, M., Parker, D.: Compositional verification of probabilistic systems using learning. In: Proc. QEST 2010, pp. 133–142. IEEE CS Press (2010)
21. Feng, L., Kwiatkowska, M., Parker, D.: Automated learning of probabilistic assumptions for compositional reasoning. In: Giannakopoulou, D., Orejas, F. (eds.) FASE 2011. LNCS, vol. 6603, pp. 2–17. Springer, Heidelberg (2011)
22. Filieri, A., Ghezzi, C., Tamburrelli, G.: Run-time efficient probabilistic model checking. In: Taylor, R.N., Gall, H., Medvidovic, N. (eds.) Proc. ICSE, pp. 341–350. ACM (2011)
23. Forejt, V., Kwiatkowska, M., Norman, G., Parker, D.: Automated verification techniques for probabilistic systems. In: Bernardo, M., Issarny, V. (eds.) SFM 2011. LNCS, vol. 6659, pp. 53–113. Springer, Heidelberg (2011)
24. Forejt, V., Kwiatkowska, M., Norman, G., Parker, D., Qu, H.: Quantitative multi-objective verification for probabilistic systems. In: Abdulla, P.A., Leino, K.R.M. (eds.) TACAS 2011. LNCS, vol. 6605, pp. 112–127. Springer, Heidelberg (2011)
25. Forejt, V., Kwiatkowska, M., Parker, D.: Pareto curves for probabilistic model checking. In: Chakraborty, S., Mukund, M. (eds.) ATVA 2012. LNCS, vol. 7561, pp. 317–332. Springer, Heidelberg (2012)
26. Forejt, V., Kwiatkowska, M., Parker, D., Qu, H., Ujma, M.: Incremental runtime verification of probabilistic systems. In: Qadeer, S., Tasiran, S. (eds.) RV 2012. LNCS, vol. 7687, pp. 314–319. Springer, Heidelberg (2013)
27. Fruth, M.: Probabilistic model checking of contention resolution in the IEEE 802.15.4 low-rate wireless personal area network protocol. In: Proc. 2nd International Symposium on Leveraging Applications of Formal Methods, Verification and Validation, ISOLA 2006 (2006)
28. Gallina, L., Han, T., Kwiatkowska, M., Marin, A., Rossi, S., Spano, A.: Automatic energy-aware performance analysis of mobile ad-hoc networks. In: Proc. IFIP Wireless Days, WD 2012 (2012)
29. Hahn, E.M., Han, T., Zhang, L.: Synthesis for PCTL in parametric Markov decision processes. In: Proc. NASA Formal Methods, pp. 146–161 (2011)
30. Hansson, H., Jonsson, B.: A logic for reasoning about time and reliability. Formal Aspects of Computing 6, 512–535 (1994)
31. Kemeny, J., Snell, J., Knapp, A.: Denumerable Markov Chains. Springer (1976)
32. Kress-Gazit, H., Fainekos, G.E., Pappas, G.J.: Where's waldo? sensor-based temporal logic motion planning. In: Proc. ICRA 2007, pp. 3116–3121. IEEE (2007)

33. Kwiatkowska, M.: Quantitative verification: Models, techniques and tools. In: Proc. ESEC/FSE 2007, pp. 449–458. ACM Press (September 2007)
34. Kwiatkowska, M., Norman, G., Parker, D.: Stochastic model checking. In: Bernardo, M., Hillston, J. (eds.) SFM 2007. LNCS, vol. 4486, pp. 220–270. Springer, Heidelberg (2007)
35. Kwiatkowska, M., Norman, G., Parker, D.: Stochastic games for verification of probabilistic timed automata. In: Ouaknine, J., Vaandrager, F.W. (eds.) FORMATS 2009. LNCS, vol. 5813, pp. 212–227. Springer, Heidelberg (2009)
36. Kwiatkowska, M., Norman, G., Parker, D.: PRISM 4.0: Verification of probabilistic real-time systems. In: Gopalakrishnan, G., Qadeer, S. (eds.) CAV 2011. LNCS, vol. 6806, pp. 585–591. Springer, Heidelberg (2011)
37. Kwiatkowska, M., Norman, G., Parker, D., Qu, H.: Assume-guarantee verification for probabilistic systems. In: Esparza, J., Majumdar, R. (eds.) TACAS 2010. LNCS, vol. 6015, pp. 23–37. Springer, Heidelberg (2010)
38. Kwiatkowska, M., Norman, G., Parker, D., Sproston, J.: Performance analysis of probabilistic timed automata using digital clocks. Formal Methods in System Design 29, 33–78 (2006)
39. Kwiatkowska, M., Norman, G., Segala, R., Sproston, J.: Automatic verification of real-time systems with discrete probability distributions. Theoretical Computer Science 282, 101–150 (2002)
40. Kwiatkowska, M., Norman, G., Sproston, J., Wang, F.: Symbolic model checking for probabilistic timed automata. Information and Computation 205(7), 1027–1077 (2007)
41. Kwiatkowska, M., Parker, D., Simaitis, A.: Strategic analysis of trust models for user-centric networks. In: Proc. SR 2013. EPTCS, vol. 112, pp. 53–60 (2013)
42. Kwiatkowska, M., Rodden, T., Sassone, V. (eds.): From computers to ubiquitous computing, by 2020, vol. 366 (1881); Philosophical Transactions of the Royal Society A (2008)
43. Lahijanian, M., Andersson, S.B., Belta, C.: Temporal logic motion planning and control with probabilistic satisfaction guarantees. IEEE Transactions on Robotics 28(2), 396–409 (2012)
44. Lakin, M., Parker, D., Cardelli, L., Kwiatkowska, M., Phillips, A.: Design and analysis of DNA strand displacement devices using probabilistic model checking. Journal of the Royal Society Interface 9(72), 1470–1485 (2012)
45. Norman, G., Parker, D., Kwiatkowska, M., Shukla, S., Gupta, R.: Using probabilistic model checking for dynamic power management. Formal Aspects of Computing 17(2), 160–176 (2005)
46. Norman, G., Parker, D., Sproston, J.: Model checking for probabilistic timed automata. Formal Methods in System Design (2012) (to appear)
47. Paparrizos, I.K., Basagiannis, S., Petridou, S.G.: Quantitative analysis for authentication of low-cost RFID tags. In: Proc. LCN, pp. 295–298 (2011)
48. Susu, A.E., Acquaviva, A., Atienza, D., Micheli, G.D.: Stochastic modeling and analysis for environmentally powered wireless sensor nodes. In: Proc. WiOpt, pp. 125–134. IEEE (2008)
49. Weiser, M.: The computer for the 21st century. SIGMOBILE Mob. Comput. Commun. Rev. 3(3), 3–11 (1999)
50. Wongpiromsarn, T., Topcu, U., Murray, R.M.: Receding horizon temporal logic planning. IEEE Trans. Automat. Contr. 57(11), 2817–2830 (2012)

Mobile Membranes: Computability and Complexity

Bogdan Aman and Gabriel Ciobanu

Romanian Academy, Institute of Computer Science, Iaşi, Romania
A.I.Cuza University, 700506 Iaşi, Romania
baman@iit.tuiasi.ro, gabriel@info.uaic.ro

Abstract. Mobile membranes represent a variant of membrane systems in which the main operations are inspired by the biological operations of endocytosis and exocytosis. We study the computational power of mobile membranes, proving an optimal computability result: three membranes are enough to have the same computational power as a Turing machine. Regarding the computational complexity, we present a semi-uniform polynomial solution for a strong NP-complete problem (SAT problem) by using only endocytosis, exocytosis and elementary division.

1 Introduction

Systems of mobile membranes are part of a larger approach defined by membrane computing. Basic membrane systems (also called P systems) together with several variants are presented in the monograph [15] and in the handbook [16]. Membrane systems were introduced as distributed, parallel and non-deterministic computing models inspired by the compartments of eukaryotic cells and their biochemical reactions. The structure of the cell is represented by a set of hierarchically embedded regions, each delimited by a surrounding boundary (called membrane), and all contained inside a skin membrane. A membrane without any other membrane inside is said to be elementary, while a membrane with other membranes inside is said to be composite. Multisets of objects are distributed inside these regions, and they can be modified or communicated between adjacent compartments.

Objects represent the formal counterpart of molecular species (ions, proteins, etc.) floating inside cellular compartments, and they are described by means of strings over a given alphabet. Evolution rules represent the formal counterpart of chemical reactions, and are given in the form of rewriting rules which operate on the objects, as well as on the structure by endocytosis, exocytosis and elementary division.

A membrane system can perform computations in the following way. Starting from an initial configuration which is defined by the multiset of objects initially placed inside the compartmentalized structure and by the sets of evolution rules, the system evolves by applying the evolution rules in a non-deterministic and maximally parallel manner (every rule that is applicable inside a region *has*

Z. Liu, J. Woodcock, and H. Zhu (Eds.): ICTAC 2013, LNCS 8049, pp. 59–75, 2013.

to be applied in that region). A rule is applicable when all the objects that appear on its left-hand side are available in the region where the rule is placed (the objects are not used by other rules applied in the same step). Due to the competition for available objects, some rules are applied non-deterministically. A halting configuration is reached when no rule can be applied anymore; the result is then given by the number of objects (in a specified region).

The first definition of mobile membranes is given in [12] where mobile membranes are presented as a variant of P systems with active membranes [15]. The new feature of mobile membranes is naturally inspired by the movement of cells, namely a membrane that is outside a neighboring membrane moves, is moved or moves by agreement inside the neighboring membrane (endocytosis, forced endocytosis or mutual endocytosis), or a membrane moves, is moved or moves by agreement outside the membrane where it is placed (exocytosis, forced exocytosis or mutual exocytosis).

A first approach regarding the computational power of a simple variant of mobile membrane systems is treated in [12]. Turing completeness is obtained by using nine membranes and the operations of endocytosis, exocytosis and elementary division (an elementary membrane is divided into two identical membranes). By using additional contextual evolution rules it is proved in [13] that four mobile membranes are enough to get the power of a Turing machine, while in [3] the number of mobile membranes is decreased to three.

The computational power of mobile membranes using endocytosis (endo), exocytosis (exo), forced endocytosis (fendo) and forced exocytosis (fexo) was studied in [9] where it is proved that twelve membranes can provide computational universality, while in [2] the result is improved by reducing the number of membranes to nine. It is worth to note that unlike the previous results, the context-free evolution of objects is not used in any of the results (proofs). Regarding $E0L$ and $ET0L$ systems [18], other results presented in [9] claim that eight membranes are enough to get the power of the ET0L systems and seven membranes for E0L systems.

Following a standard approach in membrane computing to look for membrane systems that are powerful enough to achieve the full power of Turing machines [15] with a minimal set of ingredients, in this paper we deal with the computability power of mobile membrane systems in which mobility is given by two more powerful operations: mutual endocytosis and mutual exocytosis. It is proved that it is enough to consider these biologically inspired operations and three membranes to get the full computational power of a Turing machine. Three membranes represents the minimum number of membranes in order to properly discuss movement by endocytosis and exocytosis: we work with two membranes inside a skin membrane. These theoretical results support the idea that systems of mobile membranes can represent the hardware part for a biological computer capable to compute all computable functions.

Many formal machine models (e.g., Turing machines) have an infinite number of memory locations, while membrane systems are computing devices of finite size having a finite description with a fixed amount of initial resources (membranes and objects). However, the biological operations allow an initial membrane system to evolve to a possibly infinite family of membrane systems obtained by division in order to solve a (decision) problem. We use notions from classical computational complexity theory adapted to membrane computing. The purpose of computational complexity theory is to provide bounds on the amount of resources necessary for any procedure (algorithm) solving a problem. Since mobile membranes are inspired by the biological endocytosis and exocytosis processes, the bounds of resources represent the quantitative requirements for solving a problem. The complexity notions related to membrane systems are presented in [17], where the authors use P systems with active membranes having associated electrical charges, membrane division and membrane creation.

According to [10], NP-complete problems are divided into weak (e.g., Partition, Subset Sum, Knapsack) and strong (e.g., SAT, Clique, Bin Packing) depending on the size of the input. In this paper we study the efficiency of mobile membranes, and present a semi-uniform polynomial solution for the best known strong NP-complete problem (SAT) by using systems that can perform only mutual endocytosis, mutual exocytosis and elementary division rules. In a previous paper [4], we also proposed a solution of a weak NP-complete problem: the Partition Problem. In order to find such a solution, mobile membranes are treated as deciding devices that respect the following conditions: (1) all computations halt, (2) two additional objects *yes* and *no* are used, and (3) exactly one of the objects *yes* (successful computation) and *no* (unsuccessful computation) appears in the halting configuration.

According to [17], a decision problem X is a pair (I_X, θ_X) such that I_X is a language over a finite alphabet (whose elements are called instances), and θ_X is a predicate over I_X. Its solvability is defined through the recognition of the language associated with it. Let M be a Turing machine with the working alphabet Γ, L a language over Γ, and the result of any halting computation is *yes* or *no*. If M is a deterministic device, it recognizes or decides L whenever, for any string u over Γ, if $u \in L$, then either M accepts u (the result on input u is *yes*), or M rejects u (the result on input u is *no*). If M is a non-deterministic device, it recognizes or decides L whenever, if for any string u over Γ, also $u \in L$ only if there exists a computation of M with input u such that the answer is *yes*.

2 Mobile Membrane Systems

Endocytosis and exocytosis are used in systems of mobile membranes [12], as well as in brane calculi [8]. In this paper we consider systems in which a movement is performed only if the involved membranes agree on the movement. This agreement is described by means of objects a and co-objects $\overline{a}$ present in the corresponding membranes involved in such a movement, with $\overline{\overline{a}} = a$. The duality relation is naturally extended over a multiset, namely $\overline{u} = \overline{a_1} \dots \overline{a_n}$ for $u = a_1 \dots a_n$. An object a marks the active part of the movement, and an object $\overline{a}$ marks the passive part. The motivation for introducing a mutual agreement in the rules of mobile membranes comes both from biology (e.g., receptor-mediated endocytosis), and from process calculi [8].

For an alphabet $V = \{a_1, \ldots, a_n\}$, we denote by V^* the set of all the strings over V; λ denotes the empty string and $V^+ = V^* \backslash \{\lambda\}$. A multiset over V is represented by a string over V (together with all its permutations), and each string precisely identifies a multiset.

Definition 1. *A* system of mobile membranes with elementary division *is a construct* $\Pi = (V, H, \mu, w_1, \ldots, w_n, R)$, *where:*

1. $n \geq 1$ *is the number of membranes in the initial configuration;* $(n \leq |H|)$
2. V *is an alphabet (its elements are called* objects*);*
3. H *is a finite set of* labels *for membranes;*
4. $\mu \subset H \times H$ *is the initial* membrane structure, *such that* $(i, j) \in \mu$ *denotes that the membrane labelled by* j *is contained in the membrane labelled by* i*; the hierarchical structure denoted by* μ *is described by brackets in our linear notation (e.g.,* $\mu = \{(m, h)\}$ *is* $[\,[\,]_h]_m$*).*
5. $w_1, \ldots, w_n \in V^*$ *are* multisets of objects *placed in the* n *regions of* μ*;*
6. R *is a finite set of* developmental rules *of the following forms, with* $h, m \in H$, $a, \overline{a} \in V$, $v, v', w, w' \in V^*$, $|v| \leq 1$, $|v'| \leq 1$, M_1 *and* M_2 *denote (possibly empty) multisets of objects, elementary and composite membranes, while* M_3 *denotes a (possibly empty) multiset of objects.*
   (a) $[av]_h[\overline{a}v']_m \to [\,[w]_h w']_m$ mutual endocytosis (mendo)

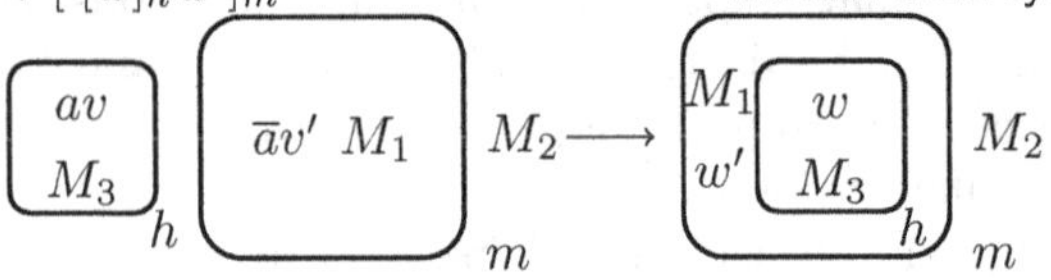

   An elementary membrane labelled h *enters the adjacent membrane labelled* m *under the control of the multisets of objects* av *and* $\overline{a}v'$*. The labels* h *and* m *remain unchanged, and the multisets of objects* av *and* $\overline{a}v'$ *are replaced by the multisets of objects* w *and* w'*, respectively.*
   (b) $[\overline{a}v'[av]_h]_m \to [w]_h[w']_m$ mutual exocytosis (mexo)

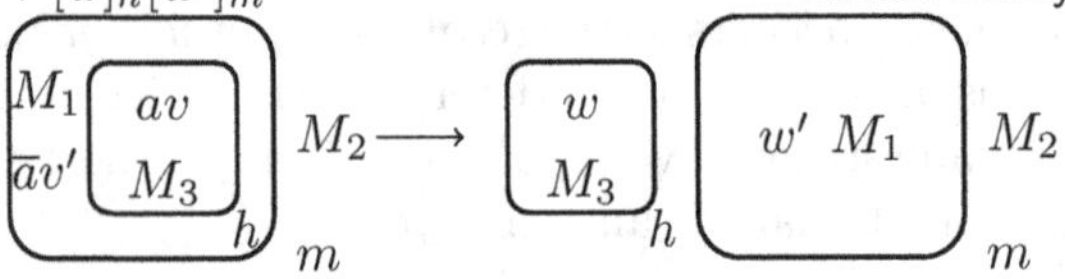

   An elementary membrane labelled h *exits a membrane labelled* m*, under the control of the multisets of objects* av *and* $\overline{a}v'$*. The labels of the two membranes remain unchanged, and the multisets of objects* av *and* $\overline{a}v'$ *are replaced by the multisets of objects* w *and* w'*, respectively.*
   (c) $[a]_h \to [w]_h[w']_h$ elementary division (ediv)

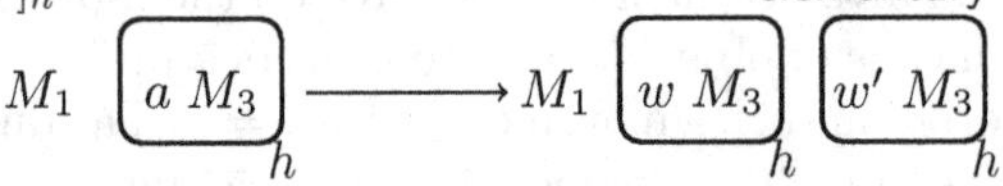

   An elementary membrane labelled h*, containing an object* a*, is divided into two membranes labelled* h*. A copy of each object from membrane* h *is placed inside the new created membranes, except for object* a *which is replaced by the multisets of objects* w *and* w'*.*

A configuration of a system with mobile membranes is a finite tree with nodes labelled by the elements of H, each node being assigned a finite multiset of objects. The rules are applied according to the following principles:

1. All the rules are applied in parallel by non-deterministically choosing the rules, the membranes and the objects in such a way that the parallelism is maximal; this means that in each step a set of rules is applied such that no further rule can be added to the set.
2. The membrane m from the rules of type $(a) - (c)$ is said to be passive (identified by the use of an object $\overline{a}$), while the membrane h is said to be active (identified by the use of an object a). In any step of a computation, any object and any active membrane can be involved in at most one rule, while passive membranes are not considered to be involved in the use of the rules (hence they can be used by several rules at the same time as passive membranes).
3. When a membrane is moved across another membrane by endocytosis or exocytosis, all objects contained in it are moved.
4. All the objects and membranes which do not evolve at a given step are passed unchanged to the next configuration of the system.

Transitions among the configurations of the system are obtained by using the rules described above. A computation is a sequence of transitions starting from the initial configuration (the initial membrane structure and the initial distribution of objects within regions). A computation is successful if it halts (it reaches a configuration where no rule can be applied). The multiplicity vector of the multiset of objects from a special membrane called the output membrane is considered as a result of the computation. Thus, the result of a halting computation consists of all the vectors describing the multiplicity of objects from the output membrane; a non-halting computation provides no output. The set of vectors of natural numbers produced in this way by a system Π is denoted by $Ps(\Pi)$.

3 Computational Power of Mobile Membranes

Several notions and notations from the field of formal languages that are used here can be found in [19]. For a string $x \in V^*$, $|x|_a$ denotes the number of occurrences of symbol a in x. For an alphabet V, the *Parikh vector* is $\psi_V : V^* \to \mathbf{N}^n$ with $\psi_V(x) = (|x|_{a_1}, \ldots, |x|_{a_n})$, for all $x \in V^*$. For a language L, the Parikh vector is $\psi_V(L) = \{\psi_V(x) \mid x \in L\}$, while for a family FL of languages, it is $PsFL = \{\psi_V(L) \mid L \in FL\}$.

Minsky introduced the concept of register machines by showing that the power of Turing machines can be achieved by such abstract machines using a finite number of registers for storing arbitrarily large non-negative integers [14]. A register machine runs a program consisting of labelled instructions which encode simple operations for updating the content of the register.

Definition 2. *An* n-register machine *is a construct* $M = (n, B, l_0, l_h, I)$, *where:*

- n *is the number of registers;* B *is a set of labels;* l_0 *and* l_h *are the labels of the initial and halting instructions;* I *is a set of labelled instructions of the form* $l_i : (op(r), l_j, l_k)$, *where* $op(r)$ *is an operation on register* r *of* M, *and* l_i, l_j, l_k *are labels from the set* B.
- *the machine is capable of the following instructions:*
  1. $l_i : (INC(r), l_j, l_k)$: *Add one to the content of register* r *and proceed, in a non-deterministic way, to instruction with label* l_j *or to instruction with label* l_k*; in the deterministic variant,* $l_j = l_k$ *and then the instruction is written in the form* $l_i : (INC(r), l_j)$.
  2. $l_i : (DEC(r), l_j, l_k)$: *If register* r *is not empty, then subtract one from its contents and go to instruction with label* l_j, *otherwise proceed to instruction with label* l_k.
  3. l_h : *halt: This instruction stops the machine and can only be assigned to the final label* l_h.

Considering the number of objects and reduction to a register machine, we prove that the family $\mathbf{N}RE$ of all the sets of natural numbers generated by arbitrary grammars is the same as the family $\mathbf{N}MM_3^{pr}(mendo, mexo)$ of all the sets of natural numbers generated by systems with three mobile membranes using *mendo* and *mexo* rules, and also a priority relation between rules (it is used when checking if some objects are present inside a membrane). The biologically motivated priority relation corresponds to the fact that certain reactions/reactants are more active than others, and can be interpreted as a competition for reactants/objects. This is calculated by looking at the cardinality of the objects in a specified *output membrane* of the mobile membrane systems at the end of a halting computation. The proof is based on the observation that each set from $\mathbf{N}RE$ is the range of a partial recursive function.

Theorem 1 ([20]). *A 3-register machine can compute any partial recursive function of one variable. It starts with the arguments in a counter, and (if it halts) leaves the answer in another counter.*

We investigate here new computability results using movement based on mutual agreements. For systems of mobile membranes using mutual endocytosis and mutual exocytosis, we get the same computation power; the next result shows that it is possible to get similar results as for register machines.

Theorem 2. $\mathbf{N}MM_3^{pr}(mendo, mexo) = \mathbf{N}RE$.

Proof. We prove only the assertion $\mathbf{N}RE \subseteq \mathbf{N}MM_3^{pr}(mendo, mexo)$; the other inclusion is based on the fact that Turing machines or type-0 grammars are able to simulate systems of mobile membranes with elementary division rules. We prove that for each partial recursive function $f : \mathbf{N} \to \mathbf{N}$, there is a mobile membrane system Π with three membranes satisfying the following condition: for any arbitrary $x \in \mathbf{N}$, the system "generates" a multiset of the form o_1^x and halts if and only if $f(x)$ is defined; if so, the result is $f(x)$.

In order to prove the assertion using similar arguments as in [11], we assume that the output register is never decremented during the computation. This happens without loss of generality. Consider a program P, which computes f, consisting of h instructions $P_1, \dots, P_h$. Let P_h correspond to the instruction HALT, and P_1 be the first instruction. The input value x is expected to be in register 1, and the output value in register 3 (we use 3 registers). We construct a mobile membrane $\Pi = (V, H, \mu, w_0, w_I, w_{op}, R)$ with output membrane I, where:

$V = \{s\} \cup \{o_r \mid 1 \le r \le 3\} \cup \{P_k, P'_k \mid 1 \le k \le h\} \cup \{\beta, \overline{\beta}, \gamma, \overline{\gamma}\}$
$\cup \{\beta_r \mid 1 \le r \le 3\}$

$H = \{0, I, op\}$ $\mu = \{(0, I), (0, op)\}$ $w_I = s\beta\overline{\gamma}$ $w_0 = \emptyset$ $w_{op} = \overline{\beta}\,\gamma$

(i) Generation of the initial contents x of register 1:
1. $[s\beta]_I[\overline{\beta}]_{op} \rightarrow [[s\beta]_I\overline{\beta}]_{op}$ (mendo)
   $[[s\beta]_I\overline{\beta}]_{op} \rightarrow [so_1\beta]_I[\overline{\beta}]_{op}$ (mexo)
2. $[[s\beta]_I\overline{\beta}]_{op} \rightarrow [P_1\beta]_I[\overline{\beta}]_{op}$ (mexo)

The rules from 1 can be used any number of times, generating a number x (o_1^x) as the initial content of register 1. Rule 2 replaces s with the initial instruction P_1, and we are ready for the simulation of the register machine.

(ii) Simulation of an add rule $P_i = (INC(r), j)$, $1 \le r \le 3, 1 \le i < h, 1 \le j \le h$
3. $[P_i\beta]_I[\overline{\beta}]_{op} \rightarrow [[P_i\beta]_I\overline{\beta}]_{op}$ (mendo)
4. $[[P_i\beta]_I\overline{\beta}]_{op} \rightarrow [P_jo_r\beta]_I[\overline{\beta}]_{op}$ (mexo)

Membrane I enters membrane *op* using rule 3, and then exits it by replacing P_i with P_jo_r (rule 4), thus simulating an addition.

(iii) Simulation of a subtract rule $P_i = (DEC(r), j, k)$, $1 \le r \le 3$, $1 \le i < h$, $1 \le j, k \le h$
5. $[[P_i\beta]_I\overline{\beta}]_{op} \rightarrow [P'_j\beta_r\beta]_I[\overline{\beta}]_{op}$ (mexo)
6. $[o_r\beta_r\beta]_I[\overline{\beta}]_{op} \rightarrow [[\beta]_I\overline{\beta}]_{op}$ (mendo)
   $[P'_j\beta_r\beta]_I[\overline{\beta}]_{op} \rightarrow [[P'_k\beta]_I\overline{\beta}]_{op}$ (mendo)
7. $[[P'_j\beta]_I\overline{\beta}]_{op} \rightarrow [P_j\beta]_I[\overline{\beta}]_{op}$ (mexo)
   $[[P'_k\beta]_I\overline{\beta}]_{op} \rightarrow [P_k\beta]_I[\overline{\beta}]_{op}$ (mexo)

To simulate a subtract instruction, we start with rule 3 having membrane I entering membrane *op*. Then rule 5 is used; P_i is replaced by $P'_j\beta_r$, and membrane I exits membrane *op*. The newly created object β_r denotes the register which has to be decreased. In order to check if there is an object o_r present in membrane I, we impose a priority relation between the two rules at item 6: the first one is applied whenever possible; only in case the first rule cannot be applied, the second one is used. If there is an o_r in membrane I, then by rule 6 the object o_r is removed together with β_r, and membrane I enters membrane *op*. This is followed by rule 7, where P'_j is replaced by P_j, and membrane I is back inside the skin membrane. If there are no o_r in membrane I, then by applying rule 6, P'_j together with β_r is replaced by P'_k. This is followed by rule 7, where P'_k is replaced by P_k and membrane I is inside the skin membrane, thus simulating a subtraction.

(iv) Halting:
8. $[\gamma]_{op}[P_h\overline{\gamma}]_I \rightarrow [[\gamma]_{op}\overline{\gamma}]_I$ (mendo)

To halt the computation, the halt instruction P_h must be simulated. Once we obtain P_h in output membrane I, membrane op enters membrane I and the computation stops (rule 8). When the system halts, the output membrane I contains o_3's, namely the content of register 3.

□

The family of all sets $Ps(\Pi)$ generated by systems of n mobile membranes using the mutual endocytosis *mendo* and the mutual exocytosis *mexo* is denoted by $PsMM_n(mendo, mexo)$. We denote by $PsRE$ the family of Turing computable sets of vectors generated by arbitrary grammars.

In Theorem 2 we have shown that systems with three mobile membranes using *mendo* and *mexo* rules generate all the sets of natural numbers. Another related result is presented in [3], namely these systems generate the recursive enumerable sets of vectors of natural numbers.

Theorem 3 ([3]). $PsMM_3(mendo, mexo) = PsRE$.

According to [18], an E0L system is a construct $G = (V, T, \omega, R)$ where V is the alphabet, $T \subseteq V$ is the terminal alphabet, $\omega \in V^*$ is the axiom, and R is a finite set of rules of the form $a \to v$ with $a \in V$ and $v \in V^*$ such that for each $a \in V$ there is at least one rule $a \to v$ in R. For $w_1, w_2 \in V^*$, we say that $w_1 \Rightarrow w_2$ if $w_1 = a_1 \ldots a_n$, $w_2 = v_1 \ldots v_n$ for $a_i \to v_i \in R$, $1 \leq i \leq n$. The generated language is $L(G) = \{x \in T^* \mid \omega \Rightarrow^* x\}$. $E0L$ denotes the family of languages generated by extended 0L grammars.

An ET0L systems is a construct $G = (V, T, \omega, R_1, \ldots R_n)$ such that each (V, T, ω, R_i) is an E0L system; each R_i is called a table, $1 \leq i \leq n$. The generated language is defined as $L(G) = \{x \in T^* \mid \omega \Rightarrow_{R_{j_1}} \cdots \Rightarrow_{R_{j_m}} w_m = x\}$, where $m \geq 0, 1 \leq j_i \leq n, 1 \leq i \leq m$. $ET0L$ denotes the family of languages generated by extended tabled 0L grammars.

If the length of the left hand side of the rules is considered, it can be shown that Proposition 1 operates with rules less complex than those occurring before.

Proposition 1. $PsET0L \subseteq PsMM_3(mendo, mexo)$.

Proof. In what follows, we use the following normal form: each language $L \in ET0L$ can be generated by $G = (V, T, \omega, R_1, R_2)$. Moreover, from [18], any derivation starts by several steps of R_1, then R_2 is used exactly once, and the process is iterated; the derivation ends by using R_2.

Let $G = (V, T, \omega, R_1, R_2)$ be an ET0L system in the normal form. We construct the mobile membrane system $\Pi = (V', H, \mu, w_0, w_1, w_2, R)$ with output membrane 0, where:

$V' = \{\dagger, \alpha, \overline{\alpha}, \beta, \overline{\beta}\} \cup \{\beta_i, \overline{\beta}_i \,|\, i = 1, 2\} \cup V \cup V_i$, with $V_i = \{a_i \,|\, a \in V\}$, $i = 1, 2$,
$H = \{0, 1, 2\}$ $\quad \mu = \{(2, 0), (2, 1)\}$ $\quad w_0 = \omega\alpha\beta_1\overline{\beta}$ $\quad w_1 = \overline{\alpha}\beta\overline{\beta}_i$

<u>*Simulation of table R_i, $i = 1, 2$*</u>

1. $[\beta_i]_0[\overline{\beta_i}]_1 \to [[\beta_i]_0\overline{\beta}_i]_1$ (mendo)
2. $[[a\beta_i]_0\overline{\beta}_i]_1 \to [w_i\beta_i]_0[\overline{\beta}_i]_1$, if $a \to w \in R_i$ (mexo)

3. $[\beta]_1[a\overline{\beta}]_0 \to [[\beta]_1\dagger\overline{\beta}]_0$ (mendo)
4. $[[a_i\beta_i]_0\overline{\beta}_i]_1 \to [a\beta_i]_0[\overline{\beta}_i]_1$ (mexo)
5. $[\beta]_1[a_i\overline{\beta}]_0 \to [[\beta]_1\dagger\overline{\beta}]_0$ (mendo)
6. $[[\beta_1\alpha]_0\overline{\alpha}]_1 \to [\beta_i\alpha]_0[\overline{\alpha}]_1$ (mexo)
   $[[\beta_2\alpha]_0\overline{\alpha}]_1 \to [\beta_1\alpha]_0[\overline{\alpha}]_1$ (mexo)
   $[[\beta_2\alpha]_0\overline{\alpha}]_1 \to [\alpha]_0[\overline{\alpha}]_1$ (mexo)
7. $[[\beta]_1\dagger\overline{\beta}]_0 \to [\beta]_1[\dagger\overline{\beta}]_0$ (mexo)
   $[\beta]_1[\dagger\overline{\beta}]_0 \to [[\beta]_1\dagger\overline{\beta}]_0$ (mendo)

In the initial configuration the string $\beta_1\omega$ is in membrane 0, where ω is the axiom and β_1 indicates that table 1 should be simulated first. The simulation begins with rule 1: membrane 0 enters membrane 1. In membrane 1, the only applicable rule is 2, by which the symbols $a \in V$ are replaced by w_1 corresponding to the rule $a \to w \in R_1$. Rules 1 and 2 can be repeated until all the symbols $a \in V$ have been replaced according to a rule in R_1, thus obtaining only objects from the alphabet V_1. In order to keep track of which table R_i of rules is simulated, each rule of the form $a \to w \in R_i$ is rewritten as $a \to w_i$.

If any symbol $a \in V$ is still present in membrane 0, i.e., if some symbol $a \in V$ has been left out from the simulation, membrane 1 enters membrane 0, replacing it with the trap symbol † (rule 3), and this triggers a never ending computation (rule 7). Otherwise, rules 1 and 4 are applied as long as required until all the symbols of V_1 are replaced by the corresponding symbols of V. Next, if any symbol $a_1 \in V_1$ has not been replaced, membrane 1 enters membrane 0 and the computation stops, replacing it with the trap symbol † (rule 5), and this triggers a never ending computation (rule 7). Otherwise, we have three possible evolutions (rule 6):

(i) if β_1 is in membrane 0, then it is replaced by β_i, and the computation continues with the simulation of table i;
(ii) if β_2 is in membrane 0, then it is replaced by β_1, and the computation continues with the simulation of table 1;
(iii) if β_2 is in membrane 0, then is deleted, and the computation stops.

Thus, all the vectors of $Ps(L(G))$ are contained in $Ps(\Pi)$; this means that $PsET0L \subseteq PsMM_3(mendo, mexo)$. □

Corollary 1. $PsE0L \subseteq PsMM_3(mendo, mexo)$.

4 Solving SAT Polynomially by Using Mobile Membranes

As stated in the introduction, we use mobile membranes as confluent deciding devices, in which all computations starting from the initial configuration agree on the result. A family $\mathbf{\Pi}$, a collection of mobile membrane systems Π, solves a decision problem if for each instance of the problem there is a member of the family able to decide on the instance. In order to define the notion of semi-uniformity, some notations are necessary:

- for a suitable alphabet Σ, each instance of the decision problem is encoded as a string w over Σ;
- $\mathbf{\Pi}(w)$ - the member of $\mathbf{\Pi}$ which solves the instance w.

Inspired from [17], for mobile membrane systems we have:

Definition 3. *Let* $X=(I_X,\theta_X)$ *be a decision problem, and* $\mathbf{\Pi}=\{\mathbf{\Pi}(w)|w\in I_X\}$ *be a family of mobile membrane systems.*

- $\mathbf{\Pi}$ *said to be is* polynomially uniform by Turing machines *if there exists a deterministic Turing machine working in polynomial time which constructs the system* $\mathbf{\Pi}(w)$ *from the instance* $w \in I_X$.
- $\mathbf{\Pi}$ *said to be* sound *with respect to* X *if the following holds: for each instance of the problem* $w \in I_X$, *if there exists an accepting computation of* $\mathbf{\Pi}(w)$, *then* $\theta_X(w) = 1$.
- $\mathbf{\Pi}$ *said to be* complete *with respect to* X *if the following holds: for each instance of the problem* $w \in I_X$, *if* $\theta_X(w) = 1$, *then every computation of* $\mathbf{\Pi}(w)$ *is an accepting computation.*

Definition 4. *A decision problem* X *is solvable in* polynomial time *by a family of mobile membrane systems* $\mathbf{\Pi} = \{\mathbf{\Pi}(w) \mid w \in I_X\}$, *if:*

- *The family* $\mathbf{\Pi}$ *is polynomially uniform by Turing machines.*
- *The family* $\mathbf{\Pi}$ *is polynomially bounded; that is, there exists a natural number* $k \in \mathbb{N}$ *such that for each instance* $w \in I_X$, *every computation of* $\mathbf{\Pi}(w)$ *performs at most* $|w|^k$ *steps.*
- *The family* $\mathbf{\Pi}$ *is sound and complete with respect to* X.

The family $\mathbf{\Pi}$ *is said to provide a* semi-uniform solution *to the problem* X.

4.1 Solving the SAT Problem

The SAT problem refers to the satisfiability of a propositional logic formula in conjunctive normal form (CNF). Let $\{x_1, x_2, \ldots, x_n\}$ be a set of propositional variables. A formula in CNF is of the form $\varphi = C_1 \wedge C_2 \wedge \cdots \wedge C_m$ where each C_i, $1 \leq i \leq m$ is a disjunction of the form $C_i = y_1 \vee y_2 \vee \cdots \vee y_r$ $(r \leq n)$, where each y_j is either a variable x_k or its negation $\neg x_k$. In this section, we propose a semi-uniform linear time solution to the SAT problem using the operations of *mendo*, *mexo* and elementary division. The maximal parallelism and movement based on mutual agreement are essential in order to obtain such a solution. The first one is used in order to check, after the generation stage, in only one step if all possible assignments of variables satisfy a certain clause C_i. The second one is also used in the checking stages in order to avoid overlapping of solutions, and also in the generation of the answer.

For any instance of SAT we construct a system of mobile membranes which solves it. Consider the formula $\varphi = C_1 \wedge C_2 \wedge \ldots C_m$ over the variables $\{x_1, \ldots, x_n\}$. Consider a system of mobile membranes having the initial configuration

$$[[c_0\ \beta]_J[\overline{\beta}]_K[c\ \overline{d}]_L[g^{n-1}g_0]_1[a_1]_0]_2$$

and working over the alphabet:

$$V = \{c, \overline{c}, d, \overline{d}, g, g_0, \beta, \overline{\beta}, yes, no\} \cup \{a_i, t_i, f_i \mid 1 \le i \le n\}$$
$$\cup\{\beta_i, \overline{\beta}_i \mid 1 \le i \le m\} \cup \{c_i \mid 0 \le i \le n + 2m + 1\}$$

We use elementary division rules to generate all the possible assignments over the variables $\{x_1, \ldots, x_n\}$. The system of mobile membranes solving the SAT problem uses the rules:

(i) $[a_i]_0 \to [t_i\ a_{i+1}]_0[f_i\ a_{i+1}]_0$, for $1 \le i \le n-1$ (div)
$[a_n]_0 \to [tn\ \beta_1]_0[f_n\ \beta_1]_0$ (div)
$[g]_1 \to [\ ]_1[\ ]_1$ (div)
$[g_0]_1 \to [\overline{\beta_1}]_1[\overline{\beta_1}]_1$ (div)
The first two rules create 2^n membranes labelled by 0 containing all the possible assignments over variables $\{x_1, \ldots, x_n\}$. In each membrane labelled by 0 is placed also a symbol β_1 . The next two rules create 2^n membranes labelled by 1 containing each an object $\overline{\beta_1}$. The symbols β_1 and $\overline{\beta_1}$ are used to determine in two steps which assignments are true for C_1.

(ii) $[t_j\ \beta_i]_0[\overline{\beta_i}]_1 \to [[t_j\ \beta_i]_0\overline{\beta_i}]_1$ (mendo)
$[[t_j\ \beta_i]_0\overline{\beta_i}]_1 \to [t_j\ \beta_{i+1}]_0[\overline{\beta_{i+1}}]_1$, $1 \le i \le m-1$, $1 \le j \le n$ (mexo)
(if clause C_i contains the literal x_j)
$[f_j\ \beta_i]_0[\overline{\beta_i}]_1 \to [[f_j\ \beta_i]_0\overline{\beta_i}]_1$ (mendo)
$[[f_j\ \beta_i]_0\overline{\beta_i}]_1 \to [f_j\ \beta_{i+1}]_0[\overline{\beta_{i+1}}]_1$, $1 \le i \le m-1$, $1 \le j \le n$ (mexo)
(if clause C_i contains the literal $\neg x_j$)
$[t_j\ \beta_m]_0[\overline{\beta_m}]_1 \to [[t_j\ \beta_m]_0\overline{\beta_m}]_1$ (mendo)
$[[t_j\ \beta_m]_0\overline{\beta_m}]_1 \to [t_j\ \overline{c}]_0[\overline{\beta_m}]_1$, $1 \le j \le n$ (mexo)
(if clause C_m contains the literal x_j)
$[f_j\ \beta_m]_0[\overline{\beta_m}]_1 \to [[f_j\ \beta_m]_0\overline{\beta_m}]_1$ (mendo)
$[[f_j\ \beta_m]_0\overline{\beta_m}]_1 \to [f_j\ \overline{c}]_0[\overline{\beta_m}]_1$, $1 \le j \le n$ (mexo)
(if clause C_m contains the literal $\neg x_j$)
If some assignments satisfy the clause C_i, $1 \le i < m$, then the objects β_i from the corresponding membranes 0 are replaced by β_{i+1}. The assignments from the membranes containing β_{i+1} satisfy the clauses $C_1, \ldots, C_i$, the object β_{i+1} marking the fact that in the next step the clause C_{i+1} is checked. If there exists assignments which satisfy all the clauses, then the membranes containing these assignments contain an object $\overline{c}$ after $n + 2m$ steps.

(iii) $[c_i\ \beta]_J[\overline{\beta}]_K \to [[c_{i+1}\ \beta]_J\overline{\beta}]_K$ (mendo)
$[[c_i\ \beta]_J\overline{\beta}]_K \to [c_{i+1}\ \beta]_J[\overline{\beta}]_K$, $0 \le i \le n + 2m$ (mexo)
$[[c_{n+2m+1}\ \beta]_J\overline{\beta}]_K \to [d\ \beta]_J[\overline{\beta}]_K$ (mexo)
$[c_{n+2m+1}\ \beta]_J[\overline{\beta}]_K \to [[c_{n+2m+1}\ \beta]_J\overline{\beta}]_K$ (mendo)
These rules determine the number of steps performed. If this number is greater than $n + 2m + 1$, then an object d is created, which will subsequently create an object *no*. The number $n + 2m + 1$ corresponds to the following steps: generating space (n steps), verifying assignments ($2m$ steps), creating a *yes* object (1 step). An additional step can be performed, such that membrane J containing the object c_{n+2m+1} becomes sibling with membrane K, thus increasing the number of steps needed to create d to $n + 2m + 2$.

(iv) $[\overline{c}]_0[c]_L \to [[yes]_L]_0$ (mendo)
$[d]_J[\overline{d}]_L \to [[no]_J]_L$ (mendo)
A *yes* object is created whenever membrane L enters some membrane 0 in the $(2m+n+1)$-th step. If no membrane 0 contains an object $\overline{c}$, then a *no* object is created, in step $(2m+n+2)$ or $(2m+n+3)$, whenever or not membrane J enters membrane L. By applying one of these two rules, the other one cannot by applied any more, so at the end of the computation the system contains either an object *yes* or an object *no*.

The number of membranes in the initial configuration is 6, and the number of objects is $n+6$. The size of the working alphabet is $4n+4m+13$. The number of rules in the above system: $n+2$ rules of type (i), $4nm$ rules of type (ii), $n+2m+3$ rules of type (iii), and 2 rules of type (iv). Hence, the size of the constructed system of mobile membranes is $\mathcal{O}(mn)$.

The fact that the computation ends in $n+2m+3$ is given by the fact that $n+2m$ is an odd number, and thus we had to perform an extra step before generating d from c_{n+2m+1}. If $n+2m$ is an even number, then d is created after $n+2m+2$ steps.

Proposition 2. *Using mobile membrane systems, SAT can be solved in a polynomial number of steps.*

Example 1. We consider 3-CNF SAT problem with $\phi = C_1 \wedge C_2 \wedge C_3$ and $X = \{x_1, x_2, x_3\}$, $C_1 = x_1 \vee \neg x_3$, $C_2 = \neg x_1 \vee \neg x_2$ and $C_3 = x_2$. In this case, $n = 3$, $m = 3$ and

$$[[c_0\ \beta]_J[\overline{\beta}]_K[c\ \overline{d}]_L[g^2 g_0]_1[a_1]_0]_2$$

Graphically, this is illustrated as:

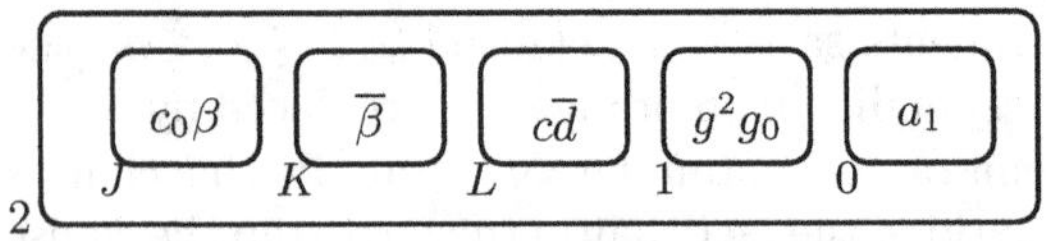

The evolution of the system is described by the following steps. The working space is created in $n = 3$ steps leading from the initial configuration 1 to configuration 4:

1. $[[c_0\ \beta]_J[\overline{\beta}]_K[c\ \overline{d}]_L[g^2 g_0]_1[a_1]_0]_2]$
2. $[[[c_1\ \beta]_J\overline{\beta}]_K[c\ \overline{d}]_L[g^2\overline{\beta_1}]_1^2[t_1\ a_2]_0[f_1\ a_2]_0]_2]$
3. $[[c_2\ \beta]_J[\overline{\beta}]_K[c\ \overline{d}]_L[g\overline{\beta_1}]_1^4[t_1\ t_2\ a_3]_0$
$[t_1\ f_2\ a_3]_0[f_1\ t_2\ a_3]_0[f_1\ f_2\ a_3]_0]_2]$
4. $[[[c_3\ \beta]_J\overline{\beta}]_K[c\ \overline{d}]_L[\overline{\beta_1}]_1^8[t_1\ t_2\ t_3\ \beta_1]_0[t_1\ t_2\ f_3\ \beta_1]_0$
$[t_1\ f_2\ t_3\ \beta_1]_0[t_1\ f_2\ f_3\ \beta_1]_0[f_1\ t_2\ t_3\ \beta_1]_0$
$[f_1\ t_2\ f_3\ \beta_1]_0[f_1\ f_2\ t_3\ \beta_1]_0[f_1\ f_2\ f_3\ \beta_1]_0]_2]$
Graphically, the working space is described by the following picture:

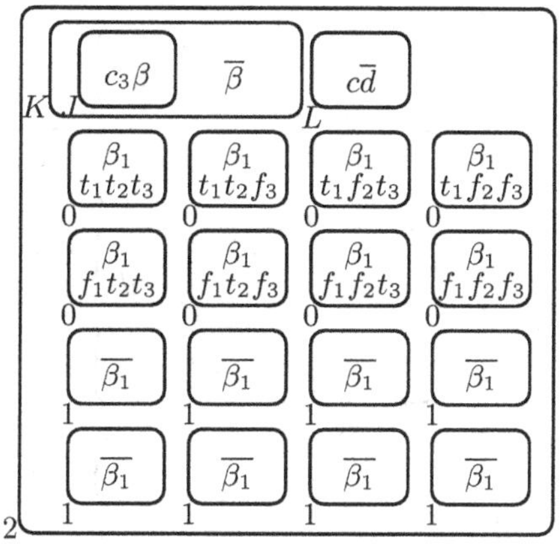

The next two steps mark the solutions of C_1 by replacing β_1 by β_2:

5. $[[c_4\ \beta]_J[\overline{\beta}]_K[c\ \overline{d}]_L[\overline{\beta_1}]_1^2[\overline{\beta_1}[t_1\ t_2\ t_3\ \beta_1]_0]_1$
$[\overline{\beta_1}[t_1\ t_2\ f_3\ \beta_1]_0]_1[\overline{\beta_1}[t_1\ f_2\ t_3\ \beta_1]_0]_1$
$[\overline{\beta_1}[t_1\ f_2\ f_3\ \beta_1]_0]_1[\overline{\beta_1}[f_1\ t_2\ f_3\ \beta_1]_0]_1$
$[\overline{\beta_1}[f_1\ f_2\ f_3\ \beta_1]_0]_1[f_1\ t_2\ t_3\ \beta_1]_0[f_1\ f_2\ t_3\ \beta_1]_0]_2]$
6. $[[[c_5\ \beta]_J\overline{\beta}]_K[c\ \overline{d}]_L[\overline{\beta_1}]_1^2[\overline{\beta_2}]_1^6[t_1\ t_2\ t_3\ \beta_2]_0$
$[t_1\ t_2\ f_3\ \beta_2]_0[t_1\ f_2\ t_3\ \beta_2]_0[t_1\ f_2\ f_3\ \beta_2]_0$
$[f_1\ t_2\ f_3\ \beta_2]_0[f_1\ f_2\ f_3\ \beta_2]_0[f_1\ t_2\ t_3\ \beta_1]_0[f_1\ f_2\ t_3\ \beta_1]_0]_2]$
The new configuration is represented graphically by:

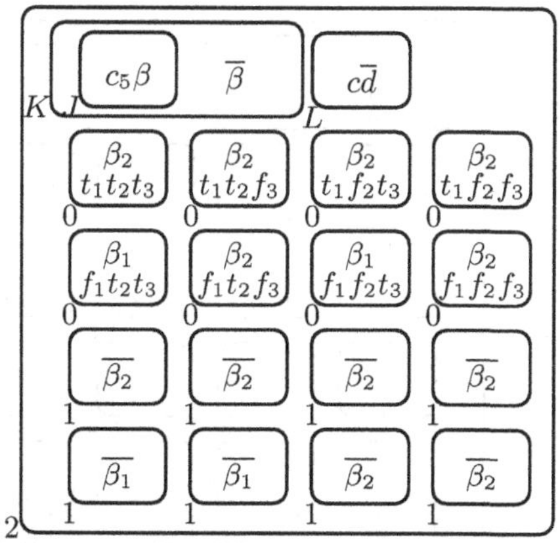

The next two steps mark the solutions of C_2 by replacing β_2 by β_3:

7. $[[c_6\ \beta]_J[\overline{\beta}]_K[c\ \overline{d}]_L[\overline{\beta_1}]_1^2[\overline{\beta_2}]_1^2[\overline{\beta_2}[t_1\ f_2\ t_3\ \beta_2]_0]_1$
$[\overline{\beta_2}[t_1\ f_2\ f_3\ \beta_2]_0]_1[\overline{\beta_2}[f_1\ t_2\ f_3\ \beta_2]_0]_1[\overline{\beta_2}[f_1\ f_2\ f_3\ \beta_2]_0]_1$
$[t_1\ t_2\ t_3\ \beta_2]_0[t_1\ t_2\ f_3\ \beta_2]_0[f_1\ t_2\ t_3\ \beta_1]_0[f_1\ f_2\ t_3\ \beta_1]_0]_2]$
8. $[[[c_7\ \beta]_J\overline{\beta}]_K[c\ \overline{d}]_L[\overline{\beta_1}]_1^2[\overline{\beta_2}]_1^2[\overline{\beta_3}]_1^4[t_1\ f_2\ t_3\ \beta_3]_0$
$[t_1\ f_2\ f_3\ \beta_3]_0[f_1\ t_2\ f_3\ \beta_3]_0[f_1\ f_2\ f_3\ \beta_3]_0[t_1\ t_2\ t_3\ \beta_2]_0$
$[t_1\ t_2\ f_3\ \beta_2]_0[f_1\ t_2\ t_3\ \beta_1]_0[f_1\ f_2\ t_3\ \beta_1]_0]_2]$
The new configuration is represented graphically by:

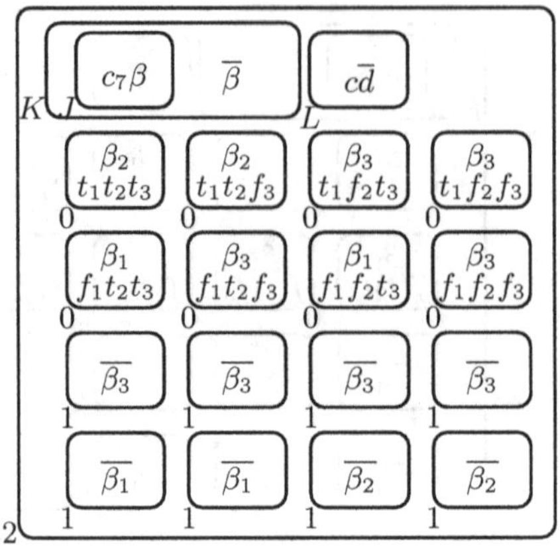

The next two steps mark the solutions of C_3 by replacing β_3 by $\overline{c}$:

9. $[[c_8\ \beta]_J[\overline{\beta}]_K[c\ \overline{d}]_L[\overline{\beta_1}]_1^2[\overline{\beta_2}]_1^2[\overline{\beta_3}]_1^3[\overline{\beta_3}[f_1\ t_2\ f_3\ \beta_3]_0]_1$
$[t_1\ f_2\ t_3\ \beta_2]_0[t_1\ f_2\ f_3\ \beta_2]_0[f_1\ f_2\ f_3\ \beta_2]_0[t_1\ t_2\ t_3\ \beta_2]_0$
$[t_1\ t_2\ f_3\ \beta_2]_0[f_1\ t_2\ t_3\ \beta_1]_0[f_1\ f_2\ t_3\ \beta_1]_0]_2]$
10. $[[[c_9\ \beta]_J\overline{\beta}]_K[c\ \overline{d}]_L[\overline{\beta_1}]_1^2[\overline{\beta_2}]_1^2[\overline{\beta_3}]_1^4[f_1\ t_2\ f_3\ \overline{c}]_0$
$[t_1\ f_2\ t_3\ \beta_3]_0[t_1\ f_2\ f_3\ \beta_3]_0[f_1\ f_2\ f_3\ \beta_3]_0[t_1\ t_2\ t_3\ \beta_2]_0$
$[t_1\ t_2\ f_3\ \beta_2]_0[f_1\ t_2\ t_3\ \beta_1]_0[f_1\ f_2\ t_3\ \beta_1]_0]_2]$
The new configuration is illustrated graphically below, where we have placed the membrane labelled by L near the membrane labelled by 0 containing the symbol $\overline{c}$ to emphasize that an interaction is possible:

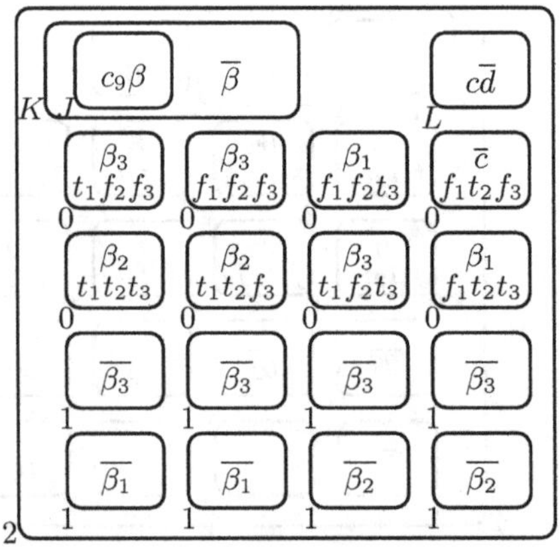

In the next step, an object *yes* is created and placed in membrane L, marking the fact that there exists an assignment such that the formula $(C_1 \wedge C_2 \wedge C_3)$ holds. The number of steps needed to create an object *yes* is $n + 2m + 1 = 3 + 6 + 1 = 10$.

11. $[[c_{10}\ \beta]_J[\overline{\beta}]_K[\overline{\beta_1}]_1^2[\overline{\beta_2}]_1^2[\overline{\beta_3}]_1^4[f_1\ t_2\ f_3\ [yes\ \overline{d}]_L]_0$
$[t_1\ f_2\ t_3\ \beta_3]_0[t_1\ f_2\ f_3\ \beta_3]_0[f_1\ f_2\ f_3\ \beta_3]_0[t_1\ t_2\ t_3\ \beta_2]_0$
$[t_1\ t_2\ f_3\ \beta_2]_0[f_1\ t_2\ t_3\ \beta_1]_0[f_1\ f_2\ t_3\ \beta_1]_0]_2]$
The new configuration is illustrated graphically as below:

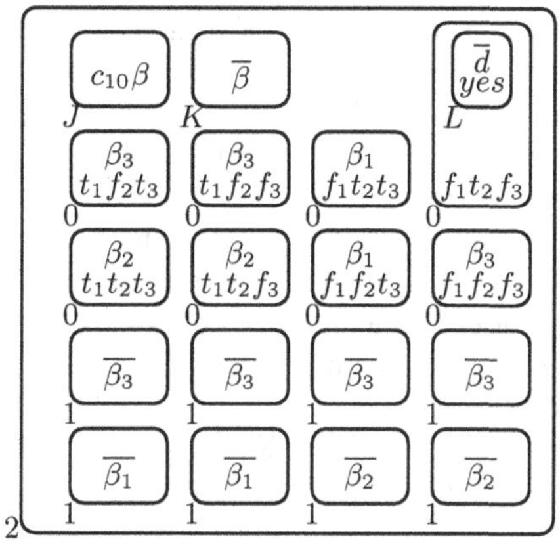

An object d used to create an object no is created after performing the steps:

12. $[[[c_{10}\ \beta]_J \overline{\beta}]_K [\overline{\beta_1}]^2_1 [\overline{\beta_2}]^2_1 [\overline{\beta_3}]^4_1 [f_1\ t_2\ f_3\ [yes\ \overline{d}]_L]_0$
$[t_1\ f_2\ t_3\ \beta_3]_0 [t_1\ f_2\ f_3\ \beta_3]_0 [f_1\ f_2\ f_3\ \beta_3]_0 [t_1\ t_2\ t_3\ \beta_2]_0$
$[t_1\ t_2\ f_3\ \beta_2]_0 [f_1\ t_2\ t_3\ \beta_1]_0 [f_1\ f_2\ t_3\ \beta_1]_0]_2]$
13. $[[d\ \beta]_J [\overline{\beta}]_K [\overline{\beta_1}]^2_1 [\overline{\beta_2}]^2_1 [\overline{\beta_3}]^4_1 [f_1\ t_2\ f_3\ [yes\ \overline{d}]_L]_0$
$[t_1\ f_2\ t_3\ \beta_3]_0 [t_1\ f_2\ f_3\ \beta_3]_0 [f_1\ f_2\ f_3\ \beta_3]_0 [t_1\ t_2\ t_3\ \beta_2]_0$
$[t_1\ t_2\ f_3\ \beta_2]_0 [f_1\ t_2\ t_3\ \beta_1]_0 [f_1\ f_2\ t_3\ \beta_1]_0]_2]$
The new configuration is illustrated graphically below, where we place the membrane labelled by J near the membrane 0 containing membrane L to emphasize that an interaction between membranes J and L is not possible, and so the computation stops after $n + 2m + 3 = 12$ steps.

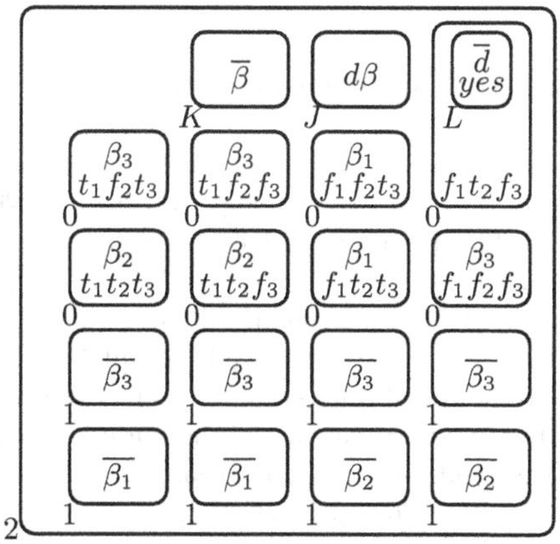

5 Conclusion

In this paper, the operations governing the mobility of mobile membrane systems are endocytosis and exocytosis. Systems of three mobile membranes have been shown to have the same computational power as a Turing machine, and two different results using different proof techniques are presented. In all these results, mutual agreement leads to a minimal number of membranes in terms of mobility: we have a skin membrane and two inner membranes able to move according to the mutual endocytosis and mutual exocytosis rules.

We showed that mobile membranes can solve computationally hard problems in polynomial time. To this aim we traded space for time as we needed to generate an exponential workspace in polynomial (if possible, linear) time, and the usual way to do it is by considering elementary division. In particular, we have taken a well-known NP-complete problem, and shown that it can be solved in linear time by systems of mobile membranes that evolve by using mutual endocytosis, mutual exocytosis and elementary division rules. The given solution is uniform in the sense that all the instances of the problem having the same size are processed by the same system of mobile membranes with an appropriate input $a_1 \dots a_n$ that depends on the specific instance.

Similar questions were addressed for mobile ambients [7], a formalism in which the key feature is given by the movement of compartments. The computational power of mobility in mobile ambients was studied in [6], while complexity aspects were tackled for the first time in [5]. The connection between mobile ambients and mobile membranes was presented in [1].

Acknowledgements. The work was supported by a grant of the Romanian National Authority for Scientific Research, CNCS-UEFISCDI, project number PN-II-ID-PCE-2011-3-0919.

References

1. Aman, B., Ciobanu, G.: On the relationship between membranes and ambients. Biosystems 91, 515–530 (2008)
2. Aman, B., Ciobanu, G.: Simple, enhanced and mutual mobile membranes. Transactions on Computational Systems Biology XI, 26–44 (2009)
3. Aman, B., Ciobanu, G.: Turing completeness using three mobile membranes. In: Calude, C.S., Costa, J.F., Dershowitz, N., Freire, E., Rozenberg, G. (eds.) UC 2009. LNCS, vol. 5715, pp. 42–55. Springer, Heidelberg (2009)
4. Aman, B., Ciobanu, G.: Solving a weak NP-complete problem in polynomial time by using mutual mobile membrane systems. Acta Informatica 48, 409–415 (2011)
5. Aman, B., Ciobanu, G.: Coordinating parallel mobile ambients to solve SAT problem in polynomial number of steps. In: Sirjani, M. (ed.) COORDINATION 2012. LNCS, vol. 7274, pp. 122–136. Springer, Heidelberg (2012)
6. Busi, N., Zavattaro, G.: On the expressive power of movement and restriction in pure mobile ambients. Theoretical Computer Science 322, 477–515 (2004)
7. Cardelli, L., Gordon, A.: Mobile ambients. Theoretical Computer Science 240, 177–213 (2000)
8. Cardelli, L.: Brane calculi. In: Danos, V., Schachter, V. (eds.) CMSB 2004. LNCS (LNBI), vol. 3082, pp. 257–278. Springer, Heidelberg (2005)
9. Ciobanu, G., Krishna, S.: Enhanced mobile membranes: computability results. Theory of Computing Systems 48, 715–729 (2011)

10. Garey, M., Johnson, D.: Computers and Intractability. A Guide to the Theory of NP-Completeness. Freeman (1979)
11. Ibarra, O., Păun, A., Păun, G., Rodríguez-Patón, A., Sosík, P., Woodworth, S.: Normal forms for spiking neural P systems. Theoretical Computer Science 372, 196–217 (2007)
12. Krishna, S., Păun, G.: P systems with mobile membranes. Natural Computing 4, 255–274 (2005)
13. Krishna, S.N.: The power of mobility: Four membranes suffice. In: Cooper, S.B., Löwe, B., Torenvliet, L. (eds.) CiE 2005. LNCS, vol. 3526, pp. 242–251. Springer, Heidelberg (2005)
14. Minsky, M.: Finite and Infinite Machines. Prentice-Hall (1967)
15. Păun, G.: Membrane Computing. An Introduction. Springer (2002)
16. Păun, G., Rozenberg, G., Salomaa, A.: The Oxford Handbook of Membrane Computing. Oxford University Press (2010)
17. Pérez-Jiménez, M., Riscos-Núñez, A., Romero-Jiménez, A., Woods, D.: Complexity - membrane division, membrane creation. In: [16] (2010)
18. Rozenberg, G., Salomaa, A.: The Mathematical Theory of L Systems. Academic Press (1980)
19. Salomaa, A.: Formal Languages. Academic Press (1973)
20. Schroeppel, R.: A Two Counter Machine Cannot Calculate 2^N. Massachusetts Institute of Technology, Artificial Intelligence Memo no.257 (1972)

Cruise Control in Hybrid Event-B

Richard Banach[1] and Michael Butler[2]

[1] School of Computer Science, University of Manchester,
Oxford Road, Manchester, M13 9PL, U.K.
banach@cs.man.ac.uk

[2] School of Electronics and Computer Science, University of Southampton,
Highfield, Southampton, SO17 1BJ, U.K.
mjb@ecs.soton.ac.uk

Abstract. A case study on automotive cruise control originally done in (conventional, discrete) Event-B is reexamined in Hybrid Event-B (an extension of Event-B that includes provision for continuously varying behaviour as well as the usual discrete changes of state). A significant case study such as this has various benefits. It can confirm that the Hybrid Event-B design allows appropriately fluent application level modelling (as is needed for serious industrial use). It also permits a critical comparison to be made between purely discrete and genuinely hybrid modelling. The latter enables application requirements to be covered in a more natural way. It also enables some inconvenient modelling metaphors to be eliminated.

1 Introduction

With the ever decreasing size and cost of computing devices today, there is a strong incentive to embed digital processors in all sorts of devices and systems, in order to improve design flexibility, performance and production cost. This has two readily discernable consequences. Firstly, since many of these systems interact directly with humans, such designs rapidly acquire a safety-critical dimension that most computing systems in the past did not have. Secondly, the profusion of such systems, their interactions with the environment and with each other, dramatically increases design complexity beyond the bounds where traditional development techniques can reliably deliver the needed level of dependability.

It is by now well accepted that formal techniques, appropriately deployed, can offer significant help with both of these issues. However, in the main, these techniques are strongly focused on purely discrete reasoning, and deal poorly with the continuous behaviours, that of necessity, are forced into the blend by the intimate coupling of computing devices to real world systems. The *hybrid* and *cyberphysical* systems we speak of (see, e.g. [20,23,2,22,6]) are poorly served by conventional formal techniques. Although they do have approaches of their own (see, e.g. [8]), most of these techniques are either limited in their expressivity, or lack rigour by comparison with most discrete techniques. An exception is KeYmaera (see [1,16]), a system that combines formal proof (of a quality commensurate with contemporary formal techniques) with continuous behaviour (as needed in the description of genuine physical systems).

Z. Liu, J. Woodcock, and H. Zhu (Eds.): ICTAC 2013, LNCS 8049, pp. 76–93, 2013.

The need for similar capabilities in systems to which the discrete Event-B methodology [3] has been applied in recent years, prompted the development of an extension, Hybrid Event-B [5], that treats discrete and continuous behaviours equally. In this paper, we apply this formalism to a case study previously done in discrete Event-B: the modelling of a cruise control system, first investigated as a component of the DEPLOY Project [9]. The motivation for doing this is: firstly, to judge the expressivity and fluency of the Hybrid Event-B formalism regarding the description of scenarios such as this (especially with a view to practical engineering use); and secondly, to readdress some of the methodological deficiencies that the original case study identified as caused by purely discrete modelling. In contrast to KeYmaera, there is at present no dedicated tool support for Hybrid Event-B. In light of this, a further benefit of the present study is to confirm that Hybrid Event-B contains the right collection of ingredients for industrial scale modelling, before more serious investment in extending the RODIN Tool for discrete Event-B [17] is made.

The rest of this paper is as follows. Section 2 overviews the cruise control system. Section 3 discusses the methodological issues raised by the previous discrete case study, and how Hybrid Event-B can address them. Section 4 overviews Hybrid Event-B itself. Sections 5, 6, 7 then take the cruise control system from a pure mode based model, through a model where continuous properties are constrained but not defined explicitly, to a model where both modes and continuous behaviour are fully defined. These models are related to one another using a sequence of refinements. Section 8 concludes.

2 Cruise Control System Overview

A cruise control system (CCS) is a software system which automatically controls the speed of a car. The CCS is part of the engine control software which controls actuators of the engine, based on the values of specific sensors. Since the CCS automatically controls the speed of the car there are some safety aspects to be considered and it needs to fulfil a number of safety properties. For example, the cruise control system must be deactivated upon request of the driver (or in case of a system fault).

The part of the CCS focused on in the DEPLOY Project, which we follow here, was the signal evaluation subsystem. For economy of space we simplify a bit from the full case study tackled in DEPLOY [12], but we take care to retain all the elements where we can demonstrate the methodological improvements discussed in Section 3 and show the advantages of our approach.

We broadly follow the description in [25,24]. In Fig. 1 we see the state transition diagram for a simplified CCS at an intermediate level of description. The CCS starts in the *OFF* state, from where it can be Switched*On* to put it into the *ON* state.

In the *ON* state several things can happen. One option for the driver is to Switch*Off* the CCS. Alternatively, the driver can *Set*the*Speed* for the CCS, which will set the target speed for the car, to be maintained by the engine control system under the guidance of the CCS. While the speed is under the control of the CCS, the speed can be *Tip*ped*Up* by the driver to increase it a little, or *Tip*ped*Down* to decrease it a little. If the driver chooses to *De*press*Br*akeor*Cl*utch while the CCS is on, then the CCS is designed to switch off since it is assumed that a hazardous condition may have been encountered.

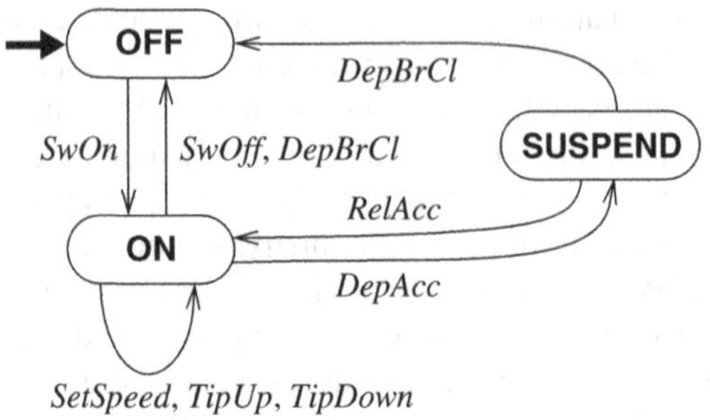

Fig. 1. The state transition diagram for a simplified cruise control system

However, if the driver chooses to *Dep*ress*Acc*elerator while the CCS is on, then it is assumed that conditions are safe, and the CCS is merely put into the *SUSPEND* state. In this state the driver controls the speed via the accelerator pedal. If in this state the driver subsequently *Rel*eases*Acc*elerator, the previous CCS state is resumed. However, use of the brake or clutch in this state switches the CCS off, in line with the assumptions mentioned earlier.

Below, we will develop a series of Hybrid Event-B machines to capture this design. Before that though, we recap some methodological issues that arose in the context of the earlier, purely discrete development, in order to focus the reader's attention on how these are handled differently in the fully hybrid formalism later.

3 Methodological Considerations

In the original discrete Event-B development of the CCS [12] the formal techniques contemplated were based round existing design practices. These produce, for any proposed application: firstly, a set of functional requirements generated by a requirements engineering process; secondly, a set of safety requirements generated by a hazard anaylsis. In relation to Event-B, the former are transformed into events, and the latter are transformed into invariants of the eventual Event-B model(s).

Typical systems in the automotive industry are embedded real time applications which contain a closed loop controller as an essential part. Closed loop controller development is done by control engineers, while their verification requires reasoning about continuous behaviour. Discrete Event-B does not support continuous behaviour, so the application of discrete Event-B to the CCS case study in [12] had to avoid its direct inclusion. Since the presence of continuous behaviour cannot be avoided in CCS, whenever such behaviour was needed in an Event-B model of [12], the modelling incorporated a function that interfaced between the continuous behaviour and the rest of the model. The function itself though, was not (and because Event-B is discrete, could not be) specified within Event-B.

The extension of discrete Event-B to Hybrid Event-B permits this deficiency to be addressed. Most closed loop controller design takes place within the frequency domain [15,10,11,4]. This is seemingly a long way away from the state based approach of techniques like Event-B, but the state based formulation of control theory (increasingly popular today, especially when supported by tools such as SIMULINK [13]), enables a direct connection with the conceptual framework of Hybrid Event-B to be made.

In our reworking of the CCS case study, we are able to incorporate the modelling of a closed loop controller as an essential element. This inclusion of the closed loop controller constitutes the first major point of departure from the earlier account.

Another issue concerns the communication of values between subsytems at different levels of a system hierarchy, especially when real time aspects are paramount. Examples include the transmission of values registered by system sensors, handled by an Event-B sensor machine, which need to be communicated to the core machine that consumes them and decides future behaviour. A corresponding situation concerns values determined by the core machine that need to be communicated to an actuator machine.

Events in the machines concerned update relevant variables with the required values. However, the fact that enabledness of events in discrete Event-B merely *permits* them to execute but does not *force* them to do so, means that when such values need to be transmitted in a timely manner, the semantics does not guarantee that this will happen. To address this, flags are introduced to prevent later events from executing before earlier events that they depend on have completed. Such techniques, essentially handshake mechanisms, are discussed in [7,12,25,24].

Handshake mechanisms are eloquent in modelling communication protocols at a high level of abstraction (see e.g. the examples in [3]). However, when the abstract level communication is continuous, such as in the coupling of a continuous controller to its plant, the low level mechanics do rather obscure the essentials of what is going on. In Hybrid Event-B, continuous behaviour is intrinsic, so the instantaneous communication of continuously changing values can be modelled directly. The capacity to directly model the communication of continuously varying values constitutes the second major point of departure from the earlier account.

4 Hybrid Event-B, A Sketch

In Fig. 2 we see a bare bones Hybrid Event-B machine, *HyEvBMch*. It starts with declarations of time and of a clock. In Hybrid Event-B time is a first class citizen in that all variables are functions of time, whether explicitly or implicitly. However time is special, being read-only, never being assigned, since time cannot be controlled by any human-designed engineering process. Clocks allow a bit more flexibility, since they are assumed to increase their value at the same rate that time does, but may be set during mode events (see below). Variables are of two kinds. There are mode variables (like u, declared as usual) which take their values in discrete sets and change their values via discontinuous assignment in mode events. There are also pliant variables (such as x, y), declared in the PLIANT clause, which take their values in topologically dense sets (normally $\mathbb{R}$) and which are allowed to change continuously, such change being specified via pliant events (see below).

Next are the invariants. These resemble invariants in discrete Event-B, in that the types of the variables are asserted to be the sets from which the variables' values *at any given moment of time* are drawn. More complex invariants are similarly predicates that are required to hold *at all moments of time* during a run.

```
MACHINE HyEvBMch
TIME t
CLOCK clk
PLIANT x, y
VARIABLES u
INVARIANTS
  x ∈ ℝ
  y ∈ ℝ
  u ∈ ℕ
EVENTS
  INITIALISATION
    STATUS ordinary
    WHEN
      t = 0
    THEN
      clk := 1
      x := x0
      y := y0
      u := u0
    END
...  ...
```

```
...  ...
  MoEv
    STATUS ordinary
    ANY i?, l, o!
    WHERE grd(x, y, u, i?, l, t, clk)
    THEN
      x, y, u, clk, o! :| BApred(x, y, u,
        i?, l, o!, t, clk, x′, y′, u′, clk′)
    END
  PliEv
    STATUS pliant
    INIT iv(x, y, t, clk)
    WHERE grd(u)
    ANY i?, l, o!
    COMPLY
      BDApred(x, y, u, i?, l, o!, t, clk)
    SOLVE
      𝒟x = φ(x, y, u, i?, l, o!, t, clk)
      y, o! := E(x, u, i?, l, t, clk)
    END
END
```

Fig. 2. A schematic Hybrid Event-B machine

Then we get to the events. The *INITIALISATION* has a guard that synchronises time with the start of any run, while all other variables are assigned their initial values in the usual way. As hinted above, in Hybrid Event-B, there are two kinds of event: mode events and pliant events.

Mode events are direct analogues of events in discrete Event-B. They can assign all machine variables (except time itself). In the schematic *MoEv* of Fig. 2, we see three parameters $i?, l, o!$, (an input, a local parameter, and an output respectively), and a guard *grd* which can depend on all the machine variables. We also see the generic after-value assignment specified by the before-after predicate *BApred*, which can specify how the after-values of all variables (except time, inputs and locals) are to be determined.

Pliant events are new. They specify the continuous evolution of the pliant variables over an interval of time. The schematic pliant event *PliEv* of Fig. 2 shows the structure. There are two guards: there is *iv*, for specifying enabling conditions on the pliant variables, clocks, and time; and there is *grd*, for specifying enabling conditions on the mode variables. The separation between the two is motivated by considerations connected with refinement.

The body of a pliant event contains three parameters $i?, l, o!$, (once more an input, a local parameter, and an output respectively) which are functions of time, defined over the duration of the pliant event. The behviour of the event is defined by the COMPLY and SOLVE clauses. The SOLVE clause specifies behaviour fairly directly. For example the behaviour of pliant variable y and output $o!$ is given by a direct assignment to the (time dependent) value of the expression $E(\ldots)$. Alternatively, the behaviour of pliant variable x is given by the solution of the first order ordinary differential equation

(ODE) $\mathcal{D}x = \phi(\ldots)$, where $\mathcal{D}$ indicates differentiation with respect to time. (In fact the sematics of the $y, o! = E$ case is given in terms of the ODE $\mathcal{D}\,y, \mathcal{D}\,o! = \mathcal{D}\,E$, so that x, y and $o!$ satisfy the same regularity properties.) The COMPLY clause can be used to express any additional constraints that are required to hold during the pliant event via its before-during-and-after predicate *BDApred*. Typically, constraints on the permitted range of values for the pliant variables, and similar restrictions, can be placed here.

The COMPLY clause has another purpose. When specifying at an abstract level, we do not necessarily want to be concerned with all the details of the dynamics — it is often sufficient to require some global constraints to hold which express the needed safety properties of the system. The COMPLY clauses of the machine's pliant events can house such constraints directly, leaving it to lower level refinements to add the necessary details of the dynamics.

Briefly, the semantics of a Hybrid Event-B machine is as follows. It consists of a set of *system traces*, each of which is a collection of functions of time, expressing the value of each machine variable over the duration of a system run. (In the case of *HyEvBMch*, in a given system trace, there would be functions for clk, x, y, u, each defined over the duration of the run.)

Time is modeled as an interval $\mathcal{T}$ of the reals. A run starts at some initial moment of time, t_0 say, and lasts either for a finite time, or indefinitely. The duration of the run $\mathcal{T}$, breaks up into a succession of left-closed right-open subintervals: $\mathcal{T} = [t_0 \ldots t_1), [t_1 \ldots t_2), [t_2 \ldots t_3), \ldots$. The idea is that mode events (with their discontinuous updates) take place at the isolated times corresponding to the common endpoints of these subintervals t_i, and in between, the mode variables are constant and the pliant events stipulate continuous change in the pliant variables.

Although pliant variables change continuously (except perhaps at the t_i), continuity alone still allows for a wide range of mathematically pathological behaviours. To eliminate these, we make the following restrictions which apply individually to every subinterval $[t_i \ldots t_{i+1})$:

I Zeno: there is a constant δ_{Zeno}, such that for all i needed, $t_{i+1} - t_i \geq \delta_{\mathsf{Zeno}}$.

II Limits: for every variable x, and for every time $t \in \mathcal{T}$, the left limit $\lim_{\delta \to 0} x(t - \delta)$ written $\overrightarrow{x(t)}$ and right limit $\lim_{\delta \to 0} x(t + \delta)$, written $\overleftarrow{x(t)}$ (with $\delta > 0$) exist, and for every t, $x(t) = \overleftarrow{x(t)}$. [N. B. At the endpoint(s) of $\mathcal{T}$, any missing limit is defined to equal its counterpart.]

III Differentiability: The behaviour of every pliant variable x in the interval $[t_i \ldots t_{i+1})$ is given by the solution of a well posed initial value problem $\mathcal{D}\,xs = \phi(xs \ldots)$ (where xs is a relevant tuple of pliant variables and $\mathcal{D}$ is the time derivative). "Well posed" means that $\phi(xs \ldots)$ has Lipschitz constants which are uniformly bounded over $[t_i \ldots t_{i+1})$ bounding its variation with respect to xs, and that $\phi(xs \ldots)$ is measurable in t.

Regarding the above, the Zeno condition is certainly a sensible restriction to demand of any acceptable system, but in general, its truth or falsehood can depend on the system's full reachability relation, and is thus very frequently undecidable.

The stipulation on limits, with the left limit value at a time t_i being not necessarily the same as the right limit at t_i, makes for an easy interpretation of mode events that happen at t_i. For such mode events, the before-values are interpreted as the left limit values, and the after-values are interpreted as the right limit values.

The differentiability condition guarantees that from a specific starting point, t_i say, there is a maximal right open interval, specified by t_{MAX} say, such that a solution to the ODE system exists in $[t_i \ldots t_{\text{MAX}})$. Within this interval, we seek the earliest time t_{i+1} at which a mode event becomes enabled, and this time becomes the preemption point beyond which the solution to the ODE system is abandoned, and the next solution is sought after the completion of the mode event.

In this manner, assuming that the *INITIALISATION* event has achieved a suitable intial assignment to variables, a system run is *well formed*, and thus belongs to the semantics of the machine, provided that at runtime:

- Every enabled mode event is feasible, i.e. has an after-state, and on its completion enables a pliant event (but does not enable any mode event).[1] (1)
- Every enabled pliant event is feasible, i.e. has a time-indexed family of after-states, and EITHER: (2)

  (i) During the run of the pliant event a mode event becomes enabled. It preempts the pliant event, defining its end. ORELSE
  (ii) During the run of the pliant event it becomes infeasible: finite termination. ORELSE
  (iii) The pliant event continues indefinitely: nontermination.

Thus in a well formed run mode events alternate with pliant events. The last event (if there is one) is a pliant event (whose duration may be finite or infinite). In reality, there are a number of semantic issues that we have glossed over in the framework just sketched. We refer to [5] for a more detailed presentation.

We note that this framework is quite close to the modern formulation of hybrid systems. (See eg. [21,16] for representative formulations, or the large literature in the *Hybrid Systems: Computation and Control* series of international conferences, and the further literature cited therein.)

5 Cruise Control — Top Level Mode Oriented Model

In this section we begin the development of the cruise control system by introducing the top level, mode oriented model of the CCS, *CruiseControl_0*. At this level, we just model the state transition diagram given in Fig. 1, i.e. we just focus on the high level user view modes of operation of the system. Regarding a more realistic engineering development, such a model would probably be agreed on first, before the details of the various submodel behaviours were determined.

Regarding the CCS model itself, we see that we model the structure of Fig. 1 using two mode variables: *mode* and *sm* (submode). The former models whether the CCS is *ON*, *OFF* or *SUSP*ended, while the latter models whether the speed has been *SET*, otherwise it is *NIL*. It is not hard to check that Fig. 3 gives a translation of Fig. 1 into

[1] If a mode event has an input, the semantics assumes that its value only arrives at a time strictly later than the previous mode event, ensuring part of (1) automatically. This used in Fig. 3.

```
MACHINE CruiseControl_0
VARIABLES mode, sm
INVARIANTS
  mode ∈ {OFF, ON, SUSP}
  sm ∈ {NIL, SET}
  sm = SET ⇒ mode ∈ {ON, SUSP}
EVENTS
  INITIALISATION
    STATUS ordinary
    BEGIN
      mode := OFF
      sm := NIL
    END
  SwOn
    STATUS ordinary
    ANY in?
    WHERE in? = swOn ∧ mode = OFF
    THEN mode := ON
         sm := NIL
    END
  SwOff
    STATUS ordinary
    ANY in?
    WHERE in? = swOff ∧ mode = ON
    THEN mode := OFF
         sm := NIL
    END
  SetSpeed
    STATUS ordinary
    ANY in?
    WHERE in? = setSpeed ∧
      mode = ON ∧ sm = NIL
    THEN sm := SET
    END
  TipUp
    STATUS ordinary
    ANY in?
    WHERE in? = tipUp ∧
      mode = ON ∧ sm = SET
    THEN skip
    END
...   ...
```

```
...   ...
  TipDown
    STATUS ordinary
    ANY in?
    WHERE in? = tipDown ∧
      mode = ON ∧ sm = SET
    THEN skip
    END
  DepAcc
    STATUS ordinary
    ANY in?
    WHERE in? = depAcc ∧
      mode = ON ∧ sm = SET
    THEN mode := SUSP
    END
  RelAcc
    STATUS ordinary
    ANY in?
    WHERE in? = relAcc ∧
      mode = SUSP ∧ sm = SET
    THEN mode := ON
    END
  DepBrCl
    STATUS ordinary
    ANY in?
    WHERE in? = depBrCl ∧
      mode ∈ {ON, SUSP}
    THEN mode := OFF
         sm := NIL
    END
  PliTrue
    STATUS pliant
    COMPLY INVARIANTS
    END
END
```

Fig. 3. Mode level description of cruise control operation

the framework of Hybrid Event-B. Aside from typing invariants, we have an invariant that only allows the *sm* to be *SET* when the CCS is active (i.e. either *ON* or *SUSP*).

One aspect of both Fig. 1 and Fig. 3 that we should comment on, is that in the real world, the pressing of any of the pedals, or of the CCS control buttons, is not restricted to when the CCS deems it permissible to do so. The car driver has these user interface elements at his disposal at all times, and can operate them whenever he wishes. Thus, we have clearly designed Fig. 1 and Fig. 3 *aggressively*, assuming events take place only when their guards are true. This implies that there is a *defensive* layer above it, deflecting inappropriately commanded events away from the core CCS functionality.

Aside from a few details, Fig. 3 is almost identical to comparable models written in discrete Event-B as described in [12] or [25,24]. The main difference between the earlier treatments and ours, is that these other treatments developed their mode level descriptions incrementally, adding a feature or two at a time via refinement, to ease automated verification. By contrast, we have presented our mode level model monolithically, so as to save space (and the reader's attention span) for the richer modelling of the continuous system behaviour between mode changes that is the main contribution of this paper.

Regarding the technical structure of Fig. 3, it differs from a discrete Event-B machine in only a couple of details. First is that each of the mode events (indicated by the 'STATUS ordinary' designation) has an input parameter whose value is (almost) the name of the event. Considering the actions of these various mode events, such parameters would be unnecessary in discrete Event-B. In Hybrid Event-B though, time is an essential feature of the modelling framework, so the timing of occurrences of mode events is an issue. The semantics of Hybrid Event-B stipulates that mode events with input parameters only become enabled when the input values become available from the environment, and it is *assumed* that they only become available at times that do not clash with other mode events. Thus the appearance of the inputs from the environment acts to schedule mode event occurrences in a way compatible with the usual interpretation of their occurrence in discrete Event-B. The only other difference from discrete Event-B that is visible in Fig. 3, is the pliant event *PliTrue*. This has a vacuous guard, and (essentially) vacuous semantics that merely insist that the INVARIANTS are maintained. Its job is simply to formally allow time to pass (according to the semantics of Hybrid Event-B) until the next mode event occurrence takes place, prompted by the appearance of the relevant parameter from the environment.

From the above, it is easy to see that a standard discrete Event-B machine, giving a mode level description of the behaviour of some desired system, could be mechanically and routinely translated to a machine of the form of Fig. 3, allowing an original discrete Event-B machine to be refined ultimately by a Hybrid Event-B machine. Alternatively, the formal semantics of UML-B [18,14,19] would enable the same job to be done starting from a more diagrammatic representation. This would enable a development process that started by focusing on just a conventional discrete Event-B mode level behaviour of the system, to be enriched with real time properties further along the development, within an integrated development activity.

6 Cruise Control — Abstract Continuous Behaviour

In this section we enhance the pure mode oriented model of Section 5 with a specification of the desired continuous behaviour in the periods between occurrences of the mode events.

The requirements that are intended to be addressed by this behaviour are relatively easy to formulate at a user level. Thus, once the CCS is in control of the car, we require that the actual speed of the car differs from the target speed that has been set by the driver by at worst a margin that is determined by the CCS design.

The car's actual behaviour may drift away from it's target value for many reasons. The target speed is set when the driver engages the CCS, and is translated into commands for the car to maintain it, but the actual behaviour is affected by many additional environmental factors. These include factors such as road slope, wind resistance, road surface characteristics, total car weight, fuel energy output, and so on. These add considerable uncertainty and complexity to the real world situation.

Control engineers cope with the vast range of environmental uncertainty by using feedback. The deviation between the actual and desired behaviour is monitored, and the difference is used to impel the controlled system towards the desired behaviour.

The low level design of a real CCS deals with the many factors that affect the car's performance, as indicated. In this paper we will restrict our attention to a simple control design addressing the user level requirements stated earlier. This illustrates how a control system design may be integrated with the modelling capabilities of Hybrid Event-B. More realistic designs will follow the same general principles as our example, and will merely exhibit increased complexity.

Our enhanced treatment of the CC system is to be found in Fig. 4, completed in Fig. 5. After the machine and refinement declarations, there is a declaration of a pliant variable v, representing the velocity of the car. In our simple approach to CCS, this single pliant variable will be sufficient.

Next come the (mode) variables. Of these, *mode* and *sm* are familiar from Fig. 3. Of the remainder, *setv* is the target velocity set by the driver of the car, while the new variable *rn* records whether a ramp up/down episode is needed after use of the accelerator prior to resuming cruising velocity. All other identifiers, occurring but not declared in Figs. 4 or 5, are constants of the system, as if they were in a Hybrid Event-B CONTEXT not included in the paper. We return to them at the end of this section.

Next come the invariants. For the real valued variables, discernable as such because of the invariants that restrict them to a real valued closed interval, e.g. $v \in [0 \ldots V_{max}]$, the restriction to the interval is mostly the only property they have to satisfy. Aside from v, these real valued variables are mode variables, so are piecewise constant during pliant transitions, despite being real valued.

The remaining invariant is CONTINUOUS(v), featuring the 'CONTINUOUS' *pliant modality*. Now, the semantics of Hybrid Event-B guarantees that in between mode transitions, the behaviour of all pliant variables must be absolutely continuous. Nevertheless, pliant variables may suffer discontinuities during mode transitions. The CONTINUOUS modality stipulates that this must not happen to v, and a simple static check on the mode events is enough to guarantee this. The global continuity of v is of course intended to contribute to the 'comfortable behaviour' requirement.

```
MACHINE CruiseControl_1
REFINES CruiseControl_0
PLIANT v
VARIABLES mode, sm, setv, rn
INVARIANTS
  v ∈ [0 ... V_max]
  CONTINUOUS(v)
  mode ∈ {OFF, ON, SUSP}
  sm ∈ {NIL, SET}
  sm = SET ⇒ mode ∈ {ON, SUSP}
  setv ∈ [VCC_min ... VCC_max]
  rn ∈ BOOL
EVENTS
  INITIALISATION
    STATUS ordinary
    REFINES INITIALISATION
    BEGIN
      v :∈ [0 ... V_max]
      setv :∈ [VCC_min ... VCC_max]
      mode := OFF
      sm := NIL
      rn := FALSE
    END
  PliDefault
    STATUS pliant
    REFINES PliTrue
    WHEN mode ∈ {OFF, SUSP} ∨
      (mode = ON ∧ sm = NIL)
    COMPLY INVARIANTS
    END
  SwOn
    STATUS ordinary
    REFINES SwOn
    ANY in?
    WHERE in? = swOn ∧ mode = OFF
    THEN mode := ON
         sm := NIL
    END
  SwOff
    STATUS ordinary
    REFINES SwOff
    ANY in?
    WHERE in? = swOff ∧ mode = ON
    THEN mode := OFF
         sm := NIL
    END
... ...
```

```
... ...
  SetSpeed
    STATUS ordinary
    REFINES SetSpeed
    ANY in?
    WHERE in? = setSpeed ∧
      v ∈ [VCC_min ... VCC_max] ∧
      mode = ON ∧ sm = NIL
    THEN sm := SET
         setv := v
    END
  Cruise
    STATUS pliant
    REFINES PliTrue
    INIT |v − setv| ≤ Δ_Cruise
    WHERE mode = ON ∧ sm = SET
    COMPLY |v − setv| ≤ Δ_Cruise ∧
      |Dv| ≤ Δ_MCA
    END
  RampUp
    STATUS pliant
    REFINES PliTrue
    INIT v − setv < −Δ_Cruise
    WHERE mode = ON ∧ sm = SET
    COMPLY |Dv − RUA| ≤ Δ_RUD
    END
  RampDown
    STATUS pliant
    REFINES PliTrue
    INIT v − setv > Δ_Cruise
    WHERE mode = ON ∧ sm = SET
    COMPLY |Dv + RDA| ≤ Δ_RUD
    END
  ResumeCruise
    STATUS convergent
    WHEN |v − setv| ≤ Δ_Cruise ∧
      mode = ON ∧ sm = SET ∧ rn
    THEN rn := FALSE
    END

  VARIANT rn
... ...
```

Fig. 4. Cruise control operation with abstract continuous behaviour, first part

... ...
TipUp
STATUS ordinary
REFINES *TipUp*
ANY *in?*
WHERE $in? = tipUp \wedge$
$mode = ON \wedge sm = SET$
THEN
$setv := min\{setv + TUD, VCC_{max}\}$
END
TipDown
STATUS ordinary
REFINES *TipDown*
ANY *in?*
WHERE $in? = tipDown \wedge$
$mode = ON \wedge sm = SET$
$setv - TUD \geq VCC_{min}$
THEN
$setv := max\{setv - TUD, VCC_{min}\}$
END
DepAcc
STATUS ordinary
REFINES *DepAcc*
ANY *in?*
WHERE $in? = depAcc \wedge$
$mode = ON \wedge sm = SET$
THEN $mode := SUSP$
END
... ...

... ...
RelAccCruise
STATUS ordinary
REFINES *RelAcc*
ANY *in?*
WHERE $in? = relAcc \wedge$
$mode = SUSP \wedge sm = SET \wedge$
$|v - setv| \leq \Delta_{\text{Cruise}}$
THEN $mode := ON$
$rn :=$ FALSE
END
RelAccRamp
STATUS ordinary
REFINES *RelAcc*
ANY *in?*
WHERE $in? = relAcc \wedge$
$mode = SUSP \wedge sm = SET \wedge$
$|v - setv| > \Delta_{\text{Cruise}}$
THEN $mode := ON$
$rn :=$ TRUE
END
DepBrCl
STATUS ordinary
REFINES *DepBrCl*
ANY *in?*
WHERE $in? = depBrCl \wedge$
$mode \in \{ON, SUSP\}$
THEN $mode := OFF$
$sm := NIL$
END
END

Fig. 5. Cruise control operation with abstract continuous behaviour, second part

The heart of the model consists of the events, the first of which is *INITIALISATION*. This intialises *mode* and *sm* as before, and sets all the real valued variables to arbitrary values in their permitted range. We examine the remaining events one by one.

PliDefault is a pliant event that refines *PliTrue* of Fig. 3. It allows the variables to vary arbitrarily via the 'COMPLY *INVARIANTS*' clause, although the invariants must be maintained. Note that the guard of *PliDefault* is stronger than that of *PliTrue* — the unconstrained behaviour is only permitted under conditions where the CCS would *not* be expected to be in control.

The events *SwOn* and *SwOff* are identical to their Fig. 3 precursors.

Event *SetSpeed* acquires new functionality, in that it now also sets the value of the demanded speed *setv* to be the car's current speed v.

The continuous control itself is handled by the next three pliant events, *Cruise*, *RampUp*, *RampDown*. We start with *Cruise*. On entry to *Cruise*, if the car's actual speed v is within a suitable margin (given by the constant Δ_{Cruise}) of the desired speed *setv*, then the event is enabled, as defined by the INIT clause $|\, v - setv \,| \le \Delta_{\text{Cruise}}$. In this case, at the present level of abstraction, the behaviour is not precisely defined, but the *Cruise* event demands that the speed remains within a suitable margin of *setv*, bounded by Δ_{Cruise} again. A further requirement is once more related to 'comfort', in that the rate of change of v should not exceed a MaximumCruise$A$cceleration, Δ_{MCA}. These stipulations are housed in the COMPLY $|\, v - setv \,| \le \Delta_{\text{Cruise}} \wedge |\, \mathcal{D}v \,| \le \Delta_{\text{MCA}}$ clause. Note that this represents a genuine *specification*, in that the COMPLY clause gives no indication of how a behaviour with the required properties is to be achieved. It also represents behaviour that trivially refines *PliTrue*, in that the latter accepts all behaviours obeying the invariants.

Similar considerations apply to *RampUp* and *RampDown*. Taking *RampUp*, it caters for the cases when, following use of the accelerator to casue some temporary variation in the car's speed, the car's actual speed v is less than the desired speed *setv* by an amount greater than Δ_{Cruise}.[2] In such a case, it is deemed that a(n approximately) constant acceleration towards the desired speed *setv* is an appropriate handling of the 'comfort' requirement. So we have a clause COMPLY $|\, \mathcal{D}v - RUA \,| \le \Delta_{\text{RUD}}$. This demands that the acceleration $\mathcal{D}v$ does not differ from the constant *RUA*, i.e. Ramp$U$pAcceleration, by more than the deviation Δ_{RUD}. Again this is specification, pure and simple. No indication is given about how to achieve the behaviour described.

Event *RampDown* is very similar to *RampUp*. It fires when, following use of the accelerator, the car's actual speed is greater than *setv* by an amount exceeding the constant Δ_{Cruise}. Now the car is required to decelerate at the (approximately) constant acceleration $-RDA$ (with the same margin as before). Again, the COMPLY clause amounts to pure specification. No indication is given about how to achieve the behaviour described.

A number of additional remarks are in order regarding *Cruise*, *RampUp*, *RampDown*. Firstly, the constants occurring in the events' INIT guards must be chosen so that the disjunction of the INIT guards can cover all permissible car speeds in the car's permitted range $[0 \ldots V_{\text{max}}]$. Otherwise, when $mode = ON \wedge sm = SET$, the relative deadlock freedom property of refinement will fail since all three events refine the unconstrained behaviour of *PliTrue*. It is clear that *Cruise*, *RampUp*, *RampDown*, as defined, meet this constraint.

Secondly, if say *RampUp* runs, then if left to continue in an unhindered manner, it will eventually cause the $v \in [0 \ldots V_{\text{max}}]$ invariant to fail, since a constant positive acceleration will eventually cause *any* upper speed limit to be exceeded. To prevent this, we have introduced a new mode event *ResumeCruise*, which runs when the car's velocity, previously differing from the set speed by more than Δ_{Cruise}, eventually gets within Δ_{Cruise} of the set speed. The main job of this mode event is to cause a reschedule, so that *RampUp* is preempted, and *Cruise* is able to run.

We only want *ResumeCruise* to only run once per resumption-of-cruise-control. In order that *ResumeCruise* disables itself upon completion, we use the new *rn* variable in its guard, and falsify it in the action of *ResumeCruise*. This causes *ResumeCruise* to

[2] The initially puzzling possibility that the car might need to *speed up* following use of the *accelerator* is explained by considering driving up a steep hill.

decrease the VARIANT *rn* (with which we interrupt the presentation of events, in order to show it at the most opportune place).

The remainder of the *CruiseControl_1* machine is in Fig. 5. Now, since *setv* is a new feature of the *CruiseControl_1* machine, and since *TipUp* and *TipDown* are intended to manipulate it, these events must be refined nontrivially in order to achieve this. The refinements therefore add or subtract the constant *TUD* from *setv*, although they must do it in a way that prevents the range of permissible cruise control speeds $[VCC_{\min} \ldots VCC_{\max}]$ from being overstepped.

Among the remaining events of *CruiseControl_1* (all mode events), *DepAcc* is as previously. Event *RelAcc* has been split in two though, depending on whether the car's speed is within the margin Δ_{Cruise} when the accelerator pedal is released. If $|\, v - setv \,| \leq \Delta_{\mathrm{Cruise}}$ holds, i.e. the car is near enough its cruise speed, then *Cruise* can be entered directly, *ResumeCruise* will not be needed, and so *RelAccCruise* sets *nr* to FALSE. If $|\, v - setv \,| \leq \Delta_{\mathrm{Cruise}}$ is false though, then a ramp up or down episode is needed, so *RelAccRamp* sets *nr* to TRUE so that *ResumeCruise* will eventually be enabled.

Finally, *DepBrCl* is as in *CruiseControl_0*.

Having covered the whole system model, we are in a position to reconsider the constants, as promised earlier. While it is natural in high level modelling to introduce, at will, constants that constrain system behaviour in desirable ways, these constants will not normally be independent, and will need to satisfy a number of properties to ensure soundness. The safest way to ensure that all needed constraints have been considered, is to attempt mechanical verification — a mechanical prover will remorselessly uncover any missing constraints, which will show up by generating unprovable subgoals.

Despite lack of dedicated tool support for Hybrid Event-B at present, the simplicity of our model here, means that a large portion of this work can be done using discrete Event-B and the existing RODIN tool. The fact that, aside from properties involving continuity and differentiability, we only have uninstantiated constants, and only use properties of reals that are also true of the integers, means that unprovability in the integers is a strong indication of falsity in the reals. Thus, regarding the details of our models, we would obviously need $0 < VCC_{\min} < VCC_{\max} < V_{\max}$. Beyond that, the mode events can be treated directly, as noted earlier. This leaves the pliant events, *Cruise*, *RampUp*, *RampDown*.

For our purposes, we can treat *Cruise* as a mode event that skips, for the following collection of reasons: it maintains its guard; $0 < \Delta_{Cruise}$ is a constant that is just used to partition the set of velocities; $\mathcal{D}v$ is a variable independent of v at any given time (and which is never tested in any guard); and $0 < \Delta_{\mathrm{MCA}}$ is a constant that occurs nowhere else. For *RampUp* and *RampDown*, aside from the obvious $0 < min\{RUA, RDA, \Delta_{\mathrm{RUD}}\}$, all of *RUA*, *RDA*, Δ_{RUD} are again constants that occur nowhere else, that only concern $\mathcal{D}v$, and thus are not further constrained. Beyond that, the behaviour of *RampUp*, *RampDown* is intended to achieve $|\, v - setv \,| \leq \Delta_{\mathrm{Cruise}}$, so for our purposes, we can replace them by mode events with action $v :|\; |\, v' - setv \,| \leq \Delta_{\mathrm{Cruise}}$. In this manner, with the help of some admittedly informal reasoning regarding continuity and differentiability, we can go quite a long way towards replicating the reachability relation of the *CruiseControl_1* machine (expressed in terms of sequences of event names that are executed and the before-/after-values of the events' variables), using a discrete

Event-B machine with the same constants obeying the same constraints. (In fact, the authors used this approach on an earlier version of the models, and uncovered a typo concerning inconsistent assumptions about the sign of *RDA*. *RDA* can be a negative constant, or alternatively, a positive constant that is negated when necessary at the point of use; but you must be consistent.)

7 Cruise Control — Continuous Behaviour Defined

In the previous section we specified the continuous behaviour of the CCS in terms of some safety properties captured in the invariants and COMPLY clauses. A real CCS though, would have to realise these properties in a specific design. In this section, we enhance *CruiseControl_1* with such a design.

Fig. 6 contains the enhancement, machine *CruiseControl_2*. This is a refinement of *CruiseControl_1* in which the vast majority of *CruiseControl_1* remains unchanged. The variable declarations show that we only introduce more refined behaviour in this machine, and even then, only in events *Cruise*, *RampUp*, *RampDown*.

We start with *Cruise*. Assuming INIT is satisfied, on entry to *Cruise*, the actual speed v may differ from *setv* by some margin since *Cruise* may have been preceded by *RampUp* or *RampDown*. And while *CruiseControl_1* tolerated a bounded deviation between these indefinitely, in *CruiseControl_2* we replace this by a more specific control law. Since *setv* is the desired speed, we drive the actual speed towards *setv* using negative feedback. The earlier *CruiseControl_1* behaviour is refined to a control law described in the SOLVE clause of the *CruiseControl_2* event. The control law sets the acceleration $\mathcal{D}v$ to be proportional to minus the excess of v over *setv*. Thus, if $v - setv$ is positive, the acceleration is negative, tending to diminish v towards *setv*, and if $v - setv$ is negative, the acceleration is positive, tending to increase v towards *setv*.

The preceding constitutes an extremely simple example of closed loop negative feedback linear control, expressed in the state space picture. The control law in the SOLVE clause, $\mathcal{D}v = -C(v - setv)$, is a simple linear ODE, and can be solved exactly, yielding $v(t) = setv + (v(\mathtt{t_L}) - setv)\, e^{-C(t-\mathtt{t_L})}$, where $\mathtt{t_L}$ is the symbol used in Hybrid Event-B to refer generically to the start time of any time interval during which a pliant event runs. It is trivial to verify that with a suitable C, this refines the behaviour permitted by the *CruiseControl_1* model, since the maximum values of both $|\,v(t) - setv\,|$ and of $|\,\mathcal{D}v\,|$ occur precisely at $t = \mathtt{t_L}$, and henceforth reduce.

In more realistic control scenarios, the overall objectives, namely to design a dynamics that behaves in an acceptable way in the face of the requirements, remains the same, but the technical details get considerably more complicated. To a large extent, frequency-based techniques using Laplace and Fourier transforms cast the reasoning into the algebraic domain, and the picture is further complicated by the use of varying criteria (often based on the properties of these frequency-based techniques) to evaluate design quality. Often, use of these techniques does not blend well with the reasoning found in state machine based formalisms like Event-B and its relatives. For this reason, resticting to state space control design techniques is recommended to achieve the optimal integration between approaches.

MACHINE *CruiseControl_2*
REFINES *CruiseControl_1*
PLIANT v
VARIABLES $mode, sm, setv, rn$
INVARIANTS
  … …
EVENTS
  INITIALISATION … …
  PliDefault … …
  SwOn … …
  SwOff … …
  SetSpeed … …
  ResumeCruise … …
  TipUp … …
  TipDown … …
  DepAcc … …
  RelAccCruise … …
  RelAccRamp … …
  DepBrCl … …
… …

… …
  Cruise
    STATUS pliant
    REFINES *Cruise*
    INIT $|v - setv| \leq \Delta_{\text{Cruise}}$
    WHERE $mode = ON \wedge sm = SET$
    SOLVE $\mathcal{D}v = -C(v - setv)$
    END
  RampUp
    STATUS pliant
    REFINES *RampUp*
    INIT $v - setv < -\Delta_{\text{Cruise}}$
    WHERE $mode = ON \wedge sm = SET$
    SOLVE $\mathcal{D}v = RUA$
    END
  RampDown
    STATUS pliant
    REFINES *RampDown*
    INIT $v - setv > \Delta_{\text{Cruise}}$
    WHERE $mode = ON \wedge sm = SET$
    SOLVE $\mathcal{D}v = -RDA$
    END
END

Fig. 6. Cruise control operation with continuous control

We turn to *RampUp* and *RampDown*. Here, the approximately linear and nondeterministic variation in speed of machine *CruiseControl_1* is replaced by a precise, deterministic linear law for the velocity, specified by a constant acceleration in the SOLVE clauses: $\mathcal{D}v = RUA$ for *RampUp* and $\mathcal{D}v = -RDA$ for *RampDown*.

In writing these deterministic dynamical laws, it is presumed that acceleration is something that can be commanded accurately by the engine management system, based on the properties of the engine, the fuel, the environmental conditions, etc., as discussed in Section 6. In truth, this is something of an exageration. In reality, there is too much uncertainty in all these environmental elements to enable the acceleration to be predicted (and therefore commanded) with complete precision. Aside form anything else, the car's sensors are severely limited regarding the type of information about the environment that they can obtain. So there will be some deviation between the acceleration that the engine management system predicts, and that which is actually achieved. On this basis we would expected to see some difference between our treatments of *Cruise*, and of *RampUp* and *RampDown*.

In the case of *Cruise*, a misjudgement of the precise acceleration that will be achieved is compensated for by the presence of negative feedback. If the car's velocity does not reduce quite as rapidly as anticipated by the engine management system, then the negative feedback will work that much harder to bring the velocity into line. The precise details of the control law can be adjusted to make allowance for such potential imprecision, without disturbing the overall structure of the behaviour. In this sense, the negative feedback makes the *Cruise* design robust against a margin of imprecision.

In the case of *RampUp* and *RampDown*, there is no feedback included in the control law. For these two events, it is the *acceleration* that might be awry, and that would need to be brought into line. There are a number of reasons why we did not include this in our models. Firstly, it would need the introduction of at least one other pliant variable into the models (to distinguish measured acceleration from commanded acceleration). Secondly, the resulting feedback law would make the control system higher order, adding unnecessary complexity. Thirdly we would lose the opportunity to illustrate the contrast between closed loop control (as in *Cruise*) and open loop control (as here, for *RampUp* and *RampDown*) in the context of Hybrid Event-B. Fourthly, if our earlier design is appropriate, then any deviation from cruise speed caused by use of the accelerator pedal will be temporary, and thus *RampUp* and *RampDown* describe *transients* of the system. The small imprecisions that may affect their behaviour will not significantly affect the quality of the CCS at the relatively simple level that we model it in this paper.

8 Conclusions

In the preceding sections, we overviewed the cruise control model examined within the DEPLOY project, and we commented on the deficiencies when formal modelling and verification are based purely on discrete Event-B, as was employed in DEPLOY. We then commented on the anticipated improvements expected when the more expressive Hybrid Event-B formalism is used instead. We continued by outlining the essential elements of Hybrid Event-B, sufficient to cater for the modelling to be done later.

We then developed a simple version of the CCS in Hybrid Event-B, through a number of relatively large scale refinements, using these refinements to illustrate the major modelling steps. Thus, we started with a pure mode oriented model, very similar to what DEPLOY achieved for CCS. The hybrid aspects of Hybrid Event-B were almost completely disregarded here by allowing the continuous behaviour to be arbitrary.

The first refinement then introduced additional structure and restrictions on the continuous behaviour. These, though nondeterministic, were deemed sufficient to express the system requirements. The next refinement then introduced specific control laws that modelled in a simple way how a real CCS might implement the continuous control.

Of course, a real system would be much more complicated than what we presented, but it would consist of a larger collection of ingredients of a similar nature to those in our design. For expository purposes then, we can claim that our presentation met the goals described in Section 3. Specifically, we showed that we could incorporate provision for closed loop controller designs unproblematically (including a brief discussion of open loop control too). Additionally, the smoothness with which our development proceeded, bore eloquent testimony to the fluency of the Hybrid Event-B formalism in tackling developments of this kind. This gives strong encouragement for the development of mechanical support for the Hybrid Event-B framework in the future.

Acknowledgement. Michael Butler is partly funded by the FP7 ADVANCE Project (http://www.advance-ict.eu).

References

1. KeYmaera, http://symbolaris.com
2. Report: Cyber-Physical Systems (2008), http://iccps2012.cse.wustl.edu/_doc/CPS_Summit_Report.pdf
3. Abrial, J.R.: Modeling in Event-B: System and Software Engineering. Cambridge University Press (2010)
4. Antsaklis, P., Michel, A.: Linear Systems. Birkhauser (2006)
5. Banach, R., Butler, M., Qin, S., Verma, N., Zhu, H.: Core Hybrid Event-B: Adding Continuous Behaviour to Event-B (2012) (submitted)
6. Barolli, L., Takizawa, M., Hussain, F.: Special Issue on Emerging Trends in Cyber-Physical Systems. J. Amb. Intel. Hum. Comp. 2, 249–250 (2011)
7. Butler, M.: Towards a Cookbook for Modelling and Refinement of Control Problems (2009), http://deploy-eprints.ecs.soton.ac.uk/108/1/cookbook.pdf
8. Carloni, L., Passerone, R., Pinto, A., Sangiovanni-Vincentelli, A.: Languages and Tools for Hybrid Systems Design. Foundations and Trends in Electronic Design Automation 1, 1–193 (2006)
9. DEPLOY: European Project DEPLOY IST-511599, http://www.deploy-project.eu/
10. Dorf, R., Bishop, R.: Modern Control Systems. Pearson (2010)
11. Dutton, K., Thompson, S., Barraclough, B.: The Art of Control Engineering. Addison-Wesley (1997)
12. Loesch, F., Gmehlich, R., Grau, K., Mazzara, M., Jones, C.: Project DEPLOY, Deliverable D19: Pilot Deployment in the Automotive Sector (2010), http://www.deploy-project.eu/pdf/D19-pilot-deployment-in-the-automotive-sector.pdf
13. MATLAB and SIMULINK, http://www.mathworks.com
14. Mermet, J.: UML-B: Specification for Proven Embedded Systems Design. Springer (2004)
15. Ogata, K.: Modern Control Engineering. Pearson (2008)
16. Platzer, A.: Logical Analysis of Hybrid Systems: Proving Theorems for Complex Dynamics. Springer (2010)
17. RODIN: European Project RODIN (Rigorous Open Development for Complex Systems) IST-511599, http://rodin.cs.ncl.ac.uk/
18. Snook, C., Butler, M.: UML-B: Formal modeling and design aided by UML. TOSEM 15, 92–122 (2006)
19. Snook, C., Oliver, I., Butler, M.: The UML-B Profile for Formal Systems Modelling in UML. UML-B Specification for Proven Embedded Systems Design (2004)
20. Sztipanovits, J.: Model Integration and Cyber Physical Systems: A Semantics Perspective. In: Butler, M., Schulte, W. (eds.) FM 2011. LNCS, vol. 6664, p. 1. Springer, Heidelberg (2011), http://sites.lero.ie/download.aspx?f=Sztipanovits-Keynote.pdf
21. Tabuada, P.: Verification and Control of Hybrid Systems: A Symbolic Approach. Springer (2009)
22. White, J., Clarke, S., Groba, C., Dougherty, B., Thompson, C., Schmidt, D.: R&D Challenges and Solutions for Mobile Cyber-Physical Applications and Supporting Internet Services. J. Internet Serv. Appl. 1, 45–56 (2010)
23. Willems, J.: Open Dynamical Systems: Their Aims and their Origins. Ruberti Lecture, Rome (2007), http://homes.esat.kuleuven.be/jwillems/Lectures/2007/Rubertilecture.pdf
24. Yeganefard, S., Butler, M.: Control Systems: Phenomena and Structuring Functional Requirement Documents. In: Proc. ICECCS-2012, pp. 39–48. IEEE (2012)
25. Yeganefard, S., Butler, M., Rezazadeh, A.: Evaluation of a Guideline by Formal Modelling of Cruise Control System in Event-B. In: Proc. 2nd NFM, NASA/CP-2010-216215, pp. 182–191. NASA (2010)

From Distributions to Probabilistic Reactive Programs

Riccardo Bresciani and Andrew Butterfield*

Foundations and Methods Group,
Trinity College Dublin,
Dublin, Ireland
{bresciar,butrfeld}@scss.tcd.ie

Abstract. We have introduced probability in the *UTP* framework by using functions from the state space to real numbers, which we term *distributions*, that are embedded in the predicates describing the different program constructs. This has allowed us to derive a probabilistic theory of designs starting from a probabilistic version of the relational theory, and continuing further down this road we can get to a theory of probabilistic reactive programs. This paper presents the route that connects these steps, and discusses the challenges lying ahead in view of a probabilistic *CSP* based on distributions.

1 Introduction

The Unifying Theories of Programming (*UTP*) aims at a semantic framework where programs and specifications can be modelled as alphabetised relational predicates, capturing the semantic models normally used for their formal description [HH98, DS06, But10, Qin10]: the advantage of this common framework is that of enabling formal reasoning on the integration of the different languages through untyped predicate calculus.

So far several theories have been given a *UTP* semantics, where programs are expressed by means of logical predicates (programs are predicates! [Heh84, Hoa85]).

In the last years the focus of our research has been how to integrate probability into the *UTP* framework: our approach is based on distributions over the state space. We use distributions to associate a probability with each state: a program can therefore be expressed by means of logical predicates involving a homogeneous relation between distributions, to account for the modifications transforming *before-distributions* into corresponding *after-distributions*. This approach gives us a framework where probabilistic choice co-exists with non-deterministic choice, so being consistent with the approach advocated in [MM04].

After having given a probabilistic *UTP* semantics to *pGCL* [BB11, BB12b] and having presented a probabilistic theory of designs [BB12a], we have started

* This work was supported, in part, by Science Foundation Ireland grant 10/CE/I1855 to Lero — the Irish Software Engineering Research Centre.

Z. Liu, J. Woodcock, and H. Zhu (Eds.): ICTAC 2013, LNCS 8049, pp. 94–111, 2013.

to look into the possibility of using our framework to have a probabilistic version of *CSP*: as the *UTP* theory of *CSP* is built on that of designs, we aim at building a theory of *pCSP* starting from that of probabilistic designs. The task turned out to be not so straightforward, posing interesting challenges which we find worthy of discussion in the present paper.

This paper is structured as follows: we describe the background to UTP, with particular focus on the standard theory of designs in that framework, and to *pCSP* (§2); introduce our probabilistic framework based on distributions over the state space (§3.1), with a brief presentation of the probabilistic theory of designs from [BB12a] (§3.2); we then discuss how to progress from this probabilistic theory of designs to a theory of reactive programs (§4); and conclude (§5).

2 Background

2.1 UTP

UTP uses second-order predicates to represent programs: they are used to express relations among a set of *observable variables* which constitute their alphabet. Observable variables usually occur as both undecorated and decorated with a dash $'$: the former refer to states before the program starts (*before-states*), whereas the latter refer to the final states reached after the program has run (*after-states*). For example, a program using two variables x and y might be characterised by having the set $\{x, x', y, y'\}$ as an alphabet, and the meaning of the assignment $x := y + 3$ would be described, in a simple relational theory, by the predicate

$$x' = y + 3 \wedge y' = y.$$

In effect *UTP* uses predicate calculus in a disciplined way to build up a relational calculus for reasoning about programs.

In addition to observations of the values of program variables, often we need to introduce observations of other aspects of program execution via so-called auxiliary variables. For example the theory of reactive programs explained below uses four auxiliary variables — namely ok, $wait$, tr, ref — to keep track of information concerning the current program run, such as termination, reach of a stable state, refusals, ...

A key notion in *UTP* is that of *healthiness conditions*: they are usually characterised as monotonic idempotent predicate transformers whose fixpoints characterise sensible (healthy) predicates. In other words they outlaw some predicates that are nonsense, e.g., $\neg ok \Rightarrow ok'$, which describes a "program" that must terminate even though not started.

This notion is closely related to that of *refinement*, defined as the universal closure[1] of reverse implication:

$$S \sqsubseteq P \triangleq [P \Rightarrow S]$$

[1] Square brackets denote universal closure, *i.e.* $[P]$ asserts that P is true for all values of its free variables.

Healthy predicates form a lattice under the ordering induced by the refinement relation. The refinement calculus enables the derivation of an implementation P from a specification S: such derivation can be proven correct if P is a valid refinement of S.

Some lines of research, including ours, are moving in the direction of introducing a probabilistic choice operator, which does not replace Dijkstra's demonic choice [Dij76] — as for example Kozen did [Koz81, Koz85] —, but rather co-exists with it, as described and motivated in [MM04]. In [HS06] the authors present an approach to unification of probabilistic choice with standard constructs, and present an axiomatic semantics to capture *pGCL* in *UTP*: the laws were justified via a Galois connection to an expectation-based semantic model. The approach presented in [CS09] is that of decomposing non-deterministic choice into a combination of pure probabilistic choice and a unary operator that accounted for its non-deterministic behaviour. It is worth underlining a comment of theirs, on how UTP theories are still unsatisfactory with respect to the issue of having co-existing probabilistic and demonic choice. The *UTP* model described in [He10], which is used to give a *UTP*-style semantics to a probabilistic BPEL-like language, relates an initial state to a final probability distribution over states.

Our approach is a *UTP*-style semantics based on predicates over probability before- and after-distributions: we see programs as *distribution-transformers* (more details in §3.1). We have previously used this to encode the semantics of *pGCL* in the *UTP* framework [BB11, BB12b]; moreover we have proposed a probabilistic theory of designs [BB12a], which we will briefly present in §3.2 after having presented the standard one.

The Standard Theory of Designs. Now that we have given a general overview of the *UTP* framework, we are going to focus on the theory of designs and present its *UTP* semantics.

The theory of designs extends the simple (relational) theory, which is only adequate for partial correctness results, into a theory of total correctness. The motivation for and details of this extension are discussed in [HH98, Chapter 3]. This extension adopts an additional "auxiliary variable" ok (along with its dashed version ok') to record start (and termination) of a program. So now, instead of just observing variable values, we can now tell when a programs has been started, or has finished.

A design (specification) consists of a precondition $\mathcal{Pre}$ that has to be met when the program starts, and if so the program terminates and establishes $\mathcal{Post}$, which can be stated as:

$$ok \wedge \mathcal{Pre} \Rightarrow ok' \wedge \mathcal{Post}$$

for which we use the following shorthand:

$$\mathcal{Pre} \vdash \mathcal{Post}$$

Note that, in general, the "pre-condition" $\mathcal{Pre}$ can mention after-values of variables and the "post-condition" $\mathcal{Post}$ can mention before-values. The usual usage

$$\begin{array}{llr} \mathsf{H1} & : \; P = (ok \Rightarrow P) & \text{(unpredictability)} \\ \mathsf{H2} & : \; P\{^{false}/_{ok'}\} \Rightarrow P\{^{true}/_{ok'}\} & \text{(possible termination)} \\ \mathsf{H3} & : \; P; \mathit{Skip} = P & \text{(dischargeable assumptions)} \\ \mathsf{H4} & : \; \exists ok', \underline{v}' \bullet P & \text{(feasibility)} \end{array}$$

Fig. 1. Design Healthiness Conditions

of designs is however to restrict the pre-conditions to only refer to the before-values of variables. The semantics of the assignment $x := y + 3$ in this theory is the following:

$$\mathit{true} \vdash x' = y + 3 \land y' = y$$

(if started, it will terminate, and the final value of x will equal the initial value of y plus three, with y unchanged).

Designs form a lattice w.r.t. the refinement ordering, whose bottom and top elements are respectively Abort and $\mathit{Miracle}$:

$$\begin{array}{lllll} \mathit{Abort} & \widehat{=} & \mathit{false} \vdash P & \equiv & \mathit{true}, \quad \text{for any predicate } P \\ \mathit{Miracle} & \widehat{=} & \mathit{true} \vdash \mathit{false} & \equiv & \neg ok \end{array}$$

It should be noted that $\mathit{Miracle}$ is a (infeasible) program that cannot be started.

There are four healthiness condition associated with designs, called H1 through H4 (see Fig. 1). The first two characterise predicates that are designs (i.e., predicates that can be written in the form $P \vdash Q$), whilst the third restricts designs to those whose pre-condition does not mention after-observations (it is defined using Skip which is described later). The first three, either individually or combined, define sublattices with Abort and $\mathit{Miracle}$ as extremal values. The fourth healthiness condition rules out infeasible predicates, such as $\mathit{Miracle}$, but breaks the lattice structure (it removes the top element, at least). Some of these conditions can be characterised by algebraic laws (H3 is defined that way):

$$\begin{array}{ll} \mathsf{H1} \;\; \mathit{true}; P = \mathit{true} \quad \text{and} \quad \mathit{Skip}; P = P \\ \mathsf{H4} \;\; P; \mathit{true} = \mathit{true} \end{array}$$

In §3.2 we present a probabilistic version of this theory based on our framework.

CSP in the UTP Framework. Reactive programs differ from ordinary sequential programs because observing them in just the initial and final states is no longer sufficient, as there are some observable intermediate steps that characterise their behaviour, i.e., their interactions with the environment. In addition to observations ok and ok', which now correspond to a process being divergence-free, we add three more observations:

$$\begin{array}{rcll} \mathit{wait}, \mathit{wait}' & : & \mathbb{B} & \text{— waiting to perform an event} \\ \mathit{tr}, \mathit{tr}' & : & \mathit{Event}\text{-seq} & \text{— history of events being performed (trace)} \\ \mathit{ref}, \mathit{ref}' & : & \mathit{Event}\text{-set} & \text{— events currently not allowed (refusals)} \end{array}$$

R1	:	$P = P \wedge (tr \le tr')$	(no time travel)
R2	:	$P = \exists s \bullet P[s, s \frown (tr' - tr)/tr, tr']$	(no direct event memory)
R3	:	$P = II \lhd wait \rhd P$	(say nothing until started)
	:	$II \triangleq (\neg ok \wedge tr \le tr') \vee (ok' \wedge tr' = tr \wedge wait' = wait \wedge ref' = ref)$	
R	:	$\bigwedge_{i \in 1,2,3} \mathsf{R}i$	

Fig. 2. Reactive Healthiness Conditions

$$\begin{aligned} Stop &= \mathsf{R}(true \vdash ok' \wedge wait' \wedge tr' = tr) \\ Skip &= \mathsf{R}(true \vdash ok' \wedge \neg wait' \wedge tr' = tr) \\ a \to Skip &= \mathsf{R}(true \vdash (ok' \wedge (a \notin ref' \lhd wait' \rhd tr' = tr \frown \langle a \rangle))) \end{aligned}$$

Fig. 3. Reactive Design semantics of CSP primitives

There are a number of associated healthiness conditions (Fig. 2). The first (R1) outlaws time travel by insisting that after-traces tr' are extensions of before-traces tr, whilst the second (R2) outlaws a process from having a direct memory of past events (any history-dependent behaviour requires some explicit state to remember some abstraction of past events). The third condition (R3) captures the fact that when not started, because some prior process is waiting ($wait = true$), we simply reflect the current behaviour of the prior process. This is captured by predicate II which requires us to propagate observations faithfully if the previous process is stable ($ok = true$). If the prior process has diverged ($ok = false$), then all we can guarantee is R1.

Originally, the theory of *communicating sequential processes* (*CSP*) was defined by adding in CSP-specific healthiness conditions CSP1–CSP2 [HH98, Chapter 8]. However a key unification result allows us to characterise CSP-healthy processes as *Reactive Designs* [OCW09]:

$$\mathsf{R}(Pre \vdash Post)$$

In other words, any CSP process can be written in the form of a design, that is "made" reactively healthy.

The semantics of some CSP constructs in this style are shown in Fig. 3.

2.2 pCSP

In §4 we are going to discuss how to create a *UTP*-friendly probabilistic variant of *CSP*. Here we look at two pieces of work regarding probabilistic *CSP*, that discuss some issues which are addressed by our theory.

In [MMSS96] we can find one of the possible definitions of *pCSP*, where probability is defined in such a way that it distributes through all operators. This leads to the surprising result that the demonic choice operator is not idempotent.

A refinement operator is defined, and the ideas of an associated probabilistic refinement calculus are discussed, where an implementation satisfies a specification with null probability. In effect we can no longer show whether an implementation satisfies a specification, but rather have to give bounds on the probability that an implementation may fail. This probability should ideally be very low, but would be expected to rise over time. In effect we have an implementation whose correctness has a life-time with some expectation value.

A different presentation is given in [Mor04], where *pCSP* is built on top of probabilistic action systems written in *pGCL* and is linked back to the relational semantics of *pGCL*. This view of the subject highlights how compositionality of probabilistic *CSP* is not straight-forward, because of the introduction of probability. Introducing probability splits a deterministic case into several possible different scenarios, and one has to take this into account when composing probabilistic programs.

They explain this using the metaphor of the colour of a child's eye: knowing the colour of the parents' eyes is not sufficient to predict that of the child. Instead we need hidden information about the alleles present and their relative dominance. In a similar fashion, in order to get accurate probabilities associated with *pCSP*, we have to track hidden information about choices that occurred in the past history.

3 Probabilistic Designs

3.1 The Distributional Framework

We are going to introduce briefly the key elements and constructs that characterise our distributional framework, in order to provide the reader with a working knowledge of it: a formal and rigorous definition can be found in [BB11], along with some soundness proofs.

Our framework relies on the concept of *distributions* over the state space, real-valued functions $\chi : \mathcal{S} \to \mathbb{R}$ that assign a *weight* x_i (a real number) to each state σ_i in the state space $\mathcal{S}$. We note the set of distributions as $\mathcal{D}$.

A state $\sigma : \mathcal{V} \to \mathcal{W}$ is a finite map from variables ($\mathcal{V}$) to values ($\mathcal{W}$). Each distribution has a weight, defined as:

$$\|\chi\| \mathrel{\widehat{=}} \sum_{\sigma \in \mathrm{dom}\,\chi} \chi(\sigma)$$

Among all distributions we distinguish *weighting distributions* π, such that $0 \leq \pi(\sigma) \leq 1$ for any state, and *probability (sub-)distributions* δ, such that $\|\delta\| \leq 1$.

Generally speaking, it is possible to operate on distributions by lifting pointwise operators such as addition, multiplication and multiplication by a scalar[2]. Analogously we can lift pointwise all traditional relations and functions on real numbers.

[2] Distributions form a vector space, which we have explored elsewhere[BB11]. We omit discussion of this aspect of our theory for clarity and brevity.

In the case of pointwise multiplication, it is interesting to see it as a way of "re-weighting" a distribution. We have a particular interest in the case when one of the operands is a weighting distribution π, as we will use this operation to give semantics to choice constructs. We opt for a postfix notation to write this operation, as this is an effective way of marking when pointwise multiplication happens in the operational flow: for example if we multiply the probability distribution δ by the weighting distribution π, we write this as $\delta\langle\pi\rangle$. We use notation ϵ and ι to denote the everywhere zero and unit distributions, respectively:

$$\epsilon(\sigma) = 0 \wedge \iota(\sigma) = 1, \qquad \text{for all } \sigma$$

Given a condition (predicate on state) c, we can define the weighting distribution that maps every state where c evaluates to *true* to 1, and every other state to 0: we overload the above notation and note this distribution as $\iota\langle c\rangle$. In general whenever we have the multiplication of a distribution by $\iota\langle c\rangle$, we can use the postfix operator $\langle c\rangle$ for short, instead of using $\langle\iota\langle c\rangle\rangle$. It is worth pointing out that if we multiply a probability distribution δ by $\iota\langle c\rangle$, we obtain a distribution whose weight $\|\delta\langle c\rangle\|$ is exactly the probability of being in a state satisfying c.

Assignment. Given a simultaneous assignment $\underline{v} := \underline{e}$, where underlining indicates that we have lists of variables and expressions of the same length, we denote its effect on an initial probability distribution δ by $\delta\{\!|\underline{e}/\underline{v}|\!\}$. The postfix operator $\{\!|\underline{e}/\underline{v}|\!\}$ reflects the modifications introduced by the assignment — the intuition behind this, roughly speaking, is that all states σ where the expression $\underline{e}$ evaluates to the same value $\underline{w} = \text{eval}_\sigma(\underline{e})$ are replaced by a single state $\sigma' = (\underline{v} \mapsto \underline{w})$ that maps to a probability that is the sum of the probabilities of the states it replaces.

$$(\delta\{\!|\underline{e}/\underline{v}|\!\})(\sigma') \triangleq (\Sigma\ \delta(\sigma) \ \mid\ \sigma' = \sigma \dagger \{\underline{v} \mapsto \text{eval}_\sigma(\underline{e})\})$$

Here we treat the state as a map, where $\dagger$ denotes map override; this operator essentially implements the concept of "push-forward" used in measure theory, and is therefore a linear operator. An example is given in Figure 4.

Assignment preserves the overall weight of a probability distribution if $\underline{e}$ can be evaluated in every state, and if not the assignment returns a sub-distribution, where the "missing" weight accounts for the assignment failing on some states (this failure prevents a program from proceeding and causes non-termination).

Programming Constructs. The semantic definitions of various programming constructs are based on a homogeneous relation between distributions and are listed in Figure 5; we will now proceed to discuss each one.

The failing program *Abort* is represented by the predicate $\|\delta'\| \le \|\delta\|$, which captures the fact that it is maximally unpredictable. However it is still guaranteed that the distribution weight cannot be increased, because that describes a program whose probability of termination is higher than that of it starting, and this is clearly impossible.

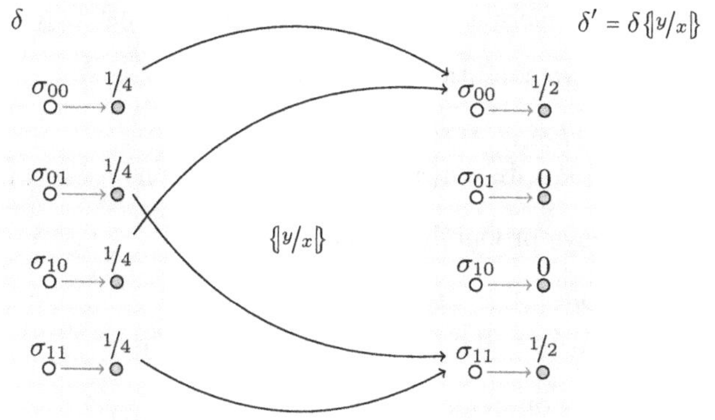

Fig. 4. The assignment $x := y$ from an initial uniform distribution on the state space $\mathcal{S} = \{0,1\} \times \{0,1\}$

$$
\begin{array}{rcl}
\mathit{Abort} & \triangleq & \|\delta'\| \le \|\delta\| \\
\mathit{Miracle} & \triangleq & (\delta = \epsilon) \wedge (\delta' = \epsilon) \\
\mathit{Skip} & \triangleq & \delta' = \delta \\
\underline{v} := \underline{e} & \triangleq & \delta' = \delta\{\!|\underline{e}/\underline{v}|\!\} \\
A;B & \triangleq & \exists \delta_m \bullet A(\delta,\delta_m) \wedge B(\delta_m,\delta') \\
\mathit{choice}(A,B,\mathcal{X}) & \triangleq & \exists \pi,\delta_A,\delta_B \bullet \pi \in \mathcal{X} \wedge A(\delta\langle\pi\rangle,\delta_A) \wedge B(\delta\langle\bar{\pi}\rangle,\delta_B) \wedge \delta' = \delta_A + \delta_B \\
c * A & \triangleq & \mathit{lfp}\, X \bullet \mathit{choice}((A;X),\mathit{Skip},\{\iota\langle c\rangle\})
\end{array}
$$

Fig. 5. UTP semantics for different programming constructs

The miraculous program $\mathit{Miracle}$ is defined as $(\delta = \epsilon) \wedge (\delta' = \epsilon)$: this is a different from the standard UTP theory, where it is simply false. This definition coincides with the standard one for most pairs of before- and after-distributions, with the exception of (ϵ, ϵ): this makes sure that $\mathit{Miracle}$ is a unit for nondeterministic choice.

Program Skip makes no changes and immediately terminates.

Assignment remaps the distribution as already discussed.

Sequential composition is characterised by the existence of a "mid-point" distribution that is the outcome of the first program, which is then fed into the second. It should be noted at this juncture that we are quantifying over function quantities, such as δ or π — this makes our logic at least second-order, even if the state spaces are finite (the range $[0,1]$ is not).

The choice operator takes a weighting distribution π, uses it with its complementary distribution $\bar{\pi} = \iota - \pi)$ to weight the distributions resulting from the left- and right-hand side respectively, and existentially quantifies it over the set of distributions $\mathcal{X} \subseteq \mathcal{D}_w$, where $\mathcal{D}_w \subset \mathcal{D}$ is the set of all weighting distributions over the program state under consideration. We have termed this operator as the *generic choice* as it generalises the standard choice constructs:

- for $\mathcal{X} = \{\iota\langle c\rangle\}$ we have conditional choice:

$$\begin{aligned} A \lhd c \rhd B &= \mathit{choice}(A, B, \{\iota\langle c\rangle\}) \\ &= \exists \delta_A, \delta_B \bullet A(\delta\langle c\rangle, \delta_A) \wedge B(\delta\langle\neg c\rangle, \delta_B) \wedge \delta' = \delta_A + \delta_B \end{aligned}$$

- for $\mathcal{X} = \{p \cdot \iota\}$ we have probabilistic choice:

$$\begin{aligned} A\ {}_p\!\oplus B &= \mathit{choice}(A, B, \{p \cdot \iota\}) \\ &= \exists \delta_A, \delta_B \bullet A(p \cdot \delta, \delta_A) \wedge B((1-p) \cdot \delta, \delta_B) \wedge \delta' = \delta_A + \delta_B \end{aligned}$$

- for $\mathcal{X} = \mathcal{D}_w$ we have non-deterministic choice:

$$\begin{aligned} A \sqcap B &= \mathit{choice}(A, B, \mathcal{D}_w) \\ &= \exists \pi, \delta_A, \delta_B \bullet A(\delta\langle\pi\rangle, \delta_A) \wedge B(\delta\langle\overline{\pi}\rangle, \delta_B) \wedge \delta' = \delta_A + \delta_B \end{aligned}$$

The usual notations for conditional, probabilistic and non-deterministic choice will be used as syntactic sugar in the remainder of this document.

Program *Abort* is a zero for non-deterministic choice, whereas the program *Miracle* is a unit.

Using the customary notation for conditional choice enlightens the definition of while-loops, which can be rewritten in a more familiar fashion as:

$$c * A \triangleq \mathit{lfp}\, X \bullet (A; X) \lhd c \rhd \mathit{Skip}$$

They are characterized as fixpoints of the appropriate functional, with respect to the ordering defined by the refinement relation, details of which can be found in [MM04, BB11] and are beyond the scope of this paper.

Healthiness Conditions. The distributional framework is characterised by the following healthiness conditions:

Dist1: the *feasibility* condition assures that the probability of termination cannot be greater than that of having started:

$$\|\delta'\| \leq \|\delta\|$$

Dist2: the *monotonicity* condition states that increasing δ implies that the resulting δ' increases as well:

$$\mathcal{P}(\delta_1, \delta_1') \wedge \mathcal{P}(\delta_2, \delta_2') \wedge \delta_2 > \delta_1 \Rightarrow \delta_2' \geq \delta_1'$$

Dist3: the *scaling* condition is about multiplication by a (not too large and non-negative[3]) constant, which distributes through commands:

$$\forall a \in \mathbb{R}^+ \wedge \|a \cdot \delta\| \leq 1 \bullet \mathcal{P}(\delta, \delta') \Leftrightarrow \mathcal{P}(a \cdot \delta, a \cdot \delta')$$

[3] Mathematically the relation holds also if this is not met, but in that case the distribution $a \cdot \delta$ may not be a probability distribution.

Dist4: the *convexity* condition poses restrictions on the space of possible program images[4], which is strictly a subset of $\wp\mathcal{D}$, the powerset of $\mathcal{D}$:

$$(\mathcal{P}_1 \sqcap \mathcal{P}_2)(\delta, \delta') \Rightarrow \delta' \geq \min\big(\mathcal{P}_1(\delta) \cup \mathcal{P}_2(\delta)\big)$$

Here $\mathcal{P}_i(\delta)$ denotes the set of all δ' that satisfy $\mathcal{P}_i(\delta, \delta')$.

We refer to this set as to the *program image* of $\mathcal{P}_i$ — we will use this concept to show the program lattice in the case of designs in Figure 6.

3.2 A Probabilistic Theory of Designs

We have used the framework above to give semantics to a probabilistic theory of designs [BB12a].

A big difference from the standard theory is that we did not need to use the auxiliary variables ok and ok': in fact the variable δ records implicitly if the program has started, as for each state it gives a precise probability that the program is in that initial state, while the variable δ' records implicitly if the program has finished, as for each state it gives a precise probability that the program is in that final state.

We can therefore relate the fact that a program has started with probability 1 with the fact that δ is a full distribution (*i.e.* $\|\delta\| = 1$): in other words the statement $ok = true$ can be translated to the statement $\|\delta\| = 1$.

Conversely a program for which $\delta = \epsilon$ is a program that has not started. Obviously there are all situations in between, where the fact of δ being a sub-distribution accounts for the program having started with probability $\|\delta\| < 1$.

Similarly if δ' is a full distribution, then the program terminates with probability 1: coherently we can translate the statement $ok' = true$ to the statement $\|\delta'\| = 1$. In general the weight of δ' is the probability of termination: if the program reaches an after-distribution whose weight is strictly less than 1, then termination is not guaranteed (and in particular if $\delta' = \epsilon$ it is certain that it will not terminate).

With these considerations in mind, it is straightforward, given a standard design $\mathcal{P}re \vdash \mathcal{P}ost$, to derive the corresponding probabilistic design:

$$\mathcal{P}re \vdash \mathcal{P}ost \equiv \|\delta(\mathcal{P}re)\| = 1 \Rightarrow \|\delta'(\mathcal{P}ost)\| = 1$$

This expression tells us that we have a valid design if whenever the before-distribution δ is a full distribution which is null everywhere $\mathcal{P}re$ is not satisfied (and therefore $\delta = \delta(\mathcal{P}re)$), then the resulting after-distribution δ' is a full distribution which is null everywhere $\mathcal{P}ost$ is not satisfied (and therefore $\delta' = \delta'(\mathcal{P}ost)$).

In other words both δ and δ' belong to the set $\mathcal{D}_p \cap \mathcal{B}(\epsilon, 1)$, which we note as $\partial\mathcal{D}_p$ (with a bit of notation abuse), where $\mathcal{D}_p \subset \mathcal{D}$ is the set of all probability distributions and $\mathcal{B}(\epsilon, 1)$ is the closed unitary ball[5] centered on the empty distribution ϵ.

---

[4] This is a consequence of the purely random non-deterministic model adopted in the distributional framework, yielding a result analogous to the set $\mathbb{H}S$ from [MM04].

[5] The norm of δ is $\|\delta\|$, and the distance function of the space is $d(\delta_1, \delta_2) \triangleq \|\delta_2 - \delta_1\|$.

In a similar way we can find a probabilistic version of other standard designs:

- assignment requires the right-hand expression to be defined everywhere in the state space, otherwise it reduces to *false*:

$$\underline{v} := \underline{e} \;\triangleq\; \|\delta\| = 1 \Rightarrow \|\delta'\| = 1 \wedge \delta' = \delta\{\!|\underline{e}/\underline{v}|\!\}$$

- the *Skip* construct preserves the before-distribution unchanged:

$$\mathit{Skip} \;\triangleq\; \|\delta\| = 1 \Rightarrow \delta' = \delta$$

- probabilistic designs form a lattice as well (with respect to the ordering induced by the $\Rightarrow$ relation). The bottom of the lattice is *Abort*, which is again *true* as in the standard theory:

$$\mathit{Abort} \;\triangleq\; \mathit{true}$$

- *Chaos* is a program that guarantees termination, but in an unspecified state[6]:

$$\mathit{Chaos} \;\triangleq\; \|\delta\| = 1 \Rightarrow \|\delta'\| = 1$$

- the top of the lattice is *Miracle*:

$$\mathit{Miracle} \;\triangleq\; \|\delta\| < 1$$

These new definitions preserve the validity of the healthiness conditions H1–H4, as on the other hand do all the constructs from the distributional framework [BB12a]: for this reason we can think of a variation and relax the constraints on the weights of the before- and after-distributions — so we use the programming constructs in Figure 5 exactly with the semantics presented there. By doing so we can fully exploit the potential of the distributional framework towards modelling situations where the probability of having started is less than 1: with a small modification we can recast the notion of total correctness by restricting Dist1 to a variant Dist1-TC (which implies Dist1), stating that:

$$\|\delta\| = \|\delta'\|$$

This requires a program to terminate with the same probability p with which it has started:

$$\|\delta\| = p \wedge \mathit{Pre} \Rightarrow \|\delta'\| = p \wedge \mathit{Post}$$

The role of preconditions and postconditions is that of restricting the range of acceptable before- and after-distributions (and therefore act as restrictions to be applied to δ and δ' respectively) — this allows us to express desirable characteristics of a program in great detail.

Through our distributional framework we therefore obtain a richer theory where corresponding healthiness conditions hold, even without the introduction of the auxiliary variables ok, ok' — the link with the standard model is discussed in [BB12a]. Moreover the use of distributions enables us to evaluate the probability both of termination and of meeting a set of arbitrary postconditions as a function of the initial distribution (which determines the probability of meeting any required precondition).

---

[6] In other words $\mathit{Chaos} \equiv \mathit{true} \vdash \mathit{Abort}_R$, where the subscript R indicates that we are talking of the relational version of *Abort*, from Figure 5.

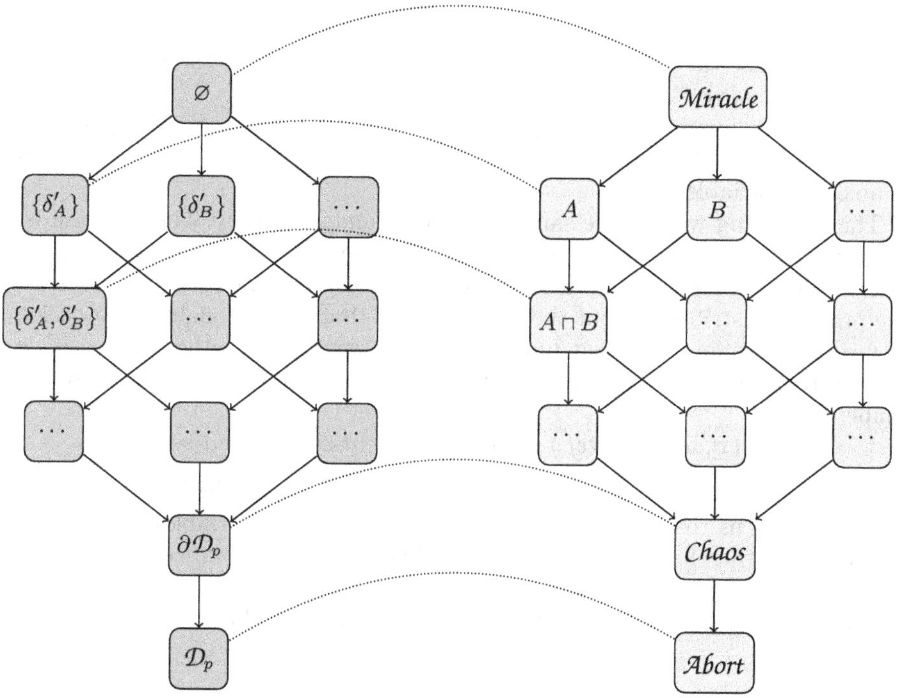

Fig. 6. Program image lattice ($\subseteq$ relation) and program lattice ($\Rightarrow$ relation) for probabilistic designs

4 Probabilistic CSP, UTP-Style

We have seen that the UTP theory of CSP is built on that of designs, with the introduction of three other pairs of auxiliary variables, notably $wait, tr, ref$ and their dashed counterparts.

We recall their roles in the theory:

- $wait, wait'$ are boolean variables recording if the program is waiting for interaction with the environment;
- tr, tr' record the list of events happened during the program run;
- ref, ref' are sets containing the event refused by the program.

They are in addition to ok, ok', already added when going from the relational theory towards the concept of designs: the distributional framework spared us from having to add these variables when creating the concept of probabilistic designs, as we do not need to use them — we have in fact argued that this information is contained implicitly in the distributions δ, δ', as their weight corresponds exactly to the probability that a particular program step has started or finished, respectively.

Information about divergent states remains implicit in the distributions: the probability of being in such a situation is precisely $(1 - \|\delta'\|)$.

In some sense the "ok" part of a distribution is mapped to the support of δ', whereas the "not-ok" part gets disregarded.

We can therefore build on the theory of probabilistic designs presented in §3.2 to get to a probabilistic theory of CSP only by adding the remaining three pairs of auxiliary variables.

Their meaning will be the same as in the standard theory. The question is: what is the best way to embed them in the probabilistic theory of designs? We may be tempted to introduce them as auxiliary variables alongside with the program distribution, but the same reasons that were brought up to decide in favour of an approach that lumps all of the variables together into a single composite observation variable, require us to work on states with the following shape:

$$\sigma : (\underline{v}, wait, tr, ref) \to \underline{\mathcal{W}} \times \mathbb{B} \times Event\text{-seq} \times Event\text{-set},$$

where $\mathcal{W}$ is the set of possible values for the program variables.

This allows us to embed all of the remaining auxiliary variables in the state domain, and therefore this simplifies the definitions of the different programming constructs and healthiness conditions, compared to the traditional reactive definitions that use $ok, wait, tr, ref$ as auxiliary variables — this is a novel approach.

4.1 R1

For example let us take the traditional R1, which states:

$$P = P \land (tr \le tr')$$

In a probabilistic world this must hold pointwise for each couple of states (σ, σ') from the before- and after-distributions that are related by the program.

If we write this in the case of a single state σ (*i.e.* we take a point distribution η_σ as the before-distribution), the trace in the before-state σ must be a prefix of the trace in all of the possible after-states σ' from the support[7] of the resulting after-distribution δ'.

This must hold true for all states in the state space, so the formulation of the probabilistic R1 is:

$$P(\delta, \delta') = P(\delta, \delta') \land \left(\forall \sigma \bullet P(\eta_\sigma, \delta') \implies (\forall \sigma' \in \text{supp}(\delta') \bullet \sigma(tr) \le \sigma'(tr))\right)$$

where we have used the functional notation $\sigma(tr)$ to stand for the evaluation of tr on σ.

From this formulation we can clearly see that divergent states do not take part in the verification of the condition R1; in addition, it is worth pointing out that, according to this definition, a totally divergent program (which yields $\delta' = \epsilon$ for any initial δ) is R1-healthy.

[7] The support of a function is the subset of its domain where the function is non-null.

4.2 R2

Healthiness condition R2 states that the initial value of tr cannot have any influence on the evolution of the program, which determines only the tail $(tr' - tr)$:

$$P(tr, tr') = \exists s \bullet P(s, s \frown (tr' - tr))$$

As we did above we first look at the case of point distributions, where a possible formulation is the following:

$$P(\eta_\sigma, \delta') = \exists s \bullet P(\eta_\sigma \{\!|{}^{s}/_{tr}|\!\}, \delta' \{\!|{}^{s \frown (tr - \sigma(tr))}/_{tr}|\!\})$$

Here we have used the remap operator to "change" the value of the trace in the spirit of R2 over all states.

This gives a sort of "substitution rule" that allows us to replace a state σ with another state ζ that differs only for the value of tr in the before-distribution, whereas in the after-distribution a part δ'_σ (accounting for the contribution of σ) is replaced by a new part δ'_ζ (accounting for the contribution of ζ):

$$P(\delta, \delta') = \forall \sigma \exists s \bullet (\zeta = \sigma\{{}^{s}/_{tr}\}) \wedge P\big((\delta - \delta_\sigma + \delta_\zeta), (\delta' - \delta'_\sigma + \delta'_\zeta)\big)$$

where δ_σ and δ_ζ are point distributions scaled down by the probability of σ, *i.e.* $\delta_\sigma = \delta(\sigma) \cdot \eta_\sigma$ and $\delta_\zeta = \delta(\sigma) \cdot \eta_\zeta$.

4.3 R3

Before getting to R3 we have to define the probabilistic version of the reactive $\mathcal{Skip}$, denoted Π.

According to the standard theory of reactive designs [HH98], Π is defined as:

$$\Pi \;\hat{=}\; (\neg ok \wedge tr \le tr') \;\vee\; (ok' \wedge tr' = tr \wedge wait' = wait \wedge ref' = ref)$$

This definition has to distinguish the case of divergence (when it does not enforce anything other than trace elongation) from the case of non-divergence (when it states that all variables are left unchanged), and as a result it is much more complicated than the pure relational skip which is simply:

$$\underline{v}' = \underline{v}$$

The choice of embedding the auxiliary variables in the state function σ (and having left all information about divergence implicit in δ, δ') starts to pay out here, as it enables us to keep such an easy definition as well:

$$\Pi \;\hat{=}\; \delta' = \delta$$

In other words all non-divergent states are preserved as they are, whereas now there is no statement on divergent states — other than the implicit one that the overall probability of divergence must be left unchanged.

R3 does not mention tr, tr':

$$P = II \lhd wait \rhd P$$

As a result this is pretty straightforward to express in a probabilistic setting, as we can use directly the semantics of the conditional construct presented in §3.1:

$$
\begin{array}{ll}
 & II \lhd wait \rhd P \\
\equiv & \quad \text{definition of conditional} \\
 & \exists \delta_A, \delta_B \bullet II(\delta\langle wait\rangle, \delta_A) \;\wedge\; P(\delta\langle \neg wait\rangle, \delta_B) \wedge \delta' = \delta_A + \delta_B \\
\equiv & \quad \text{definition of } II \\
 & \exists \delta_A, \delta_B \bullet II(\delta\langle wait\rangle, \delta_A) \wedge \delta_A = \delta\langle wait\rangle \;\wedge\; P(\delta\langle \neg wait\rangle, \delta_B) \wedge \delta' = \delta_A + \delta_B \\
\equiv & \quad \text{one-point rule on } \delta_A \\
 & \exists \delta_B \bullet II(\delta\langle wait\rangle, \delta\langle wait\rangle) \;\wedge\; P(\delta\langle \neg wait\rangle, \delta_B) \wedge \delta_B = \delta' - \delta\langle wait\rangle \\
\equiv & \quad \text{one-point rule on } \delta_B \\
 & II(\delta\langle wait\rangle, \delta\langle wait\rangle) \;\wedge\; P(\delta\langle \neg wait\rangle, \delta' - \delta\langle wait\rangle)
\end{array}
$$

And therefore.

$$P(\delta, \delta') = II(\delta\langle wait\rangle, \delta\langle wait\rangle) \;\wedge\; P(\delta\langle \neg wait\rangle, \delta' - \delta\langle wait\rangle)$$

We split the before-distribution into two parts, one where $wait$ is true and that equals the corresponding after-distribution, and one where it is not and that has evolved into the difference of the total after-distribution δ' and the part $\delta\langle wait\rangle$ that did not evolve.

This can be simplified down to:

$$P(\delta, \delta') = P(\delta\langle \neg wait\rangle, \delta' - \delta\langle wait\rangle).$$

4.4 CSP1 and CSP2

At this stage the readers with prior knowledge of *CSP* in the *UTP* framework may be surprised that the end of this paper is approaching and yet we have not mentioned two other healthiness conditions, namely CSP1 and CSP2.

The reason for our omission is that another advantage of the distributional framework is that compliance with these healthiness conditions is subsumed by other conditions, as we are now going to show.

In standard *CSP*, CSP1 states that:

$$P = P \vee (\neg ok \wedge tr \leq tr')$$

As all information about divergent states is kept implicit in distributions, we can argue that this healthiness condition is stripped down to the identity $P = P$.

In some sense, all states which are "ok" evolve from the support of the before-distribution towards a state in the support of the after-distribution, which is "ok′", or diverge to a state, which is "not-ok′" and is not part of the support of the after-distribution, effectively getting out of the game; on the other hand all states which are "not-ok" are not part of the support of the before-distribution and have no means to get back in the game.

Probabilistic reactive programs are therefore CSP1-healthy by design, as $P(\delta, \delta')$ already states that either a state evolves according to what is described by δ, δ' or diverges.

Our formalism does not allow us to express the trace-elongation property for divergent states, but after all it is not crucial information — they diverge, that's already bad enough!

The other healthiness condition, CSP2, states that:

$$P; J = P$$

where

$$J \triangleq \underline{v}' = \underline{v} \wedge (ok \Rightarrow ok') \wedge tr' = tr \wedge wait' = wait \wedge ref' = ref$$

In the probabilistic world based on distribution this reduces to:

$$P; \mathit{II} = P$$

which is nothing but H3. In fact:

$$\begin{aligned} J &\triangleq (\underline{v}' = \underline{v} \wedge (ok \Rightarrow ok') \wedge tr' = tr \wedge wait' = wait \wedge ref' = ref) \\ &\equiv (\underline{v}' = \underline{v} \wedge ok' \wedge tr' = tr \wedge wait' = wait \wedge ref' = ref) \vee \\ &\qquad\qquad \vee (\underline{v}' = \underline{v} \wedge \neg ok \wedge tr' = tr \wedge wait' = wait \wedge ref' = ref) \\ &\equiv \mathit{II} \vee (\underline{v}' = \underline{v} \wedge \neg ok \wedge tr' = tr \wedge wait' = wait \wedge ref' = ref) \end{aligned}$$

And again the part with $\neg ok$ gets disregarded, thus the reactive program J in the probabilistic world coincides with II — and there we have that CSP2 collapses to H3.

5 Conclusion

We have built a framework using the notion of distributions on the state space: through distributions we are able to associate a probability with each state.

If we use predicates stating relations among distributions we can build a *UTP* theory of programs that naturally embeds probability, so that probabilistic choice and non-deterministic choice can co-exist in the same framework.

We have extended this theory first to generalise the standard *UTP* theory of designs, and then we have built on that a theory of reactive programs.

The peculiarity of this approach is that divergent states are implicitly accounted for by sub-distributions, where the weight is strictly less than one: a divergent state does not belong to the domain of a distribution (in some sense all states which are "not-ok" are disregarded), and the overall probability of being in a divergent state is equal to the difference between 1 and the distribution weight.

Probabilistic versions of healthiness conditions R1, R2 and R3 hold in the probabilistic theory, whereas healthiness conditions CSP1 and CSP2 are subsumed by the framework.

References

[BB11] Bresciani, R., Butterfield, A.: Towards a UTP-style framework to deal with probabilities. Technical Report TCD-CS-2011-09, FMG, Trinity College Dublin, Ireland (August 2011)

[BB12a] Bresciani, R., Butterfield, A.: A probabilistic theory of designs based on distributions. In: Wolff, B., Gaudel, M.-C., Feliachi, A. (eds.) UTP 2012. LNCS, vol. 7681, pp. 105–123. Springer, Heidelberg (2013)

[BB12b] Bresciani, R., Butterfield, A.: A UTP semantics of pGCL as a homogeneous relation. In: Derrick, J., Gnesi, S., Latella, D., Treharne, H. (eds.) IFM 2012. LNCS, vol. 7321, pp. 191–205. Springer, Heidelberg (2012)

[But10] Butterfield, A. (ed.): UTP 2008. LNCS, vol. 5713. Springer, Heidelberg (2010)

[CS09] Chen, Y., Sanders, J.W.: Unifying probability with nondeterminism. In: Cavalcanti, A., Dams, D.R. (eds.) FM 2009. LNCS, vol. 5850, pp. 467–482. Springer, Heidelberg (2009)

[Dij76] Dijkstra, E.W.: A Discipline of Programming. Prentice-Hall (1976)

[DS06] Dunne, S., Stoddart, B. (eds.): UTP 2006. LNCS, vol. 4010. Springer, Heidelberg (2006)

[He10] He, J.: A probabilistic BPEL-like language. In: Qin [Qin 2010], pp. 74–100 (2010)

[Heh84] Hehner, E.C.R.: Predicative programming — Part I & II. Commun. ACM 27(2), 134–151 (1984)

[HH98] Hoare, C.A.R., He, J.: Unifying Theories of Programming. Prentice Hall International Series in Computer Science (1998)

[Hoa85] Hoare, C.A.R.: Programs are predicates. In: Proceedings of a discussion meeting of the Royal Society of London on Mathematical Logic and Programming Languages, Upper Saddle River, NJ, USA, pp. 141–155. Prentice-Hall (1985)

[HS06] He, J., Sanders, J.W.: Unifying probability. In: Dunne and Stoddart [DSO 2006], pp. 173–199 (2006)

[Koz81] Kozen, D.: Semantics of probabilistic programs. J. Comput. Syst. Sci. 22(3), 328–350 (1981)

[Koz85] Kozen, D.: A probabilistic PDL. J. Comput. Syst. Sci. 30(2), 162–178 (1985)

[Mis00] Mislove, M.W.: Nondeterminism and probabilistic choice: Obeying the laws. In: Palamidessi, C. (ed.) CONCUR 2000. LNCS, vol. 1877, pp. 350–365. Springer, Heidelberg (2000)

[MM04] McIver, A., Morgan, C.: Abstraction, Refinement and Proof for Probabilistic Systems. Monographs in Computer Science. Springer (2004)

[MMSS96] Morgan, C., McIver, A., Seidel, K., Sanders, J.W.: Refinement-oriented probability for CSP. Formal Asp. Comput. 8(6), 617–647 (1996)

[Mor04] Morgan, C.: Of probabilistic *Wp* and *CSP*—and compositionality. In: Abdallah, A.E., Jones, C.B., Sanders, J.W. (eds.) CSP 2004. LNCS, vol. 3525, pp. 220–241. Springer, Heidelberg (2005)

[OCW09] Oliveira, M., Cavalcanti, A., Woodcock, J.: A UTP semantics for Circus. Formal Asp. Comput 21(1-2), 3–32 (2009)

[Qin10] Qin, S. (ed.): UTP 2010. LNCS, vol. 6445. Springer, Heidelberg (2010)

HOL-TestGen/fw

An Environment for Specification-Based Firewall Conformance Testing

Achim D. Brucker[1], Lukas Brügger[2], and Burkhart Wolff[3]

[1] SAP AG, Vincenz-Priessnitz-Str. 1, 76131 Karlsruhe, Germany
achim.brucker@sap.com
http://www.brucker.ch/

[2] Information Security, ETH Zurich, 8092 Zurich, Switzerland
lukas.a.bruegger@gmail.com

[3] LRI, Université Paris-Sud, 91405 Orsay Cedex, France
wolff@lri.fr
http://www.lri.fr/~wolff

Abstract. The HOL-TestGen environment is conceived as a system for modeling and *semi-automated* test generation with an emphasis on expressive power and generality. However, its underlying technical framework Isabelle/HOL supports the customization as well as the development of highly automated add-ons working in specific application domains.

In this paper, we present HOL-TestGen/fw, an add-on for the test framework HOL-TestGen, that allows for testing the conformance of firewall implementations to high-level security policies. Based on generic theories specifying a security-policy language, we developed specific theories for network data and firewall policies. On top of these firewall specific theories, we provide mechanisms for policy transformations based on derived rules and adapted code-generators producing test drivers. Our empirical evaluations shows that HOL-TestGen/fw is a competitive environment for testing firewalls or high-level policies of local networks.

Keywords: symbolic test case generations, black box testing, theorem proving, network security, firewall testing, conformance testing.

1 Introduction

HOL-TestGen [6, 7] (http://www.brucker.ch/projects/hol-testgen/) is a generic model-based testing environment. Built as an extension of the Isabelle framework [15], HOL-TestGen inherits, among other things, the front-end PIDE, the Isar language for HOL specifications and proofs, and code- and documentation generators from the Isabelle framework. HOL-TestGen extends the framework by an infrastructure to develop formal *test plans*, i.e., descriptions of test goals, their decomposition into abstract test partitions, and their transformation to concrete tests with the help of constraint solvers like Z3 [12]. Finally, customized code-generators produce code of concrete test drivers which can be run against real implementations following a black-box testing approach.

Z. Liu, J. Woodcock, and H. Zhu (Eds.): ICTAC 2013, LNCS 8049, pp. 112–121, 2013.

HOL-TESTGEN as such is conceived as an interactive, flexible environment that draws from the abundant expressive power and generality of HOL; test plans are therefore typically mixtures of very powerful automated partitioning and selection tactics, their configurations, and intermediate small-step tactics that help to turn the results into a suitable form for the next step. HOL-TESTGEN was used successfully in large case studies from various domains, see [7] for details.

In this paper, we present the novel HOL-TESTGEN/FW environment, which is an add-on of HOL-TESTGEN for a specific problem domain: the specification-based conformance test of network components. Such components can be stateless packet filters, stateful firewalls, routers, devices performing network address translation (NAT), etc. In the sequel we just refer to them as firewalls. We describe the underlying generic theories for modeling network data and firewall policies using a generic security-policy language called the *Unified Policy Framework* (UPF) [3, 8], mechanisms for policy transformations (for which formal proofs of correctness have been established [2]) and adapted code-generators producing test drivers. We present application scenarios as well as experimental evaluations which show HOL-TESTGEN/FW as a competitive environment for testing firewalls or high-level policies of networks.[1]

2 The HOL-TESTGEN/FW Workflow

HOL-TESTGEN/FW is an environment for the specification-based conformance testing of firewalls.

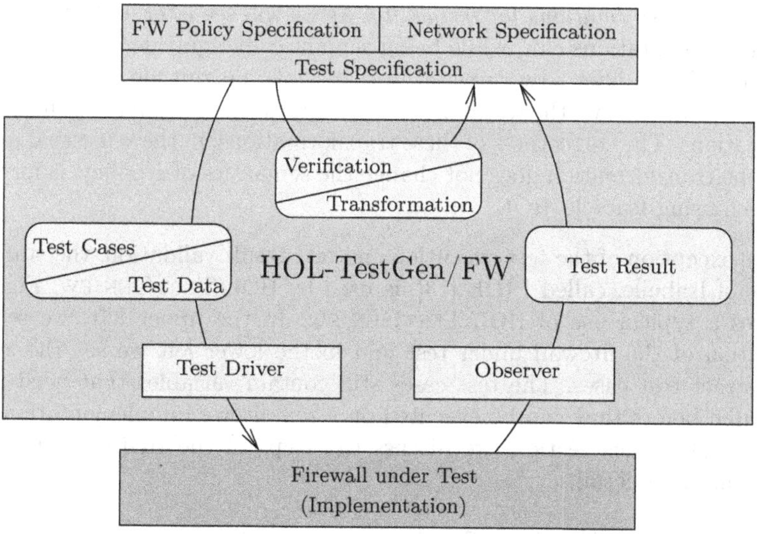

Fig. 1. The HOL-TESTGEN/FW Architecture

[1] HOL-TESTGEN/FW (including case studies) is, since version 1.7.1, part of the HOL-TESTGEN distribution. HOL-TESTGEN is available from: `http://www.brucker.ch/projects/hol-testgen/`.

Figure 1 illustrates the standard workflow, respectively the main components of HOL-TestGen/fw:

1. *Firewall policy specification, network specification, and test specification:* HOL-TestGen/fw provides an instantiation of the Unified Policy Framework (UPF) [3, 8] that allows to specify networks and security policies for those networks in a user-friendly way. The test specification, i. e., the properties that should be tested, also need to be specified here.
2. *Test case and test data generation:* In this phase, the abstract *test cases* as well as the concrete *test data* are generated. The test cases still contain constraints: a test case actually represents a section of the test space. By choosing ground instances for these constraints, we obtain test data that can be executed on an actual firewall implementation.
3. *Test execution and test result validation:* Finally, the test data is injected (using the *test driver*) into a real network and the behavior of the firewall under test is observed (using an *observer* or monitor) and compared to the test specification.

In its essence, this resembles the standard model-based testing workflow applied to firewalls (or any other network components controlling network traffic). In addition, HOL-TestGen/fw also supports:

- *Verification of (security) properties:* Both the specification of the security policy as well as the network specification can be analyzed and properties can be verified formally using the full reasoning power of Isabelle/HOL.
- *Verified transformations for testability:* As we will see later, different syntactical representations can, while being semantically equivalent, result in test efforts that differ by several orders of magnitude. Thus, using HOL-TestGen/fw, the testability can be improved by applying policy transformations. The correctness of these transformations, in the sense that applying the transformation does not change the semantics of a policy, is formally proven using Isabelle/HOL.

With the exception of the test execution and test result validation, the standard interface of Isabelle, called PIDE [13], is used by HOL-TestGen/fw. Figure 2 illustrates a typical use of HOL-TestGen/fw: In the upper left, we see the specification of the firewall under test and in the lower left we see the generated abstract test cases. The test cases still contain variables that need to be instantiated before they can be executed on a real firewall implementation.

In the rest of this section, we discuss the steps of the HOL-TestGen/fw workflow in more detail.

2.1 System and Test Specification

The Language: UPF with Firewall-Policy-Combinators. HOL is a typed λ-calculus and its foundational type are total functions $\alpha \Rightarrow \alpha'$. Using the provided infrastructure, the usual data-types like α option or α list can be defined. *Partial* functions ($\alpha \rightharpoonup \alpha'$) are introduced as synonym to $\alpha \Rightarrow (\alpha'$ option). They

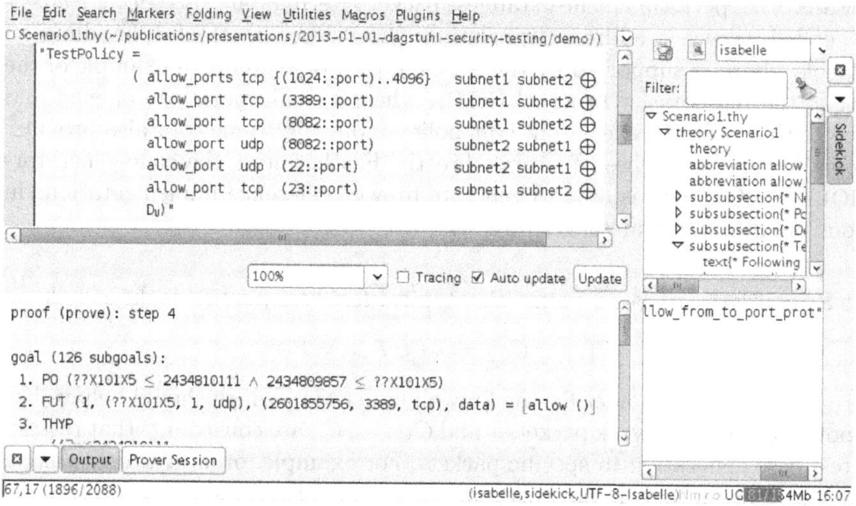

Fig. 2. A HOL-TestGen/fw Session using the PIDE/jEdit User Interface

are used to model the fundamental concept of UPF: *policies* as partial decision functions:

$$(\alpha, \beta)\ \text{policy} = \alpha \rightharpoonup (\beta\ \text{decision})$$

The decision datatype is defined as α decision = allow α | deny α. Thus, policies are three-valued: allow, deny, or $\bot$ (i. e., "don't know"). They can map input data to output data, refer to state, or be a policy-transforming policy.

Several combinators are defined in the UPF library providing definitions for families of *override* ($\_ \oplus \_$), *sequential composition* ($\_ \circ \_$), and *parallel composition* ($\_ \otimes \_$) of policies. These operators enjoy a wealth of algebraic properties like associativity, quasi-commutativity, or distributivity. We provide formal proofs, using Isabelle/HOL, for these properties.

The UPF is instantiated within HOL-TestGen/fw by concrete formats for TCP/IP packets, standard policies such as allow_all or deny_all, as well as combinators such as allow_port.

Network and Policy Models. Stateless firewall policies are modeled similar to common firewall configuration tools (see Brucker et al. [4] for details). After definitions of the relevant sub-networks (subsets of IP addresses modeling, e. g., the *demilitarized zone* dmz), it is for example straightforward to build a composition of elementary rules to be executed from left to right using the UPF override combinator. For example, we define a firewall policy P allowing only traffic by tcp from the internet to the dmz on port 25 or on port 80 formally:

$$P = \text{allow\_port internet dmz tcp } 25 \oplus \text{allow\_port internet dmz tcp } 80 \oplus \text{deny\_all}$$

Firewalls often perform not just stateless packet filtering, but also *packet translation* called network address translation (NAT), or a stateful handling of protocols—both is supported by HOL-TESTGEN/FW as well. An example of the latter is the file transfer protocol (FTP), where specific ports are opened and closed during protocol execution. Our policy modeling framework also provides support for modeling these concepts directly. Furthermore, the code-generators of HOL-TESTGEN/FW is able to generate firewall reference implementations in various programming languages directly.

Test Specification. For a policy P, a typical *test specification* looks as follows:

$$[\![C_1; \ldots ; C_n]\!] \Longrightarrow FUT\ x = P\,x$$

where FUT is a placeholder for the firewall under test, which should behave like the policy P for all network packets x and $C_1, \ldots, C_n$ are constraints that restrict the test case generation to specific packets. For example, often it is desirable to exclude test cases that do not send packets across different sub-networks, or we might want to restrict testing to specific protocols.

2.2 Test Case and Test Data Generation

HOL-TESTGEN/FW can generate abstract test cases as well as concrete test data. This involves both normal form computations (resulting in test cases), and constraint solving (resulting in instantiations of the test cases, i. e., the concrete test data). While generic tactics for any models are available, the policy tactic library allows for a more *efficient* processing by using domain-specific knowledge. As a result of this phase, we obtain descriptions of network packets together with the desired decision, possibly extended by transformed packets. For our example policy P shown above, we state the *test specification*:

$$FUT\ x = P\,x$$

From this test specification, 24 test cases are generated automatically. Among them:

1. $FUT(12, (?X100, \mathrm{tcp}, 6), (?X101, \mathrm{tcp}, 80), \mathrm{content}) = \lfloor \mathrm{deny}\ () \rfloor$
2. $FUT(8, (?X102, \mathrm{tcp}, 12), (?X103, \mathrm{tcp}, 25), \mathrm{content}) = \lfloor \mathrm{accept}\ () \rfloor$

The variables starting with a question mark (e. g., $?X100$) are meta-variables representing a network address. In a separate step, we infer the actual test data from the test cases by finding ground instances that fulfill the constraints. For our two exemplary test cases, we might obtain the following test data:

1. $FUT(12, ((154, 23, 43, 2), \mathrm{tcp}, 6), ((172, 0, 5, 3), \mathrm{tcp}, 80), \mathrm{content}) = \lfloor \mathrm{deny}\ () \rfloor$
2. $FUT(8, ((154, 23, 43, 2), \mathrm{tcp}, 12), ((172, 0, 5, 3), \mathrm{tcp}, 25), \mathrm{content}) = \lfloor \mathrm{accept}\ () \rfloor$

We see that in our model, the description of a network packet is a tuple consisting of an identifier, a source address, a destination address and a content. Both the source and destination address consist of an IP address, a protocol, and a port number.

2.3 Test Execution and Test Result Validation

Next, the test data is injected into a network containing the firewall (or multiple firewalls) to be tested. The packet injection, the probing of the behavior, and the validation of the results are supported by the HOL-TestGen/fw test execution environment (see Figure 3). In more detail, the test execution environment consists of a test execution manager, a result analysis module, a set of endpoints, and a set of probes.

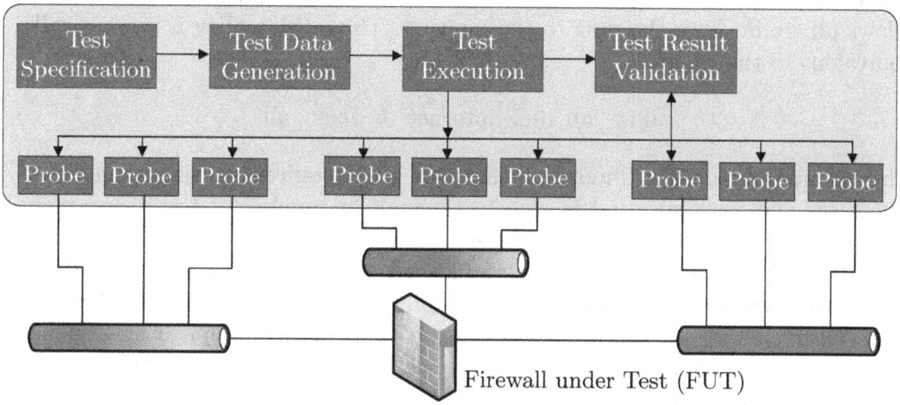

Fig. 3. A Framework for testing firewalls or routers

Internally, the HOL-TestGen/fw execution environment uses an adapted version of fwtest (`http://user.cs.tu-berlin.de/~seb/fwtest/`) for injecting and observing network packets. Thus, the test data generated by HOL-TestGen is converted automatically to the input format of fwtest. As an example:

```
12:154.23.43.2: 6:172.0.5.3:80:S:TCP:10
 8:154.23.43.2:12:172.0.5.3:25:S:TCP:10
```

Here, the meaning of the individual parts (separated by a colon) is as follows: packet id, source IP, source port, destination IP, destination port, TCP flags, and the time to live. The test execution as well as the transformation of the input data is automated. Just some further information about the network topology that is not part of the model used to generate the test cases (e. g., IP addresses of the devices where the probes should be installed) has to be provided by the test engineer.

2.4 Verified Policy Transformations

The naïve approach presented so far does not scale very well in many cases and application domains; in many practical scenarios, the method takes too long and generates far too many tests resulting in a very long time for test execution.

There is an obvious need for speeding up both the test data generation as well as the test execution.

Our environment offers a solution to this problem called *verified policy transformations*, where a firewall policy is transformed into one that is easier to test but semantically equivalent, for example by eliminating redundant rules. As an example, consider the policy

$$\text{allow\_all dmz internet} \oplus \text{deny\_port dmz internet 21} \oplus \text{deny\_all}$$

which, as the rule deny_port dmz internet 21 is overridden by the first rule, allows all traffic from the dmz to the internet. Thus, this policy is semantically equivalent to the policy:

$$\text{allow\_all dmz internet} \oplus \text{deny\_all}$$

The second policy is much more efficient to test: it requires less time to generate test cases and test data and is, due to the smaller number of test cases, more efficient during the test execution phase.

Motivated by this and similar examples, we developed a rich theory of policy transformations that improve the testability of firewall policies (see Brucker et al. [2] for detail). A specific set of these transformations applied in sequence constitute a default normalization of firewall policies. All of these transformations are formally verified (using Isabelle/HOL) to be semantically correct and, as we will see in the next section, the normalization can increase the performance by several orders of magnitude.

3 Case Studies and Evaluations

We used HOL-TestGen/fw in a large number of case studies. Those also included "real policies," for example some drawn from the network of ETH Zurich as well as some coming from collaborations with partners from industry. These large and complex policies revealed immediately the need for optimizations of the naïve approach and motivated us to develop the verified policy transformation approach presented above. Using the policy transformation, we were able to apply HOL-TestGen/fw in all our case studies successfully.

We analyzed the scalability issues as well as the impact of the policy transformation by applying HOL-TestGen/fw to randomly generated policies. This allowed us to estimate the correlation between the size of a policy and the generation time of tests, and to study the influence of various parameters of this correlation (e. g., different representations of network packets, number of networks) and, of course, the impact of our optimization. We discussed our generated policies as well as the generated test data before and after the optimization with experts from industry to ensure that our evaluation fulfills their needs.

In more detail, we applied HOL-TestGen/fw in the following scenarios that cover both industrial case studies as well as randomly generated policies to study for example the effect of different modeling variants.

- *Packet Filter with Varying Number of Rules and Networks.* We tested "personal firewalls" of various sizes and network complexity. While for rules with low complexity, the naïve approaches works quite well (Figure 4a), it fails even for small policies with complex rules (Figure 4b). This observation motivated the development of our verified policy transformation approach.

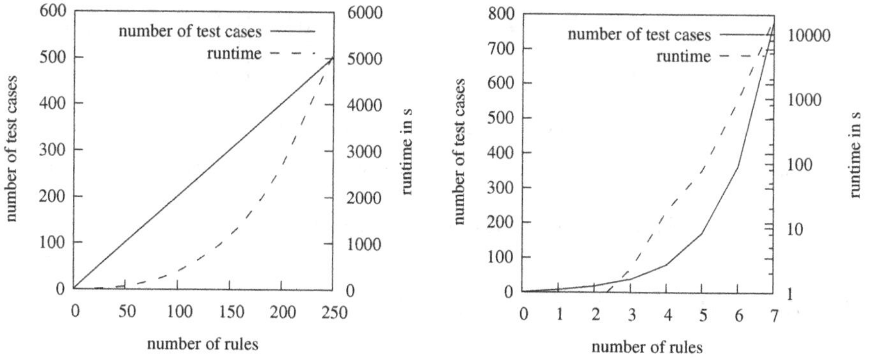

(a) Rules with low complexity. (b) Rules of larger internal complexity

Fig. 4. Policy Complexity

- *Effect of Address Representation.* Our firewall models support different formalizations of network addresses. To study the effect of a more complex representation, we carried out the personal firewall scenarios with different address representations. From this experiment, we concluded that representing addresses as integers is the most efficient approach [7].
- *Packet Filter and NAT.* Motivated by needs from industry, we implemented support for network address translation (NAT). Technically, this is modeled as a parallel composition of a filtering and a translating policy. In practice, this does only add moderate overhead to test case generation as the translating policies are usually rather small.
- *Policy Transformation.* To address the scalability problem, we implemented a policy transformation approach which increases the efficiency of the naïve approach by several orders of magnitude (see Figure 5). In more detail, the transformation reduces the time required for generating the test cases and the test data (Figure 5b), as well as their number (Figure 5a). The latter also reduces the time required for test execution and validation.
- *Stateful Firewalls.* Several protocols, such as the file transfer protocol (FTP), Voice over IP (VoIP), or protocols for streaming multimedia data have an internal state; thus they are stateful. Such protocols require an (application-level) stateful firewall. HOL-TestGen/fw tests stateful firewalls by generating sequences of input network packets. Overall, this works quite efficiently; see Brucker and Wolff [5] for details.

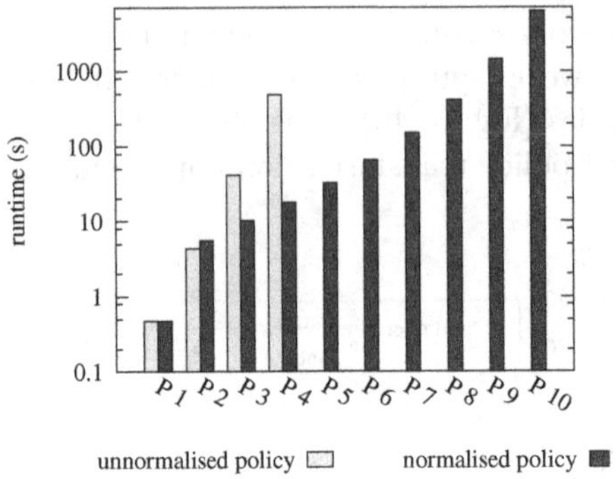

(a) Policy transformation (time)

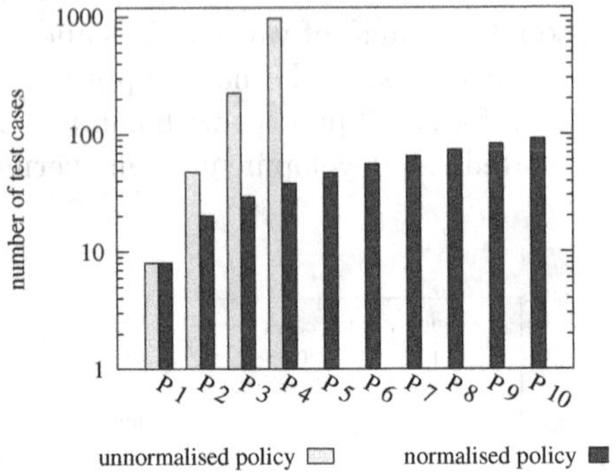

(b) Policy transformation (test cases)

Fig. 5. Effect of the policy transformation

4 Related Work and Conclusion

Widely used tools for "testing" firewalls and other network components fall, broadly, into three categories:

1. Policy management and analysis tools, e. g., for optimizing polices or deploying the same policy to firewalls of different vendors. An example of this category is the Firewall Analyzer from AlgoSec (`http://www.algosec.com/`).
2. Tools that help to manage and analyze logs of firewalls, e. g., for detecting or analyzing security breaches. The Network Intelligence Engine from Network Intelligence (`http://www.network-intelligence.com/`) is an example for this category.
3. Tools that test for common misconfigurations (e. g., forwarding NetBIOS requests) or well-known vulnerabilities (e. g., exploitable buffer overflows of a specific firewall system). Examples for this categories are nmap (`http://www.nmap.org`) or OpenVAS (`http://www.openvas.org`).

These tools test for generic and well-known misconfigurations and security problems. In contrast to our approach, they do not base their test on the actual firewall policy. Thus, these tools complement HOL-TestGen/fw.

HOL-TestGen/fw supports the model-based conformance testing of firewalls. These conformance tests ensure both the correctness of the firewall implementation as well as the actual configuration of the firewall. The underlying foundations of the system as well as a more detailed report on the case studies is provided elsewhere [4].

Close to our work are tools that test for a firewall's conformance to a given policy. For example, [9, 10] present a policy segmentation technique to create the test cases. [11] also proposes a specification-based testing of firewalls, however the policies are restricted to stateless packet filters. Finally, [1, 14] present a framework for testing firewalls at the implementation level.

References

[1] von Bidder, D.: Specification-based firewall testing. Ph.d. thesis, ETH Zurich, ETH Dissertation No. 17172. Diana von Bidder's maiden name is Diana Senn (2007)

[2] Brucker, A.D., Brügger, L., Kearney, P., Wolff, B.: Verified firewall policy transformations for test-case generation. In: Third International Conference on Software Testing, Verification, and Validation (ICST) , pp. 345–354. IEEE Computer Society (2010), doi:10.1109/ICST.2010.50

[3] Brucker, A.D., Brügger, L., Kearney, P., Wolff, B.: An approach to modular and testable security models of real-world health-care applications. In: ACM Symposium on Access Control Models and Technologies (SACMAT), pp. 133–142. ACM Press (2011), doi:10.1145/1998441.1998461

[4] Brucker, A.D., Brügger, L., Wolff, B.: Formal firewall testing: An exercise in test and proof. Submitted for publication (2013)

[5] Brucker, A.D., Wolff, B.: Test-sequence generation with Hol-TestGen with an application to firewall testing. In: Gurevich, Y., Meyer, B. (eds.) TAP 2007. LNCS, vol. 4454, pp. 149–168. Springer, Heidelberg (2007)

[6] Brucker, A.D., Wolff, B.: HOL-TESTGEN. In: Chechik, M., Wirsing, M. (eds.) FASE 2009. LNCS, vol. 5503, pp. 417–420. Springer, Heidelberg (2009)

[7] Brucker, A.D., Wolff, B.: On theorem prover-based testing. Formal Aspects of Computing, FAC (2012), doi:10.1007/s00165-012-0222-y

[8] Brügger, L.: A framework for modelling and testing of security policies. Ph.D. thesis, ETH Zurich, ETH Dissertation No. 20513 (2012)

[9] El-Atawy, A., Ibrahim, K., Hamed, H., Al-Shaer, E.: Policy segmentation for intelligent firewall testing. In: NPSec 2005, pp. 67–72. IEEE Computer Society (2005)

[10] El-Atawy, A., Samak, T., Wali, Z., Al-Shaer, E., Lin, F., Pham, C., Li, S.: An automated framework for validating firewall policy enforcement. In: POLICY 2007, pp. 151–160. IEEE Computer Society (2007)

[11] Jürjens, J., Wimmel, G.: Specification-based testing of firewalls. In: Bjørner, D., Broy, M., Zamulin, A.V. (eds.) PSI 2001. LNCS, vol. 2244, pp. 308–316. Springer, Heidelberg (2001)

[12] de Moura, L., Bjørner, N.S.: Z3: An efficient SMT solver. In: Ramakrishnan, C.R., Rehof, J. (eds.) TACAS 2008. LNCS, vol. 4963, pp. 337–340. Springer, Heidelberg (2008)

[13] PIDE (2013), `http://fortesse.lri.fr/index.php?option=com_content&id=91&Itemid=60#PlatformDevelopment`

[14] Senn, D., Basin, D.A., Caronni, G.: Firewall conformance testing. In: Khendek, F., Dssouli, R. (eds.) TestCom 2005. LNCS, vol. 3502, pp. 226–241. Springer, Heidelberg (2005)

[15] Wenzel, M., Wolff, B.: Building formal method tools in the Isabelle/Isar framework. In: Schneider, K., Brandt, J. (eds.) TPHOLs 2007. LNCS, vol. 4732, pp. 352–367. Springer, Heidelberg (2007)

Random Walks on Some Basic Classes of Digraphs

Wen-Ju Cheng[1], Jim Cox[1], and Stathis Zachos[1,2]

[1] Computer Science Department, CUNY Graduate Center, New York, USA
[2] CS Dept, School of ECE, NTUA, Greece

Abstract. Reingold has shown that L=SL, that s-t connectivity in a poly-mixing digraph is complete for promise-RL, and that s-t connectivity for a poly-mixing out-regular digraph with known stationary distribution is in L. However, little work has been done on identifying structural properties of digraphs that effect cover times. We examine the complexity of random walks on a basic parameterized family of unbalanced digraphs called Strong Chains (which model weakly symmetric computation), and a special family of Strong Chains called Harps. We show that the worst case hitting times of Strong Chain families vary smoothly with the number of asymmetric vertices and identify the necessary condition for non-polynomial cover time. This analysis also yields bounds on the cover times of general digraphs. Our goal is to use these structural properties to develop space efficient digraph modification for randomized search and to develop derandomized search strategies for digraph families.

Keywords: complexity, space bounded complexity classes, random walks, digraph search, reachability, strong connectivity, symmetric computation, L, RL, NL, BPL.

1 Introduction

The complexity of random walks on digraphs has important implications for log space bounded complexity classes and efficient derandomization. Recall that L (respectively NL) is the class of languages accepted by deterministic (respectively nondeterministic) log space bounded Turing machines (space bounded by $O(\log n)$). Recall also that RL is the class of languages accepted by probabilistic log space bounded Turing machines with one-sided error. It is well known that STCON, the problem of determining if there exists a path between two specified vertices, s and t, in a given directed graph is complete for NL. Symmetric Logspace (SL) was first introduced by Lewis and Papadimitriou in 1982 [LP]. They defined SL as the class of all languages accepted by a log space bounded symmetric Turing machine. USTCON is the restriction of STCON to undirected graphs. They showed that USTCON is complete for SL, and thus proved that $L \subseteq SL \subseteq NL$, since it was not at the time how to search an undirected graph in deterministic log space. Aleliunas et. al. [AKLLR] introduced a randomized log-space algorithm for undirected graph reachability and thus showed that USTCON $\in$ RL. The well-known Savitch's Theorem [Savitch] can be used to show that $NL \subseteq L^2$ (deterministic $O(\log^2 n)$ space). Nisan, Szemeredi, and Wigderson

Z. Liu, J. Woodcock, and H. Zhu (Eds.): ICTAC 2013, LNCS 8049, pp. 122–140, 2013.

[NSW] showed that USTCON is in $L^{3/2}$, thus showing $SL \subseteq L^{3/2}$. Saks and Zhou [SZ] showed the stronger result that any randomized space S machine can be simulated by a deterministic space $S^{3/2}$ machine, implying that $BPL \subseteq L^{3/2}$, where BPL is the class of languages accepted by probabilistic log space machines with bounded two-sided error (i.e. Monte Carlo algorithms). In 1997, Armoni, et. al. [ATWZ] improved this deterministic simulation to give a $O(\log^{4/3} n)$-space algorithm for USTCON. The relation between SL and L had remained open until 2005, when Reingold showed the surprising result that any undirected graph can be searched deterministically in log space, thereby establishing that SL = L. Other interesting recent results concern unambiguous log space machines with only a polynomial number of computation paths, e.g., ReachFewL = ReachUL [GSTV]. Summarizing the above facts we now know that:

$L = SL \subseteq RL \subseteq NL = \text{Co-NL} \subseteq L^2$
and
$RL \subseteq BPL \subseteq L^{3/2}$

Reingold showed how to transform any graph (using log space) into an expander with constant degree. Rozenman and Vadhan [RV] showed how to accomplish this transformation, without increasing the size of the graph, by the use of what they call pseudo-randomized graph squaring. Research on extending Reingold's original algorithm to the directed case has been undertaken by Chung, Reingold and Vadhan [CRV], in an attempt to prove RL = L. Recall that the mixing time of a random walk on a graph is the number of steps needed to converge sufficiently close to the stationary distribution of the associated Markov chain. They call a digraph poly-mixing if s and t have non-negligible probability (the reciprocal of a polynomial in the number of vertices) and a random walk from s has polynomial mixing time. Their best result shows that STCON on a poly-mixing digraph with a known stationary distribution is in L. They also show that STCON on a poly-mixing digraph is complete for Promise-RL [RTV]. The complexity of searching such a digraph, without knowing the stationary distribution, remains open. This, and similar recent work, has primarily focused on analyzing the search problem for either general digraphs or digraphs with a restricted structure so that they "look like" undirected graphs. Moreover, the promise of a polynomial mixing time together with a high probability of reaching t is precisely that; no examination of the structure that leads to this behavior is made.

If NL is not equal to L, and if RL = L, as is generally believed, then there is a large gap between RL and NL. We begin by examining the complexity of random walks on some simple families of digraphs, with the goal of elucidating the structural properties and identifying the boundary between polynomial and non-polynomial cover times. It is known that STCONN on topologically ordered digraphs [HIM], and STCONN on 3-page digraphs are both complete for NL [PRV]. As we observe below, solving STCONN on a single strongly connected digraph component with bounded degree and a pseudo-topological order on the vertices, is sufficient to capture NL. We remark that lazy random walks from s on these digraphs can be shown to have polynomial mixing time (using Lemma A.1 of [RTV]), but the target vertex t may, in general, have an exponentially small probability of being reached from s.

We define a parameterized family of digraphs, called Strong Chains, which will represent some simple nondeterministic computations. We investigate random walks on these digraphs. We analyze the structure of the family of digraphs by introducing several notions of degree of symmetry. Related work by Li and Zhang [LZ] has applied a notion of asymmetry to digraphs, by relating it to the probability assigned to the edges of an essentially regular digraph. In contrast, our definitions are related to the actual digraph structure. We then define another parameterized family of special Strong Chains called Harps, which are in a sense "complete" for Strong Chains. For given parameters, the hitting time of a random walk on the family of Harps will dominate the corresponding family of Strong Chains. The Harps have a very simple structure that embodies the asymmetry of families of Strong Chains. We use the Harps to identify the most relevant symmetry parameter, the number of asymmetric vertices, and to identify the values of this parameter that provide a necessary condition for non-polynomial cover time. We use this analysis to construct a three level stratification of strongly connected digraphs. It is our hope in initiating this study of digraph structure that it will also help in identifying opportunities for derandomization.

2 Weakly Symmetric Classes

We now motivate our decision to consider only strongly connected digraphs with the following discussion. We note that there is a simple construction that reduces RL (or NL) to a search on a single strongly connected digraph component (see [CRV]), but we wish to retain the property that each node of G has bounded degree. We call an order on the vertices of a digraph pseudo-topological if the removal of the edges to the least vertex makes it a topological order. We observe that every NL computation can be simulated by a "weakly symmetric" machine M, in the following manner. We may assume w.l.o.g. that all computation paths lead to terminal configurations and that there is a unique accepting configuration. From each non-accepting terminal configuration of the original machine, the simulating machine M erases the work tapes, rewinds the input tape and returns to the start configuration S. Given an upper bound b on the number of distinct configurations of M on input x, we can construct a strongly connected computation graph for M with a pseudo-topological order. The nodes will consist of the pair $(0, S)$, where S is the start configuration and the pair $T=(b, A)$, where A is the accepting configuration, together with all pairs (t, C), where $0 < t \leq b$ is an integer time step and $C \neq S$ is a configuration. There is an edge from a node (t, C_i) to $(t+1, C_j)$ iff there is a valid transition of M from configuration C_i to C_j or $C_i = C_j = A$, and an edge from (t, C_i) to $(0, S)$ iff there is a transition from C_i to S. Since we may assume a bound on the number of nondeterministic choices machines can make (typically two) the resulting computation graph has out-degree bounded by 2, and the subgraph consisting of the nodes reachable from $(0, S)$ has in-degree bounded by a constant, depending on the machine and the alphabet size. The natural order on these pairs becomes a topological order on the nodes if the edges to $(0, S)$ are removed, and thus it is pseudo-topological.

2.1 Strong Chains

Any successful computation path can be represented as a directed path in a graph. For this initial study of computation graphs we will focus on these paths. Following all computation paths of a weakly symmetric machine will yield a single Strong Chain, but one with exponential size and redundancy. The actual computation graph, without this redundancy, will be a union of Strong Chains, and have polynomial size. The study of Strong Chains provides a good tool for the analysis of strongly connected digraphs, and we are able to transfer some of our analysis to general digraphs.

The vertex $v(0)$ is the initial state, and the vertex $v(n)$ is the successful terminal state.

Definition: A *Strong Chain* is a simple strongly connected directed graph which contains a directed Hamiltonian path as a subgraph.

A random walk is a stochastic (Markov) process that starts from a given vertex, and then selects one of its out-neighbors, uniformly at random, to visit next. Our first goal is to estimate the hitting time from $v(0)$ to $v(n)$ for a given digraph. For this purpose we define some terminology for Strong Chains.

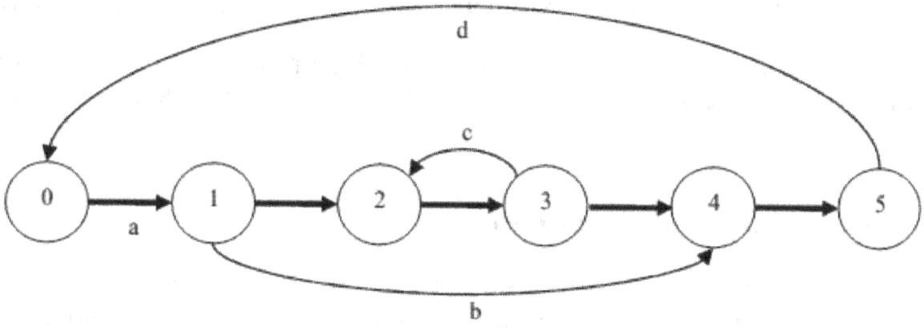

Fig. 1.

Definition: *Strong Chain(V, F, B)*

1. A set V of vertices, labeled from 0 to n.
2. The directed Hamiltonian path of length n, called *base*, consists of directed edges from $v(i)$ to $v(i+1)$ for $0 \leq i < n$.
3. The edge distance of an edge from $v(i)$ to $v(j)$ is $|i - j|$.
4. A forward edge is an edge from $v(i)$ to $v(j)$ where $i < j$.
5. The set F of directed forward edges (e.g. edges a and b in Figure 1) satisfies $|F| \geq n$. The forward edges of distance 1 are called "*to next*" (edge a).
6. F_0 is the *base*, the set of the edges of "*to next*", and $|F_0| = n$.
7. A back edge is an edge from $v(i)$ to $v(j)$ where $i > j$.
8. A set B of directed back edges (edges c and d). The back edges of distance 1 are called "*back to previous*" (edge c).
9. A back edge from $v(i)$ to $v(0)$ (edge d) is called "*back to root*".
10. *Hit(i, j)* is the expected number of steps taken by a random walk on a Strong Chain starting from $v(i)$ and reaching $v(j)$.

11. The hitting time of digraph G, $Hit(G)$, is the maximum of $Hit(v, w)$ over all pairs of vertices of G. For a Strong Chain C, $Hit(0, n) \leq Hit(C)$.
12. The cover time of digraph G, $Cover(G)$, is the maximum over all vertices v of G, of the expected time for a random walk started from v to visit all vertices.

2.2 Strong Chain Symmetry

Definition: for a directed graph $G(V, E)$

1. A directed edge is *symmetric* if its inverse edge also belongs to G. That is, $edge(u, v)$ and $edge(v, u) \in E$.
2. A vertex is *symmetric* if all of its edges are *symmetric*.
3. A vertex is *balanced* if its out-degree is equal to its in-degree.
4. G is *symmetric* if all of its edges are *symmetric*. A directed symmetric graph is equivalent to the corresponding undirected graph.
5. G is *balanced* if all of its vertices are *balanced*, and is called a *pseudo-symmetric* digraph. A connected *balanced* digraph is called an *Eulerian Circuit* digraph, and it contains a directed Eulerian circuit.
6. G is *regular* if the in-degree and out-degree of all vertices are equal. A *regular* digraph has symmetry (but is not a symmetric digraph in the sense defined above).

We note that using these definitions for connected digraphs, *symmetric* implies *balanced*, *balanced* implies *Eulerian Circuit*, and *regular* implies *balanced* and *Eulerian Circuit.*

2.3 Symmetric and Asymmetric Graphs

We begin our analysis of Strong Chains by noting the effect of adding back edges to the base. This analysis will be important in demonstrating the domination property of Harps in the next section, and in illustrating the reason for our choice of symmetry property. We then perform a similar analysis for the Line digraph, defined below. We then transfer this analysis to Strong Chains.

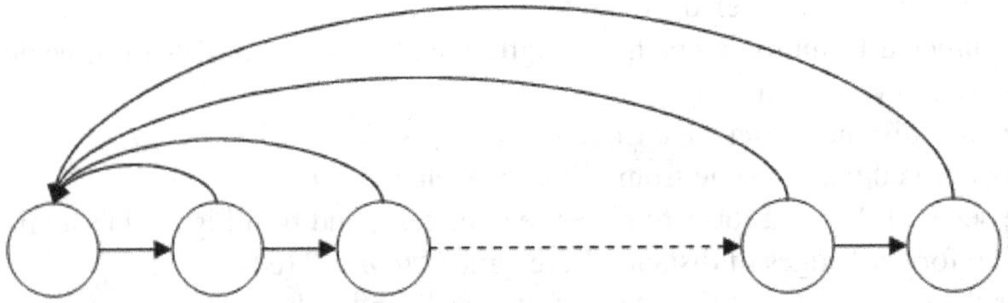

Fig. 2. Harp Strings Digraph

The following simple Lemma will be useful.

Lemma 1: For a given Strong Chain C,

$$Hit(0,n) \leq Cover(C) \leq \sum_{i=0}^{n-1} Hit(i,i+1).$$

Equality is only satisfied when the forward edges satisfy $F = F_0$.

The digraph in Figure 2 we will call the *Harp Strings* digraph, in anticipation of our definition of the Harp digraph in the next section. In addition to the base, each vertex $v(i)$, $i > 0$, has a "back to root" edge.

Lemma 2: For the *Harp Strings* digraph G, $Hit(0,n) = Cover(G) = \theta(2^n)$.

Proof: The probabilities of advancing from $v(i)$ to $v(i+1)$ or returning to the start are both ½. $Hit(0,n)$ is thus the expected time of a run of n successes in a Bernoulli process, which by solving the well-known recurrence is $\theta(2^n)$. □

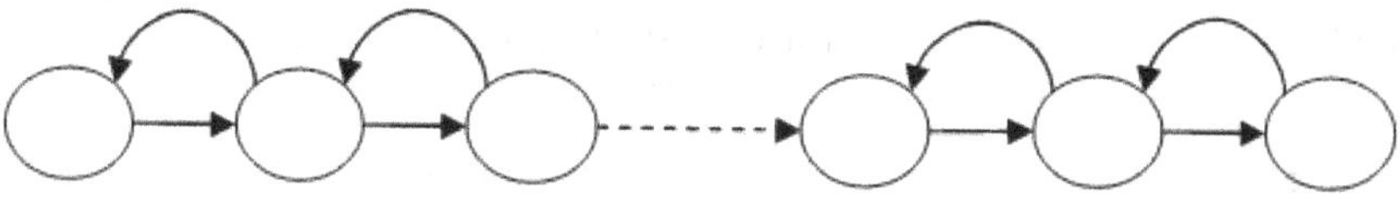

Fig. 3. Line Digraph

The *Line* graph consists of a single simple path from s to t and has diameter n-1. The *Line* digraph, Figure 3, is obtained from the Line graph by replacing each undirected edge with two directed edges, and thus also has diameter n-1.

Lemma 3: For the *Line* digraph G, $Hit(0,n) = Cover(G) = n^2$.

Proof: This is also a well-known simple recurrence.

$\mathrm{Hit}(0,1) = 1$

$\mathrm{Hit}(i,i+1) = \frac{1}{2} \times 1 + \frac{1}{2}(1 + Hit(i-1,i) + Hit(i,i+1)), for\ 1 \le i < n$

$\mathrm{Hit}(i,i+1) = 2 + \mathrm{Hit}(i-1,i) = 2i + 1$

From Lemma 1, we have $\mathrm{Hit}(0,n) = \sum_{i=0}^{n-1} Hit(i,i+1)$ where $F = F_0$ then $\mathrm{Hit}(0,n) = \sum_{i=0}^{n-1}(2i+1) = n^2$ □

It is not necessary to have all back edges back to root, or a badly unbalanced digraph to have exponential hitting time. A connected directed graph has an Eulerian path if and only if at most one vertex has out-degree – in-degree = 1, at most one vertex has in-degree – out-degree = 1 and every other vertex is balanced. If we modify the Line digraph by changing each back edge to be distance 2 (see Figure 4) then we obtain a Strong Chain C_E, which is an Eulerian path digraph with bad behavior.

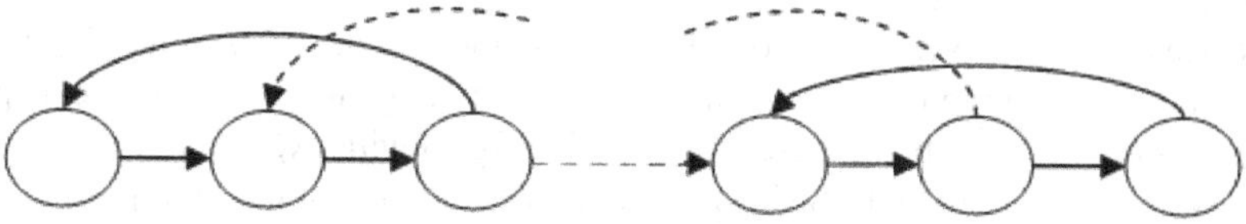

Fig. 4. Eulerian Path Digraph

Lemma 4: For C_E, $Hit(0,n) = Cover(C_E) = \Theta(\varphi^n)$, where φ is the golden ratio.

Proof:

$\mathrm{Hit}(0,1) = \mathrm{Hit}(1,2) = 1$

$\mathrm{Hit}(i,i+1) = \frac{1}{2} \times 1 + \frac{1}{2}(1 + \mathrm{Hit}(i-2,i-1) + \mathrm{Hit}(i-1,i) + \mathrm{Hit}(i,i+1))$, for $2 < i < n$

$\mathrm{Hit}(i,i+1) = 2 + \mathrm{Hit}(i-2,i-1) + \mathrm{Hit}(i-1,i)$

From Lemma 1, we have $\text{Hit}(0,n) = \sum_{i=0}^{n-1} Hit(i,i+1)$ where $F = F_0$. $Hit(i,i+1)$ grows in proportion to the well known Fibonacci sequence, so that $Hit(0,n)$ grows as the sum of the first n Fibonacci numbers, yielding: $\text{Hit}(0,n) = \Theta(\varphi^{n+2}) = \Theta(\varphi^n)$. □

Notice that although C_E has only two unbalanced vertices, half of the back edges are not included in any maximal balanced subgraph. This observation is the basis of our symmetry measure. C_E also illustrates that some badly behaved digraphs can be easily balanced in a way that removes the bad behavior. If we add a single long forward edge of length n-2 on the two unbalanced vertices to C_E we obtain an Eulerian Circuit digraph C_E' with polynomial hitting and cover time.

Lemma 5: For C_E' the hitting and cover time is polynomial in n.

Proof: A bound on the cover time follows directly from a result of [Chung], which states that a strongly connected Eulerian directed graph G with m edges has a lazy random walk with the rate of convergence no more than $m^2 \log m$. The hitting time is thus also bounded by a polynomial. □

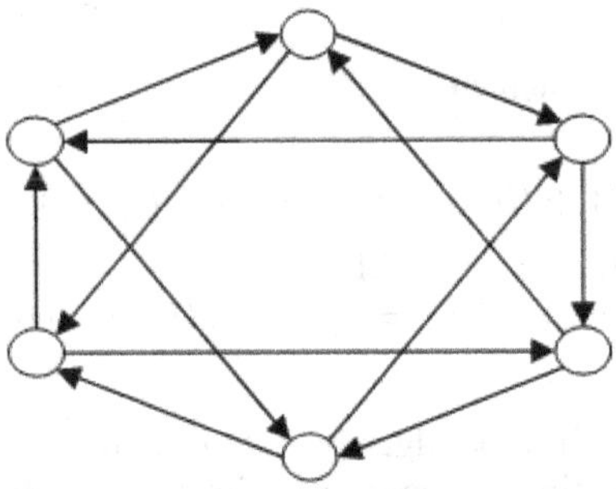

Fig. 5. 2-regular digraph

In Figure 5 we see an example of a 2-regular digraph. We mention that Chung has demonstrated that the rate of convergence for a k-regular strongly connected digraph is no more than $k^2 n^2 \log n$.

Next we compare several ways of adding the same number of asymmetric directed edges to the Line digraph. If we add a "back to root" edge to each vertex, except for $v(0)$, $v(1)$, and $v(n)$, we obtain a graph L_1 (see Figure 6) with exponential hitting time. The analysis is similar to Harp Strings digraph. We remark that the hitting time of any Strong Chain (and any digraph in general) with maximal out degree d will be bounded by $O(d^n)$. This is because the waiting time for n consecutive successes in a Bernoulli experiment, with the probability of success $1/d$, is $\Theta(d^n)$ [CS]. We remark that if we add to each vertex of the base both a "back to root" edge and an edge to $v(1)$, we will achieve this worst case behavior of $\Theta(3^n)$, for out-degree 3. If we add all possible back edges to the base we get $\Theta(n!)$ hitting time.

We summarize this discussion with the following lemmas.

Lemma 6: For any n+1 vertex Strong Chain C, with vertices $v(0),\ldots,v(n)$ and with the out-degree of $v(i)$ denoted by d_i, $Hit(C) = O(n\prod_{j=0}^{n-1} d_j))$. If, for all i, $d_i \le D$, then we have that $Hit(C) = O(nD^{n-1})$, since d_0=1. If the bound D is constant then in the worst case $Hit(C) = \Omega(\prod_{j=0}^{n-1} d_j + n)$.

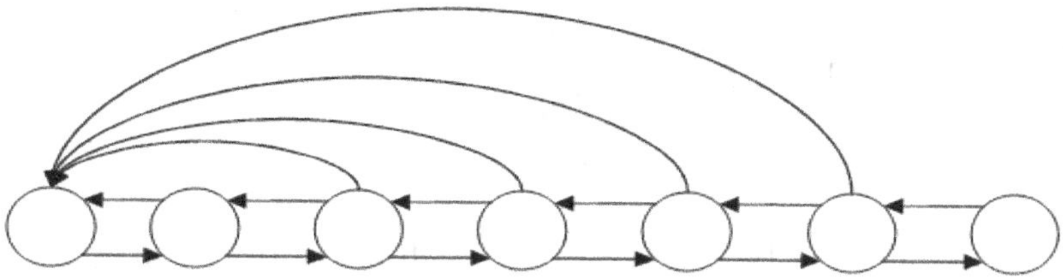

Fig. 6. Line digraph modification L_1

Proof: The proof of the upper bound is by induction on n, one less than the number of vertices in the Strong Chain. The worst case hitting time will be obtained when each forward edge is to next. The probability of advancing from $v(i)$ to $v(i+1)$ is $1/d_i$. For the worst case the d_n-1 back edges from $v(n)$ go to $v(0),\ldots,v(d_i\text{-}2)$. Since $F = F_0$, by Lemma 1 we have that for all $0 < i < n$, $Hit(i,n) < Hit(0,n)$. For this upper bound proof, we shall use this fact by replacing the term contributed by the d_n-1 back edges from $v(n)$ in the recurrence by $(d_n\text{-}1)Hit(0,n)$.

Let G_i be a Strong Chain with i+1 vertices $v(0),\ldots,v(i)$. and let Hit_i denote the hitting time of G_i.

For the base case $Hit(G_1) = 1$.

The inductive hypothesis:

$\mathrm{Hit}(G_n) \le n\prod_{j=0}^{n-1} d_j$

Inductive Step:

We add vertex $v(n+1)$ to G_n, which adds a to next edge to $v(n)$.

$\mathrm{Hit}_{n+1}(0,n) = \mathrm{Hit}(G_n)$.

$\mathrm{Hit}(G_{n+1}) = \mathrm{Hit}_{n+1}(0,n) + \mathrm{Hit}_{n+1}(n,n+1)$ from Lemma 1

$$\begin{aligned}
\mathrm{Hit}_{n+1}(n,n+1) &\le \frac{1}{d_n}\times 1 + \frac{d_{n-1}}{d_n}(1 + \mathrm{Hit}_{n+1}(0,n) + \mathrm{Hit}_{n+1}(n,n+1))\\
&= d_n + (d_n - 1)(\mathrm{Hit}_{n+1}(0,n)).\\
\mathrm{Hit}_{n+1}(0,n+1) &= \mathrm{Hit}_{n+1}(0,n) + \mathrm{Hit}_{n+1}(n,n+1)\\
&= \mathrm{Hit}(G_n) + d_n + d_{n-1}\mathrm{Hit}(G_n)\\
&= \mathrm{Hit}(G_n) + d_n + d_{n-1}\mathrm{Hit}(G_n)\\
&= d_n\mathrm{Hit}(G_n) + d_n\\
&\le d_n n(\textstyle\prod_{j=0}^{n-1} d_j) + d_n \text{ (by the inductive hypothesis)}\\
&= n\textstyle\prod_{j=0}^{n} d_j + d_n\\
&\le n\textstyle\prod_{j=0}^{n} d_j + \prod_{j=0}^{n} d_j\\
&= (n+1)\textstyle\prod_{j=0}^{n} d_j
\end{aligned}$$

The proof of the lower bound when *D* is constant is also by induction on *n*.

The base case $Hit(G_1) = 1$.

The inductive hypothesis:

$\mathrm{Hit}(G_n) \geq \prod_{j=0}^{n-1} d_j + n$

Inductive Step:

In case $d_n = 1$

$$\begin{aligned}\mathrm{Hit}_{n+1}(n, n+1) &= 1 + \mathrm{Hit}(G_n)\\ &\geq 1 + \prod_{j=0}^{n-1} d_j + n\\ &= \prod_{j=0}^{n} d_j + n + 1\end{aligned}$$

Else $d_n \geq 2$

$$\begin{aligned}\mathrm{Hit}_{n+1}(n, n+1) &= \left(\frac{1}{d_n} \times 1 + \frac{1}{d_n} \sum_{j=0}^{d_n-2} \mathrm{Hit}_{n+1}(j, n) + \mathrm{Hit}_{n+1}(n, n+1)\right)\\ &= d_n + \sum_{j=0}^{d_n-2} \mathrm{Hit}_{n+1}(j, n)\\ &= d_n + (d_n - 1)\mathrm{Hit}(0, n) - \sum_{j=0}^{d_n-2} \mathrm{Hit}_{n+1}(0, j)\\ \mathrm{Hit}_{n+1}(0, n+1) &= \mathrm{Hit}_{n+1}(0, n) + \mathrm{Hit}_{n+1}(n, n+1)\\ &= \mathrm{Hit}(G_n) + d_n + (d_n - 1)\mathrm{Hit}(G_n) - \sum_{j=0}^{d_n-2} \mathrm{Hit}(G_j)\\ &= d_n \mathrm{Hit}(G_n) + d_n - \sum_{j=0}^{d_n-2} \mathrm{Hit}(G_j)\\ &\geq d_n\left(\prod_{j=0}^{n-1} d_j + n\right) + d_n - \sum_{j=0}^{d_n-2} \mathrm{Hit}(G_j)\\ &\geq d_n\left(\prod_{j=0}^{n-1} d_j + n\right) + d_n - D^{D-1}\\ &\geq \prod_{j=0}^{n} d_j + d_n n - D^{D-1}\\ &\geq \prod_{j=0}^{n} d_j + 2n - D^{D-1} \quad (\text{since } d_n \geq 2)\\ &\geq \prod_{j=0}^{n} d_j + n + 1 \quad (\text{since D is constant so that } D^{D-1} < n-1)\end{aligned}$$

□

In the following let G_0 be the Line digraph.

Lemma 7: Let G_1 be obtained by adding a single back edge from *v*(*i*) to G_0, then in the worst case $Hit(G_1) = n^2 + (n-i)(i^2) = \Theta(Hit(G_0) + (n-i)(i^2))$. For $i = n/2$, this is $\Theta(n\, Hit(G_0))$.

Proof: For the worst case we add a back to root edge from *v*(*i*). We observe that adding a "back to root" edge from *v*(*i*) will leave $Hit(0, i)$ unchanged.

$$\mathrm{Hit}_1(i, i+1) = \frac{1}{3}(1 + \mathrm{Hit}_0(0, i) + \mathrm{Hit}_1(i, i+1)) + \frac{1}{3}(1 + \mathrm{Hit}_0(i-1, i) + \mathrm{Hit}_1(i, i+1)) + \frac{1}{3}$$

$$\mathrm{Hit}_1(i, i+1) = 1 + \mathrm{Hit}_0(0, i) + 1 + \mathrm{Hit}_0(i-1, i) + 1$$

$$\mathrm{Hit}_1(j, j+1) = 1 + \mathrm{Hit}_0(0, i) + 2 + \mathrm{Hit}_0(j-1, j), \text{for } i \leq j \leq n-1$$

$$\mathrm{Hit}_1(0, n) = \mathrm{Hit}_0(0, i) + \mathrm{Hit}_1(i, n) = \mathrm{Hit}_0(0, n) + (n-i)(1 + \mathrm{Hit}_0(0, i))$$

It is easy to see that this recurrence grows most rapidly when $i = n/c$, for constant $c > 1$.

Let $i = n/2$, then

$$\mathrm{Hit}_1(0, n) = n^2 + (n-i)(1 + i^2) = n^2 + \frac{n}{2}\left(1 + \frac{n^2}{4}\right) = \Theta(n^3)$$

Thus from Lemma 3,
$\mathrm{Hit}_1(0, n) = \Theta(n\,\mathrm{Hit}(G_0)) = \Theta(n^3)$ □

Lemma 8: Let G be a graph obtained by adding a single back edge from each of k distinct vertices of G_0, the Line digraph. Then in the worst case, we have for $1 \le k < n/2$,

$$\mathrm{Hit}(G) = O\left(\left(\frac{2n}{k+1}\right)^k \mathrm{Hit}(G_0) + \mathrm{Hit}(G_0)\right) = O\left(\left(\frac{2n}{k+1}\right)^{k+2}\right) \text{ and } \mathrm{Hit}(G) = \Omega\left(\left(\frac{n}{k+1}\right)^k\right).$$

Proof: We obtain the worst case by adding "back to root" edges to G_0. For a given k we add "back to root" edges from each of the vertices $v(i_1)$, …, $v(i_k)$ of G_0 and let G_k be the induced subgraph consisting of the vertices $v(j)$, j=0,…,i_k. To simplify the analysis we will assume, w.l.o.g., that n is a multiple of $k + 1$. We first show by induction on k that

$\mathrm{Hit}(G_k) = O(\mathrm{Hit}(G_0)) + \prod_{j=1}^{k} 2(i_j - i_{j-1})\,\mathrm{Hit}(G_0))$, where we assume that i_0=0.

Base Case:

$\mathrm{Hit}\,(G_1) = \mathrm{Hit}_0(0, i_1) = {i_1}^2 \le \mathrm{Hit}(G_0) \le \mathrm{Hit}(G_0) + 2(i_1 - 0)\mathrm{Hit}(G_0)$.

For the inductive hypothesis we assume

$\mathrm{Hit}(G_m) \le \mathrm{Hit}(G_0) + \prod_{j=1}^{m} 2(i_j - i_{j-1})\mathrm{Hit}(G_0)$

Inductive Step:

$$\begin{aligned}
\mathrm{Hit}_{m+1}(i_m, i_m + 1) &= 1 + \mathrm{Hit}_{m+1}(0, i_m) + 1 + \mathrm{Hit}_{m+1}(i_m - 1, i_m) \\
&\le 2 + 2\mathrm{Hit}(G_m) \qquad \text{since } \mathrm{Hit}_{m+1}(i_m - 1, i_m) \le \mathrm{Hit}(G_m) \\
\mathrm{Hit}'(j, j+1) &= 2 + \mathrm{Hit}(j-1, j) \text{ for } j = i_m + 1 \text{ to } i_{m+1} \\
\mathrm{Hit}(G_{m+1}) &= \mathrm{Hit}(G_m) + \mathrm{Hit}(i_m, i_{m+1}) \\
&\le \mathrm{Hit}(G_m) + 2(i_{m+1} - i_m)\,\mathrm{Hit}(G_m) + (i_{m+1} - i_m)^2 \\
&= \prod_{j=1}^{m+1} 2(i_j - i_{j-1})\,\mathrm{Hit}(G_0) + \mathrm{Hit}(G_0)
\end{aligned}$$

Maximizing the solution to this recurrence is equivalent to maximizing the product of the distances between the added back edges, subject to the constraint that the total distance is at most n. This is just the problem of finding the hyperbox of maximum volume, subject to a bound on the total side lengths, and the well known solution is the hypercube [Kazarinoff]. Thus the solution is asymptotically maximal when the distances are the same length. So to prevent adding asymmetric edges to $v(0)$ or $v(n)$ we choose $i_m = \frac{mn}{k+1}$. This yields $\mathrm{Hit}(G_k) = \left(\frac{2n}{k+1}\right)^k O(\mathrm{Hit}(G_0) + O(\mathrm{Hit}(G_0)) = O\left(\left(\frac{2n}{k+1}\right)^{k+2}\right)$, since the hitting time of the Line digraph G_0 is n^2. One can also prove by induction that $\mathrm{Hit}(G_k) = \Omega\left(\left(\frac{n}{k+1}\right)^k\right)$ by replacing the base case by $\mathrm{Hit}(G_1) \ge 1$ and the inductive hypothesis by $\mathrm{Hit}(G_m) \ge \prod_{j=1}^{m}(i_j - i_{j-1})$. □

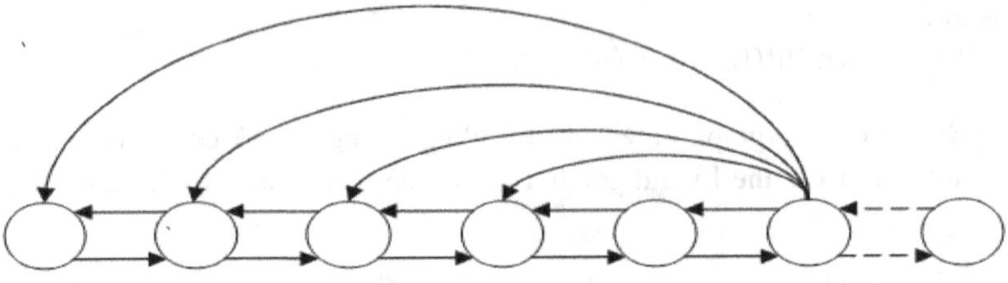

Fig. 7. Line digraph modification L_2

It is easy to see that when k is constant, the constant of proportionality in the hitting time is maximized if all asymmetric edges are equally spaced in the last half of the Line digraph. However, when k is large, the effect of $Hit(G_0)$ becomes negligible. Next we consider the effect of adding d back edges from the single vertex $v(i)$ of G_0 to obtain the digraph L_2.

Lemma 9: In the worst case, L_2 has $Hit(0,n) = \Theta(n(d\,Hit(G_0))) = \Theta(n(dn^2))$.

Proof: We analyze the worst case by adding long edges. We add back edges from $v(i)$ to each of the vertices $v(0)$, …, $v(d\text{-}1)$.

$$\begin{aligned}
\mathrm{Hit}(i,i+1) &= \tfrac{1}{d+1}\textstyle\sum_{j=0}^{d-1}(1+\mathrm{Hit}(j,i)+\mathrm{hit}(i,i+1)) + \tfrac{1}{d+1} \\
&= d + \textstyle\sum_{j=0}^{d-1}\mathrm{Hit}(j,i) \\
&= d + \textstyle\sum_{j=0}^{d-1}(\mathrm{Hit}(0,i) - \mathrm{Hit}(0,j)) \\
\mathrm{Hit}(j,j+1) &= 2 + \mathrm{Hit}(j-1,j), \text{for all } j \neq i \\
\mathrm{Hit}(0,n) &= \mathrm{Hit}(0,i) + \mathrm{Hit}(i,n) \\
&= i^2 + (n-i)(d + \textstyle\sum_{j=i}^{d-1}(\mathrm{Hit}(0,i) - \mathrm{Hit}(0,j)))
\end{aligned}$$

Let $d = n\text{–}2$, so that $i = n\text{–}1$

$$\begin{aligned}
\mathrm{Hit}(0,n) &= (n-1)^2 + n - 2 + \textstyle\sum_{j=0}^{n-3}(\mathrm{Hit}(0,n-1) - \mathrm{Hit}(0,j)) \\
&= (n-1)^2 + n - 2 + (n-2)(n-1)^2 - \textstyle\sum_{j=0}^{n-3} j^2 \\
&= (n-1)^2 + n - 2 + (n-2)(n-1)^2 - 1/6(n-3)(n-2)(2n-5) \\
&= \Theta(n^3)
\end{aligned}$$

Let $d = n/2$ - 1, and $i = n/2$

$$\begin{aligned}
\mathrm{Hit}(0,n) &= \frac{n^2}{2} + \frac{n}{2}\left(\frac{n}{2} - 1 + \sum_{j=0}^{\frac{n}{2}-2}\left(\mathrm{Hit}\left(0,\frac{n}{2}\right) - \mathrm{Hit}(0,j)\right)\right) \\
&= \frac{n^2}{2} + \frac{n}{2}\left(\frac{n}{2} - 1\right) + \frac{n}{2}\left(\frac{n}{2} - 1\right)\frac{n^2}{2} - \frac{1}{24}(n-4)(n-3)(n-2) \\
&= \Theta(nd(n^2)) \\
&= \Theta(n^4)
\end{aligned}$$

□

We can also add d back edges from each of k vertices, in the same manner, to yield L_3.

Lemma 10: For natural $d \geq 1$, and for $k < n/2$, L_3 has worst case hitting time $\mathrm{Hit}(0,n) = O\left(\left(\frac{(d+1)n}{k+1}\right)^k \mathrm{Hit}(G_0)\right) = O\left(\left(\frac{(d+1)n}{k+1}\right)^k n^2\right)$.

Proof: The proof is by induction on k, and it is a straightforward combination of the analysis in the proofs of Lemma 8 and Lemma 9. □

We remark that the upper bound in this theorem is not tight for non-constant k, however, if we allow $k = \Omega(n)$ in Lemma 8 and Lemma 10, the lower bounds for the worst case will be at least $\Omega(3^{O(k)})$ and $\Omega((d+2)^{O(k)})$, respectively. In the following we will assume w.l.o.g. that n is divisible by $2k$.

Definition: Let G be a balanced Strong Chain with out-degree bounded by D, constructed as follows: Let vertices $v(0),\ldots,v(n/2-1)$ be a D-regular Strong Chain (called the ***frame***) and $v(n/2),\ldots,v(n)$ be a Line digraph (called the ***handle***). We form G by uniting the frame and the handle by adding the two directed edges between $v(n/2-1)$ to $v(n/2)$. We call G the ***Mirror Frame digraph*** because it is reminiscent of a mirror with a handle.

Property 11: Let G be a *Mirror Frame* digraph with out-degree bounded by D.
1. G has $Dn/2 + 2(n/2 + 1)$ directed edges.
2. G has diameter $= \Omega(n)$.
3. $Hit(G) = \Theta(Dn^2)$ [Chung].

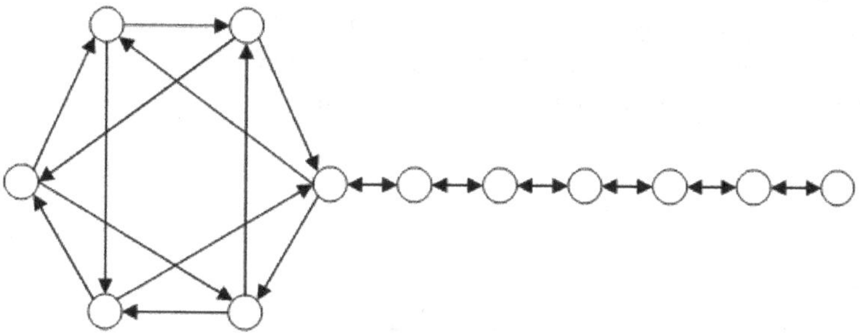

Fig. 8. Mirror Frame digraph

The Mirror Frame digraph is similar to the undirected lollipop graph [Feige], and it achieves the asymptotic upper bound on the hitting time for balanced digraphs. The handle part of the digraph guarantees that the diameter is $\Omega(n)$. The best case is obtained when the frame is a d-expander, for constant d. The worst case is when the frame is a complete digraph, so that G is just the digraph version of the lollipop. If D is bounded by some constant, then we can get a result similar to Lemmas 7, 8, 9 and 10, since the Line digraph is basically a Mirror Frame digraph (where $D = 2$) with a "broken" frame.

Theorem 12: Let G be a Mirror Frame digraph with out-degree bounded by constant D, $Hit(G) = \Theta(Dn^2)$.

Let $v(f)$ be the frame vertex of greatest distance from $v(n)$ (see Figure 9), so that the shortest path between $v(n)$ and $v(f)$, achieves the diameter of G. The following new digraphs are obtained by adding asymmetric back edges from the k handle vertices $v(n/2),\ldots,v\left(\frac{(k-1)n}{2k}\right)$ to vertices in the set $(v(f - d/2), \ldots, v(f + d/2))$.

1. Let G_1 be obtained by adding a single back edge to G. $\mathrm{Hit}(G_1) = O(n\,\mathrm{Hit}(G))$.
2. Let G_2 be obtained by adding a single back edge from each of k distinct vertices of the handle of G. $\mathrm{Hit}(G_2) = \mathrm{Hit}(G) = O\left(\left(\frac{2n}{2k}\right)^k \mathrm{Hit}(G) + \mathrm{Hit}(G)\right)$.
3. Let G_3 be obtained by adding d back edges from a single vertex of G, where $d < D$-1. $\mathrm{Hit}(G_3) = \Theta(n(d\,\mathrm{Hit}(G)))$.
4. Let G_4 be obtained from G by adding d back edges to each of k handle vertices, where $d = D$-2. $\mathrm{Hit}(G_4) = O\left(\left(\frac{(d+1)n}{2k}\right)^k \mathrm{Hit}(G)\right)$.

Proof: We can apply the analysis of the Line digraph directly to the Mirror Frame digraph. To see this, we first transform the first half of the Line digraph G_0 into a cycle by adding both directed edges between $v(n/2 - 1)$ and $v(0)$, to form the frame. The handle is then the Line digraph from vertex $v(n/2)$ to $v(n)$. The hitting times for the Line digraph (the handle) and the cycle (the frame) are the same. The hitting time for any frame formed by adding up to (the constant) D-2 edges to each vertex of this 2-regular cycle is still $O(n^2)$ (the same as the Line digraph), by Property 11. Back edges from the handle to the frame will be the longest back edges (edge distance $\Omega(n)$) and thus produce the greatest increase in hitting time. Adding these edges increases the hitting time by an amount proportional to the increase when adding the long back edges to the Line digraph (to $v(0)$). We conclude that we may apply the results of Lemmas 7 through 10 directly, by replacing $\mathrm{Hit}(G_0)$ with $\mathrm{Hit}(G)$. □

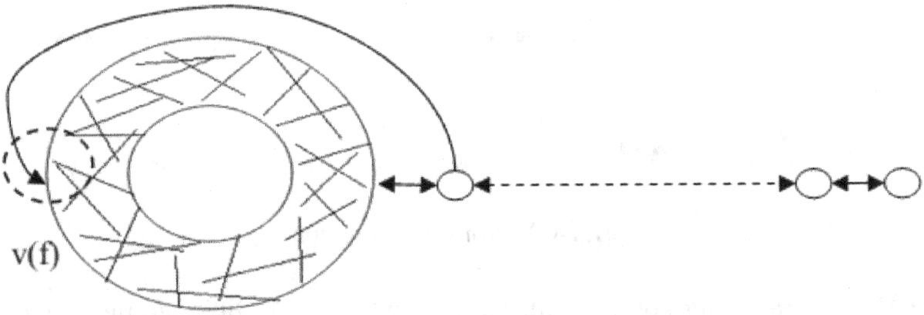

Fig. 9.

Theorem 13: Let G be a balanced strongly connected digraph with out-degree bounded by constant D. Let G have diameter = $\Omega(n)$. Let G have $\Omega(Dn)$ edges and $Hit(G) = \Theta(Dn^2)$.

1. Let G_1 be obtained by adding a single back edge from a vertex v, where *degree*(v) $< D$. $\mathrm{Hit}(G_1) = O(n\,\mathrm{Hit}(G))$.
2. Let G_2 be obtained by adding a single back edge from each of k distinct vertices of G. $\mathrm{Hit}(G_2) = O\left(\left(\frac{2n}{k+1}\right)^k \mathrm{Hit}(G) + \mathrm{Hit}(G)\right)$.
3. Let G_3 be obtained by adding d back edges from a single vertex v of G, where $d \leq D - degree(v)$. $\mathrm{Hit}(G_3) = \Theta(n(d\,\mathrm{Hit}(G)))$.

4. Let G_4 be obtained from G by adding d_i back edges from each of k distinct vertices $v(i)$ of G, for $i = 1$ to k, where $d_i < D - degree(v(i))$.
$$\mathrm{Hit}(G_4) = O\left(\left(\frac{(D-1)n}{k+1}\right)^k \mathrm{Hit}(G)\right).$$

Proof: The proofs of statements 1-4 are by induction, and they follow the proofs of Lemmas 7 to 9, with $\mathrm{Hit}(G_0)$ replaced by $\mathrm{Hit}(G)$. We begin by labeling the vertices of G as $v(0)$ through $v(n)$, in the following manner: We select $v(0)$ and $v(n)$ so that the shortest path from $v(0)$ to $v(n)$ (the distance) is maximal (is equal to the diameter of G). We iteratively label the vertices from $v(n\text{-}1)$ to $v(1)$. In step k, we have labeled k-1 vertices as $v(n)$ through $v(n\text{-}k\text{-}1)$, and from the unlabeled vertices we select a vertex v of maximal distance from $v(0)$ and label it as $v(n\text{-}k)$.

We may now proceed with the proofs by induction by using this labeling of G in the same manner as the (natural) labeling of the Strong Chains. By our construction of the labeling of G, and by the assumption that the diameter of G is $\Omega(n)$, distances between corresponding pairs of vertices of G_0 and G will be proportional, that is, the distance between $v(i)$ and $v(j)$ in G will be at least $c_1|i\text{-}j|$ and at most $c_2|i\text{-}j|$, for some constants c_1 and c_2 . In the inductive step of each of these proofs, we have use the fact that adding a back edge to the Line digraph increases the hitting time at most (or at least) by an amount that is a multiplicative function of the distance between the incident vertices. Substituting the corresponding distances for G will yield the stated results. □

We remark that if out-degree of G is bounded by some constant, the hitting time is affected only by the number of vertices that are made unbalanced by the addition of the new edges. (i.e., the size of k in Theorem 13). We will use a similar measure of how "far" a digraph is from being balanced in the next section.

3 Categorizing Strong Chains

3.1 Harp Directed Graphs

A *Harp* is a directed graph whose vertices can be divided into two parts: a *balanced* part and an *asymmetric* part. The balanced part is called the *head* or *body* and the asymmetric part is called the *tail* or *string*.

Definition: *Harp(k, ℓ)*:

The *Harp* is a Strong Chain with a balanced part (*body*) containing k vertices and an asymmetric part (*tail*) containing ℓ vertices, where $\ell + k = n+1$, the number of vertices in the Strong Chain. The vertices of body are labeled $b(0)$ to $b(k\text{-}1)$ and the vertices of the strings are labeled s(0) to $s(\ell\ \text{-}1)$. Each vertex of the strings is incident on two directed edges: a "to next" edge and a "back to root" edge. There is no directed edge from any vertex of body to the vertices of strings.

If the body consists of the first k vertices v(*0*)...v(k-1) then the *Harp* is called ***simple***.

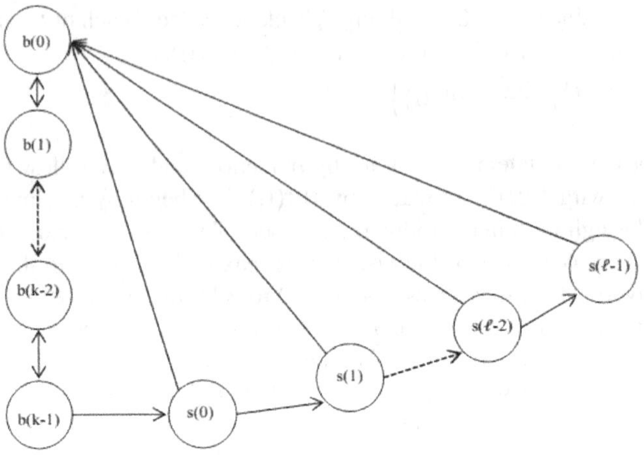

Fig. 10. An example of a *simple Harp*

Lemma 14: Hitting Time of the simple *Harp(k, ℓ)* = $\Theta(k^c 2^\ell)$, for some constant $c \geq 1$.

Proof: From the results of [Feige] and [Chung] we know that the hitting time of the body part is Θ(poly *k*) (we can force it to be at least linear, for example the cycle). Replacing the edge from *v*(0) to *v*(1) in the Harp Strings digraph of Lemma 2 by the body of *Harp(k, ℓ)*, yields a simple recurrence, with a solution that establishes $\text{Hit}(Harp(k,\ell)) = \Theta(k^c 2^\ell)$. □

In this paper we will consider only simple Harps. In the following definitions the parameters *k*, *ℓ*, and τ are assumed to be functions of *n* = *k* + *ℓ*, the number of vertices in the *Harp*.

Definition: *Simple Harp Families - Harp(k, ℓ, τ)*

These are the families of simple Harps with hitting times that are bounded from above by *τ*. Using Lemma 14 we have:

Theorem 15: The following bounds on *ℓ* hold:

1. For Harp(*k*, *ℓ*, poly(*n*)), *ℓ* is O(log *n*).
2. For Harp(*k*, *ℓ*, $n^{\log n}$), *ℓ* is $O(\log^2 n)$.
3. For Harp(*k*, *ℓ*, 2^n), $\ell = \omega(\log^2 n)$, that is, for all $c > 0$, $\lim_{n \to \infty} \frac{\ell}{c \log^2 n} = \infty$.

3.2 Parameterized Complexity of Strong Chains

Definition:

1. Let *G* and *G′* be Strong Chains. We say that *G′* dominates *G* if Hit(G′) = Ω(Hit(G)). A family of Strong Chains is a collection $F = \cup S_n$, for all $n > 0$, where each S_n is a set of *n*-vertex Strong Chains. We say that a family $F' = \cup S'_n$ dominates family *F* if for all *n*, there exists an *m* = poly(*n*), so that for all $G \in S_n$, every $G' \in S'_m$ dominates *G*.

2. *Maximal Balanced Subgraphs*: Let $G = (V, E)$ be a digraph. Let $G' = (V, E') \subseteq G$ be balanced. If for all balanced $G'' = (V, E'') \subseteq G$, $|E'| \geq |E''|$ then G' is a maximal balanced subgraph of G. Let G be a Strong Chain, and $G' = (V, E') \subseteq G$ be balanced with $F_0 \subseteq E'$. We say that G' is a *maximal balanced subgraph with base* if $F_0 \subseteq E'$ and for all balanced $G'' = (V, E'') \subseteq G$ such that $F_0 \subseteq E''$, we have that $|E'| \geq |E''|$.
3. *Asymmetric Vertices*: Let G' be a *maximal balanced subgraph* of G. If vertex v has more out edges in G than in G', then we call v an *asymmetric vertex* relative to G'.

The reason for this definition is that the edges that are not in G' and the number of vertices that they are incident upon as out edges, determines the worst case complexity of G. Note that a balanced vertex may become asymmetric relative to a choice of maximal balanced subgraph. The number of asymmetric vertices, however, is independent of the choice of maximal balanced subgraph.

Theorem 16: For any Strong Chain C, $|V_c| = n + 1$, $|E_c| = m$. Let d_i be the out-degree of $v(i)$ in C. There is a *simple Harp* $H(k, \ell)$ that dominates C, where $k = n + 1$, and $\ell = \sum_{i=0}^{n-1} \lceil \log d_i \rceil < m$.

Proof: We assume, without loss of generality, that C contains a back edge from $v(n)$ to $v(0)$, as this edge will clearly have no effect on the hitting time. This edge will now insure that the base is part of a balanced subgraph of C.

Let C_b be a *maximal balanced subgraph of C with base*. Let H be the simple Harp obtained by adding $\ell = \sum_{i=0}^{n-1} \lceil \log d_i \rceil$ string vertices to C_b. From Lemma 6 we have $Hit(C) = O(n \prod_i d_i) = O(n2^{\sum_i \lceil \log d_i \rceil}) = O(n2^{\ell})$. By Lemma 14, $\mathrm{Hit(H)} = \Theta\left(2^{\ell}\mathrm{Hit(C_b)}\right)$. Thus we conclude that $\mathrm{Hit(H)} = \Omega(2^{\ell}\mathrm{Hit(C_b)}) = \Omega(2^{\ell}\mathrm{n}) = \Omega(\mathrm{Hit(C)})$.

□

The construction of Theorem 16 is somewhat pessimistic, since we only needed to show the existence of a dominating Harp. The number of string vertices required to dominate a Strong Chain is a function of the number of asymmetric vertices. A technical issue is that a maximal balanced subgraph of C will not, in general, be strongly connected. However, this is easily remedied by adding just enough edges.

Theorem 17: Let $C = (V_C, E_C)$ be a Strong Chain with out-degree bounded by some constant D. There is a simple Harp $\mathrm{H}(k, \ell)$ that dominates C, where $k = |V_C|$, and $\ell = |\mathrm{V_A}| \log\left\lceil (\mathrm{D}-1)^{\frac{|\mathrm{V_C}|-1}{|\mathrm{V_A}|+1}} \right\rceil$, where V_A is a set of asymmetric vertices of C.

Proof: Let *Bal* be a maximal balanced subgraph of C. If *Bal* is a strongly connected digraph, then let G equal *Bal*. Otherwise, let G be a balanced connected digraph obtained as follows:

Let E_F be a minimal subset of F_0 in C, such that $Bal \cup E_F$ is a connected digraph.

Let E_b be a minimal set of back edges such that $G = Bal \cup E_F \cup E_b$ is a balanced strongly connected digraph. Note that $|E_F| \leq |V_C| - 1$ and $|E_b| \leq |E_F|$.

Let $C' = C \cup E_b$. Clearly $\mathrm{Hit(C)} \leq \mathrm{Hit(C')}$. Let V_A be the set of asymmetric vertices of C' relative to G. Let H be the simple Harp obtained by adding ℓ string vertices to G, where $\ell = |\mathrm{V_A}| \log\left\lceil (\mathrm{D}-1)^{\frac{|\mathrm{V_C}|-1}{|\mathrm{V_A}|+1}} \right\rceil$.

Let $j = |V_A|$ and $n = |V_C| - 1$, then $\ell = \mathrm{j}\log\left\lceil(\mathrm{D}-1)\frac{n}{\mathrm{j}+1}\right\rceil$. From Theorem 13 we have

$$\begin{aligned} Hit(C') &= O\left(\left(\frac{(D-1)n}{j+1}\right)^{j} Hit(G)\right) \\ &= O(2^{\mathrm{j}\log\left\lceil\frac{(\mathrm{D}-1)\mathrm{n}}{\mathrm{j}+1}\right\rceil} Hit(G)) \\ &= O(2^{\ell} Hit(G)). \end{aligned}$$

By Lemma 14, $\mathrm{Hit(H)} = \Theta(2^{\ell}\mathrm{Hit(G)})$. Thus we conclude that

$$\mathrm{Hit(H)} = \Omega(2^{\ell}\mathrm{Hit(G)}) = \Omega(\mathrm{Hit(C')}) = \Omega(\mathrm{Hit(C)}).$$

□

The number of asymmetric vertices also provides a lower bound for more general digraphs.

Theorem 18: The family of n-vertex strongly connected digraphs with maximum in-degree and out-degree d+1 and ℓ asymmetric vertices has worst case cover time $\Omega((n - \ell)\, d^{\ell})$. This gives:

1. If $\ell = O(\log n)$ the worst case cover time is $\Omega(n^{O(\log d)})$, which is $\Omega(\mathrm{poly}(n))$ for constant d.
2. If $\ell = \omega(\log n)$ the worst case cover time is super-polynomial.
3. If $\ell = \Theta(\log^2 n)$ the worst case cover time is $\Omega(\mathrm{n}^{O(\log d \log n)})$, which is $\Omega(\mathrm{n}^{O(\log n)})$ for constant d.
4. If $\ell = \omega(\log^2 n)$ the worst case cover time is $\Omega(d^{\mathrm{poly}(n)})$.

Proof: We will modify the simple (out-degree 1) ordered cycle. We add d back edges to each of the last ℓ vertices of the cycle, with the destinations distributed evenly among first ℓ vertices of the cycle. The resulting digraph will have in-degree and out-degree bounded by d+1. The lower bound now follows directly from the previously mentioned Bernoulli bound [CS], and the fact that the hitting time is less than or equal to the cover time. □

Since the hitting time and cover time for simple Harps are equal we divide digraphs into classes based on their cover times using the Harps:

Definition: Consider all digraphs that are strongly connected, have bounded degree, and have a pseudo-topological order. We divide them into the following three families :

1. **WS[1] (Weakly Symmetric[1])** – those dominated by **Harp(k, ℓ, $poly(n)$).**
2. **WS[2] (Weakly Symmetric[2])** – those dominated by **Harp(k, ℓ, $n^{\log n}$).**
3. **WS[3] (Weakly Symmetric[3])** – those dominated by **Harp(k, ℓ, $2^{poly(n)}$).**

WS[1] is contained in RL (?=L), and WS[3] is contained in NL ($\subseteq \mathrm{L}^2$). We conjecture that WS[2] is an intermediate class, between RL and PL. We could, of course, refine this hierarchy, but we are primarily interested in polynomial versus non-polynomial hitting times.

4 Conclusion and Future Work

We have begun the study of the structure of unbalanced digraphs and we have identified a simple class of digraphs called Strong Chains, which facilitate this analysis. We have identified an asymmetry parameter, V_A, the number of asymmetric vertices. We show matching upper and lower bounds on the worst case hitting time of Strong Chains as a function of V_A. We have identified the threshold that is a necessary condition for non-polynomial cover time. We have shown that V_A provides lower bounds on the worst case cover time for families of general strongly connected digraphs.

In the next phase of our work we will study the polynomial sized union of Strong Chains, the digraph families that more closely model the more general pseudo-topologically ordered NL computation graphs. Moreover, we will work on the combination of simple Harps (complex Harp families) which can dominate the union of Strong Chains. For example, Reingold discusses digraphs with good stationary distributions, having only a few "bad" vertices. This seems to us, in general, to be somewhat unrealistic, as there will be more of a smooth transition between "good" and "bad" vertices. The vertices can be grouped by stationary distribution. The stationary distribution is more strongly related to the number of groups than the diameter, which gives only a rather loose bound (Max $\pi(v) \leq k^D$ Min $\pi(v)$, where k = out-degree and D = diameter [Chung]).

We are currently working on applying the nice properties of the Eulerian circuit to unbalanced digraphs which are close to being balanced, by combining cycles in a union of Strong Chains. Another approach is to choose a bound b for a digraph, and develop an algorithm to determine if a vertex is b-reachable, that is, Hit$(s,v) \leq b$. We are attempting to use this algorithm to construct universal traversal sequences for the subgraph consisting of all b-reachable vertices. The goal is an RL algorithm that terminates on digraphs that are not poly-mixing, but succeeds on poly-mixing digraphs. Another line of attack is to add edges to attempt to "balance" a digraph, which can create false paths. Bounding the probability of following a false path may lead to a BPL algorithm for classes of non poly-mixing digraphs. Finally, we are especially interested in the relation between RL and ReachUL.

Acknowledgements. This research was supported by the project AlgoNow, co-financed by the European Union (European Social Fund - ESF) and Greek national funds, through the Operational Program "Education and Lifelong Learning" of the National Strategic Reference Framework (NSRF) - Research Funding Program: THALES, investing in knowledge society through the European Social Fund.

References

[AKLLR] Aleliunas, R., Karp, R.M., Lipton, R.J., Lovász, L., Rackoff, C.: Random Walks, Universal Traversal Sequences, and the Complexity of Maze Problems. In: 20th IEEE Symp. on Found. of Computer Science (FOCS 1979), pp. 218–223 (1979)

[ATWZ] Armoni, R., Ta-Shma, A., Wigderson, A., Zhou, S.: An $O(\log(n)^{4/3})$ space algorithm for (s, t) connectivity in undirected graphs. J. ACM 47(2), 294–311 (2000)

[CS] Chaves, L.M., de Souza, D.J.: Waiting Time for a Run of N Success in Bernoulli Sequences. Rev. Bras. Biom (2007)

[Chung] Chung, F.R.K.: Laplacians and the cheeger inequality for directed graphs. Annals of Combinatorics 9, 1–19 (2005)

[CRV] Chung, K.-M., Reingold, O., Vadhan, S.: S-T Connectivity on Digraphs with a Known Stationary Distribution. ACM Transactions on Algorithms 7(3), Article 30 (2011)

[Feige] Feige, U.: A tight upper bound on the cover time for random walks on graphs. Random Structures and Algorithms 6, 51–54 (1995)

[GSTV] Garvin, B., Stolee, D., Tewari, R., Vinodchandran, N.V.: ReachFewL = ReachUL. Electronic Colloquium on Computational Complexity (ECCC) 18, 60 (2011)

[HIM] Hartmanis, J., Immerman, N., Mahaney, S.: One-way Log-tape Reductions. In: Proc. IEEE FOCS, pp. 65–71 (1978)

[Kazarinoff] Kazarinoff, N.D.: Analytic inequalities. Holt, Rinehart and Winston, New York (1961)

[LP] Lewis, H.R., Papadimitriou, C.H.: Symmetric space-bounded computation. Theoretical Computer Science. pp.161-187 (1982)

[LZ] Li, Y., Zhang, Z.-L.: Digraph Laplacian and the Degree of Asymmetry. Invited for submission to a Special Issue of Internet Mathematics (2011)

[NSW] Nisan, N., Szemeredi, E., Wigderson, A.: Undirected connectivity in $O(\log^{1.5n})$ space. In: 33rd Annual Symposium on Foundations of Computer Science, Pittsburgh, Pa, October 1992. IEEE (1992)

[PRV] Pavan, A., Tewari, R., Vinodchandran, N.V.: On the Power of Unambiguity in Logspace. Technical Report TR10-009, Electronic Colloquium on Computational Complexity, To appear in Computational Complexity (2010)

[Reingold] Reingold, O.: Undirected ST-connectivity in log-space. In: STOC 2005, pp. 376–385 (2005)

[RTV] Reingold, O., Trevisan, L., Vadhan, S.P.: Pseudorandom walks on regular digraphs and the RL vs. L Problem. In: STOC 2006, pp. 457–466 (2006)

[RV] Rozenman, E., Vadhan, S.: Derandomized Squaring of Graphs. In: Chekuri, C., Jansen, K., Rolim, J.D.P., Trevisan, L. (eds.) APPROX and RANDOM 2005. LNCS, vol. 3624, pp. 436–447. Springer, Heidelberg (2005)

[Savitch] Savitch, W.J.: Relationships Between Nondeterministic and Deterministic Tape Complexityies. J. Comput. Syst. Sci. 4(2), 177–192 (1970)

[SZ] Saks, M.E., Zhou, S.: BPHSpace(S) $\subseteq$ DSPace($S^{3/2}$). J. Comput. Syst. Sci. 58(2), 36–403 (1999)

A Probabilistic Logic for pTiMo

Gabriel Ciobanu and Armand Rotaru

Romanian Academy, Institute of Computer Science
Blvd. Carol I no.8, 700505 Iaşi, Romania
gabriel@info.uaic.ro, armand@iit.tuiasi.ro

Abstract. In this paper we present pTiMo, a process algebra in which migrations and interactions depend upon timers and have probabilities. The semantics of the calculus is given in terms of labeled, discrete-time Markov chains. The existing quantitative tools do not explicitly support properties which make use of local clocks, multisets of transitions (generated by the maximal progress policy in pTiMo) and transition provenance (the location at which a transition originates, and the processes that participate in the transition). In order to study such properties, we introduce a probabilistic temporal logic PLTM for pTiMo, and provide an algorithm for verifying PLTM properties. These properties can be checked over states and/or transitions, and encompass both transient and steady-state behaviors. We also provide a verification algorithm for PLTM properties, and analyze its time complexity.

In some previous articles, we have introduced a formalism called TiMo with processes able to migrate between different explicit locations of a distributed environment defined by a number of spatially distinct locations. Timing constraints are used to control migration and communication; we use local clocks and local maximal parallelism of actions. Two processes may communicate if they are present at the same location. We are not aware of any approach combining all the features of TiMo. However, TiMo is related to a large body of literature describing process algebras. TiMo is derived as a simpler version of tDpi [6]. The distributed π-calculus [10] has an explicit notion of location, and deals with static resources access by using a type system. The paper [2] studies a π-calculus extension with a timer construct, and then enriches it with locations. Some prototype languages have been designed and experimental implementations derived from process calculi like Klaim [7] and Acute [14]; these prototype languages did not become a real practical programming language.

This paper is devoted to a quantitative extension for TiMo. In fact we use the same syntax, and give the semantics in terms of labeled, discrete-time Markov chains. Quantitative tools (e.g., the PRISM model checker [13]) do not support properties which make use of local clocks, and of multisets of transitions generated by the maximal progress policy in pTiMo. These properties could be described by a probabilistic temporal logic PLTM given for pTiMo. We describe pTiMo and PLTM, focusing on their new features. Moreover, we provide a model-checking algorithm to verify PLTM properties of pTiMo processes.

Z. Liu, J. Woodcock, and H. Zhu (Eds.): ICTAC 2013, LNCS 8049, pp. 141–158, 2013.

1 Probabilistic Timed Mobility

Process calculi are used to model distributed systems. Various features were introduced to obtain such formalisms, including explicit locations in distributed π-calculus [10], and explicit migration and timers in timed distributed π-calculus [6]. Papers considering time assume the existence of a global clock; however, there are several applications and distributed systems for which considering a global clock would be inappropriate. As a solution, the process algebra TiMo [1] is a formalism for mobile systems in which it is possible to add timers to control process mobility and interaction. A local clock is assigned to each location [4]; each local clock determines the timing of actions executed at the corresponding location. Inspired by TiMo, a flexible software platform supporting the specification of agents and allowing a timed migration in a distributed environment is presented in [3]. Timing constraints for migration allow one to specify a temporal interval after which a mobile process must move to another location. A timer denoted by $\Delta 3$ associated to a migration action $\mathsf{go}^{\Delta 3} work$ indicates that the process moves to location *work* after 3 time units. It is also possible to constrain the waiting period for a communication on a channel; if a communication action does not happen before a deadline, the process gives up and switches its operation to an alternative. E.g., a timer $\Delta 5$ associated to an output action $a^{\Delta 5}!\langle 10\rangle$ makes the channel available for communication only for a period of 5 time units. We assume suitable data sets including a set *Loc* of locations and a set *Chan* of communication channels. We use a set *Id* of process identifiers, and each $id \in Id$ has the arity m_{id}. In what follows, we use $\boldsymbol{x}$ to denote a finite tuple of elements $(x_1, \ldots, x_k)$ whenever it does not lead to confusion.

Table 1. TiMo Syntax

Processes	$P ::= a^{\Delta lt}!\langle \boldsymbol{v}\rangle$ then P else P' ❘	(output)
	$a^{\Delta lt}?(\boldsymbol{u}{:}\boldsymbol{X})$ then P else P' ❘	(input)
	$\mathsf{go}^{\Delta lt}\ l$ then P ❘	(move)
	$P \mid P'$ ❘	(parallel)
	0 ❘	(termination)
	$id(\boldsymbol{v})$	(definition)
	ⓈP	(stalling)
Located processes	$L ::= l[\![P]\!]$	
Networks	$N ::= L$ ❘ $L \mid N$	

The syntax of TiMo is given in Table 1, where P are processes, L, located processes, and N, networks [4]. For each $id \in Id$ there is a unique definition of the form $id(u_1, \ldots, u_{m_{id}} : X_1^{id}, \ldots, X_{m_{id}}^{id}) = P_{id}$, where P_{id} is a process expression, the u_i's are distinct variables playing the role of parameters, and the X_i^{id}'s are data types. In the syntax, $a \in Chan$ is a channel; $lt \in \mathbb{N} \cup \{\infty\}$ is a deadline, where lt stands for *local time*; each v_i in $\boldsymbol{v}$ is an expression built from data values and variables; each u_i in $\boldsymbol{u}$ is a variable, and each X_i in $\boldsymbol{X}$ is a data type; l is a location or a location variable; and Ⓢ is a special symbol used to state that a process is temporarily 'stalled' and will be re-activated after a time progress.

The only variable binding constructor is $a^{\Delta lt}?(\boldsymbol{u}{:}\boldsymbol{X})$ then P else P', which binds the variables $\boldsymbol{u}$ within P (but *not* within P'). We use $fv(P)$ to denote the free variables of a process P (and similarly for networks). For a process definition, we assume that $fv(P_{id}) \subseteq \{u_1, \ldots, u_{m_{id}}\}$, and so the free variables of P_{id} are parameter bound. Processes are defined up to α-conversion, and $\{v/u, \ldots\}P$ is obtained from P by replacing all free occurrences of a variable u by v, etc, possible after α-converting P in order to avoid clashes. Moreover, if $\boldsymbol{v}$ and $\boldsymbol{u}$ are tuples of the same length then $\{\boldsymbol{v}/\boldsymbol{u}\}P$ denotes $\{v_1/u_1, v_2/u_2, \ldots, v_k/u_k\}P$.

Intuitively, a process $a^{\Delta lt}!\langle \boldsymbol{v} \rangle$ then P else P' attempts to send a tuple of values $\boldsymbol{v}$ over channel a for lt time units. If successful, it continues as process P; otherwise, it continues as process P'. Similarly, $a^{\Delta lt}?(\boldsymbol{u}{:}\boldsymbol{X})$ then P else P' is a process that attempts for lt time units to input a tuple of values of type $\boldsymbol{X}$ and substitute them for the variables $\boldsymbol{u}$. Mobility is implemented by a process $\mathsf{go}^{\Delta lt}\, l$ then P which moves from the current location to the location l after exactly lt time units. Note that since l can be a variable, and so its value is assigned dynamically through the communication with other processes, migration actions support a flexible scheme for the movement of processes from one location to another. By delaying the migration to another location, we can model in a simple way the movement time of processes within the network which is, in general, outside the control of a system designer. Processes are further constructed from the (terminated) process 0 and parallel composition $P|P'$. A located process $l[\![P]\!]$ specifies a process P running at location l, and networks are composed of located processes. A network N is *well-formed* if there are no free variables in N, there are no occurrences of the special symbol Ⓢ in N, and assuming that id is as in the recursive definition of a process, for every $id(\boldsymbol{v})$ occurring in N or on the right hand side of any recursive equation, the expression v_i is of type corresponding to X_i^{id}. The set of processes is denoted by $\mathcal{P}$, the set of located processes by $\mathcal{L}$, and the set of networks by $\mathcal{N}$.

Using the commutativity and the associativity of parallel composition in TiMo, one can always transform a given network N into a finite parallel composition of located processes of the form $l_1[\![P_1]\!] \mid \ldots \mid l_n[\![P_n]\!]$ such that no process P_i has the parallel composition operator at its topmost level, and then apply the action rules given in Table 2. Each located process $l_i[\![P_i]\!]$ is called a component of N, and the parallel composition is called a *component decomposition* of the network N. Note that these notions are well defined since component decomposition is unique up to the permutation of the components. This follows from the rule (Call) which treats recursive definitions as function calls that take a unit of time. Another consequence of such a treatment is that it is impossible to execute an infinite sequence of action steps without executing any time actions.

Table 2 presents two kinds of rules: $N \xrightarrow{\lambda} N'$ and $N \xrightarrow{\surd_l} N'$. The former is an execution of an action λ; the latter is a time step at location l.

Table 2. TiMo Operational Semantics

(Move)	$l[\![\mathsf{go}^{\Delta lt} l' \text{ then } P]\!] \xrightarrow{l'@l} l'[\![\circledS P]\!]$
(Com)	$\dfrac{v_1 \in X_1 \ \ldots\ v_k \in X_k}{l[\![a^{\Delta lt}!\langle \boldsymbol{v}\rangle \text{ then } P \text{ else } Q \mid a^{\Delta lt'}?(\boldsymbol{u}{:}\boldsymbol{X}) \text{ then } P' \text{ else } Q']\!] \xrightarrow{a\langle \boldsymbol{v}\rangle @l} l[\![\circledS P \mid \circledS\{\boldsymbol{v}/\boldsymbol{u}\}P']\!]}$
(Call)	$l[\![id(\boldsymbol{v})]\!] \xrightarrow{id@l} l[\![\circledS\{\boldsymbol{v}/\boldsymbol{u}\}P_{id}]\!]$
(Par)	$\dfrac{N \xrightarrow{\lambda} N'}{N \mid N'' \xrightarrow{\lambda} N' \mid N''}$
(Time)	$\dfrac{N \not\rightarrow_l}{N \xrightarrow{\surd_l} \phi_l(N)}$

In the rule (Time), $N \not\rightarrow_l$ means that the rules (Call) and (Com) as well as (Move) with $\Delta lt = \Delta 0$ **cannot** be applied to N for location l. Moreover, $\phi_l(N)$ is obtained by taking the component decomposition of N and simultaneously replacing all components:

$$l[\![a^{\Delta lt}\omega \text{ then } P \text{ else } Q]\!] \quad \text{by} \quad \begin{cases} l[\![a^{\Delta lt-1}\omega \text{ then } P \text{ else } Q]\!] & \text{if } lt > 0 \\ l[\![Q]\!] & \text{if } lt = 0 \end{cases}$$

$$l[\![\mathsf{go}^{\Delta lt} l' \text{ then } P]\!] \quad \text{by} \quad l[\![\mathsf{go}^{\Delta lt-1} l' \text{ then } P]\!]$$

where ω stands for $!\langle \boldsymbol{v}\rangle$ or $?(\boldsymbol{u}{:}\boldsymbol{X})$. After that, all the occurrences of the symbol Ⓢ in N are erased since processes that were unfolded or interacted with other processes or migrated need to be activated (note that the number of the symbols Ⓢ to be erased cannot exceed the number of the components of the network).

The rules of Table 2 express executions of individual actions. A complete computational step is captured by a derivation of the form $N \overset{\Lambda@l}{\Longrightarrow} N'$, where $\Lambda = \{\lambda_1, \ldots, \lambda_m\}$ ($m \geq 0$) is a finite multiset of actions for some location l (i.e., actions λ_i of the form $l'@l$ or $a\langle v\rangle@l$ or $id@l$) such that

$$N \xrightarrow{\lambda_1} N_1 \ldots N_{m-1} \xrightarrow{\lambda_m} N_m \xrightarrow{\surd_l} N'.$$

That means that a derivation represents a sequence of individual actions followed by a clock tick, all happening at the same location. Intuitively, this captures the cumulative effect of the concurrent execution of the multiset of actions Λ at location l, and so we write $N \overset{\Lambda@l}{\Longrightarrow} N'$.

pTiMo Semantics. The new process calculus pTiMo is a quantitative, probabilistic extension of TiMo, and it has the same syntax as TiMo. However, unlike in TiMo, we decided that it would be more realistic to give networks a large degree of freedom in deciding when a process is allowed to move from the current active location. We achieve this by assuming that any pTiMo process $\mathsf{go}^{\Delta lt} l$ then P can move to location l after at most lt time units (and not necessarily after exactly lt time units). In order to define the semantics for pTiMo, we note that the behavior of a well-formed network N consists of an alternating sequence of derivations (i.e., complete computational steps, in which a maximally parallel multiset of actions is performed at a certain location) and location selections (i.e., choosing the location at which the next complete computational step takes place). As a means of simplifying the description of pTiMo, we have decided to combine derivations, followed by location selections, into unitary computational steps, referred to as complete transitions (i.e., as opposed to individual actions and location selections, which are referred to as elementary transitions). Within a complete transition, both derivations and location selections can be seen as forms of nondeterministic choice. In the case of derivations, the nondeterminism originates in the fact that moving processes can "choose" either to stay at the current location or to move to a new location. Furthermore, there are multiple possible outcomes when more than one sender and one receiver have the possibility of communicating over a certain channel, at the same time. For location selections, the nondeterminism is caused by the fact that the semantics of TiMo does not include any rule regarding the selection. Therefore, we can obtain a probabilistic version of TiMo just by turning all the aforementioned nondeterministic choices into corresponding probabilistic, independent choices. More specifically, when switching from TiMo to pTiMo we find it useful to treat each source of nondeterminism separately. We impose this condition of independence because we assume that the movements performed by certain processes should not affect the communications between other processes, that communication channels are isolated from one another, and that process behavior at a certain location does not influence the choice of the next active location. Whenever necessary, alternative semantics for pTiMo can be obtained, for instance, by dropping this condition and by assigning the probability of each complete transition in a holistic manner.

When describing the semantics of pTiMo, we will employ the notation $N@l$ to indicate that the next complete transition for the network N will take place at location l. Moreover, if the network N, which is active at location l, can make a complete computational step $N \overset{tr_c}{\Longrightarrow} N'$, after which N' becomes active at location l', we will denote this unified transition by $N@l \overset{tr_c, l'}{\Longrightarrow} N'@l'$. Let $\mathcal{T}_v$ refer to the set of all valid complete transitions, starting from a valid state, and let $\mathcal{T}(N@l)$ denote the set of complete transitions immediately available at $N@l$, meaning that $\mathcal{T}(N@l) = \{(tr_c, l', N'@l') \mid N@l \overset{tr_c, l'}{\Longrightarrow} N'@l' \in \mathcal{T}_v\}$. Additionally, let us denote by $\mathcal{S}$ and $\mathcal{T}$ the sets containing the states and the complete transitions of N, respectively.

In order to assign probabilities to complete transitions in a meaningful manner, we will first introduce a number of additional notations, as to separate movements from communications. Let $Dist_{fin}(X)$ denote the set of all the finite, discrete probability distributions over the set X. Also, let $[M]N@l$ and $[C, a]N@l$ refer to the network N, active at location l, restricted exactly to those (located) processes which, as their next action, can perform a movement, or a communication over channel a, respectively. Furthermore, we define the following two sets:

$$[M]TR(N@l) = \{(tr_c^1, l_1', N_1'@l_1') \mid [M]N@l \xrightarrow{tr_c^1, l_1'} N_1'@l_1' \in \mathcal{T}_v\}$$
$$[C,a]TR(N@l) = \{(tr_c^2, l_2', N_2'@l_2') \mid [C,a]N@l \xrightarrow{tr_c^2, l_2'} N_2'@l_2' \in \mathcal{T}_v\}$$

By employing the sets $[M]N@l$, $[C,a]N@l$, $[M]TR(N@l)$, and $[C,a]TR(N@l)$, we can easily solve the nondeterminism created by movements and communications. In the case of movements, the set $[M]TR(N@l)$ captures all the possible combinations of movements that originate in $[M]N@l$ (and, implicitly, in $N@l$). Similarly, the set $[C,a]TR(N@l)$ describes all the possible communications that can be generated by $[C,a]N@l$ (and, implicitly, by $N@l$). Now, we can transform nondeterministic choices into probabilistic choices simply by associating probabilities to the elements of $[M]TR(N@l)$ and $[C,a]TR(N@l)$, through the use of finite, discrete probability distributions. More specifically, we can choose two distributions $Dist_{fin}^M(N@l) \in Dist_{fin}^M([M]TR(N@l))$ and $Dist_{fin}^{C,a}(N@l) \in Dist_{fin}([C,a]TR(N@l))$, such that $Dist_{fin}^M(N@l)$ and $Dist_{fin}^{C,a}(N@l)$ quantify the probability of each complete transition arising from $[M]N@l$ and $[C,a]N@l$, respectively. Let $Dist_{fin}^M(\mathcal{S}) = \bigcup_{N@l \in \mathcal{S}} Dist_{fin}([M]TR(N@l))$ and

$$Dist_{fin}^{C,a}(\mathcal{S}) = \bigcup_{N@l \in \mathcal{S}} Dist_{fin}([C,a]TR(N@l)),$$

for any $a \in Chan$. In the general case, for solving all forms on nondeterminism (including the nondeterminism involved in selecting the next active location) we employ the functions $sch_M \in SCH_M$, $sch_C^a \in SCH_C^a$ and $sch_L \in SCH_L$, where $SCH_M = \{f : \mathcal{S} \to Dist_{fin}^M(\mathcal{S}) \mid \forall N@l \in \mathcal{S}, f(N@l) \in Dist_{fin}([M]TR(N@l))\}$,

$SCH_C^a = \{g : \mathcal{S} \to Dist_{fin}^{C,a}(\mathcal{S}) \mid \forall N@l \in \mathcal{S}, g(N@l) \in Dist_{fin}([C,a]TR(N@l))\}$,

and $SCH_L = \{h : \mathcal{S} \to Dist_{fin}(Loc)\}$.

Definition 1. *Starting from the previously defined functions, the probability* $P(tr_c, l')$ *of any complete transition* $N@l \xrightarrow{tr_c, l'} N'@l'$ *can be computed as* $P(tr_c, l') = P_M(tr_c) \cdot P_C(tr_c) \cdot (sch_L(N@l))(l')$*, where:*

$$P_M(tr_c) = (sch_M(N@L))(tr_c, l', N'@l')$$
$$P_C(tr_c) = \prod_{a \in Chan} (sch_C^a(N@L))(tr_c, l', N'@l')$$

Once probabilities have been assigned to all the complete transitions in a TiMo network, the resulting structure is a pTiMo network.

Definition 2. *In the general case, a* pTiMo *network is a quadruple*

$$N_p = \left(N@l, sch_M, \left\{ \bigcup_{a \in Chan} sch_C^a \right\}, sch_L \right)$$

where $N@l$ *is a* TiMo *network that is active at location* l*, corresponding to the initial state of* N_p*, and, as mentioned earlier,* $sch_M \in SCH_M$*,* $sch_C^a \in SCH_C^a$*, for any* $a \in Chan$*, and* $sch_L \in SCH_L$.

After eliminating all the nondeterminism found in a TiMo model, as shown in Definition 1, the resulting structure is a (labeled) discrete-time Markov chain. The syntax of pTiMo is the same as that of TiMo. As mentioned before, any state of a pTiMo network includes the currently active location for that particular state (or network), and derivations are replaced by complete transitions, which consist of a complete computational step and a new active location. The actual difference between the two formalisms is in terms of semantics, namely in the fact that complete transitions are associated with probabilities, and that processes have a greater freedom of movement.

Travel Agency Example in pTiMo. In order to illustrate the syntax and the semantics of pTiMo networks, we provide a running example involving an understaffed travel agency. We assume that the agency has a central office and six local offices. However, due to massive layoffs, the staff of the agency consists only of three travel agents, whose jobs are to recommend specific travel destinations to potential customers, and two executives, in charge of assigning the travel agents to the local offices of the agency. Also, there are two potential customers, who are interested in the recommendations made by the agency. We assume that the behaviors of the agency staff and of the potential customers are cyclic and can be described as follows, in the form of pTiMo processes.

The first agent (i.e., process $A1$) leaves home (i.e., location $home_{A1}$) and goes to the central office of the agency (i.e., location $office$); there, he/she is assigned a certain local office for the day (i.e., location $newloc$); the agent then moves to the given location and advertises (over channel a) the first destination on the agency's list (i.e., location $dest_1$), in the form of a holiday pack for 100 monetary units; finally, the agent returns home. The second and the third agent (i.e., processes $A2$ and $A3$) are similar to the first, but they different home (i.e., locations $home_{A2}$ and $home_{A3}$), and advertise different destinations (i.e., locations $dest_2$ and $dest_3$), in the form of holiday packs for 200 and 300 monetary units, respectively. Formally, we have:

$AX(home_{AX} : Loc) = \mathsf{go}^{\Delta 0}\ office\ \mathsf{then}\ AX(office : Loc)$
$AX(office : Loc) = b^{\Delta 0}?(newloc : Loc)\ \mathsf{then}\ (\mathsf{go}^{\Delta 1}\ newloc\ \mathsf{then}\ AX(newloc : Loc))\ \mathsf{else}\ AX(office : Loc)$
$AX(office_i : Loc) = a^{\Delta 1}!\langle dest_X, 100 \cdot X\rangle\ \mathsf{then}\ \mathsf{go}^{\Delta 0}\ home_{AX}\ \mathsf{then}\ AX(home_{AX} : Loc)$, for $1 \leq i \leq 6$

where $X \in \{1, 2, 3\}$ refers to the number of the agent.

The two executives (i.e., processes $E1$ and $E2$) reside at the central office (i.e., location $office$), and each chooses a local office (i.e., in a cyclic manner, from the locations $office_1$, $office_3$, for process $E1$, and the locations $office_2$, $office_4$, for process $E2$) that will be assigned to the next agent that comes to the central office (over channel b). Formally, we have:

$E1(office_1 : Loc) = b^{\Delta 0}!\langle office_1\rangle\ \mathsf{then}\ E1(office_3 : Loc)\ \mathsf{else}\ E1(office_1 : Loc)$
$E1(office_3 : Loc) = b^{\Delta 0}!\langle office_3\rangle\ \mathsf{then}\ E1(office_5 : Loc)\ \mathsf{else}\ E1(office_3 : Loc)$
$E1(office_5 : Loc) = b^{\Delta 0}!\langle office_5\rangle\ \mathsf{then}\ E1(office_1 : Loc)\ \mathsf{else}\ E1(office_5 : Loc)$

$E2(office_2 : Loc) = b^{\Delta 0}!\langle office_2\rangle$ then $E2(office_4 : Loc)$ else $E2(office_2 : Loc)$
$E2(office_4 : Loc) = b^{\Delta 0}!\langle office_4\rangle$ then $E2(office_6 : Loc)$ else $E2(office_4 : Loc)$
$E2(office_6 : Loc) = b^{\Delta 0}!\langle office_6\rangle$ then $E2(office_2 : Loc)$ else $E2(office_6 : Loc)$

The first customer (i.e., process $C1$) leaves home (i.e., location $home_{C1}$) and visits the three local offices of the agency that are closest to his/her home (i.e., locations $office_1$, $office_2$, and $office_3$), in order, receives travel offers from the agents, and chooses a travel destination; then, he/she goes to the desired destination, spends a certain amount of time there, after which he/she returns home. The second customer (i.e., process $C2$) resembles the first, except that he/she initially has a different home (i.e., location $home_{C2}$), and the offices closest to his/her home are locations $office_4$, $office_5$, and $office_6$. Formally, we have:

$C1(home_{C1} : Loc) = \mathsf{go}^{\Delta 1}\ office_1$ then $C1(office_1 : Loc)$
$C1(office_1 : Loc) = a^{\Delta 1}?(dest : Loc, cost : \mathbb{N})$ then $(\mathsf{go}^{\Delta 0}\ dest$ then $C1(dest : Loc))$ else $(\mathsf{go}^{\Delta 0}\ office_2$ then $C1(office_2 : Loc))$
$C1(office_2 : Loc) = a^{\Delta 1}?(dest : Loc, cost : \mathbb{N})$ then $(\mathsf{go}^{\Delta 0}\ dest$ then $C1(dest : Loc))$ else $(\mathsf{go}^{\Delta 0}\ office_3$ then $C1(office_3 : Loc))$
$C1(office_3 : Loc) = a^{\Delta 1}?(dest : Loc, cost : \mathbb{N})$ then $(\mathsf{go}^{\Delta 0}\ dest$ then $C1(dest : Loc))$ else $(\mathsf{go}^{\Delta 0}\ home_{C1}$ then $C1(home_{C1} : Loc))$
$C1(dest_i : Loc) = \mathsf{go}^{\Delta i}\ home_{C1}$ then $C1(home_{C1} : Loc)$, for $1 \leq i \leq 3$

$C2(home_{C2} : Loc) = \mathsf{go}^{\Delta 1}\ office_4$ then $C2(office_4 : Loc)$
$C2(office_4 : Loc) = a^{\Delta 1}?(dest : Loc, cost : \mathbb{N})$ then $(\mathsf{go}^{\Delta 0}\ dest$ then $C2(dest : Loc))$ else $(\mathsf{go}^{\Delta 0}\ office_5$ then $C2(office_5 : Loc))$
$C2(office_5 : Loc) = a^{\Delta 1}?(dest : Loc, cost : \mathbb{N})$ then $(\mathsf{go}^{\Delta 0}\ dest$ then $C2(dest : Loc))$ else $(\mathsf{go}^{\Delta 0}\ office_6$ then $C2(office_6 : Loc))$
$C2(office_6 : Loc) = a^{\Delta 1}?(dest : Loc, cost : \mathbb{N})$ then $(\mathsf{go}^{\Delta 0}\ dest$ then $C2(dest : Loc))$ else $(\mathsf{go}^{\Delta 0}\ home_{C2}$ then $C2(home_{C2} : Loc))$
$C2(dest_i : Loc) = \mathsf{go}^{\Delta i}\ home_{C2}$ then $C2(home_{C2} : Loc)$, for $1 \leq i \leq 3$

The initial state of the corresponding pTiMo network is:

$$\begin{aligned} N = {} & home_{A1}[[A1(home_{A1})]] \mid home_{A2}[[A2(home_{A2})]] \mid home_{A3}[[A3(home_{A3})]] \mid \\ & \mid office[[E1(office_1)]] \mid office[[E2(office_2)]] \mid \\ & \mid home_{C1}[[C1(home_{C1})]] \mid home_{C2}[[C2(home_{C2})]] \end{aligned}$$

Also, the initial active location for the N is $l = home_{A1}$.

While the description presented so far is sufficient in order to construct the underlying TiMo network, we still have to solve the inherent non-determinism of the network, before we can obtain a proper pTiMo specification. In the case of the movement of the agents from the central office to the local offices, and of the movement of the customers from their homes to the local offices, each agent or customer will move at either $\Delta 1$ or $\Delta 0$, with equal probability (i.e., $p = 0.5$). When it comes to the movement of the customers from their travel destinations to their homes, we assume that the holiday packs have different (maximum) durations, such that any customer can stay at location $dest_i$ for a number of at most i steps. The first customer is rather moody, which means that he/she can leave at any time before Δi, with equal probability (i.e., $p = 1/(i+1)$). However, the second customer is always satisfied, which means that he/she will leave only at $\Delta 0$. Next, in the case of the communication between the agents and the executives, all the possible combinations of senders and receivers have the same probability. For the communication between the customers and the agents, the first customer has a preference for expensive holiday packs, which means that the probability of choosing a certain offer is directly proportional to the cost of that offer, while the second customer typically opts for cheaper packs, which means that the probability of choosing a certain offer is inversely proportional to the cost of that offer. Finally, we assume that the next active location is always chosen deterministically, in the following cyclic order: $home_{A1}$, $home_{A2}$, $home_{A3}$, $office$, $home_{C1}$, $home_{C2}$, $office_1$, $office_2$, $office_3$, $office_4$, $office_5$, $office_6$, $dest_1$, $dest_2$, $dest_3$. Due to reasons of space, we do not include here the values of all the probabilities resulting from the previous, informal description of system behavior. For the interested reader, the complete version of this example can be found in [5][1]. However, we illustrate some of these probabilities by taking the case of the communication between client $C2$ and the agents $A1$, $A2$, and $A3$. To simplify the description of the aforementioned probabilities, we use the following process identifiers:

$$AX_{b0?}(office) = b^{\Delta 0}?(newloc : Loc) \text{ then } (\text{go}^{\Delta 1}\ newloc \text{ then } AX(newloc : Loc)) \text{ else } AX(office : Loc)$$

$$AX_{g1}(newloc) = \text{go}^{\Delta 1}\ newloc \text{ then } AX(newloc : Loc)$$
$$AX_{g0}(newloc) = \text{go}^{\Delta 0}\ newloc \text{ then } AX(newloc : Loc)$$
$$AX_{a1!}(office_i) = a^{\Delta 1}!\langle dest_X, 100 \cdot X\rangle \text{ then go}^{\Delta 0}\ home_{AX} \text{ then } AX(home_{AX} : Loc) \text{ for } 1 \le i \le 6$$
$$AX_{a0!}(office_i) = a^{\Delta 0}!\langle dest_X, 100 \cdot X\rangle \text{ then go}^{\Delta 0}\ home_{AX} \text{ then } AX(home_{AX} : Loc) \text{ for } 1 \le i \le 6$$
$$C2_{ah?}(office_4) = a^{\Delta h}?(dest : Loc, cost : \mathbb{N}) \text{ then } (\text{go}^{\Delta 0}\ dest \text{ then } C2(dest : Loc)) \text{ else } (\text{go}^{\Delta 0}\ office_5 \text{ then } C2(office_5 : Loc))$$
$$C2_{ah?}(office_5) = a^{\Delta h}?(dest : Loc, cost : \mathbb{N}) \text{ then } (\text{go}^{\Delta 0}\ dest \text{ then } C2(dest : Loc)) \text{ else } (\text{go}^{\Delta 0}\ office_6 \text{ then } C2(office_6 : Loc))$$
$$C2_{ah?}(office_6) = a^{\Delta h}?(dest : Loc, cost : \mathbb{N}) \text{ then } (\text{go}^{\Delta 0}\ dest \text{ then } C2(dest : Loc)) \text{ else } (\text{go}^{\Delta 0}\ home_{C2} \text{ then } C2(home_{C2} : Loc))$$

where $X \in \{1, 2, 3\}$ and $h \in \{0, 1\}$.

Let $SEND_1$, $SEND_2$, and $SEND_3$ denote the ordered sets $SEND_1 = \{Ai_{ah_1!}(office_q)\}$, $SEND_2 = \{Ai_{ah_1!}(office_q), Aj_{ah_2!}(office_q)\}$, and $SEND_3 = \{Ai_{ah_1!}(office_q), Aj_{ah_2!}(office_q), Ak_{ah_3!}(office_q)\}$, where $1 \le q \le 6$, $h_1, h_2, h_3 \in \{0, 1\}$, and $1 \le i \le 3$, $1 \le i < j \le 3$, $1 \le i < j < k \le 3$,

[1] The semantics given in the current paper is a streamlined version of that defined in [5] and used in the example. However, although the two semantics involve different notations and levels of detail, they are identical from a practical point of view.

respectively. For any communication between the second customer and the travel agents, we have the following probabilities:

$$P(\{(Ai, C2)\} \mid SEND_1, C2_{ah?}(office_q)) = 1$$

$$P(\{(Ai, C2)\} \mid SEND_2, C2_{ah?}(office_q)) = j/(i+j)$$
$$P(\{(Aj, C2)\} \mid SEND_2, C2_{ah?}(office_q)) = i/(i+j)$$

$$P(\{(Ai, C2)\} \mid SEND_3, C2_{ah?}(office_q)) = jk/(ij+jk+ki)$$
$$P(\{(Aj, C2)\} \mid SEND_3, C2_{ah?}(office_q)) = ki/(ij+jk+ki)$$
$$P(\{(Ak, C2)\} \mid SEND_3, C2_{ah?}(office_q)) = ij/(ij+jk+ki).$$

2 A Probabilistic Logic for Timed Mobility

The main reason for creating a probabilistic extension of TiMo is to gain the ability to verify quantitative properties of pTiMo networks, such as the probability that a certain transient or steady-state behavior occurs. Therefore, it is natural to have a probabilistic temporal logic for expressing such properties over networks of located processes. Unfortunately, we have not been able to find a quantitative logic (such as PCTL [9] or aPCTL [12]) which is immediately compatible with all or most of the distinguishing features of pTiMo, such as explicit locations, local clocks, and the maximally parallel execution of processes at a given location. As a result, starting from the PCTL family of quantitative logics, we define a novel logic for pTiMo networks, namely PLTM (Probabilistic Logic for Timed Mobility), which includes features such as:

- properties for transient and steady-state behavior,
- explicit references to locations and (named) processes,
- temporal constraints over local clocks, both finite and infinite,
- complex action guards over multisets of actions (i.e., structured transitions).

By using PLTM, one can express properties such as "with probability greater than 0.5, the process P_1 will communicate at location l_1, on channels a_1 or a_3, before 3 time steps have elapsed at location l_1, and 4 time steps have elapsed at location l_2", and "the long-run probability that no movement occurs during a complete transition is less than 0.3". For the travel agency, we can have properties such as "with probability greater than 0.5, the customers $C1$ and $C2$ will meet at location $dest_3$, before 6 time steps have elapsed at each location", or "the long-run probability that agents $A1$ and $A3$ are at home is less than 0.4". If we employ rewards, we can query whether "the average amount of money that customer $C2$ spends on vacations, before 30 time steps have elapsed at location $home_{C2}$, is equal to 400 monetary units", or whether "the average number of times that agent $A2$ has to visit the local office $office_1$, before he/she will find customer $C1$ waiting there, is greater than 5".

In order to introduce the formal syntax and semantics of PLTM, we first describe the notions of guards and temporal constraints. A guard is a logical expression over a set of quantitative properties, which refer to the multiplicity of the elementary transitions that belong to a complete transition. For instance, a guard can be specified as $g = \neg(\#(a_1\langle v_1\rangle) = 1) \vee ((\#(\texttt{MOVE}\,\texttt{at}\,l_1) < 5) \wedge (\#(a_2\langle\texttt{MSG}\rangle) \geq \#(a_3\langle\texttt{MSG}\rangle)))$. For the travel agency, one such guard could be $g = (\#(b\langle dest_1\rangle < dest_1 >) = 1) \wedge (\#(\texttt{MOVE}\,\texttt{at}\,office) > 0)$. In the first case, a complete transition (tr_c, l') satisfies the guard g iff tr_c either does not involve exactly one COM transition rule with the message v_1 (i.e., $\neg(\#(a_1\langle v_1\rangle) = 1)$), or it includes strictly less than 5 MOVE transition rules at location l_1 (i.e., $\#(MOVE\ \texttt{at}\ l_1) < 5$) and the total number of COM transition rules over the channel a_2 is greater than or equal to the number of COM transition rules over the channel a_3 (i.e., $\#(a_2\langle MSG\rangle) \geq \#(a_3\langle MSG\rangle)))$. The complete syntax for guards is given in Table 3.

The (fully specified) elementary matchers l' and $a\langle v\rangle$ are compatible with a movement to location l', and a communication of the message v over the channel a, respectively. Additionally, the (partially specified) elementary matchers $\texttt{MOVE}$, $a\langle\texttt{MSG}\rangle$, $\texttt{COM}\langle v\rangle$ and $\texttt{COM}\langle\texttt{MSG}\rangle$ are compatible with a generic movement, a communication over the channel a (regardless of message content), a communication involving the message v (regardless of channel), and a generic communication, respectively. A further level of detail is added by the enhanced matchers $tran$ $\texttt{at}$ l, $tran$ $\texttt{by}$ P and $tran$ $\texttt{by}$ P $\texttt{at}$ l, which denote an elementary transition $tran$ that is performed at a specific location l or by a specific process P. The arithmetic operators are used to generate arithmetic expressions, involving real constants (i.e., cst) and the total number of elementary (enhanced) transitions $tran$ ($tran_e$) that are performed during a complete transition, as indicated by the corresponding matchers. Next, comparison expressions allow the numerical values returned by arithmetic expressions to be compared either between themselves, or with respect to given real constants. Finally, guards are specified as logical expressions, created by applying logical operators to comparison expressions.

Table 3. Action Guard Syntax

Elementary matchers	$tran ::= l' \mid a\langle v\rangle \mid \texttt{MOVE} \mid a\langle\texttt{MSG}\rangle \mid \texttt{COM}\langle v\rangle \mid \texttt{COM}\langle\texttt{MSG}\rangle$
Enhanced matchers	$tran_e ::= tran\ \texttt{at}\ l \mid tran\ \texttt{by}\ P \mid tran\ \texttt{by}\ P\ \texttt{at}\ l$
Arithmetic operators	$\phi_{arit} ::= + \mid - \mid *$
Comparison operators	$\phi_{cmp} ::= < \mid > \mid = \mid \leq \mid \geq$
Logical operators	$\phi_{log} ::= \neg \mid \wedge \mid \vee$
Arithmetic expressions	$arit ::= cst \mid \#(tran) \mid \#(tran_e) \mid arit_1\ \phi_{arit}\ arit_2$
Comparison expressions	$cmp ::= arit\ \phi_{cmp}\ const \mid arit_1\ \phi_{cmp}\ arit_2$
Logical expressions (guards)	$log ::= \texttt{true} \mid cmp \mid log_1\ \phi_{log}\ log_2$

Moving on to temporal constraints, let us note that the passage of discrete time in pTiMo is localized, i.e., while a complete transition is performed at a given location, taking one time step, the processes at all the other locations are inactive. Assuming that we start with a network $N_0@l_0$ and have a finite path $\sigma_f = N_0@l_0 \xrightarrow{tr_{c1},l_1} N_1@l_1 \ldots N_{m-1}@l_{m-1} \xrightarrow{tr_{cm},l_m} N_m@l_m$, we can define the local time $t_i@l_i$ after the completion of σ_f simply as the number of time steps that were performed at location l_i (i.e., the number of complete transitions that originated in l_i). More generally, for each state $N_i@l_i$, with i between 0 and m, we can define the network time as the set consisting of the local time for each $l \in Loc$, which is written as a vector $t(N_i@l_i) = (t_1@l_1, \ldots, t_n@l_n)$, with $\sum_{j=1}^{n} t_j@l_j = i$. It is now straightforward to define a partial order for the set of network times, such that $t(N_a@l_a) \leq t(N_b@l_b)$ iff $t_{loc_j}(N_a@l_a) \leq t_{loc_j}(N_b@l_b)$, for any j between 1 and n. This partial order offers the possibility of specifying temporal constraints on the expressions under verification. For example, given an initial network N consisting of two locations, namely loc_1 and loc_2, and a logical formula ϕ_P, we can ask whether ϕ_P becomes true with a probability of at least p, before three time steps have passed at loc_1 and four time steps have elapsed at loc_2, by employing the formula $\phi = [\texttt{true}\mathbf{U}\phi_P]_{\geq p}^{\leq 3@loc_1, 4@loc_2}$. For the travel agency, we could ask whether agent $A3$ reaches location $office_4$, before 8 time steps have elapsed at location $office$, with probability greater than 0.75. However, in order to facilitate the formulation of temporal constraints, it is not necessary to set an upper bound for each and every local time: one can indicate temporal restrictions only for a number of relevant locations (e.g., all the locations are considered to be relevant in our previous example), which means that no conditions are imposed on the remaining locations (i.e., formally, the upper bounds for these locations are set to ∞). Thus, given a set of locations $L = \{l_1, \ldots, l_n\}$, a temporal bound (i.e., a set of temporal constraints $B_1, \ldots, B_n$) can be expressed simply as an element of the set $\mathbb{T} = \{(B_1@l_1, \ldots, B_n@l_n) \mid B_1, \ldots, B_n \in \mathbb{N} \cup \infty\}$, where B_i indicates the maximum local time allowed at l_i, for i between 1 and n. Also, for ease of reference, given any $t \in \mathbb{T}$ with $t = (b_1@l_1, \ldots, b_n@l_n)$, let $t@l_i = b_i$ denote the temporal bound at location l_i.

Definition 3. *Using guards and temporal constraints, we can now define the syntax of the probabilistic temporal logic PLTM as follows:*

$$\phi_P ::= \textit{true} \mid \textit{prop} \mid \neg\phi_P \mid \phi_{P1} \wedge \phi_{P2} \mid [\phi_{P1}\mathbf{U}_{\phi_A}\phi_{P2}]_{\geq p}^{\leq t} \mid [\phi_{P1}\mathbf{U}_{\phi_A}\phi_{P2}]_{>p}^{\leq t}$$
$$\phi_S ::= [\mathbf{S}\phi_P]_{\geq p} \mid [\mathbf{S}\phi_P]_{>p} \mid [\mathbf{S}\phi_A]_{\geq p} \mid [\mathbf{S}\phi_A]_{>p}$$

where $prop \in AP$ is an atomic proposition (i.e., a Boolean property that can be defined over each of the states in $\mathcal{S}$), p is a probability in the interval $[0, 1]$, ϕ_A is a guard over complete transitions, t is a set of temporal constraints over localized complete transitions, ϕ_{cmp} is a comparison operator as described in Table 3. The connectives $\neg$ (negation) and $\wedge$ (conjunction) have their usual, classical logic interpretation. The term $[\phi_{P1}\mathbf{U}_{\phi_A}\phi_{P2}]_{>p\ (\geq p)}^{\leq t}$ expresses that, with probability greater than (or equal to) p, both ϕ_{P2} becomes true before t complete transitions have been performed, and ϕ_{P1} holds until ϕ_{P2} becomes true, with the additional constraint that each transition up to ϕ_2 becoming true has to satisfy ϕ_A. The term $[\mathbf{S}\phi_P]_{>p\ (\geq p)}$ denotes that, according to the steady-state behavior of the system, the probability of being in a state which satisfies ϕ_P is greater than (or equal to) p. Similarly, $[\mathbf{S}\phi_A]_{>p\ (\geq p)}$ expresses that, with probability greater than (or equal to) p, the system performs a complete transition for which ϕ_A is true.

Before presenting the formal semantics of PLTM, we introduce a number of useful concepts, adapted from the description of PCTL [9]. Given an initial network $N_0@l_0$, a path σ is an infinite sequence $\sigma = N_0@l_0 \xrightarrow{tr_{c1},l_1} N_1@l_1 \xrightarrow{tr_{c2},l_2} N_2@l_2 \xrightarrow{tr_{c3},l_3} \ldots$ of states and transitions, starting from $N_0@l_0$. Furthermore, a finite path σ_f is a finite sequence of states and transitions, originating in $N_0@l_0$, and ending either in a state or in a transition. The n-th state and the n-th transition in a path are denoted as $\sigma[n]$ and $\tau[n]$, respectively. Also, let $\sigma \uparrow_s n$ and $\sigma \uparrow_t n$ represent the finite paths starting in $N_0@l_0$, and ending in $\sigma[n]$ and $\tau[n]$, respectively. Moving to probabilities, let $paths^N_{N_0@l_0}$ denote the set of paths in N whose first state is $N_0@l_0$, and $\mu^N_{N_0@l_0}$ the probability measure over the sets from $paths^N_{N_0@l_0}$ induced by the probabilities of the complete transitions[2].

We can now define the semantics of PLTM. We start with action guards ϕ_A, since they are some of the basic elements of our logic. For the purpose of facilitating the description of their semantics, we represent any complete computational step $N@l \xrightarrow{tr_c,l'} N'@l'$ as a multiset of triplets $TR = TR_{MOVE} \cup TR_{COM}$. The multisets TR_{MOVE} and TR_{COM} are defined as follows:

- $TR_{MOVE} = \{\langle P, l, l_{new}\rangle \mid P \in Proc,\ l, l_{new} \in Loc,\ l_{new}@l \in tr_c$, such that $N \equiv l[[P]]|N^*$ and $l[[P]] \xrightarrow{l_{new}@l} l_{new}[[\circledS P']]\}$, and
- $TR_{COM} = \{\langle \{P_1, P_2\}, l, a\langle v\rangle \mid P_1, P_2 \in Proc,\ l \in Loc,\ a\langle v\rangle\rangle@l \in tr_c$, such that $N \equiv l[[P_1]]|l[[P_2]]|N^*$ and $l[[P_1]]|l[[P_2]] \xrightarrow{a\langle v\rangle@l} l[[\circledS P_1']]|l[[\circledS P_2']]\}$.

Basically, each triple $\langle P, l, act\rangle$ corresponds to an elementary transition from tr_c, for which source data has been added (i.e., the location at which the transition is performed, and the processes that generate the transition).

Definition 4 (Action Guards). *By using the multisets TR_{MOVE} and TR_{COM}, the semantics of the guards ϕ_A can now be defined inductively. The resulting semantics is described in Table 4. Formally, a complete transition TR satisfies an action guard ϕ_A, denoted by $TR \vDash \phi_A$, iff $\phi_A(TR) =$ **true**.*

As expected, guards are Boolean functions which operate over complete transitions. Since PLTM is a quantitative logic, the basic element of a guard is the total number of elementary transitions that satisfy a certain arithmetic expression over elementary matchers or enhanced matchers. Thus, guards verify quantitative relations over certain sets of elementary transitions (i.e., comparison expressions over arithmetic terms, or, at the highest level, logical formulas.

Once the guards have been properly defined, we can now present the semantics for probability queries ϕ_P. In doing so, we rely on the auxiliary formula $[\phi_{P1} \mathbf{U}_{\phi_A} \phi_{P2}]^{\leq t}$, which is a path formula (unlike all the other formulas in PLTM, which operate over states or complete transitions).

Definition 5 (Path Properties). *In order to formalize the notion that a state $N_x@l_x$ (reached by the network $N = N_0@l_0$) satisfies the path query ϕ_P, denoted*

[2] This probability measure is discussed in more detail on page 20 of [5].

Table 4. Satisfiability of Action Guards

Elementary matchers:	
$l'(TR)$	$= \{\langle Pr, loc, act\rangle \in TR_{MOVE} \mid act = l'\}$
$MOVE(TR)$	$= TR_{MOVE}$
$a\langle v\rangle(TR)$	$= \{\langle Pr, loc, act\rangle \in TR_{COM} \mid act = a\langle v\rangle\}$
$a\langle MSG\rangle(TR)$	$= \{\langle Pr, loc, act\rangle \in TR_{COM} \mid channel(act) = a\}$
$COM\langle v\rangle(TR)$	$= \{\langle Pr, loc, act\rangle \in TR_{COM} \mid message(act) = v\}$
$COM\langle MSG\rangle(TR)$	$= TR_{COM}$
Enhanced matchers:	
$(tran\ \mathtt{at}\ l)(TR)$	$= \{\langle Pr, loc, act\rangle \in tran(TR) \mid loc = l\}$
$(tran\ \mathtt{by}\ P)(TR)$	$= \{\langle Pr, loc, act\rangle \in tran(TR) \mid Pr = P \text{ or } P \in Pr\}$
$(tran\ \mathtt{by}\ P\ \mathtt{at}\ l)(TR)$	$= \{\langle Pr, loc, act\rangle \in tran(TR) \mid (Pr = P \text{ or } P \in Pr) \text{ and } loc = l\}$
Arithmetic expressions:	
$const(TR)$	$= const$
$(\#(tran))(TR)$	$= \lvert tran(TR)\rvert$
$(\#(tran_e))(TR)$	$= \lvert tran_e(TR)\rvert$
$(arit_1\ \phi_{arit}\ arit_2)(TR)$	$= arit_1(TR)\ \phi_{arit}\ arit_2(TR)$
Comparison expressions:	
$(arit\ \phi_{cmp}\ const)(TR)$	$= arit(TR)\ \phi_{cmp}\ const(TR)$
$(arit_1\ \phi_{cmp}\ arit_2)(TR)$	$= arit_1(TR)\ \phi_{cmp}\ arit_2(TR)$
Logical expressions:	
$\mathtt{true}(TR)$	$= \mathtt{true}$
$(log_1\ \phi_{log}\ log_2)(TR)$	$= log_1(TR)\ \phi_{log}\ log_2(TR)$

by $N_x@l_x \vDash_N \phi_P$, we use induction on ϕ_P and define two satisfaction relations, namely $\vDash_N$ and $\vdash_N$, in Table 5.

We employ the notation $P(N, N_x@l_x, [\phi_{P1}\mathbf{U}_{\phi_A}\phi_{P2}]^{\leq t})$ to refer to the term $\mu^N_{N_x@l_x}(\sigma \mid \sigma[0] = N_x@l_x$ and $\sigma \vdash_N [\phi_{P1}\mathbf{U}_{\phi_A}\phi_{P2}]^{\leq t})$, where σ is a path and t is a network time. Based on the semantics for ϕ_A and ϕ_P, we can define the semantics for the steady-state queries ϕ_S, by extending the satisfaction relation $\vDash_N$.

Definition 6 (Steady-State Properties). *The steady-state probability of a network N being in state $N_y@l_y$, after having started in the state $N_x@l_x$, can be computed as*

$$SS_{N_x@l_x}(N_y@l_y) = \lim_{n\to\infty} \mu^N_{N_x@l_x}(\sigma \mid \sigma[n] = N_y@l_y \text{ and } \sigma[0] = N_x@l_x)^3.$$

[3] We restrict our definition of steady-state measures to pTiMo networks which generate finite, ergodic discrete-time Markov chains, for which the limiting behavior of the networks is guaranteed to exist and can be computed easily [8]. Like in the case of other process algebras (e.g., PEPA [11]), it is the task of the modeler to make sure that a network has the required properties.

Table 5. Satisfiability of Probability Properties

$N_x@l_x \models_N prop$	iff $prop \in labels(N_x@l_x)$
$N_x@l_x \models_N \neg\phi_P$	iff not $N_x@l_x \models_N \phi_P$
$N_x@l_x \models_N \phi_{P1} \wedge \phi_{P2}$	iff $N_x@l_x \models_N \phi_{P1}$ and $N_x@l_x \models_N \phi_{P2}$
$\sigma \vdash_N [\phi_{P1}\mathbf{U}_{\phi_A}\phi_{P2}]^{\leq t}$	iff there exists $i \in \mathbb{N}$ such that $t(\sigma[i]) \leq t$ and $\sigma[i] \models_N \phi_{P2}$ and $\sigma[j] \models_N \phi_{P1}$, for all j between 0 and $i-1$, and $\tau[k] \models \phi_A$, for all k between 1 and i
$N_x@l_x \models_N [\phi_{P1}\mathbf{U}_{\phi_A}\phi_{P2}]^{\leq t}_{\geq p}$	iff $\mu^N_{N_x@l_x}(\sigma \mid \sigma[0] = N_x@l_x,\ \sigma \vdash_N [\phi_{P1}\mathbf{U}_{\phi_A}\phi_{P2}]^{\leq t}) \geq p$
$N_x@l_x \models_N [\phi_{P1}\mathbf{U}_{\phi_A}\phi_{P2}]^{\leq t}_{>p}$	iff $\mu^N_{N_x@l_x}(\sigma \mid \sigma[0] = N_x@l_x,\ \sigma \vdash_N [\phi_{P1}\mathbf{U}_{\phi_A}\phi_{P2}]^{\leq t}) > p$

The steady-state probability of the network N performing a complete transition (tr_c, l'), after having started in the state $N_x@l_x$, can be derived as

$$SS_{N_x@l_x}(tr_c, l') = \lim_{n\to\infty} \mu^N_{N_x@l_x}(\sigma \mid \tau[n] = (tr_c, l') \text{ and } \sigma[0] = N_x@l_x) =$$
$$= \sum_{N_y@l_y, N'@l'} SS_{N_x@l_x}(N_y@l_y) \cdot P(N_y@l_y \xrightarrow{tr_c, l'} N'@l').$$

The satisfaction relation $\models_N$ for ϕ_S is defined inductively, in Table 6.

Table 6. Satisfiability of Steady-State Properties

$N_x@l_x \models_N [\mathbf{S}\phi_P]_{\geq p\ (>p)}$	iff $\sum_{N_y@l_y \models_N \phi_P} SS_{N_x@l_x}(N_y@l_y) \geq p\ (> p)$
$N_x@l_x \models_N [\mathbf{S}\phi_A]_{\geq p\ (>p)}$	iff $\sum_{(tr_c, l') \models \phi_A} SS_{N_x@l_x}(tr_c, l') \geq p\ (> p)$

A simple model checking algorithm for PLTM can be obtained by adapting the standard algorithm for verifying PCTL; our algorithm is based on the approach described in [13]. We do not include a proof of soundness and completeness for our algorithm, for reasons of brevity and due to the fact that it can be easily derived from the corresponding proof for PCTL. The algorithm takes as inputs a pTiMo network N, in the form of a discrete-time Markov chain $\mathcal{D} = (\mathcal{S}, N_0@l_0, \mathcal{T})$, a labeling function L, and a PLTM formula ϕ, where $\phi = \phi_P$ or $\phi = \phi_A$. The output produced by the algorithm is the set $Sat(\phi) = \{N_x@l_x \in \mathcal{S} \mid N_x@l_x \models_N \phi\}$, which means that $N_x@l_x \models_N \phi$ iff $N_x@l_x \in Sat(\phi)$ for any state $N_x@l_x \in \mathcal{S}$. The algorithm first involves generating the parse tree for the property ϕ, in which every subtree is labeled with a subproperty of ϕ, the root node is labeled with the complete property ϕ, and the leaves are labeled with atomic propositions and `true`. Starting from the leaves of the tree, the algorithm recursively determines all the states that satisfy each subproperty of ϕ, until it reaches the root node and

Table 7. Conditions for Property Satisfaction

$$Sat(\mathtt{true}) = \mathcal{S}$$
$$Sat(prop) = \{N_x@l_x \in \mathcal{S} \mid prop \in L(N_x@l_x)\}$$
$$Sat(\neg\phi_P) = \mathcal{S} \setminus Sat(\phi_P)$$
$$Sat(\phi_{P1} \wedge \phi_{P2}) = Sat(\phi_{P1}) \cap Sat(\phi_{P2})$$
$$Sat([\phi_{P1}\mathbf{U}_{\phi_A}\phi_{P2}]^{\leq t}_{\geq p\ (>p)}) = \{N_x@l_x \in \mathcal{S} \mid P(N, N_x@l_x, [\phi_{P1}\mathbf{U}_{\phi_A}\phi_{P2}]^{\leq t}) \geq p\ (> p)\}$$
$$Sat([\mathbf{S}\phi_P]_{\geq p\ (>p)}) = \{N_x@l_x \in \mathcal{S} \mid \sum_{N_y@l_y \in Sat(\phi_P)} SS_{N_x@l_x}(N_y@l_y) \geq p\ (> p)\}$$
$$Sat([\mathbf{S}\phi_A]_{\geq p\ (>p)}) = \{N_x@l_x \in \mathcal{S} \mid \sum_{(tr_c, l') \in \mathcal{T}[\phi_A]} SS_{N_x@l_x}(tr_c, l') \geq p\ (> p)\}$$

produces the set $Sat(\phi)$. Considering $\mathcal{T}[\phi_A] = \{(tr_c, l') \in \mathcal{T} \mid (tr_c, l') \vDash \phi_A\}$, the set $Sat(\phi)$ can be constructed according to Table 7.

Properties of the form $\mathtt{true}$, *prop*, $\neg\phi_P$ and $\phi_{P1} \wedge \phi_{P2}$ can be checked easily, through elementary set operations. In order to verify properties of the form $[\phi_{P1}\mathbf{U}_{\phi_A}\phi_{P2}]^{\leq t}_{\geq p}$ or $[\phi_{P1}\mathbf{U}_{\phi_A}\phi_{P2}]^{\leq t}_{>p}$, it is enough to determine the probability $P(N, N_x@l_x, [\phi_{P1}\mathbf{U}_{\phi_A}\phi_{P2}]^{\leq t})$, which is used in defining these two types of queries. To simplify the notation, let $t \ominus l_x$ denote the temporal bound such that $(t \ominus l_x)@l_x = t@l_x - 1$, and $(t \ominus l_x)@l_y = t@l_y$, for any location $l_y \neq l_x$. Furthermore, in keeping with the meaning of the bound, we assume that if $t@l_x = \infty$, then $(t \ominus l_x)@l_x = \infty$, and also, that $(t \ominus l_x)@l_x$ is undefined if $t@l_x = 0$. The standard approach (employed, for example, in PRISM [13]) is to compute the probabilities $P(N, N_x@l_x, [\phi_{P1}\mathbf{U}_{\phi_A}\phi_{P2}]^{\leq t})$ for all the states $N_x@l_x \in \mathcal{S}$, by solving a certain set of linear equations. More precisely, the value of $P(N, N_x@l_x, [\phi_{P1}\mathbf{U}_{\phi_A}\phi_{P2}]^{\leq t})$ is expressed recursively in terms of the values for $P(N, N_y@l_y, [\phi_{P1}\mathbf{U}_{\phi_A}\phi_{P2}]^{\leq t \ominus l_x})$, where $N_y@l_y$ is a state that can be reached from $N_x@l_x$ by performing a complete transition. This procedure is based on the following property of the satisfaction relation $\vdash_N$:

Proposition 1. *For any path σ and $t \in \mathbb{T}$, we have $\sigma \vdash_N [\phi_{P1}\mathbf{U}_{\phi_A}\phi_{P2}]^{\leq t}$ iff:*

- *$t@l_x = 0$ and $\sigma[0] \vDash_N \phi_{P2}$, or*
- *$t@l_x > 0$ and $\sigma[0] \vDash_N \phi_{P1}$ and $\tau[1] \in \mathcal{T}[\phi_A]$ and $\sigma' \vdash_N [\phi_{P1}\mathbf{U}_{\phi_A}\phi_{P2}]^{\leq t \ominus l_x}$, where $\sigma'[i] = \sigma[i+1]$, for $i \geq 0$, $\tau'[j] = \tau[j+1]$, for $j \geq 1$, and $\sigma[0] = N_x@l_x$*

The proof follows immediately from the conditions for $\sigma \vdash_N [\phi_{P1}\mathbf{U}_{\phi_A}\phi_{P2}]^{\leq t}$. By using this property and the probability measures defined earlier, the computation of $P(N, N_x@l_x, [\phi_{P1}\mathbf{U}_{\phi_A}\phi_{P2}]^{\leq t})$ is equivalent to finding the unique solution of the following set of equations:

$P(N, N_x@l_x, [\phi_{P1}\mathbf{U}_{\phi_A}\phi_{P2}]^{\leq t'}) =$

- 1, if $N_x@l_x \in Sat(\phi_{P2})$, else
- 0, if $N_x@l_x \in Sat(\neg\phi_{P1} \wedge \neg\phi_{P2})$, or $t'@l_x = 0$, or $\mathcal{T}[\phi_A] = \emptyset$, else
- $\sum_{tr \in \mathcal{T}[\phi_A]} P(tr)P(dest(tr), [\phi_{P1}\mathbf{U}_{\phi_A}\phi_{P2}]^{\leq t' \ominus l_x})$, otherwise.

for any $N_x@l_x \in \mathcal{S}$ and $t' \leq t$, where $dest(tr)$ denotes the state entered by the network after performing the complete transition tr.

Finally, checking properties of the form $[\mathbf{S}\phi_P]_{\geq p}$, $[\mathbf{S}\phi_P]_{>p}$, $[\mathbf{S}\phi_A]_{\geq p}$ and $[\mathbf{S}\phi_A]_{>p}$ is straightforward, once the equilibrium (i.e., steady-state) distribution for $\mathcal{D}$ and the sets $Sat(\phi_P)$ and $\mathcal{T}[\phi_A]$ have been computed. Finding the set $\mathcal{T}[\phi_A]$ involves recursively applying the definitions given in Table 4, for each complete transition from $\mathcal{T}$.

To estimate the computational complexity of the model checking algorithm, we first define the auxiliary functions $fs : \mathbb{T} \to \mathbb{N}$ and $steps : (\mathbb{N} \cup \infty) \to \mathbb{N}$, such that $fs(t) = \prod_{i=1}^{|Loc|} steps(t@loc_i)$, where $steps(n) = n + 1$ for any $n \in \mathbb{N}$, and $steps(\infty) = 1$. Moreover, let $length(\phi)$ denote the length of the property ϕ, as defined in [9], which is equal to the total number of logical and temporal operators from ϕ plus the sum of the sizes of all the temporal operators from ϕ (i.e., $size([\phi_{P1}\mathbf{U}_{\phi_A}\phi_{P2}]^{\leq t}_{\geq p} = size([\phi_{P1}\mathbf{U}_{\phi_A}\phi_{P2}]^{\leq t}_{>p}) = fs(t))$. In the case of probability properties (i.e., if $\phi = \phi_P$), the most computationally expensive stages of the algorithm are those which involve solving the sets of linear equations generated by properties of the form $[\phi_{P1}\mathbf{U}_{\phi_A}\phi_{P2}]^{\leq t}_{\geq p}$ or $[\phi_{P1}\mathbf{U}_{\phi_A}\phi_{P2}]^{\leq t}_{>p}$. Each such stage requires at most $\mathcal{O}(fs(t) \cdot |\mathcal{S}| \cdot |\mathcal{T}|)$ elementary operations to complete, given that the associated system contains $fs(t) \cdot |\mathcal{S}|$ linear equations, involving $|\mathcal{T}|$ elementary operations each. Therefore, the overall time complexity for checking ϕ is at most $\mathcal{O}(length(\phi) \cdot size_{max} \cdot |\mathcal{S}| \cdot |\mathcal{T}|)$, where $size_{max}$ denotes the maximum value for $fs(t)$, over all the temporal bounds t which appear in ϕ. However, in the case of steady-state properties (i.e., if $\phi = \phi_A$), the most time-consuming operation is deriving the equilibrium distribution for $\mathcal{D}$, which involves solving a set of $\mathcal{S}$ linear equations with at most $\mathcal{S}$ variables, requiring at most $\mathcal{O}(|\mathcal{S}|^3)$ elementary operations to complete.

Proposition 2. *The overall time complexity for verifying ϕ is at most $\mathcal{O}(|\mathcal{S}|^3 + length(\phi) \cdot size_{max} \cdot |\mathcal{S}| \cdot |\mathcal{T}|)$, where $length(\phi)$ is the length of the property ϕ.*

3 Conclusion

This paper presents a probabilistic extension for the process calculus TiMo. The new formalism, namely pTiMo, assigns probabilities to the complete transitions that describe the behavior of TiMo networks, by solving the nondeterminism involved in the movement and in the communication of processes, as well as in the selection of active locations. Also, process movements are redefined such that they can now occur anytime before a deadline (i.e., not only at deadline expiration).

The main contribution of the paper is the introduction of the probabilistic temporal logic PLTM, which is inspired by the existing logic PCTL [9], but includes a number of features not commonly found in other logics, such as the ability to check properties which make explicit reference to specific locations and/or processes, to impose temporal constraints over local clocks (i.e., finite or infinite upper bounds, for each location independently), and to define complex action guards over multisets of actions. Given that PLTM operates at the level of discrete-time Markov chains, it can also be adapted for and applied to other process algebras which involve locations, timers, process movements and communications, as well as non-atomic, structured transitions. Finally, we sketch a verification algorithm for PLTM, and determine its time complexity.

As further work, we intend to study the properties of certain behavioral equivalences defined over pTiMo networks, as well as to develop a software tool for PLTM, in order to demonstrate the practical utility of this logic.

Acknowledgements. The work was supported by a grant of the Romanian National Authority for Scientific Research CNCS-UEFISCDI, project number PN-II-ID-PCE-2011-3-0919.

References

1. Aman, B., Ciobanu, G., Koutny, M.: Behavioural Equivalences over Migrating Processes with Timers. In: Giese, H., Rosu, G. (eds.) FORTE/FMOODS 2012. LNCS, vol. 7273, pp. 52–66. Springer, Heidelberg (2012)
2. Berger, M.: Towards Abstractions For Distributed Systems. PhD thesis, Imperial College, Department of Computing (2002)
3. Ciobanu, G., Juravle, C.: A Software Platform for Timed Mobility and Timed Interaction. In: Lee, D., Lopes, A., Poetzsch-Heffter, A. (eds.) FMOODS/FORTE 2009. LNCS, vol. 5522, pp. 106–121. Springer, Heidelberg (2009)
4. Ciobanu, G., Koutny, M.: Timed mobility in process algebra and Petri nets. J. Log. Algebr. Program. 80(7), 377–391 (2011)
5. Ciobanu, G., Rotaru, A.: A Probabilistic Query Language for Migrating Processes with Timers. Technical Report FML-12-01, Formal Methods Laboratory, Institute of Computer Science, Romanian Academy (2012)
6. Ciobanu, G., Prisacariu, C.: Timers for distributed systems. Electron. Notes Theor. Comput. Sci. 164(3), 81–99 (2006)
7. De Nicola, R., Ferrari, G., Pugliese, R.: KLAIM: A Kernel Language for Agents Interaction and Mobility. IEEE T. Software Eng. 24(5), 315–329 (1998)
8. Feller, W.: An Introduction to Probability Theory and Its Applications, 3rd edn., vol. 1. Wiley (1968)
9. Hansson, H., Jonsson, B.: A logic for reasoning about time and reliability. Form. Asp. Comput. 6(5), 512–535 (1994)
10. Hennessy, M.: A distributed π-calculus. Cambridge University Press (2007)
11. Hillston, J.: A Compositional Approach to Performance Modelling. Cambridge University Press (1996)
12. Huth, M.: The interval domain: a matchmaker for aCTL and aPCTL. Electron. Notes Theor. Comput. Sci. 14, 134–148 (1998)
13. Kwiatkowska, M., Norman, G., Parker, D.: Stochastic Model Checking. In: Bernardo, M., Hillston, J. (eds.) SFM 2007. LNCS, vol. 4486, pp. 220–270. Springer, Heidelberg (2007)
14. Sewell, P., et al.: Acute: High-Level Programming Language Design for Distributed Computation. J. Funct. Program. 17, 547–612 (2007)

An Interface Model of Software Components*

Ruzhen Dong[1,2], Naijun Zhan[3], and Liang Zhao[4]

[1] Dipartmento di Informatica, Università di Pisa, Italy
[2] UNU-IIST, Macau
ruzhen@iist.unu.edu
[3] State Key Lab. of Computer Science, Institute of Software, Chinese Academy of Sciences
znj@ios.ac.cn
[4] Institute of Computing Theory and Technology, Xidian University
lzhao@xidian.edu.cn

Abstract. We present an automata-based model for describing the behaviors of software components. This extends our previous work by allowing internal behaviors. In order to improve the techniques for checking if two component can be composed without causing deadlocks, we develop an interface model, called input deterministic automata, that define all the non-blockable traces of invocation to services provided by a component. We also present an algorithm that, for any given component automaton, generates the interface model that has the same input deterministic behaviors as the original automaton. Properties of the algorithm with respect to component refinement and composition are studied as preliminary results towards a theory of software component interfaces.

1 Introduction

In component-based software engineering [25,10], large software systems are composed/decomposed from/into components with clearly stated interfaces in order to facilitate a sound development process across different teams of developers exploiting existing software components. An interface theory [1,12,4] should then define the basic principles for composing several software components based on their interfaces, as the concrete implementation of the components is invisible to its environment. On the other hand, an interface theory should also define a refinement relation that if component C' refines component C then C' can substitute C in any context. This means that components can be treated as black-boxes, and the theory allows for independent implementation, substitution, and deployment [2,24,17].

In our previous work [7], we studied the interface model of components that comprise *provided* and *required* interface that describes which services the

* Part of the work of the second author was done during his visit to UNU-IIST in February 2013 and he wishes to thank the support from project PEARL funded by Macau Science and Technology Development Fund, and the work of the third author was mainly done when he was working at UNU-IIST as a postdoctoral research fellow supported by PEARL.

Z. Liu, J. Woodcock, and H. Zhu (Eds.): ICTAC 2013, LNCS 8049, pp. 159–176, 2013.

component offers to its environment and specifies what services the component needs to call in order to provide the services on its provided interface, respectively. *Run-to-completeness* is assumed in our model, which means that an invocation of a provided service either is not executed at all, or has to be completed, cannot be interrupted by its environment during the execution.

In this paper, component models we considered in [7] are extended with *internal actions* which are invisible to the environment. Components are adapted with some provided services internalized to restrict these services from being called by the environment for safety or privacy reasons. The interface model should still guarantee provided services non-blockable whenever these provided services are called. So, we show that the interface model is *input-deterministic*, meaning that any invocation to the provided service according to the interface model is guaranteed to be non-blockable.

In order to construct an interface model for any given execution model with internal behaviors, we first study what kinds of provided services are *nonrefusal* at a given state, that is, the provided services are never blocked by the component when the environment calls at the state. Then we study whether sequence of provided services with possible internal behaviors interleaved is blocked or not. A provided service m is nonrefusal at state s if m is available at all the internally reachable stable states at which there are no internal behaviors available. Based on these, we revise the algorithm in [7] to get an algorithm that generates an interface model, whose non-blockable behavior is same as the considered component.

Two components are composed by service invocation, which is event synchronization in the automata-based model. Service invocation fails if the service declared in the provided interface is not available when it is called by the environment or the component also needs services from the environment to provide the service called by the environment.

We define a refinement relation based on state simulation [21,5], and show that a component can be substituted by any its refinement as far as nonrefusal provided services at each state are concerned. The intuitive idea of refinement is that a refined component can provide more services while requiring less.

Related Work. The work is based on the rCOS unified model of components [12,3,17,4] that define components in terms of their provided and required interface interaction behaviors, data model and local data functionality (including those models in OO programming [11]). This paper focuses on the interface interaction behaviors and aims to develop an interface theory based on I/O automata.

There are two main well known approaches to interface theories, the Input/Output(I/O) Automata [19,18] and the Interface Automata [5,1,6]. And there are also some works extending these with modalities [16,22,23,20].

As argued in [7], our approach is positioned in between these existing approaches. I/O automata are defined by Lynch and Tuttle to model concurrent and distributed discrete event systems. The main features of the I/O automata are *input-enabledness* and *pessimistic* compatibility. The input-enabledness requires that all the input actions should be available at any state. The pessimism is that two components are compatible if there is no deadlock in the composition for any environment. On the contrary, our interface model does not require that all inputs are always enabled, because there are guards for provided services in software components, while the interface model is input-deterministic to guarantee that all the sequences of provided services with possible internal behaviors interleaved can never be blocked when the environment calls.

Alfaro and Henzinger introduce interface automata to model reactive components that have an assume-guarantee relation with the environment. Two components are compatible in an optimistic way in the sense that two components are compatible if there exists one environment that can make the composition avoid deadlock. This compatibility condition may be too relaxed since the usability of the provided service of a component depends not only on the components to be composed with and also the environment for the composition. To this end, Giannalopoulou et al [8,9] develop assume-guarantee rules and tools to reason about compatibility and weakest assumptions for any given interface automaton, while Larson et al [15] present interface models for any given I/O automaton by splitting assumptions from guarantees. In contrast to these approaches, we present an interface model that directly specifies the non-blockable sequences of provided services independent of the environment and develop an algorithm to generate such interface model based on the execution model of any given component.

Summary of Contributions. The contributions of this paper are (1) a new interface model ensuring non-blockable provided services of software components with internal behaviors under any environment. (2) a revised algorithm to generate the interface model of a component based on its execution model with internal behaviors. (3) composition operators. (4) a refinement relation, which provides a criterion for substitution of components.

Outline of the Paper. The rest of the paper is organized as follows. In Sect. 2, we introduce component automata and related concepts. In Section 3, we show non-blockable sequences of provided events and the algorithm to generate the interface model from the execution model. In Section 4, we present the composition operators. In Section 5, we define a refinement relation based on state simulation and prove compositional results. In Section 6, we conclude the paper and discuss future work.

2 Component Automata

We start with a general execution model of components. This model is used by the component designers who needs to know how the and from what (composite) component is composed. They need to use the model to verify the safety and livelock of the component. Thus it contains the full information about the determinisms and non-determinism of the component. Before we define this model. we first introduce some notations that will be used.

2.1 Preliminary Definitions

For any $w_1, w_2 \in \mathcal{L}^*$, the sequence concatenation of w_1 and w_2 is denoted as $w_1 \circ w_2$ and extended to sets of sequences, that is, $A \circ B$ is $\{w_1 \circ w_2 \mid w_1 \in A,\ w_2 \in B\}$ where $A, B \subseteq \mathcal{L}^*$ are two sets of sequences of elements from $\mathcal{L}$. Given $a \in L$, we use $w_1 \circ a$ as $w_1 \circ \langle a \rangle$. Given a sequence of sets of sequences $\langle A_1, \ldots, A_k \rangle$ with $k \geq 0$, we denote $A_1 \circ \cdots A_k$ as $conc(\langle A_1, \ldots, A_k \rangle)$. We use ϵ as notion of empty sequence, that is, $\epsilon \circ w = w \circ \epsilon = w$. Given a sequence w, we use $last(w)$ to denote the last element of w.

Let ℓ be a pair (x, y), we denote $\pi_1(\ell) = x$ and $\pi_2(\ell) = y$. Given any sequence of pairs $tr = \langle \ell_1, \ldots, \ell_k \rangle$ and a set of sequences of pairs T, it is naturally extended that $\pi_i(tr) = \langle \pi_i(\ell_1), \ldots, \pi_i(\ell_k) \rangle$, $\pi_i(T) = \{\pi_i(tr) \mid tr \in T\}$ where $i \in \{1, 2\}$.

Let $tr \in A$ and $\Sigma \subseteq \mathcal{L}$, $tr\lfloor_\Sigma$ is a sequence obtained by removing all the elements that are not in Σ from tr. And we extend this to a set of sequences $T\lfloor_\Sigma = \{tr\lfloor_\Sigma \mid tr \in T\}$.

Given a sequence of pairs tr, $tr\lfloor^1_P$ is a sequence obtained by removing the elements whose first entry is not in P. For a sequence of elements $\alpha = \langle a_1, \cdots, a_k \rangle$, $pair(\alpha) = \langle (a_1, \{a_1\}), \cdots, (a_k, \{a_k\}) \rangle$.

2.2 Execution Model of a Component

In this part, we introduce our formal model describing interaction behaviors of components. Provided and required services are modeled as provided and required events, respectively. Internal actions are modeled as internal events. The invocation of a provided service or an internal action will trigger invoking services provided by other components, so the label on a transition step in the formal model consists a provided or internal event and a set of sequences of required events.

Definition 1. *A tuple $C = (S, s_0, f, P, R, A, \delta)$ is called a* component automaton *where*

- *S is a finite set of states, and $s_0 \in S$ is the initial state, $f \in S$ is the error state;*
- *P, R, and A are disjoint and finite sets of provided, required, and internal events, respectively;*
- *$\delta \subseteq (S \setminus \{f\}) \times \Sigma(P, R, A) \times (S \cup \{f\})$ is the transition relation, where the set of labels is defined as $\Sigma(P, R, A) = (P \cup A) \times (2^{R^*} \setminus \emptyset)$.*

Whenever there is $(s, \ell, s') \in \delta$ with $\ell = (w, T)$, we simply write it as $s \xrightarrow{w/T} s'$ and call it a provided transition step if $w \in P$, otherwise internal transition step. We call $s \xrightarrow{a/T} f$ a failure transition, which will be discussed in detail in Section 4. We write $s \xrightarrow{w/} s'$ for $s \xrightarrow{w/\{\epsilon\}} s'$. The internal events are prefixed with ; to differentiate them from the provided events. We use τ to represent any internal event when it causes no confusion. For a state s we use $out(s)$ denote $\{w \in P \cup A \mid \exists s', w, T.s \xrightarrow{w/T} s'\}$ and $out^\bullet(s) = out(s) \cap P$ and $out^\circ(s) = out(s) \cap A$. We write $s \xrightarrow{w/\bullet} s'$ for $s \xrightarrow{w/T} s'$, when T is not essential.

An alternating sequence of states and labels of the form

$$e = \langle s_1, \ell_1, \ldots, s_k, \ell_k, s_{k+1} \rangle$$

is denoted as $s_1 \xRightarrow{\ell_1, \cdots, \ell_k} s_{k+1}$ with $k > 0$ and $s_i \xrightarrow{\ell_i} s_{i+1}$ for all i with $0 < i \leq k$.

It is called an *execution* of the component automaton C, if s_1 is the initial state s_0. The set $\{\langle \ell_1, \ldots, \ell_k \rangle \mid s \xRightarrow{\ell_1, \ldots, \ell_k} s' \text{ is an execution}\}$ is denoted as $\mathcal{T}(s)$. An element in $\mathcal{T}(s_0)$ is called a *trace* of component automaton C and $\mathcal{T}(s_0)$ is also written as $\mathcal{T}(C)$.

$\{\pi_1(tr)\downharpoonright_P \mid tr \in \mathcal{T}(s)\}$ is denoted as $\mathcal{T}_p(s)$ and $pt \in \mathcal{T}_p(s_0)$ is called a *provided trace* of component automaton C, so $\mathcal{T}_p(s_0)$ is also written as $\mathcal{T}_p(C)$. Given a provided trace pt, we write $s \xRightarrow{pt} s'$, if there exists $tr \in \mathcal{T}(s)$ that $s \xRightarrow{tr} s'$ with $\pi_1(tr)\downharpoonright_P$.

For a provided trace pt of C, the set $\mathcal{T}_r(pt)$ of required traces for pt is defined as $\mathcal{T}_r(pt) = \{conc(\pi_2(tr)) \mid \pi_1(tr)\downharpoonright_P = pt, \text{ and } last(\pi_1(tr)) \in P\}$.

Next, we will use the example shown in [7] with *wifi* hidden as an internal behavior, which means that the component automatically connects *wifi* internally.

Example 1. As a demonstrating example, we consider a simple internet-connection component presented in Fig. 1. It provides the services *login*, *print*, and *read* available to the environment and there is an internal service ; *wifi*. The services model the logging into the system, invocation of printing a document, an email service, and automatically connecting the wifi, respectively. The component calls the services *unu1*, *unu2*, *cserv*, *cprint*, and *senddoc*. The first three of them model the searching for a wifi router nearby, connecting to the *unu1* or *unu2* wireless network, and connecting to an application server, respectively. The *cprint* and *senddoc* are services that connect to the printer, sends the document to print and start the printing job. The *print* service is only available for the wifi network *unu1* and *read* can be accessed at both networks.

In the component model of Fig. 1 we can perform e.g.

$$e = \langle 0, (login/\{\epsilon\}), 1, (;\, wifi/\{unu1\}), 2, (print/\{cprint \cdot senddoc\}), 2 \rangle \ .$$

Now $pt = \langle login, print \rangle$ is a provided trace of the execution e and the set of required traces of pt is $\mathcal{T}_r(pt) = \{unu1 \cdot cprint \cdot senddoc\}$. This example will be used throughout this paper to show the features of our model.

3 Interface Model

The execution model of a component describes how the component interacts with the environment by providing and requiring services. However, some provided transition or execution may fail due to non-determinism or transitions to the error state. In this section, we will discuss about non-blockableness of provided events and traces.

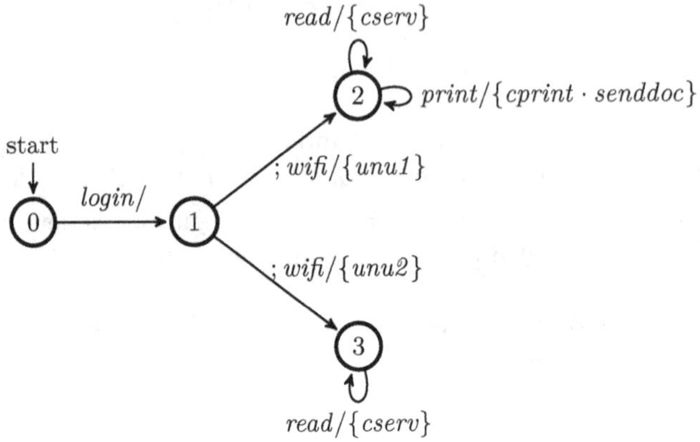

Fig. 1. Execution model of internet connection component C_{ic}

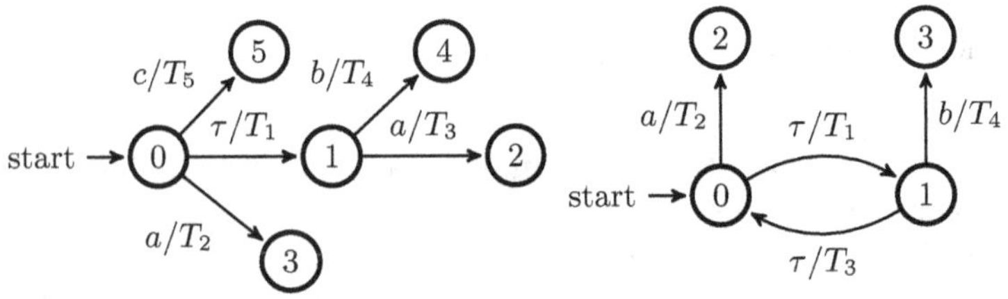

Fig. 2.

We call a state s *divergent* if there exists a sequence of internal transitions to s from s or s can transit to such kinds of states via a sequence of internal transitions.

Definition 2 (divergent state). *A state s is* divergent, *if there exists tr with $\pi_1(tr) \in A^+$ such that $s \stackrel{tr}{\Longrightarrow} s$ or there exists s', $tr_1 \in A^+$ and $tr_2 \in A^+$ such that $s \stackrel{tr_1}{\Longrightarrow} s'$ and $s' \stackrel{tr_2}{\Longrightarrow} s'$.*

A state s is *stable*, if $out(s) \subseteq P$, that is, there is no internal transition from state s. Internally reachable states of state s is $\{s' \mid s \stackrel{tr}{\Longrightarrow} s' \text{ with } \pi_1(tr) \in A^*\}$, written as $intR^\circ(s)$. We use $intR^\bullet(s)$ to denote the set of internally reachable stable states, which is empty if there exists a divergent state s' with $s' \in intR^\circ(s)$, otherwise $intR^\bullet(s) = \{s' \text{ is stable } \mid s' \in intR^\circ(s)\}$.

Definition 3 (nonrefusal provided event). *Given a component automaton $C = (S, s_0, f, P, R, A, \delta)$, for any $s \in S$, the set of nonrefusal provided events of s is $\mathcal{N}(s) = \bigcap_{r \in intR^\bullet(s)} out^\bullet(r) \setminus \{a \mid s \stackrel{a}{\Longrightarrow} f\}$.*

Intuitively, a provided event a being *nonrefusal* at state s means that any invocation to it is not possible to be blocked when the component automaton is at state s. For example, consider state 0 of the component automaton shown on the left of Fig. 2. From the viewpoint of the environment, the component automaton may be at 0 or 1, because there is an internal transition from 0 to 1. We assume that after some time, the component will eventually move to state 1, because 0 is not a stable state. So we can see that event $c \in out^\bullet(0)$, c is not *nonrefusal* at state 0, because $c \notin out^\bullet(1)$. However, if the environment requires b, the component can react to this invocation successfully, that is, b is nonrefusal at state 0. The nonrefusal provided events are determined by internally reachable stable states. In the component automaton shown on the right part of Fig. 2, there are no internally reachable stable states from state 0, therefore the set of its nonrefusal provided events is empty. We also make events from a given state, if it may lead the component automaton to the error state f.

The nonrefusal provided events assure non-blockableness of a single provided event at a given state. Next, we will introduce non-blockable provided traces which can never be blocked by the component when the environment calls such provided traces.

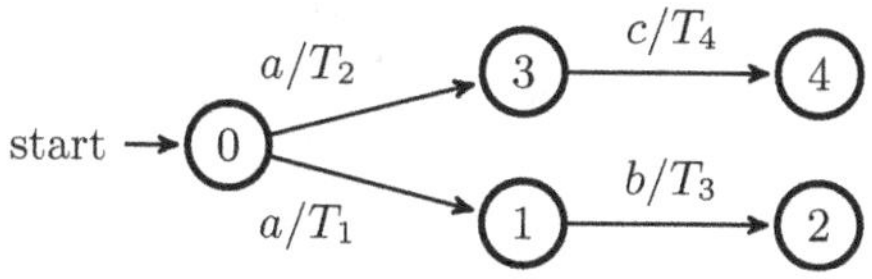

Fig. 3.

Let's consider the component automaton shown in Fig. 3. We can see that a is nonrefusal at state 0, but, after the invocation of a, the component determines whether to move to state 1 or 3. So both of b and c may be blocked after a.

A sequence of provided events $\langle a_1, \cdots, a_k \rangle$ with $k \geq 0$ is *non-blockable* at state s, if $a_i \in \mathcal{N}(s')$ for any $1 \leq i \leq k$ and s' such that $s \stackrel{tr}{\Longrightarrow} s'$ with $\pi_1(tr)\downharpoonright_P = \langle a_1, \cdots, a_{i-1} \rangle$. A sequence of pairs tr is *non-blockable* at s, if $\pi_1(tr)\downharpoonright_P$ is non-blockable at s. We use $\mathcal{T}_{up}(s)$ and $\mathcal{T}_u(s)$ to denote the set of all non-blockable provided traces and non-blockable traces at state s, respectively. $\mathcal{T}_{up}(s)$ and $\mathcal{T}_u(s)$ are also written as $\mathcal{T}_{up}(C)$ and $\mathcal{T}_u(C)$, respectively, when s is the initial state.

3.1 Component Interface Automata

In this part, we will introduce input-deterministic component automaton of which all traces are non-blockable and the error state is not reachable from the initial state. We present an algorithm that constructs an input-deterministic component automaton $\mathcal{I}(C)$ for any given component automaton C, such that $\mathcal{I}(C)$ and C have the same non-blockable traces, in particular, $\mathcal{I}(C)$ is a refinement w.r.t. the refinement relation defined in Section 5.

Definition 4 (input-determinism).
A component automaton $C = (S, s_0, f, P, R, A, \delta)$ *is* input-deterministic *if* f *is not reachable from* s_0 *and for any* $s_0 \stackrel{tr_1}{\Longrightarrow} s_1$ *and* $s_0 \stackrel{tr_2}{\Longrightarrow} s_2$ *with* $\pi_1(tr_1)\lfloor_P = \pi_1(tr_2)\lfloor_P$*, implies* $\mathcal{N}(s_1) = \mathcal{N}(s_2)$*.*

The following theorem states that all the traces of an input-deterministic component automaton are non-blockable.

Theorem 1. *A component automaton* C *is input-deterministic iff* $\mathcal{T}_p(C) = \mathcal{T}_{up}(C)$*.*

Proof. $\mathcal{T}_p(C) = \mathcal{T}_{up}(C)$ means every provided trace of C is non-blockable actually.

First, we prove the direction from left to right. From the input-determinism of C follows that for each provided trace $pt = (a_0, \ldots, a_k)$ and for each state s with $s_0 \stackrel{tr}{\Longrightarrow} s$ and $\pi_1(tr) = \langle a_0, \ldots, a_i \rangle$ for $0 \leq i \leq k-1$, the set $\mathcal{N}(s)$ is the same. Since pt is a provided trace, so $a_{i+1} \in \mathcal{N}(s)$. This shows that all provided traces are non-blockable, and so all traces are non-blockable too.

Second, we prove the direction from right to left by contraposition. We assume that C is not input-deterministic, so there exist traces tr_1 and tr_2 with $\pi_1(tr_1)\lfloor_P = \pi_1(tr_2)\lfloor_P$ and $s_0 \stackrel{tr_1}{\Longrightarrow} s_1$, $s_0 \stackrel{tr_2}{\Longrightarrow} s_2$ such that $\mathcal{N}(s_1) \neq \mathcal{N}(s_2)$.

Without loss of generality, we assume that there is a provided event a such that $a \in \mathcal{N}(s_1)$ and $a \notin \mathcal{N}(s_2)$. Now $\pi_1(tr_1) \circ \langle a \rangle$ is a provided trace of C that is blockable. □

Hereafter, we simply call *component interface automaton*(or *interface automaton*) if it is input-deterministic.

In the following, we present an algorithm (see given in Algorithm 1) that, given component automaton C, constructs an interface automaton $\mathcal{I}(C)$ which share the same non-blockable trace with C, and refines C in the sense of the refinement relation defined in Section 5.

The basic idea of Algorithm 1 is quite similar to the one given in [7]. If the error state f can be reached from the initial state s_0, then the algorithm exits with an empty component automaton. Each state of $\mathcal{I}(C)$ is of the form (Q, r), where Q is a subset of states of C and r is a state of C with $r \in Q$ and the initial state is (Q_0, s_0) with $Q_0 = \{s' \mid s' \in intR^{\circ}(s_0)\}$. Q records all reachable states from each state $s' \in Q'$, (suppose (Q', r') has been added as a state of $\mathcal{I}(C)$), by executing a provided event a, where $a \in \bigcap_{s' \in Q'} \mathcal{N}(s')$. By inductive way, we can see that all traces of $\mathcal{I}(C)$ are non-blockable. On the other hand, all the states that can be reached from states in Q' via each provided event $b \in \bigcap_{s' \in Q'} \mathcal{N}(s')$ with possible internal events before/after b will consist a Q such that (Q, r) is one state of $\mathcal{I}(C)$. So all non-blockable traces of C are also contained in $\mathcal{I}(C)$ by inductive way. Correctness of Algorithm 1 is given formally in the following theorem.

Theorem 2 (correctness of Algorithm 1). *The following properties holds for Algorithm 1, for any component automaton* C*:*

1. *The algorithm always terminates and the error state f is not reachable from the initial state,*
2. *$\mathcal{I}(C)$ is an input deterministic automaton,*
3. *$\mathcal{T}_u(C) = \mathcal{T}_u(\mathcal{I}(C))$.*

Proof. 1. The termination of the algorithm can be obtained because *todo* will be eventually empty, the set *done* increases for each iteration of the loop in the algorithm, and the union of *done* and *todo* is bounded.

By the definition of $\mathcal{N}(s)$ for any given state s, we clearly see that f is not reachable from s_0.

2. We show that for each provided trace pt of $\mathcal{I}(C)$, if $(Q_0, s_0) \stackrel{pt}{\Longrightarrow} (Q, r)$, then $Q = \{s' \mid s_0 \stackrel{pt}{\Longrightarrow} s'\}$. This can be proved by induction on the length of pt. The base case follows that $Q_0 = s' \mid s' \in intR^{\circ}(s_0)$. Consider $(Q_0, s_0) \stackrel{pt \circ a}{\Longrightarrow} (Q, r)$, then $(Q_0, s_0) \stackrel{pt}{\Longrightarrow} (Q', r')$ and $(Q', r') \stackrel{a}{\Longrightarrow} (Q, r)$. From Line 5-19 of Algorithm 1, $Q = \{s' \mid s \in Q'.s \stackrel{a}{\Longrightarrow} s'\}$. By induction hypothesis, $Q' = \{s' \mid s_0 \stackrel{pt}{\Longrightarrow} s'\}$, so $Q = \{s' \mid (Q_0, s_0) \stackrel{pt \circ a}{\Longrightarrow} (Q, r)\}$. From Line 5 of Algorithm 1, for any $r \in Q$, $\mathcal{N}(Q, r) = \bigcap_{s \in Q} \mathcal{N}(s)$. From above, we see that $\mathcal{I}(C)$ is input deterministic.

3. First, we show $\mathcal{T}_u(C) \subseteq \mathcal{T}_u(\mathcal{I}(C))$ by proving that for each non-blockable provided trace pt of C, if $s_0 \stackrel{tr}{\Longrightarrow} r$ with $\pi_1(tr)\lfloor_P = pt$, then there exists $(Q_0, s_0) \stackrel{tr}{\Longrightarrow} (Q, r)$ where $Q = \{s' \mid s_0 \stackrel{pt}{\Longrightarrow} s'\}$ by induction on the length of pt. The base case follows directly by Line 15-19 of Algorithm 1. Consider $s_0 \stackrel{tr_1 \circ tr_2}{\Longrightarrow} r$ where $tr_1 \circ tr_2$ is non-blockable and $\pi_1(tr_2)\lfloor_P = a$. Then $s_0 \stackrel{tr_1}{\Longrightarrow} r'$ and $r' \stackrel{tr_2}{\Longrightarrow} r$. By induction hypothesis, $(Q_0, r_0) \stackrel{tr_1}{\Longrightarrow} (Q', r')$ where $Q' = \{s' \mid s_0 \stackrel{\pi_1(tr_1)\lfloor_P}{\Longrightarrow} s'\}$. Because $tr_1 \circ tr_2$ is non-blockable, so $a \in \bigcap_{s \in Q'} \mathcal{N}(s)$. By Line 5 of Algorithm 1, $Q = s' \mid s \in Q'.s \stackrel{a}{\Longrightarrow} s'$. Then $(Q', r') \stackrel{tr_2}{\Longrightarrow} (Q, r)$. So $(Q_0, s_0) \stackrel{tr_1 \circ tr_2}{\Longrightarrow} (Q, r)$.

Second, we show $\mathcal{T}_u(\mathcal{I}(C)) \subseteq \mathcal{T}_u(C)$. During the proof of Item 1, we have for each $pt \in \mathcal{T}_p(\mathcal{I}(C))$ there exists $Q = \{s' \mid s_0 \stackrel{pt}{\Longrightarrow} s'\}$. We prove that pt is non-blockable in C by induction on length of pt. The base case follows directly. Consider pt' is non-blockable in C, then $pt' \circ a$ is also non-blockable, since $a \in \bigcap_{s' \in Q'} \mathcal{N}(s')$ where $Q' = \{s' \mid s_0 \stackrel{pt'}{\Longrightarrow} s'\}$ by induction hypothesis. So $pt' \circ a$ is non-blockable in C, which implies $\mathcal{T}_p(\mathcal{I}(C)) \subseteq \mathcal{T}_p(C)$. It is clear to see that $\mathcal{T}(\mathcal{I}(C)) \subseteq \mathcal{T}(C)$. And $\mathcal{T}(\mathcal{I}(C)) = \mathcal{T}_u(\mathcal{I}(C))$ by Item 1, so $\mathcal{T}_u(\mathcal{I}(C)) \subseteq \mathcal{T}_u(C)$.

From above, we see that $\mathcal{T}_u(\mathcal{I}(C)) = \mathcal{T}_u(C)$.

Example 2. In the internet connection component automaton 1, the provided trace $\langle login, read\rangle$ are non-blockable but $\langle login, print\rangle$ may be blocked during execution, because after *login* is called, the component may transit to state 3 at which *print* is not available. We use Algorithm 1 to generate the interface model of C_{ic}, shown in Fig. 4.

Algorithm 1. Construction of Interface Automaton $\mathcal{I}(C)$

Input: $C = (S, s_0, f, P, R, A, \delta)$
Output: $\mathcal{I}(C) = (S_I, (Q_0, s_0), f, P, R, A, \delta_I)$, where $S_I \subseteq 2^S \times S$
if $f \in intR^\circ(s_0)$ **then**
  exit with $\delta_I = \emptyset$
end if
Initialization: $S_I := \{(Q_0, s_0)\}$ **with** $Q_0 = \{s' \mid s' \in intR^\circ(s_0)\}$; $\delta_I := \emptyset$; $todo := \{(Q_0, s_0)\}$; $done := \emptyset$
while $todo \neq \emptyset$ **do**
  choose $(Q, r) \in todo$; $todo := todo \setminus \{(Q, r)\}$; $done := done \cup \{(Q, r)\}$
  for each $a \in \bigcap_{s \in Q} \mathcal{N}(s)$ **do**
    $Q' := \bigcup_{s \in Q} \{s' \mid s \stackrel{tr}{\Longrightarrow} s', \pi_1(tr)\downharpoonleft_P = \langle a \rangle\}$
    for each $(r \xrightarrow{a/T} r') \in \delta$ **do**
      if $(Q', r') \notin (todo \cup done)$ **then**
        $todo := todo \cup \{(Q', r')\}$
        $S_I := S_I \cup \{(Q', r')\}$
      end if
      $\delta_I := \delta_I \cup \{(Q, r) \xrightarrow{a/T} (Q', r')\}$
    end for
  end for
  for each $r \xrightarrow{w/T} r'$ **with** $r' \in Q$ **and** $w \in A$ **do**
    $\delta_I := \delta_I \cup \{(Q, r) \xrightarrow{w/T} (Q, r')\}$
  end for
end while

Given a component automaton C, for each state s of C, there may be several sets Q such that (Q, r) is a state of $\mathcal{I}(C)$. Then, we call $\mathcal{N}(s) \setminus \bigcup_{(Q,s) \in S_I} \mathcal{N}(Q, s)$ *the refusal set* at s, denoted by $\mathcal{F}(s)$. Intuitively, any execution of a method in $\mathcal{F}(s)$ may result in deadlock, which is quite similar to the notion of refusal set in CSP[1].

Obviously, for a non-blockable component automaton, the refusal set at each of its states is empty.

4 Composition Operators

In this section, we will present how two components are composed. Components interact with each other by service invocation, that is, component automata synchronize on the events that are provided by one and required by the other.

[1] In our setting, a deadlock of a provided action at a state may be caused by the execution of some provided methods at one of its predecessor, therefore, such action should not be in the refusal set in CSP, but it is indeed in the refusal set according to our definition.

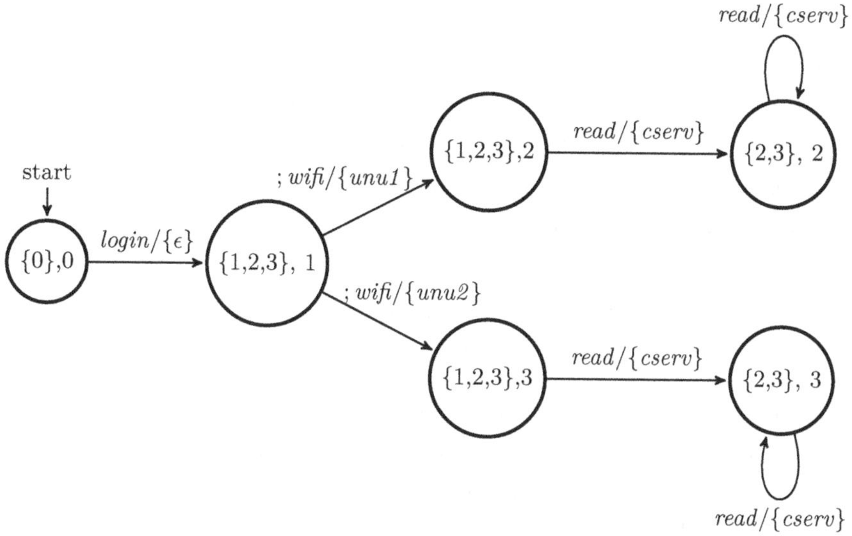

Fig. 4. Interface model of internet connection component C_{ic}

To this end, we firstly define the synchronization rules between a component automaton and a finite state machine which represents the set of required traces.

In a component automaton $C_1 = (S, s_0, f, P, R, A, \delta)$, for any transition $s_1 \xrightarrow{a/T} s_2$, there is a minimal deterministic finite state machine recognizing T [14], denoted by $\mathcal{M}(T)$. $\mathcal{M}(T)$ is of the form $(Q, \Sigma, \sigma, q_0, F)$, where Q is the finite set of states, Σ is the input alphabet, $\sigma : Q \times \Sigma \mapsto Q$ is the next-state function, q_0 is the initial state, and F is the set of final states.

Suppose a component automaton C_1 with a transition $s_1 \xrightarrow{a/T} s_2$, which means C_1 requires all the traces in T in order to provide a, and another component automaton C_2 that can provide these required services in T. When composing C_1 and C_2 together, all methods appearing in T should be synchronized. To this end, we define *internal product* between $\mathcal{M}(T)$ and C_2 to implement the synchronization of C_1 and C_2 on T.

Given a set of sequences of elements T or a sequence of elements α, we use *events*(T) and *events*(α) to denote all the elements appearing in T, respectively. If the component automaton C can synchronize with M under E successfully, we denote $C \models_E M$.

Definition 5 (internal product)
Given a component automaton $C = (S, s_0, f, P, R, A, \delta)$ and a finite state machine $M = (Q, \Sigma, \sigma, q_0, F)$, the composition of C and M under E, denoted by $C \lhd_E M$, is defined as $(Q', \Sigma', \sigma', q_0, F')$, where

- $Q' = S \times Q$, $q_0' = (s_0, q_0)$;
- $\Sigma' = 2^R \cup 2^{\Sigma^*}$;

- σ' *is the smallest set given by the following rules: Suppose* $(r_1, t_1) \in Q'$ *with* $t_1 \notin F$ *and* $r_1 \notin \{r \mid out(r) = \emptyset\}$, *and* $r_1 \xrightarrow{a/T} r_2$ *with* $a \in E \cup A$ *and* $t_1 \xrightarrow{b} t_2$. $C \models_E M$ *as default. Then,*
  - *if* $events(T) \cap E \neq \emptyset$ *or* $b \in E \wedge b \notin \mathcal{N}(r_1)$, *then* $C \not\models_E M$;
  - *otherwise if* $a \in A$, $(r_1, t_1) \xrightarrow{T} (r_2, t_1) \in \sigma'$;
  - *otherwise if* $b \notin E$, $(r_1, t_1) \xrightarrow{\{b\}} (r_1, t_2) \in \sigma'$;
  - *otherwise if* $a == b$, $(r_1, t_1) \xrightarrow{T} (r_2, t_2) \in \sigma'$;
- $F' = \{(r, t) \mid r \in S, t \in F\}$.

where E is a set of shared events of C and M.

Intuitively, the first clause expresses that if the current states of M and C are q and s, respectively and there exists transition $q \xrightarrow{a} q'$ with $a \in E$ of finite state machine M, then C should provide a. However, if $a \notin \mathcal{N}(s)$, this causes the request of a fail. If $a \in \mathcal{N}(s)$, but there exists transition $s \xrightarrow{a/T} s'$ that T also requires services of E, the invocation of a also fails, because this is deadlock caused by cyclic invocation.

The above definition can be extended to a sequence of transitions $t \xRightarrow{\alpha} t'$ and $r \xRightarrow{tr} r'$, where $\pi_1(tr)\downharpoonright_P = \alpha\downharpoonright_P$ and $events(\pi_2(tr)) \cap E = \emptyset$, then $(r, t) \xRightarrow{\pi_2(tr')} (r', t')$, where $tr'\downharpoonright^1_{R\setminus E} = pair(\alpha\downharpoonright_{R\setminus E})$, $tr'\downharpoonright^1_{P\cup A} = tr\downharpoonright^1_{P\cup A}$, $last(\pi_1(tr') \in R)$.

Next, We present the conditions of $C \models_E M$.

Lemma 1. $C \models_E M$ *iff* $T\downharpoonright_P \subseteq \mathcal{T}_{up}(C)$ *where* T *is* $\mathcal{L}(M)$ *and* $events(\alpha) \cap E = \emptyset$ *where* $\forall \alpha \in \mathcal{T}_r(pt)$ *with* $\forall pt \in T\downharpoonright_P$.

Proof. First, we prove the direction " $\Longrightarrow$ " by contraposition. There exists β and $\pi_1(tr)\downharpoonright_P = \beta$ that $s_0 \xRightarrow{tr} s$ and $t_0 \xRightarrow{\beta} t$. If (s, t) is reachable and $a \notin \mathcal{N}(s)$ and $t \xrightarrow{a} t'$, so $C \not\models_E M$. If $s \xrightarrow{a/T} s'$ with $events(T) \cap E \neq \emptyset$, so $C \not\models_E M$.

Next we show " $\Longleftarrow$ " by contraposition too. If $C \not\models_E M$, there exists reachable state (r, t) that $r \xrightarrow{a/T} r'$ where $events(T)\ E \neq \emptyset$, then there exists $pt \in T\downharpoonright_P$ and $\alpha \in \mathcal{T}_r(pt)$ that $events(\alpha) \cap E \neq \emptyset$. Or $t \xrightarrow{b} t'$ with $b \in E$, but $b \notin \mathcal{N}(r)$, then there exists $\beta \in T\downharpoonright_P$ but $\beta \notin \mathcal{T}_{up}(C)$. □

Given a component automaton $C = (S, s_0, f, P, R, A, \delta)$, we use $C(s)$ with $s \in S$ to denote the component automaton $(S, s, f, P, R, A, \delta)$ with s as the initial state.

$C_1 = (S_1, s_0^1, f, P_1, R_1, A_1, \delta_1)$ and $C_2 = (S_2, s_0^2, f, P_2, R_2, A_2, \delta_2)$ are *composable*, if $(P_1 \cup R_1) \cap A_2 = (P_2 \cup R_2) \cap A_1 = \emptyset$ and $P_1 \cap P_2 = R_1 \cap R_2 = \emptyset$.

Definition 6 (product)
For two composable component automata $C_1 = (S_1, s_0^1, f, P_1, R_1, A_1, \delta_1)$ *and* $C_2 = (S_2, s_0^2, f, P_2, R_2, A_2, \delta_2)$, *let* $E = (P_1 \cap R_2) \cup (P_2 \cap R_1)$, *then the product* $C_1 \otimes C_2 = (S, s_0, f, P, R, A, \delta)$ *is defined as:*

- $S = S_1 \times S_2$, $s_0 = (s_0^1, s_0^2)$, f *is the error state;*
- $P = (P_1 \cup P_2)$;

- *$R = (R_1 \cup R_2) \setminus (P_1 \cup P_2)$;*
- *$A = A_1 \cup A_2$;*
- *δ is defined as follows:*
  - *For any reachable state $(s_1, s_2) \in S$ and $s_1 \xrightarrow{w/T} s_1' \in \delta_1$ where $f \notin intR^\circ(s_1')$ we write (Q, R, σ, q_0, F) as the internal product $C_2(s_2) \lhd_E \mathcal{M}(T)$.*
    - *if $C \not\models_E \mathcal{M}(T)$, then $(s_1, s_2) \xrightarrow{w/} f \in \delta$;*
    - *otherwise $\{(s_1, s_2) \xrightarrow{w/T'} (s_1', s_2') \mid s_2' \in S_2, T' = \{conc(\ell) \mid q_0 \overset{\ell}{\Longrightarrow} (s_2', t) \text{ with } (s_2', t) \in F\}\} \subseteq \delta$.*
  - *Symmetrically, for any reachable state $(s_1, s_2) \in S$ and $s_2 \xrightarrow{w/T} s_2' \in \delta_2$, we add some transitions to δ similarly to the above.*

Next, we show how two components are composed by traces, or we can also say how T' is obtained directly by traces without internal product. This is inspired by how traces of interleaving and parallel composition operators are defined in CSP [13].

Lemma 2. *If $C_2(s_2) \models_{shared} \mathcal{M}(T)$ in the product, T' can also be defined as $T' = \{\pi_2(tr') \mid \alpha \in T, s_2 \overset{tr}{\Longrightarrow} s_2',\ \text{with } \pi_1(tr){\downharpoonleft_{P_2}} == \alpha{\downharpoonleft_{P_2}}, tr'{\downharpoonleft^1_R} = pair(\alpha{\downharpoonleft_R}), tr'{\downharpoonleft^1_{P_2 \cup A_2}} = tr^1{\downharpoonleft_{P_2 \cup A_2}}, last(\pi_1(tr') \in R_1)\}$.*

Composition of Component Interface Automata. From [7], the product of two component interface automata may contain blockable traces. This means the product operator is not closed in the domain of component interface automata. So we introduce a composition operator of component interface automata based on operator product and Algorithm 1.

Definition 7 (composition). *Given two component interface automata I_1 and I_2, the composition, written as $I_1 \parallel I_2$, is $\mathcal{I}(I_1 \otimes I_2))$.*

Hiding. In the following, we introduce the hiding operator, which is used to internalize certain provided services.

Definition 8 (hiding). *Given a component automaton $C = (S, s_0, f, P, R, A, \delta)$ and a set of provided events $E \subseteq P$, hiding E from C, written as $C \backslash E$ is $(S, s_0, f, P \setminus E, R, A \cup E, \delta)$.*

5 Refinement

In this section, we study refinement relation between component automata. Refinement is one of the key issues in component based development. It is mainly for substitution at interface level. We define a refinement relation by state simulation technique [21]. The intuitive idea is a state s' simulates s, if at state s' more provided events are nonrefusal, less required traces are required and the next states following the transitions keep the simulation relation, which is similar to alternating simulation in [5].

Let C be a component automaton, some nonrefusal provided events at a given state s may also be refused. For example, provided event c at state 3 may be refused shown in Fig. 3, which is caused by non-determinism after provided event a is called. Therefore, the refusal set at s, i.e., $\mathcal{F}(s)$, defined in Section 3, is a subset of $\mathcal{N}(s)$. Therefore, the refusal set by our definition is a little different from the one in CSP.

Definition 9 (simulation). *A binary relation R over the set of states of a component automaton is a simulation iff whenever $s_1 R s_2$:*

- *if $s_1 \xrightarrow{w/T} s_1'$ with $w \in A \cup \mathcal{N}(s_1) \setminus \mathcal{F}(s_1)$ and $f \notin intR^\circ(s_1')$, there exists s_2' and T' such that $s_2 \xrightarrow{w/T'} s_2'$ where $T' \subseteq T$ and $s_1' R s_2'$;*
- *for any transitions $s_2 \xrightarrow{w/T'} s_2'$ with $w \in A \cup \mathcal{N}(s_1) \setminus \mathcal{F}(s_1)$ and $f \notin intR^\circ(s_2')$, then there exists s_1' and T such that $s_1 \xrightarrow{w/T} s_1'$ where $T' \subseteq T$ and $s_1' R s_2'$;*
- *$\mathcal{F}(s_2) \subseteq \mathcal{F}(s_1)$;*
- *if $s_2 \xrightarrow{w/} f$ with $w \in A \cup P_1$, then $s_1 \xrightarrow{w/} f$.*

We say that s_2 simulates s_1, written $s_1 \lesssim s_2$, if $(s_1, s_2) \in R$. C_2 refines *C_1, if there exists a simulation relation R such that $s_1^0 R s_2^0$ and $P_1 \subseteq P_2$ and $R_2 \subseteq R_1$.*

Remark 1. The above definition is quite similar to the alternating simulation given in [5]. But they are different, and main differences include: first of all, in our definition, we only require a pair of states keep the simulation relation w.r.t. the provided services that could not result in deadlock; in addition, we also require a refinement should have smaller refusal sets at each location, which is similar to the stable failures model of CSP. Also notice that our refinement is not comparable with the failure refinement nor the failure-divergence refinement of CSP, because of the different requirements on the simulation of provided methods and required methods. However, if we suppose no required methods, our definition is stronger than the failure refinement as well as failure-divergence refinement as we explained above.

The following theorem indicates the component interface automaton constructed by Algorithm 1 is a refinement of the considered component automaton w.r.t. the above definition, which justifies that we can safely use the resulted component interface instead of the component at the interface level.

Theorem 3. *Given any component automaton C, $C \sqsubseteq \mathcal{I}(C)$. And consider two component automata C_1 and C_2, if $C_1 \sqsubseteq C_2$, then $\mathcal{I}(C_1) \sqsubseteq \mathcal{I}(C_2)$.*

Proof. Let $R = \{(s, (Q, s)) \mid s \in S, (Q, s) \in S_I\}$. We show R is a simulation relation.

For any $sR(Q, s)$,

- $s \xrightarrow{a/T} s'$ with $a \in \mathcal{N}(s)$ and $a \notin \mathcal{F}(s)$. Then $a \in \mathcal{N}(Q, s)$ and $(Q, s) \xrightarrow{a/T} (Q', s')$. $s \xrightarrow{;w/T} s'$ with $;w \in A$, then $(Q, s) \xrightarrow{;w/T} (Q, s')$.

– for any $(Q, s) \xrightarrow{e/T} (Q', s')$ with $e \in A \cup \mathcal{N}(s) \setminus \mathcal{F}(Q, s)$. Then $s \xrightarrow{e/T} s'$ and $s' R (Q', s')$.
– $\mathcal{F}(Q, s) \subseteq \mathcal{F}(s)$.

From above, we see R is a simulation relation. So $C \sqsubseteq \mathcal{I}(C)$, because $s_0 R(\{s_0\}, s_0)$.

Now we prove the second part of the theorem. Let R_O be a simulation for $C_1 \sqsubseteq C_2$, then we show $R'_O = \{((Q_1, s_1), (Q_2, s_2)) \mid (s_1, s_2) \in R_O, \forall r_1 \in Q_1 \exists r_2 \in Q_2.(r_1, r_2) \in R_O, \forall r_2 \in Q_2 \exists r_1 \in Q_1.(r_1, r_2) \in R_O\} \cap (S_I^1 \times S_I^2)$. For any $(Q_1, s_1) R'_O (Q_2, s_2)$, then $\mathcal{N}(Q_1) \subseteq \mathcal{N}(Q_2)$ and $\mathcal{F}(Q_1, s_1) = \mathcal{F}(Q_2, s_2) = \emptyset$. Consider $(Q_1, s_1) \xrightarrow{w/T} (Q'_1, s'_1)$ with $w \in A_1 \cup \mathcal{N}(Q_1, s_1) \setminus \mathcal{F}(Q_1, s_1)$, then $s_1 \xrightarrow{w/T} s'_1$. By simulation relation R_O, there exists $s_2 \xrightarrow{w/T'} s'_2$ with $T' \subseteq T$.

For all $(Q_2, s_2) \xrightarrow{w/T'} (Q'_2, s'_2)$ with $w \in A_1 \cup \mathcal{N}(Q_1, s_1) \setminus \mathcal{F}(Q_1, s_1)$, there exists $s_2 \xrightarrow{w/T'} s'_2$, then there exists s'_1 and T such that $s_1 \xrightarrow{w/T} s'_1$ with $T' \subseteq T$ by simulation R_O. Then $(Q_1, s_1) \xrightarrow{w/T} (Q'_1, s'_1)$ and $(Q'_1, s'_1) R'_O (Q'_2, s'_2)$ by the definition of R'_O. From above we see that R'_O is a simulation relation and it is clear that $(\{s_0^1\}, s_0^1) R'_O (\{s_0^2\}, s_0^2)$. So $\mathcal{I}(C_1) \sqsubseteq \mathcal{I}(C_2)$. □

The next theorem shows that the trace inclusion properties.

Theorem 4. *Given two component interface automata C_1 and C_2, if $C_1 \sqsubseteq C_2$, then $\mathcal{T}_{up}(C_1) \subseteq \mathcal{T}_{up}(C_2)$, and for any non-blockable provided trace $pt \in \mathcal{T}_p(C_1)$, $\mathcal{T}_r^2(pt) \subseteq \mathcal{T}_r^1(pt)$.*

Proof. This can be proved by induction on the length of pt. □

The following theorem states that the refinement relation is preserved by the composition operator over component automata.

Theorem 5. *Given a component automaton C and two non-blockable component automata C_1 and C_2 such that $C_1 \sqsubseteq C_2$, then $C_1 \otimes C \sqsubseteq C_2 \otimes C$.*

Proof. Assume the simulation relation of $C_1 \sqsubseteq C_2$ is R. We prove the relation $R' = \{((s_1, s), (s_2, s)) \mid (s_1, s_2) \in R \text{ and } s \in S\}$ be a simulation relation. Let $(s_1, r)\mathcal{R}'(s_2, r)$. By Lemma 1, (s_2, r) leads to the error state implies (s_1, r) leads to the error states. We prove by considering the following two cases.

First, C_1 and C_2 requires services from C. If $(s_1, r) \xrightarrow{w/T'_1} (s'_1, r')$, we assume that $s_1 \xrightarrow{w/T_1} s'_1$ and $r \xRightarrow{tr} r'$. C_1 and C_2 are non-blockable component automata, so $w \in A \cup \mathcal{N}(s_1)$ and $w \notin \mathcal{F}(s_1)$. By simulation, there exists $s_2 \xrightarrow{w/T_2} s'_2$ that $T'_2 \subseteq T'_1$. Then $(s_2, r) \xrightarrow{w/T'_2} (s'_2, r)$ that $T'_2 \subseteq T'_1$, by Lemma 2.

For any $(s_2, r) \xrightarrow{w/T'_2} (s'_2, r')$ with $w \in A \cup \mathcal{N}(s_2)$ and $w \notin \mathcal{F}(s_1, r)$, then there exists $s_2 \xrightarrow{w/T_2} s'_2$, $r \xRightarrow{tr} r'$. Then $w \in A \cup \mathcal{N}(s_1)$ and $w \notin \mathcal{F}(s_1)$. By simulation relation, there exists $s_1 \xrightarrow{w/T_1} s'_1$ with $T_2 \subseteq T_1$. Then $(s_1, r) \xrightarrow{(w/T'_1)} (s'_1, r')$ where $T'_2 \subseteq T'_1$ by Lemma 2.

Second, C require services from C_1 and C_2, respectively. If $(s_1, r) \xrightarrow{w/T_1'} (s_1', r')$, we assume that $s_1 \overset{tr_1}{\Longrightarrow} s_1'$ and $r \overset{w/T}{\Longrightarrow} r'$. Because C_1 and C_2 are two non-blockable component automata, there exists $s_2 \overset{tr_2}{\Longrightarrow} s_2'$ that $\pi_2(tr_2) \subseteq \pi_2(tr_1)$ and $\pi_1(tr_2)\lfloor_{P_2} = \pi_1(tr_1)\lfloor_{P_1}$ by simulation. Then $(s_2, r) \xrightarrow{w/T_2'} (s_2', r')$ that $T_2' \subseteq T_1'$, by Lemma 2.

For any $(s_2, r) \xrightarrow{w/T_2'} (s_2', r')$, then there exists $s_2 \overset{tr_2}{\Longrightarrow} s_2'$ and $r \xrightarrow{w/T} r'$. Because C_1 and C_2 are non-blockable component automata, there exists $s_1 \overset{tr_1}{\Longrightarrow} s_1'$ that $\pi_2(tr_2) \subseteq \pi_2(tr_1)$ and $\pi_1(tr_2)\lfloor_{P_2} = \pi_1(tr_1)\lfloor_{P_1}$ by simulation. Then $(s_1, r) \xrightarrow{(w/T_1')} (s_1', r')$ where $T_2' \subseteq T_1'$ by Lemma 2.

$\mathcal{F}(s_2) \subseteq \mathcal{F}(s_1)$, then $\mathcal{F}(s_2, r) \subseteq \mathcal{F}(s_1, r)$.

For both cases, $s_1' R s_2'$, so $(s_1', r')\mathcal{R}'(s_2', r')$, this implies that $\mathcal{R}'$ is an simulation relation.

□

The following corollary is immediate.

Corollary 1. *Given two component interface automata C_1 and C_2, if $C_1 \sqsubseteq C_2$, then $C_1 \parallel C \sqsubseteq C_2 \parallel C$.*

6 Conclusion and Future Work

We presented an execution model of components, which extends our previous work by allowing internal behaviors of components. Then we considered how to constructed its interface model, which share the same non-blockable behavior, so that all operations on the component can be done over the obtained interface model instead. Thus, the usage of the component according to the interface model is guaranteed to be safe, that is, no deadlock whenever it is used in any environment.

Furthermore, in order to discuss the substitutivity of components at the interface level, which is very important in component-based methods, we define a revised alternating simulation, which provides a criterion how to substitute one component for another one at the interface level freely. In particular, we proved the derived interface model indeed is a refinement of the original component according to the revised alternating simulation.

Future Work. There are several open problems left for future work. Firstly, the components discussed in this paper provide services in a passive way, that is, the components only triggers invocation of services when provided services are called by the environment or when some internal behaviors are available. The kind of components used for actively coordinating the behaviors of multi-components is needed. Secondly, algebraic properties of composition such as associative, commutative, distributive of coordination over composition are also important. The third research direction is development of execution and interface models for components with timing characteristics, which support timing, deadlock, and scheduling analysis of applications in the presence of timed requirement.

Acknowledgments. This work has been supported by the Projects GAVES and PEARL funded by Macau Science and Technology Development Fund and grants from the Natural Science Foundation of China NSFC-61103013 and NSFC-91118007. We thank Zhiming Liu for his inspiring comments and discussions. We also thank the anonymous reviewers for the feedback and our colleges Stephan Arlt, Johannes Faber, and Nafees Qamar for their comments and discussions.

References

1. de Alfaro, L., Henzinger, T.A.: Interface theories for component-based design. In: Henzinger, T.A., Kirsch, C.M. (eds.) EMSOFT 2001. LNCS, vol. 2211, pp. 148–165. Springer, Heidelberg (2001)
2. Arbab, F.: Reo: a channel-based coordination model for component composition. Mathematical Structures in Computer Science 14, 329–366 (2004), http://portal.acm.org/citation.cfm?id=992032.992035
3. Chen, X., Liu, Z., Mencl, V.: Separation of concerns and consistent integration in requirements modelling. In: van Leeuwen, J., Italiano, G.F., van der Hoek, W., Meinel, C., Sack, H., Plášil, F. (eds.) SOFSEM 2007. Part I. LNCS, vol. 4362, pp. 819–831. Springer, Heidelberg (2007)
4. Chen, Z., Liu, Z., Ravn, A.P., Stolz, V., Zhan, N.: Refinement and verification in component-based model-driven design. Science of Computer Programming 74(4), 168–196 (2009),http://www.sciencedirect.com/science/article/pii/S0167642308000890, special Issue on the Grand Challenge
5. De Alfaro, L., Henzinger, T.: Interface automata. ACM SIGSOFT Software Engineering Notes 26(5), 109–120 (2001)
6. De Alfaro, L., Henzinger, T.: Interface-based design. Engineering Theories of Software-intensive Systems 195, 83–104 (2005)
7. Dong, R., Faber, J., Liu, Z., Srba, J., Zhan, N., Zhu, J.: Unblockable compositions of software components. In: Proceedings of the 15th ACM SIGSOFT Symposium on Component Based Software Engineering, CBSE 2012, pp. 103–108. ACM, New York (2012), http://doi.acm.org/10.1145/2304736.2304754
8. Emmi, M., Giannakopoulou, D., Păsăreanu, C.S.: Assume-guarantee verification for interface automata. In: Cuellar, J., Maibaum, T., Sere, K. (eds.) FM 2008. LNCS, vol. 5014, pp. 116–131. Springer, Heidelberg (2008), http://dx.doi.org/10.1007/978-3-540-68237-0_10
9. Giannakopoulou, D., Pasareanu, C.S., Barringer, H.: Assumption generation for software component verification. In: ASE, pp. 3–12. IEEE Computer Society (2002), http://doi.ieeecomputersociety.org/10.1109/ASE.2002.1114984
10. Jifeng, H., Li, X., Liu, Z.: Component-based software engineering. In: Van Hung, D., Wirsing, M. (eds.) ICTAC 2005. LNCS, vol. 3722, pp. 70–95. Springer, Heidelberg (2005)
11. He, J., Li, X., Liu, Z.: rcos: A refinement calculus of object systems. Theor. Comput. Sci. 365(1-2), 109–142 (2006)
12. He, J., Li, X., Liu, Z.: A theory of reactive components. Electr. Notes Theor. Comput. Sci. 160, 173–195 (2006)
13. Hoare, C.: Communicating sequential processes. Communications of the ACM 21(8), 666–677 (1978)
14. Hopcroft, J., Motwani, R., Ullman, J.: Introduction to Automata Theory, Languages, and Computation, vol. 2. Addison-Wesley (1979)

15. Larsen, K.G., Nyman, U., Wąsowski, A.: Interface input/output automata. In: Misra, J., Nipkow, T., Sekerinski, E. (eds.) FM 2006. LNCS, vol. 4085, pp. 82–97. Springer, Heidelberg (2006), http://dx.doi.org/10.1007/11813040_7
16. Larsen, K.G., Nyman, U., Wąsowski, A.: Modal I/O automata for interface and product line theories. In: De Nicola, R. (ed.) ESOP 2007. LNCS, vol. 4421, pp. 64–79. Springer, Heidelberg (2007), http://dx.doi.org/10.1007/978-3-540-71316-6_6
17. Liu, Z., Morisset, C., Stolz, V.: rCOS: Theory and tool for component-based model driven development. In: Arbab, F., Sirjani, M. (eds.) FSEN 2009. LNCS, vol. 5961, pp. 62–80. Springer, Heidelberg (2010)
18. Lynch, N.A., Tuttle, M.R.: Hierarchical correctness proofs for distributed algorithms. In: PODC, pp. 137–151 (1987)
19. Lynch, N.A., Tuttle, M.R.: An introduction to input/output automata. CWI Quarterly 2(3), 219–246 (1989)
20. Lüttgen, G., Vogler, W.: Modal interface automata. In: Baeten, J.C.M., Ball, T., de Boer, F.S. (eds.) TCS 2012. LNCS, vol. 7604, pp. 265–279. Springer, Heidelberg (2012), , http://dx.doi.org/10.1007/978-3-642-33475-7_19
21. Milner, R.: Communication and concurrency. Prentice Hall International (UK) Ltd., Hertfordshire (1995)
22. Raclet, J., Badouel, E., Benveniste, A., Caillaud, B., Legay, A., Passerone, R.: Modal interfaces: unifying interface automata and modal specifications. In: Proceedings of the Seventh ACM International Conference on Embedded software, pp. 87–96. ACM (2009)
23. Raclet, J.B., Badouel, E., Benveniste, A., Caillaud, B., Legay, A., Passerone, R.: A modal interface theory for component-based design. Fundam. Inf. 108(1-2), 119–149 (2011), http://dl.acm.org/citation.cfm?id=2362088.2362095
24. Sifakis, J.: A framework for component-based construction. In: Third IEEE International Conference on Software Engineering and Formal Methods, SEFM 2005, pp. 293–299. IEEE (2005)
25. Szyperski, C.: Component Software: Beyond Object-Oriented Programming. Addison-Wesley (1997)

A High-Level Semantics for Program Execution under Total Store Order Memory

Brijesh Dongol[1,*], Oleg Travkin[2], John Derrick[1,*], and Heike Wehrheim[2]

[1] Department of Computer Science
The University of Sheffield, S1 4DP, UK
[2] Fakultät für Elektrotechnik, Informatik und Mathematik
The University of Paderborn, Germany
B.Dongol@sheffield.ac.uk, oleg82@zitmail.uni-paderborn.de,
J.Derrick@dcs.shef.ac.uk, wehrheim@mail.uni-paderborn.de

Abstract. Processor cores within modern multicore systems often communicate via shared memory and use (local) store buffers to improve performance. A penalty for this improvement is the loss of Sequential Consistency to weaker memory guarantees that increase the number of possible program behaviours, and hence, require a greater amount of programming effort. This paper formalises the effect of Total Store Order (TSO) memory — a weak memory model that allows a write followed by a read in the program order to be reordered during execution. Although the precise effects of TSO are well-known, a high-level formalisation of programs that execute under TSO has not been developed. We present an interval-based semantics for programs that execute under TSO memory and include methods for fine-grained expression evaluation, capturing the non-determinism of both concurrency and TSO-related reorderings.

1 Introduction

Approaches to reasoning about concurrency usually assume *Sequentially Consistent* (SC) memory models, where program instructions are executed by the hardware in the order specified by the program [19], i.e., under SC memory, execution of the sequential composition $S_1\ ;\ S_2$ of statements S_1 and S_2 must execute S_2 after S_1. Fig. 1 shows a multicore architecture idealised by the SC memory model, where processor cores interact directly with shared memory. In such an architecture, contention for shared memory becomes a bottleneck to efficiency, and hence, modern processors often utilise additional local buffers within which data may be stored (e.g., the processor cores in Fig. 2 use local write buffers). Furthermore, modern processors implement weaker memory models than sequential consistency and allow the order in which instructions are executed to differ from the program order in a restricted manner [1], e.g., *Write* $\rightarrow$ *Read*, *Write* $\rightarrow$ *Write*, *Read* $\rightarrow$ *Write*, *Read* $\rightarrow$ *Read*. Here *Write* $\rightarrow$ *Read* means that a *Write* instruction to an address a followed by a *Read* instruction to an address b in the program order are allowed to be reordered if $a \neq b$. As a result, a programmer must perform additional reasoning to ensure that the actual (executed) behaviour of a program is consistent with the expected behaviour.

* This research is supported by EPSRC Grant EP/J003727/1.

Z. Liu, J. Woodcock, and H. Zhu (Eds.): ICTAC 2013, LNCS 8049, pp. 177–194, 2013.

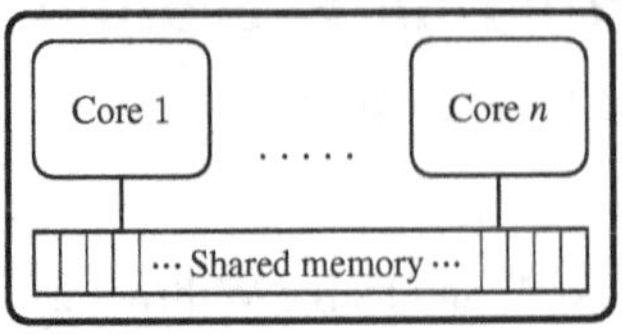

Fig. 1. Idealised multicore architecture

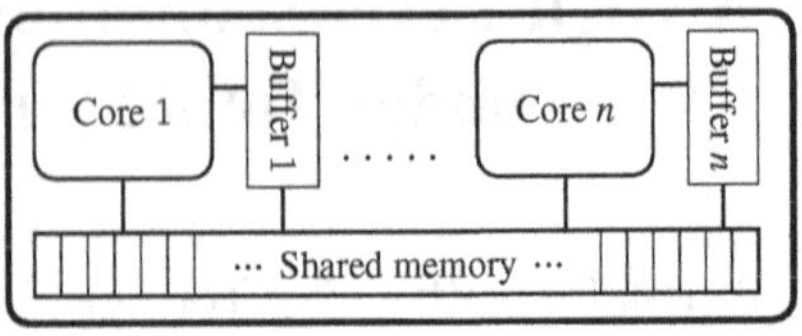

Fig. 2. Multicore architecture with write buffers

In this paper, we study the high-level behaviour of the common x86 multicore processor architecture. Each core uses a write buffer (as shown in Fig. 2), which is a FIFO queue that stores pending writes. A processor core performing a write may enqueue the write in the buffer and continue computation without waiting for the write to be committed to memory. Pending writes do not become visible to other cores until the buffer is flushed, which commits (some or all) pending writes. Thus, x86 architectures allow *Write* → *Read* reordering. Furthermore, using a technique known as *Intra-Process Forwarding* (IPF) [16] a processor core may read pending writes from its own (local) write buffer, i.e., without accessing shared memory. The combination of *Write* → *Read* reordering and IPF forms the *Total Store Order* (TSO) memory model [1, 24].

Existing approaches to memory-model-aware reasoning, e.g. Alglave et al [2], formalise several different orders that are imposed by a specific memory model. Applying these orders to a program yields all possible behaviour that can be observed with respect to the applied memory model. Executable memory models like the x86-TSO [23, 24] have been defined to observe the impact of a memory model on a program's execution. Such models can be used for state space exploration, but this quickly becomes infeasible due to the exponential explosion in the complexity of the state space. Burckhardt et al use an approach [6] in which the memory model is defined axiomatically and combined with a set of axioms modelling a program written in a low-level language. The combination of both is used to feed a SAT-solver to check for program properties like linearisability [15]. Each of the approaches [2, 6, 23, 24] is focused on the use of a low-level language instead of the high-level language in which programs are often written. Hence, to perform a verification, programs need to be observed and understood in their low-level representation, which is a complex task because at this level of abstraction, programs are verbose in their representation and use additional variables to implement high-level language instructions.

Although there are many approaches dealing with the influence of memory models for low-level languages [2–4, 23, 24], we are not aware of any approach that tries to lift such memory model effects to a higher level of abstraction. Our work here is hence unique in this sense. The basic idea is to think of high-level statements as being executed over an interval of time or an execution window. Such execution windows can overlap, if programs are executed concurrently. Under TSO memory, the execution windows can even overlap within a single process. Overlapping windows correspond to program instructions that can be executed in any order, representing the effect of concurrent executions and reorderings due to TSO. Furthermore, overlapping execution windows may also interfere with each other and fixing the outcome of an execution within a window can influence the outcome within another.

Initially: $x = 0 \wedge y = 0 \wedge z \neq 0$

Process p	Process q
p_1: $x := 1$;	q_1: $y := 1$;
p_2: **if** $y = 0 \wedge z = 0$	q_2: $z := x$
p_3: **then** *statement*$_1$	
p_4: **else** *statement*$_2$	

Fig. 3. SC does not allow execution of *statement*$_1$, TSO does

Initially: $x = 0 \wedge y = 0 \wedge z \neq 0$

Process p	Process q
p_1: $write(x, 1)$;	q_1: $write(y, 1)$;
$p_{2.1}$: $\big(read(y, r1_p)$;	$q_{2.1}$: $read(x, r_q)$;
$p_{2.2}$: $read(z, r2_p)\big)$	$q_{2.2}$: $write(z, r_q)$;
$\sqcap$	
$p_{2.3}$: $\big(read(z, r2_p)$;	
$p_{2.4}$: $read(y, r1_p)\big)$;	
$p_{2.5}$: **if** $r1_p = 0 \wedge r2_p = 0 \ldots$	

Fig. 4. Low-level representation of program in Fig. 3

Section 2 introduces the TSO memory model and its influence on a program's behaviour. Section 3 presents our interval-based framework for reasoning about different memory models, an abstract programming language, and a parameterised semantics for the language. In Section 4, we formalise instantaneous and actual states evaluation under SC memory, a restricted form of TSO that allows *Write* $\rightarrow$ *Read* reordering without allowing IPF, and *Write* $\rightarrow$ *Read* with IPF to fully cover TSO behaviour.

2 Effect of Total Store Order on Program Behaviour

On top of the non-determinism inherent within concurrent programs, TSO memory allows additional relaxations that enable further reordering of program instructions within a process via *Write* $\rightarrow$ *Read* reordering and IPF, complicating their analysis [4]. We describe these concepts and their effects on program behaviour using the examples in Sections 2.1 and 2.2. Note that *Write* $\rightarrow$ *Read* reordering is not implemented without IPF by any current processor, but we find it useful to consider its effects separately.

2.1 *Write* $\rightarrow$ *Read* Reordering

Fig. 3 shows a program with two concurrent processes p and q that use shared variables x, y and z. A low-level representation of Fig. 3 is given in Fig. 4, which uses additional local registers $r1_p$, $r2_p$ and r_q.[1] Evaluation of the guard at p_2 is split into a number of atomic steps, where the order in which y and z are read is chosen non-deterministically. That is, after execution of p_1, either $p_{2.1}$; $p_{2.2}$ or $p_{2.3}$; $p_{2.4}$ is executed. For both choices, under SC memory, process p will never execute *statement*$_1$ because whenever control of process p is at $p_{2.5}$, either $r1_p$ or $r2_p$ is non-zero, and hence, the guard at $p_{2.5}$ always evaluates to *false*. In particular, for SC memory, if $r1_p = 0$ holds, then either $p_{2.1}$ or $p_{2.4}$ must have been executed before q_1 (otherwise $r1_p$ would equal 1), and hence, by the program order (which is preserved by the execution order), p_1 must have been executed before q_1. Thus, if $r1_p = 0$ holds, then $r2_p \neq 0$ must hold, and hence, the guard at

[1] Note that implementation of the **if** statement in process p uses additional local variables and goto/jump instructions, whose details have been elided.

$p_{2.5}$ must evaluate to *false*. Furthermore, if $r2_p = 0$ holds at $p_{2.5}$, then $q_{2.2}$ must have been executed before p_1 (otherwise z with value 1 would be loaded as the value of r_2). Therefore, due to the program order, q_1 must also have been executed before p_1, and hence, before both $p_{2.1}$ and $p_{2.4}$. However, this means $r1_p = 1$ must hold at $p_{2.5}$.

Now consider a *restricted TSO* (RTSO) memory model that allows *Write* → *Read* reordering but without IPF. For example, RTSO allows $p_{2.1}$ in Fig. 4 to be executed before p_1 even though p_1 occurs before $p_{2.1}$ in the program order. All other program orders are preserved, including a write to a variable followed by a read to the same variable. Execution of the program in Fig. 4 under RTSO allows execution of $statement_1$ if process p chooses branch $p_{2.1}$; $p_{2.2}$ (i.e., p reads y then z) to evaluate the guard at p_2. This occurs if both:

1. p_1 ; $p_{2.1}$; $p_{2.2}$; $p_{2.5}$ is reordered to $p_{2.1}$; p_1 ; $p_{2.2}$; $p_{2.5}$, which can happen if the write to x (i.e., instruction p_1) is stored in p's write buffer, but committed to memory before execution of $p_{2.2}$, and
2. q_1 ; $q_{2.1}$; $q_{2.2}$ is reordered to $q_{2.1}$; q_1 ; $q_{2.2}$, which can happen if the write to y (i.e., q_1) is stored in q's write buffer.

After the reordering, the concurrent execution of p and q may execute $p_{2.1}$ (setting $r1_p = 0$), then $q_{2.1}$; q_1 ; $q_{2.2}$ (setting $z = 0$), and then $p_{2.2}$ (setting $r2_p = 0$).

Note that it is also possible for none of the instructions to be re-ordered, in which case execution under RTSO would be identical to execution under SC memory. Furthermore, if process p chooses branch $p_{2.3}$; $p_{2.4}$, $statement_1$ cannot be executed despite any reorderings within p and q. Finally, RTSO does not allow re-orderings such as $p_{2.2}$; $p_{2.1}$ because they are both read instructions (i.e., *Read* → *Read* ordering is preserved), $q_{2.2}$; q_1 because both $q_{2.2}$ and q_1 are write instructions (i.e., *Write* → *Write* ordering is preserved), and $q_{2.2}$; $q_{2.1}$ because $q_{2.1}$ is a read and $q_{2.2}$ is a write (i.e., *Read* → *Write* ordering is preserved). A write to a variable that is followed by a read to the same variable in the program order must not be reordered (e.g., in Fig. 6, reordering $p_{2.1}$; p_1 is disallowed).

2.2 Total Store Order

TSO extends RTSO by including IPF, allowing a process to read pending writes from its own buffer, and hence, obtaining values that are not yet globally visible to other processes. To observe the effect of IPF, consider the program in Fig. 5 and its corresponding low-level representation in Fig. 6. Process p can never execute $statement_1$ under RTSO memory because the read at $p_{2.1}$ cannot be reordered with the write at p_1 due to the variable dependency. Furthermore, because *Read* → *Read* ordering is preserved, $p_{2.1}$ prevents reads to y at $p_{3.1}$ and $p_{3.4}$ from being executed before the write instruction at p_1 even though both reorderings $p_{3.1}$; $p_{2.2}$ and $p_{3.3}$; $p_{3.4}$; $p_{2.2}$ are possible. Similarly, $q_{2.1}$ prevents $q_{3.1}$ from being executed before q_1 even though $q_{2.2}$ may be reordered with $q_{3.1}$. Because SC memory is a special case of RTSO in which no reorderings are possible, it is also not possible for p to reach $statement_1$ under SC memory.

In contrast, TSO allows execution of $statement_1$ because IPF enables reads to occur from the write buffer. For the program in Fig. 6, the value written by $write(x, 1)$ at p_1 could still be in p's write buffer, which could be used by $p_{2.1}$ before the write at p_1 is committed to memory. Then $write(u, r0_p)$ at $p_{2.2}$ may become a pending write, and

Initially: $x = 0 \wedge y = 0 \wedge z \neq 0$

Process p	Process q
p_1: $x := 1$;	q_1: $y := 1$;
p_2: $u := x$;	q_2: $v := y$;
p_3: **if** $y = 0 \wedge z = 0$	q_3: $z := x$
p_4: **then** *statement*$_1$;	
p_5: **else** *statement*$_2$	

Fig. 5. Neither SC nor RTSO cause execution of *statement*$_1$, TSO does

Initially: $x = 0 \wedge y = 0 \wedge z \neq 0$

Process p	Process q
p_1: $write(x, 1)$;	q_1: $write(y, 1)$;
$p_{2.1}$: $read(x, r0_p)$;	$q_{2.1}$: $read(y, r0_q)$;
$p_{2.2}$: $write(u, r0_p)$;	$q_{2.2}$: $write(v, r0_q)$;
$p_{3.1}$: $\big(read(y, r1_p)$;	$q_{3.1}$: $read(x, r1_q)$;
$p_{3.2}$: $read(z, r2_p)\big)$	$q_{3.2}$: $write(z, r1_q)$
$\sqcap$	
$p_{3.3}$: $\big(read(z, r2_p)$;	
$p_{3.4}$: $read(y, r1_p)\big)$;	
$p_{3.5}$: **if** $r1_p = 0 \wedge r2_p = 0 \ldots$	

Fig. 6. Low-level representation of program in Fig. 5

then $read(y, r1_p)$ and $read(z, r2_p)$ (at $p_{3.1}$ and $p_{3.2}$, respectively) may be executed. By fetching values from memory before the pending $write(x, 1)$ at p_1 has been committed, the reads at $p_{3.1}$ and $p_{3.2}$, can appear as if they were executed before $p_{2.1}$. The same arguments apply to process q where $read(y, r0_q)$ at $q_{2.1}$ can read the value of y from q's write buffer, and hence, execution of $q_{2.1}$ and $q_{3.1}$ appear to be reordered. A concurrent execution after reordering that allows control to reach p_4 is:

$$p_{3.1} \,;\, q_{3.1} \,;\, q_1 \,;\, q_{2.1} \,;\, q_{2.2} \,;\, q_{3.2} \,;\, p_1 \,;\, p_{2.1} \,;\, p_{2.2} \,;\, p_{3.2}$$

This example shows that TSO allows *Read* $\rightarrow$ *Read* reordering in a restricted manner and in fact that the IPF relaxation can be viewed as such [3].

3 Interval-Based Reasoning

The programs in Figs. 4 and 6 have helped explain TSO concepts, however, reasoning about interleavings at such a low level of abstraction quickly becomes infeasible. Instead, we use a framework that considers the intervals in which a program execute [9], which enables both non-deterministic evaluation [13] and compositional reasoning [17]. We present interval predicates in Section 3.1, fractional permissions (to model conflicting accesses) in Section 3.2, and a programming language as well as its generalised interval-based semantics in Section 3.3.

3.1 Interval Predicates

We use interval predicates to formalise the interval-based semantics due to the generality they provide over frameworks that consider programs as relations between pre/post states. An *interval* is a contiguous set of integers (denoted $\mathbb{Z}$), and hence the set of all intervals is $Intv \mathrel{\widehat{=}} \{\Delta \subseteq \mathbb{Z} \mid \forall t_1, t_2 \colon \Delta \bullet \forall t \colon \mathbb{Z} \bullet t_1 \leq t \leq t_2 \Rightarrow t \in \Delta\}$. Using '.' for function application (i.e., $f.x$ denotes $f(x)$), we let $\mathsf{lub}.\Delta$ and $\mathsf{glb}.\Delta$ denote the *least upper* and *greatest lower* bounds of an interval Δ, respectively. We define $\mathsf{lub}.\varnothing \mathrel{\widehat{=}} -\infty$, $\mathsf{glb}.\varnothing \mathrel{\widehat{=}} \infty$, $\mathsf{inf}.\Delta \mathrel{\widehat{=}} (\mathsf{lub}.\Delta = \infty)$, $\mathsf{fin}.\Delta \mathrel{\widehat{=}} \neg\mathsf{inf}.\Delta$, and $\mathsf{empty}.\Delta \mathrel{\widehat{=}} (\Delta = \varnothing)$.

One must often reason about two *adjoining* intervals, i.e., intervals that immediately precede or follow a given interval. For $\Delta_1, \Delta_2 \in \mathit{Intv}$, we say Δ_1 *adjoins* Δ_2 iff $\Delta_1 \propto \Delta_2$ holds, where $\Delta_1 \propto \Delta_2 \mathrel{\widehat{=}} (\Delta_1 \cup \Delta_2 \in \mathit{Intv}) \wedge (\forall t_1{:}\, \Delta_1, t_2{:}\, \Delta_2 \bullet t_1 < t_2)$. Thus, $\Delta_1 \propto \Delta_2$ holds iff Δ_2 immediately follows Δ_1. Note that adjoining intervals Δ_1 and Δ_2 must be both contiguous and disjoint, and that both $\Delta \propto \varnothing$ and $\varnothing \propto \Delta$ trivially hold.

Given that variable names are taken from the set *Var*, a *state space* over a set of variables $V \subseteq \mathit{Var}$ is given by $\mathit{State}_V \mathrel{\widehat{=}} V \to \mathit{Val}$ and a *state* is a member of State_V, i.e., a state is a total function mapping variables in V to values in *Val*. A *stream* of behaviours over V is given by the total function $\mathit{Stream}_V \mathrel{\widehat{=}} \mathbb{Z} \to \mathit{State}_V$, which maps each time in $\mathbb{Z}$ to a state over V. A *predicate* over type T is a total function $\mathcal{P}T \mathrel{\widehat{=}} T \to \mathbb{B}$ mapping each member of T to a Boolean. For example $\mathcal{P}\mathit{State}_V$ and $\mathcal{P}\mathit{Stream}_V$ denote state and stream predicates, respectively. To facilitate reasoning about specific parts of a stream, we use *interval predicates*, which have type $\mathit{IntvPred}_V \mathrel{\widehat{=}} \mathit{Intv} \to \mathcal{P}\mathit{Stream}_V$. A stream predicate defines the behaviour of a system over all time, and an interval predicate defines the behaviour of a system with respect to a given interval [9, 10]. We assume pointwise lifting of operators on stream and interval predicates in the normal manner, e.g., if g_1 and g_2 are interval predicates, Δ is an interval and s is a stream, we have $(g_1 \wedge g_2).\Delta.s = (g_1.\Delta.s \wedge g_2.\Delta.s)$.

We define two operators on interval predicates: *chop* (to model sequential composition), and *k*- and ω-*iteration* (to model loops), i.e.,

$$(g_1 \,;\, g_2).\Delta.s \mathrel{\widehat{=}} \begin{pmatrix} \exists \Delta_1, \Delta_2{:}\, \mathit{Intv} \bullet (\Delta = \Delta_1 \cup \Delta_2) \wedge \\ (\Delta_1 \propto \Delta_2) \wedge g_1.\Delta_1.s \wedge g_2.\Delta_2.s \end{pmatrix} \vee (\mathsf{inf}.\Delta \wedge g_1.\Delta.s)$$

$$g^0 \mathrel{\widehat{=}} \mathsf{empty} \qquad g^{k+1} \mathrel{\widehat{=}} g^k \,;\, g \qquad g^\omega \mathrel{\widehat{=}} \nu z \bullet (g \,;\, z) \vee \mathsf{empty}$$

The *chop* operator ';' is a basic operator on two interval predicates [21, 10], where $(g_1 \,;\, g_2).\Delta.s$ holds iff either interval Δ may be split into two adjoining parts Δ_1 and Δ_2 so that g_1 holds for Δ_1 and g_2 holds for Δ_2 in s, or the least upper bound of Δ is ∞ and g_1 holds for Δ in s. Inclusion of the second disjunct $\mathsf{inf}.\Delta \wedge g_1.\Delta.s$ enables g_1 to model an infinite (divergent or non-terminating) program. Iteration g^k defines the k-fold iteration of g and g^ω is the greatest fixed point of $\lambda z \bullet (g \,;\, z) \vee \mathsf{empty}$, which allows both finite and infinite iterations of g [12]. We use

$$(\ominus g).\Delta.s \mathrel{\widehat{=}} \exists \Omega{:}\, \mathit{Intv} \bullet \Omega \propto \Delta \wedge g.\Omega.s$$

to denote that g holds in some interval Ω that immediately precedes Δ.

We define the following operators to formalise properties over an interval using a state predicate c over an interval Δ in stream s.

$$(\boxdot c).\Delta.s \mathrel{\widehat{=}} \forall t{:}\, \Delta \bullet c.(s.t) \qquad (\Diamond c).\Delta.s \mathrel{\widehat{=}} \exists t{:}\, \Delta \bullet c.(s.t)$$

$$\overrightarrow{c}.\Delta.s \mathrel{\widehat{=}} (\mathsf{lub}.\Delta \in \Delta) \wedge c.(s.(\mathsf{lub}.\Delta))$$

That is $(\boxdot c).\Delta.s$ holds iff c holds for each state $s.t$ where $t \in \Delta$, $(\Diamond c).\Delta.s$ holds iff c holds in some state $s.t$ where $t \in \Delta$, and $\overrightarrow{c}.\Delta.s$ holds iff c holds in the state corresponding to the end of Δ. Note that $\boxdot c$ trivially holds for an empty interval, but $\Diamond c$ and $\overrightarrow{c}$ do not. A variable v is stable over interval Δ in stream s iff $\mathsf{stable}.v.\Delta.s$ holds, where $\mathsf{stable}.v.\Delta.s \mathrel{\widehat{=}} \exists k{:}\, \mathit{Val} \bullet \ominus(\overrightarrow{v = k}) \wedge \boxdot(v = k)$.

3.2 Fractional Permissions

The behaviour of a process executing a command is formalised by an interval predicate, and the behaviour of a parallel execution over an interval is given by the conjunction of these behaviours over the same interval. Because the state-spaces of the two processes often overlap, there is a possibility that a process writing to a variable conflicts with a read or write to the same variable by another process. To ensure that such conflicts do not take place, we follow Boyland's idea of mapping variables to a *fractional permission* [5], which is *rational* number between 0 and 1. A process has write-only access to a variable v if its permission to access v is 1, has read-only access to v if its permission to access v is above 0 but below 1, and has no access to v if its permission to access v is 0. Note that a process may not have both read and write permission to a variable. Because a permission is a rational number, read access to a variable may be split arbitrarily (including infinitely) among the processes of the system. However, at most one process may have write permission to a variable in any given state.

We assume that every state contains a *permission* variable Π whose value in state $\sigma \in State_V$ is a function of type $V \to Proc \to \{n{:}\, \mathbb{Q} \mid 0 \leq n \leq 1\}$, where *Proc* denotes the type of a process identifier. Note that it is possible for permissions to be distributed differently within states σ_1, σ_2 even if the values of the normal variables in σ_1 and σ_2 are identical. Process $p \in Proc$ has *write-permission* to variable v in state σ iff $\mathscr{W}_p.v.\sigma \mathrel{\widehat{=}} (\sigma.\Pi.v.p = 1)$, has *read-permission* to v in σ iff $\mathscr{R}_p.v.\sigma \mathrel{\widehat{=}} (0 < \sigma.\Pi.v.p < 1)$, and has *no-permission* to access v in σ iff $\mathscr{D}_p.v.\sigma \mathrel{\widehat{=}} (\sigma.\Pi.v.p = 0)$ holds. In the context of a stream s, for any time $t \in \mathbb{Z}$, process p may only write to and read from v in the transition step from $s.(t-1)$ to $s.t$ if $\mathscr{W}_p.v.(s.t)$ and $\mathscr{R}_p.v.(s.t)$ hold, respectively. Thus, $\mathscr{W}_p.v.(s.t)$ does not grant process p permission to write to v in the transition from $s.t$ to $s.(t+1)$ (and similarly $\mathscr{R}_p.v.(s.t)$). We introduce two assumptions on streams using fractional permissions that formalise our assumptions on the underlying hardware.

HC1. If no process has write access to v within an interval, then the value of v does not change within the interval, i.e., for any interval Δ and stream s,
$(\boxdot(\forall p{:}\, Proc \bullet \neg \mathscr{W}_p.v) \Rightarrow \mathsf{stable}.v).\Delta.s$

HC2. The sum of the permissions of the processes on any variable v is at most 1, i.e., for any interval Δ and stream s, $(\boxdot((\Sigma_{p \in Proc} \Pi.v.p) \leq 1)).\Delta.s$

For the rest of this paper, we assume that the streams and intervals under consideration satisfy both **HC1** and **HC2**. Further restrictions may explicitly be introduced to the programs if required. In essence, both **HC1** and **HC2** are implicit *rely* conditions of the programs that we develop [9, 17].

3.3 A Programming Language

To formalise common programming constructs, we present a language inspired by the refinement calculus [20], extended to enable reasoning about concurrency. The syntax closely matches program code, which simplifies translation from an implementation to the model. For a state predicate b, variable v, expression e and set of processes $P \subseteq Proc$, the abstract syntax of commands is given by *Cmd* below, where $BC \in BasicCmd$ and $C, C_1, C_2, C_p \in Cmd$.

$$BasicCmd ::= \mathsf{Idle} \mid [b] \mid v := e$$
$$Cmd ::= BC \mid \mathsf{Empty} \mid \mathsf{Magic} \mid \mathsf{Chaos} \mid \mathsf{fin\_Idle} \mid \mathsf{inf\_Idle} \mid$$
$$C_1 ; C_2 \mid C_1 \sqcap C_2 \mid C^\omega \mid \|_{p:P} C_p \mid \textsc{Init}\, b \bullet C$$

Thus, a basic command may either be Idle, a guard $[b]$ or an assignment $v := e$. A command may either be a basic command, Empty (representing the empty program), Magic (an infeasible command that has no behaviours), Chaos (a chaotic command that allows any behaviour), fin_Idle (a finite idle), inf_Idle (an infinite idle), sequential composition $(C_1 ; C_2)$, non-deterministic choice $C_1 \sqcap C_2$, iteration C^ω, parallel composition $\|_{p:P} C_p$, or a command with an initialisation $\textsc{Init}\, b \bullet C$.

Using this syntax, the programs in Fig. 3 and Fig. 5 are modelled by the commands in Fig. 7 and Fig. 8, respectively, where the labels in Figs. 3 and 5 have been omitted. For Fig. 3, the initialisation is modelled using the INIT construct, and the main command consists of the parallel composition between C_p and C_q, which model processes p and q, respectively. Command C_p is the sequential composition of the assignment followed by a non deterministic choice between Ct_p and Cf_p, which respectively model the true and false evaluations of the guard at p_2 in Fig. 3.

We define an interval-based semantics for this language, which is used to formalise program execution in RTSO ($\mathcal{R}$) and TSO ($\mathcal{T}$) memory models. Like [9], we split SC executions into instantaneous ($\mathcal{I}$) and apparent states ($\mathcal{S}$) evaluation, where the apparent states stem from non-atomic expression evaluation, i.e., by observing different variables of an expression at different times [9, 13].

To simplify comparison of the different memory models on program execution, we present a generalised semantics where the behaviour function is parameterised by the memory model under consideration. In particular, the generalised semantics for commands in a memory model $\mathcal{M} \in \{\mathcal{I}, \mathcal{S}, \mathcal{R}, \mathcal{T}\}$ is given by function $[\![\cdot]\!]_P^{\mathcal{M}}$ in Fig. 9, which for a given command returns an interval predicate that formalises the behaviour of the command with respect to $P \subseteq Proc$. A basic command BC is assumed to be executed by a single process p and its behaviour over an interval with respect to memory model $\mathcal{M}$ is defined by $(\!| BC |\!)_p^{\mathcal{M}}$, which requires that we instantiate interval predicates $\mathsf{idle}_p^{\mathcal{M}}$, $\mathsf{eval}_p^{\mathcal{M}}$ and $\mathsf{update}_p^{\mathcal{M}}$. Note that the behaviour of an assignment consists of two portions, an evaluation portion, where the expression e is evaluated to some value k, followed by an interval in which the variable v is updated to a new value k.

Note that the behaviours of each of the commands except for basic commands and parallel composition decompose for each of the memory models in the same way. The behaviour of Empty, Magic and Chaos are always empty, *false* and *true*, respectively, sequential composition is defined by the chop operator, and non-deterministic choice is defined by disjunction. The behaviour of command iteration C^ω is defined as iteration of

$$Ct_p \mathrel{\widehat{=}} [y = 0 \wedge z = 0] ; \mathit{statement}_1$$
$$Cf_p \mathrel{\widehat{=}} [y \neq 0 \vee z \neq 0] ; \mathit{statement}_2$$
$$C_p \mathrel{\widehat{=}} x := 1 ; (Ct_p \sqcap Cf_p)$$
$$C_q \mathrel{\widehat{=}} y := 1 ; z := x$$
$$C \mathrel{\widehat{=}} \textsc{Init}\, x = 0 \wedge y = 0 \wedge z \neq 0 \bullet C_p \| C_q$$

Fig. 7. Formalisation of program in Fig. 3

$$Dt_p \mathrel{\widehat{=}} [y = 0 \wedge z = 0] ; \mathit{statement}_1$$
$$Df_p \mathrel{\widehat{=}} [y \neq 0 \vee z \neq 0] ; \mathit{statement}_2$$
$$D_p \mathrel{\widehat{=}} x := 1 ; u := x ; (Dt_p \sqcap Df_p)$$
$$D_q \mathrel{\widehat{=}} y := 1 ; v := y ; z := x$$
$$D \mathrel{\widehat{=}} \textsc{Init}\, x = 0 \wedge y = 0 \wedge z \neq 0 \bullet D_p \| D_q$$

Fig. 8. Formalisation of program in Fig. 5

$$(\!|\, \mathsf{Idle} \,|\!)_p^{\mathcal{M}} \mathrel{\widehat{=}} \mathsf{idle}_p^{\mathcal{M}}.\mathit{Var} \qquad (\!|\, [b] \,|\!)_p^{\mathcal{M}} \mathrel{\widehat{=}} \mathsf{eval}_p^{\mathcal{M}}.b \qquad (\!|\, v := e \,|\!)_p^{\mathcal{M}} \mathrel{\widehat{=}} \exists k{:}\, \mathit{Val} \bullet \mathsf{eval}_p^{\mathcal{M}}.(e = k) \,;\, \mathsf{update}_p^{\mathcal{M}}(v, k)$$

$$[\![BC]\!]_{\{p\}}^{\mathcal{N}} \mathrel{\widehat{=}} (\!| BC |\!)_p^{\mathcal{N}} \qquad [\![\mathsf{Magic}]\!]_P^{\mathcal{M}} \mathrel{\widehat{=}} \mathit{false} \qquad [\![C_1 \,;\, C_2]\!]_P^{\mathcal{M}} \mathrel{\widehat{=}} [\![C_1]\!]_P^{\mathcal{M}} \,;\, [\![C_2]\!]_P^{\mathcal{M}}$$

$$[\![\mathsf{Empty}]\!]_P^{\mathcal{M}} \mathrel{\widehat{=}} \mathsf{empty} \qquad [\![\mathsf{Chaos}]\!]_P^{\mathcal{M}} \mathrel{\widehat{=}} \mathit{true} \qquad [\![C_1 \sqcap C_2]\!]_P^{\mathcal{M}} \mathrel{\widehat{=}} [\![C_1]\!]_P^{\mathcal{M}} \vee [\![C_2]\!]_P^{\mathcal{M}}$$

$$[\![C^{\omega}]\!]_P^{\mathcal{M}} \mathrel{\widehat{=}} ([\![C]\!]_P^{\mathcal{M}})^{\omega}$$

$$[\![\mathsf{fin\_Idle}]\!]_P^{\mathcal{M}} \mathrel{\widehat{=}} \mathsf{fin} \wedge \textstyle\bigwedge_{p:P} [\![\mathsf{Idle}]\!]_p^{\mathcal{M}} \qquad [\![\mathsf{inf\_Idle}]\!]_P^{\mathcal{M}} \mathrel{\widehat{=}} \mathsf{inf} \wedge \textstyle\bigwedge_{p:P} [\![\mathsf{Idle}]\!]_p^{\mathcal{M}}$$

$$[\![\textsc{Init}\, b \bullet C]\!]_P^{\mathcal{M}} \mathrel{\widehat{=}} \ominus \overrightarrow{b} \Rightarrow [\![C]\!]_P^{\mathcal{M}}$$

$$\begin{aligned} \mathit{term}.S.T \mathrel{\widehat{=}}\; & S \in \{\mathsf{fin\_Idle}, \mathsf{inf\_Idle}\} \wedge T \in \{\mathsf{fin\_Idle}, \mathsf{inf\_Idle}\} \wedge \\ & (S = \mathsf{inf\_Idle} \Rightarrow T \neq \mathsf{inf\_Idle}) \end{aligned}$$

$$\begin{aligned} [\![\,\|_{p:P}\, C_p]\!]_P^{\mathcal{N}} \mathrel{\widehat{=}}\; & \textbf{if } P = \varnothing \textbf{ then } \mathit{true} \textbf{ elseif } P = \{p\} \textbf{ then } [\![C_p]\!]_{\{p\}}^{\mathcal{M}} \\ & \textbf{else } \exists Q, R, S, T \bullet (Q \cup R = P) \wedge (Q \cap R = \varnothing) \wedge Q \neq \varnothing \wedge R \neq \varnothing \wedge \\ & \quad \mathit{term}.S.T \wedge [\![(\|_{p:Q}\, C_p) \,;\, S]\!]_Q^{\mathcal{M}} \wedge [\![(\|_{p:R}\, C_p) \,;\, T]\!]_R^{\mathcal{M}} \end{aligned}$$

Fig. 9. General semantics for interval-based reasoning

the behaviour of C, and the behaviour of the $\textsc{Init}\, b \bullet C$ is the behaviour of C assuming that b holds at the end of some immediately preceding interval.

Assuming $\mathcal{N} \mathrel{\widehat{=}} \mathcal{M} \backslash \{\mathcal{T}\}$, the behaviour of a basic command $[\![BC]\!]_{\{p\}}^{\mathcal{N}}$ is defined as the basic behaviour $(\!| BC |\!)_{\{p\}}^{\mathcal{N}}$. Behaviour $[\![\,\|_{p:P}\, C_p]\!]_P^{\mathcal{N}}$ is *true* if the set P is empty and discards the parallel composition operator if P is a singleton set. If P contains at least two elements, $[\![\,\|_{p:P}\, C_p]\!]_P^{\mathcal{N}}$ holds if P can be split into two non-empty disjoint subsets Q and R such that both $[\![\,\|_{p:Q}\, C_p \,;\, S]\!]_Q^{\mathcal{N}}$ and $[\![\,\|_{p:R}\, C_p \,;\, T]\!]_R^{\mathcal{N}}$ hold, where S and T denote possible idling. This idling is necessary because $\|_{p:Q}\, C_p$ and $\|_{p:R}\, C_p$ may terminate at different times [9] and idling may sometimes be infinite because a component may not terminate. Within a parallel composition, fractional permissions together with assumptions **HC1** and **HC2**, restrict access to shared variables, and hence, how processes may affect each other [9]. The behaviours of both $[\![BC]\!]_{\{p\}}^{\mathcal{T}}$ and $[\![\,\|_{p:P}\, C_p]\!]_P^{\mathcal{T}}$ (i.e., for TSO memory) are defined in Section 4.4.

4 Program Semantics under Different Memory Models

We present a semantics for instantaneous evaluation (where an entire expression is evaluated in a single atomic step) in Section 4.1 and apparent states evaluation (where variables are assumed to be read one at a time) is given in Section 4.2. This work has appeared in [9], but we present it here once again for completeness and to simplify comparisons with RTSO (Section 4.3) and TSO memory (Section 4.4).

4.1 Sequentially Consistent Instantaneous Evaluation Semantics

The simplest execution model we consider is $\mathcal{I}$ (instantaneous evaluation), where expressions are evaluated under SC in one of the actual states that occur in an interval of evaluation [13]. Given that an expression e is evaluated in an interval Δ of stream s and that S is the set of states of s that occur within Δ, this form of expression evaluation returns a value of e for some state of S. To formalise this, we define interval predicate

$$\mathsf{idle}_p.V \mathrel{\widehat{=}} \forall v\colon V \bullet \boxdot \neg \mathscr{W}_p.v$$

i.e., p does not write to any variable of V. To complete the instantaneous evaluation semantics for our language, we instantiate interval predicates $\mathsf{idle}_p^{\mathcal{I}}$, $\mathsf{eval}_p^{\mathcal{I}}$ and $\mathsf{update}_p^{\mathcal{I}}$ as follows, where c is a state predicate, v is a variable and k is a value. We let $vars.c$ denote the set of free variables of c.

$$\mathsf{idle}_p^{\mathcal{I}} \mathrel{\widehat{=}} \mathsf{idle}_p \qquad \mathsf{eval}_p^{\mathcal{I}}.c \mathrel{\widehat{=}} \circledcirc(c \wedge (\forall v\colon vars.c \bullet \mathscr{R}_p.v)) \wedge \mathsf{idle}_p.Var$$
$$\mathsf{update}_p^{\mathcal{I}}(v,k) \mathrel{\widehat{=}} \boxdot((v = k) \wedge \mathscr{W}_p.v) \wedge \neg\mathsf{empty} \wedge \mathsf{idle}_p.(Var \backslash \{v\})$$

The semantics of $\mathsf{idle}_p^{\mathcal{I}}$ is straightforward. Evaluation of c in a stream s within interval Δ is given by $\mathsf{eval}_p^{\mathcal{I}}.c.\Delta.s$, which holds iff (a) there is a time $t \in \Delta$ such that $c.(s.t)$ holds and p has permission to read the variables of c in $s.t$, and (b) p does not write to any variable within Δ. Updating the value of v to k (in shared memory) within interval Δ of stream s is modelled by $\mathsf{update}_p^{\mathcal{I}}(v,k).\Delta.s$, which holds iff (a) throughout Δ, v has value k and p has write permission to v, (b) Δ is non-empty and (c) p does not write to any other variable. We must ensure that $\neg\mathsf{empty}$ holds because $\boxdot c$ is trivially true for an empty interval.

4.2 Sequentially Consistent Apparent States Evaluation Semantics

Instantaneous evaluation is not problematic for expressions in which at most one variable of the expression is unstable [9, 13]. For more complex expressions (e.g., the guard of p_2 in Fig. 3), instantaneous evaluation will be unimplementable because hardware will seldom be able to guarantee that all variables of an expression can be read in a single atomic step. That is, instantaneous evaluation does not reflect the fact that implementations can read at most one variable atomically. Hence, we consider a second method of evaluation that returns a value in the states apparent to a process.

For each expression evaluation, we assume that each variable is read at most once, and that the same value is used for each occurrence of the variable in an expression[2]. We assume that a compiler non-deterministically chooses an ordering of read instructions when evaluating an expression. For example, in the low-level program in Fig. 4, the order of reads of the variables of p_2 in Fig. 3 is non-deterministically chosen.

The $apparent_{p,W}^{\mathcal{S}}$ function generates a set of states that may not exist in the stream, but can be observed by a process that reads variables one at a time. For example, eliding details of the permission variable, if over an interval Δ, a stream s has actual states $\{x \mapsto 0, y \mapsto 0\}, \{x \mapsto 1, y \mapsto 0\}, \{x \mapsto 1, y \mapsto 1\}$, a possible observable state within Δ in s is $\{x \mapsto 0, y \mapsto 1\}$. To generate the set of states apparent to process p, one must ensure that p has the appropriate read permissions. Using the $apparent_{p,W}^{\mathcal{S}}$ function, we define the *possibly* operator $\circledS_p$, which evaluates state predicates over a set of apparent states with respect to a given interval and stream.

$$apparent_{p,W}^{\mathcal{S}}.\Delta.s \mathrel{\widehat{=}} \{\sigma\colon State_W \mid \forall v\colon W \bullet \exists t\colon \Delta \bullet (\sigma.v = s.t.v) \wedge \mathscr{R}_p.v.(s.t)\}$$
$$(\circledS_p c).\Delta.s \mathrel{\widehat{=}} \exists \sigma\colon apparent_{p,vars.c}^{\mathcal{S}}.\Delta.s \bullet c.\sigma$$

[2] It is possible to define evaluators that, for example, (re)read a variable for each occurrence of the variable, and hence, potentially returns false for $v = v$ if the value of v changes during the observation interval [18, 13].

To complete the program semantics for sequentially consistent apparent states evaluation, we must instantiate predicates $\mathsf{idle}_p^{\mathcal{S}}$, $\mathsf{eval}_p^{\mathcal{S}}$ and $\mathsf{update}_p^{\mathcal{S}}$ for a process p.

$$\mathsf{idle}_p^{\mathcal{S}} \mathrel{\widehat{=}} \mathsf{idle}_p \qquad \mathsf{eval}_p^{\mathcal{S}}.c \mathrel{\widehat{=}} (\circledS_p c) \wedge \mathsf{idle}_p^{\mathcal{I}}.\mathit{Var} \qquad \mathsf{update}_p^{\mathcal{S}}(v,k) \mathrel{\widehat{=}} \mathsf{update}_p^{\mathcal{I}}(v,k)$$

Except for $\mathsf{eval}_p^{\mathcal{S}}.c$, these interval predicates are identical to memory model $\mathcal{I}$. Interval predicate $\mathsf{eval}_p^{\mathcal{S}}.c$ uses $\circledS$ evaluation, which models the fact that the variables of c are read one at a time and at most once in the interval of evaluation, capturing the non-determinism due to fine-grained concurrency, e.g., Fig. 4. We ask the reader to consult [9, 13] for further details on instantaneous and apparent states evaluation under SC memory.

4.3 Restricted TSO

As described in Section 2.1, RTSO weakens SC memory by relaxing *Write* $\rightarrow$ *Read* ordering, but a read from a variable with a pending write must wait for the pending write to be committed to memory. RTSO is not implemented by any hardware, however, we use it as a stepping stone to formalisation of the more complicated TSO model in Section 4.4, which is implemented by several mainstream processors [7, 16, 22].

As with apparent states evaluation in Section 4.2, the semantics of a program under RTSO is defined by instantiating interval predicates $\mathsf{idle}_p^{\mathcal{R}}$, $\mathsf{eval}_p^{\mathcal{R}}$ and $\mathsf{update}_p^{\mathcal{R}}$ for a process p, which requires that we formalise expression evaluation with respect to the reorderings RTSO memory may cause. Like SC apparent states evaluation (Section 4.2), we assume that the variables of an expression may be read in any order, but that each variable is read at most once per evaluation. We define an apparent states evaluator $\mathit{apparent}_{p,W}^{\mathcal{R}}.\Delta.s$, where Δ is the interval of execution in the *program order* in stream s. Because SC is not guaranteed, the interval in which an expression is evaluated (i.e., the *execution order*) extends beyond Δ (see Fig. 10). We use *write/read barrier* variables $WB_p \notin \mathit{Var}$ and $RB_p \notin \mathit{Var}$ for each process p, which describe how far the interval of evaluation may extend. By selecting placement of the barriers, one can control the reorderings allowed by RTSO. We assume that a write barrier for each variable is placed at initialisation, and hence, a variable's value prior to initialisation cannot be read.

Like permission variable Π, we implicitly assume that each state of the program includes barrier variables WB_p and RB_p for each process p. A write barrier for variable v in process p prevents reorderings of reads to variable v within p, and hence, its value is a function of type $\mathit{Var} \rightarrow \mathbb{B}$. Process p places a write barrier to a variable v whenever the value of v is updated, i.e., committed to memory (see definition of $\mathsf{update}_p^{\mathcal{R}}$ below). This prevents future reads to v in process p from being reordered with the write to v.

Read barriers must allow variables that are part of the same expression to be read in any order, but must disallow reorderings from expressions that are evaluated later in the program order. Hence, one is required to uniquely identify each expression occurrence. The value of a read RB_p variable is hence of type $\mathbb{Z} \rightarrow \mathit{Var} \rightarrow \mathbb{B}$, where the integer component is used to identify the corresponding expression evaluation. In particular, we identify an evaluation using the least upper bound of the interval of evaluation. Hence, whenever a process p reads a variable v in an interval Δ as part of an expression evaluation, p places a read barrier for v with identifier $\mathsf{lub}.\Delta$ at the time at which v is

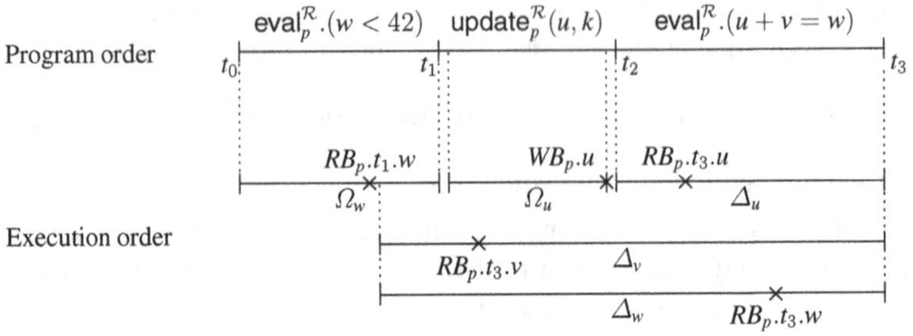

Fig. 10. Extending apparent states evaluation

read. This prevents any reads that are part of future expression evaluations from being reordered with the read to v in Δ, and hence, from reading outdated values. We define apparent states evaluation for RTSO as follows, where $id \in \mathbb{Z}$, $v \in Var$, $p \in Proc$, $s \in Stream$, $W \subseteq Var$ and $\Delta \in Intv$.

$$extendedIntv.id.v.p.s \mathrel{\widehat{=}} \left\{ \Omega{:}\, Intv \;\middle|\; \begin{array}{l} (\mathsf{lub}.\Omega = id) \wedge \\ \boxdot(\neg WB_p.v \wedge (\forall t{:}\, \mathbb{Z}, u{:}\, Var \bullet RB_p.t.u \Rightarrow t \geq id)).\Omega.s \end{array} \right\}$$

$$apparent^{\mathcal{R}}_{p,W}.\Delta.s \mathrel{\widehat{=}} \left\{ \sigma{:}\, State \;\middle|\; \begin{array}{l} \forall v{:}\, W \bullet \exists \Omega{:}\, extendedIntv.(\mathsf{lub}.\Delta).v.p.s \bullet \exists t{:}\, \Omega \bullet \\ \qquad (\sigma.v = s.t.v) \wedge \mathscr{R}_p.v.(s.t) \wedge RB_p.(\mathsf{lub}.\Delta).v.(s.t) \end{array} \right\}$$

Hence, $extendedIntv.id.v.p.s$ returns a set of extended intervals within which p may read v with respect to stream s as part of the expression identified by id. Each interval within $extendedIntv.id.v.p.s$ must not contain a write barrier to v or a read barrier to any variable with identifier t such that $t < id$. An example of such extended intervals is given in Fig. 10, where intervals Δ_v and Δ_w (corresponding to the evaluation of $u + v = w$) are disallowed from extending beyond the read barrier $RB_p.t_1.w$, which marks the point at which w was read in Ω_w. Interval Δ_u is disallowed from extending beyond time t_2, due to the write barrier for u ($WB.u$) within Ω_u that is placed by the update to u. The write barrier $WB.u$ in Ω_u does not affect Δ_v and Δ_w because $u \neq v$ and $u \neq w$, and hence, allows v and w to be evaluated before u is updated. The read barriers in Δ_u, Δ_v and Δ_w do not affect each other, because they each have the same identifier t_3, i.e., are part of the same expression evaluation. However, note that any evaluations that occur after t_3 in the program order would be disallowed from extending beyond the latest read barrier identified by t_3, which in the example above is $RB_p.t_3.w$ within Δ_w.

The apparent states for RTSO are defined by $apparent^{\mathcal{R}}_{p,W}$, where extended intervals are used for evaluation of each variable. To generate a state σ apparent to process p, for each variable $v \in W$, we pick an extended interval Ω corresponding to v, then pick a time t from Ω such that p has permission to read v at t, and set the value of v in σ to $(s.t).v$. Process p places a read barrier to v with identifier $\mathsf{lub}.\Delta$ at t to prevent future reads to any variable in the program order from being reordered with the read to v at time t in the execution order.

Using the set of apparent states, we define $(\circledR_p c).\Delta.s$ which holds iff state predicate c holds in some state apparent to process p in interval Δ and stream s with respect to RTSO memory.

$$(\circledR_p c).\Delta.s \mathrel{\widehat{=}} \exists \sigma\colon apparent^{\mathcal{R}}_{p,vars.c}.\Delta.s \bullet c.\sigma$$

In addition to the effect of each command on the read/write permissions, we must also specify the effect of each command on the read/write barriers. We define the following interval predicates for a process p, set of variables V, interval Δ and stream s.

$$\begin{aligned} \mathsf{wBar}_p.V.\Delta.s &\mathrel{\widehat{=}} \forall v\colon V \bullet \boxdot \neg WB_p.v.\Delta.s \\ \mathsf{rBar}_p.V.\Delta.s &\mathrel{\widehat{=}} \forall v\colon V \bullet \boxdot \neg RB_p.(\mathsf{lub}.\Delta).v.\Delta.s \end{aligned}$$

Hence, $\mathsf{wBar}_p.V.\Delta.s$ states that p does not place any write barriers to any of the variables of V within Δ and $\mathsf{rBar}_p.V.\Delta.s$ states that p does not place any read barrier to any of the variables of V with identifier $\mathsf{lub}.\Delta$ within Δ.

This now allows one to complete the semantics of programs that execute under RTSO memory, which is achieved by the following instantiations:

$$\begin{aligned} \mathsf{idle}^{\mathcal{R}}_p.V &\mathrel{\widehat{=}} (\mathsf{idle}_p \wedge \mathsf{rBar}_p \wedge \mathsf{wBar}_p).V \\ \mathsf{eval}^{\mathcal{R}}_p.c &\mathrel{\widehat{=}} \circledR_p c \wedge (\mathsf{idle}_p \wedge \mathsf{wBar}_p).Var \wedge \mathsf{rBar}_p.(Var \backslash vars.c) \\ \mathsf{update}^{\mathcal{R}}_p(v,k) &\mathrel{\widehat{=}} \mathsf{update}^{\mathcal{I}}_p(v,k) \wedge \overrightarrow{WB_p.v} \wedge \mathsf{wBar}_p.(Var \backslash \{v\}) \wedge \mathsf{rBar}_p.Var \end{aligned}$$

Hence, $\mathsf{idle}^{\mathcal{R}}_p.\Delta.s$ holds iff p does not write to any variable and does not introduce any read/write barriers. Interval predicate $\mathsf{eval}^{\mathcal{R}}_p.c.\Delta.s$ holds iff c holds in some apparent state generated by $apparent^{\mathcal{R}}_{p,vars.c}.\Delta.s$, process p does not write to any variable, and introduces no barriers except for the read barriers for variables used in c. Finally, a variable update to v behaves in the same manner as $\mathsf{update}^{\mathcal{I}}_p(v,k)$ and additionally places a write barrier to v at the end of execution. An update does not introduce any other barriers except for the one to v.

Example. We apply our RTSO semantics to our running example program from Fig. 3 using the encoding from Fig. 7. Instead of unrolling the full details of our definitions, we consider Fig. 11, which shows a possible interval of execution of processes $C_p \parallel C_q$ that leads to execution of $statement_1$. Note that details regarding disjointness at the boundary between adjoining intervals have been elided from the diagram. The top of Fig. 11 shows process p and its corresponding basic commands, obtained by unfolding the language definitions in Fig. 9. Below this, we present the actual intervals of execution allowed by the weak memory model; corresponding intervals of the program and execution orders are connected by dotted lines. Representation of process q is vertically inverted. The time line shows the times at which the actual reads/writes of each basic command occur in terms of the low-level instructions from Fig. 4. The intervals in which the updates occur in both p and q are preserved by the execution order. However, the intervals in which $\mathsf{eval}^{\mathcal{T}}_p(y = 0 \wedge z = 0)$ and $\mathsf{eval}^{\mathcal{T}}_q(k_x = x)$ (which is part of the behaviour of $z := x$) execute extend beyond their respective intervals in the program order. As a result of the extension, process p may read $y = 0$, process q may write $z = 0$, which allows process p to read $z = 0$. Note that the intervals in which the reads occur also contain a fuzzy portion depicting an interval in which read permission is not available due to a write in the other process. Furthermore, our framework allows

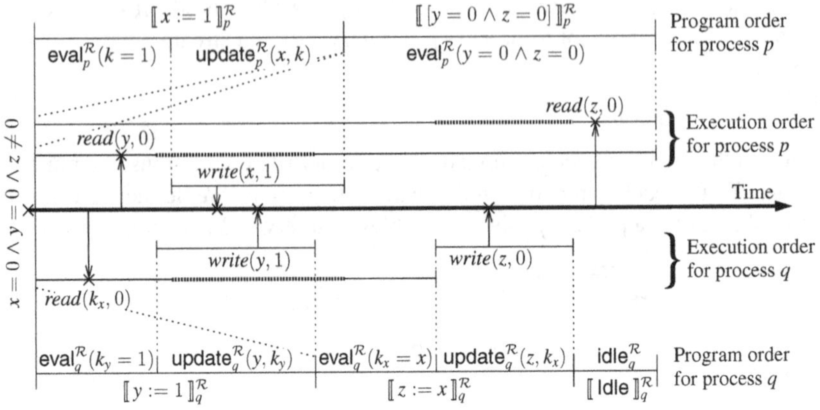

Fig. 11. A possible RTSO execution of $C_p \parallel C_q$ from Fig. 7

truly concurrent non-conflicting reads and writes to take place. Conflicts are avoided by fractional permissions together with assumptions **HC1** and **HC2**.

4.4 Total Store Order Semantics

The TSO memory model extends RTSO by allowing a process to read values from its own write buffer early without waiting for the pending writes to be committed to memory. Hence, in the TSO memory model, a read to a variable v returns the pending value of v in the write buffer (if a pending write exists) and the value of v from memory (if there are no pending writes to v). It is possible for a buffer to contain multiple pending writes to v, i.e. the same variable occurs more than once in a write buffer; in this case, a read must return the most recent pending write.

We let seq.T denote sequences of type T, assume sequences are indexed from 0 onward, let $\langle a_0, \ldots, a_{n-1}\rangle$ denote a sequence with n elements and use '$\frown$' to denote sequence concatenation. To formalise the semantics of a program under TSO, we further extend the state and explicitly include a variable $Buffer_p$ whose value is of type seq.$(Var \times Val)$ and models the write buffer of process p. Each $Buffer_p$ is a sequence containing pending writes with its new value. Hence, we define two state predicates for a variable v, process p, value k, and state σ. We assume dom.f and ran.f return the domain and range of function f, respectively.

$$\begin{aligned} inBuffer.v.p.\sigma &\mathrel{\widehat=} \exists k \bullet (v, k) \in \mathrm{ran}.(\sigma.Buffer_p) \\ bufferVal.v.k.p.\sigma &\mathrel{\widehat=} \exists i \bullet \sigma.Buffer_p.i = (v, k) \wedge \\ &\qquad \forall j{:}\, \mathrm{dom}.(\sigma.Buffer_p), l{:}\, Val \bullet j > i \Rightarrow \sigma.Buffer_p.j \neq (v, l) \end{aligned}$$

Hence, $inBuffer.v.p.\sigma$ holds iff there is a pending write to v in the write buffer of p in state σ, and $bufferVal.v.k.p.\sigma$ holds iff the latest value of v in $Buffer_p$ of state σ is k.

We define the set of states apparent to a process p under TSO memory with respect to set of variables W as follows, assuming that the evaluation takes place in stream s within interval Δ in the program order.

$$apparent^{\mathcal{T}}_{p,W}.\Delta.s \mathrel{\widehat{=}} \left\{ \sigma{:}\,State \;\middle|\; \begin{array}{l} \forall v{:}\,W \bullet \textbf{if } inBuffer.v.p.(s.(\mathsf{glb}.\Delta)) \\ \quad \textbf{then } bufferVal.v.(\sigma.v).p.(s.(\mathsf{glb}.\Delta)) \\ \quad \textbf{else } \exists \gamma{:}\, apparent^{\mathcal{R}}_{p,W}.\Delta.s \bullet \sigma.v = \gamma.v \end{array} \right\}$$

As with the other memory models, we generate an apparent state by mapping each variable in W to a possible value over the evaluation interval. If $v \in W$ is in p's write buffer, the value of v is taken from the most recent write to v within the write buffer. Otherwise, we return a possible value with respect to RTSO evaluation.

Using $apparent^{\mathcal{T}}_{p,vars.c}$, we define an operator that formalises whether a state predicate holds in some apparent state with respect to an interval Δ and stream s as follows.

$$(\textcircled{\scriptsize T}_p c).\Delta.s \mathrel{\widehat{=}} \exists \sigma{:}\, apparent^{\mathcal{T}}_{p,vars.c}.\Delta.s \bullet c.\sigma$$

To complete the program semantics, we instantiate functions $\mathsf{idle}^{\mathcal{T}}_p$, $\mathsf{eval}^{\mathcal{T}}_p$ and $\mathsf{update}^{\mathcal{T}}_p$ for a process p as follows.

$$\begin{aligned} \mathsf{idle}^{\mathcal{T}}_p.V &\mathrel{\widehat{=}} \mathsf{idle}^{\mathcal{R}}_p.V \wedge \mathsf{stable}.Buffer_p \\ \mathsf{eval}^{\mathcal{T}}_p.c &\mathrel{\widehat{=}} \textcircled{\scriptsize T}_p c \wedge (\mathsf{idle}_p \wedge \mathsf{wBar}_p).Var \wedge \mathsf{rBar}_p.(Var \backslash vars.c) \wedge \mathsf{stable}.Buffer_p \\ \mathsf{update}^{\mathcal{T}}_p(v,k) &\mathrel{\widehat{=}} \left(\exists buf \bullet \ominus(\overrightarrow{buf = Buffer_p}) \wedge \boxdot(Buffer_p = buf \frown \langle (v,k) \rangle)\right) \wedge \\ &\qquad \mathsf{idle}^{\mathcal{R}}_p.Var \wedge \neg \mathsf{empty} \end{aligned}$$

Command $\mathsf{idle}^{\mathcal{T}}_p$ behaves as $\mathsf{idle}^{\mathcal{R}}_p.V$ and in addition ensures that $Buffer_p$ is not modified. Interval predicate $\mathsf{eval}^{\mathcal{T}}_p.c$ holds iff c holds in some apparent state using TSO evaluation, and in addition, does not modify any variable (including $Buffer_p$), place a write barrier to any variable, or place a read barrier to any variable outside of $vars.c$. Finally, $\mathsf{update}^{\mathcal{T}}_p(v,k)$ adds the pair (v,k) to the end of $Buffer_p$, which is obtained from the state at the end of an immediately preceding interval, and behaves as $\mathsf{idle}^{\mathcal{R}}_p.Var$, i.e., does not modify the value or barrier of any variable. Interval predicate $\mathsf{update}^{\mathcal{T}}_p(v,k)$ also ensures that the interval under consideration is non-empty to guarantee that the buffer is actually updated.

Unlike $\mathcal{I}$, $\mathcal{S}$ and $\mathcal{R}$, local writes in a process p are not visible to other concurrent processes as long as the writes are stored in the buffer of p. To make these local writes globally visible, p must commit any pending writes to shared memory, which is achieved via a *flush* command. Buffers must be flushed in a FIFO order. Note that a flush does not necessarily commit the contents of the entire buffer, and may also not commit any elements from the buffer. Hence, we define an interval predicate commit_p, which commits the first pending write from $Buffer_p$ to memory, then extend the language with a basic command Flush, which for a process p, commits the first k elements of $Buffer_p$, where the value of k is chosen non-deterministically.

$$\begin{aligned} \mathsf{commit}_p &\mathrel{\widehat{=}} \exists buf, v, k \bullet \ominus(\overrightarrow{buf = Buffer_p \wedge (v,k) = buf.0}) \wedge \\ &\qquad [\![\mathsf{fin\_Idle}]\!]^{\mathcal{T}}_p \,;\, (\mathsf{update}^{\mathcal{R}}_p(v,k) \wedge \boxdot(Buffer_p = tail.buf)) \\ [\![\mathsf{Flush}]\!]^{\mathcal{T}}_p &\mathrel{\widehat{=}} \exists k{:}\, \mathrm{dom}.Buffer_p \cup \{-1\} \bullet \mathsf{commit}^{k+1} \end{aligned}$$

Hence, $\mathsf{commit}^{\mathcal{T}}_p$ instantiates buf to be the value of $Buffer_p$ at the end of the previous interval and sets the pair (v,k) to be the first element of buf. It then performs some finite idling, then the value of p is updated in the same manner as for RTSO and the value of the $Buffer_p$ is set to be $tail.buf$, which is the remaining write buffer excluding the first element of *buf*. Using $\mathsf{update}_p^{\mathcal{R}}(v,k)$ in order to commit elements to memory ensures that the required write barriers to v are placed appropriately. Note that empty implies finite idling, and hence, elements from the buffer may also be committed immediately. The behaviour of $[\![\,\mathsf{Flush}\,]\!]_p^{\mathcal{T}}$ commits 0 or more pending writes (upto the number of elements in the buffer). If the buffer is empty, the only possible behaviour of Flush is $\mathsf{commit}^0 \equiv \mathsf{empty}$.

Processes under TSO may non-deterministically choose to commit contents from their write buffer to memory, therefore, the semantics of a basic command BC allows an arbitrary number of Flush commands after the execution of BC.

$$[\![\,BC\,]\!]_p^{\mathcal{T}} \mathrel{\widehat{=}} (\!|\,BC\,|\!)_p^{\mathcal{T}} \ ; \ [\![\,\mathsf{Flush}\,]\!]_p^{\mathcal{T}}$$

Note that $[\![\,BC_1\,]\!]_p^{\mathcal{T}} \ ; \ [\![\,BC_2\,]\!]_p^{\mathcal{T}}$ is a possible behaviour of $[\![\,BC_1 \ ; \ BC_2\,]\!]_p^{\mathcal{T}}$, where BC_1 and BC_2 are both basic commands because $[\![\,\mathsf{Flush}\,]\!]_p^{\mathcal{T}}$ may be instantiated to commit^0, which is equivalent to empty and $(g_1 \ ; \ \mathsf{empty} \ ; \ g_2) \equiv (g_1 \ ; \ g_2)$ for any interval predicates g_1 and g_2. That is, a buffer flush may not occur in between two consecutive commands. TSO guarantees that the buffer is eventually flushed. This is incorporated into our semantics by modifying the behaviour of parallel composition so that the entire buffer is flushed when the processes terminate.

$$\begin{aligned}
&[\![\,\mathsf{FlushAll}\,]\!]_P^{\mathcal{T}} \mathrel{\widehat{=}} \textstyle\bigwedge_{p:P} \mathsf{commit}^{\#\mathrm{dom}.\mathit{Buffer}_p} \\
&[\![\,\|_{p:P}\, C_p\,]\!]_P^{\mathcal{T}} \mathrel{\widehat{=}} \textbf{if } P = \varnothing \textbf{ then } \mathit{true} \textbf{ elseif } P = \{p\} \textbf{ then } [\![\,C_p\,]\!]_{\{p\}}^{\mathcal{T}} \\
&\qquad\qquad \textbf{else } \exists Q,R,S,T \bullet (Q \cup R = P) \wedge (Q \cap R = \varnothing) \wedge Q \neq \varnothing \wedge R \neq \varnothing \wedge \\
&\qquad\qquad\qquad \mathit{term}.S.T \wedge [\![\,(\|_{p:Q}\, C_p) \ ; \ \mathsf{FlushAll} \ ; \ S\,]\!]_Q^{\mathcal{T}} \wedge \\
&\qquad\qquad\qquad [\![\,(\|_{p:R}\, C_p) \ ; \ \mathsf{FlushAll} \ ; \ T\,]\!]_R^{\mathcal{T}}
\end{aligned}$$

Example. An example execution under TSO is given in Fig. 12, where the E_p and U_p abbreviate $\mathsf{eval}_p^{\mathcal{T}}$ and $\mathsf{update}_p^{\mathcal{T}}$, respectively, FA denotes execution of a $\mathsf{FlushAll}$ command, and $\mathit{pend}(v,k)$ denotes an enqueuing of a pending write to the buffer of the corresponding process. Like Fig. 11, execution intervals are shown below the program order of process p (above q, respectively). In the depicted execution, each U adds a pending write to the local buffer, and hence, the new value cannot be observed by the other process. Because pending values are read first, execution of $\mathsf{E}_p(k_u = x)$ reads the value of x from the buffer. The effects of $\mathsf{U}_p(x,k)$, $\mathsf{E}_p(k_u = x)$ and $\mathsf{U}_p(u,k_u)$ are local, and hence, do not place any read barriers. This allows the interval of execution of $[y = 0 \wedge z = 0]$ to be extended as depicted. Following a similar behaviour in process q, variables y and x can be read early in processes p and q, enabling $[y = 0 \wedge z = 0]$ in process p to evaluate to *true*. One can also see that $[y = 0 \wedge z = 0]$ can never evaluate to *true* under RTSO memory because the intervals of evaluation cannot be extended beyond preceding evaluation intervals.

Note that the pending writes are eventually are committed to memory, which is only shown in Fig. 12 for process q, but is omitted for process p due to lack of space. The example also shows how memory efficiency has been improved by avoiding a read of x in process p and a read of y in process q. Furthermore, by storing pending writes in a buffer, the processes are able to wait until contention for shared memory has reduced before committing their writes.

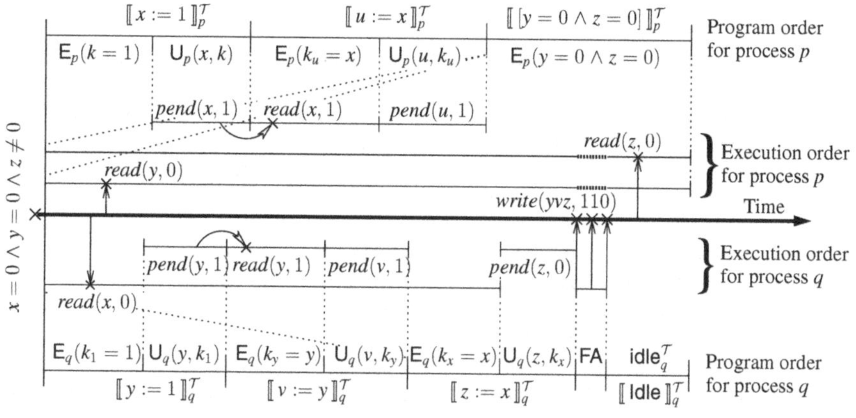

Fig. 12. A possible TSO execution of $D_p \parallel D_q$ from Fig. 8

5 Conclusions and Future Work

This paper presents a high-level formalisation of a program's behaviour under Total Store Order memory using an interval-based semantics. We enable reasoning about the fine-grained atomicity of expression evaluation that not only captures the inherent non-determinism due to concurrency, but also due to the memory read/write policy of the underlying hardware. Our formalisation is presented at a level of abstraction that avoids compilation to low-level language. Hence, tedious transformations steps (e.g. encoding of additional control-flow due to reorderings) are not necessary, and therefore, compares favourably to the existing low-level formalisations in the literature. The presented semantics is modular in the sense that the underlying memory model is a parameter to the behaviour function. The separation of program specification and language semantics that our framework achieves is beneficial in the sense that it reduces the specification effort.

We aim to use the semantics from this paper to reason about concurrent programs using interval-based rely/guarantee reasoning [8, 9]. In particular, to show that a program modelled by C executed by a set of processes P under memory model $\mathcal{M}$ satisfies a property g (expressed as an interval predicate), one would need to prove a formula of the form $[\![C]\!]_P^{\mathcal{M}} \Rightarrow g$. If C is a parallel composition $\|_{p:P}\, C_p$, one can decompose proofs of $[\![\|_{p:P}\, C_p]\!]_P^{\mathcal{M}} \Rightarrow g$ into proofs $[\![\|_{p:Q}\, C_p]\!]_Q^{\mathcal{M}} \Rightarrow r$ and $[\![\|_{p:R}\, C_p]\!]_R^{\mathcal{M}} \wedge r \Rightarrow g$ where Q and R are disjoint sets such that $Q \cup R = P$ and r is an interval predicate that represents a rely condition [9, 11, 17].

Using our formalisation it is possible to prove relationships between different memory models, e.g., that SC is a special case of RTSO, which in turn is a special case of TSO, but we leave these proofs as future work. Other future work includes mechanisation of the language semantics in a theorem prover, and the development of high-level semantics for other weak memory models such as PSO [7] and transactional memory [14], together with proofs that relate the various semantics.

References

1. Adve, S.V., Gharachorloo, K.: Shared memory consistency models: A tutorial. IEEE Computer 29(12), 66–76 (1996)
2. Alglave, J., Kroening, D., Nimal, V., Tautschnig, M.: Software verification for weak memory via program transformation. CoRR, abs/1207.7264 (2012)
3. Arvind, A., Maessen, J.-W.: Memory model = instruction reordering + store atomicity. SIGARCH Comput. Archit. News 34(2), 29–40 (2006)
4. Atig, M.F., Bouajjani, A., Burckhardt, S., Musuvathi, M.: On the verification problem for weak memory models. In: POPL, pp. 7–18. ACM, New York (2010)
5. Boyland, J.: Checking interference with fractional permissions. In: Cousot, R. (ed.) SAS 2003. LNCS, vol. 2694, pp. 55–72. Springer, Heidelberg (2003)
6. Burckhardt, S., Alur, R., Martin, M.M.K.: Checkfence: Checking consistency of concurrent data types on relaxed memory models. In: PLDI, pp. 12–21 (2007)
7. Inc. CORPORATE SPARC International. The SPARC architecture manual: version 8. Prentice-Hall, Inc., Upper Saddle River, NJ, USA (1992)
8. Dongol, B., Derrick, J.: Proving linearisability via coarse-grained abstraction. CoRR, abs/1212.5116 (2012)
9. Dongol, B., Derrick, J., Hayes, I.J.: Fractional permissions and non-deterministic evaluators in interval temporal logic. ECEASST 53 (2012)
10. Dongol, B., Hayes, I.J.: Deriving real-time action systems controllers from multiscale system specifications. In: Gibbons, J., Nogueira, P. (eds.) MPC 2012. LNCS, vol. 7342, pp. 102–131. Springer, Heidelberg (2012)
11. Dongol, B., Hayes, I.J.: Rely/guarantee reasoning for teleo-reactive programs over multiple time bands. In: Derrick, J., Gnesi, S., Latella, D., Treharne, H. (eds.) IFM 2012. LNCS, vol. 7321, pp. 39–53. Springer, Heidelberg (2012)
12. Dongol, B., Hayes, I.J., Meinicke, L., Solin, K.: Towards an algebra for real-time programs. In: Kahl, W., Griffin, T.G. (eds.) RAMICS 2012. LNCS, vol. 7560, pp. 50–65. Springer, Heidelberg (2012)
13. Hayes, I.J., Burns, A., Dongol, B., Jones, C.: Comparing degrees of non-determinism in expression evaluation. The Computer Journal (2013) (accepted January 04, 2013)
14. Herlihy, M., Moss, J.E.B.: Transactional memory: Architectural support for lock-free data structures. In: Jay Smith, A. (ed.) ISCA, pp. 289–300. ACM (1993)
15. Herlihy, M.P., Wing, J.M.: Linearizability: a correctness condition for concurrent objects. ACM Trans. Program. Lang. Syst. 12(3), 463–492 (1990)
16. Intel, Santa Clara, CA, USA. Intel 64 and IA-32 Architectures Software Developer's Manual Volume 3A: System Programming Guide, Part 1 (May 2012)
17. Jones, C.B.: Tentative steps toward a development method for interfering programs. ACM Trans. Prog. Lang. and Syst. 5(4), 596–619 (1983)
18. Jones, C.B., Pierce, K.: Elucidating concurrent algorithms via layers of abstraction and reification. Formal Aspects of Computing 23, 289–306 (2011)
19. Lamport, L.: How to make a multiprocessor computer that correctly executes multiprocess programs. IEEE Trans. Computers 28(9), 690–691 (1979)
20. Morgan, C.: Programming from Specifications. Prentice-Hall (1990)
21. Moszkowski, B.C.: A complete axiomatization of Interval Temporal Logic with infinite time. In: LICS, pp. 241–252 (2000)
22. AMD64 Architecture Programmer's Manual Volume 2: System Programming (2012), `http://support.amd.com/us/Processor_TechDocs/24593_APM_v2.pdf`
23. Park, S., Dill, D.L.: An executable specification, analyzer and verifier for RMO (relaxed memory order). In: SPAA, pp. 34–41 (1995)
24. Sewell, P., Sarkar, S., Owens, S., Nardelli, F.Z., Myreen, M.O.: x86-TSO: A rigorous and usable programmer's model for x86 multiprocessors. Commun. ACM 53(7), 89–97 (2010)

Preemptive Type Checking in Dynamically Typed Languages

Neville Grech*, Julian Rathke, and Bernd Fischer

Electronics and Computer Science, University of Southampton
{n.grech,jr2,b.fischer}@ecs.soton.ac.uk

Abstract. We describe a type system that identifies potential type errors in dynamically typed languages like Python. The system uses a flow-sensitive static analysis on bytecodes to compute, for every variable and program point, over-approximations of the variable's present and future use types. If the future use types are not subsumed by the present types, the further program execution may raise a type error, and a narrowing assertion is inserted; if future use and present types are disjoint, it will raise a type error, and a type error assertion is inserted. We prove that the assertions are inserted in optimal locations and thus preempt type errors earlier than dynamic, soft, and gradual typing. We describe the details of our type inference and assertion insertion, and demonstrate the results of an implementation of the system with a number of examples.

1 Introduction

Dynamically typed languages such as Python are among the most widely used languages [25]. In these languages, the principle type of any variable in a program is determined through runtime computations and can change throughout the execution and between different runs. Type checking is typically carried out as the program is executing and type errors manifest themselves as runtime errors or exceptions rather than being detected before execution. However, type errors are an indication that the code has latent computation errors and is therefore potentially dangerous. For example, the Mars climate orbiter crashed into the atmosphere due to *metric mixup* [1]. The earlier type errors are detected, the earlier the code can be fixed.

Fig. 1 shows a small example program with type errors. In a dynamically typed language, the program will fail at either line 15 or line 17, depending on whether arguments are passed to the program. Using the standard Python interpreter we can get for example the following trace:

```
$ python foo.py
enter initial value: 45
Traceback (most recent call last):
  File "foo.py", line 21, in <module>
  File "foo.py", line 15, in main
TypeError: bad operand type for abs(): 'str'
```

* The research work disclosed in this publication is partially funded by a Strategic Educational Pathways Scholarship (Malta). The scholarship is part-financed by the European Union – European Social Fund (ESF).

Z. Liu, J. Woodcock, and H. Zhu (Eds.): ICTAC 2013, LNCS 8049, pp. 195–212, 2013.

```
1  from sys import argv
2
3  def compute(x1=None,x2=None,x3=None):
4      global initial
5      if initial%5==0:
6          fin=int(input('enter final value: '))
7          return x1+x2+x3+fin
8      else:
9          initial-=1
10         return compute(x2,x3,initial)
11
12 def main():
13     global initial
14     if len(argv)<2:
15         initial=abs(input('enter initial value: '))
16     else:
17         initial=abs(argv[1])
18     print('outcome:',compute())
19
20 if __name__=='__main__':
21     main()
```

Fig. 1. Dynamically typed program with type errors in lines 15 and 17

We can see that the program only raises a type error when it executes line 15, after the user input has already been taken. We cannot see from the error trace, however, that the program actually contains another type error, i.e., at line 17, which in cases when the modulus of the entered number with 5 is less than 3. To discover this error, we are reliant on sufficient testing.

Our goal here is the development of a *preemptive type checking* system that statically analyses the program, and inserts type checking assertions that preempt (i.e., force the termination of) the program execution as soon as a type error becomes inevitable. In contrast, under the existing dynamic, gradual [18,19] or soft [7] typing systems, these errors are only caught at the point that a value of an incorrect type is used. In the example, preemptive type checking finds both errors and presents the same error traces as shown above. Moreover, it inserts a type error assertion at the beginning of the `main` function that prevents the program from executing at all, since *all* program executions will lead to a type error:

```
def main():
    raise TypeError('Type mismatch at lines 15, 17: expected Number, found str')
    ...
```

Now we assume that the user "fixes" this bug and manually inserts explicit type casts into the `main` function:

```
def main():
    global initial
    if len(argv)<2:
        initial=abs(int(input('enter initial value: ')))
    else:
        initial=abs(int(argv[1]))
    print('outcome:',compute())
```

However, when this program is run without preemptive type checking, the program will, depending on the input, either raise a type error or work as expected, for example:

```
$ python foo.py
enter initial value: 3
enter final value: 3
outcome: 6

$ python foo.py
enter initial value: 2
enter final value: 3
...
TypeError: unsupported operand type(s) for +: 'NoneType' and 'int'
```

As we can see, the manual debugging process is time consuming, and relies on the right combination of inputs to find the type errors. With preemptive type checking we can minimise this effort and find and correct type errors much quicker. Our analysis *statically* infers that `x1` and `x2` are either of type `NoneType` or integers, depending on the control flow taken by the program. It also concludes that `x1` and `x2` need to be integers for the program not to raise type errors:

```
Failure 1 - partial Traceback:
  File "foo.py", line 18, in main
  File "foo.py", line 6, in compute
Variable x1 expected Number but found NoneType

Failure 2 - partial Traceback:
  File "foo.py", line 18, in main
  File "foo.py", line 10, in compute
  File "foo.py", line 6, in compute
Variable x1 expected Number but found NoneType

Failure 3 - partial Traceback:
  File "foo.py", line 18, in main
  File "foo.py", line 10, in compute
  File "foo.py", line 10, in compute
  File "foo.py", line 6, in compute
Variable x1 expected Number but found NoneType
```

Note that it is difficult and expensive to determine the possible types of `x1` and `x2`. For example, using data flow analysis techniques, the fact that `x1` can be an integer is only discovered on a path that inlines function `compute` three times. We thus introduce an effective technique that uses *trails* to perform a flow sensitive type inference.

Preemptive type checking also transforms the `compute` function so that the type errors are preempted (see Fig. 2). The inserted assertions contain all details to identify the source of the type error, in particular the variable causing the type error, the location where the type error would be raised and the present type there. Hence, the user can correct the program with minimal debugging. Note that the assertions cannot be inserted any earlier (i.e., before the if-statement) because there are possible control flow paths that do not raise type errors.

Preemptive type checking identifies potential type errors in advance through a flow-sensitive static analysis. It computes, for every variable and every program point, an over-approximation of the types of the values that have last been assigned to a variable (its "present types") as well as the types with which it is next used in any reachable program point (its "future use types"). If the future use types are not subsumed by the present types, the further program execution *may* raise a type error, and a corresponding narrowing assertion is inserted; if future use types and present types are disjoint, the

```
def compute(x1=None,x2=None,x3=None):
    global initial
    if initial%5==0:
        if not isinstance(x1, Number):           # start inserted type check
            raise TypeError(...)
        if not isinstance(x2, Number):
            raise TypeError(...)                 # end inserted type check
        fin=int(input('enter final value: '))
        return x1+x2+x3+fin
    else:
        initial-=1
        return compute(x2,x3,initial)
```

Fig. 2. Transformed version of the `compute` function

further program execution *will* raise a type error, and a corresponding type error assertion is inserted. We prove that the assertions are inserted in optimal locations and thus preempt type errors earlier than dynamic typing, gradual typing [18,19], and soft typing [7]. We further show that these assertions do not change the semantics of programs that do not raise type errors. We proceed by formalising the type system and corresponding bytecode level type inference. Although the theory is presented for μPython, a dynamically typed Python-like core language, the techniques presented are applicable for any similar dynamically typed language such as Ruby or JavaScript, or indeed larger subsets of Python as in our implementation. Finally, we describe an implementation of preemptive type checking, including assertion insertion, for a subset of Python bytecodes, and evaluate it on a some benchmarks.

2 The μPython Language

In this section we define μPython as a dynamically typed core language modelled on Python. It is a bytecode based language with dynamically typed variables and dynamically bound functions. Although small, the language is still sufficiently expressive to require a rich static type analysis.

High-Level Syntax. We present the high-level syntax of μPython in Fig. 3 for illustrative purposes only, as our type analysis is exclusively performed at the bytecode level. The base types of the language are standard except perhaps for the types Un of uninitialised variables and Fn of functions. μPython supports function definitions, conditional statements, assignments, and while loops. In μPython, expressions are either function calls, constants, or variables. Valid expressions are also valid statements. There are three built-in functions. isInst is a reflection operator to check the dynamic type of an expression, and always returns a boolean. intOp and strOp represent prime integer and string operations, which implicitly raise a type error if their argument is of the wrong type. Note that conditional statements and function calls will also implicitly raise a type error when their guard or function expressions do not evaluate to boolean or function types respectively. This contrasts with the raise operation that will immediately raise an *explicit* exception error to terminate execution.

Statements:		Expressions:	
$s ::=$ def $f(x)$: s	(function definition)	$e ::= x$	(variable)
| return e	(function return)	| c	(constant)
| e	(expression)	| $e(e)$	(function application)
| pass	(empty statement)	| intOp(e)	(prime integer function)
| raise	(exception)	| strOp(e)	(prime string function)
| $x = e$	(assignment)	| isInst(e, τ)	(instance check)
| if e : s else : s	(conditional)		
| while e : s	(loop)	Types:	$\tau ::=$ Int | Str | Bool | Un | Fn
| $s; s$	(sequence)	Constants:	$c ::= n \mid str \mid$ true | false

Fig. 3. Syntax of the μPython language

We have a single namespace $\mathbb{V}$ that comprises both variable and function names and use the metavariables x, y (respectively f, g) to denote names that are intended to represent variables (respectively functions). In μPython, all variables have global scope. Function definitions are semantically just assignments of anonymous, single argument functions to variable names. Functions can be redefined at any point and within any control flow structure or scope. μPython supports higher order functions, where functions are first class citizens.

Bytecode. Our type analysis is defined on the μPython bytecode. This is based on a simplified machine model consisting of a store (for mapping variables to constants), an integer-valued program counter and a single accumulator acc. The full Python VM is a stack based machine and for presentation purposes we replace the evaluation stack with an accumulator acc. Our implementation of preemptive type checking supports full evaluation stacks. We use the metavariables u, v to range over names including acc. Similar to the high-level syntax, we choose a subset of actual Python bytecodes, albeit with minor modifications, sufficient to represent the challenges involved with static type analysis in a dynamically typed language. We reuse the namespace $\mathbb{V}$ for variable and function names but, in order to model functions, we extend the set of constants to now include constants of type Fn made of finite sequences of bytecode instructions. For technical convenience we also add a constant U of type Un.

$instr ::=$ LC c	(load constant)	| JP n	(unconditional jump)	| intOp	
| LG x	(load global)	| JIF n	(jump if false)	| strOp	
| SG x	(store global)	| CF f	(call function)	| isInst τ	
		| RET	(return from call)	| raise	

Fig. 4. The μPython bytecodes

The actual bytecodes we use are given in Fig. 4. Loading places constant values in the accumulator, storing moves a constant to store from the accumulator. We assume well-formed bytecode where jumps only refer to actual program locations and every program has a RET-instruction at its final location. Note that JIF consumes the accumulator value as part of its test. The instructions intOp, strOp and raise echo the

$$
\begin{array}{ll}
\langle \Sigma, \varepsilon \rangle \rightarrow \langle \Sigma_I, \langle M, 0 \rangle :: \varepsilon \rangle & \\
\langle \Sigma, \langle P, pc \rangle :: S \rangle \rightarrow \mathsf{End} & \text{if } P_{pc} = \mathsf{RET}, S = \varepsilon \\
\langle \Sigma, \langle P, pc \rangle :: S \rangle \rightarrow \langle \Sigma, S \rangle & \text{if } P_{pc} = \mathsf{RET}, S \neq \varepsilon \\
\langle \Sigma, \langle P, pc \rangle :: S \rangle \rightarrow \langle \Sigma \oplus (acc \mapsto c), \langle P, pc+1 \rangle :: S \rangle & \text{if } P_{pc} = \mathsf{LC}\ c \\
\langle \Sigma, \langle P, pc \rangle :: S \rangle \rightarrow \langle \Sigma \oplus (acc \mapsto \Sigma(x)), \langle P, pc+1 \rangle :: S \rangle & \text{if } P_{pc} = \mathsf{LG}\ x \\
\langle \Sigma, \langle P, pc \rangle :: S \rangle \rightarrow & \text{if } P_{pc} = \mathsf{SG}\ x \\
\quad \langle \Sigma \oplus (x \mapsto \Sigma(acc)) \oplus (acc \mapsto \mathsf{U}), \langle P, pc+1 \rangle :: S \rangle & \\
\langle \Sigma, \langle P, pc \rangle :: S \rangle \rightarrow \langle \Sigma, \langle P, pc' \rangle :: S \rangle & \text{if } P_{pc} = \mathsf{JP}\ pc' \\
\langle \Sigma, \langle P, pc \rangle :: S \rangle \rightarrow \langle \Sigma \oplus (acc \mapsto \mathsf{U}), \langle P, n \rangle :: S \rangle & \text{if } P_{pc} = \mathsf{JIF}\ n, \Sigma(acc) = \mathsf{false} \\
\langle \Sigma, \langle P, pc \rangle :: S \rangle \rightarrow \langle \Sigma \oplus (acc \mapsto \mathsf{U}), \langle P, pc+1 \rangle :: S \rangle & \text{if } P_{pc} = \mathsf{JIF}\ n, \Sigma(acc) = \mathsf{true} \\
\langle \Sigma, \langle P, pc \rangle :: S \rangle \rightarrow \mathsf{TypeError} & \text{if } P_{pc} = \mathsf{JIF}\ n, \neg\Sigma(acc) : \mathsf{Bool} \\
\langle \Sigma, \langle P, pc \rangle :: S \rangle \rightarrow \langle \Sigma, \langle P', 0 \rangle :: \langle P, pc+1 \rangle :: S \rangle & \text{if } P_{pc} = \mathsf{CF}\ f, \Sigma(f) = P' \\
\langle \Sigma, \langle P, pc \rangle :: S \rangle \rightarrow \mathsf{TypeError} & \text{if } P_{pc} = \mathsf{CF}\ f, \neg\Sigma(f) : \mathsf{Fn} \\
\langle \Sigma, \langle P, pc \rangle :: S \rangle \rightarrow \langle \Sigma \oplus (acc \mapsto \mathsf{U}), \langle P, pc+1 \rangle :: S \rangle & \text{if } P_{pc} = \mathsf{intOp}, \Sigma(acc) : \mathsf{Int} \\
\langle \Sigma, \langle P, pc \rangle :: S \rangle \rightarrow \langle \Sigma \oplus (acc \mapsto \mathsf{U}), \langle P, pc+1 \rangle :: S \rangle & \text{if } P_{pc} = \mathsf{strOp}, \Sigma(acc) : \mathsf{Str} \\
\langle \Sigma, \langle P, pc \rangle :: S \rangle \rightarrow \mathsf{TypeError} & \text{if } P_{pc} = \mathsf{intOp}, \neg\Sigma(acc) : \mathsf{Int} \\
\langle \Sigma, \langle P, pc \rangle :: S \rangle \rightarrow \mathsf{TypeError} & \text{if } P_{pc} = \mathsf{strOp}, \neg\Sigma(acc) : \mathsf{Str} \\
\langle \Sigma, \langle P, pc \rangle :: S \rangle \rightarrow \langle \Sigma \oplus (acc \mapsto \mathsf{true}), \langle P, pc+1 \rangle :: S \rangle & \text{if } P_{pc} = \mathsf{isInst}\ \tau, \Sigma(acc) : \tau \\
\langle \Sigma, \langle P, pc \rangle :: S \rangle \rightarrow \langle \Sigma \oplus (acc \mapsto \mathsf{false}), \langle P, pc+1 \rangle :: S \rangle & \text{if } P_{pc} = \mathsf{isInst}\ \tau, \neg\Sigma(acc) : \tau \\
\langle \Sigma, \langle P, pc \rangle :: S \rangle \rightarrow \mathsf{Exn} & \text{if } P_{pc} = \mathsf{raise}
\end{array}
$$

Fig. 5. Semantics of the μPython Bytecode

corresponding high-level expressions of the same names and isInst writes a boolean into the accumulator depending on whether it contains a value of the given type. The CF f instruction is of interest: to execute this the machine finds the sequence of instructions P' mapped from f in the store and pushes this program on to the call stack with program counter 0.

Reduction Semantics. We formalise this semantics by the rules for single execution steps of the abstract machine shown in Fig. 5. The states of the machine, $State^{\rightarrow}$, are of the form $\langle \Sigma, S \rangle$ (where the *environment* Σ is a mapping from names, including acc, to constants and S is a *call stack* of $\langle$program, program counter$\rangle$ pairs) or one of the termination states TypeError, Exn, or End. We assume that the machine begins in state $\langle \Sigma, \varepsilon \rangle$. The step applicable at this point loads $\langle M, 0 \rangle :: \varepsilon$ onto the call stack, where M is the initial, or main, program. This step also sets the store to Σ_I, an initial store that contains mappings for built-ins and that maps all other names to U. We write P_n to refer to the bytecode instruction at location n in program P. We write $\Sigma(u)$ to denote lookup in Σ and $\Sigma \oplus (u \mapsto c)$ to denote the environment Σ updated with the mapping $u \mapsto c$. We also write $\Sigma(u) : \tau$ whenever Σ maps u to a constant of principal type τ.

3 Type Inference for μPython

A key characteristic of our dynamically typed core language is that the types of variables may change during execution. Therefore, to determine whether a type error may occur we need to establish, for any given point of execution, two pieces of information: the type a variable actually has and the type a variable may be used as in the future.

We call these the *present* and *future use* types. To establish the former we perform a traditional forwards analysis over the execution points of the program; the present type of a variable depends on the instructions that have previously been executed. Obviously the precise present runtime type of a variable cannot be statically determined so our analysis uses an over-approximation of this. In order to represent the different type possibilities for a given variable, we make use of the familiar concept of union types. These come equipped with a natural subtyping order. We extend the grammar of types to be

$$\tau ::= \mathsf{Int} \mid \mathsf{Str} \mid \mathsf{Bool} \mid \mathsf{Un} \mid \mathsf{Fn} \mid \bot \mid \top \mid \tau \sqcup \tau$$

and define the subtyping order <: inductively

$$\frac{}{\tau <: \tau} \qquad \frac{\tau <: \tau' \quad \tau' <: \tau''}{\tau <: \tau''} \qquad \frac{}{\bot <: \tau} \qquad \frac{}{\tau <: \top}$$

$$\frac{\tau <: \tau'}{\tau <: \tau' \sqcup \tau''} \qquad \frac{\tau <: \tau''}{\tau <: \tau' \sqcup \tau''} \qquad \frac{\tau <: \tau'' \quad \tau' <: \tau''}{\tau \sqcup \tau' <: \tau''}$$

Dual to the analysis of present types we establish the future use type using a backwards analysis so that the future use type depends on the next instructions that will be executed. At any given program execution point we will check that the present and future use types are compatible, by which we simply mean that the present type is a subtype of the future use type.

3.1 Execution Points and Trails

A naive idea of a program execution point might be a simple code location but because variables can change type during execution, the entire call stack is important in determining their current types. In principle, program execution points must therefore be full call stacks. The control flow graph (CFG) of a μPython program is then a relation $S \to S'$ between call stacks. This is unfortunate because, even for finite programs, the CFG of all possible program execution points could then be infinite. This has drastic consequences for a static analysis.

We address this issue by over-approximating the CFG via the simple means of *truncating* call stacks. Specifically, given a call stack S, and an integer $N \geq 1$, we write $\lfloor S \rfloor_N$ to mean the equivalence class of all call stacks whose prefix of length N is the same as that of the stack S. We typically omit N as this is fixed throughout. We refer to these equivalence classes as *truncated execution points* and it is clear that, for each program, they form a finite, truncated CFG as follows:

$$\lfloor S \rfloor \to \lfloor S' \rfloor \text{ if and only if } S_0 \to S_0' \text{ for some } S_0 \in \lfloor S \rfloor, S_0' \in \lfloor S' \rfloor$$

We will use a shorthand notation in the remainder by writing s to mean $\lfloor S \rfloor$, similarly for s' for $\lfloor S' \rfloor$. We will also make extensive use of the following two functions: given a truncated execution point s we write $\text{prev}(s)$ for the set of nodes from which s can be reached in the truncated CFG of the program. Similarly, $\text{next}(s)$ denotes the set of nodes which can be reached from s.

At the heart of our analysis is the forwards/backwards traversal of the truncated CFG using the $\mathrm{prev}(s)$ and $\mathrm{next}(s)$ functions in order to find the present and future use types of variables. Of course, these CFGs may contain cycles so we must take care to terminate our analysis in cases where we have reached a point that we have previously visited. This motivates the following: the type inferencer is expressed using two independent inductively defined relations written

$$\langle s, \mathcal{T} \rangle \vdash_p u : \tau \quad \text{and} \quad \langle s, \mathcal{T} \rangle \vdash_f u : \tau$$

where s is a truncated execution point and $\mathcal{T}$ is a *trail*. A trail is a set of pairs $\langle s, u \rangle$ of truncated execution points and variables. They represent the previously visited execution points (together with the variables that triggered the visit) and are used to ensure termination of the inferencer, as explained in the next section. The judgement $\langle s, \mathcal{T}_\emptyset \rangle \vdash_p u : \tau$ (where $\mathcal{T}_\emptyset$ is the empty trail) denotes that u will have type τ *after* the current instruction has been executed. The judgement $\langle s, \mathcal{T}_\emptyset \rangle \vdash_f u : \tau$ denotes that the variable u is required to have type τ in order to execute the instructions from the current instruction onwards without raising a TypeError.

3.2 Type Inference Rules

The type inferencer is expressed as inference rules, given in Fig. 6 and Fig. 7. The *leaf rules* in Fig. 6 for inferring $\vdash_p$ account for situations in which the present type is fully determined by the current instruction. For example, after loading a constant (Rule pLC) the accumulator is known to have the type of the constant that has just been loaded. The non-leaf rules all follow a shared pattern: the types of *relevant* variables in each previous state are calculated and the present type of a specific variable is the union across the types from each previous state. The relevant variables are instruction dependent. For example, in Rule pSG1 for the instruction SG x the type of x depends on the type of *acc* in the previous states.

Again, for the rules for $\vdash_f$ in Fig. 7 we have leaf rules and non-leaf rules. Many of the leaf rules assign an f-type of $\top$ to a variable. This follows in cases where that variable is just about to be overwritten (Rules fSET/SG1). Otherwise, the immediate uses are recorded in the type (Rules fJIF/STR/INT). Two interesting rules are fLG1 and fCF1. In these a variable is used but its contents remain intact so there may be future uses also. We define a *meet* operation on types, written as $\boxdot$, in the following rules (applied in top-down order):

$$\begin{aligned} \tau \boxdot (\tau_1 \sqcup \tau_2) &= (\tau \boxdot \tau_1) \sqcup (\tau \boxdot \tau_2) \\ (\tau_1 \sqcup \tau_2) \boxdot \tau &= (\tau_1 \boxdot \tau) \sqcup (\tau_2 \boxdot \tau) \\ \tau \boxdot \top = \tau &\qquad \top \boxdot \tau = \tau \\ \tau \boxdot \tau = \tau &\qquad \tau_1 \boxdot \tau_2 = \bot \end{aligned}$$

It is worth noting that the trail sets $\mathcal{T}$ are finitely bounded. This is due to the fact that call stacks are truncated to a fixed depth and that, for a given program, there are finitely many code locations and finitely many variables. For a given program, we write $\mathcal{T}_U$ to denote the maximum trail containing all truncated execution point/variable pairs. In fact, by virtue of the fact that trail sizes strictly decrease in non-leaf rules, that all rules have finitely many hypotheses, and by König's Lemma, it is guaranteed that the

Leaf rules:

$$\frac{\Sigma_I(u) : \tau}{\langle \varepsilon, \mathcal{T}\rangle \vdash_p u : \tau}\text{pINIT} \qquad \frac{\langle s, u\rangle \in \mathcal{T}}{\langle s, \mathcal{T}\rangle \vdash_p u : \bot}\text{pTRAIL} \qquad \frac{\langle s, u\rangle \notin \mathcal{T} \quad P_{pc} = \mathsf{raise}}{\langle s, \mathcal{T}\rangle \vdash_p u : \bot}\text{pRAISE}$$

$$\frac{\langle s, acc\rangle \notin \mathcal{T} \quad P_{pc} = \mathsf{LC}\ c \quad c : \tau}{\langle s, \mathcal{T}\rangle \vdash_p acc : \tau}\text{pLC} \qquad \frac{\langle s, acc\rangle \notin \mathcal{T} \quad P_{pc} = \mathsf{isInst}\ \tau}{\langle s, \mathcal{T}\rangle \vdash_p acc : \mathsf{Bool}}\text{pINST}$$

$$\frac{\langle s, acc\rangle \notin \mathcal{T} \quad P_{pc} \in \{\mathsf{SG}\ x, \mathsf{JIF}\ n, \mathsf{strOp}, \mathsf{intOp}\}}{\langle s, \mathcal{T}\rangle \vdash_p acc : \mathsf{Un}}\text{pUSE}$$

Non-leaf rules:

$$\frac{\langle s, x\rangle \notin \mathcal{T} \quad P_{pc} = \mathsf{SG}\ x \quad \langle s_i, \mathcal{T} \cup \{\langle s, x\rangle\}\rangle \vdash_p acc : \tau_i}{\langle s, \mathcal{T}\rangle \vdash_p x : \bigsqcup \tau_i}\text{pSG1} \qquad \frac{\langle s, acc\rangle \notin \mathcal{T} \quad P_{pc} = \mathsf{LG}\ x \quad \langle s_i, \mathcal{T} \cup \{\langle s, acc\rangle\}\rangle \vdash_p x : \tau_i}{\langle s, \mathcal{T}\rangle \vdash_p acc : \bigsqcup \tau_i}\text{pLG1}$$

$$\frac{\langle s, y\rangle \notin \mathcal{T} \quad P_{pc} = \mathsf{SG}\ x \quad x \neq y \quad \langle s_i, \mathcal{T} \cup \{\langle s, y\rangle\}\rangle \vdash_p y : \tau_i}{\langle s, \mathcal{T}\rangle \vdash_p y : \bigsqcup \tau_i}\text{pSG2} \qquad \frac{\langle s, y\rangle \notin \mathcal{T} \quad P_{pc} = \mathsf{LG}\ x \quad \langle s_i, \mathcal{T} \cup \{\langle s, y\rangle\}\rangle \vdash_p y : \tau_i}{\langle s, \mathcal{T}\rangle \vdash_p y : \bigsqcup \tau_i}\text{pLG2}$$

$$\frac{\langle s, u\rangle \notin \mathcal{T} \quad P_{pc} \in \{\mathsf{RET}, \mathsf{JP}\ pc', \mathsf{CF}\ f\} \quad \langle s_i, \mathcal{T} \cup \{\langle s, u\rangle\}\rangle \vdash_p u : \tau_i}{\langle s, \mathcal{T}\rangle \vdash_p u : \bigsqcup \tau_i}\text{pRET/JP/CF} \qquad \frac{\langle s, x\rangle \notin \mathcal{T} \quad P_{pc} \in \{\mathsf{LC}\ c, \mathsf{JIF}\ pc', \mathsf{strOp}, \mathsf{intOp}, \mathsf{isInst}\ \tau\} \quad \langle s_i, \mathcal{T} \cup \{\langle s, x\rangle\}\rangle \vdash_p x : \tau_i}{\langle s, \mathcal{T}\rangle \vdash_p x : \bigsqcup \tau_i}\text{p*}$$

Fig. 6. Inference rules for the $\vdash_p$ judgement. Unless stated otherwise, s is assumed to be of the form $\langle P, pc\rangle :: \ldots$ and s_i ranges over $\text{prev}(s)$.

application of the type inference rules terminates and thus, for any s, u, the judgements $\langle s, \mathcal{T}_\emptyset\rangle \vdash_p u : \tau$ and $\langle s, \mathcal{T}_\emptyset\rangle \vdash_f u : \tau'$ hold for some τ, τ'.

4 Correctness

We now show that the type inference rules are correct. We give proof sketches for the main results. Full proofs can be found in [11]. The notion of soundness for p-types should be clear. Given a derivation $\langle s, \mathcal{T}_\emptyset\rangle \vdash_p u : \tau$ we expect that the actual runtime type of the constant stored at u in the Σ store after the current instruction in s has been executed to be a subtype of τ. This is formally expressed in the next theorem.

Theorem 1 (Soundness of p-types). *Suppose*

$$\langle \Sigma, \varepsilon\rangle \to^* \langle \Sigma, S\rangle \to \langle \Sigma', S'\rangle \quad \textit{and} \quad \langle \lfloor S \rfloor, \mathcal{T}_\emptyset\rangle \vdash_p x : \tau_p$$

and suppose τ_r is such that $\Sigma'(x) : \tau_r$. Then $\tau_r <: \tau_p$.

Proof. (Sketch) The proof proceeds by induction on the number of reduction steps taken to reach $\langle \Sigma, S\rangle$. For the base case we know that $\langle \Sigma, S\rangle$ is of the form $\langle \Sigma, \varepsilon\rangle$

Leaf rules:

$$\frac{}{\langle \varepsilon, \mathcal{T}\rangle \vdash_f u : \top}\,\textsf{fINIT} \qquad \frac{P_{pc} = \textsf{RET}}{\langle\langle P, pc\rangle :: \varepsilon, \mathcal{T}\rangle \vdash_f u : \top}\,\textsf{fEND} \qquad \frac{P_{pc} = \textsf{SG}\ x \quad \langle s, x\rangle \notin \mathcal{T}}{\langle s, \mathcal{T}\rangle \vdash_f x : \top}\,\textsf{fSG1}$$

$$\frac{\langle s, x\rangle \in \mathcal{T}}{\langle s, \mathcal{T}\rangle \vdash_f u : \bot}\,\textsf{fTRAIL} \qquad \frac{P_{pc} = \textsf{raise} \quad \langle s, u\rangle \notin \mathcal{T}}{\langle s, \mathcal{T}\rangle \vdash_f u : \top}\,\textsf{fRAISE} \qquad \frac{P_{pc} \in \{\textsf{LC}\ c, \textsf{LG}\ x, \textsf{isInst}\ \tau\} \quad \langle s, acc\rangle \notin \mathcal{T}}{\langle s, \mathcal{T}\rangle \vdash_f acc : \top}\,\textsf{fSET}$$

$$\frac{P_{pc} = \textsf{JIF}\ pc' \quad \langle s, acc\rangle \notin \mathcal{T}}{\langle s, \mathcal{T}\rangle \vdash_f acc : \textsf{Bool}}\,\textsf{fJIF} \qquad \frac{P_{pc} = \textsf{strOp} \quad \langle s, acc\rangle \notin \mathcal{T}}{\langle s, \mathcal{T}\rangle \vdash_f acc : \textsf{Str}}\,\textsf{fSTR} \qquad \frac{P_{pc} = \textsf{intOp} \quad \langle s, acc\rangle \notin \mathcal{T}}{\langle s, \mathcal{T}\rangle \vdash_f acc : \textsf{Int}}\,\textsf{fINT}$$

Non-leaf rules:

$$\frac{\langle s, x\rangle \notin \mathcal{T} \quad P_{pc} = \textsf{LG}\ x \quad \langle s_i, \mathcal{T} \cup \{\langle s, x\rangle\}\rangle \vdash_f acc : v_i \quad \langle s_i, \mathcal{T} \cup \{\langle s, x\rangle\}\rangle \vdash_f x : \nu_i}{\langle s, \mathcal{T}\rangle \vdash_f x : \bigsqcup(v_i \dot{\sqcap} \nu_i)}\,\textsf{fLG1}$$

$$\frac{s = \langle P, pc\rangle :: \langle P', n\rangle :: \ldots \quad \langle s, u\rangle \notin \mathcal{T} \quad P_{pc} = \textsf{RET} \quad \langle s_i, \mathcal{T} \cup \{\langle s, u\rangle\}\rangle \vdash_f u : \tau_i}{\langle s, \mathcal{T}\rangle \vdash_f u : \bigsqcup \tau_i}\,\textsf{fRET}$$

$$\frac{\langle s, acc\rangle \notin \mathcal{T} \quad P_{pc} = \textsf{SG}\ x \quad \langle s_i, \mathcal{T} \cup \{\langle s, acc\rangle\}\rangle \vdash_f x : \tau_i}{\langle s, \mathcal{T}\rangle \vdash_f acc : \bigsqcup \tau_i}\,\textsf{fSG2} \qquad \frac{\langle s, y\rangle \notin \mathcal{T} \quad P_{pc} \in \{\textsf{LG}\ x, \textsf{SG}\ x\} \quad x \neq y \quad \langle s_i, \mathcal{T} \cup \{\langle s, y\rangle\}\rangle \vdash_f y : \tau_i}{\langle s, \mathcal{T}\rangle \vdash_f y : \bigsqcup \tau_i}\,\textsf{fLG2/SG3}$$

$$\frac{\langle s, f\rangle \notin \mathcal{T} \quad P_{pc} = \textsf{CF}\ f \quad \langle s_i, \mathcal{T} \cup \{\langle s, f\rangle\}\rangle \vdash_f f : \tau_i}{\langle s, \mathcal{T}\rangle \vdash_f f : \bigsqcup(\tau_i \dot{\sqcap} \textsf{Fn})}\,\textsf{fCF1} \qquad \frac{\langle s, u\rangle \notin \mathcal{T} \quad P_{pc} = \textsf{CF}\ f \quad u \neq f \quad \langle s_i, \mathcal{T} \cup \{\langle s, u\rangle\}\rangle \vdash_f u : \tau_i}{\langle s, \mathcal{T}\rangle \vdash_f u : \bigsqcup \tau_i}\,\textsf{fCF2}$$

$$\frac{\langle s, u\rangle \notin \mathcal{T} \quad P_{pc} = \textsf{JP}\ n \quad \langle s_i, \mathcal{T} \cup \{\langle s, u\rangle\}\rangle \vdash_f u : \tau_i}{\langle s, \mathcal{T}\rangle \vdash_f u : \bigsqcup \tau_i}\,\textsf{fJP} \qquad \frac{P_{pc} \in \{\textsf{LC}\ c, \textsf{JIF}\ n, \textsf{intOp}, \textsf{strOp}, \textsf{isInst}\ \tau\} \quad \langle s, x\rangle \notin \mathcal{T} \quad \langle s_i, \mathcal{T} \cup \{\langle s, x\rangle\}\rangle \vdash_f x : \tau_i}{\langle s, \mathcal{T}\rangle \vdash_f x : \bigsqcup \tau_i}\,\textsf{f*}$$

Fig. 7. Inference rules for the $\vdash_f$ judgement. Unless stated otherwise, s is assumed to be of the form $\langle P, pc\rangle :: \ldots$ and s_i ranges over $\text{prev}(s)$.

and that there is a unique reduction step from this state whose target has store Σ_I (cf. Fig. 5). The type rule pINIT then guarantees the desired result. The inductive case requires a case analysis on the last type rule used to derive type τ_p. The leaf rules all follow from the definition of reduction but the non-leaf rules require use of the inductive hypothesis along with the following lemma that relates the types of variables as the trail sets are increased. □

Lemma 1 (Bounding). *For all u, v, s, s' and all $\mathcal{T}' \subseteq \mathcal{T}$ such that $\langle s, \mathcal{T}'\rangle \vdash_p u : \tau'$ and $\langle s', \mathcal{T} \cup \{\langle s, u\rangle\}\rangle \vdash_p v : \tau''$ then $\tau <: \tau' \sqcup \tau''$ whenever $\langle s', \mathcal{T}\rangle \vdash_p v : \tau$.*

Intuitively, the lemma states that the most type information that can be gained for u in the absence of the trail assumption $\langle s, v\rangle$ is what can be established for u, with the assumption in place, along with any possible contribution to the type from v itself.

The correctness criteria for f-types are more subtle. The f-types describe constraints on future uses of a variable and we will use these constraints to report type errors preemptively by raising type error exceptions. So correctness in this case must mean that, supposing we execute the program in a preemptive type checked semantics, if we raise a type error exception then the same program running in the non-preemptive semantics would continue executing to reach an actual type error. In addition, we must also allow for the possibility that the program in the non-preemptive semantics could diverge before reaching the detected future error.

In order to formalise the above, we will need to define the preemptive type checked semantics and a predicate on states that holds whenever a future divergence or type error is guaranteed. We begin by defining the diverge-error predicate coinductively:

Definition 1. *A relation $R^{\Uparrow}$ on $State^{\rightarrow}$ is called a diverge-error relation if whenever $\langle \Sigma, S \rangle \in R^{\Uparrow}$ then*

$$\langle \Sigma, S \rangle \rightarrow \langle \Sigma', S' \rangle \wedge \langle \Sigma', S' \rangle \in R^{\Uparrow} \quad \text{or} \quad \langle \Sigma, S \rangle \rightarrow \mathsf{TypeError}.$$

Let $\Uparrow$ be the largest diverge-error relation.

It follows that a state in a diverge-error relation cannot reach the state End or Exn.

Definition 2. *The state compatibility predicate SC holds at $\langle \Sigma, S \rangle$ if for all variables u such that $\langle s, \mathcal{T}_{\emptyset} \rangle \vdash_f u : \tau_f$ and $\Sigma(u) : \tau_r$ then $\tau_r <: \tau_f$, where $s = \lfloor S \rfloor$.*

The next proposition demonstrates that this simple predicate would already by sufficient for preemptive type checking. However, we will see in the next section that SC may be refined to make better use of static type information.

Proposition 1 (Soundness of f-types). *If $\langle \Sigma, S \rangle \notin SC$ then $\langle \Sigma, S \rangle \in \Uparrow$.*

Proof. (Sketch) We use coinduction here by proving that the complement of SC is itself a diverge-error relation. To do this we suppose that $\langle \Sigma, S \rangle \notin SC$ to see that there is some u for which $\Sigma(u) : \tau_r$, and $\langle s, \mathcal{T}_{\emptyset} \rangle \vdash_f u : \tau_f$ and $\tau_r \not<: \tau_f$. We perform a case analysis on the last rule used to derive the type τ_f and see that, for all applicable leaf rules, then state $\langle \Sigma, S \rangle$ reduces to TypeError. For all non-leaf rules, a lemma analogous to Lemma 1 is used to show that where $\langle \Sigma, S \rangle$ reduces to some $\langle \Sigma', S' \rangle$ then $\langle \Sigma', S' \rangle \notin SC$ as required. □

4.1 Checked μPython Semantics

The naive runtime type check SC above simply checks whether the current runtime type of a variable is a subtype of the statically inferred f-type. However, we have also statically calculated the p-types as a sound approximation of the runtime types and we can leverage this to obtain a type check that can be partially evaluated statically. This predicate is defined on edges in the truncated CFG.

Definition 3. *The edge compatibility predicate EC holds at $\langle s, s', \Sigma' \rangle$ if for all variables u, such that*

$$\langle s, \mathcal{T}_{\emptyset} \rangle \vdash_f u : \tau_f \quad \langle s', \mathcal{T}_{\emptyset} \rangle \vdash_f u : \tau_f' \quad \langle s, \mathcal{T}_{\emptyset} \rangle \vdash_p u : \tau_p \quad \Sigma'(u) : \tau_r'$$

then

$$\tau_f = \tau'_f \quad or \quad \tau_p <: \tau'_f \quad or \quad \tau'_r <: \tau_p \sqcap \tau'_f$$

Essentially this says that, if the program moves from a state s to a state s' then the f-types report no error if there is no change in the future use constraints, if the statically approximated runtime type is a subtype of future uses, or if the actual new runtime type of a variable is within the future use set (modulated by the present type). Clearly only the latter of these requires the inspection of the runtime types and even then, where the meet $\tau_p \sqcap \tau'_f$ is $\bot$, we know statically that the predicate must fail as there are no constants of type $\bot$. The predicate *EC* is used extensively in our checked μPython semantics, as is the following predicate that allows type incompatibilities to be propagated backwards through the CFG.

Definition 4. *The fail edge predicate FE holds at* $\langle s, s' \rangle$ *if* $s \in \text{prev}(s')$ *and either* $\forall \Sigma' \cdot \langle s, s', \Sigma' \rangle \notin EC'$ *or* $\{\langle s', s'' \rangle \mid s'' \in \text{next}(s')\} \subseteq FE$.

Definition 5. *The checked semantics is defined as a binary relation* $\rightsquigarrow$ *on the set of states,* $State^{\rightsquigarrow}$ *comprised of* $\langle \Sigma, S \rangle$ *states,* End, *and* Exn *such that:*

$$\begin{array}{lll}
\langle \Sigma, S \rangle \rightsquigarrow \mathsf{End} & \text{if} \langle \Sigma, S \rangle \rightarrow \mathsf{End} \\
\langle \Sigma, S \rangle \rightsquigarrow \mathsf{Exn} & \text{if} \langle \Sigma, S \rangle \rightarrow \mathsf{Exn} \\
\langle \Sigma, S \rangle \rightsquigarrow \mathsf{Exn} & \text{if} \langle \Sigma, S \rangle \rightarrow \langle \Sigma', S' \rangle \wedge \langle s, s', \Sigma' \rangle \notin EC \\
\langle \Sigma, S \rangle \rightsquigarrow \mathsf{Exn} & \text{if} \langle \Sigma, S \rangle \rightarrow \langle \Sigma', S' \rangle \wedge \langle s, s' \rangle \in FE \\
\langle \Sigma, S \rangle \rightsquigarrow \langle \Sigma', S' \rangle & \text{if} \langle \Sigma, S \rangle \rightarrow \langle \Sigma', S' \rangle \; otherwise
\end{array}$$

Definition 6. *A relation* $R^{\lesssim}$ *on* $State^{\rightarrow} \times State^{\rightsquigarrow}$*, which relates only identical non-terminating states (i.e., if* $\langle \Sigma, S \rangle R^{\lesssim} \langle \Sigma_1, S_1 \rangle$ *then* $\Sigma = \Sigma_1$ *and* $S = S_1$*) is called an error-preserving simulation if the following holds:*

- $\langle \Sigma, S \rangle \not\rightarrow$ TypeError
- *If* $\langle \Sigma, S \rangle \rightarrow$ End *then* $\langle \Sigma, S \rangle \rightsquigarrow$ End.
- *If* $\langle \Sigma, S \rangle \rightarrow$ Exn *then* $\langle \Sigma, S \rangle \rightsquigarrow$ Exn.
- *If* $\langle \Sigma, S \rangle \rightarrow \langle \Sigma', S' \rangle$ *then either*
  - $\langle \Sigma, S \rangle \rightsquigarrow \langle \Sigma', S' \rangle \wedge \langle \Sigma', S' \rangle \in R^{\lesssim}$ *or*
  - $\langle \Sigma, S \rangle \rightsquigarrow$ Exn $\wedge \langle \Sigma', S' \rangle \in \Uparrow$

Let $\lesssim$ *be the largest error-preserving simulation.*

Theorem 2. *Let* R^{SC} *be defined as*

$$\{\langle \Sigma, S \rangle, \langle \Sigma, S \rangle \mid \langle \Sigma_I, \langle M, 0 \rangle :: \varepsilon \rangle \rightarrow^* \langle \Sigma, S \rangle \wedge \langle \Sigma, S \rangle \in SC\}$$

Then R^{SC} *is an error-preserving simulation and hence* $R^{SC} \subseteq \lesssim$.

Proof. (Sketch) It is easy to see that states $\langle \Sigma, S \rangle$ in R^{SC} preserve termination steps. To show that $\langle \Sigma, S \rangle \not\rightarrow$ TypeError we use proof by contradiction by assuming a type error and analyse all possible reduction steps that could cause this. In each case the inferred types must contradict the hypothesis that $\langle \Sigma, S \rangle \in SC$. To show that transitions are preserved by matching checked transitions or exceptions that guarantee future divergence we consider the possible derivations of the checked semantics. In case that $\langle s, s', \Sigma' \rangle \notin EC$ we note $\tau_r' \not<: \tau_p \sqcap \tau_f'$ and thus, using Theorem 1 and Proposition 1, we have $\langle \Sigma', S' \rangle \in \Uparrow$. In case $\langle s, s', \Sigma' \rangle \in EC$ we analyse each type rule to show that $\langle \Sigma', S' \rangle \in SC$. □

Corollary 1. *Suppose* $\langle \Sigma_I, \langle M, 0 \rangle :: \varepsilon \rangle \leadsto^* N \not\leadsto$*. Then* N *is either* End *or* Exn.

Proof. We note immediately that $\langle \Sigma, \varepsilon \rangle \in SC$ holds by virtue of rule fINIT of Fig. 7. Therefore we have $\langle \Sigma, \varepsilon \rangle R^{SC} \langle \Sigma, \varepsilon \rangle$ and hence by the above theorem we have $\langle \Sigma, \varepsilon \rangle \lesssim \langle \Sigma, \varepsilon \rangle$. Now, suppose for contradiction that N is neither End or Exn. Then we must have N being some $\langle \Sigma, S \rangle$ such that $\langle \Sigma, S \rangle \lesssim \langle \Sigma, S \rangle$. This tells us that $\langle \Sigma, S \rangle \not\to$ TypeError and, by the definition of $\to$ we must have $\langle \Sigma, S \rangle \to \langle \Sigma', S' \rangle$ for some $\langle \Sigma', S' \rangle$. This means that $N \leadsto N'$ for some N' also, contradicting maximality. □

4.2 Optimality

Now that we have shown the correctness of our type inferencer, we would like to establish that our type inference system is optimal in the sense that the checked semantics report an Exn as soon as the control flow reaches a point where all possible further execution steps in the unchecked semantics lead to state TypeError. Since our analysis considers variables individually, we can only prove that our inference system satisfies a milder form of optimality in general, along execution sequences in which there are no branches of control flow.

Definition 7. *A reduction step* $\langle \Sigma, S \rangle \to \langle \Sigma', S' \rangle$ *is called linear if* $\mathrm{next}(s) = \{s'\}$*. A sequence* $\langle \Sigma, S \rangle \to^* \langle \Sigma', S' \rangle$ *is called linear if each step in the sequence is linear.*

Theorem 3 (Linear optimality). *Suppose* $\langle \Sigma, \varepsilon \rangle \leadsto^* \langle \Sigma, S \rangle$ *such that there is a linear reduction sequence* $\langle \Sigma, S \rangle \to^*$ TypeError*. Then* $\langle \Sigma, S \rangle \leadsto$ Exn.

Proof. (Sketch) This is proved by assuming for contradiction that $\langle \Sigma, S \rangle \leadsto \langle \Sigma', S' \rangle$ and $\langle \Sigma', S' \rangle \leadsto$ Exn. We consider the cases that derive the latter step and can quickly rule out $\langle \Sigma', S' \rangle$ being the source of a fail edge because the assumption of linearity guarantees that $\langle s, s', \Sigma' \rangle \in FE$ in this case, which contradicts our assumption. Therefore we must have $\langle s', s'', \Sigma'' \rangle \notin EC$. We then consider the type rules used to derive the f-type in state $\langle \Sigma', S' \rangle$ and use these to derive a contradiction. □

Linear optimality is not as restrictive as it might seem: the fail edge predicate FE propagates guaranteed type errors backwards even over control flow splits.

4.3 Type Checks Insertion

We now describe an algorithm that transforms bytecode programs by inserting type checks and explicit errors in such a way that the transformed program implements the checked semantics. An important point to note, however, is that the checked semantics is defined in terms of edges of the truncated CFG and that nodes in this graph do not correspond uniquely to program locations. That is, each program location may occur

```
P' ⟵ ε
for pc ⟵ 0..size(P) − 1:
  s ⟵ ⌊⟨P, pc⟩ :: s⌋_N
  for s' ∈ next(s):
    if P_pc = JIF pc' ∧ s' = ⟨P, pc'⟩ :: ... ∧ ⟨s, s'⟩ ∈ FE: extend(P', failIfFalse)
    if P_pc = JIF pc' ∧ s' = ⟨P, pc + 1⟩ :: ... ∧ ⟨s, s'⟩ ∈ FE: extend(P', failIfTrue)
    if ⟨ε, s⟩ ∈ FE: extend(P', raise)
    if P_pc ∉ {JIF pc', CF f, JP pc'}: extend(P', P_pc)
    for x ∈ 𝕍:
      let ⟨s, T_∅⟩ ⊢_p x : τ_p   ⟨s, T_∅⟩ ⊢_f x : τ_f   ⟨s', T_∅⟩ ⊢_f x : τ'_f
      if ¬(τ_f = τ'_f ∨ τ_p <: τ'_f):
        if P_pc = JIF pc' ∧ s' = ⟨P, pc'⟩ :: ...: extend(P', checkIfFalse(x, τ_p ⊓ τ'_f))
        if P_pc = JIF pc' ∧ s' = ⟨P, pc + 1⟩ :: ...: extend(P', checkIfTrue(x, τ_p ⊓ τ'_f))
        if P_pc ≠ JIF pc': extend(P', check(x, τ_p ⊓ τ'_f))
    if P_pc = CF f:
      ⟨Q, 0⟩ :: ... ⟵ s'
      extend(P', call(specialise(Q, s)))
  if P_pc = JIF pc' ∨ P_pc = JP pc': extend(P', P_pc)
```

Fig. 8. Algorithm for inserting type checks in μPython programs, expressed as a function specialise(P, s) that returns an updated program P'

many times as the currently executing instruction in different nodes of the graph. For this reason, the bytecode transformation takes as a parameter the particular truncated call stack against which we are inserting checks. Where the same program is reached with a different call stack, a specialised copy of the program bytecode is created with the relevant assertions for that different call stack inserted. Of course, call sites must be updated to call these specialised programs also.

The algorithm (see Fig. 8) iterates over every instruction of the program, extending the call stack with this instruction as the current one. It then considers edges in the truncated CFG from this point in order to implement the *FE* and *EC* predicates. The algorithm uses bytecode macros that are underlined in the algorithm and implemented as a sequence of μPython bytecode instructions. Procedure extend takes a program and a list of instructions and appends the instructions to the end of the given program.

5 Implementation

We have implemented the system as a Python library for a subset of Python 3.3. We suppport both local and global variables, which helps make the system scalable as most variables in typical programs are local. Our implementation handles 40 bytecodes in total. In particular, we support extra bytecodes for arithmetic, more control structures such as while-loops, local variables, some built-in data structures and polyadic functions.

Architecture. In Python the load path for individual modules can sometimes only be resolved at runtime, and the bytecode for a module that requires type checking may not be available statically. We therefore postpone our analysis until the program has stabilised. Hence, during initialisation, the full power of Python can be used, including metaclasses, `eval` and dynamic code loading. The entry point to the type checking mechanism is the analysis in the class `Analyser`. This takes a `callable` object such as the main function, and an integer truncation level N. By starting the analysis once the environment has stabilised, we obtain a more accurate type analysis.

Analysis. As our system is built upon a static control flow analysis, we need an implementation for this. Our type inference and its correctness are independent of the particular choice, as long as the analysis returns an over-approximation of the actual control flow at runtime. Similarly, our implementation is parametric in the implementation of the control flow analysis. As a proof of concept, we use a simplified version of next(.) and prev(.) in which we assume that all function definitions are declared once.

The `Analyser` first constructs the truncated CFG and then iterates over all nodes in order to calculate the p and f-types for the accumulator. This triggers recursive computations for other variables. All runtime type errors arise due to an ill-typed accumulator value and therefore, to just *identify* the type errors, the type of the accumulator is sufficient. However, in order to *preempt* type errors, the types of all other variables that feed into the computation are necessary as well. All type calculations are cached during the iteration across the CFG so that p and f types for all necessary variables in all states are established. An implementation of specialise as in Fig. 8 is then used to transform the program so that it implements preemptive type checking. This is carried out on the given callable object, such as `main`, and all other functions it may call. Then, calling the specialised `main` activates the preemption to catch any runtime type errors.

The `Analyser` class can also statically issue messages explaining the potential type failures in the given function. This includes partial stack traces with the expected type errors. Along with the expected and actual types. This information is derived from our internal representation of execution points and types.

Full Evaluation Stacks. The Python virtual machine is a stack based machine. The *evaluation stack* serves as working memory and is read and manipulated by a large portion of bytecode instructions. For example, load operations push a single element on to the stack while store operations pop a single element from it. In general, bytecode instructions may displace stack elements by a number of positions, which can be determined statically. Although the theory outlined above uses a single element evaluation stack (i.e. the accumulator), the implementation *already* supports the full stack model. We adjust the inference rules above to cater for a full stack machine simply by statically calculating how much the stack is shifted for every instruction and factoring that in to identify the particular variables that we need to analyse in the type inference rules.

6 Evaluation

We tested our implementation on a number of Python benchmarks and examples from the Computer Language Benchmarks Game [2]. In order to run the benchmarks we had to manually provide type information for external functions such as `cout`. Some benchmarks in this suite have been ported from original code in statically typed languages and therefore type errors should be rare. One of the benchmarks that we analysed is `mandelbrot`, which plots the Mandelbrot set on a bitmap. This raises a type error when this is run with certain parameters due to a tuple of bytes being used instead of a byte string by function `cout`. With our tool, failure assertions are inserted at two different points, which preempt the type error. Warnings are also statically displayed, which indicate the type errors.

The largest benchmark that we tested is `meteor-contest`, where the C++ version of this is 500 lines of code. A number of type checks were inserted, especially since some type information is lost, such as when heterogenous objects are placed into lists and subsequently retrieved. When running this benchmark no type errors were encountered, with or witout preemptive type checking. A possible failure was however statically inferred by our analyser in function `findFreeCell`:

```
45  def findFreeCell(board):
46      for y in range(height):
47          for x in range(width):
48              if board & (1 << (x + width*y)) == 0:
49                  return x,y
```

We can see that if no free cells are found in a board, this function will not return anything, so by default this would return `None`. In this case, a type error would occur as `None` cannot be unpacked, like a tuple. The programmer is therefore assuming an invariant that asserts that a "free cell" will always be found in the "board". The invariant that the loop will never terminate without returning is explicitly inserted by our tool. If this program is run using preemptive type checking, a preemptive type checking error is raised as soon as the loop at line 47 exits.

Preemptive type checking can be successfully scaled to medium sized programs. For example, the benchmark `meteor-contest` with a maximum execution point depth of 4 yields a control flow graph with over 30k nodes. In this case, it took under half an hour to analyse the program and 15 seconds to transform it on a standard workstation. The same program however takes under ten seconds to analyse and transform when the maximum execution point depth is set to 1. Optimality is still guaranteed in both cases, however more error information can be presented to the user with a larger execution point depth.

Preemptive type checking can be also particularly helpful for less experienced programmers and so we also tested our implementation on code in a question posed by a Python beginner on stackoverflow.com.[1] Our implementation statically produces warnings that corroborate the answer given to this question by Python developers.

7 Related Work

Combinations of static and dynamic typing have been proposed, which enable statically typed code to interact with dynamically typed code. The initial work focused on increasing the degree of dynamic typing in statically typed languages. Abadi et al. [3] introduced the type Dyn to model finite disjoint unions or subclassing in object-oriented languages. The use of dynamic types is constrained (values of type Dyn can only be used in a typecase-construct) and therefore casting is made explicit. In Gradual typing [18], type consistency $\backsim$ (a reflective, symmetric but non-transitive relation) is used to relate Dyn with static types, and Dyn is statically consistent with any type. Gradual typing can support type inferance [19,24] and can be applied to object oriented languages

[1] `http://stackoverflow.com/questions/320827/python-type-error-issue`

[24]. Intermediaries between Dyn and static types are introduced by Flanagan [9] (*Hybrid types*) and by Wrigstad [23] (*like* types). The type systems discussed here do not perform any type error preemption.

As in preemptive type checking, soft typing [7] uses union types to approximate static types in an untyped language and inserts type narrowers to prevent implicit type error exceptions. However, the original work [7] did not handle assignments, so there is no notion of preemption. Soft typing was extended to support Scheme [22] and to handle assignments, but all occurrences of the assigned variable have to have the same type, which makes it impossible to successfully typecheck even the simple example from Fig. 1. Soft typing has also been applied to Python [15] and Erlang [13]. In the latter, the author also bases the type system on a data flow analysis, but does not distinguish between p and f types. Bracha introduces the notion of pluggable type systems [5]. Since preemptive type checking does not affect the semantics of μPython in runtime executions that terminate without raising type errors (Section 4) and no type annotations are required, our type system meets this definition.

We now look at static type inference mechanisms, which turn dynamically typed languages into statically typed subsets. Strongtalk [6] is a subset of Smalltalk with features such as polymorphic signatures, protocol based inheritance, generics and parametric polymorphism. This language also supports the typecase construct. This work however does not define a formal type system or describe how omitted type annotations are treated. Felleisen and Tobin-Hochstadt [21] propose the notion of *occurrence typing* for implementing a statically typed version of Scheme. A translation of the simple example in Fig. 1 is statically rejected by this system. Similarly, statically typed subsets of Python [4] and Ruby [10] have been proposed. These however do not catch all type errors statically, and limit the expressiveness of the language by flagging false positives. Recency types [20] deal with object initialisation patterns in JavaScript, where members are assigned dynamically. The concept of a recency type is similar to the *present types* in our work. Present types are however more sophisticated as these can change throughout intraprocedural paths of control flow rather than blocks.

Lastly, we look at control flow analysis for dynamically typed languages. k-CFA [16] is an algorithm to perform inter-procedural control flow analysis on Scheme by abstract interpretation. Unfortunately, some variants of k-CFA are intractable [17].

8 Conclusions and Future Work

In this paper, we introduce a new method for type checking dynamically typed programs that combines elements of both static and dynamic type checking. It is described as *preemptive type checking* since the type checking happens much earlier than in dynamic typing. Preemptive type checking tries to detect type errors as early as possible and guarantees that any program that can run to completion under dynamic typing without raising a type error will also work with preemptive type checking. We also evaluate an implementation for a subset of Python.

In the future, we plan to add features such as classes and objects, possibly using structural types [14]. This can be complemented with a control flow analysis algorithm such as k-CFA [16]. We also intend to investigate how preemptive type checking can be applied to other popular dynamically typed languages such as JavaScript. Finally, we intend to support metaprogramming by going back and forth between type checking and runtime whenever a new part of the running program is generated.

References

1. Mars Climate Orbiter Mishap Investigation Board Phase I Report. NASA (1999)
2. The Computer Language Benchmarks Game, `http://shootout.alioth.debian.org/`
3. Abadi, M., Cardelli, L., Pierce, B., Plotkin, G.: Dynamic typing in a statically typed language. ACM Transactions on Programming Languages and Systems 13(2), 237–268 (1991)
4. Ancona, D., Ancona, M., Cuni, A., Matsakis, N.: RPython: A step towards reconciling dynamically and statically typed OO languages. In: DLS, pp. 53–64 (2007)
5. Bracha, G.: Pluggable type systems. Revival of Dynamic Languages (2004)
6. Bracha, G., Griswold, D.: Strongtalk: Typechecking Smalltalk in a production environment. In: OOPSLA, pp. 215–230 (1993)
7. Cartwright, R., Fagan, M.: Soft typing. In: PLDI, pp. 278–292 (1991)
8. Findler, R., Felleisen, M.: Contracts for higher-order functions. In: ICFP, pp. 48–59 (2002)
9. Flanagan, C.: Hybrid type checking. In: POPL, pp. 245–256 (2006)
10. Furr, M., An, J., Foster, J., Hicks, M.: Static type inference for Ruby. In: Symposium on Applied Computing, pp. 1859–1866 (2009)
11. Grech, N.: Preemptive Type Checking in Dynamically Typed Languages. PhD thesis, University of Southampton (submitted)
12. Might, M., Smaragdakis, Y., Horn, D.: Resolving and Exploiting the k-CFA Paradox. In: PLDI, pp. 305–315 (2010)
13. Nyström, S.: A soft-typing system for Erlang. In: Erlang Workshop, pp. 56–71 (2003)
14. Pierce, B.: Nominal and Structural Type Systems. In: Types and Programming Languages, ch. 19, pp. 247–264 (2002)
15. Salib, M.: Starkiller: A Static Type Inferencer and Compiler for Python. Thesis, MIT (2004)
16. Shivers, O.: Control-flow analysis in Scheme. In: PLDI, pp. 164–174 (1988)
17. Shivers, O.: Higher-order control-flow analysis in retrospect: lessons learned, lessons abandoned. ACM SIGPLAN Notices 39(4), 257–269 (2004)
18. Siek, J., Taha, W.: Gradual typing for functional languages. In: Scheme and Functional Programming Workshop (2006)
19. Siek, J., Vachharajani, M.: Gradual typing with unification-based inference. In: DLS (2008)
20. Heidegger, P., Thiemann, P.: Recency Types for Dynamically-Typed, Object-Based Languages. In: FOOL (2009)
21. Tobin-Hochstadt, S., Felleisen, M.: The design and implementation of typed scheme. In: POPL, pp. 395–406 (2008)
22. Wright, A., Cartwright, R.: A practical soft type system for scheme. ACM Transactions on Programming Languages and Systems 19, 87–152 (1997)
23. Wrigstad, T., Nardelli, F., Lebresne, S., Östlund, J., Vitek, J.: Integrating typed and untyped code in a scripting language. In: POPL, pp. 377–388 (2010)
24. Rastogi, A., Chaudhuri, A., Hosmer, B.: The Ins and Outs of gradual type inference. In: POPL, pp. 481–494 (2012)
25. TIOBE Programming Community Index (2013), `www.tiobe.com`

On Refinements of Boolean and Parametric Modal Transition Systems

Jan Křetínský[1,2,*] and Salomon Sickert[1,**]

[1] Institut für Informatik, Technische Universität München, Germany
[2] Faculty of Informatics, Masaryk University, Brno, Czech Republic

Abstract. We consider the extensions of modal transition systems (MTS), namely Boolean MTS and parametric MTS and we investigate the refinement problems over both classes. Firstly, we reduce the problem of modal refinement over both classes to a problem solvable by a QBF solver and provide experimental results showing our technique scales well. Secondly, we extend the algorithm for thorough refinement of MTS providing better complexity than via reductions to previously studied problems. Finally, we investigate the relationship between modal and thorough refinement on the two classes and show how the thorough refinement can be approximated by the modal refinement.

1 Introduction

Due to the ever increasing complexity of software systems and their re-use, component-based design and verification have become crucial. Therefore, having a specification formalism that supports *component-based* development and *step-wise refinement* is very useful. In such a framework, one can start from an initial specification, proceed with a series of small and successive refinements until eventually a specification is reached from which an implementation can be extracted directly. In each refinement step, we can replace a single component of the current specification with a more concrete/implementable one. The correctness of such a step should follow from the correctness of the refinement of the replaced component, so that the methodology supports *compositional* verification.

Modal transition systems (MTS) were introduced by Larsen and Thomsen [LT88] in order to obtain an operational, yet expressive and manageable specification formalism meeting the above properties. Their success resides in natural combination of two features. Firstly, the simplicity of labelled transition systems, which have proved appropriate for behavioural description of systems as well as their compositions; MTS as their extension inherit this appropriateness. Secondly, as opposed to e.g. temporal logic specifications, MTS can be easily *gradually refined* into implementations while preserving the desired behavioural

* The author is partially supported by the Czech Science Foundation, project No. P202/10/1469.

** The author is partially funded by the DFG project "Polynomial Systems on Semirings: Foundations, Algorithms, Applications".

Z. Liu, J. Woodcock, and H. Zhu (Eds.): ICTAC 2013, LNCS 8049, pp. 213–230, 2013.

properties. In this work, we focus on checking the refinement between MTS and also their recent extensions.

The formalism of MTS has proven to be useful in practice. Industrial applications are as old as [Bru97] where MTS have found use for an air-traffic system at Heathrow airport. Besides, MTS are advocated as an appropriate base for interface theories in [RBB+09] and for product line theories in [Nym08]. Further, MTS based software engineering methodology for design via merging partial descriptions of behaviour has been established in [UC04]. Moreover, the tool support is quite extensive, e.g. [BLS95, DFFU07, BML11, BČK11].

MTS consist of a set of states and two transition relations. The *must* transitions prescribe which behaviour has to be present in every refinement of the system; the *may* transitions describe the behaviour that is allowed, but need not be realized in the refinements. This allows for underspecification of non-critical behaviour in the early stage of design, focusing on the main properties, verifying them and sorting out the details of the yet unimplemented non-critical behaviour later.

Over the years, many extensions of MTS have been proposed. While MTS can only specify whether or not a particular transition is required, some extensions equip MTS with more general abilities to describe what *combinations* of transitions are possible. Disjunctive MTS (DMTS) [LX90] can specify that at least one of a given set of transitions is present. One selecting MTS [FS08] allow to choose exactly one of them. Boolean MTS (BMTS) [BKL+11] cover all Boolean combinations of transitions. The same holds for acceptance automata [Rac07] and Boolean formulae with states [BDF+], which both express the requirement by listing all possible sets instead of a Boolean formula. Parametric MTS (PMTS) [BKL+11] add parameters on top of it, so that we can also express persistent choices of transitions and relate possible choices in different parts of a system. This way, one can model hardware dependencies of transitions and systems with prices [BKL+12].

Our Contribution. In this paper, we investigate extensions of MTS with respect to two notions of refinement. The *modal refinement* is a syntactically defined notion extending on the one hand bisimulation and on the other hand simulation. Similarly to bisimulation having a counterpart in trace equivalence, here the counterpart of modal refinement is the *thorough refinement.* It is the corresponding semantically defined notion relating (by inclusion) the sets of implementations of the specifications.

We focus both on theoretical and practical complexity of the refinement problems. While modal refinement on MTS and disjunctive MTS can be decided in polynomial time, on BMTS and PMTS it is higher in the polynomial hierarchy (Π_2 and Π_4, respectively). The huge success of SAT and also QBF solvers inspired us to reduce these refinement problems to problems solvable by a QBF solver. We have also performed experiments showing that this solution scales well in the size of the system as well as in the number of parameters, while a direct naive solution is infeasible.

Furthermore, we extend the decision algorithm for thorough refinement checking over MTS [BKLS12] and DMTS [BČK10] to the setting of BMTS and PMTS. We show how PMTS can be translated to BMTS and BMTS can then be transformed to DMTS. As we can decide the problem on DMTS in EXPTIME, this shows decidability for BMTS and PMTS, but each of the translations is inevitably exponential. However, we show better upper bounds than doubly and triply exponential. To this end, we give also a direct algorithm for showing the problem is in NEXPTIME for BMTS and 2-EXPTIME for PMTS.

Since the thorough refinement is EXPTIME-hard for already MTS, it is harder than the modal refinement, which is in P for DMTS and in Π_4 for PMTS. Therefore, we also investigate how the thorough refinement can be approximated by the modal refinement. While underapproximation is easy, as modal refinement implies thorough refinement, overapproximation is more difficult. Here we extend our method of the deterministic hull for MTS [BKLS09] to both BMTS and PMTS. We prove that for BMTS modal and thorough refinements coincide if the refined system is deterministic, which then yields an overapproximation via the deterministic hull. Finally, in the case with PMTS, we need to overapproximate the behaviour dependent on the parameters, because the coincidence of the refinements on deterministic systems fails for PMTS.

Our contribution can be summarized as follows:

- We reduce the problem of modal refinement over BMTS and PMTS to a problem solvable by a QBF solver. We provide promising experimental results showing this solution scales well.
- We extend the algorithm for thorough refinement on MTS and DMTS to BMTS and PMTS providing better complexity then via translation of these formalisms to DMTS. This also shows (together with results on modal refinement) that we can make use of the more compact representation used in the formalisms of BMTS and PMTS.
- We investigate the relationship between modal and thorough refinement on BMTS and PMTS. We introduce approximation methods for the thorough refinement on BMTS and PMTS through the modal refinement.

Related Work. There are various other approaches to deal with component *refinements*. They range from subtyping [LW94] over Java modelling language [JP01] to interface theories close to MTS such as interface automata [dAH01]. Similarly to MTS, interface automata are behavioural interfaces for components. However, their composition works very differently. Furthermore, its notion of refinement is based on alternating simulation [AHKV98], which has been proved strictly less expressive than MTS refinement—actually coinciding on a subclass of MTS—in the paper [LNW07], which combines MTS and interface automata based on I/O automata [Lyn88]. The compositionality of this combination is further investigated in [RBB$^+$11].

Further, alternatively to the design of correct software where an abstract verified MTS is transformed into a concrete implementation, one can consider checking correctness of software through *abstracting* a concrete implementation into a coarser system. The use of MTS as abstractions has been advocated e.g. in [GHJ01]. While usually overapproximations (or underapproximations) of systems are constructed and thus only purely universal (or existential) properties can be checked, [GHJ01] shows that using MTS one can check mixed formulae (arbitrarily combining universal and existential properties) and, moreover, at the same cost as checking universal properties using traditional conservative abstractions. This advantage has been investigated also in the context of systems equivalent or closely related to MTS [HJS01, DGG97, Nam03, DN04, CGLT09, GNRT10].

MTS can also be viewed as a fragment of mu-calculus that is "graphically representable" [BL90, BDF+]. The graphical representability of a variant of alternating simulation called covariant-contravariant simulation has been recently studied in [AFdFE+11].

Outline of the Paper. In Section 2, we recall the formalism of MTS and the extensions discussed and in Section 3 the modal refinement problem is restated. We then reduce it to a QBF problem in Section 4. In Section 5, we give a solution to the thorough refinement problems. Section 6 investigates the relationship of the two refinements and how modal refinement can approximate the thorough refinement. We conclude in Section 7.

2 Modal Transition Systems and Boolean and Parametric Extensions

In this section, we introduce the studied formalisms of modal transition systems and their Boolean and parametric extensions. We first recall the standard definition of MTS:

Definition 2.1. *A* modal transition system (MTS) *over an action alphabet* Σ *is a triple* $(S, \dashrightarrow, \longrightarrow)$*, where* S *is a set of* states *and* $\longrightarrow \subseteq \dashrightarrow \subseteq S \times \Sigma \times S$ *are* must *and* may *transition relations, respectively.*

The MTS are often drawn as follows. Unbroken arrows denote the must (and underlying may) transitions while dashed arrows denote may transitions where there is no must transition.

Example 2.2. The MTS on the right is adapted from [BKL+11] and models traffic lights of types used e.g. in Europe and North America. In state *green* on the left there is a must transition under *ready* to state *yellow* from which there is must transition to *red*. Here transitions to *yellowRed* and back to *green* are may transition. Intuitively, this means that any final implementation may have either one, both or none of the transitions. In contrast, the must transitions are present in all implementations.

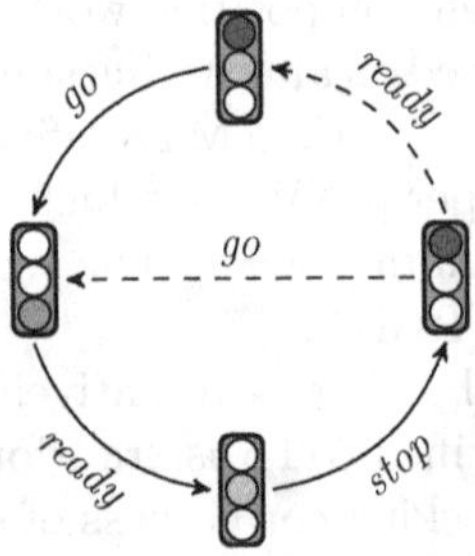

Note that using MTS, we cannot express the set of implementations with exactly one of the transitions in *red*. For that, we can use Boolean MTS [BKL+11] instead, which can express not only arbitrary conjunctions and disjunctions, but also negations and thus also exclusive-or. However, in Boolean MTS it may still happen that an implementation alternates transitions to *green* and *yellowRed* between two traffic lights cycles. To make sure the choice will remain the same in the whole implementation, parametric MTS have been introduced [BKL+11] extending the Boolean MTS.

Before we define the most general class - the parametric MTS - and derive other classes as special cases, we first recall the standard propositional logic. A Boolean formula over a set X of atomic propositions is given by the following abstract syntax

$$\varphi ::= \mathbf{tt} \mid x \mid \neg\varphi \mid \varphi \wedge \psi \mid \varphi \vee \psi$$

where x ranges over X. The set of all Boolean formulae over the set X is denoted by $\mathcal{B}(X)$. Let $\nu \subseteq X$ be a valuation, i.e. a set of variables with value true, then the satisfaction relation $\nu \models \varphi$ is given by $\nu \models \mathbf{tt}$, $\nu \models x$ iff $x \in \nu$, and the satisfaction of the remaining Boolean connectives is defined in the standard way. We also use the standard derived operators like exclusive-or $\varphi \oplus \psi := (\varphi \wedge \neg\psi) \vee (\neg\varphi \wedge \psi)$, implication $\varphi \Rightarrow \psi := \neg\varphi \vee \psi$ and equivalence $\varphi \Leftrightarrow \psi := (\neg\varphi \vee \psi) \wedge (\varphi \vee \neg\psi)$.

We can now proceed with the definition of parametric MTS. In essence, it is a labelled transition system, in which we can specify which transitions can be present depending on values of some fixed parameters.

Definition 2.3. *A* parametric modal transition system (PMTS) *over an action alphabet Σ is a tuple (S, T, P, Φ) where*

- *S is a set of* states*,*
- *$T \subseteq S \times \Sigma \times S$ is a* transition relation*,*
- *P is a finite set of* parameters*, and*
- *$\Phi : S \to \mathcal{B}((\Sigma \times S) \cup P)$ is an* obligation function *over the outgoing transitions and parameters. We assume that whenever (a, t) occurs in $\Phi(s)$ then $(s, a, t) \in T$.*

A Boolean modal transition system (BMTS) *is a PMTS with the set of parameters P being empty. A* disjunctive MTS (DMTS) *is a BMTS with the obligation function in conjunctive normal form and using no negation. An* implementation *(or* labelled transition system*) is a BMTS with $\Phi(s) = \bigwedge_{(s,a,t)\in T}(a, t)$ for each $s \in S$.*

An MTS is then a BMTS with $\Phi(s)$ being a conjunction of positive literals (some of the outgoing transitions), for each $s \in S$. More precisely, $\dashrightarrow$ is the same as T, and $(s, a, t) \in\ \longrightarrow$ if and only if (a, t) is one of the conjuncts of $\Phi(s)$.

Example 2.4. A PMTS which captures the traffic lights used in Europe for cars and pedestrians is depicted below. Depending on the valuation of parameter *reqYellow*, we either always use the yellow light between the red and green lights, or we never do. The transition relation is depicted using unbroken arrows.

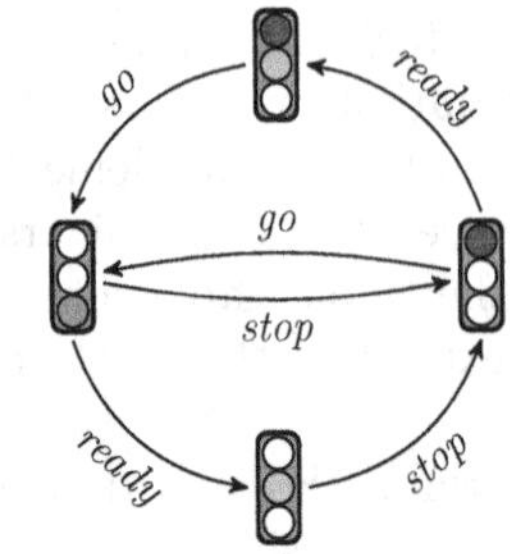

Parameters: $P = \{reqYellow\}$

Obligation function:

$$\Phi(green) = ((stop, red) \oplus (ready, yellow)) \wedge (reqYellow \Leftrightarrow (ready, yellow))$$
$$\Phi(yellow) = (stop, red)$$
$$\Phi(red) = ((go, green) \oplus (ready, yellowRed)) \wedge (reqYellow \Leftrightarrow (ready, yellowRed))$$
$$\Phi(yellowRed) = (go, green)$$

3 Modal Refinement

A fundamental advantage of MTS-based formalisms is the presence of *modal refinement* that allows for a step-wise system design (see e.g. [AHL+08]). We start with the standard definition of modal refinement for MTS and then discuss extensions to BMTS and PMTS.

Definition 3.1 (MTS Modal Refinement). *For states s_0 and t_0 of MTS $(S_1, \longrightarrow_1, \dashrightarrow_1)$ and $(S_2, \longrightarrow_2, \dashrightarrow_2)$, respectively, we say that s_0* modally refines *t_0, written $s_0 \leq_{\mathrm{m}} t_0$, if (s_0, t_0) is contained in a relation $R \subseteq S_1 \times S_2$ satisfying for every $(s,t) \in R$ and every $a \in \Sigma$:*

1. *if $s \overset{a}{\dashrightarrow}_1 s'$ then there is a transition $t \overset{a}{\dashrightarrow}_2 t'$ with $(s', t') \in R$, and*
2. *if $t \overset{a}{\longrightarrow}_2 t'$ then there is a transition $s \overset{a}{\longrightarrow}_1 s'$ with $(s', t') \in R$.*

Intuitively, $s \leq_{\mathrm{m}} t$ iff whatever s can do is allowed by t and whatever t requires can be done by s. Thus s is a refinement of t, or t is an abstraction of s. Furthermore, an *implementation of* s is a state i of an implementation (labelled transition system) with $i \leq_{\mathrm{m}} s$.

In [BKL+11], the modal refinement has been extended to PMTS (and thus BMTS) so that it coincides with the standard definition in the MTS case. We first recall the definition for BMTS. To this end, we set the following notation. Let (S, T, P, Φ) be a PMTS and $\nu \subseteq P$ be a valuation. For $s \in S$, we write $T(s) = \{(a,t) \mid (s,a,t) \in T\}$ and denote by

$$\mathrm{Tran}_\nu(s) = \{E \subseteq T(s) \mid E \cup \nu \models \Phi(s)\}$$

the set of all admissible sets of transitions from s under the fixed truth values of the parameters. In the case of BMTS, we often write Tran instead of $\mathrm{Tran}_\emptyset$.

Definition 3.2 (BMTS Modal Refinement). *For states s_0 and t_0 of BMTS $(S_1, T_1, \emptyset, \Phi_1)$ and $(S_2, T_2, \emptyset, \Phi_2)$, respectively, we say that s_0* modally refines *t_0, written $s_0 \leq_{\mathrm{m}} t_0$, if (s_0, t_0) is contained in a relation $R \subseteq S_1 \times S_2$ satisfying for every $(s,t) \in R$:*

$$\forall M \in \mathrm{Tran}(s) : \exists N \in \mathrm{Tran}(t) : \begin{array}{l} \forall (a,s') \in M : \exists (a,t') \in N : (s',t') \in R \ \wedge \\ \forall (a,t') \in N : \exists (a,s') \in M : (s',t') \in R \ . \end{array}$$

For PMTS, we propose here a slightly altered definition, which corresponds more to the intuition, is closer to the semantically defined notion of thorough refinement, but still keeps the same complexity as established in [BKL+11]. We use the following notation. For a PMTS $\mathcal{M} = (S, T, P, \Phi)$, a valuation $\nu \subseteq P$ of parameters induces a BMTS $\mathcal{M}^\nu = (S, T, \emptyset, \Phi')$ where each occurrence of $p \in \nu$ in Φ is replaced by **tt** and of $p \notin \nu$ by $\neg$**tt**, i.e. $\Phi'(s) = \Phi(s)[\mathbf{tt}/p \text{ for } p \in \nu, \mathbf{ff}/p \text{ for } p \notin \nu]$ for each $s \in S$. We extend the notation to states and let s^ν denote the state of $\mathcal{M}^\nu$ corresponding to the state s of $\mathcal{M}$.

Definition 3.3 (PMTS Modal Refinement). *For states s_0 and t_0 of PMTS (S_1, T_1, P_1, Φ_1) and (S_2, T_2, P_2, Φ_2), we say that s_0* modally refines *t_0, written $s_0 \leq_{\mathrm{m}} t_0$, if for every $\mu \subseteq P_1$ there exists $\nu \subseteq P_2$ such that $s_0^\mu \leq_{\mathrm{m}} t_0^\nu$.*

Before we comment on the difference to the original definition, we illustrate the refinement on an example of [BKL+11] where both definitions coincide.

Example 3.4. Consider the rightmost PMTS below. It has two parameters, namely *reqYfromG* and *reqYfromR* whose values can be set independently and it can be refined by the system in the middle of the figure having only one parameter *reqYellow*. This single parameter simply binds the two original parameters to the same value. The PMTS in the middle can be further refined into the implementations where either yellow is always used in both cases, or never at all as discussed in the previous example. Up to bisimilarity, the *green* state of this system only has the two implementations on the left.

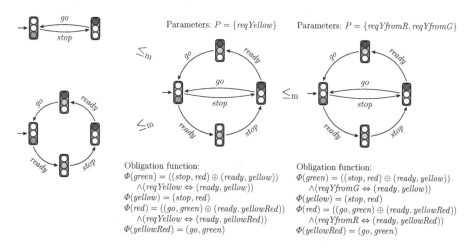

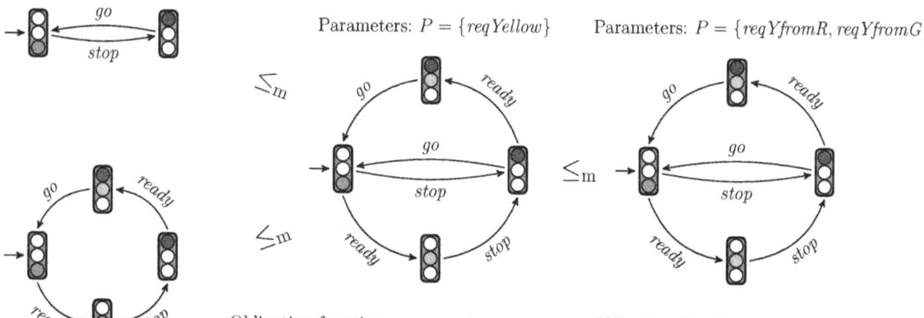

Obligation function:
$\Phi(green) = ((stop, red) \oplus (ready, yellow))$
$\quad \wedge (reqYellow \Leftrightarrow (ready, yellow))$
$\Phi(yellow) = (stop, red)$
$\Phi(red) = ((go, green) \oplus (ready, yellowRed))$
$\quad \wedge (reqYellow \Leftrightarrow (ready, yellowRed))$
$\Phi(yellowRed) = (go, green)$

Obligation function:
$\Phi(green) = ((stop, red) \oplus (ready, yellow))$
$\quad \wedge (reqYfromG \Leftrightarrow (ready, yellow))$
$\Phi(yellow) = (stop, red)$
$\Phi(red) = ((go, green) \oplus (ready, yellowRed))$
$\quad \wedge (reqYfromR \Leftrightarrow (ready, yellowRed))$
$\Phi(yellowRed) = (go, green)$

The original version of [BKL+11] requires for $s_0 \leq_{\mathrm{m}} t_0$ to hold that there be a *fixed* $R \subseteq S_1 \times S_2$ such that for every $\mu \subseteq P_1$ there exists $\nu \subseteq P_2$ satisfying for each $(s, t) \in R$

$$\forall M \in \mathrm{Tran}_\mu(s) : \exists N \in \mathrm{Tran}_\nu(t) : \; \forall (a, s') \in M : \exists (a, t') \in N : (s', t') \in R \;\wedge$$
$$\forall (a, t') \in N : \exists (a, s') \in M : (s', t') \in R \,.$$

Clearly, the original definition is stronger: For any two PMTS states, if $s_0 \leq_m t_0$ holds according to [BKL+11] it also holds according to Definition 3.3. Indeed, the relation for any sets of parameters can be chosen to be the fixed relation R. On the other hand, the opposite does not hold.

Example 3.5. Consider the PMTS on the left with parameter set $\{p\}$ and obligation $\Phi(s_0) = (a, s_1)$, $\Phi(s_1) = (b, s_2) \Leftrightarrow p$, $\Phi(s_2) = \mathbf{tt}$ and the PMTS on the right with parameter set $\{q\}$ and obligation $\Phi(t_0) = ((a, t_1) \Leftrightarrow q) \wedge ((a, t_1') \Leftrightarrow \neg q)$, $\Phi(t_1) = (a, t_2)$, $\Phi(t_2) = \Phi(t_1') = \mathbf{tt}$. On the one hand, according to our definition $s_0 \leq_m t_0$, we intuitively agree this should be the case (and note they also have the same set of implementations). On the other hand, the original definition does not allow to conclude modal refinement between s_0 and t_0. The reason is that depending on the value of p, s_1 is put in the relation either with t_1 (for p being true and thus choosing q true, too) or with t_1' (for p being false and thus choosing q false, too). In contrast to the original definition, our definition allows us to pick different relations for different parameter valuations.

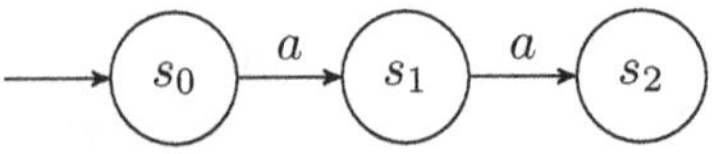

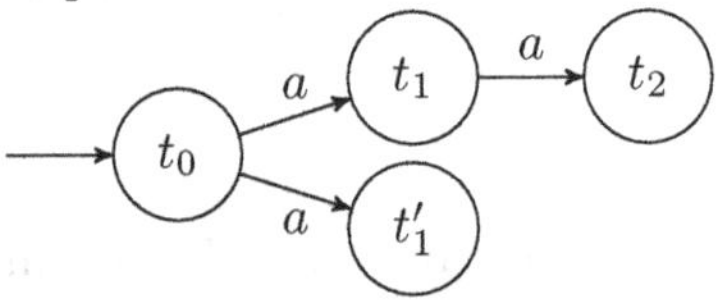

We propose our modification of the definition since it is more intuitive and for all considered fragments of PMTS has the same complexity as the original one. Note that both definitions coincide on BMTS. Further, on MTS they coincide with Definition 3.1 and on labelled transition systems with bisimulation.

4 Modal Refinement Checking

In this section, we show how to solve the modal refinement problem on BMTS and PMTS using QBF solvers. Although modal refinement is Π_2-complete (the second level of the polynomial hierarchy) on BMTS and Π_4-complete on PMTS (see [BKL+11]), this way we obtain a solution method that is practically fast. We have implemented the approach and document its scalability with experimental results.

As mentioned, in order to decide whether modal refinement holds between two states, a reduction to a quantified boolean formula will be used. First, we recall the QBF decision problems.

Definition 4.1 (QBF_n^Q). *Let Ap be a set of atomic propositions, which is partitioned into n sets with $Ap = \bigcup_{i=0}^{n} X_i$, and $\phi \in \mathcal{B}(Ap)$ a boolean formula over this set of atomic propositions. Let $Q \in \{\forall, \exists\}$ be a quantifier and $\overline{} : \{\forall \mapsto \exists, \exists \mapsto \forall\}$ a function. Then a formula*

$$QX_1\overline{Q}X_2QX_3\ldots\widetilde{Q}X_n\phi \quad \text{with } \widetilde{Q} = \begin{cases} Q & \text{if } n \text{ is odd} \\ \overline{Q} & \text{if } n \text{ is even} \end{cases}$$

is an instance of QBF_n^Q if it is satisfiable.

Satisfiability means that if e.g. $Q = \exists$ there is some partial valuation for the atomic propositions in X_1, such that for all partial valuations for the elements of X_2, there is another partial valuation for the propositions of X_3 and so on up to X_n, such that ϕ is satisfied by the union of all partial valuations. It is well known that these problems are complete for the polynomial hierarchy: For each $i \geq 1$, $QBF_i^\exists$ is Σ_i-complete and $QBF_i^\forall$ is Π_i-complete.

4.1 Construction for BMTS

Due to the completeness of QBF problems and the results of [BKL+11], it is possible to polynomially reduce modal refinement on BMTS to $QBF_2^\forall$. However, we would then have to perform a fixpoint computation to compute the refinement relation causing numerous invocations of the external QBF solver. Additionally this approach is not applicable in the PMTS case, hence we reduce modal refinement to $QBF_3^\exists$.

Let $s \in S_1$ and $t \in S_2$ be processes of two arbitrary BMTSs $\mathcal{M}_1 = (S_1, T_1, \emptyset, \Phi_1)$ and $\mathcal{M}_2 = (S_2, T_2, \emptyset, \Phi_2)$. Furthermore let

$$Ap = \underbrace{(S_1 \times S_2)}_{X_R} \uplus \underbrace{T_1}_{X_{T1}} \uplus \underbrace{(S_1 \times T_2)}_{X_{T2}}$$

be a set of atomic propositions. The intended meaning is that $(u, v) \in X_R$ is assigned **tt** if and only if it is also contained in the modal refinement relation R. Further, X_{T1} and X_{T2} are used to talk about the transitions. The prefix S_1 is attached to the set T_2 because $N \in \text{Tran}(t)$ with $t \in S_2$ must be chosen independently for different states of S_1. This enables us to move the $\exists$ quantification.

We now construct a formula $\Psi_{s,t} \in \mathcal{B}(Ap)$ satisfying

$$s \leq_m t \quad \textit{iff} \quad \exists X_R \forall X_{T1} \exists X_{T2} \Psi_{s,t} \in QBF_3^\exists \tag{1}$$

To this end, we shall use a macro $\psi_{u,v}$ capturing the condition which has to be satisfied by any element $(u, v) \in R$. Furthermore, we ensure that (s, t) is assigned **tt** by every satisfying assignment for the formula by placing it directly in the conjunction:

$$\Psi_{s,t} = (s, t) \wedge \bigwedge_{(u,v) \in X_R} ((u, v) \Rightarrow \psi_{u,v}) \tag{2}$$

It remains to define the macro $\psi_{u,v}$. We start with the modal refinement condition as a blueprint:

$$\begin{aligned} \forall M \in \text{Tran}(u) : \exists N \in \text{Tran}(v) : \; & \forall (a, u') \in M : \exists (a, v') \in N : (u', v') \in R \; \wedge \\ & \forall (a, v') \in N : \exists (a, u') \in M : (u', v') \in R \, . \end{aligned}$$

As M and N are subsets of $T_1(u)$ and $T_2(v)$, respectively, and are finite, the inner quantifiers can be expanded causing only a polynomial growth of the formula size (see [KS13]). Further, Tran sets are replaced by the original definition and the outer quantifiers are moved in front of $\Psi_{s,t}$. As the state obligations are defined over a different set of atomic propositions ($\Phi(v) \in \mathcal{B}((\Sigma \times S) \cup P) \not\subseteq \mathcal{B}(Ap)$), a family of mapping functions π_p is introduced.

$$\begin{aligned} \pi_p : \mathcal{B}(\Sigma \times S) &\to \mathcal{B}(Ap) \\ \mathbf{tt} &\mapsto \mathbf{tt} \\ (a, x) &\mapsto (p, a, x) \quad \text{with } a \in \Sigma,\, x \in S \\ \neg\varphi &\mapsto \neg\, \pi_p(\varphi) \\ \varphi_1 \wedge \varphi_2 &\mapsto \pi_p(\varphi_1) \wedge \pi_p(\varphi_2) \\ \varphi_1 \vee \varphi_2 &\mapsto \pi_p(\varphi_1) \vee \pi_p(\varphi_2) \end{aligned} \tag{3}$$

Applying these steps to the blueprint yields the following result:

$$\psi_{u,v} = \pi_u\left(\Phi_1(u)\right) \Rightarrow \pi_{u,v}\left(\Phi_2(v)\right) \wedge \varphi_{u,v} \tag{4}$$

$$\begin{aligned} \varphi_{u,v} = &\bigwedge_{\substack{u^* \in X_{T1} \\ u^* = (u,a,u')}} \Big(u^* \Rightarrow \bigvee_{\substack{v^* \in X_{T2} \\ v^* = (u,v,a,v')}} (v^* \wedge (u', v'))\Big) \\ \wedge &\bigwedge_{\substack{v^* \in X_{T2} \\ v^* = (u,v,a,v')}} \Big(v^* \Rightarrow \bigvee_{\substack{u^* \in X_{T1} \\ u^* = (u,a,u')}} (u^* \wedge (u', v'))\Big) \end{aligned} \tag{5}$$

Theorem 4.2. *For states s, t of a BMTS, we have*

$$s \leq_m t \quad \textit{iff} \quad \exists X_R \forall X_{T1} \exists X_{T2} \Psi_{s,t} \in QBF_3^{\exists}$$

Due to space constraints, the technical proof can be found in [KS13].

4.2 Construction for PMTS

We now reduce the modal refinement on PMTS to $QBF_4^{\forall}$, which now corresponds directly to the complexity established in [BKL+11]. Nevertheless, due to the first existential quantification in ∀∃∀∃ alternation sequence, we can still guess the refinement relation using the QBF solver rather than compute the lengthy fixpoint computation.

In the PMTS case, we have to find for all parameter valuations for the system of s a valuation for the system of t, such that there exists a modal refinement relation containing (s, t). We simply choose universally a valuation for the parameters of the left system (the underlying system of s) and then existentially for the right system (the underlying system of t). Prior to checking modal refinement, the valuations are fixed, so the PMTS becomes a BMTS. This is accomplished by extending Ap with P_1 and P_2 and adding the necessary quantifiers to the formula. Thus we obtain the following:

Theorem 4.3. *For states s, t of a PMTS, we have*

$$s \leq_m t \quad \textit{iff} \quad \forall P_1 \exists P_2 \exists X_R \forall X_{T1} \exists X_{T2} \Psi_{s,t} \in QBF_4^{\forall}$$

4.3 Experimental Results

We now show how our method performs in practice. We implemented the reduction and linked it to the QBF solver Quantor. In order to evaluate whether our solution scales, we generate random samples of MTS, disjunctive MTS, Boolean MTS and parametric MTS with different numbers of parameters (as displayed in tables below in parenthesis). For each type of system and the number of reachable states (25 to 200 as displayed in columns), we generate several pairs of systems and compute the average time to check modal refinement between them. While the systems in Table 1 are generated independently, the refining systems in Table 2 are refinements of the abstract systems.

We show several sets of experiments. In Table 1, we consider (1) systems with alphabet of size 2 and all states with branching degree 2, and (2) systems with alphabet of size 10 and all states with branching degree 10. Further, in Table 2, we consider systems with alphabet of size 2 and all states with branching degree 5. Here we first consider the systems as above, i.e. with edges generated randomly so that they create a tree and with some additional "noise" edges thus making the branching degree constant. Second, we consider systems where we have different "clusters", each of which is interconnected with many edges. Each of these clusters has a couple of "interface" states, which are used to connect to other clusters. We use this class of systems to model system descriptions with more organic structure.

The entries in the tables are average running times in seconds. The standard deviation in our experiments was around 30-60%. The experiments were run on an Intel Core 2 Duo CPU P9600 2.66GHz with 3.8 GB RAM using Java 1.7. For more details, see [KS13].

Table 1. Experimental results: systems over alphabet of size 2 with branching degree 2 in the upper part, and systems over alphabet of size 10 with branching degree 10 in the lower part

	25	50	75	100	125	150	175	200
MTS	0.03	0.15	0.29	0.86	0.87	0.96	1.88	2.48
DMTS	0.04	0.22	0.39	0.91	1.13	1.34	2.61	3.19
BMTS	0.03	0.15	0.30	0.62	0.83	0.87	1.61	2.17
PMTS(1)	0.03	0.20	0.37	0.84	0.97	1.23	2.44	3.15
PMTS(5)	0.04	0.22	0.42	0.91	1.26	1.59	2.83	3.66
MTS	0.18	0.84	2.12	3.88	5.63	7.64	10.30	14.18
DMTS	0.44	2.23	5.31	8.59	10.13	14.14	13.96	66.92
BMTS	0.21	1.08	2.65	4.58	6.70	9.63	12.44	17.06
PMTS(1)	0.26	1.12	2.74	4.57	7.58	10.31	11.26	16.41
PMTS(5)	0.25	1.17	2.94	6.36	7.80	10.01	11.90	36.51

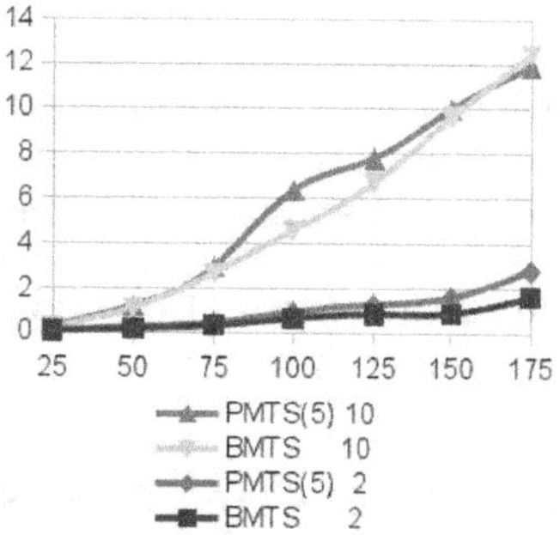

On the one hand, observe that the number of parameters does not play any major role in the running time. The running times on PMTS with 5 parameters are very close to BMTS, i.e. PMTS with zero parameters, as can be seen in the graph. Therefore, the greatest theoretical complexity threat—the number of parameters allowing in general only for searching all exponentially many combinations—is in practice eliminated by the use of QBF solvers.

Table 2. Experimental results: systems over alphabet of size 2 with branching degree 5; systems with random structure in the upper part, and systems with organic structure in the lower part; the refining system is identical to the abstract system, besides a stronger obligation

	25	50	75	100	125	150	175	200
BMTS	0.32	1.57	3.46	7.18	10.24	15.18	20.6	27.05
PMTS(1)	0.34	1.57	3.21	8.25	12.46	19.88	24.53	31.01
PMTS(5)	0.33	1.65	4.48	8.21	13.14	21.5	20.55	25.82
BMTS	0.01	0.03	0.18	0.22	0.3	0.48	0.73	1.02
PMTS(1)	0.01	0.07	0.14	0.22	0.43	0.43	0.72	0.83
PMTS(5)	0.01	0.05	0.1	0.17	0.31	0.43	0.88	1.39

On the other hand, observe that the running time is more affected by the level of non-determinism. For branching degree 10 over a 10-letter alphabet, there are more likely to be more outgoing transitions under the same letter than in the case with branching degree 2 over a 2-letter alphabet, but still less than for branching degree 5 over a 2-letter alphabet. However, the level of non-determinism is often quite low [BKLS09], hence this dependency does not pose a serious problem in practice. Further, even this most difficult setting with a high level of non-determinism allows for fast analysis if systems with natural organic structure are considered, cf. upper and lower part of Table 2.

A more serious problem stems from our use of Java. With sizes around 200, the running times often get considerably longer, as the automatic memory management takes its toll. However, this problem should diminish in a garbage-collection-free setting.

5 Thorough Refinement Checking

While modal refinement has been defined syntactically, there is also a corresponding notion defined semantically. The semantics of a state s of a PMTS is the set of its implementations $[\![s]\!] := \{i \mid i \text{ is an implementation and } i \leq_{\mathrm{m}} s\}$.

Definition 5.1 (Thorough Refinement). *For states s_0 and t_0 of PMTS, we say that s_0* thoroughly refines *t_0, written $s_0 \leq_{\mathrm{t}} t_0$, if $[\![s_0]\!] \subseteq [\![t_0]\!]$.*

5.1 Transforming PMTS to BMTS and DMTS

The thorough refinement problem is EXPTIME-complete for MTS [BKLS12] and also for DMTS [BČK11] (for proof, see [BČK10]). First, we show how to transform PMTS to BMTS and DMTS and thus reduce our problems to the already solved one.

For a PMTS, we define a system where we can use any valuation of the parameters:

Definition 5.2. *For a PMTS $\mathcal{M} = (S, T, P, \Phi)$ with initial state s_0, we define a BMTS called* de-parameterization $\mathcal{M}^B = (\{s_0^B\} \cup S \times 2^P, T', \emptyset, \Phi')$ *with initial state s_0^B and*

- $T' = \{(s_0^B, a, (s, \nu)) \mid (s_0, a, s) \in T, \nu \subseteq P\} \cup \{((s, \nu), a, (s', \nu) \mid (s, a, s') \in T\}$,
- $\Phi'(s_0^B) = \bigoplus_{\nu \subseteq P} \Phi(s_0)[\mathbf{tt}/p \text{ for } p \in \nu, \mathbf{ff}/p \text{ for } p \notin \nu, (s, \nu)/s]$,
- $\Phi'((s, \nu)) \ = \ \Phi(s)[\mathbf{tt}/p \text{ for } p \in \nu, \mathbf{ff}/p \text{ for } p \notin \nu, (s, \nu)/s]$.

The de-parameterization is a BMTS having exactly all the implementations of the PMTS and only one (trivial) valuation.

Proposition 5.3. *Let s_0 be a PMTS state. Then $[\![s_0]\!] = [\![s_0^B]\!]$ and $s_0 \leq_{\mathrm{m}} s_0^B$.*

Proof. For any parameter valuation ν we match it with $\emptyset$ and the modal refinement is achieved in the copy with ν fixed in the second component. Clearly, any implementation of s_0^B corresponds to a particular parameter valuation and thus also to an implementation of s_0. □

Remark 5.4. The price we have to pay is a blowup exponential in $|P|$. This is, however, inevitable. Indeed, consider a PMTS $(\{s_0, s_1, s_2\}, \{(s_0, p, s_1), (s_1, p, s_2) \mid p \in P\}, P, \{s_0, s_1 \mapsto \bigwedge_{p \in P}(p, s) \Leftrightarrow p, s_2 \mapsto \mathbf{tt}\})$. Then in every equivalent BMTS we need to remember the transitions of the first step so that we can repeat exactly these in the following step. Since there are exponentially many possibilities, the result follows.

Further, similarly to Boolean formulae with states in [BDF+], we can transform every BMTS to a DMTS.

Definition 5.5. *For a BMTS $\mathcal{M} = (S, T, \emptyset, \Phi)$ with initial state s_0, we define a DMTS called* de-negation $\mathcal{M}^D = (S', T', \emptyset, \Phi')$

- $S' = \{M \in \mathrm{Tran}(s) \mid s \in S\}$,
- $\Phi'(M) = \bigwedge_{(a,s') \in M} \bigvee_{M' \in \mathrm{Tran}(s')}(a, M')$,

and T' minimal such that for each $M \in S'$ and each occurrence of (a, M') in $\Phi(M)$, we have $(M, a, M') \in T'$.

However, this DMTS needs to have more initial states in order to be equivalent to the original BMTS:

Lemma 5.6. *For a state s_0 of a BMTS, $[\![s_0]\!] = \bigcup_{M \in \mathrm{Tran}(s_0)} [\![M]\!]$ (where M are taken as states of the de-negation).*

Note that both transformations are exponential. The first one in $|P|$ and the second one in the branching degree. Therefore, their composition is still only singly exponential, yielding a state space where each state has two components: a valuation of original parameters and Tran of the original state under this valuation.

Theorem 5.7. *Thorough refinement on PMTS is in 2-EXPTIME.*

Proof. Recall that thorough refinement on DMTS is in EXPTIME. Further, note that we have reduced the PMTS and BMTS thorough refinement problems to the one on DMTS with more initial states. However, this does not pose a problem. Indeed, let s_0 and t_0 be states of a BMTS. We want to check whether $s_0 \leq_{\mathrm{t}} t_0$. According to [BČK10] where DMTS only have one initial state, we only need to check whether for each $M \in \mathrm{Tran}(s_0)$ we have $(M, \mathrm{Tran}(t_0)) \notin \mathit{Avoid}$ (defined in [BČK10]), which can clearly still be done in exponential time. □

5.2 Direct Algorithm

We now extend the approach for MTS and DMTS to the BMTS case. Before proceeding, one needs to prune all inconsistent states, i.e. those with unsatisfiable obligation. This is standard and the details can be found in [KS13].

We define a set *Avoid*, which contains pairs consisting of one process and one set of processes. A pair is contained in the relation if there exists an implementation refining the single process, but none of the other processes. This approach is very similar to [BKLS12], but the rules for generating *Avoid* are much more complex.

Definition 5.8. (Avoid) *Let $(S, T, \emptyset, \Phi)$ be a globally consistent BMTS over the action alphabet Σ. The set of* avoiding *states of the form $(s, \mathcal{T})$, where $s \in S$ and $\mathcal{T} \subseteq S$, is the smallest set Avoid such that $(s, \mathcal{T}) \in \mathit{Avoid}$ whenever $\mathcal{T} = \emptyset$ or there exists an admissible set of transitions $M \in \mathrm{Tran}(s)$ and sets $\mathit{later}_{a,u,f} \subseteq S$ for every $a \in \Sigma$, $u \in S$, $f \in \bigcup_{t \in \mathcal{T}} \mathrm{Tran}(t)$ such that*

$$\begin{aligned} \forall t \in \mathcal{T} : \forall N_t \in \mathrm{Tran}(t) : \ \exists a \in \Sigma : & \\ & \exists t_a \in N_t(a) : \forall s_a \in M(a) : \forall f \in \bigcup_{t \in \mathcal{T}} \mathrm{Tran}(t) : t_a \in \mathit{later}_{a,s_a,f} \\ \vee \quad & \exists s_a \in M(a) : \forall t_a \in N_t(a) : t_a \in \mathit{later}_{a,s_a,N_t} \end{aligned}$$

and

$$\forall f \in \bigcup_{t \in \mathcal{T}} \mathrm{Tran}(t) : \forall (a, s_a) \in M : (s_a, \mathit{later}_{a,s_a,f}) \in \mathit{Avoid}$$

hold.

Lemma 5.9. *Given processes $s, t_1, t_2 \ldots t_n$ of some finite, global-consistent BMTS, there exists an implementation I such that $I \leq_{\mathrm{m}} s$ and $I \not\leq_{\mathrm{m}} t_i$ for all $i \in [1, n]$ if $(s, \{t_1, t_2 \ldots t_n\}) \in \mathit{Avoid}$.*

Theorem 5.10. *Thorough refinement checking on BMTS is in NEXPTIME.*

Proof. For deciding $s \leq_{\mathrm{t}} t$ the *Avoid* relation has to be computed, whose size grows exponentially with the size of the underlying system. Moreover, in each step of adding a new element is added to *Avoid*, the sets $\mathit{later}_{a,s,f}$ need to be guessed. □

6 Thorough vs. Modal Refinement

In this section, we discuss the relationship of the two refinements. This missing proofs can be found in [KS13]. Firstly, the modal refinement is a sound approximation to the thorough refinement.

Proposition 6.1. *Let s_0 and t_0 be states of PMTS. If $s_0 \leq_{\rm m} t_0$ then $s_0 \leq_{\rm t} t_0$.*

Proof. For any $i \in [\![s_0]\!]$, we have $i \leq_{\rm m} s_0$ and due to transitivity of $\leq_{\rm m}$, $i \leq_{\rm m} s_0 \leq_{\rm m} t_0$ implies $i \leq_{\rm m} t_0$, hence $i \in [\![t_0]\!]$. □

The converse does not hold even for MTS as shown in the following classical example ([BKLS09]) where $s_0 \leq_{\rm t} t_0$, but $s_0 \not\leq_{\rm m} t_0$.

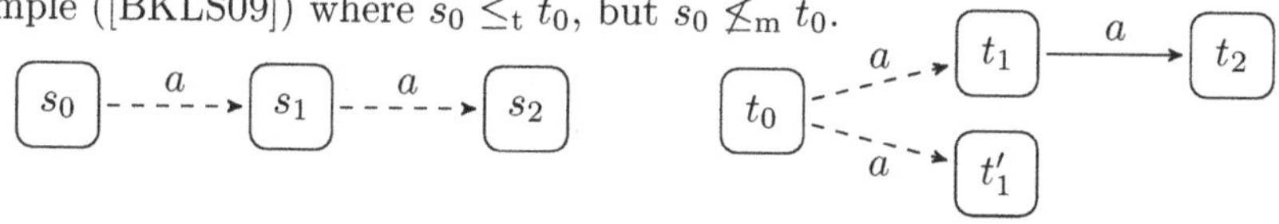

However, provided the refined MTS is deterministic, the approximation is also complete [BKLS09]. This holds also for BMTS and is very useful as deterministic system often appear in practice [BKLS09] and checking modal refinement is computationally easier than the thorough refinement. Formally, a PMTS (S, T, P, Φ) is called deterministic if for every $(s, a, t), (s, a, t') \in T$ we have $t = t'$.

Proposition 6.2. *Let s_0 be a PMTS state and t_0 a deterministic BMTS state. If $s_0 \leq_{\rm t} t_0$ then $s_0 \leq_{\rm m} t_0$.*

However, the completeness fails if the refined system is deterministic but with parameters:

Example 6.3. Consider a BMTS $(\{s_0, s_1\}, \{s_0, a, s_1\}, \emptyset, \{s_0 \mapsto \mathbf{tt}, s_1 \mapsto \mathbf{tt}\})$ and a deterministic PMTS $(\{t_0, t_1\}, \{(t_0, a, t_1)\}, \{p\}, \{t_0 \mapsto a \Leftrightarrow p, t \mapsto \mathbf{tt}\})$ below. Obviously $[\![s_0]\!] = [\![t_0]\!]$ contains the implementations with no transitions or one step a-transitions. Although $s_0 \leq_{\rm t} t_0$, we do not have $s_0 \leq_{\rm m} t_0$ as we cannot match with any valuation of p.

$$\Phi(t_0) = a \Leftrightarrow p$$

Corollary 6.4. *There is a state s_0 of a PMTS and a state t_0 of a deterministic PMTS such that $s_0 \leq_{\rm t} t_0$ but $s_0 \not\leq_{\rm m} t_0$.*

In the previous example, we lacked the option to match a system with different parameter valuations at once. However, the de-parameterization introduced earlier is non-deterministic even if the original system was deterministic. Hence the modal refinement is not guaranteed to coincide with the thorough refinement. In [BKLS09], we defined the notion of deterministic hull, the best deterministic overapproximation of a system. The construction on may transitions was the standard powerset construction and a must transition was created if all states of a macrostate had one. Here we extend this notion to PMTS, which allows to over- and under-approximate the thorough refinement by the modal refinement.

Definition 6.5. *For a PMTS* $\mathcal{M} = (S, T, P, \Phi)$ *with initial state* s_0*, we define a PMTS called* deterministic hull $\mathcal{D}(\mathcal{M}) = (2^S \setminus \emptyset, T', P, \Phi')$ *with initial state* $\mathcal{D}(s_0) := \{s_0\}$ *and*

- $T' = \{(X, a, X_a)\}$ *where* X_a *denotes all* a*-successors of elements of* X*, i.e.* $X_a = \{s' \mid \exists s \in X : (s, a, s') \in T)\}$,
- $\Phi'(X)$ *is such that* $\mathrm{Tran}(X) = \bigcup_{s \in X} \mathrm{Tran}(s)[(a, X_a)/(a, s)$ *for every* $a, s]$.

Proposition 6.6. *For a PMTS state* s_0, $\mathcal{D}(s_0)$ *is deterministic and* $s_0 \leq_{\mathrm{m}} \mathcal{D}(s_0)$.

We now show the minimality of the deterministic hull.

Proposition 6.7. *Let* s_0 *be a PMTS state. Then*

- *for every deterministic PMTS state* t_0*, if* $s_0 \leq_{\mathrm{m}} t_0$ *then* $\mathcal{D}(s_0) \leq_{\mathrm{m}} t_0$*;*
- *for every deterministic BMTS state* t_0*, if* $s_0 \leq_{\mathrm{t}} t_0$ *then* $\mathcal{D}(s_0) \leq_{\mathrm{m}} t_0$.

The next transformation allows for removing the parameters without introducing non-determinism.

Definition 6.8. *For a PMTS* $\mathcal{M} = (S, T, P, \Phi)$ *with initial state* s_0*, we define a BMTS called* parameter-free hull $\mathcal{P}(\mathcal{M}) = (S, T, \emptyset, \Phi')$ *with initial state* $\mathcal{P}(s_0) := s_0$ *and*

$$\Phi'(s) = \bigvee_{\nu \subseteq P} \Phi(s)[\mathbf{tt}/p \text{ for } p \in \nu, \mathbf{ff}/p \text{ for } p \notin \nu]$$

Lemma 6.9. *For a PMTS state* s_0, $s_0 \leq_{\mathrm{m}} s_0^B \leq_{\mathrm{m}} \mathcal{P}(s_0)$.

The parameter-free deterministic hull now plays the rôle of the deterministic hull for MTS.

Corollary 6.10. *For PMTS states* s_0 *and* t_0*, if* $s_0 \leq_{\mathrm{t}} t_0$ *then* $s_0 \leq_{\mathrm{m}} \mathcal{P}(\mathcal{D}(t_0))$.

Proof. Since $s_0 \leq_{\mathrm{t}} t_0$, we also have $s_0 \leq_{\mathrm{t}} \mathcal{D}(t_0)$ by Propositions 6.6 and 6.1. Therefore, $s_0 \leq_{\mathrm{t}} \mathcal{P}(\mathcal{D}(t_0))$ by Proposition 6.9 and thus $s_0 \leq_{\mathrm{m}} \mathcal{P}(\mathcal{D}(t_0))$ by Proposition 6.2. □

7 Conclusions

We have investigated both modal and thorough refinement on boolean and parametric extension of modal transition systems. Apart from results summarized in the table below, we have shown a practical way to compute modal refinement and use it for approximating thorough refinement. Closing the complexity gap for thorough refinement, i.e. obtaining matching lower bounds or improving our algorithm remains as an open question.

	MTS	BMTS	PMTS
$\leq_{\mathrm{t}}\ \in$	EXPTIME	NEXPTIME	2-EXPTIME
$s \leq_{\mathrm{t}} t$, t deterministic	$\leq_{\mathrm{m}} = \leq_{\mathrm{t}}$	$\leq_{\mathrm{m}} = \leq_{\mathrm{t}}$	$\leq_{\mathrm{m}} \neq \leq_{\mathrm{t}}$

References

[AFdFE+11] Aceto, L., Fábregas, I., de Frutos-Escrig, D., Ingólfsdóttir, A., Palomino, M.: Graphical representation of covariant-contravariant modal formulae. In: EXPRESS, pp. 1–15 (2011)

[AHKV98] Alur, R., Henzinger, T.A., Kupferman, O., Vardi, M.Y.: Alternating refinement relations. In: Sangiorgi, D., de Simone, R. (eds.) CONCUR 1998. LNCS, vol. 1466, pp. 163–178. Springer, Heidelberg (1998)

[AHL+08] Antonik, A., Huth, M., Guldstrand Larsen, K., Nyman, U., Wasowski, A.: 20 years of modal and mixed specifications. Bulletin of the EATCS 95, 94–129 (2008)

[BČK10] Beneš, N., Černá, I., Křetínský, J.: Disjunctive modal transition systems and generalized LTL model checking. Technical report FIMU-RS-2010-12, Faculty of Informatics, Masaryk University, Brno (2010)

[BČK11] Beneš, N., Černá, I., Křetínský, J.: Modal transition systems: Composition and LTL model checking. In: Bultan, T., Hsiung, P.-A. (eds.) ATVA 2011. LNCS, vol. 6996, pp. 228–242. Springer, Heidelberg (2011)

[BDF+] Beneš, N., Delahaye, B., Fahrenberg, U., Křetínský, J., Legay, A.: Hennessy-milner logic with maximal fixed points as a specification theory (to appear in CONCUR 2013)

[BKL+11] Beneš, N., Křetínský, J., Guldstrand Larsen, K., Møller, M.H., Srba, J.: Parametric modal transition systems. In: Bultan, T., Hsiung, P.-A. (eds.) ATVA 2011. LNCS, vol. 6996, pp. 275–289. Springer, Heidelberg (2011)

[BKL+12] Beneš, N., Křetínský, J., Guldstrand Larsen, K., Møller, M.H., Srba, J.: Dual-priced modal transition systems with time durations. In: Bjørner, N., Voronkov, A. (eds.) LPAR-18 2012. LNCS, vol. 7180, pp. 122–137. Springer, Heidelberg (2012)

[BKLS09] Beneš, N., Křetínský, J., Guldstrand Larsen, K., Srba, J.: On determinism in modal transition systems. Theor. Comput. Sci. 410(41), 4026–4043 (2009)

[BKLS12] Beneš, N., Křetínský, J., Guldstrand Larsen, K., Srba, J.: Exptime-completeness of thorough refinement on modal transition systems. Inf. Comput. 218, 54–68 (2012)

[BL90] Boudol, G., Guldstrand Larsen, K.: Graphical versus logical specifications. In: Arnold, A. (ed.) CAAP 1990. LNCS, vol. 431, pp. 57–71. Springer, Heidelberg (1990)

[BLS95] Børjesson, A., Larsen, K.G., Skou, A.: Generality in design and compositional verification using TAV. Formal Methods in System Design 6(3), 239–258 (1995)

[BML11] Bauer, S.S., Mayer, P., Legay, A.: MIO workbench: A tool for compositional design with modal input/output interfaces. In: Bultan, T., Hsiung, P.-A. (eds.) ATVA 2011. LNCS, vol. 6996, pp. 418–421. Springer, Heidelberg (2011)

[Bru97] Bruns, G.: An industrial application of modal process logic. Sci. Comput. Program. 29(1-2), 3–22 (1997)

[CGLT09] Campetelli, A., Gruler, A., Leucker, M., Thoma, D.: *Don't know* for multi-valued systems. In: Liu, Z., Ravn, A.P. (eds.) ATVA 2009. LNCS, vol. 5799, pp. 289–305. Springer, Heidelberg (2009)

[dAH01] de Alfaro, L., Henzinger, T.A.: Interface automata. In: ESEC/SIGSOFT FSE, pp. 109–120 (2001)

[DFFU07] D'Ippolito, N., Fischbein, D., Foster, H., Uchitel, S.: MTSA: Eclipse support for modal transition systems construction, analysis and elaboration. In: ETX, pp. 6–10 (2007)

[DGG97] Dams, D., Gerth, R., Grumberg, O.: Abstract interpretation of reactive systems. ACM Trans. Program. Lang. Syst. 19(2), 253–291 (1997)

[DN04] Dams, D., Namjoshi, K.S.: The existence of finite abstractions for branching time model checking. In: LICS, pp. 335–344 (2004)

[FS08] Fecher, H., Schmidt, H.: Comparing disjunctive modal transition systems with an one-selecting variant. J. Log. Algebr. Program. 77(1-2), 20–39 (2008)

[GHJ01] Godefroid, P., Huth, M., Jagadeesan, R.: Abstraction-based model checking using modal transition systems. In: Larsen, K.G., Nielsen, M. (eds.) CONCUR 2001. LNCS, vol. 2154, pp. 426–440. Springer, Heidelberg (2001)

[GNRT10] Godefroid, P., Nori, A.V., Rajamani, S.K., Tetali, S.: Compositional must program analysis: unleashing the power of alternation. In: POPL, pp. 43–56 (2010)

[HJS01] Huth, M., Jagadeesan, R., Schmidt, D.A.: Modal transition systems: A foundation for three-valued program analysis. In: Sands, D. (ed.) ESOP 2001. LNCS, vol. 2028, pp. 155–169. Springer, Heidelberg (2001)

[JP01] Jacobs, B., Poll, E.: A logic for the java modeling language JML. In: Hussmann, H. (ed.) FASE 2001. LNCS, vol. 2029, pp. 284–299. Springer, Heidelberg (2001)

[KS13] Křetínský, J., Sickert, S.: On refinements of boolean and parametric modal transition systems. CoRR, abs/1304.5278 (2013)

[LNW07] Guldstrand Larsen, K., Nyman, U., Wąsowski, A.: Modal I/O automata for interface and product line theories. In: De Nicola, R. (ed.) ESOP 2007. LNCS, vol. 4421, pp. 64–79. Springer, Heidelberg (2007)

[LT88] Guldstrand Larsen, K., Thomsen, B.: A modal process logic. In: LICS, pp. 203–210 (1988)

[LW94] Liskov, B., Wing, J.M.: A behavioral notion of subtyping. ACM Trans. Program. Lang. Syst. 16(6), 1811–1841 (1994)

[LX90] Guldstrand Larsen, K., Xinxin, L.: Equation solving using modal transition systems. In: LICS, pp. 108–117 (1990)

[Lyn88] Lynch, N.: I/O automata: A model for discrete event systems. In: 22nd Annual Conference on Information Sciences and Systems, pp. 29–38. Princeton University (1988)

[Nam03] Namjoshi, K.S.: Abstraction for branching time properties. In: Hunt Jr., W.A., Somenzi, F. (eds.) CAV 2003. LNCS, vol. 2725, pp. 288–300. Springer, Heidelberg (2003)

[Nym08] Nyman, U.: Modal Transition Systems as the Basis for Interface Theories and Product Lines. PhD thesis, Aalborg Universitet (2008)

[Rac07] Raclet, J.-B.: Quotient de spécifications pour la réutilisation de composants. PhD thesis, Université de Rennes I (December 2007) (in French)

[RBB+09] Raclet, J.-B., Badouel, E., Benveniste, A., Caillaud, B., Passerone, R.: Why are modalities good for interface theories? In: ACSD. IEEE Computer Society Press (2009)

[RBB+11] Raclet, J.-B., Badouel, E., Benveniste, A., Caillaud, B., Legay, A., Passerone, R.: A modal interface theory for component-based design. Fundamenta Informaticae 108(1-2), 119–149 (2011)

[UC04] Uchitel, S., Chechik, M.: Merging partial behavioural models. In: SIGSOFT FSE, pp. 43–52 (2004)

Proof Theory of a Multi-Lane Spatial Logic*

Sven Linker and Martin Hilscher

Department of Computing Science, University of Oldenburg, Germany
{linker,hilscher}@informatik.uni-oldenburg.de

Abstract. We extend the Multi-lane Spatial Logic MLSL, introduced in previous work for proving the safety (collision freedom) of traffic maneuvers on a multi-lane highway, by length measurement and dynamic modalities. We investigate the proof theory of this extension, called EMLSL. To this end, we prove the undecidability of EMLSL but nevertheless present a sound proof system which allows for reasoning about the safety of traffic situations. We illustrate the latter by giving a formal proof for a lemma we could only prove informally before.

Keywords: Spatial logic, undecidability, labelled natural deduction.

1 Introduction

In our previous work [1] we proposed a multi-dimensional spatial logic MLSL inspired by Moszkowski's interval temporal logic (ITL) [2], Zhou, Hoare and Ravn's Duration Calculus (DC) [3] and Schäfer's Shape Calculus [4] for formulating the purely spatial aspects of safety of traffic maneuvers on highways. In MLSL we modeled the highway as one continuous dimension, i.e., in the direction along the lanes and one discrete dimension, the different lanes. We illustrated MLSL's usefulness by proving safety of two variants of lane change maneuvers on highways. The safety proof establishes that the braking distances of no two cars intersecting is an inductive invariant of a transition system capturing the dynamics of cars and controllers.

In this paper we introduce EMLSL which extends MLSL by length measurement and dynamic modalities. In comparison to MLSL, where we are only able to reason about qualitative spatial properties, i.e., topological relations between cars, EMLSL also allows for quantitative reasoning, e.g., on braking distances. To further the practicality of EMLSL, we define a proof system based on ideas of Basin et al. [5], who presented systems of labelled natural deduction for a vast class of typical modal logics. Rasmussen [6] refined their work to interval logics with binary chopping modalities. Since EMLSL incorporates both unary as well as chopping modalities, our proof system is strongly related to both approaches.

Besides providing a higher expressiveness, extending MLSL enables us to formulate and prove the invariance of the spatial safety property *inside* EMLSL

* This research was partially supported by the German Research Council (DFG) in the Transregional Collaborative Research Center SFB/TR 14 AVACS.

Z. Liu, J. Woodcock, and H. Zhu (Eds.): ICTAC 2013, LNCS 8049, pp. 231–248, 2013.

and its deductive proof system. We demonstrate this by conducting a formal proof of the so called *reservation lemma* [1], which informally states that no car changes lanes without having set the turn signal beforehand.

Further on, we show undecidability of a subset of EMLSL. We adapt the proof of Zhou et al. [7] for DC and reduce the halting problem of two counter machines to satisfiability of EMLSL formulas. Due to the restricted set of predicates EMLSL provides, this is non-trivial.

The *contributions* of this paper are as follows:

- we extend MLSL with lengths measurements and dynamic modalities (Sec. 2);
- we show the spatial fragment of EMLSL to be undecidable (Sec. 3);
- we present a suited proof system and derive the reservation lemma (Sec. 4).

2 Extended MLSL Syntax and Semantics

The purpose of EMLSL is to reason about highway situations. To this end, we first present the formal model of a *traffic snapshot* capturing the position and speed of every car on the highway at a given point in time. In addition a traffic snapshot comprises the lane a given car is driving on, which we call a *reservation*. Every car usually holds one reservation, i.e., drives on one lane, but may, during lane change maneuvers, hold up to two reservations on adjacent lanes. Furthermore, we capture the indication that a given car wants to change to a adjacent lane by the notion of a *claim* which is an abstraction of setting the turn signal. Every car may only hold claims while not engaged in a lane change.

To formally define a traffic snapshot, we assume a countably infinite set of globally unique *car identifiers* $\mathbb{I}$ and an arbitrary but fixed set of lanes $\mathbb{L} = \{0, \ldots, N\}$, for some $N \geq 1$. Throughout this paper we will furthermore make use of the notation $\mathcal{P}(X)$ for the powerset of X, and the override notation $\oplus$ from Z for function updates [8], i.e., $f \oplus \{x \mapsto y\}(z) = y$ if $x = z$ and $f(z)$ otherwise.

Definition 1 (Traffic snapshot). *A* traffic snapshot $\mathcal{TS}$ *is a structure* $\mathcal{TS} = (res, clm, pos, spd, acc)$, *where* res, clm, pos, spd, acc *are functions*

- $res : \mathbb{I} \to \mathcal{P}(\mathbb{L})$ *such that* $res(C)$ *is the set of lanes the car* C *reserves,*
- $clm : \mathbb{I} \to \mathcal{P}(\mathbb{L})$ *such that* $clm(C)$ *is the set of lanes the car* C *claims,*
- $pos : \mathbb{I} \to \mathbb{R}$ *such that* $pos(C)$ *is the position of the car* C *along the lanes,*
- $spd : \mathbb{I} \to \mathbb{R}$ *such that* $spd(C)$ *is the current speed of the car* C*,*
- $acc : \mathbb{I} \to \mathbb{R}$ *such that* $acc(C)$ *is the current acceleration of the car* C*.*

Furthermore, we require the following sanity conditions *to hold for all* $C \in \mathbb{I}$*.*

1. $res(C) \cap clm(C) = \emptyset$
2. $1 \leq |res(C)| \leq 2$
3. $0 \leq |clm(C)| \leq 1$
4. $1 \leq |res(C)| + |clm(C)| \leq 2$
5. $clm(C) \neq \emptyset$ *implies* $\exists n \in \mathbb{L} \bullet res(C) \cup clm(C) = \{n, n+1\}$
6. $|res(C)| = 2$ *or* $|clm(C)| = 1$ *holds only for finitely many* $C \in \mathbb{I}$*.*

We denote the set of all traffic snapshots by $\mathbb{TS}$*.*

The kinds of transitions are twofold. First, we have discrete transitions defining the possibilities to create, mutate and remove claims and reservations. The other type of transitions handles abstractions of the dynamics of cars, i.e., they allow for instantaneous changes of accelerations and for the passing of time, during which the cars move according to a simple model of motion. For the results presented subsequently, we only require the changes of positions to be continuous.

Definition 2 (Transitions). *The following* transitions *describe the changes that may occur at a traffic snapshot* $\mathcal{TS} = (res, clm, pos, spd, acc)$.

$$\begin{aligned}
\mathcal{TS} \xrightarrow{\mathsf{c}(C,n)} \mathcal{TS}' \quad &\Leftrightarrow \quad \mathcal{TS}' = (res, clm', pos, spd, acc) \\
&\quad \wedge |clm(C)| = 0 \wedge |res(C)| = 1 \\
&\quad \wedge res(C) \cap \{n+1, n-1\} \neq \emptyset \\
&\quad \wedge clm' = clm \oplus \{C \mapsto \{n\}\} && (1) \\
\mathcal{TS} \xrightarrow{\mathsf{wd\ c}(C)} \mathcal{TS}' \quad &\Leftrightarrow \quad \mathcal{TS}' = (res, clm', pos, spd, acc) \\
&\quad \wedge clm' = clm \oplus \{C \mapsto \emptyset\} && (2) \\
\mathcal{TS} \xrightarrow{\mathsf{r}(C)} \mathcal{TS}' \quad &\Leftrightarrow \quad \mathcal{TS}' = (res', clm', pos, spd, acc) \\
&\quad \wedge clm' = clm \oplus \{C \mapsto \emptyset\} \\
&\quad \wedge res' = res \oplus \{C \mapsto res(C) \cup clm(C)\} && (3) \\
\mathcal{TS} \xrightarrow{\mathsf{wd\ r}(C,n)} \mathcal{TS}' \quad &\Leftrightarrow \quad \mathcal{TS}' = (res', clm, pos, spd, acc) \\
&\quad \wedge res' = res \oplus \{C \mapsto \{n\}\} \\
&\quad \wedge n \in res(C) \wedge |res(C)| = 2 && (4) \\
\mathcal{TS} \xrightarrow{t} \mathcal{TS}' \quad &\Leftrightarrow \quad \mathcal{TS}' = (res, clm, pos', spd', acc) \\
&\quad \wedge \forall C \in \mathbb{I} \colon pos'(C) = pos(C) + spd(C) \cdot t + \tfrac{1}{2} acc(C) \cdot t^2 \\
&\quad \wedge \forall C \in \mathbb{I} \colon spd'(C) = spd(C) + acc(C) \cdot t && (5) \\
\mathcal{TS} \xrightarrow{\mathsf{acc}(C,a)} \mathcal{TS}' \quad &\Leftrightarrow \quad \mathcal{TS}' = (res, clm, pos, spd, acc') \\
&\quad \wedge acc' = acc \oplus \{C \mapsto a\} && (6)
\end{aligned}$$

We also combine passing of time and changes of accelerations to *evolutions*.

$$\mathcal{TS} \overset{t}{\Rightarrow} \mathcal{TS}' \Leftrightarrow \mathcal{TS} = \mathcal{TS}_0 \xrightarrow{t_0} \mathcal{TS}_1 \xrightarrow{\mathsf{acc}(C_0,a_0)} \dots \xrightarrow{t_n} \mathcal{TS}_{2n-1} \xrightarrow{\mathsf{acc}(C_n,a_n)} \mathcal{TS}_{2n} = \mathcal{TS}',$$

where $t = \sum_{i=0}^{n} t_i$, $a_i \in \mathbb{R}$ and $C_i \in \mathbb{I}$ for all $0 \leq i \leq n$.

The transitions preserve the sanity conditions in Def. 1.

Lemma 1 (Preservation of Sanity). *Let* $\mathcal{TS}$ *be a snapshot satisfying the constraints given in Def. 1. Then, each structure* $\mathcal{TS}'$ *reachable by a transition is again a traffic snapshot satisfying Def. 1.*

EMLSL restricts the parts of the motorway perceived by each car to so called *views*. Each view comprises a set of lanes and a real-valued interval, its length.

Definition 3 (View). *For a given traffic snapshot $\mathcal{TS}$ with a set of lanes $\mathbb{L}$, a* view *V is defined as a structure $V = (L, X, E)$, where*

- *$L = [l, n] \subseteq \mathbb{L}$ is an interval of lanes that are visible in the view,*
- *$X = [r, t] \subseteq \mathbb{R}$ is the extension that is visible in the view,*
- *$E \in \mathbb{I}$ is the identifier of the car under consideration.*

A subview *of V is obtained by restricting the lanes and extension we observe. For this we use sub- and superscript notation: $V^{L'} = (L', X, E)$ and $V_{X'} = (L, X', E)$, where L' and X' are subintervals of L and X, respectively.*

Sensor Function. Subsequently we will use a car dependent sensor function $\Omega_E : \mathbb{I} \times \mathbb{TS} \to \mathbb{R}_+$ which, given a car identifier and a traffic snapshot, provides the length of the corresponding car, as perceived by E.

Abbreviations. For a given view $V = (L, X, E)$ and a traffic snapshot $\mathcal{TS} = (res, clm, pos, spd, acc)$ we use the following abbreviations:

$$res_V : \mathbb{I} \to \mathcal{P}(L) \text{ with } C \mapsto res(C) \cap L \tag{7}$$
$$clm_V : \mathbb{I} \to \mathcal{P}(L) \text{ with } C \mapsto clm(C) \cap L \tag{8}$$
$$len_V : \mathbb{I} \to \mathcal{P}(X) \text{ with } C \mapsto [pos(C), pos(C) + \Omega_E(C, \mathcal{TS})] \cap X \tag{9}$$

The functions (7) and (8) are restrictions of their counterparts in $\mathcal{TS}$ to the sets of lanes considered in this view. The function (9) gives us the part of the view occupied by a car C.[1]

Definition 4 formalizes the partitioning of discrete intervals. We need this slightly intricate notion to have a clearly defined chopping operation, even on the empty set of lanes.

Definition 4 (Chopping discrete intervals). *Let I_D be a discrete interval, i.e., $I_D = [l, n]$ for some $l, n \in \mathbb{L}$ or $I_D = \emptyset$. Then $I_D = I_D^1 \ominus I_D^2$ if and only if $I_D^1 \cup I_D^2 = I_D$, $I_D^1 \cap I_D^2 = \emptyset$, and both I_D^1 and I_D^2 are discrete convex intervals, which implies $\max(I_D^1) + 1 = \min(I_D^2)$ or $I_D^1 = \emptyset$ or $I_D^2 = \emptyset$.*

We define the following relations on views to have a consistent description of vertical and horizontal chopping operations.

Definition 5 (Relations of Views). *Let V_1, V_2 and V be views of a snapshot $\mathcal{TS}$. Then $V = V_1 \ominus V_2$ if and only if $V = (L, X, E)$, $L = L_1 \ominus L_2$, $V_1 = V^{L_1}$ and $V_2 = V^{L_2}$. Furthermore, $V = V_1 \oplus V_2$ if and only if $V = (L, [r, t], E)$ and there is an $s \in [r, t]$ such that $V_1 = V_{[r,s]}$ and $V_2 = V_{[s,t]}$.*

[1] This presentation differs slightly from our previous work in two ways. First, we do not restrict the set of identifiers anymore to the cars "visible" to E. Since the functions for the reservations, claims or length return the empty set for cars outside of V, such cars cannot satisfy the corresponding atomic formulas. The definition of res_V and clm_V was altered due to a technical mistake in the previous form.

To abstract from the borders of intervals during the definition of the semantics, we define the following norm giving the length of an interval. This notion coincides with the length measurement of DC [3].

Definition 6 (Measure of a real-valued interval). *Let $I_R = [r, t]$ be a real-valued interval, i.e. $r, t \in \mathbb{R}$. The* measure *of I_R is the norm $\|I_R\| = t - r$.*

We employ three sorts of variables. The set of variables ranging over car identifiers is denoted by CVar, with typical elements c and d. For referring to lengths and quantities of lanes, we use the sorts RVar and LVar ranging over real numbers and elements of the set of lanes $\mathbb{L}$, respectively. The set of all variables is denoted by Var. To refer to the car owning the current view, we use the special constant ego. Furthermore we use the syntax ℓ for the length of a view, i.e., the length of the extension of the view and ω for the width, i.e., the number of lanes. For simplicity, we only allow for addition between correctly sorted terms. However, it is straightforward to augment the definition with further arithmetic operations.

Definition 7 (Syntax). *We use the following definition of* terms.

$$\theta ::= n \mid r \mid \mathrm{ego} \mid u \mid \ell \mid \omega \mid \theta_1 + \theta_2,$$

where $n \in \mathbb{L}$, $r \in \mathbb{R}$ and $u \in$ Var and θ_i are both of the same sort, and not elements of $\mathrm{CVar} \cup \{\mathrm{ego}\}$. *We denote the set of terms with Θ. The syntax of the* extended multi-lane spatial logic EMLSL *is given as follows.*

$$\phi ::= \bot \mid \theta_1 = \theta_2 \mid re(c) \mid cl(c) \mid \phi_1 \rightarrow \phi_2 \mid \forall z \bullet \phi_1 \mid \phi_1 \frown \phi_2 \mid \begin{matrix}\phi_2\\ \phi_1\end{matrix} \mid M\phi$$

where $M \in \{\Box_{\mathsf{r}(c)}, \Box_{\mathsf{c}(c)}, \Box_{\mathsf{wd\ c}(c)}, \Box_{\mathsf{wd\ r}(c)}, \Box_{\mathcal{T}}\}$, $c \in \mathrm{CVar} \cup \{\mathrm{ego}\}$, $z \in \mathrm{Var}$, and $\theta_1, \theta_2 \in \Theta$ are of the same sort. We denote the set of all EMLSL formulas by Φ.

Definition 8 (Valuation and Modification). *A* valuation *is a function $\nu \colon \mathrm{Var} \cup \{\mathrm{ego}\} \rightarrow \mathbb{I} \cup \mathbb{R} \cup \mathbb{L}$. We silently assume valuations and their modifications to respect the sorts of variables. For a view $V = (L, X, E)$, we lift ν to a function ν_V evaluating terms, where variables and* ego *are interpreted as in ν, and $\nu_V(\ell) = \|X\|$ and $\nu_V(\omega) = |L|$. The function $+$ is interpreted as addition.*

Definition 9 (Semantics). *In the following, let θ_i be terms of the same sort, $c \in \mathrm{CVar} \cup \{\mathrm{ego}\}$ and $z \in \mathrm{Var}$. The* satisfaction *of formulas with respect to a traffic snapshot $\mathcal{TS}$, a view $V = (L, X, E)$ and a valuation ν with $\nu(\mathrm{ego}) = E$ is defined inductively as follows:*

$$
\begin{aligned}
&\mathcal{TS}, V, \nu \not\models \bot && \text{for all } \mathcal{TS}, V, \nu\\
&\mathcal{TS}, V, \nu \models \theta_1 = \theta_2 && \Leftrightarrow\ \nu_V(\theta_1) = \nu_V(\theta_2)\\
&\mathcal{TS}, V, \nu \models re(c) && \Leftrightarrow\ |L| = 1 \text{ and } \|X\| > 0 \text{ and}\\
& && \quad\ res_V(\nu(c)) = L \text{ and } X = len_V(\nu(c))\\
&\mathcal{TS}, V, \nu \models cl(c) && \Leftrightarrow\ |L| = 1 \text{ and } \|X\| > 0 \text{ and}
\end{aligned}
$$

$$\begin{aligned}
& && clm_V(\nu(c)) = L \text{ and } X = len_V(\nu(c)) \\
& \mathcal{TS}, V, \nu \models \phi_1 \rightarrow \phi_2 && \Leftrightarrow \mathcal{TS}, V, \nu \models \phi_1 \text{ implies } \mathcal{TS}, V, \nu \models \phi_2 \\
& \mathcal{TS}, V, \nu \models \forall z \bullet \phi && \Leftrightarrow \forall \alpha \in \mathbb{I} \cup \mathbb{R} \cup \mathbb{L} \bullet \mathcal{TS}, V, \nu \oplus \{z \mapsto \alpha\} \models \phi \\
& \mathcal{TS}, V, \nu \models \phi_1 \frown \phi_2 && \Leftrightarrow \exists V_1, V_2 \bullet V = V_1 \oplus V_2 \text{ and} \\
& && \quad \mathcal{TS}, V_1, \nu \models \phi_1 \text{ and } \mathcal{TS}, V_2, \nu \models \phi_2 \\
& \mathcal{TS}, V, \nu \models \begin{matrix} \phi_2 \\ \phi_1 \end{matrix} && \Leftrightarrow \exists V_1, V_2 \bullet V = V_1 \ominus V_2 \text{ and} \\
& && \quad \mathcal{TS}, V_1, \nu \models \phi_1 \text{ and } \mathcal{TS}, V_2, \nu \models \phi_2 \\
& \mathcal{TS}, V, \nu \models \Box_{\mathsf{r}(c)} \phi && \Leftrightarrow \forall \mathcal{TS}' \bullet \mathcal{TS} \xrightarrow{\mathsf{r}(\nu(c))} \mathcal{TS}' \text{ implies } \mathcal{TS}', V, \nu \models \phi \\
& \mathcal{TS}, V, \nu \models \Box_{\mathsf{c}(c)} \phi && \Leftrightarrow \forall \mathcal{TS}', n \bullet \mathcal{TS} \xrightarrow{\mathsf{c}(\nu(c),n)} \mathcal{TS}' \text{ implies } \mathcal{TS}', V, \nu \models \phi \\
& \mathcal{TS}, V, \nu \models \Box_{\mathsf{wd\ c}(c)} \phi && \Leftrightarrow \forall \mathcal{TS}' \bullet \mathcal{TS} \xrightarrow{\mathsf{wd\ c}(\nu(c))} \mathcal{TS}' \text{ implies } \mathcal{TS}', V, \nu \models \phi \\
& \mathcal{TS}, V, \nu \models \Box_{\mathsf{wd\ r}(c)} \phi && \Leftrightarrow \forall \mathcal{TS}', n \bullet \mathcal{TS} \xrightarrow{\mathsf{wd\ r}(\nu(c),n)} \mathcal{TS}' \text{ implies } \mathcal{TS}', V, \nu \models \phi \\
& \mathcal{TS}, V, \nu \models \Box_{\tau} \phi && \Leftrightarrow \forall \mathcal{TS}', t \bullet \mathcal{TS} \overset{t}{\Rightarrow} \mathcal{TS}' \text{ implies } \mathcal{TS}', V, \nu \models \phi
\end{aligned}$$

In addition to the standard abbreviations of the remaining Boolean operators and the existential quantifier, we use $\top \equiv \neg\bot$. An important derived modality of our previous work [1] is the *somewhere* modality

$$\langle \phi \rangle \equiv \top \frown \begin{pmatrix} \top \\ \phi \\ \top \end{pmatrix} \frown \top.$$

Further, we use its dual operator *everywhere*. We abbreviate the modality *somewhere along the extension of the view* with the operator $\Diamond_\ell$, similar to the *on some subinterval* modality of DC.

$$[\phi] \equiv \neg \langle \neg\phi \rangle \qquad \Diamond_\ell \phi \equiv \top \frown \phi \frown \top \qquad \Box_\ell \phi \equiv \neg \Diamond_\ell \neg \phi$$

Likewise, abbreviations can be defined to express the modality *on some lane*. Furthermore, we define the diamond modalities for the transitions as usual, i.e., $\Diamond_* \phi \equiv \neg \Box_* \neg \phi$, where $* \in \{\mathsf{r}(c), \mathsf{c}(c), \mathsf{wd\ r}(c), \mathsf{wd\ c}(c), \tau\}$.

In the first definition of MLSL, we included the atom *free* to denote free space on the road, i.e., space which is neither occupied by a reservation nor by a claim. It was not possible to derive this atom from the others, since we were unable to express the existence of exactly one lane and a non-zero extension in the view. However, in the current presentation, *free* can be defined within EMLSL. Observe that a view of non-zero extension can be characterized by $\ell > 0 \equiv \neg(\ell = 0)$.

$$\mathit{free} \equiv \ell > 0 \wedge \omega = 1 \wedge \forall c \bullet \Box_\ell (\neg cl(c) \wedge \neg re(c))$$

Furthermore, we can define $\ell < r \equiv \neg(\ell = r \frown \top)$ and use the superscript φ^r to abbreviate the schema $\varphi \wedge \ell = r$. For reasons of clarity, we will not always use this abbreviation and write out the formula instead, to emphasize the restriction.

As an example, the following formula defines the behavior of a safe distance controller, i.e., as long as the car starts in a situation with free space in front of it, the formula demands that after an arbitrary time, there is still free space left.

$$\forall x, y \bullet \Diamond_\ell \begin{pmatrix} \omega = x \\ re(\text{ego}) \frown \mathit{free} \\ \omega = y \end{pmatrix} \rightarrow \Box_\tau \left(\Diamond_\ell \begin{pmatrix} \omega = x \\ re(\text{ego}) \frown \mathit{free} \\ \omega = y \end{pmatrix} \right)$$

We have to relate the lane in both the antecedent and the conclusion by the atoms $\omega = x$ and $\omega = y$ respectively. If we simply used $\langle re(\text{ego}) \frown \mathit{free} \rangle$, it would be possible for the reservations to be on different lanes, and hence, we would not ensure that free space is in front of each of ego's reservations at every point in time. However, the formula does not constrain how the situations may change, whenever reservations or claims are created or withdrawn.

Observe that it is crucial to combine acceleration and time transitions into a single modality $\Box_\tau$. Let ego drive on lane m with a velocity of v. If we only allowed for the passing of time, this formula would require all cars on m in front of ego to have a velocity $v_f \geq v$, while all cars behind ego had to drive with $v_b \leq v$. Hence the evolutions allow for more complex behavior in the underlying model.

Like for ITL [2] or DC [3], we call a formula *flexible* whenever its satisfaction is dependent on the current traffic snapshot and view. Otherwise the formula is *rigid*. However, since the spatial dimensions of EMLSL are not directly interrelated, we also distinguish *horizontally rigid* and *vertically rigid* formulas. The satisfaction of the former is independent of the extension of views, while for the latter, the amount of lanes in a view is of no influence. If a formula is only independent of the current traffic snapshot, we call it *dynamically rigid*.

Definition 10 (Types of Rigidity). *Let ϕ be a formula of EMLSL. We call ϕ* dynamically rigid, *if it does not contain any spatial atom, i.e., $re(c)$ or $cl(c)$ as a subformula. Furthermore, we call ϕ* horizontally rigid, *if it is dynamically rigid and in addition does not contain ℓ as a term. Similarly, ϕ is* vertically rigid, *if it is dynamically rigid and does not contain ω as a term. If ϕ is both vertically and horizontally rigid, it is simply* rigid.

Lemma 2. *Let ϕ by dynamically rigid and ϕ_H (ϕ_V) be horizontally (vertically) rigid. Then for all traffic snapshots $\mathcal{TS}$, $\mathcal{TS}'$, views V, V_1, V_2 and valuations ν,*

1. $\mathcal{TS}, V, \nu \models \phi$ *iff* $\mathcal{TS}', V, \nu \models \phi$
2. *Let* $V = V_1 \oplus V_2$. *Then* $\mathcal{TS}, V, \nu \models \phi_H$ *iff* $\mathcal{TS}, V_i, \nu \models \phi_H$ *(for* $i \in \{1, 2\}$*).*
3. *Let* $V = V_1 \ominus V_2$. *Then* $\mathcal{TS}, V, \nu \models \phi_V$ *iff* $\mathcal{TS}, V_i, \nu \models \phi_V$ *(for* $i \in \{1, 2\}$*).*

Proof. By induction on the structure of EMLSL formulas.

3 Undecidability of Pure MLSL

In this section we give an undecidability result for the spatial fragment of EMLSL, i.e., we do not need the modalities for the discrete state changes of the model or the evolutions. We will call this fragment *spatial MLSL*, subsequently. We reduce the halting problem of two-counter machines, which is known to be undecidable [9], to satisfaction of spatial MLSL formulas.

Intuitively, a two counter machine executes a branching program which manipulates a (control) state and increments and decrements two different counters c_1 and c_2. Formally, two counter machines consist of a set of states $Q = \{q_0, \dots, q_m\}$, distinguished initial and final states $q_0, q_{fin} \in Q$ and a set of instructions I of the form shown in Tab. 1 (the instructions for the counter c_2 are analogous). The instructions mutate configurations of the form $s = (q_i, c_1, c_2)$, where $q_i \in Q$ and $c_1, c_2 \in \mathbb{N}$ into new configurations:

Table 1. Instructions for counter c_1 of a two-counter machine

s	Instruction	s'
(q, c_1, c_2)	$q \xrightarrow{c_1^+} q_j$	$(q_j, c_1 + 1, c_2)$
$(q, 0, c_2)$	$q \xrightarrow{c_1^-} q_j, q_n$	$(q_j, 0, c_2)$
$(q, c+1, c_2)$	$q \xrightarrow{c_1^-} q_j, q_n$	(q_n, c, c_2)

An *run from the initial configuration* of a two-counter machine (Q, q_0, q_{fin}, I) is a sequence of configurations $(q_0, 0, 0) \xrightarrow{i_0} \dots \xrightarrow{i_p} (q_{p+1}, c_{p+1}, c'_{p+1})$, where each i_j is an instance of an instruction within I. If $q_{p+1} = q_{fin}$, the run is *halting*.

We follow the approach of Zhou et al. [7] for DC. They encode the configurations in recurring patterns of length $4k$, where the first part constitutes the current state, followed by the contents of the first counter. The third part is filled with a marker to distinguish the counters, and is finally followed by the contents of the second counter. Each of these parts is exactly of length k.

Zhou et al. could use distinct observables for the state of the machine, counters and separating delimiters, since DC allows for the definition of arbitrary many observable variables. We have to modify this encoding since within spatial MLSL we are restricted to two predicates for reservations and claims, and the derived predicate for free space, respectively. Furthermore, due to the constraints on EMLSL models in Def. 1, we cannot use multiple occurrences of reservations of a unique car to stand, e.g., for the values of one counter. Hence we have to existentially quantify all mentions of reservations and claims. We will never reach an upper limit of existing cars, since we assume $\mathbb{I}$ to be countably infinite.

The current state of the machine q_i is encoded by the number of lanes below the current configuration, the states of the counters is described by a sequence of reservations, separated by a single claim. To safely refer to the start of a configuration, we also use an additional marker consisting of a claim, an adjacent reservation and again a claim. Each part of the configurations is assumed to have length k. Free space separates the reservations within one counter from each other and from the delimiters. Intuitively, a configuration is encoded as follows:

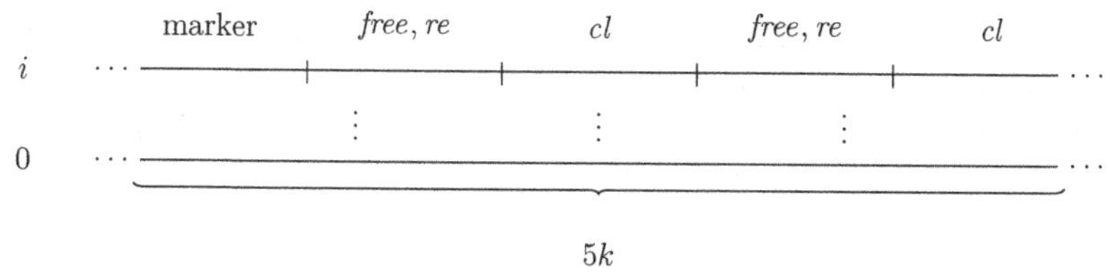

To enhance the readability of our encoding, we use the abbreviation marker $\equiv \exists c \bullet cl(c) \frown \exists c \bullet re(c) \frown \exists c \bullet cl(c)$ to denote the start of a configuration.

Like Zhou et al., we ensure that reservations and claims are mutually exclusive. We do not have to consider *free*, since it is already defined as the absence of both reservations and claims. Observe that we use the square brackets to denote the *everywhere* modality (cf. Section 2).

$$\text{mutex} = \forall c, d \bullet [cl(c) \rightarrow \neg re(d)) \wedge (re(c) \rightarrow \neg cl(d)] \,.$$

The initial marking $(q_0, 0, 0)$ is then defined by the following formula.

$$\text{init} = \left(\begin{array}{c} [\neg \exists c \bullet cl(c)] \\ \text{marker}^k \frown \mathit{free}^k \frown (\exists c \bullet cl(c))^k \frown \mathit{free}^k \frown (\exists c \bullet cl(c))^k \\ \omega = 0 \end{array} \right) \frown \top$$

We have to ensure that the configurations occur periodically after every $5k$ spatial units. Therefore, we use the following schema $Per(\mathcal{D})$. Observe that we only require that the lanes surrounding the formula $\mathcal{D}$ do not contain claims. This ensures on the one hand that no configuration lies in parallel with the formula $\mathcal{D}$, since well-defined configurations have to include claims. On the other hand, it allows for satisfiability of the formula, since we do not forbid the occurrence of reservations, which are needed for the claims within the configurations.

$$Per(\mathcal{D}) = \left[\left(\begin{array}{c} [\neg \exists c \bullet cl(c)] \\ \mathcal{D} \\ [\neg \exists c \bullet cl(c)] \end{array} \frown \ell = 5k \right) \rightarrow \left(\ell = 5k \frown \begin{array}{c} [\neg \exists c \bullet cl(c)] \\ \mathcal{D} \\ [\neg \exists c \bullet cl(c)] \end{array} \right) \right]$$

Note that we did not constrain on which lane the periodic behavior occurs. This will be defined by the encoding of the operations.

Now we may define the periodicity of the delimiters and the counters. Here we also have to slightly deviate from Zhou et al.: we are not able to express the statement "almost everywhere *free* or $re(c)$ holds," directly. We have to encode it by ensuring that on every subinterval with a length greater than zero, we can find another subinterval which satisfies *free* or $re(c)$. This expresses in particular, that no claim may occur, due to the mutual exclusion property.

$$\begin{aligned} \text{periodic} = \; & Per((\Box_\ell(\ell > 0 \rightarrow \top \frown (\mathit{free} \vee \exists c \bullet re(c)) \frown \top) \wedge \omega = 1)^k) \\ & \wedge Per((\exists c \bullet cl(c))^k) \wedge Per(\text{marker}^k) \end{aligned}$$

We turn to the encoding of the operation $q_i \xrightarrow{c_1^+} q_j$, i.e., the machine goes from q_i to q_j and increments the first counter by one. Similar to Zhou et al., we use encodings of the form $\neg(\mathcal{D}_1 \frown \neg\mathcal{D}_2)$, meaning "whenever the beginning of the view satisfies $\mathcal{D}_1$, the next part satisfies $\mathcal{D}_2$."

The formula F_1 copies the reservations of counter one of state q_i to the corresponding places in counter one in state q_j.

$$F_1 = \neg\left(\left(\begin{array}{c}\top \\ \text{marker}^k \frown \ell < k \frown \exists c \bullet \mathit{re}(c) \frown ((\exists c \bullet \mathit{re}(c) \frown \top) \land \ell = 5k) \\ \omega = i\end{array}\right) \frown \right.$$
$$\left. \neg\left(\begin{array}{c}\top \\ \ell = 0 \lor (\exists c \bullet \mathit{re}(c) \frown \top) \\ \omega = j\end{array}\right)\right)$$

We use a similar formula F_{free} to copy the free space before the reservations.

The formulas F_2 and F_3 handle the addition of another reservation to the counter. We have to distinguish between an empty counter and one already containing reservations.

$$F_2 = \left(\begin{array}{c}\top \\ \text{marker}^k \frown \mathit{free}^k \frown \ell = 5k \\ \omega = i\end{array}\right) \to \left(\begin{array}{c}\top \\ \top \frown (\mathit{free} \frown \exists c \bullet \mathit{re}(c) \frown \mathit{free})^k \\ \omega = j\end{array}\right)$$

$$F_3 = \left(\begin{array}{c}\top \\ \text{marker}^k c \frown \ell < k \frown \exists c \bullet \mathit{re}(c) \frown (\mathit{free} \frown \exists c \bullet \mathit{cl}(c) \frown \top) \land \ell = 6k \\ \omega = i\end{array}\right) \to$$
$$\left(\begin{array}{c}\top \\ \top \frown (\mathit{free} \frown \exists c \bullet \mathit{re}(c) \frown \mathit{free} \frown \exists c \bullet \mathit{cl}(c))^k \\ \omega = j\end{array}\right)$$

In addition, we need formulas which copy of contents of the second counter to the new configuration, similar to F_1.

Let I_C be the set of the machine's instructions and $F(i)$ be the conjunction of the formulas encoding operation i and q_{fin} its final state. Then

$$\text{halt}(C) = \text{init} \land \text{periodic} \land \text{mutex} \land \bigwedge_{i \in I_C} \Box_\ell F(i) \land \Diamond_\ell \left(\begin{array}{c}\top \\ \exists c \bullet \mathit{cl}(c) \\ \omega = \mathit{fin}\end{array}\right).$$

If and only if halt(C) is satisfiable, the machine contains a halting run. This holds since only configurations may contain claims (as defined in the formalization of periodicity), and whenever the machine reaches its final state, it halts. Hence the halting problem of two counter machines with empty initial configuration reduces to satisfiability of spatial MLSL formulas.

Proposition 1. *Let C be a two counter machine. Then C has a halting run if and only if* halt(C) *is satisfiable.*

The main theorem of this section is a corollary of Prop. 1.

Theorem 1. *The satisfiability problem of spatial MLSL is undecidable.*

Even though we used the full power of spatial MLSL in the proof, i.e., we used both ℓ and ω, the proof would be possible without using the latter. For that, we would not be able to encode the state of the configuration in the lanes, but by a similar way to the markers in the formulas. For example, the formula $(\exists c \bullet cl(c) \frown \exists c \bullet re(c) \frown \exists c \bullet cl(c))^k$ would denote the state q_0, and with another iteration of $re(c)$, it would denote q_1 and so on. If we remove the references to more than one lane in each of the formulas above, the reservations and claims would already imply that only one lane exists, and hence, the use of ω within the abbreviation *free* could be omitted. This shows that spatial MLSL is already undecidable even if we only use ℓ.

4 Labelled Natural Deduction for EMLSL

Despite the negative decidability result of the previous section, we define a system of labelled natural deduction [10,5,11] for the full logic EMLSL. That is, the rules of the deduction system do not operate on formulas ϕ, but on *labelled formulas* $w\colon \phi$, where w is a term of a *labelling algebra* and ϕ is a formula of EMLSL. They may connect the derivations of formulas and relations between the terms w to allow for a tighter relationship between both. The labelling algebra is more involved than for standard modal logics, since EMLSL is in essence a multi-dimensional logic, where the modalities are not interdefinable. Obviously, the spatial modalities can not be defined by the dynamic modalities and vice versa. Furthermore, neither can the dynamic modalities be defined by each other in general. Consider, e.g., the modalities $\Box_{\mathsf{r}(c)}$ and $\Box_{\mathsf{c}(c)}$. Both of these modalities rely on different transitions between the models, which are only indirectly related.

The labels of the algebra consist of tuples $\mathcal{TS}, V$, where similar to the semantics, $\mathcal{TS}$ is the name of a traffic snapshot and V a view. The algebra is then twofold. The relations of the form $V = V_1 \oplus V_2$ and $V = V_1 \ominus V_2$ define ternary reachability relations between views for the spatial modalities. Relations between snapshots, e.g., $\mathcal{TS} \xrightarrow{\mathsf{r}(C)} \mathcal{TS}'$ describe the behavior of transitions. The relations within the labelling algebra for traffic snapshots directly correspond to the dynamic modalities. For example, we have $\mathcal{TS} \xrightarrow{\mathsf{c}(C)} \mathcal{TS}'$, whenever there exists an $n \in \mathbb{N}$ such that $\mathcal{TS} \xrightarrow{\mathsf{c}(C,n)} \mathcal{TS}'$.

We do not give a deduction system for the transitions between snapshots, since the conditions needed to hold between them are of a very complex nature, i.e., they are definable only with the power of full first-order logic with functions, identity and arithmetic. Hence we would not achieve a system with a nice distinction between the relational deductions and the deductions of labelled formulas [5,11]. Instead we simply assume the existence of the relations between snapshots whenever needed. That is, we will often have, e.g., the existence of a transition in our set of assumptions. However, we give simple rules defining that chopping of a view into two subviews is always possible.

Definition 11 (Labelled Formulas and Relational Formulas). *Let $\mathcal{TS}$ be a name for a traffic snapshot, V a name for a view and ϕ a formula according to Definition 7. Then $\mathcal{TS}, V \colon \phi$ is a* labelled formula *of EMLSL. Furthermore, we call $\mathcal{TS} \xrightarrow{*} \mathcal{TS}'$, $V = V_1 \oplus V_2$ and $V = V_1 \ominus V_2$* relational formulas, *where $\xrightarrow{*}$ is a relation of the labelling algebra.*

To have a meaningful soundness result of the calculus, we give the relation of the semantics of labelled formulas and normal formulas. Observe that we do not define a completely independent notion of models, but only use a valuation for this purpose. This is due to the semantic information which is still comprised within the views and traffic snapshots.

Definition 12 (Satisfaction of Labelled Formulas). *We say that a valuation ν* satisfies *a labelled formula $\mathcal{TS}, V \colon \phi$, written $\nu \models \mathcal{TS}, V \colon \phi$ if and only if $\mathcal{TS}, V, \nu \models \phi$. Furthermore,*

$$\begin{aligned}
\nu \models \mathcal{TS}_1 \xrightarrow{\mathsf{r}(c)} \mathcal{TS}_2 \quad &\Leftrightarrow \quad \mathcal{TS}_1 \xrightarrow{\mathsf{r}(\nu(c))} \mathcal{TS}_2,\\
\nu \models \mathcal{TS}_1 \xrightarrow{\mathsf{wd\ r}(c)} \mathcal{TS}_2 \quad &\Leftrightarrow \quad \exists n \bullet \mathcal{TS}_1 \xrightarrow{\mathsf{wd\ r}(\nu(c),n)} \mathcal{TS}_2,\\
\nu \models \mathcal{TS}_1 \xrightarrow{\mathsf{c}(c)} \mathcal{TS}_2 \quad &\Leftrightarrow \quad \exists n \bullet \mathcal{TS}_1 \xrightarrow{\mathsf{c}(\nu(c),n)} \mathcal{TS}_2\\
\nu \models \mathcal{TS}_1 \xrightarrow{\mathsf{wd\ c}(c)} \mathcal{TS}_2 \quad &\Leftrightarrow \quad \mathcal{TS}_1 \xrightarrow{\mathsf{wd\ c}(\nu(c))} \mathcal{TS}_2\\
\nu \models \mathcal{TS}_1 \xrightarrow{\tau} \mathcal{TS}_2 \quad &\Leftrightarrow \quad \exists t \bullet \mathcal{TS}_1 \overset{t}{\Rightarrow} \mathcal{TS}_2
\end{aligned}$$

The relational formulas $V = V_1 \oplus V_2$ and $V = V_1 \ominus V_2$ are independent of the valuation at hand, and hence are satisfied whenever V_1 and V_2 combined according to Definition 5 result in V.

Definition 13 (Derivation). *A* derivation *of a labelled formula $\mathcal{TS}, V \colon \phi$ from a set of labelled formulas Γ and a set of relational formulas Δ is a tree, where the root is $\mathcal{TS}, V \colon \phi$, each leaf is an element of Γ or Δ and each node within the tree is a result of an application of one of the rules defined subsequently. We denote the existence of such a derivation by $\Gamma, \Delta \vdash \mathcal{TS}, V \colon \phi$.*

Following Rasmussen [6], we define predicates for chop-freeness of formulas and rigidity of terms and formulas. To increase the deducible theorems, we differentiate between *vertical* and *horizontal* chop-freeness and rigidity. These properties are especially important for the correct instantiation of terms, i.e., for the elimination of universal quantifiers.

Example 1. Consider the formula

$$\forall x \bullet \left(\begin{matrix} \ell = x \\ \ell = x \end{matrix} \rightarrow \ell = x \right),$$

which is a theorem of MLSL, since the length of a view is not changed by chopping vertically. If we use classical universal quantifier instantiation and substitute the vertically flexible term ω for x, then we would get

$$\begin{array}{c}\ell = \omega\\ \ell = \omega\end{array} \rightarrow \ell = \omega. \tag{10}$$

Now let V be a view satisfying the antecedent of (10). Then V can be vertically chopped such that its length equals its width on both subviews. Now let $\ell = c$. Then also $\omega = c$ for both subviews. Since V consists of both these subviews, V satisfies $\omega = 2c$. But the conclusion of (10) states that V should satisfy $\omega = \ell = c$. However, we could of course substitute x by the vertically rigid term ℓ.

We denote vertical (horizontal) chop-freeness by the predicate vcf (hcf) and vertical (horizontal) rigidity by vri (hri). The rules for the definition of all four predicates are straightforward, since both rigidity and chop-freeness are syntactic properties. All atomic formulas are vertically and horizontally chop-free. For $\oslash$ being a Boolean operator or the horizontal chop $\frown$, the following rules give vertical chop-freeness.

$$\frac{\mathrm{vcf}(\phi) \quad \mathrm{vcf}(\psi)}{\mathrm{vcf}(\phi \oslash \psi)}\ \mathrm{vcf} \oslash \mathrm{I} \qquad \frac{\mathrm{vcf}(\phi \oslash \psi)}{\mathrm{vcf}(\phi)}\ \mathrm{vcf} \oslash \mathrm{E} \qquad \frac{\mathrm{vcf}(\phi \oslash \psi)}{\mathrm{vcf}(\psi)}\ \mathrm{vcf} \oslash \mathrm{E}$$

The rules for quantifiers and the horizontal rules are defined similarly.

For terms, ℓ is vertically rigid and ω is horizontally rigid. The spatial atoms $re(c)$, $cl(c)$ and *free* are neither horizontally nor vertically rigid, since they require the view to possess an extension greater than zero and exactly one lane. Equality is both vertically and horizontally rigid, as long as both compared terms are rigid. Below, we show some exemplary rules, where $\otimes$ is an arbitrary binary operator.

$$\frac{\mathrm{hri}(\phi) \quad \mathrm{hri}(\psi)}{\mathrm{hri}(\phi \otimes \psi)}\ \mathrm{hri} \otimes \mathrm{I} \qquad \frac{\mathrm{hri}(\phi \otimes \psi)}{\mathrm{hri}(\phi)}\ \mathrm{hri} \otimes \mathrm{E} \qquad \frac{\mathrm{hri}(\phi \otimes \psi)}{\mathrm{hri}(\psi)}\ \mathrm{hri} \otimes \mathrm{E}$$

$$\frac{}{\mathbb{E}V', V''(V = V' \ominus V'')}\ \mathrm{VDec}$$

$$\frac{\mathbb{E}V', V''(V = V' \ominus V'') \qquad \begin{array}{c}[V = V_2 \ominus V_2]\\ \vdots \\ \mathcal{TS}, V_3 \colon \phi\end{array}}{\mathcal{TS}, V_3 \colon \phi}\ \mathbb{E}\mathrm{E}$$

We have only two simple rules for the relations between views. First, we state that each view V is decomposable into two subviews. This is true, since we allow for the empty view, i.e., the view without lanes or with a point-like extension. We use $\mathbb{E}$ to denote existential quantification over views. To use the relations between views, we have to be able to instantiate views, i.e., we have to introduce a rule for *elimination of existential quantifiers over views.* As a side condition for this elimination rule, we require that $\mathcal{TS}, V_3 \colon \phi$ is not dependent on any assumption including V_1 or V_2 as a label, except for $V = V_1 \ominus V_2$. The rule itself is a straightforward adaptation of the classical rule. Again, we only show the case for the vertical relations.

The intuition of rigidity is formalized in the following rules. Whenever a formula is horizontally rigid, the formula holds on all views horizontally reachable from the current view. Observe that the traffic snapshot may change arbitrarily, since horizontally rigid formulas are also dynamically rigid. The rules for vertically rigidity are similar.

$$\frac{\mathcal{TS}, V\colon \phi \qquad \mathrm{hri}(\phi) \qquad V = V_1 \oplus V_2}{\mathcal{TS}', V_1\colon \phi}\, R_H \qquad \frac{\mathcal{TS}, V\colon \phi \qquad \mathrm{hri}(\phi) \qquad V = V_1 \oplus V_2}{\mathcal{TS}', V_2\colon \phi}\, R_H$$

$$\frac{\mathcal{TS}, V_1\colon \phi \qquad \mathrm{hri}(\phi) \qquad V = V_1 \oplus V_2}{\mathcal{TS}', V\colon \phi}\, R_H \qquad \frac{\mathcal{TS}, V_2\colon \phi \qquad \mathrm{hri}(\phi) \qquad V = V_1 \oplus V_2}{\mathcal{TS}', V\colon \phi}\, R_H$$

For the first-order operators, we use the typical definitions of labelled natural deduction rules [5]. The only difference lies in the rules for quantification. We may instantiate an universally quantified variable with a horizontally (vertically) rigid, if the formula is vertically (horizontally) chop-free. If the formula is completely chop-free, we may instantiate the variable with an arbitrary term. Similarly, rigid terms may instantiate x in arbitrary formulas. In all cases, a side condition for the instantiation is that s respects the sort of x.

$$\frac{\mathcal{TS}, V\colon \forall x \bullet \phi \qquad \mathrm{hcf}(\phi) \quad \mathrm{vri}(s)}{\mathcal{TS}, V\colon \phi[x \mapsto s]}\, \forall\mathrm{E} \qquad \frac{\mathcal{TS}, V\colon \forall x \bullet \phi \qquad \mathrm{vcf}(\phi) \quad \mathrm{hri}(s)}{\mathcal{TS}, V\colon \phi[x \mapsto s]}\, \forall\mathrm{E}$$

$$\frac{\mathcal{TS}, V\colon \forall x \bullet \phi \qquad \mathrm{hcf}(\phi) \quad \mathrm{vcf}(\phi)}{\mathcal{TS}, V\colon \phi[x \mapsto s]}\, \forall\mathrm{E} \qquad \frac{\mathcal{TS}, V\colon \forall x \bullet \phi \qquad \mathrm{hri}(s) \quad \mathrm{vri}(s)}{\mathcal{TS}, V\colon \phi[x \mapsto s]}\, \forall\mathrm{E}$$

$$\frac{\mathcal{TS}, V_1\colon \phi \qquad \mathcal{TS}, V_2\colon \psi \qquad V = V_1 \oplus V_2}{\mathcal{TS}, V\colon \phi \frown \psi}\, \frown\mathrm{I}$$

$$\frac{\mathcal{TS}, V\colon \phi \frown \psi \qquad \begin{array}{c}[\mathcal{TS}, V_1\colon \phi]\\ [\mathcal{TS}, V_2\colon \psi]\\ [V = V_1 \oplus V_2]\\ \vdots \\ \mathcal{TS}', V'\colon \chi\end{array}}{\mathcal{TS}', V'\colon \chi}\, \frown\mathrm{E}$$

The elimination and introduction rules for the chop modalities are adopted from Rasmussen [6], and resemble the rules for existential quantification. We only show the case for the horizontal chop, the rules for vertical chopping are obtained straightforwardly, by replacing horizontal modalities and relations by the vertical ones.

The chopping of intervals is not ambiguous, i.e., there is a unique view of a certain length at the beginning of a view. This is the *single decomposition property* [12] of interval logics and captured in the following rules. Hence when there are two vertical chops of a view, and the upper parts are of equal width, we can derive that the same formulas hold on the lower parts. Even though we only show the vertical set of rules, similar rules hold for the horizontal chopping of views.

$$\frac{\mathcal{TS}, V_1\colon \phi \qquad \mathcal{TS}, V_2\colon \omega = s \quad \mathcal{TS}, V_2'\colon \omega = s \qquad \mathrm{vri}(s) \quad V = V_1 \ominus V_2 \quad V = V_1' \ominus V_2'}{\mathcal{TS}, V_1'\colon \phi}\, VD$$

$$\frac{\mathcal{TS}, V_2\colon \phi \qquad \mathcal{TS}, V_1\colon \omega = s \quad \mathcal{TS}, V_1'\colon \omega = s \qquad \mathrm{vri}(s) \quad V = V_1 \ominus V_2 \quad V = V_1' \ominus V_2'}{\mathcal{TS}, V_2'\colon \phi}\, VD$$

The additivity of length and width can be formalized by the following rules.

$$\frac{\mathcal{TS}, V_1 \colon \omega = s \quad \mathcal{TS}, V_2 \colon \omega = t \quad \text{vri}(s) \quad \text{vri}(t) \quad V = V_1 \ominus V_2}{\mathcal{TS}, V \colon \omega = s + t} V + \text{I}$$

$$\frac{\mathcal{TS}, V \colon \omega = s + t \quad \text{vri}(s) \quad \text{vri}(t) \quad \begin{matrix} [\mathcal{TS}, V_1 \colon \omega = s] \\ [\mathcal{TS}, V_2 \colon \omega = t] \\ [V = V_1 \ominus V_2] \\ \vdots \\ \mathcal{TS}', V' \colon \phi \end{matrix}}{\mathcal{TS}', V' \colon \phi} V + \text{E}$$

$$\frac{\mathcal{TS} \xrightarrow{*} \mathcal{TS}' \quad \mathcal{TS}, V \colon \Box_* \phi}{\mathcal{TS}', V \colon \phi} \Box_* \text{E}$$

$$\frac{\begin{matrix} [\mathcal{TS} \xrightarrow{*} \mathcal{TS}'] \\ \vdots \\ \mathcal{TS}', V \colon \phi \end{matrix}}{\mathcal{TS}, V \colon \Box_* \phi} \Box_* \text{I}$$

The dynamic modalities are defined along the lines of Basin et al. [5]. If a transition from the current snapshot is possible, the box modalities may be eliminated and if we can prove that under the assumption of a transition $*$, ϕ holds on the now reachable snapshot, $\Box_* \phi$ holds.

Finally, we have to define how the spatial atoms behave with respect to occurring transitions. There are two types of rules in general, *stability rules* and *activity rules*. Stability rules define which atoms stay true after a snapshot changes according to a certain transition. The truth of all reservation and claims of cars not involved in the transition are unchanged. Only one stability rule for creating reservations includes the car which is the source of the transition. We will show this rule and one example for typical stability. The *activity rules* state how the reservations and claims of cars will change according to the transitions.

The following stability rules show that whenever a car creates a new claim, the reservations and claims of other cars are unchanged. We have similar stability rules for the other types of transitions.

$$\frac{\mathcal{TS}, V \colon cl(c) \quad \mathcal{TS} \xrightarrow{\mathsf{c}(d)} \mathcal{TS}' \quad \mathcal{TS}, V \colon c \neq d}{\mathcal{TS}', V \colon cl(c)} \xrightarrow{\mathsf{c}(c)} \text{S}$$

$$\frac{\mathcal{TS}, V \colon re(c) \quad \mathcal{TS} \xrightarrow{\mathsf{c}(d)} \mathcal{TS}' \quad \mathcal{TS}, V \colon c \neq d}{\mathcal{TS}', V \colon re(c)} \xrightarrow{\mathsf{c}(c)} \text{S}$$

The activity rule for $\mathsf{c}(c)$ implies two properties. First, a claim may only be created when only one reservation exists. Second, the newly created claim resides on one side of the existing reservation. Observe that the negations in the antecedent would allow for empty views on both sides of the reservation, but this case is prohibited by the antecedent that the view V is two lanes wide.

$$\frac{\mathcal{TS}, V \colon \begin{matrix} \neg(re(c) \lor cl(c)) \\ re(c) \\ \neg(re(c) \lor cl(c)) \end{matrix} \quad \mathcal{TS} \xrightarrow{\mathsf{c}(d)} \mathcal{TS}' \quad \mathcal{TS}, V \colon c = d \quad \mathcal{TS}, V \colon \omega = 2}{\mathcal{TS}', V \colon \begin{matrix} re(c) \\ cl(c) \end{matrix} \lor \begin{matrix} cl(c) \\ re(c) \end{matrix}} \xrightarrow{\mathsf{c}(c)} \text{A}$$

Rules for the creation of reservations in between traffic snapshots are:

$$\frac{\mathcal{TS}, V\colon cl(c) \qquad \mathcal{TS} \xrightarrow{\mathsf{r}(d)} \mathcal{TS}' \qquad \mathcal{TS}, V\colon c = d}{\mathcal{TS}', V\colon re(c)} \xrightarrow{\mathsf{r}(c)}\mathrm{A}$$

$$\frac{\mathcal{TS}, V\colon re(c) \qquad \mathcal{TS} \xrightarrow{\mathsf{r}(d)} \mathcal{TS}' \qquad \mathcal{TS}, V\colon c = d}{\mathcal{TS}', V\colon re(c)} \xrightarrow{\mathsf{r}(c)}\mathrm{S}$$

The following activity rules define the withdrawal of reservations and claims.

$$\frac{\mathcal{TS}, V\colon \begin{matrix} re(c) \\ re(c) \end{matrix} \qquad \mathcal{TS} \xrightarrow{\mathsf{wd\ r}(d)} \mathcal{TS}' \qquad \mathcal{TS}, V\colon c = d}{\mathcal{TS}', V\colon \begin{matrix} re(c) \\ \neg re(c) \end{matrix} \vee \begin{matrix} \neg re(c) \\ re(c) \end{matrix}} \xrightarrow{\mathsf{wd\ r}(c)}\mathrm{A}$$

$$\frac{\mathcal{TS}, V\colon cl(c) \qquad \mathcal{TS} \xrightarrow{\mathsf{wd\ c}(d)} \mathcal{TS}' \qquad \mathcal{TS}, V\colon c = d}{\mathcal{TS}', V\colon \neg cl(c)} \xrightarrow{\mathsf{wd\ c}(c)}\mathrm{A}$$

We also have rules for "backwards" reasoning, i.e., if our current snapshot is reachable from another, we may draw conclusions about the originating snapshot. Again, we differentiate between activity and stability rules (omitted here).

$$\frac{\mathcal{TS}', V\colon re(c) \qquad \mathcal{TS} \xrightarrow{\mathsf{r}(d)} \mathcal{TS}' \qquad \mathcal{TS}, V\colon c = d}{\mathcal{TS}, V\colon re(c) \vee cl(c)} \xleftarrow{\mathsf{r}}\mathrm{A}$$

$$\frac{\mathcal{TS}', V\colon cl(c) \qquad \mathcal{TS} \xrightarrow{\mathsf{c}(d)} \mathcal{TS}' \qquad \mathcal{TS}, V\colon c = d}{\mathcal{TS}, V\colon \neg cl(c)} \xleftarrow{\mathsf{c}}\mathrm{A}$$

Observe that we can not reason backwards along withdrawal transitions, since these may be taken without changing any reservations and claims (cf. Def. 2).

Theorem 2. *The calculus of labelled natural deduction for EMLSL is sound.*

As an example, we derive a variant of the *reservation lemma*, which we proved informally in our previous work [1].

Lemma 3 (Reservation). *A reservation of a car c observed directly after c created it, was either already present or is due to a previously existing claim. I.e., assuming $\mathcal{TS} \xrightarrow{\mathsf{r}(c)} \mathcal{TS}'$, the formula $(re(c) \vee cl(c)) \leftrightarrow \Box_{\mathsf{r}(c)} re(c)$ holds. Hence*

$$\{\mathcal{TS} \xrightarrow{\mathsf{r}(c)} \mathcal{TS}'\} \vdash \mathcal{TS}, V\colon (re(c) \vee cl(c)) \leftrightarrow \Box_{\mathsf{r}(c)} re(c).$$

Proof. The existence of the transition is of major importance for the elimination of the box modality in the proof using the backwards reasoning rule. For reasons of simplicity, we use a variant of the stability rules and activity rules, where d in the transition has been replaced by c, and hence we do not need the extra assumption of $\mathcal{TS}, V\colon c = d$. We use two auxiliary derivations, which allow us to infer the existence of a reservation on the snapshot after taking a transition.

$$\Pi_{\mathrm{S}}\colon \frac{[\mathcal{TS}, V\colon re(c)]_1 \qquad [\mathcal{TS} \xrightarrow{\mathsf{r}(c)} \mathcal{TS}']_2}{\mathcal{TS}', V\colon re(c)} \qquad \Pi_{\mathrm{A}}\colon \frac{[\mathcal{TS}, V\colon cl(c)]_1 \qquad [\mathcal{TS} \xrightarrow{\mathsf{r}(c)} \mathcal{TS}']_2}{\mathcal{TS}', V\colon re(c)}$$

Derivation of $\vdash \mathcal{TS}, V\colon (re(c) \vee cl(c)) \rightarrow \Box_{\mathsf{r}(c)} re(c)$.

$$\dfrac{\dfrac{\dfrac{\dfrac{\Pi_{\mathrm{S}}}{\mathcal{TS}', V\colon re(c)} \qquad \dfrac{\Pi_{\mathrm{A}}}{\mathcal{TS}', V\colon re(c)} \qquad [\mathcal{TS}, V\colon re(c) \vee cl(c)]_3}{\mathcal{TS}', V\colon re(c)}\,\vee\mathrm{E}_1}{\mathcal{TS}, V\colon \Box_{\mathsf{r}(c)} re(c)}\,\Box_{\mathsf{r}(c)}\mathrm{I}_2}{\mathcal{TS}, V\colon (re(c) \vee cl(c)) \rightarrow \Box_{\mathsf{r}(c)} re(c)}\,\rightarrow \mathrm{I}_3$$

Derivation of $\{\mathcal{TS} \xrightarrow{\mathsf{r}(c)} \mathcal{TS}'\} \vdash \mathcal{TS}, V\colon \Box_{\mathsf{r}(c)} re(c) \rightarrow (re(c) \vee cl(c))$.

$$\dfrac{\dfrac{\dfrac{[\mathcal{TS}, V\colon \Box_{\mathsf{r}(c)} re(c)]_1 \qquad \mathcal{TS} \xrightarrow{\mathsf{r}(c)} \mathcal{TS}'}{\mathcal{TS}', V\colon re(c)}\,\Box_{\mathsf{r}(c)}\mathrm{E} \qquad \mathcal{TS} \xrightarrow{\mathsf{r}(c)} \mathcal{TS}'}{\mathcal{TS}, V\colon re(c) \vee cl(c)}\,\xleftarrow{\mathsf{r}(c)}}{\mathcal{TS}, V\colon \Box_{\mathsf{r}(c)} re(c) \rightarrow (re(c) \vee cl(c))}\,\rightarrow \mathrm{I}_1$$

□

Since models of EMLSL are based on the real numbers, we cannot hope for a complete deduction system.

5 Related and Future Work

Most related work on spatial logics is focused on purely qualitative spatial reasoning [13], e.g., the expressible properties concern topological relations [14]. Logics expressing quantitative spatial properties are rare, an example is Schäfer's Shape Calculus (SC) [4], which is a very general extension of DC. Contrasting SC, the focus of EMLSL lies on a restricted field of application, i.e., highway traffic. EMLSL is an instance of a multi-dimensional and multi-modal logic [15], since it consists of various different modal operators, which are not interdefinable. It is also a combination of binary modalities, i.e., the chopping operations, and unary box-like modalities, i.e., the dynamic modal operators. Labelled natural deduction for (multi-)modal logics has been studied intensely recently. E.g., when the rules for relational formulas can be defined with horn clauses as antecedents, nice meta-theoretical properties like normalization of proofs can be established [5,11]. In intuitionistic modal logic, similar results are obtained, when the relational theory is defined using only geometric sequents [16]. Unfortunately, even with our restricted set of rules for view relations, these results do not carry over to our setting, since we made use of existential quantification on views. Still we would like to explore how rules for the manipulation of traffic snapshots could blend in. However, due to the complex internal structure of traffic snapshots, we do not expect such rules to be definable by horn clauses. Rasga et al. investigated the fibring [17] of labelled deductive systems [18]. We assume that the deduction system of Sec. 4 is an instance of such a fibring, where the Boolean operators are shared between all deduction systems involved. A further classification of EMLSL (or a suitable subset) and its proof system within the framework of fibring and multi-dimensional logics would be of interest in order to use preservation results concerning, e.g., decidability. Finally, an implementation within a general theorem prover like Isabelle [19] similar to implementations for modal or interval logics [5,11,6] would increase the usefulness of the proof system.

References

1. Hilscher, M., Linker, S., Olderog, E.-R., Ravn, A.P.: An abstract model for proving safety of multi-lane traffic manoeuvres. In: Qin, S., Qiu, Z. (eds.) ICFEM 2011. LNCS, vol. 6991, pp. 404–419. Springer, Heidelberg (2011)
2. Moszkowski, B.: A temporal logic for multilevel reasoning about hardware. Computer 18, 10–19 (1985)
3. Chaochen, Z., Hoare, C.A.R., Ravn, A.P.: A calculus of durations. Information Processing Letters 40, 269–276 (1991)
4. Schäfer, A.: A calculus for shapes in time and space. In: Liu, Z., Araki, K. (eds.) ICTAC 2004. LNCS, vol. 3407, pp. 463–477. Springer, Heidelberg (2005)
5. Basin, D., Matthews, S., Viganó, L.: Natural deduction for non-classical logics. Studia Logica 60, 119–160 (1998)
6. Rasmussen, T.M.: Labelled natural deduction for interval logics. In: Fribourg, L. (ed.) CSL 2001. LNCS, vol. 2142, pp. 308–323. Springer, Heidelberg (2001)
7. Zhou Chaochen, M.R., Hansen, Sestoft, P.: Decidability and undecidability results for duration calculus. In: Enjalbert, P., Finkel, A., Wagner, K.W. (eds.) STACS 1993. LNCS, vol. 665, pp. 58–68. Springer, Heidelberg (1993)
8. Woodcock, J., Davies, J.: Using Z – Specification, Refinement, and Proof. Prentice Hall (1996)
9. Minsky, M.L.: Computation: finite and infinite machines. Prentice-Hall, Inc. (1967)
10. Gabbay, D.M.: Labelled deductive systems. vol. 1. Oxford University Press (1996)
11. Viganò, L.: Labelled Non-Classical Logics. Kluwer Academic Publishers (2000)
12. Dutertre, B.: Complete proof systems for first order interval temporal logic. In: Proceedings of the 10th Annual IEEE Symposium on Logic in Computer Science, LICS 1995, p. 36. IEEE Computer Society, Washington, DC (1995)
13. van Benthem, J., Bezhanishvili, G.: Modal logics of space. In: Aiello, M., Pratt-Hartmann, I., Benthem, J. (eds.) Handbook of Spatial Logics, pp. 217–298. Springer (2007)
14. Randell, D.A., Cui, Z., Cohn, A.G.: A Spatial Logic based on Regions and Connection. In: Proc. 3rd Int'l Conf. on Knowledge Representation and Reasoning (1992)
15. Gabbay, D.M., Kurucz, A., Wolter, F., Zakharyaschev, M.: Many-dimensional modal logics: theory and applications. Studies in Logic and the Foundations of Mathematics, vol. 148. Elsevier (2003)
16. Simpson, A.K.: The Proof Theory and Semantics of Intuitionistic Modal Logic. PhD thesis, University of Edinburgh (1994)
17. Caleiro, C., Sernadas, A., Sernadas, C.: Fibring logics: Past, present and future. In: We Will Show Them! Essays in Honour of Dov Gabbay, vol. 1, pp. 363–388 (2005)
18. Rasga, J., Sernadas, A., Sernadas, C., Viganó, L.: Fibring labelled deduction systems. Journal of Logic and Computation 12, 443–473 (2002)
19. Paulson, L.: Isabelle: A Generic Theorem Prover. Springer (1994)

Counterexample-Preserving Reduction for Symbolic Model Checking*

Wanwei Liu**, Rui Wang, Xianjin Fu, Ji Wang, Wei Dong, and Xiaoguang Mao

School of Computer Science,
National University of Defense Technology,
Changsha, P.R. China, 410073
wwliu@nudt.edu.cn

Abstract. The cost of LTL model checking is highly sensitive to the length of the formula under verification. We observe that, under some specific conditions, the input LTL formula can be reduced to an easier-to-handle one before model checking. In our reduction, these two formulae need not to be logically equivalent, but they share the same counterexample set w.r.t the model. In the case that the model is symbolically represented, the condition enabling such reduction can be detected with a lightweight effort (e.g., with SAT-solving). In this paper, we tentatively name such technique "CounterExample-Preserving REduction" (CEPRE, for short), and the proposed technique is experimentally evaluated by adapting NuSMV.

1 Introduction

LTL [12] is one of the most frequently used specification languages in model checking (cf. [15]). It designates properties over a linear structure, which can be viewed as an execution of the program. The task of LTL model checking is to search the state space (explicitly or implicitly), with the goal of detecting the existence of feasible traces violating the specification. If such traces exist, the model checker will report one of them as a "counterexample"; otherwise, the model checker will give an affirmative report.

It can be shown that the complexity of LTL model checking for $M \models \varphi$ is in $\mathcal{O}(|M| \times 2^{|\varphi|})$, meanwhile, the nesting depth of temporal operators might be the major factor affecting the cost in compiling LTL formulae.

Hence, it is reasonable to simplify the specification before conducting model checking. For example, in [13], Somenzi and Bloem provided a set of rewriting schemas for simplifying LTL specifications, and these rewriting schemas preserve logical equivalence.

* This work is supported by NSFC under Grant No. 61103012, 91118007; the 863 Program under Grant No. 2011AA010106, 2012AA011201; the Program for New Century Excellent Talents in University.

** Corresponding author.

Z. Liu, J. Woodcock, and H. Zhu (Eds.): ICTAC 2013, LNCS 8049, pp. 249–266, 2013.

One may argue that "a majority of LTL formulae used in real applications are simple, succinct rather than complicated", but, we might want to notice the following facts:

- Some LTL formula, for example $\mathbf{F}(p\mathbf{U}q)$, is usually considered to be a "simple" one. Nevertheless, it can be further simplified to $\mathbf{F}q$, and this fact tends to be ignored.[1]
- Indeed, people do use complicate specifications in the real industrial field, as well in some standard benchmark (cf. [2]).
- Last but not least, not all specifications are designated manually. Actually, some formulae are generated by specification-generaton-tools (e.g., ProSpec). Indeed, one may find that lots of these machine-generated specifications can be simplified.

Symbolic model checking [11] is one of the most significant breakthrough in model checking, and two major fashions of symbolic model checking are widely used: one is the BDD-based manner [6], and the other is SAT-based manner, such as BMC [1].

Instead of using an explicit representation, the symbolic approach represents state space with a series of Boolean formulae. This enables implicit manipulation of the verification process and it usually leads to an efficient implementation [3]. Meanwhile, the symbolic encoding of transitions and invariants of the model provides heuristic information to simplify the specification. For example:

- The formulae $p\mathbf{U}q$ and $(r\mathbf{U}p)\mathbf{U}q$ can be respectively reduced as q and $(r\mathbf{U}p)\vee q$, if we know that $p \rightarrow q$ holds everywhere in the model.
- Each occurrence of $\mathbf{G}\theta$ in the specification can be replaced with $\top$ (i.e., logically true), if we can inductively infer that the Boolean formula θ holds at each reachable state in the model.

Actually, we can make certain of these conditions with the following efforts.

- To ensure that "$p \rightarrow q$ holds everywhere in the model", one possible way is to make sure that $p \rightarrow q$ is an *invariant* in the model — i.e., just to examine if $\rho\wedge\neg(p \rightarrow q)$ is unsatisfiable (we in the later denote it as $\rho \vdash p \rightarrow q$), where ρ is the Boolean encoding of the model's transition relation.
- Likely, to justify that θ holds at each reachable state[2], it suffices to ensure that $\theta_0 \vdash \theta$ and $\rho \vdash \theta \rightarrow \theta'$, where θ_0 is the initial condition of the model.

We could do this because the component ρ should be satisfied at each transition step. Hence, it encloses both "local invariants" and "transitional invariants". For example, if $\rho = p\wedge(q \rightarrow q')$, then we may consider p as a local invariant, whereas $q \rightarrow q'$ as a transitional invariant.

---

[1] On one hand, $p\mathbf{U}q$ implies $\mathbf{F}q$, and hence $\mathbf{F}(p\mathbf{U}q)$ implies $\mathbf{FF}q$ (i.e., $\mathbf{F}q$); on the other hand, q implies $p\mathbf{U}q$, and hence $\mathbf{F}q$ implies $\mathbf{F}(p\mathbf{U}q)$.

[2] Note that a "dead-end" has no infinite path starting from it, hence we may safely omit dead-ends in the model when doing this.

Hence, this provides an opportunity to replace the specification with a simpler one, accompanied with some lightweight extra task of condition detection. Even if such detection fails, the overhead is usually negligible. More importantly, such reductions can be performed before starting model checking.

In this paper, we systematically investigate the above idea, and tentatively name this technique *CounterExample-Preserving REduction* (CePRe , for short). To justify it, we have extended NuSMV and implemented CePRe as an up-front option for LTL model checking. Subsequently, we conduct experiments over both industrial benchmarks and randomly generated cases. Experimental results show that CePRe can improve the efficiency significantly.

This paper is organized as follows: Section 2 revisits some basic notions. Section 3 introduces the CePRe technique and gives the performance analysis. In Section 4, the experimental results over industrial benchmarks and over random generated cases are given. We summarize the whole paper with Section 5.

2 Preliminaries

We presuppose a countable set $\mathcal{P}$ of *atomic propositions*, ranging over p, q, etc, and for each proposition $p \in \mathcal{P}$, we create a *primed version* p' (not belonging to $\mathcal{P}$) for it. For each set $\mathcal{V} \subseteq \mathcal{P}$, we define $\mathcal{V}' \triangleq \{p' \mid p \in \mathcal{V}\}$. We use $\mathbf{B}(\mathcal{V})$ to denote the set of Boolean formulae over $\mathcal{V}$. Similarly, we denote by $\mathbf{B}(\mathcal{V} \cup \mathcal{V}')$ the set of Boolean formulae built up from $\mathcal{V} \cup \mathcal{V}'$. The scope of the *prime* operator can be naturally lifted to Boolean formulae over $\mathbf{B}(\mathcal{V})$, by defining

$$\top' = \top \qquad \bot' = \bot \qquad (\neg\theta)' \triangleq \neg\theta' \qquad (\theta_1 \to \theta_2)' \triangleq \theta_1' \to \theta_2'$$

An *assignment* is a subset $\mathcal{V}$ of $\mathcal{P}$. Intuitively, it assigns 1 (or, true) to the propositions belonging to $\mathcal{V}$, and assigns 0 (or, false) to the other propositions. For each $\mathcal{V} \subseteq \mathcal{U} \subseteq \mathcal{P}$ and $\theta \in \mathbf{B}(\mathcal{U})$, we denote by $\mathcal{V} \Vdash \theta$ if θ is evaluated to 1 under the assignment $\mathcal{V}$.

A *united assignment* is a pair $(\mathcal{V}_1, \mathcal{V}_2)$, where both $\mathcal{V}_1$ and $\mathcal{V}_2$ are subsets of $\mathcal{P}$. It assigns 1 to the propositions belonging to $\mathcal{V}_1 \cup \mathcal{V}_2'$, and assigns 0 to the other propositions. Suppose that $\mathcal{V}_1, \mathcal{V}_2 \subseteq \mathcal{U} \subseteq \mathcal{P}$ and $\theta \in \mathbf{B}(\mathcal{U} \cup \mathcal{U}')$, we also write $(\mathcal{V}_1, \mathcal{V}_2) \Vdash \theta$ if θ is evaluated to 1 under the united assignment $(\mathcal{V}_1, \mathcal{V}_2)$.

LTL formulae can be inductively defined as follows.

- $\bot$ and $\top$ are LTL formulae.
- Each proposition $p \in \mathcal{P}$ is an LTL formula.
- If both φ_1 and φ_2 are LTL formulae, so does $\varphi_1 \to \varphi_2$.
- If φ is an LTL formula, then $\mathbf{X}\varphi$ and $\mathbf{Y}\varphi$ are LTL formulae.
- If φ_1 and φ_2 are LTL formulae, then both $\varphi_1\mathbf{U}\varphi_2$ and $\varphi_1\mathbf{S}\varphi_2$ are LTL formulae.

Semantics of an LTL formula is defined w.r.t. a *linear structure* $\pi \in (2^{\mathcal{P}})^\omega$ (i.e., π is an infinite word over the alphabet $2^{\mathcal{P}}$) and a position $i \prec \omega$. Inductively:

- $\pi, i \models \top$ and $\pi, i \not\models \bot$;
- $\pi, i \models p$ iff $\pi(i) \Vdash p$ (where $\pi(i)$ is the i-th letter of π, which can be viewed as an assignment);
- $\pi, i \models \varphi_1 \to \varphi_2$ iff either $\pi, i \not\models \varphi_1$ or $\pi, i \models \varphi_2$;
- $\pi, i \models \mathbf{X}\varphi$ iff $\pi, i+1 \models \varphi$;
- $\pi, i \models \mathbf{Y}\varphi$ iff $i > 0$ and $\pi, i-1 \models \varphi$;
- $\pi, i \models \varphi_1 \mathbf{U} \varphi_2$ iff there is some $j \geq i$, s.t. $\pi, j \models \varphi_2$ and $\pi, k \models \varphi_1$ for each $i \leq k < j$;
- $\pi, i \models \varphi_1 \mathbf{S} \varphi_2$ iff there is some $j \leq i$, s.t. $\pi, j \models \varphi_2$ and $\pi, k \models \varphi_1$ for each $i \geq k > j$.

For the sake of convenience, we may directly write $\pi, 0 \models \varphi$ as $\pi \models \varphi$.

As usual, we employ some derived Boolean connectives such as

$$\neg\varphi \triangleq \varphi \to \bot \qquad \varphi \vee \psi \triangleq \neg\varphi \to \psi \qquad \varphi \wedge \psi \triangleq \neg(\neg\varphi \vee \neg\psi)$$

and derived temporal operators such as

$$\begin{array}{ccc} \mathbf{F}\varphi \triangleq \top\mathbf{U}\varphi & \mathbf{Z}\varphi \triangleq \neg\mathbf{Y}\neg\varphi & \mathbf{O}\varphi \triangleq \top\mathbf{S}\varphi \\ \mathbf{G}\varphi \triangleq \neg\mathbf{F}\neg\varphi & & \mathbf{H}\varphi \triangleq \neg\mathbf{O}\neg\varphi \\ \varphi\mathbf{R}\psi \triangleq \neg(\neg\varphi\mathbf{U}\neg\psi) & & \varphi\mathbf{T}\psi \triangleq \neg(\neg\varphi\mathbf{S}\neg\psi) \end{array}$$

We say that '$\top$ and $\bot$', '$\wedge$ and $\vee$', '**F** and **G**', '**O** and **H**', '**Y** and **Z**', '**X** and **X** itself', '**U** and **R**', '**T** and **S**' are pairwise the *dual operators*.

Temporal operators like **X**, **U**, **F**, **G**, **R** are called *future operators*, whereas **Y**, **Z**, **S**, **O**, **H** and **T** are called *past operators*. An LTL formula is said to be *pure future* (resp. *pure past*) if it involves no past (resp. future) operators.

Theorem 1 **([8]).** *Each LTL formula has an equivalent pure future expression.*

Theorem 1 tells the fact that past operators do not add any expressive power to LTL formulae. Nevertheless, with these, we can give a much more succinct description in defining specifications.

Given an LTL formula φ, we denote by $sub(\varphi)$ the set constituted with subformulae of φ. Particularly, we respectively denote by $sub_{\mathbf{U}}(\varphi)$ and $sub_{\mathbf{S}}(\varphi)$ the set consisting of "**U**-subformulae" and "**S**-subfomulae" of φ, where an **U**-formula (resp. **S**-formula) is a formula rooted at **U** (resp. **S**). [3]

A *model* is a tuple $M = \langle \mathcal{V}, \rho, \theta_0, \mathcal{F} \rangle$, where:

- $\mathcal{V} \subseteq \mathcal{P}$, is a finite set of atomic propositions.
- $\rho \in \mathbf{B}(\mathcal{V} \cup \mathcal{V}')$, is the *transition relation*.
- $\theta_0 \in \mathbf{B}(\mathcal{V})$, is the *initial condition*.
- $\mathcal{F} \subseteq \mathbf{B}(\mathcal{V})$, is a set of *fairness constraints*.

[3] Note that $\mathbf{F}\varphi$ is also an **U**-formula whereas $\mathbf{G}\varphi$ is not.

A *derived linear structure* of M is an infinite word $\pi \in (2^{\mathcal{V}})^{\omega}$, such that

1. $\pi(0) \Vdash \theta_0$;
2. $(\pi(i), \pi(i+1)) \Vdash \rho$ for each $i \prec \omega$;
3. for each $\varphi \in \mathcal{F}$, there are infinitely many i's having $\pi(i) \Vdash \varphi$.

We denote by $\mathbf{L}(M)$ the set of derived linear strctures of M, call it the *language* of M.

For a model M and an LTL formula φ, we denote as $M \models \varphi$ if $\pi \models \varphi$ for each $\pi \in \mathbf{L}(M)$. Meanwhile, we define

$$\mathbf{CE}(\varphi, M) \triangleq \{\pi \in \mathbf{L}(M) \mid \pi \not\models \varphi\}$$

and call it the *counterexample set* of φ w.r.t. M.

3 Counterexample-Preserving Reduction

We describe the CePRe technique in this section, but first of all, let us fix the components of the model, and just let M be $\langle \mathcal{V}, \rho, \theta_0, \mathcal{F} \rangle$ in the following.

For M, we are particularly concerned about formulae having the same counterexample set — we say that φ and ψ are *inter-reduce-able* w.r.t. M if and only if $\mathbf{CE}(\varphi, M) = \mathbf{CE}(\psi, M)$, denoted as $\varphi \approx_M \psi$. Hence, $\varphi \approx_M \psi$ implies that $M \models \varphi \Leftrightarrow M \models \psi$.

The central part of CePRe is a series of *reduction rules* being of the form

$$\text{Cond} \ \rhd \ \varphi \approx_M \psi \quad (\text{NAME})$$

where "Cond" is called the *additional condition.*

Though the relation $\approx_M$ is, actually symmetric, we always write the reduced formula on the righthand of the "$\approx$" sign in a reduction rule. Since the model M is fixed, in this section, we omit it from the subscript. In addition, if the additional condition trivially holds, we will discard this part and directly write the rule as $\varphi \approx \psi$, and in this case we say that this rule is "*model-independent*"; otherwise, we say that the underlying reduction rule is "*model-dependent*".

3.1 The Reduction Rules

First of all, we have some elementary reduction rules as depicted in Figure 1. For the rules (Init), (Ind) and (Trans), the notation "$\vdash$" occurring in the condition part stands for the "*inferring*" relation in propositional logic ($\rho \vdash \theta$ iff $\rho \wedge \neg\theta$ is unsatisfiable), and we here require that $\theta, \theta_1, \theta_2 \in \mathbf{B}(\mathcal{V})$.

Subsequently, let us define a partial order "$\sqsubseteq$" over unary temporal operators (and their combinations) as follows:

$$\begin{array}{c} \mathbf{F} \sqsubseteq \mathbf{GF} \sqsubseteq \mathbf{FG} \sqsubseteq \mathbf{G} \\ \mathbf{F} \sqsubseteq \mathbf{X}^i \sqsubseteq \mathbf{G} \quad (i \prec \omega) \\ \mathbf{O} \sqsubseteq \mathbf{HO} \sqsubseteq \mathbf{OH} \sqsubseteq \mathbf{H} \end{array}$$

where $\mathbf{X}^0\varphi \triangleq \varphi$ and $\mathbf{X}^{i+1}\varphi \triangleq \mathbf{X}(\mathbf{X}^i\varphi)$.

$$\theta_0 \vdash \theta \ \triangleright \ \theta \approx \top \ \ (\textsc{Init}) \qquad \rho \vdash \theta \ \triangleright \ \mathbf{G}\theta \approx \top \ \ (\textsc{Trans})$$

$$\theta \in \mathcal{F} \ \triangleright \ \mathbf{GF}\theta \approx \top \ \ (\textsc{Fair}) \qquad \theta_0 \vdash \theta;\ \rho \vdash \theta \to \theta' \ \triangleright \ \mathbf{G}\theta \approx \top \ \ (\textsc{Ind})$$

Fig. 1. Elementary reduction rules

Assume that $\mathbf{P}^w, \mathbf{P}^s \in \{\mathbf{F}, \mathbf{FG}, \mathbf{GF}, \mathbf{G}, \mathbf{O}, \mathbf{HO}, \mathbf{OH}, \mathbf{H}\} \cup \{\mathbf{X}^i \mid i \prec \omega\}$ and $\mathbf{P}^w \sqsubseteq \mathbf{P}^s$, then we have two model-indenpendent rules, as depicted in Figure 2. Though these rules seem to be trivial, they are useful in doing combinational reductions (see the example given in Section 3.2).

$$(\mathbf{P}^w\varphi \wedge \mathbf{P}^s\varphi) \approx \mathbf{P}^s\varphi \ \ (\textsc{Conj}) \qquad (\mathbf{P}^w\varphi \vee \mathbf{P}^s\varphi) \approx \mathbf{P}^w\varphi \ (\textsc{Disj})$$

Fig. 2. Reduction rules of (Conj) and (Disj)

Figure 3 provides some reduction rules that can be used to simplify nested temporal operators. Moreover, we may immediately get such a rule's "*past version*" by switching **U** and **S**, **R** and **T**, etc. For example, we may obtain the rule (OS) (i.e., $\mathbf{O}(\varphi\mathbf{S}\psi) \approx \mathbf{O}\psi$) from (FU) .

$$\mathbf{F}(\varphi\mathbf{U}\psi) \approx \mathbf{F}\psi \ \ (\mathrm{FU}) \qquad \varphi\mathbf{U}(\mathbf{F}\psi) \approx \mathbf{F}\psi \ (\mathrm{U_F})$$

$$\mathbf{FF}\varphi \approx \mathbf{F}\varphi \ (\mathrm{FF}) \qquad \mathbf{GFG}\varphi \approx \mathbf{FG}\varphi \ (\mathrm{GFG})$$

Fig. 3. Reduction rules for formulae involving nested pure future operators

Meanwhile, we also have the *Duality Principle* for model-independent rules: "by switching each operator with its dual operator, then we may get a new reduction rule". For the rules listed in Figure 3, we may obtain the corresponding rules such as (GR), ($\mathrm{R_G}$), (GG) and (FGF). As an example, the rule (GG) is just $\mathbf{GG}\varphi \approx \mathbf{G}\varphi$.

$$\mathbf{Y}\varphi \approx \bot \ (\mathrm{Y}) \qquad \mathbf{O}\varphi \approx \varphi \ (\mathrm{O}) \qquad \varphi\mathbf{S}\psi \approx \varphi \ (\mathrm{S})$$

Fig. 4. Reduction rules for formulae involving (outermost) past operators

Since we always stand at the starting point when doing model checking (i.e., the goal is to check if $\pi, 0 \models \varphi$ for each $\pi \in \mathbf{L}(M)$), we can sometimes "erase" the outermost past operators, as depicted in Figure 4. Note that we can also acquire the rules (Z), (H) and (T) by applying the Duality Principle.

$$\mathbf{XY}\varphi \approx \varphi \text{ (XY)} \qquad \mathbf{FH}\varphi \approx \mathbf{H}\varphi \text{ (FH)}$$

$$\mathbf{FO}\varphi \approx \mathbf{F}\varphi \vee \mathbf{O}\varphi \text{ (FO)} \qquad \mathbf{F}(\varphi\mathbf{S}\psi) \approx \mathbf{F}\psi \vee \varphi\mathbf{S}\psi \text{ (FS)}$$

Fig. 5. Reduction rules for formulae involving adjacent past and future operators

Figure 5 introduces a series of rules handing formulae involving adjacent past and future temporal operators. Remind that the rules (XZ), (GO), (GH) and (GT) are also immediately available.

$$\rho \vdash \theta_1 \vee \theta_2 \rhd \theta_1\mathbf{U}\theta_2 \approx \mathbf{F}\theta_2 \text{ (U)}$$

$$\rho \vdash \theta_2 \to \theta_1 \vee \theta_2' \rhd \theta_1\mathbf{R}\theta_2 \approx \theta_2 \quad \text{(R)}$$

Fig. 6. Reduction rules of (U) and (R)

From now on, we let $\theta_1, \theta_2, \ldots$ range over $\mathbf{B}(\mathcal{V})$, and let $\varphi_1, \varphi_2, \ldots$ be arbitrary LTL formulae. We have some model-dependent rules. The first group of such rules is listed in Figure 6.

Figure 7 provides another set of model-dependent reduction rules, and these rules are mainly concerned with LTL formulae involving adjacent **U**-operators. Note that when applying the Duality Principle to this group of rules, besides switching the operators, we also need to exchange the *antecedent* and *subsequent* in the righthand of $\vdash$ in the condition part. As an example, we may obtain the reduction rule

$$\rho \vdash \theta_3 \to \theta_2 \;\rhd\; (\varphi_1\mathbf{R}\theta_2)\mathbf{R}\theta_3 \approx \theta_3 \wedge (\varphi_1\mathbf{R}\theta_2) \quad (\mathrm{R}^{\mathrm{R}}[3 \to 2])$$

by applying the Duality Principle to $(\mathrm{U}^{\mathrm{U}}[2 \to 3])$.

Lastly, Figure 8 provides some reduction rules that can be used to simplify formulae with mixed usage of **U** and **R**. Similarly, by switching dual operators and inverting the corresponding part in the additional condition, one may obtain the reduction rules for formulae in which **R** appears (adjacently) out of **U**.

$$\rho \vdash \theta_1 \to \theta_2 \rhd \theta_1 \mathbf{U} \theta_2 \approx \theta_2 \qquad (\mathrm{U}[1 \to 2])$$

$$\rho \vdash \theta_1 \to \theta_3 \rhd (\theta_1 \mathbf{U} \varphi_2)\mathbf{U}\theta_3 \approx \varphi_2 \mathbf{U} \theta_3 \qquad (\mathrm{U}^{\mathrm{U}}[1 \to 3])$$

$$\rho \vdash \theta_2 \to \theta_3 \rhd (\varphi_1 \mathbf{U} \theta_2)\mathbf{U}\theta_3 \approx \theta_3 \vee (\varphi_1 \mathbf{U} \theta_2) \qquad (\mathrm{U}^{\mathrm{U}}[2 \to 3])$$

$$\rho \vdash \theta_3 \to \theta_2 \rhd (\varphi_1 \mathbf{U} \theta_2)\mathbf{U}\theta_3 \approx (\varphi_1 \vee \theta_2)\mathbf{U}\theta_3 \qquad (\mathrm{U}^{\mathrm{U}}[3 \to 2])$$

$$\rho \vdash \theta_2 \to \theta_3' \rhd (\varphi_1 \mathbf{U} \theta_2)\mathbf{U}\theta_3 \approx (\varphi_1 \vee \theta_2)\mathbf{U}\theta_3 \qquad (\mathrm{U}^{\mathrm{U}}[2 \to 3'])$$

$$\rho \vdash \neg\theta_2 \to \theta_3 \rhd (\varphi_1 \mathbf{U} \theta_2)\mathbf{U}\theta_3 \approx \mathbf{F}\theta_3 \qquad (\mathrm{U}^{\mathrm{U}}[\neg 2 \to 3])$$

$$\rho \vdash \theta_1 \to \theta_2 \rhd \theta_1 \mathbf{U}(\theta_2 \mathbf{U} \varphi_3) \approx \theta_2 \mathbf{U} \varphi_3 \qquad (\mathrm{U}_{\mathrm{U}}[1 \to 2])$$

$$\rho \vdash \theta_1 \to \theta_3 \rhd \theta_1 \mathbf{U}(\varphi_2 \mathbf{U} \theta_3) \approx \varphi_2 \mathbf{U} \theta_3 \qquad (\mathrm{U}_{\mathrm{U}}[1 \to 3])$$

$$\rho \vdash \theta_2 \to \theta_1 \rhd \theta_1 \mathbf{U}(\theta_2 \mathbf{U} \varphi_3) \approx \theta_1 \mathbf{U} \varphi_3 \qquad (\mathrm{U}_{\mathrm{U}}[2 \to 1])$$

Fig. 7. Reduction rules for formulae involving adjacent **U** operators

$$\rho \vdash \theta_1 \to \theta_3 \rhd (\theta_1 \mathbf{R} \varphi_2)\mathbf{U}\theta_3 \approx ((\theta_1 \mathbf{R} \varphi_2) \vee \theta_3) \wedge \mathbf{F}\theta_3 \qquad (\mathrm{U}^{\mathrm{R}}[1 \to 3])$$

$$\rho \vdash \neg\theta_1 \to \theta_3 \rhd (\theta_1 \mathbf{R} \varphi_2)\mathbf{U}\theta_3 \approx \varphi_2 \mathbf{U} \theta_3 \qquad (\mathrm{U}^{\mathrm{R}}[\neg 1 \to 3])$$

$$\rho \vdash \theta_1 \to \theta_3 \rhd \theta_1 \mathbf{U}(\varphi_2 \mathbf{R} \theta_3) \approx \varphi_2 \mathbf{R} \theta_3 \qquad (\mathrm{U}_{\mathrm{R}}[1 \to 3])$$

Fig. 8. Reduction rules for formulae involving adjacent **U** and **R** operators

3.2 Reduction Strategy

We show the usage of CePRe reduction rules by illustrating the reduction process of $M \models (\theta_1 \mathbf{U} \theta_2)\mathbf{U}\theta_3$:

1. We may first try with the rule $(\mathrm{U}^{\mathrm{U}}[1 \to 3])$ by inquiring the SAT-solver if $\rho \vdash \theta_1 \to \theta_3$ holds.
2. If the SAT-solver returns "unsatisfiable" with the input $\rho \wedge \theta_1 \wedge \neg\theta_3$, then it implies that the additional condition is stated, and we may replace the specification with $\theta_2 \mathbf{U} \theta_3$.
3. Otherwise, we will try with another reduction rule, such as $(\mathrm{U}^{\mathrm{U}}[2 \to 3])$.

In fact, these rules can also be "*locally applied*" to subformulae. For example, to make a local reduction of (FU), we may replace each occurrence of $\mathbf{F}(\varphi \mathbf{U} \psi)$ in the specification with $\mathbf{F}\psi$. The only exception is for the group of rules listed in Figure 4: observe that we have $\mathbf{Y}\varphi \approx \bot$ according to (Y), yet this does not imply that $\mathbf{FY}\varphi \approx \mathbf{F}\bot$ holds. Hence, these rules have an "implicit condition" when doing local application: the subformula to be reduced must occur "*temporally outermost*" in the specification — i.e., the target subformula does not occur in the scope of any temporal operators in the specification.

Input: The original specification φ.
Output: The reduced specification.

1 **let** $\Gamma := \emptyset$; /* Γ memorizes the sub-formulae with infeasible condition */
2 **let** $\Delta := \{\psi \in (sub(\varphi) \setminus \Gamma)$ such that ψ matches some reduction rule(s)$\}$;
3 **foreach** $\psi_1, \psi_2 \in \Delta$ *s.t.* $\psi_1 \neq \psi_2$ **do**
4   **if** $\psi_1 \in sub(\psi_2)$ **then**
5         $\Delta := \Delta \setminus \{\psi_1\}$; /* i.e., we only proceed "max" subformulae */
6   **end**
7 **end**
8 **if** $\Delta = \emptyset$ **then**
9   **return** φ;
10 **end**
11 **foreach** $\psi \in \Delta$ **do**
12   **let** $\Theta :=$ the set of rules that can be applied to ψ;
13   /* note that we have $|\Theta| \leq 5$ for each ψ */
14   **while** $\Theta \neq \emptyset$ **do**
15   **choose** $R := (\text{Cond} \rhd \psi \approx \eta)$ **in** Θ ;
16   **if** Cond *is stated* **then**
17             $\varphi := \varphi^{\psi}_{\eta}$; /* φ^{ψ}_{η} is obtained from φ by replacing ψ with η */
18   **break**;
19   **end**
20         $\Theta := \Theta \setminus \{R\}$;
21   **end**
22     $\Delta := \Delta \setminus \{\psi\}$;
23   **if** $\Theta = \emptyset$ **then**
24         $\Gamma := \Gamma \cup \{\psi\}$; /* ψ would be excluded in the next iteration */
25   **end**
26 **end**
27 **goto** 2;

Algorithm 1. The "max-match" rule-selection strategy

Compositional use of reduction rules may lead to a more aggressive reduction. For example:

1. For the task of model checking $M \models \mathbf{FO}p$, we may firstly change the goal as $M \models \mathbf{F}p \vee \mathbf{O}p$, according to the rule (FO).
2. Now, the subformula $\mathbf{O}p$ is a temporally outermost one, hence we may make a local application of (O), and then the goal becomes $M \models \mathbf{F}p \vee p$.
3. Finally, we may change the model checking problem into $M \models \mathbf{F}p$ via the rule (Disj).

In the real implementation, we perform a "*max-match*" rule-selection strategy, as depicted in Algorithm 1. In Line 15, for a rule "Cond $\rhd\ \psi \approx \eta$", the simplerCond is, and the shorter η is, the higher priority to be chosen it has. Hence, a model-independent rule always has a higher priority than a model-dependent one. We can see that the reduction can be accomplished within $\mathcal{O}(|\varphi|)$ iterations.

3.3 Performance Analysis of the Reduction

We now try to answer the question "why we can gain a better performance during verification if CEPRE is conducted first". To give a rigorous explanation, we briefly revisit the implementation of symbolic model checking algorithms.

The core procedure of BDD-based LTL symbolic model checking algorithm is to construct a *tableau* for the (negated) property. In the following, we refer the tableau of $\neg\varphi$ as $T_{\neg\varphi}$, and we would give an analysis on its major components affecting the cost of model checking.

State Space: The state space of $T_{\neg\varphi}$ consists of subsets of $el(\varphi)$, and the set $el(\varphi)$ can be inductively computed as follows.

- $el(\top) = el(\bot) = \emptyset$.
- $el(p) = \{p\}$ if $p \in \mathcal{P}$.
- $el(\varphi_1 \to \varphi_2) = el(\varphi_1) \cup el(\varphi_2)$.
- $el(\mathbf{X}\psi) = \{\mathbf{X}\psi\} \cup el(\psi)$, and $el(\mathbf{Y}\psi) = \{\mathbf{Y}\psi\} \cup el(\psi)$.
- $el(\varphi_1\mathbf{U}\varphi_2) = el(\varphi_1)\cup el(\varphi_2)\cup\{\mathbf{X}(\varphi_1\mathbf{U}\varphi_2)\}$ and $el(\varphi_1\mathbf{S}\varphi_2) = el(\varphi_1)\cup el(\varphi_2)\cup \{\mathbf{Y}(\varphi_1\mathbf{S}\varphi_2)\}$.

We can see from the definition that $el(\varphi) = el(\neg\varphi)$ holds. With symbolic representation, each formula $\psi \in el(\varphi)$ corresponds to a proposition in building the tableau. Moreover, if $\psi \in \mathcal{P}$, then no new proposition need to be introduced (since it has already been introduced in building the symbolic representation of M), otherwise, a fresh proposition p_ψ is required. Hence the total number of newly introduced propositions equals to $|el(\varphi) \setminus \mathcal{P}|$. From an induction over formula's structure, we have the following claim.

Proposition 1. *$|el(\varphi) \setminus \mathcal{P}|$ equals to the number of temporal operators in φ.*

Transitions: The transition relation of $T_{\neg\varphi}$ is a conjunction of a set of constraints, and each constraint is either of the form $p_{\mathbf{X}\psi} \leftrightarrow (\sigma(\psi))'$ or $p'_{\mathbf{Y}\eta} \leftrightarrow \sigma(\eta)$, where $\mathbf{X}\psi, \mathbf{Y}\eta \in el(\varphi)$, and the function σ can inductively defined as follows.

- $\sigma(\bot) = \bot$ and $\sigma(\top) = \top$.
- $\sigma(p) = p$ for each $p \in \mathcal{P}$.
- $\sigma(\psi_1 \to \psi_2) = \sigma(\psi_1) \to \sigma(\psi_2)$.
- $\sigma(\mathbf{X}\psi_1) = p_{\mathbf{X}\psi_1}$ and $\sigma(\mathbf{Y}\psi_2) = p_{\mathbf{Y}\psi_2}$.
- $\sigma(\psi_1\mathbf{U}\psi_2) = \sigma(\psi_2) \vee \sigma(\psi_1) \wedge p_{\mathbf{X}(\psi_1\mathbf{U}\psi_2)}$ and $\sigma(\psi_1\mathbf{S}\psi_2) = \sigma(\psi_2) \vee \sigma(\psi_1) \wedge p_{\mathbf{Y}(\psi_1\mathbf{U}\psi_2)}$.

According to the definition of el, we can see that each $\psi \in sub(\varphi)$ rooted at a future (reps. past) temporal operator exactly produces one formula $\mathbf{X}\eta$ (resp. $\mathbf{Y}\eta$) in $el(\varphi)$, and hence a new proposition $p_{\mathbf{X}\eta}$ (resp. $p_{\mathbf{Y}\eta}$) would be introduced. Subsequently, each such $p_{\mathbf{X}\eta}$ (reps. $p_{\mathbf{Y}\eta}$) adds exactly one constraint to the transition relation. Hence, we have the following claim.

Proposition 2. *The number of constraints in the transition relation of $T_{\neg\varphi}$ equals to the number of temporal operators occurring in φ (alternatively, $|el(\varphi) \setminus \mathcal{P}|$).*

Fairness Constraints: According to the tableau construction, each $\psi \in sub_{\mathbf{U}}(\neg\varphi)$ would impose a fairness constraint to $T_{\neg\varphi}$. Hence, the number of fairness constraints equals to $|sub_{\mathbf{U}}(\neg\varphi)|$.

With a case-by-case checking, we can show the following theorem.

Theorem 2. *Let "Cond $\rhd \varphi \approx \psi$" be a reduction rule, then we have $|el(\psi)\setminus\mathcal{P}| \leq |el(\varphi) \setminus \mathcal{P}|$ and $|sub_{\mathbf{U}}(\psi)| \leq |sub_{\mathbf{U}}(\neg\varphi)|$.*

In contrast, the cost of BMC is quite sensitive to the encoding approach. In a broad sense, we can categorize the encoding approaches into two fashions.

Syntactic encodings: Such kind of encodings are inductively produced w.r.t. the formula's structure. The very original one is presented in [1], and this is improved in [4] by observing some properties of that encoding. In [9,10], a linear incremental syntactic encoding is suggested. And see [16] for a recent translation for ECTL*.

Semantic encodings: In [5], an alternative BMC technique is provided: it mimics the tableau-based model checking process, but it expresses the fair-path detection upon the product model with Boolean formula.[4]

For the semantic encodings, the reason that we can benefit from CePRe is exactly the same as that for BDD-based approach. Because, the encoding is a conjunction of a k-step unrolling of M and a k-step unrolling of $T_{\neg\varphi}$ (an unrolling is either a partial derived linear structure, or a one ending with a lasso). The former is usually in a fixed pattern, and for the latter, we need $k \times |el(\varphi)\setminus\mathcal{P}|$ new propositions, and the sizes of Boolean formulae w.r.t the transition and fairness constraints[5] are respectively $\mathcal{O}(k \times |el(\varphi) \setminus \mathcal{P}|)$ and $\mathcal{O}(k^2 \times |sub_{\mathbf{U}}(\neg\varphi)|)$.

For a syntactic BMC encoding, one need to generate a Boolean formula of the form $E_M^k \wedge E_{\neg\varphi}^k$, where E_M^k is the unrolling of M with k steps, and $E_{\neg\varphi}^k$ describes that such k-step unrolling would cause a violation of φ. In general, E_M^k is almost the same in all kinds of syntactic encodings, and the key factor affecting the cost lies in $E_{\neg\varphi}^k$.

Given a subformula ψ of φ, if we use $||E_\psi^k||$ to denote the max length of the Boolean formula describing that ψ is initially satisfied upon a k-step unrolling, then it can be inductively computed as follows.

- $||E_\perp^k|| = ||E_\top^k|| = 0$. [6]
- $||E_p^k|| = 1$ for each $p \in \mathcal{P}$.

[4] In [7], a "fixpoint"-based encoding is proposed, and it can also be subsumed to semantic encodings.

[5] Note that the part w.r.t. fairness constraints can be linearized.

[6] This is just for the case when $\perp$ or $\top$ appears as a subformula in the specification, and hence can be optimized; otherwise, we have $||E_\perp^k|| = ||E_\top^k|| = 1$.

- $||E^k_{\varphi_1 \to \varphi_2}|| = ||E^k_{\varphi_1}|| + ||E^k_{\varphi_2}|| + 1$.
- $||E^k_{\mathbf{X}\psi}|| = ||E^k_{\mathbf{Y}\psi}|| = ||E^k_{\psi}||$.
- $||E^k_{\varphi_1 \mathbf{U} \varphi_2}|| = ||E^k_{\varphi_1 \mathbf{S} \varphi_2}|| = L(k) \times ||E^k_{\varphi_1}|| + k \times ||E^k_{\varphi_2}||$. [7]

Here, $L(k)$ is some polynomial about k, related to the encoding approach. For example, with the technique proposed in [1,4], we have $L(k) \in \mathcal{O}(k^2)$, whereas $L(k) \in \mathcal{O}(k)$ in [9,10]. This partly explains the reason that we tend to change temporal nestifications with Boolean combinations, as done in ($\mathrm{U}^{\mathrm{U}}[3 \to 2]$) etc.

Another feature affecting the cost is the scale of propositions required for the encoding. If we denote by $var_k(\varphi)$ the set of additional propositions which only takes part in the encoding of $E^k_{\neg\varphi}$, then we have the following conclusions.

- For the techniques proposed in [1] and [4], we have $var_k(\varphi) = 0$. i.o.w., all propositions required in encoding $E^k_{\neg}\varphi$ can be shared with those for E^k_M.
- In term of the encoding presented in [10], we need to add $\mathcal{O}(k)$ new propositions to $var_k(\varphi)$ for each **U**-subformula and for each **S**-subformula.

Theorem 3. *Let "Cond $\rhd$ $\varphi \approx \psi$" be a reduction rule, then we have $||E^k_{\psi}|| \leq ||E^k_{\varphi}||$ and $|var_k(\psi)| \leq |var_k(\varphi)|$ in syntactic encodings.*

4 Experimental Results

We have implemented CEPRE as an upfront option in NUSMV[8], and we have also conducted experiments upon both industrial benchmarks and randomly generated cases in terms of both BDD-based and bounded model checking. The BMC encoding approach here we adapt is that proposed in [4], which is the current BMC implementation of NUSMV.

We conduct the experiments under such platform: CPU - Intel Core Duo2 E4500 2.2GHz, Mem - 2G Bytes, OS - Ubuntu 10.04 Linux, Cudd -v2.4.1.1, Zchaff -v2007.3.12.

4.1 Experiments upon Industrial Benchmarks

The benchmarks we choose in this paper are suggested in [2], and most of them come from real hardware verification.

Table 1 provides the experimental results for BDD-based LTL symbolic model checking. The field #Time is the executing time totally elapsed, and the field #R.S. refers to the number of reachable states. For the experiments "with CEPRE", both the overheads of time and space are the summations of preprocessing and model checking. For Table 1, we have the following remarks:

[7] Note that this case does not imply that further blow-up would be caused with deeper nesting of temporal operators. For example, in [10], by introducing fresh propositions and reusing, it still leads to a linear encoding for the whole formula.

[8] The tool is available in `http://sourceforge.net/projects/nusmvwithcepre`, and all SMV manuscripts for experiments can be found in the folder of `/files/benchmark` and `/files/random` from that site.

Table 1. Comparative results of BDD-based MC with/without CePRe

Model	Spec.	Without CePRe			With CePRe		
		#BDD--Nodes	#R.S.	#Time (sec.)	#BDD--Nodes	#R.S.	#Time (sec.)
srg5	Ptimo.ltl	7946	720	0.024	2751	720	0.016
	Pti.gnv.ltl	29704	11460	0.058	5712	2880	0.012
	Pti.g.ltl	64749	130048	0.048	8119	32768	0.016
abp4	P2false.ltl	99577	559104	0.200	99625	559104	0.202
	P2true.ltl	61209	904384	0.066	56494	419296	0.064
	Pold.ltl	52301	353536	0.060	52349	353536	0.064
	Ptimo.ltl	78098	219616	0.080	78146	219616	0.088
	Pti.g.ltl	8385	200704	0.060	8433	200704	0.062
dme3	P0.ltl	889773	35964	5.756	527983	26316	5.096
	P1.ltl	455148	8775	0.460	409432	5505	0.374
dme5	Mdl.ltl	793942	8.64316e+06	167.346	814494	3.2097e+06	114.599
	Wat.ltl	412867	1.79217e+07	302.005	967033	1.12567e+07	286.850
	Ptimo.neg	508036	1.26202e+06	3.260	508081	1.26202e+06	3.280
msi_w-trans	Sched.ltl	2275558	7.31055e+07	6.612	2275655	7.31055e+07	6.632
	Safety.ltl	1213308	3.6528e+07	7.568	1213460	3.6528e+07	7.644
	Seq.ltl	1921973	3.5946e+07	93.570	1702585	1.7973e+07	94.085

1. 8 out of 16 specifications could be reduced with CePRe (and these specifications have been highlighted).
2. For the specifications that can be reduced, considerable improvements are made during verification. For example, for the specification Pit.g.ltl, with CePRe, the number of BDD nodes are decreased to 12.5% of that without using CePRe.
3. When a specification cannot be reduced with CePRe, it spends a very low extra overheads for doing preprocessings.
4. Something noteworthy we do not provide here is that: in the case that a violated LTL specification can be reduced, the newly generated counterexample is usually shorter than that of before. Among 8 specifications that can be reduced, counterexample-lengths of Pti.nuv.ltl, Pit.g.ltl, P0.ltl and Seq.ltl are respectively shortened to 15, 10 and 194, opposing to the original values 16, 12 and 217. Meanwhile, counterexample-lengths of others are kept unchanged.

Table 2 gives the experimental results for BMC-based model checking, and we here give some comments on that.

1. With NuSMV, we need to preset a max-bound when doing bounded model checking. The column #Max-bound gives such values — a "star mark" means that this bound does not reach the completeness threshold. The field #N.O.C. designates the number of clauses generated during model checking.

Table 2. Experimental results of BMC-based MC with/without CEPRE

Model	Spec.	Without CePRe #N.O.C.	Without CePRe #Time (sec.)	With CePRe #N.O.C.	With CePRe #Time (sec.)	#Max-bound
srg5	Ptimo.ltl	272567	67.391	1371	0.143	20
	Pti.gnv.ltl	2101	0.116	299	0.024	6
	Pti.g.ltl	21	0.016	21	0.016	1
abp4	P2false.ltl	7532	3.972	7532	3.972	17
	P2true.ltl	12639	8.145	9369	7.753	20*
	Pold.ltl	7499	9.087	7499	9.488	20*
	Ptimo.ltl	6332	2.500	6332	2.512	16
	Pti.g.ltl	11952	0.841	11952	0.976	20*
dme3	P0.ltl	–	–	35102	524.207	62
	P1.ltl	216	0.036	167	0.048	1
dme5	Mdl.ltl	90	0.044	90	0.048	0
	Wat.ltl	367	0.048	274	0.052	1
	Ptimo.neg	367	0.050	277	0.058	1
msi_w-trans	Sched.ltl	14235	1.076	14235	1.078	20*
	Safety.ltl	12439	8.441	12439	8.448	20*
	Seq.ltl	1907	0.064	81	0.052	3

2. From Table 2, we can see that without CEPRE the specification Pti.gnv.ltl generates 2101 clauses when the verification stops, in contrast, it only produces 299 clauses if CEPRE is switched on.
3. Another comparison is for P0.ltl upon dme3: If we don't do any reduction, the SAT-solver reports a SEGMENTATION FAULT at Step 35. In contrast, using CEPRE, a counterexample could be found at Step 62.
4. Since the encoding approach we adapt is taken from [4], propositions used in the encoding are only determined by the model and the bound, thus the number of required propositions does not change. For this reason, the corresponding experimental results on proposition numbers are not provided.

Note that both model-independent and model-dependent rules contribute to the reductions. For example, for the model srg5 and the specification Pti.g.ltl, the rules (FS) and (S) are applied; meanwhile, for the model msi_wtrans and the specification Seq.ltl, the application of $(\mathrm{U}^{\mathrm{U}}[\neg 2 \rightarrow 3])$ is invoked.

4.2 Experiments w.r.t. Random Models and Specifications

We have also performed experiments upon randomly generated models and specifications with the tool LBTT [14] and with the methodology suggested in [10].

For each $3 \leq \ell \leq 7$, we randomly generate 40 specifications having length ℓ. Subsequently, for each specification, we generate two models respectively for the BDD-based model checking and for BMC. Hence, we totally have 200 specifications and 400 models.

For the BDD-based model checking, we give the comparative results on 1) the scale of BDD-nodes, 2) the number of reachable states, 3) the time consumed, and the experimental results are respectively shown in Figure 9 – Figure 11. For bounded model checking, we have set the max-bound to 20 and we have compared: 1) the number of clauses, and 2) the executing time, the results are respectively shown in Figure 12 and Figure 13. Each value here we provide is the average of the 40 executions.

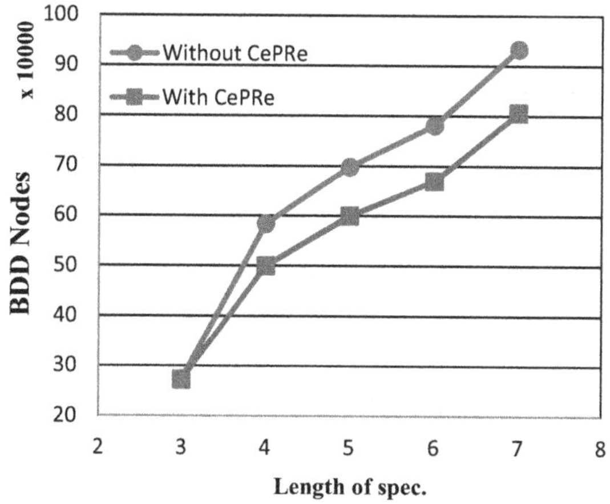

Fig. 9. Results on the scale of BDD nodes in random BDD-MC experiments

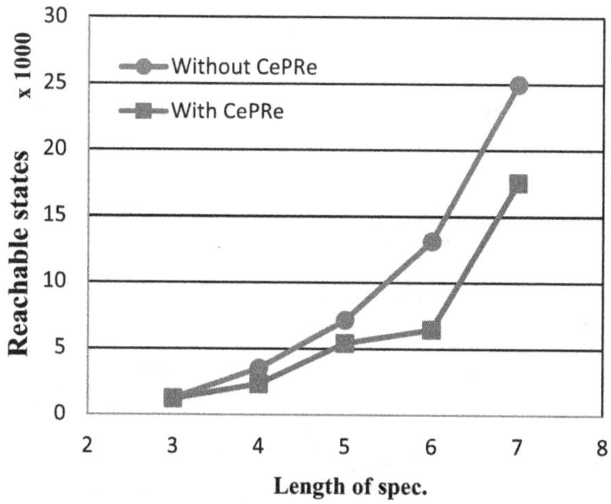

Fig. 10. Results on reachable states in random BDD-MC experiments

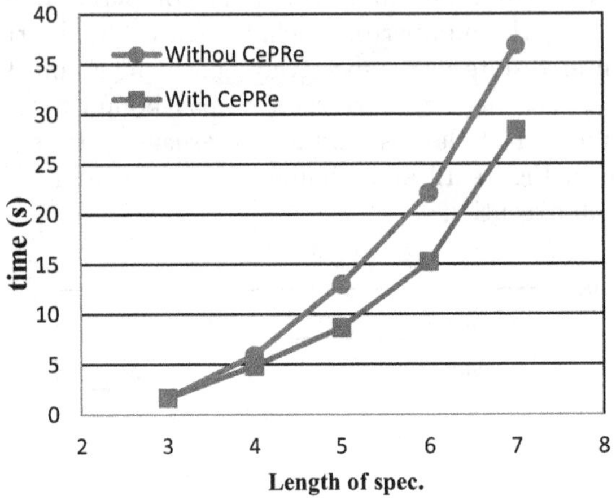

Fig. 11. Time overhead in random BDD-MC experiments

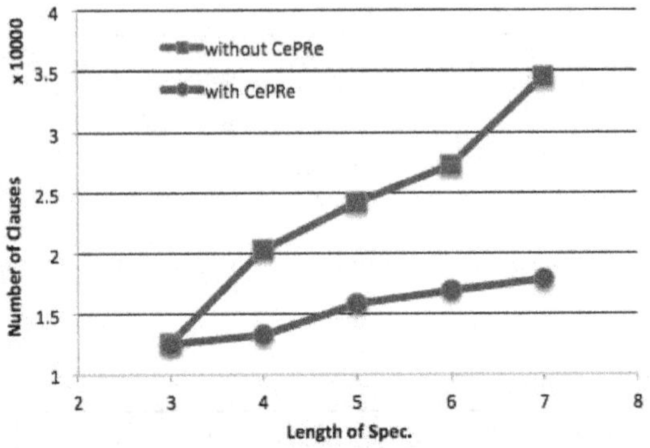

Fig. 12. The scale of clauses in random BMC experiments

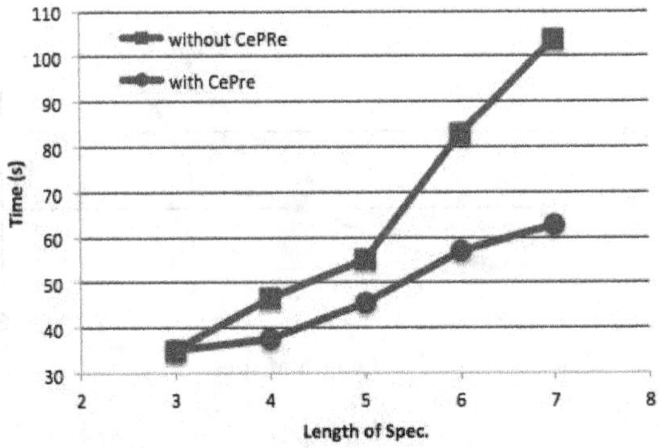

Fig. 13. Time overhead in random BMC experiments

For the BDD-based model checking, there are 123 (out of 200) specifications can be reduced, wheras for bounded model checking, the number of specifications that can be reduced is 118. Note that in this experiment, when CePRe is switched on, extra overheads (such as time) have also been taken into account.

5 Concluding Remarks

In this paper, we present a new technique to reduce LTL specifications' complexity towards symbolic model checking, namely, CePRe. The novelty in this technique is that the reduced formula needs not to be logically equivalent with the original one, but just preserves the counterexample set. Moreover, the condition enabling such a reduction can be usually detected with lightweight approaches, such as SAT-solving. Hence, this technique could leverage the power of SAT-solvers.

The central part of CePRe is a set of reduction rules, and soundness of these reduction rules are fairly easy to check. For the model dependent rules, additional conditions mainly concern about the invariants and transitions, and we do not make a sufficient use of other features, such as fairness. In this paper, the rules are given by enumerating all possible combinations of (at most two) temporal operators. Indeed, there might be some other reduction schemas we are not aware.

From the experimental results, we can see that, in a statistical perspective, a better performance and lower overhead can be achieved with CePRe.

References

1. Biere, A., Cimatti, A., Clarke, E., Zhu, Y.: Symbolic model checking without bDDs. In: Cleaveland, W.R. (ed.) TACAS 1999. LNCS, vol. 1579, pp. 193–207. Springer, Heidelberg (1999)
2. Biere, A., Heljanko, K., Junttila, T., Latvala, T., Schuppan, V.: Linear encodings of bounded LTL model checking. Logical Methods in Computer Science 2(5:5), 1–64 (2006)
3. Burch, J.R., Clarke, E.M., McMillan, K.L., Dill, D.L., Hwang, L.J.: Symbolic model checking 10^{20} states and beyond. Information and Computation 98(2), 142–170 (1992)
4. Cimatti, A., Pistore, M., Roveri, M., Sebastiani, R.: Improving the encoding of LTL model checking into SAT. In: Cortesi, A. (ed.) VMCAI 2002. LNCS, vol. 2294, pp. 196–207. Springer, Heidelberg (2002)
5. Clarke, E., Kroning, D., Ouaknine, J., Strichman, O.: Completeness and complexity of bounded model checking. In: Steffen, B., Levi, G. (eds.) VMCAI 2004. LNCS, vol. 2937, pp. 85–96. Springer, Heidelberg (2004)
6. Clarke, E.M., Grumberg, O., Hamaguchi, K.: Another look at LTL model checking. In: Dill, D.L. (ed.) CAV 1994. LNCS, vol. 818, pp. 415–427. Springer, Heidelberg (1994)
7. Frisch, A., Sheridan, D., Walsh, T.: A fixpoint encoding for bounded model checking. In: Aagaard, M.D., O'Leary, J.W. (eds.) FMCAD 2002. LNCS, vol. 2517, pp. 238–255. Springer, Heidelberg (2002)

8. Gabbay, D.: The declarative past and imperative future: Executable temporal logic for interactive systems. In: Banieqbal, B., Pnueli, A., Barringer, H. (eds.) Temporal Logic in Specification. LNCS, vol. 398, pp. 431–448. Springer, Heidelberg (1989)
9. Latvala, T., Biere, A., Heljanko, K., Junttila, T.A.: Simple bounded LTL model checking. In: Hu, A.J., Martin, A.K. (eds.) FMCAD 2004. LNCS, vol. 3312, pp. 186–200. Springer, Heidelberg (2004)
10. Latvala, T., Biere, A., Heljanko, K., Junttila, T.A.: Simple is better: Efficient bounded model checking for past LTL. In: Cousot, R. (ed.) VMCAI 2005. LNCS, vol. 3385, pp. 380–395. Springer, Heidelberg (2005)
11. McMillan, K.L.: Symbolic Model Checking, An Approach to the State Explosion Problem. PhD thesis, Carnegie Mellon University, Kluwer Academic Publishers (1993)
12. Pnueli, A.: The temporal logic of programs. In: Proc. of 18th IEEE Symposium on Foundation of Computer Science (FOCS 1977), pp. 46–57. IEEE Computer Society (1977)
13. Somenzi, F., Bloem, R.: Efficient Büchi automata from LTL formulae. In: Emerson, E.A., Sistla, A.P. (eds.) CAV 2000. LNCS, vol. 1855, pp. 53–65. Springer, Heidelberg (2000)
14. Taurainen, H., Heljanko, K.: Testing LTL formula translation into Büchi automata. STTT 4, 57–70 (2002)
15. Vardi, M.Y.: Branching vs. Linear time: Final showdown. In: Margaria, T., Yi, W. (eds.) TACAS 2001. LNCS, vol. 2031, pp. 1–22. Springer, Heidelberg (2001)
16. Zbrzezny, A.: A new translation from ETCL* to SAT. In: Szczuka, M., et al. (eds.) Proceedings of the International Workshop CS&P 2011, pp. 589–600 (September 2011)

A Transformation from p-π to MSVL *

Ling Luo and Zhenhua Duan**

Institute of Computing Theory and Technology,
Xidian University, Xi'an, P.R. China
lingluo@stu.xidian.edu.cn, zhhduan@mail.xidian.edu.cn

Abstract. A structural transformation from p-π processes to MSVL programs is proposed in this paper. To this end, channel and communication primitives are firstly defined in MSVL. Further, based on these definitions, a mapping function Υ which transforms p-π processes into MSVL programs is formalized. As a result, p-π can provide a mechanism to model, simulate and verify concurrent systems by means of the techniques of MSVL. Finally, a case study is given to illustrate how the transformation is used in practice.

Keywords: process algebra, temporal logic, π-calculus, MSVL, verification.

1 Introduction

Following CCS [1], CSP [2] and ACP [3], lots of variations of process algebras were proposed for different purposes. For example, with the development of new network computing technologies, e.g. SaaS [4], SOA [5] and Cloud Computing [6], π-calculus is such a variation widely used in practice to ensure the correctness of systems with dynamic properties. However, with π-calculus [7–11], the time duration of an action and the residence time of a system at a state are not taken into account. Thus, π-calculus is not convenient for modeling time-dependent systems. p-π[23] is an extension of π-calculus for specifying time-dependent mobile systems, which augments the action prefixes of π-calculus by adding interval action prefixes. Although p-π provides plenty of algebraic ways to specify concurrent time-dependent systems, it is difficult to verify systems by model checking or theorem proving.

On the other hand, Projection Temporal Logic (PTL) [12–14] offers abundant mechanisms such as model checking, equivalence reasoning and theorem proving for modeling and reasoning about concurrent time-dependent systems. MSVL[15, 18, 19], an executable subset of PTL, is a modeling, simulation and verification language. Further, an interpreter for MSVL has been developed and it can work in three modes: modeling, simulation and verification.

In this paper, we are motivated to investigate the relationship between p-π and MSVL so that we can take advantage of techniques of MSVL to verify properties of time-dependent systems modeled by p-π. Precisely, we present a structural transformation Υ which can translate a given p-π process into an MSVL program.

* This research is supported by the NSFC Grant Nos. 61133001, 61272118, 61272117, 61202038, 91218301 and National Program on Key Basic Research Project (973 Program) Grant No. 2010CB328102.

** Corresponding author.

Z. Liu, J. Woodcock, and H. Zhu (Eds.): ICTAC 2013, LNCS 8049, pp. 267–281, 2013.

For iteration and more complex (non-regular) patterns of recursion processes, they can be expressed in two manners in original π-calculus. One is by !P and the other is by $A\langle a_1, .., a_n\rangle$. In [8], $A\langle a_1, .., a_n\rangle$ is employed and in [7], both $A\langle a_1, .., a_n\rangle$ and !P are used. !*P* means an unlimited number of copies of *P* is able to run concurrently and *P* is dynamically created by the law "$!P \equiv P|!P$". However, the use of !*P* is only for the succinctness of the syntax, but not for the practice of the modeling. As a result, many examples in [7] are expressed by $A\langle a_1, .., a_n\rangle$. Especially, in section "9.5" of the book, how to express recursive definitions by both $A\langle a_1, .., a_n\rangle$ and !*P* is presented. For our calculus p-π, we employ $A\langle a_1, .., a_n\rangle$. The main consideration is for the practice in the modeling. Since $A\langle a_1, .., a_n\rangle$ can express iteration/recursion, p-π is not restrictive. However, recursive definitions in p-π would make reachability/safety verification of p-π undecidable. For decidability of the verification of p-π, we restrict the form of p-π processes. For the transformation, we just take into account the processes which are decidable. Precisely, to transform process instances, we consider only process instances without recursive calls in their definitions and process instances with recursive calls in the definitions which can be in a specific form. For these process instances, their least fixed points exist. To transform each of them, we employ a recursion procedure to get the fixed point. Moreover, for process instances with recursive calls in the definitions which cannot be in the given form, their behavior may not be convergent so that we cannot directly transform them into MSVL.

In the literature, Zhou et al present a language, called HCSP, to describe hybrid systems [16]. The semantics of the language is given in terms of Extended Duration Calculus [17]. Our translation is defined in a way much as how the semantics is given. Comparing with their work, we focus on only discrete processes rather than both discrete and continuous processes. Further, the messages passed by channels in HCSP are discrete or continuous variables while in p-π the messages can be channels.

However, the communication mechanisms used in MSVL and p-π are different. In fact, MSVL involves shared variables whereas p-π uses communication channels (or names). Therefore, to transform p-π, the channel and communication primitives need to be defined in MSVL. The contribution of this paper is two-fold: (1) A structural transformation Υ is provided to transform p-π processes into MSVL programs. (2) The channel and communication primitives are defined in MSVL to smooth the transformation.

The rest of the paper is organized as follows. The syntax and semantics of p-π are briefly introduced in section 2. In section 3, firstly the syntax and semantics of MSVL are shortly presented; further, the channel and communication primitives are formally defined. Section 4 is devoted to demonstrating the structural transformation from p-π processes to MSVL programs. Moreover, a case study is given in section 5. Finally, conclusions are drawn in Section 6.

2 Extended π-Calculus: p-π

p-π [23] is an extension of π-calculus and has two types of action prefixes: instantaneous and interval ones. The instantaneous action prefixes are executed without time-consuming whereas the execution of interval action prefixes takes one time unit.

2.1 Syntax of p-π

Let $\mathcal{N}$ be an infinite countable set of names, *PR* a countable set of propositions, and $\mathbb{N}$ the set of non-negative integers. The syntax of p-π processes is given as follows:

$$\pi ::= x(y) \mid \overline{x}\langle y\rangle \mid \tau \mid I_p \mid skip \mid \varepsilon$$
$$P ::= 0 \mid \pi.P \mid P_1 + P_2 \mid P_1|P_2 \mid [a_1 = a_2]P \mid \nu a\ P \mid A\langle a_1, ..., a_n\rangle$$

where x, y, a, and a_i (i is an integer from 1 to $n \in \mathbb{N}$) are names ranging over $\mathcal{N}$.

The action prefix π falls into two categories: instantaneous action prefix and interval action prefix. An instantaneous action prefix represents either sending (denoted by $\overline{x}\langle y\rangle$) or receiving (denoted by $x(y)$) a message, or executing a silent τ or empty transition ε. An interval action prefix represents either I_p=$\{p_1 \wedge skip, ..., p_k \wedge skip\}$ or $skip$. Here $p_i \in PR$ (i is an integer from 1 to $k \in \mathbb{N}$), and $skip$ is a special proposition indicating a time unit. For convenience, we use $\tilde{p}_i$ to represent $p_i \wedge skip$ and $\overline{x}$ (or x) to denote $\overline{x}\langle\rangle$ (or $x()$). Note that $\overline{x}()$ (or $x()$) means an action prefix without message.

A process (or process expression) can be an empty process 0, an action prefix guarded process $\pi.P$, summation of two processes $P_1 + P_2$, parallel composition of two processes $P_1|P_2$, a match structure $[a_1{=}a_2]P$, a restriction structure $\nu a\ P$, or a process instance $A\langle a_1, ..., a_n\rangle$. $P_1 + P_2$ means a nondeterministic choice. $[a_1{=}a_2]P$ indicates that P is executed if $a_1{=}a_2$. $\nu a\ P$ behaves as P except that the communication on the bound name a is forbidden. A in $A\langle a_1, ..., a_n\rangle$ is a process identifier defined by an equation $A(x_1, ..., x_n) \stackrel{\text{def}}{=} P_A$ and $A\langle a_1, ..., a_n\rangle$=$\{\vec{a}/\vec{x}\}P_A$ where $\vec{a}$ and $\vec{x}$ are the vectors of $a_1, ..., a_n$ and $x_1, ..., x_n$, respectively. For succinctness, .0 can be omitted. For instance, we write $a(b)$ instead of $a(b).0$. Also we often write $\nu\ a\ \nu\ b\ P$ as $\nu\ a, b\ P$. Usually, prefixed operations ($\pi.$, $\nu\ a$ and $[a{=}b]$) have priority over summation and composition operations. For example, $\nu\ a\ a(b).P|Q$ means $(\nu\ a\ a(b).P)|Q$, but not $\nu\ a\ (a(b).P|Q)$.

The abbreviations about $skip$ and $await$ are defined as follows.

Skip_0 $\quad skip^0 \stackrel{\text{def}}{=} \varepsilon$

Skip_n $\quad skip^n \stackrel{\text{def}}{=} skip.skip^{n-1} (n \geq 1)$

Await_d $\quad await(P) \stackrel{\text{def}}{=} \varepsilon.P + skip.P + ... + skip^n.P (n \geq 0)$

where $n \in \mathbb{N}$ is a finite integer. P in $await(P)$ is a sending (or receiving) prefix guarded process.

The set of names in a process $n(P)$ consists of bound names $bn(P)$ and free names $fn(P)$. That is $n(P)$=$bn(P) \cup fn(P)$. Names, say a, appearing in (a) or $\nu a\ P$ are bound names while others are free names.

2.2 Semantics of p-π

Definition 1. *Let $\cong$ be an equivalence relation over the set of p-π processes $\mathcal{P}$. $\cong$ is called a process congruence, iff if $P \cong Q$, then*

$$\pi.P \cong \pi.Q, \qquad P + R \cong Q + R,$$
$$R + P \cong R + Q, \qquad P|R \cong Q|R,$$
$$R|P \cong R|Q, \qquad [a_1 = a_2]P \cong [a_1 = a_2]Q,$$
$$\nu aP \cong \nu aQ.$$

Definition 2. *Let $\equiv$ be an equivalence relation over $\mathcal{P}$ defined by the sixteen equations below. $\equiv$ is called a structural congruence iff $\equiv$ is a process congruence.*

$$
\begin{array}{ll}
S1: \nu x\, P \equiv \nu y\, \{y/x\}P \text{ if } y \notin fn(P) & S2: P+Q \equiv Q+P \\
S3: x(y).P \equiv x(z).\{z/y\}P \text{ if } z \notin fn((y)P) & S4: P|0 \equiv P \\
S5: P|Q \equiv Q|P & S6: (P|Q)|R \equiv P|(Q|R) \\
S7: \nu x\,(P|Q) \equiv P|\nu x\, Q, \text{ if } x \notin fn(P) & S8: \nu x\, 0 \equiv 0 \\
S9: [x=y]P \equiv 0, \text{ if } x \neq y & S10: \nu xy\, P \equiv \nu yx\, P \\
S11: A\langle a_1,...,a_n\rangle \equiv \{\vec{a}/\vec{x}\}P_A \text{ if } A(x_1,...,x_n) \stackrel{\text{def}}{=} P_A & S12: \varepsilon.P \equiv P \\
S13: skip.P + skip.Q \equiv skip.(P+Q) & S14: P+0 \equiv P \\
S15: P+(Q+R) \equiv (P+Q)+R & S16: \nu x\, \overline{x}\langle y\rangle.P \equiv 0
\end{array}
$$

It has been proved that $\equiv$ is a process congruence. That is $\equiv$ is a structural congruence over the set of p-π processes $\mathcal{P}$. Two process expressions $P, Q \in \mathcal{P}$ are structurally congruent, written as $P \equiv Q$, if one can be transformed into the other by using the equations in Definition 2 in either direction.

Operational Rules. To define the operational rules of p-π, we firstly specify the observable actions as follows:

$$
\begin{aligned}
\pi_o &::= \overline{x}\langle y\rangle \mid x(z) \mid \overline{x}(z) \mid \tau \mid I_p \mid skip \\
\pi_c &::= \overline{x}\langle y\rangle \mid x(z) \mid \overline{x}(z) \mid \tau \\
\pi_t &::= I_p \mid skip
\end{aligned}
$$

where x and y are free names in $fn(\pi_o)$ or $fn(\pi_c)$. z is a bound name in $bn(\pi_o)$ or $bn(\pi_c)$. Here, $\overline{x}(z)$ is defined by $\nu z\, \overline{x}\langle z\rangle$.

In Fig.1, *late* operational semantics of p-π is defined. A transition in the form of $P \xrightarrow{\pi_o} Q$ in p-π means that P can evolve into Q after performing action π_o.

Definition 3. ***Weakly-guarded** [8]: A process identifier is weakly-guardedly defined if each occurrence of the process instance of this process identifier within its definition is action prefix guarded.*

The definition is used to guarantee that the behavior of a process instance will be unfolded uniquely [8]. It is a prerequisite for us to transform p-π processes into MSVL programs.

3 Modeling, Simulation and Verification Language

In this section, the syntax and semantics of a Modeling, Simulation and Verification Language MSVL are briefly introduced. Further, the channel and communication primitives are defined.

3.1 Syntax and Semantics

MSVL consists of expressions and statements. Let N_0 be a set of non-negative integers. D denotes all data including integers, lists, sets, etc. Expressions can be regarded as

$$\text{Tau:}\frac{}{\tau.P \xrightarrow{\tau} P} \qquad \text{In:}\frac{}{x(z).P \xrightarrow{x(w)} \{w/z\}P}(w \notin fn((z)P))$$

$$\text{Out:}\frac{}{\bar{x}\langle y\rangle.P \xrightarrow{\bar{x}\langle y\rangle} P} \qquad \text{Par:}\frac{P_1 \xrightarrow{\pi_c} P_1'}{P_1|P_2 \xrightarrow{\pi_c} P_1'|P_2}(bn(\pi_c) \cap fn(P_2) = \emptyset)$$

$$\text{Sum:}\frac{P_1 \xrightarrow{\pi_c} P_1'}{P_1{+}P_2 \xrightarrow{\pi_c} P_1'} \qquad \text{Close:}\frac{P_1 \xrightarrow{\bar{x}(y)} P_1' \;\; P_2 \xrightarrow{x(y)} P_2'}{P_1|P_2 \xrightarrow{\tau} \nu y\,(P_1'|P_2')}$$

$$\text{Com:}\frac{P_1 \xrightarrow{\bar{x}\langle y\rangle} P_1' \;\; P_2 \xrightarrow{x(z)} P_2'}{P_1|P_2 \xrightarrow{\tau} P_1'|\{y/z\}P_2'} \qquad \text{Mat:}\frac{P \xrightarrow{\pi_o} P'}{[a_1 = a_2]P \xrightarrow{\pi_o} P'}(a_1 = a_2)$$

$$\text{Open:}\frac{P \xrightarrow{\bar{x}\langle y\rangle} P'}{\nu y\, P \xrightarrow{\bar{x}(z)} \{z/y\}P'} \;(x \neq y, z \notin fn(\nu y P'))$$

$$\text{Res:}\frac{P \xrightarrow{\pi_o} P'}{\nu x P \xrightarrow{\pi_o} \nu x P'}(x \notin n(\pi_o)) \qquad \text{Ide:}\frac{\{\vec{a}/\vec{x}\}P_A \xrightarrow{\pi_o} P'}{A\langle\vec{a}\rangle \xrightarrow{\pi_o} P'}(A(\vec{x}) \stackrel{\text{def}}{=} P_A)$$

$$\text{Act}_t\text{:}\frac{}{\pi_t.P \xrightarrow{\pi_t} P} \qquad \text{Sum}_{t_1}\text{:}\frac{P_1 \xrightarrow{skip} P_1' \;\; P_2 \xrightarrow{skip} P_2'}{P_1{+}P_2 \xrightarrow{skip} P_1'{+}P_2'}$$

$$\text{Act}_\varepsilon\text{:}\frac{P \xrightarrow{\pi_c} P'}{\varepsilon.P \xrightarrow{\pi_c} P'} \qquad \text{Await:}\frac{\varepsilon.P{+}skip.await(P) \xrightarrow{\pi_o} P'}{await(P) \xrightarrow{\pi_o} P'}$$

$$\text{Com}_{idle}\text{:}\frac{P_1 \xrightarrow{\pi_t} P_1' \;\; P_2 \equiv 0}{P_1|P_2 \xrightarrow{\pi_t} P_1'} \qquad \text{Sum}_{t_2}\text{:}\frac{P_1 \xrightarrow{\pi_t} P_1'}{P_1{+}P_2 \xrightarrow{\pi_t} P_1'}(P_1{+}P_2 \not\xrightarrow{skip})$$

$$\text{Com}_t\text{:}\frac{P_1 \xrightarrow{\pi_{t_1}} P_1' \;\; P_2 \xrightarrow{\pi_{t_2}} P_2'}{P_1|P_2 \xrightarrow{\pi_{t_1} \cup \pi_{t_2}} P_1'|P_2'}(\pi_{t_1} \cap \pi_{t_2} - skip = \emptyset, P_1|P_2 \not\xrightarrow{\tau})$$

Fig. 1. Operational semantics of p-π

PTL terms and statements as PTL formulas. The arithmetic expression *e* and boolean expression *b* of MSVL are inductively defined as follows:

$$e ::= c \mid x \mid \&x \mid *x \mid \bigcirc x \mid \odot x \mid e_0 \; op \; e_1 \qquad (op ::= + \mid - \mid * \mid /)$$
$$b ::= \mathsf{true} \mid \mathsf{false} \mid \neg b \mid b_0 \wedge b_1 \mid e_0{=}e_1 \mid e_0 < e_1$$

where $c \in D$ is a constant, *x* a variable. A dynamic variable x is said to be framed in program prog if $\mathsf{frame}(x)$ or $\mathsf{lbf}(x)$ is contained in prog.

A framed program in MSVL can be formalized by the sixteen elementary statements in Figure 2. As usual, *x* denotes a variable, *e* stands for an arbitrary arithmetic expression, *b* represents a boolean expression, and $p_1, \ldots, p_m$, p and *q* are general framed programs.

ε is the termination statement, which simply states that the current state is the final state of the interval over which a program is executed. The $next$ statement $\bigcirc p$ means that p holds at the immediate successor state. $\Box p$ implies that p holds in all the states from now on. The sequential statement $p \;\; ; \;\; q$ signifies that p holds from the current state until some point in the future at which it terminates and *q* will start executing from that point.

Termination :	ε	Basic Assignment :	$x = e$
Pointer Assignment :	$*x = e$	State Frame :	$\mathsf{lbf}(x)$
Interval Frame :	$\mathsf{frame}(x)$	Conjuction :	$p \wedge q$
Selection :	$p \vee q$	Next Statement :	$\bigcirc p$
Always Statement :	$\Box p$	Conditional Statement:	$\texttt{if}\ b\ \texttt{then}\ p\ \texttt{else}\ q$
Existential Quantification :	$\exists x : p(x)$	Sequential Statement :	$p\ ;\ q$
Parallel :	$p \parallel q$	While Statement :	$\texttt{while}\ b\ \texttt{do}\ p$
Synchronized Communication :	$\mathsf{await}(b)$	Projection :	$(p_1, \ldots, p_m)\ \mathsf{prj}\ q$

Fig. 2. MSVL statements

$x = e$ is the assignment statement meaning that the value of variable x is equal to the value of expression e. If e is evaluated a constant c and x has not been specified before (or it was specified to have the same value as e), then we say c is assigned to x. In this case, the equality $x = e$ is satisfied otherwise it is false. In other words, x is unified with e. Similarly, $*x = e$ is the assignment associated with the pointer. Unlike variable assignment, the evaluation for pointer assignment involves both interpretation of the pointer and the expression [22]. The unit assignment $x := e$ is defined as $x := e \stackrel{\text{def}}{=} skip \wedge \bigcirc x = e$.

$\mathsf{lbf}(x)$ means that, when a variable is framed at a state, its value remains unchanged if no assignment is encountered at that state while $\mathsf{frame}(x)$ implies that a variable is framed over an interval if it is framed at every state over the interval.

The conditional statement $\texttt{if}\ b\ \texttt{then}\ p\ \texttt{else}\ q$ first evaluates the boolean expression; if b is true, then the process p is executed, otherwise q is executed.

The iteration $\texttt{while}\ b\ \texttt{do}\ p$ allows process p to be repeatedly executed a finite (or infinite) number of times over a finite (resp. infinite) interval as long as the condition b is satisfied at the beginning of each execution. If b becomes false, then the $\texttt{while}$ statement terminates.

The selection statement $p \vee q$ represents that p or q will be executed.

The conjunction statements $p \wedge q$ declares that the processes p and q are executed concurrently sharing all the states and variables during the mutual execution.

The parallel construction $p \parallel q$, shows another concurrent computation manner. The difference between $p \parallel q$ and $p \wedge q$ is that the former allows both p and q to be able to specify their own intervals while the latter does not. E.g., $\mathsf{len}(2) \parallel \mathsf{len}(3)$ holds but $\mathsf{len}(2) \wedge \mathsf{len}(3)$ is obviously false.

The statement $\mathsf{await}(b)$ is used to synchronize communication between parallel processes in a concurrent program with the shared variable mode. It does not change any variables, but waits until the condition b becomes true, at which point it terminates.

Projection can be regarded as a special parallel computation which is executed on different time scales. $(p_1, \ldots, p_m)\ \mathsf{prj}\ q$ claims that q is executed in parallel with $p_1, \ldots, p_m$ over an interval obtained by taking the endpoints of the intervals over which p_i's$(1 \leq i \leq m)$ are executed. The construct permits the processes $p_1, \ldots, p_m, q$ to be autonomous, each process having the right to specify the interval over which it is executed. In particular, the sequence of p_i's and q may terminate at different time points.

The existential quantification statement $\exists x : p(x)$ intends to hide the variable x within the process p. We use a renaming method to reduce this kind of programs. Consider a formula $\exists x : p(x)$ with a bound name x. The existential quantification $(\exists x)$ is removed from $\exists x : p(x)$ to obtain an equivalent formula $p(y)$ with a free variable y by renaming x as y. To do so, we require that: (1) y do not occur (free or bound) in the whole program such as $(q \wedge \exists x : p(x))$; (2) y and x both are either dynamic or static; (3) y substitutes for x only within the bound scope of x in $\exists x : p(x)$. In this case, we call $p(y)$ a *renamed formula* of $\exists x : p(x)$.

3.2 Channel and Communication Primitives

There are two significant kinds of communication modes between concurrent processes: by shared variables and by channels. In MSVL, such a communication is based on shared variables, whereas, in π-calculus, it is by channels. For smoothness of transformation, the channel and communication primitives are defined in MSVL. Actually, in π-calculus, the identification of many apparently different things, such as labels, channels, pointers, variables etc, is simply as one thing: names (or channels) [7]. Therefore, mobility can be treated by passing names (or channels) between concurrent processes. To model mobility, a channel should be capable of being passed as a message. Further, to implement the name-substituting of p-π, an auxiliary channel will be used as the substituted channel. Here, the key nodus is how to guarantee the substituted channel and the substituting channel point to the same channel instance. To this end, the channel is formalized as a pointer referring to a tripe in definition 4 and communication primitives are specified in Definition 5.

Definition 4

$$C_x \stackrel{\text{def}}{=} \&X$$
$$X \stackrel{\text{def}}{=} (w, r, v)$$

where w and r are boolean variables declaring whether or not channel C_x is waiting for sending a message or receiving a message. v is a channel variable representing the message (the message is a channel) to be sent by C_x. Notice that, X is a triple connected with channel C_x as its channel instance and cannot be used for other purposes.

Definition 5

$$\begin{array}{ll}
\text{write}(C_x) & \stackrel{\text{def}}{=} \Pi_1(*C_x) = \mathsf{true} \\
\text{read}(C_x) & \stackrel{\text{def}}{=} \Pi_2(*C_x) = \mathsf{true} \\
\text{send}(C_x, C_y) & \stackrel{\text{def}}{=} \text{write}(C_x) \wedge \Pi_3(*C_x) = C_y \wedge \varepsilon \\
\text{receive}(C_x, C_y) & \stackrel{\text{def}}{=} \text{read}(C_x) \wedge C_y = \Pi_3(*C_x) \wedge \varepsilon \\
\text{wait_send}(C_x, C_y) & \stackrel{\text{def}}{=} \text{write}(C_x) \wedge await(\text{read}(C_x)); (\Pi_3(*C_x) = C_y \wedge \varepsilon) \\
\text{wait_receive}(C_x, C_y) & \stackrel{\text{def}}{=} \text{read}(C_x) \wedge await(\text{write}(C_x)); (C_y = \Pi_3(*C_x) \wedge \varepsilon)
\end{array}$$

Here, projection function $\Pi_i (1 \leq i \leq 3)$ is used as usual to obtain the components of a multi-component. For instance, to get the first component from $X \stackrel{\text{def}}{=} (w, r, v)$, we have

$\Pi_1(X) = \Pi_1(w, r, v) = w$. *write*$(C_x)$ denotes a sending action occurring via channel C_x and *read*(C_x) a receiving action occurring via channel C_x. The communication can be synchronous or asynchronous. *send*(C_x, C_y) represents asynchronous sending, *receive*(C_x, C_y) asynchronous receiving, *wait_send*(C_x, C_y) synchronous sending and *wait_receive*(C_x, C_y) synchronous receiving. Asynchronous sending and receiving will execute writing or reading instantaneously while synchronous sending and receiving will wait for some actions from its partner. For *wait_send*(C_x, C_y), since *write*$(C_x) \wedge$ $await($*read*$(C_x)) \equiv ($*write*$(C_x) \wedge$ *read*$(C_x) \wedge \varepsilon) \vee ($*write*$(C_x) \wedge \neg$*read*$(C_x) \wedge \bigcirc await($ *read*$(C_x))$, its behavior is nondeterministic. In other words, it will communicate with its partner instantaneously, i.e., *write*$(C_x) \wedge$ *read*$(C_x) \wedge \varepsilon; \Pi_3(*C_x) = C_y \wedge \varepsilon \equiv$ *write*$(C_x) \wedge$ *read*$(C_x) \wedge \Pi_3(*C_x) = C_y \wedge \varepsilon$ or waits for some actions from its partner, i.e., *write*$(C_x) \wedge \neg$*read*$(C_x) \wedge \bigcirc await($*read*$(C_x)); (C_u = \Pi_3(*C_x) \wedge \varepsilon))$. The behavior of *wait_receive*(C_x, C_y) is analogous to that of *wait_send*(C_x, C_y) but assigns C_y to the message which is sent by the channel C_x.

4 Transformation from p-π to MSVL

Although p-π and MSVL describe concurrent systems fundamentally in different ways, we can show that each weakly-guardedly defined p-π process can be transformed into an MSVL program by the mapping function $\Upsilon : \{p\text{-}\pi\ process\} \to \{\text{MSVL}\ program\}$, which is defined as follows. $\Upsilon(P)$ transforms P by the induction on its structures.

4.1 Transformation of Names and Propositions

For easy of discussion, in the following, according to the set of names $n(P)$ and propositions PR_P appearing in a p-π process P, the set of channels $CH_{\Upsilon(P)}$ and propositional (or boolean) variables $V_{\Upsilon(P)}$ of a corresponding MSVL program are obtained. For instance, if $n(P)$=$\{a, b, c\}$ and PR_P=$\{p_1, p_2, p_3\}$, we have that,

$$\begin{aligned} CH_{\Upsilon(P)} &= \{C_a, C_b, C_c\}, \\ V_{\Upsilon(P)} &= \{x_{p_1}, x_{p_2}, x_{p_3}\}. \end{aligned}$$

4.2 Transformation of Processes

Empty Process

$$\Upsilon(0) \stackrel{\text{def}}{=} \varepsilon$$

Empty process 0 means doing nothing, so it can naturally be mapped to ε in MSVL.

Output Action Prefix

$$\Upsilon(\bar{x}\langle y\rangle.P) \stackrel{\text{def}}{=} send(C_x, C_y); \Upsilon(P)$$

Output action prefix guarded process $\bar{x}\langle y\rangle.P$ means it sends y through x and then behaves as P. Since $\bar{x}\langle y\rangle$ is an instantaneous action prefix without waiting for its partner, the process can be mapped to *send*$(C_x, C_y); \Upsilon(P)$ where *send*(C_x, C_y) is an asynchronous sending. C_x and C_y are the corresponding MSVL channels of x and y.

Input Action Prefix

$$\Upsilon(x(y).P) \stackrel{\text{def}}{=} \exists C_y : (\mathsf{frame}(C_y) \wedge (\mathit{receive}(C_x, C_y); \Upsilon(P)))$$

Input action prefix guarded process $x(y).P$ indicates it will accept z from x and then behaves as $\{z/y\}P$. It should be mapped to $\exists C_y : (\mathsf{frame}(C_y) \wedge (\mathit{receive}(C_x, C_y); \Upsilon(P)))$. Here, since y is a bound name and will be substituted later, it should consequently be translated to a local channel. Therefore, the existing quantifier $\exists$ is brought in. Further, $\mathsf{frame}(C_y)$ guarantees that the channel C_y always keeps its old value (or refers to the old channel instance) over an interval if no assignment to C_y is encountered. What accurately happens is that C_y will be assigned the message sent by channel C_x. We assume the message is C_z so that C_y will refer to the same channel instance as C_z. Analogous to $\bar{x}\langle y \rangle$, $x(y)$ is translated into an asynchronous receiving.

Await

$$\Upsilon(await(\bar{x}\langle y \rangle.P)) \stackrel{\text{def}}{=} \mathit{wait\_send}(C_x, C_y); \Upsilon(P)$$
$$\Upsilon(await(x(y).P)) \stackrel{\text{def}}{=} \exists C_y : (\mathsf{frame}(C_y) \wedge (\mathit{wait\_receive}(C_x, C_y); \Upsilon(P)))$$

For derived process $await(P)$ where P is a sending (or receiving) prefix guarded process, since the communication is synchronous, its transformation involves synchronous sending $\mathit{wait\_send}(C_x, C_y)$ and receiving $\mathit{wait\_receive}(C_x, C_y)$. Except for the different communication modes, the transformations of $await\ (\bar{x}\langle y \rangle.P)$ and $await(x(y).P)$ are similar to those of $\bar{x}\langle y \rangle.P$ and $x(y).P$ respectively.

Internal Action Prefix

$$\Upsilon(\tau.P) \stackrel{\text{def}}{=} p_I \wedge \varepsilon; \Upsilon(P)$$

Internal action prefix guarded process $\tau.P$ performs an internal action τ and then behaves as P. It can be mapped to $p_I \wedge \varepsilon; \Upsilon(P)$ in which p_I is a special proposition used to indicate whether or not an internal action takes place.

Property Action Prefix

$$\Upsilon(I_p.P) \stackrel{\text{def}}{=} x_{p_1} = \mathsf{true} \wedge ... \wedge x_{p_n} = \mathsf{true} \wedge skip; \Upsilon(P)$$

where $I_p = \{\tilde{p}_1, ..., \tilde{p}_n\}$. The property action prefix guarded process $I_p.P$ satisfies $p_i (1 \leq i \leq n)$ in the first time unit and then behaves as P. Intuitively, it can be mapped to x_{p_1}=$\mathsf{true} \wedge ... \wedge x_{p_n}$=$\mathsf{true} \wedge skip; \Upsilon(P)$. Here, x_{p_1}, ..., and x_{p_n} are the corresponding boolean variables of p_1, ..., and p_n, respectively.

Time Unit Action Prefix

$$\Upsilon(skip.P) \stackrel{\text{def}}{=} skip; \Upsilon(P)$$

Time unit action prefix guarded process $skip.P$ declares that it will idle in the first time unit and then behave as P. Its transformation is straightforward and it can be mapped to $skip; \Upsilon(P)$.

Empty Action Prefix

$$\Upsilon(\varepsilon.P) \stackrel{\text{def}}{=} \varepsilon; \Upsilon(P)$$

For empty action prefix guarded process $\varepsilon.P$, it will execute an empty transition and then behave as P. Similar to $skip.P$, it is directly translated into $\varepsilon; \Upsilon(P)$.

Nondeterministic Choice

$$\Upsilon(P_1 + P_2) \stackrel{\text{def}}{=} \Upsilon(P_1) \vee \Upsilon(P_2)$$

Structure $P_1 + P_2$ shows that P_1 and P_2 will proceed nondeterminately, so that it can naturally be expressed by a disjunction statement.

Parallel

$$\Upsilon(P_1 \mid P_2) \stackrel{\text{def}}{=} \Upsilon(P_1) \mid\mid \Upsilon(P_2)$$

Parallel composition structure $P_1 \mid P_2$ manifests that P_1 and P_2 execute concurrently and will directly be transformed into a parallel statement.

Match

$$\Upsilon([a_1 = a_2]P) \stackrel{\text{def}}{=} \texttt{if } C_{a_1} = C_{a_2} \texttt{ then } \Upsilon(P) \texttt{ else } \varepsilon$$

Matching structure $[a_1 = a_2]P$ tells us that if a_1 and a_2 are the same name, the process will behave as P, otherwise 0. Its transformation is defined based on the conditional statement and C_{a_1} and C_{a_2} are the corresponding transformed channels of a_1 and a_2, respectively.

Restriction

$$\Upsilon(\nu a\ P) \stackrel{\text{def}}{=} \exists C_a : (\mathsf{frame}(C_a) \wedge \Upsilon(P))$$

Restriction structure $\nu a\ P$ means that the process will behave as P except that the communication by bound name a is forbidden. The bound name will be mapped to local channel C_a so that restriction structure $\nu a\ P$ can be defined by $\exists C_a : (\mathsf{frame}(C_a) \wedge \Upsilon(P))$, where frame is used as in the transformation of the input action prefix guarded structure .

Process Instance

For process instance $A\langle a_1, ..., a_n\rangle$, we assume that $A(x_1, ..., x_n)$ is defined by P_A, so that $A\langle a_1, ..., a_n\rangle = \{\vec{a}/\vec{x}\}P_A$. To transform process instance, we firstly claim a theorem below.

Theorem 1. *Let process* $A(x_1, ..., x_n) \stackrel{\text{def}}{=} P_A$ *and* $A\langle a_1, ..., a_n\rangle = \{\vec{a}/\vec{x}\}P_A$*. If A is recursively called in* P_A *and each A is in the form of* $\pi_1^s + ... + \pi_i^s + \pi_1^{'s}.A\langle x_1, ..., x_n\rangle + ... + \pi_m^{'s}.A\langle x_1, ..., x_n\rangle$*, where,* π_j^s $(1 \leq j \leq i)$ *and* $\pi_k^{'s}$ $(1 \leq k \leq m)$ *denote* $\pi_{j_1}.....\pi_{j_{nj}}$, $\pi_{k_1}.....\pi_{k_{nk}}$*, respectively, then, there exists the least fixed point* $L_{fix}\langle a_1, ..., a_n\rangle$ *of* $A\langle a_1, ..., a_n\rangle$ *such that* $A\langle a_1, ..., a_n\rangle = L_{fix}\langle a_1, ..., a_n\rangle$.

In particular, for a simple definition $A(x_1, ..., x_n) = \pi_1^s + \pi^s.A\ \langle x_1, ..., x_n\rangle$, the least fixed point of $A\langle a_1, ..., a_n\rangle$ is $\{\vec{a}/\vec{x}\}\pi^{s*}.\pi_1^s$. However, in practise, the iterative number of times is deterministic. Therefore, to transform $A\langle a_1, ..., a_n\rangle$ into MSVL, we can specify an arbitrary integer N as number of iteration times to control the recursion. For $A(x_1, ..., x_n)$=$\pi_1^s + ... + \pi_i^s + \pi_1^{'s}.A\langle x_1, ..., x_n\rangle + ... + \pi_m^{'s}.A\langle x_1, ..., x_n\rangle$, the transformation is similar.

Since a process instance can be defined with recursive calls in p-π, its transformation will be divided into three cases:

1. Without recursive calls in the definition of A:

$$\Upsilon(A\langle a_1, ..., a_n\rangle) \stackrel{\text{def}}{=} \{\overrightarrow{C_a}/\overrightarrow{C_x}\}\Upsilon(P_A)$$

   For this kind of process instance, it will be directly translated by substitution. $\overrightarrow{C_a}$ and $\overrightarrow{C_x}$ are the corresponding MSVL channel vectors of $\vec{a}$ and $\vec{x}$. Here, we use a substituting method $\{\overrightarrow{C_a}/\overrightarrow{C_x}\}$ to substitute $\overrightarrow{C_a}$ for $\overrightarrow{C_x}$ so that each C_{x_i} will be substituted by C_{a_i} within the bound scope of $C_{x_i}(1 \leq i \leq n)$ in $\Upsilon(P_A)$.
2. With recursive calls in the definition of A and $A(x_1, ..., x_n)$=π_1^s+$\pi^s.A\langle x_1, ..., x_n\rangle$:

$$\begin{aligned}\Upsilon(A\langle a_1, ..., a_n\rangle) \stackrel{\text{def}}{=} \; & j := 0;\\ & \Upsilon(A_{-1}\langle a_1, ..., a_n\rangle) := \varepsilon;\\ & \Upsilon(A_0\langle a_1, ..., a_n\rangle) := \{\overrightarrow{C_a}/\overrightarrow{C_x}\}\Upsilon(\pi_1^s);\\ & \texttt{while}\ (j < N)\\ & \texttt{do}\ (j := j + 1;\\ & \Upsilon(A_j\langle a_1, ..., a_n\rangle) :=\\ & \{\overrightarrow{C_a}/\overrightarrow{C_x}\}\Upsilon(\pi_1^s) \vee (\{\overrightarrow{C_a}/\overrightarrow{C_x}\}\Upsilon(\pi^s); \Upsilon(A_{j-1}\langle a_1, ..., a_n\rangle)))\end{aligned}$$

   Where N is a constant integer. For this kind process instance, by Theorem 1, a least fixed point can be obtained. In practise, we employ a recursion procedure to get an arbitrary given times iteration result of $A\langle a_1, ..., a_n\rangle$. For process instances with recursive calls in the definition of A and $A(x_1, ..., x_n) = \pi_1^s + ... + \pi_i^s + \pi_1^{'s}.A\langle x_1, ..., x_n\rangle + ... + \pi_m^{'s}.A\langle x_1, ..., x_n\rangle$, the corresponding MSVL programs can be obtained in the same way.
3. With recursive calls in the definition of A but A is not in the form stated in Theorem 1: For this kind process identifier, its behavior may not be convergent so that we cannot directly transform them into MSVL. Further, the following theorem can be proved.

Theorem 2. *The transformation is sound.*

5 Case Study

In this section, we employ a simple time-dependent mobile system modeled by p-π. By the transformation Υ, it will be mapped to an MSVL program and hence verified by techniques of MSVL.

5.1 System Specification

The system consists of a server process S, a client C (the system can be scaled up by increasing the number of clients) and two data service processes D_1 and D_2. The server can communicate with the client and the two data services by sc, sd_1 and sd_2 respectively (in the process identifier definitions, sc', sd_1' and sd_2' are parameters and will be replaced by sc, sd_1 and sd_2). The client utilizes a local channel r to get access to the objective data service (D_1 or D_2) nondeterministically. Each data service process has a local channel d_i(i=1,2) representing the relevant data source. This kind of examples are usually used to explain the mobility of π-calculus. But the existing versions does not consider the time-dependent aspects. Here, we incorporate I_p and $skip$ to model these aspects. Let *PR*= $\{p, w\}$ be the set of propositions where p represents occupying the printer and w the writer.

The system needs to satisfy several time-dependent constraints: (1) A process will be idle if it does nothing (or occupies nothing) for a time unit (denoted by $skip$ in p-π); (2) the usage of the printer and the writer which are shared resources will occupy an interval with one time unit; (3) the usage of the same resource is exclusive, which means a printer (or writer) cannot be occupied by two processes at the same time; (4) the usage of different resources is compatible. For instance, a printer and a writer are able to be used by two processes at the same time.

The system is modeled in p-π as follows.

$$
\begin{aligned}
& \nu\, sc, sd_1, sd_2\ (S\langle sc, sd_1, sd_2\rangle \mid C\langle sc\rangle \mid D_1\langle sd_1\rangle \mid D_2\langle sd_2\rangle) \\
S(sc', sd_1', sd_2') & \stackrel{\text{def}}{=} await(sc'(r_x).(await(\overline{sd_1'}\langle r_x\rangle.\{\tilde{p}\}.skip.S\langle sc', sd_1', sd_2'\rangle)))+ \\
& \quad\ await(sc'(r_x).(await(\overline{sd_2'}\langle s_x\rangle.\{\tilde{p}\}.skip.S\langle sc', sd_1', sd_2'\rangle))) + \tau \\
C(sc') & \stackrel{\text{def}}{=} \nu\, r\ (await(\overline{sc'}\langle r\rangle.await(r(d).\{\tilde{w}\}.skip.C\langle sc'\rangle))) + \tau \\
D_i(sd_i') & \stackrel{\text{def}}{=} \nu\, d_i\ (await(sd_i'(r_y).await(\overline{r_y}\langle d_i\rangle.skip.skip.D_i\langle sd_i'\rangle))) + \tau \\
& \quad\ (i{=}1, 2)
\end{aligned}
$$

In the system, the client sends a service request to the server and the server chooses one data service to link to the client by an abstract channel r_x which will be replaced by channel r. In this way the client can communicate with the objective data service through channel r. Subsequently, the server will occupy the printer for an interval with one time unit($\{\tilde{p}\}$) and the client will occupy the writer for an interval with one time unit ($\{\tilde{w}\}$). Afterwards, the system will idle for a time unit. And then, the system repeatedly execute the procedure or perform an internal action to stop.

5.2 Transformation

By the transformation rules given in section 4, the system will be translated as follows.

$\Upsilon(\nu\ sc, sd_1, sd_2\ S\langle sc, sd_1, sd_2\rangle \mid C\langle sc\rangle \mid D_1\langle sd_1\rangle \mid D_2\langle sd_2\rangle)$
$\equiv \mathsf{prog}_1 \wedge \Upsilon(S\langle sc, sd_1, sd_2\rangle \mid C\langle sc\rangle \mid D_1\langle sd_1\rangle \mid D_2\langle sd_2\rangle)$
$\equiv \mathsf{prog}_1 \wedge (\Upsilon(S\langle sc, sd_1, sd_2\rangle) \mid\mid \Upsilon(C\langle sc\rangle) \mid\mid \Upsilon(D_1\langle sd_1\rangle) \mid\mid \Upsilon(D_2\langle sd_2\rangle))$
$\equiv \mathsf{prog}_1 \wedge ($
$j_1 :=0;$
$\Upsilon(S_{-1}\langle sc, sd_1, sd_2\rangle) :=\varepsilon;$
$\Upsilon(S_0\langle sc, sd_1, sd_2\rangle) :=(p_I \wedge \varepsilon);$
$\texttt{while}\ (j_1 < N_1)$
$\texttt{do}\ (j_1 :=j_1 + 1;$
$\Upsilon(S_{j_1}\langle sc, sd_1, sd_2\rangle) :=$
$(p_I \wedge \varepsilon) \vee (\mathsf{frame}(C_{r_x}) \wedge (\mathit{wait\_receive}(C_{sc}, C_{r_x}); (\mathit{wait\_send}(C_{sd_1}, C_{r_x}); x_p=$
$\mathsf{true} \wedge skip; skip)); \Upsilon(S_{j_1-1}\langle sc, sd_1, sd_2\rangle)) \vee (\mathsf{frame}(C_{r_x}) \wedge (\mathit{wait\_receive}(C_{sc},$
$C_{r_x}); (\mathit{wait\_send}(C_{sd_2}, C_{r_x}); x_p=\mathsf{true} \wedge skip; skip)); \Upsilon(S_{j_1-1}\langle sc, sd_1, sd_2\rangle)))$
$\mid\mid j_2 :=0;$
$\Upsilon(C_{-1}\langle sc\rangle) :=\varepsilon;$
$\Upsilon(C_0\langle sc\rangle) :=(p_I \wedge \varepsilon);$
$\texttt{while}\ (j_2 < N_2)$
$\texttt{do}\ (j_2 :=j_2 + 1;$
$\Upsilon(C_{j_2}\langle sc\rangle) :=$
$(p_I \wedge \varepsilon) \vee (\exists C_r : (\mathsf{frame}(C_r) \wedge (\mathit{wait\_send}(C_{sc}, C_r); \exists C_d : (\mathsf{frame}(C_d) \wedge ($
$\mathit{wait\_receive}(C_r, C_d); x_w=\mathsf{true} \wedge skip; skip)))); \Upsilon(C_{j_2-1}\langle sc\rangle)))$
$\mid\mid j_3 :=0;$
$\Upsilon(D_{1-1}\langle sd_1\rangle) :=\varepsilon;$
$\Upsilon(D_{11}\langle sd_1\rangle) :=(p_I \wedge \varepsilon);$
$\texttt{while}\ (j_3 < N_3)$
$\texttt{do}\ (j_3 :=j_3 + 1;$
$\Upsilon(D_{1j_3}\langle sd_1\rangle) :=$
$(p_I \wedge \varepsilon) \vee (\exists C_{d_1} : (\mathsf{frame}(C_{d_1}) \wedge (\exists C_{r_y} : (\mathsf{frame}(C_{r_y}) \wedge (\mathit{wait\_receive}(C_{sd_1},$
$C_{r_y}); \mathit{wait\_send}(C_{r_y}, C_{d_1}); skip; skip)))); \Upsilon(D_{1j_3-1}\langle sd_1\rangle)))$
$\mid\mid j_4 :=0;$
$\Upsilon(D_{2-1}\langle sd_2\rangle) :=\varepsilon;$
$\Upsilon(D_{21}\langle sd_2\rangle) :=(p_I \wedge \varepsilon);$
$\texttt{while}\ (j_4 < N_4)$
$\texttt{do}\ (j_4 :=j_4 + 1;$
$\Upsilon(D_{2j_4}\langle sd_2\rangle) :=$
$(p_I \wedge \varepsilon) \vee (\exists C_{d_2} : (\mathsf{frame}(C_{d_2}) \wedge (\exists C_{r_y} : (\mathsf{frame}(C_{r_y}) \wedge (\mathit{wait\_receive}(C_{sd_2},$
$C_{r_y}); \mathit{wait\_send}(C_{r_y}, C_{d_2}); skip; skip)))); \Upsilon(D_{2j_4-1}\langle sd_2\rangle))))$
(where prog_1 denotes $\exists C_{sc}, C_{sd_1}, C_{sd_2} : \mathsf{frame}(C_{sc}, C_{sd_1}, C_{sd_2})))$

Where $N_i (1 \leq i \leq 4)$ is a constant integer. According to the obtained MSVL programs, we can verify properties of time–dependent systems modeled in p-π by the modeling, simulation and verification tool based on MSVL. The tool can work in three modes: (1) in the modeling mode, given the MSVL program p of a system, the state space of the system can explicitly be given as an NFG (Normal Form Graph) of p [20]; (2) with the simulation mode, an execution path of the NFG of the system is presented as the output with respect to operational semantics of MSVL [19]; (3) under the verification mode, given a system model described by an MSVL program p, and a property specified by a PPTL (Propositional PTL) formula ϕ, it can automatically check whether the system satisfies the property or not [21]. Limited to the length of the paper, the details of the verification is omitted here.

6 Conclusion

In this paper, we proposed a transformation Υ from p-π processes to MSVL programs. This enables us to make use of the theories and techniques of MSVL to analyze p-π processes. More precisely, p-π is able to model, simulate and verify its processes by means of MSVL. In the future, we will further investigate the possibility for transforming MSVL programs into p-π processes so that a tight relationship between MSVL and p-π could be established. Moreover, several case studies with more practical examples are also required. In addition, supporting tools for transformation between p-π processes and MSVL programs are needed.

References

1. Milner, R.: A Calculus of Communication Systems. LNCS, vol. 92. Springer, Heidelberg (1980)
2. Hoare, C.A.R.: Communicating sequential processes. Prentice-Hall (1985)
3. Bergstra, J.A., Klop, J.W.: Algebra of communicating processes with abstraction. Journal of Theoretical Computer Science 37, 77–121 (1985)
4. Autoren, D., Buxmann, P., Hess, T.: Software as a Service (2008), doi:10.1007/s11576-008-0095-0
5. Ibrahim, M., Holley, K., Josuttis, N.M.: The Future of SOA: What worked, what didn't, and where is it going from here? In: Proceeding of OOPSLA, pp. 21–25 (2007)
6. Armbrust, M., Fox, A., Griffith, R., et al.: Above the Clouds: A Berkeley View of Cloud Computing. Technical Report No. UCB/EECS-2009-28 (2009)
7. Milner, R.: Communicating and Mobile Systems: The π-Calculus. Cambridge University Press (1999)
8. Milner, R., Parrow, J., Walker, D.: A calculus of mobile processes. Inf. Comput. 100, 1–77 (1992)
9. Milner, R., Parrow, J., Walker, D.: Modal logics for mobile processes. Theoret. Comp. Sci. 114, 149–171 (1993)
10. Sangiorgi, D., Walker, D.: The π-calculus: a Theory of Mobile Processes. Cambridge University Press (2002)
11. Sangiorgi, D.: A theory of bisimulation for the π-calculus. In: Best, E. (ed.) CONCUR 1993. LNCS, vol. 715, pp. 127–142. Springer, Heidelberg (1993)
12. Duan, Z., Koutny, M., Holt, C.: Projection in temporal logic programming. In: Pfenning, F. (ed.) LPAR 1994. LNCS, vol. 822, pp. 333–344. Springer, Heidelberg (1994)
13. Duan, Z.: An extended interval temporal logic and a framing technique for temporal logic programming. Ph.D. Thesis, University of Newcastle upon Tyne (1996)
14. Duan, Z.: Temporal logic and temporal logic programming. Science Press, Beijing (2006) ISBN:7-03-016651-5/TP. 3158
15. Duan, Z., Yang, X., Koutny, M.: Framed temporal logic programming. Journal of Science of Computer Programming 70, 31–61 (2008)

16. Zhou, C., Wang, J., Ravn, A.: A formal description of hybrid systems. In: Alur, R., Sontag, E.D., Henzinger, T.A. (eds.) HS 1995. LNCS, vol. 1066, pp. 511–530. Springer, Heidelberg (1996)
17. Zhou, C., Rays, A.P., Hansen, M.R.: An extended duration calculus for hybrid systems. In: Grossman, R.L., Ravn, A.P., Rischel, H., Nerode, A. (eds.) HS 1991 and HS 1992. LNCS, vol. 736, pp. 36–59. Springer, Heidelberg (1993)
18. Yang, X., Duan, Z., Ma, Q.: Axiomatic semantics of projection temporal logic programs. Mathematical Structures in Computer Science 20(5), 865–914 (2010)
19. Yang, X., Duan, Z.: Operational semantics of framed tempura (2008), doi:10. 1016/j. jlap. 2008. 08. 001
20. Duan, Z., Tian, C., Zhang, L.: A decision procedure for propositional projection temporal logic with infinite models. Acta Informatica 45(1), 43–78 (2008)
21. Duan, Z., Tian, C.: A unified model checking approach with projection temporal logic. In: Liu, S., Araki, K. (eds.) ICFEM 2008. LNCS, vol. 5256, pp. 167–186. Springer, Heidelberg (2008)
22. Wang, X., Duan, Z.: Pointers in framing projection temporal logic programming languages. Journal of Xidian University 35(6), 1069–1074 (2008)
23. Luo, L., Duan, Z.: An extended π-calculus. In: Proceeding of CNSI 2012, pp. 632–637 (2012)

On Slicing of Programs with Input Statements*

Härmel Nestra

Institute of Computer Science, University of Tartu
J. Liivi 2, 50409 Tartu, Estonia
harmel.nestra@ut.ee

Abstract. This paper studies program slicing in the presence of input statements. If unnecessary input statements are sliced away, the remaining input statements are assumed to read the same data as within the entire program. For specifying the relation of one program being a slice of another under this assumption, one needs a formalism for treating "stages of computation". This paper presents an approach where stages of computation, called run points, are encoded by rational numbers. Run points of the slice and the corresponding run points of the whole program are encoded by equal numbers. We adapt a program analysis used by a classic slicing algorithm to our setting, in order to prove correctness of the slicing algorithm.

1 Introduction

Program slicing is a program transformation technique for cutting out all code lines that do not contribute to the computation of some special values of interest. These values are specified by a *slicing criterion* which is formally a set of variables coupled together with the program points at which their values are interesting. The result of slicing a program is called a *slice*.

For a standard example, the program in the right is a slice of the program in the left w.r.t. the variable sum at the final program point:

```
sum := 0 ;
prod := 1 ;
i := 0 ;
while i < n do (
  i := i + 1 ;
  sum := sum + i ;
  prod := prod * i
)
```

$\longrightarrow$

```
sum := 0 ;

i := 0 ;
while i < n do (
  i := i + 1 ;
  sum := sum + i

)
```

Namely, all lines that do not contribute to the computation of sum are omitted.

Program slicing is widely used in different branches of software engineering, e.g. debugging. Overviews of program slicing and its numerous applications can be found in Tip [16] or Binkley and Gallagher [2].

* This work was partially supported by the Estonian Science Foundation grant no. 7543, from research theme IUT2-1 and by European Regional Development Fund through the Estonian Center of Excellence in Computer Science (EXCS).

Z. Liu, J. Woodcock, and H. Zhu (Eds.): ICTAC 2013, LNCS 8049, pp. 282–300, 2013.

1.1 Motivation

A slice of a program may be defined as a selection of given lines of code such that, whenever both the given program and the subset are executed under equal circumstances, the sequences of observations (or updates) of the important variables at the important program points are equal. For example, if the two programs above are both executed in the same initial state then both runs give rise to the same 1-element sequence of values of `sum` at the final program point.

We are interested in slicing of programs that consume input during their run, e.g. from keyboard, random number generators, etc. In this case, one must reckon with run-time input when specifying "equal execution circumstances".

Observe that treating the inputs as non-deterministic choices and applying the bisimulation approach, widely used in the works on multi-threaded program slicing (first time in [7]; used also for single-threaded programs, see [17,18]), is not suitable here. In that approach, the updates of important variables during any execution of the original program are required to occur in the same order during at least one possible execution of the slice starting from the same initial state, and vice versa. However, suppose that we slice a program with an input statement as follows, w.r.t. variable `out` at the final point:

```
in := input() ;
in := in + 1 ;
out := in
```

⟶

```
in := input() ;

out := in
```

This "slicing" is clearly flawed as it changes the functional dependence of the important variable `out` on the input. Yet it turns out to be correct in the bisimulation approach, since each value obtained by the variable `out` by the end of executing the first program can also occur as the final value of that variable in the second program (for an input larger by 1) and, similarly, vice versa.

Sivagurunathan et al. [15] treat the whole input stream as an extension of the initial state of program execution. On the other hand, classic algorithms enable the following transformation as slicing w.r.t. variable `out` at the final point:

```
x := input() ;
y := input() ;
out := y
```

⟶

```
y := input() ;
out := y
```

Since `x` is not used for computing `out`, the line defining `x` is omitted. However, if the programs are executed with equal input streams as the approach in [15] assumes, the variable `y` in the slice takes the value that would be spent on `x` by the original program. The programs end up with different values of `out`, whence the second program fails to meet the condition of being a slice of the first one.

The truth is that this transformation may be correct or not, depending on the intended meaning of variable `y`. It is correct if the meaning of `y` does not rely on the previous input of `x`. In this case, the classic approach is preferred to that of [15] as it removes more lines. The approach of [15] applies if `y` is meant to be, say, the second line of the input stream.

In this paper, we assume the first possibility, i.e. that different inputs have independent meaning. Firstly, this case seems to occur quite often in practice. Secondly, this meets the needs that appear in our work on program slicing in the context of transfinite semantics. In transfinite semantics [8,6,12], program execution traces continue after infinite loops from some limit states, and if there is no natural way of determining the value of a variable in a limit state, we specify the value as a random input.

Our idea is to interpret "equal execution circumstances" in the definition of slice as the conjunction of two conditions: (1) the initial states coincide, and (2) the consumed inputs are equal at each "computation stage", or "run points" as we prefer to say, passed through by both runs. The notion of run point is to be defined in a way that makes evident the correspondence of run points of a program and that of its subset programs.

There seems to be a lack of good formalisms for treating computation stages. "Relative points" in Collard [3] capture the idea of computation stage by distinguishing visits of program points during different iterations, but their labels involve program elements, which means that expressing the correspondence of these points in different programs is not easy. Our work makes two contributions:

- Developing a simple mathematical view of run points that identifies the corresponding run points in a program and its subset programs;
- Proving in this setting that a classic slicing method (based on data and control flow analysis, similar to that given by Weiser [19]) is correct.

In the paper, proof details are omitted due to space constraints.

Transfinite semantics is used to ensure the above notion of slice being in accordance with the classic algorithms that can slice away infinite loops [6,9]. In standard semantics, a program that results from removing an infinite loop could visit important program points more times than the original program and the condition of slice would not be satisfied. (For the same reason, other approaches require the sequence of observations of important values during the run of the original program be a prefix of, rather than equal to, the sequence of observations arising from the corresponding run of the slice, so weakening the notion.)

Since standard semantics traces are obtained by truncating the corresponding execution traces in transfinite semantics after the first ω steps, classic correctness of slicing (w.r.t. standard semantics, assuming the classic definition of slice) is a direct consequence of correctness w.r.t. transfinite semantics.

1.2 A Brief Overview of Our Approach

We will denote run points by rational numbers from the interval $[0;1]$. In our opinion, rational numbers are excellently serving the ambition for a simple correspondence between run points of different programs, and they are easier to manipulate than, for example, labels in [3]. In program execution traces, the states will be explicitly indexed by run points. For a toy example, the execution trace of program `z := x ; (x := y ; y := z)` at the initial state

$\left\{\begin{array}{l}\mathtt{x}\mapsto 1\\ \mathtt{y}\mapsto 2\\ \mathtt{z}\mapsto 0\end{array}\right\}$ consists of associations

$$0\mapsto\left\{\begin{array}{l}\mathtt{x}\mapsto 1\\ \mathtt{y}\mapsto 2\\ \mathtt{z}\mapsto 0\end{array}\right\},\quad \frac{1}{2}\mapsto\left\{\begin{array}{l}\mathtt{x}\mapsto 1\\ \mathtt{y}\mapsto 2\\ \mathtt{z}\mapsto 1\end{array}\right\},\quad \frac{3}{4}\mapsto\left\{\begin{array}{l}\mathtt{x}\mapsto 2\\ \mathtt{y}\mapsto 2\\ \mathtt{z}\mapsto 1\end{array}\right\},\quad 1\mapsto\left\{\begin{array}{l}\mathtt{x}\mapsto 2\\ \mathtt{y}\mapsto 1\\ \mathtt{z}\mapsto 1\end{array}\right\},$$

where 0, $\frac{1}{2}$, $\frac{3}{4}$ and 1 are the run points.

Semantics of this kind are called *fractional* in our previous work [10,12]. Whenever a trace is composed of two pieces, the first and second piece are uniformly compressed to the line segments $[0;\frac{1}{2}]$ and $[\frac{1}{2};1]$, respectively. This way, the natural ordering of numbers coincides with the execution order.

Observe that the ordered set of run points of any program with loops is transfinite, even if all run points appear in finite executions. For example, the program **while** `x < 0` **do** `x := x + 1` never runs infinitely, but its run points are $0, \frac{1}{2}, \frac{3}{4}, \frac{7}{8}$, etc. (the largest fraction in use depends on the initial value of x), together with 1. This set corresponds to the transfinite ordinal number $\omega+1$.

In transfinite semantics, the run points beyond a loop are engaged even if the loop runs infinitely. For instance, the consituents of the trace of the program (**while** `true` **do** **skip**) ; `x := x - 1` at the initial state $\{\mathtt{x}\mapsto 1\}$ are $\frac{1}{2}-\frac{1}{2^{i+1}}\mapsto\{\mathtt{x}\mapsto 1\}$ for every $i=0,1,2,\ldots$ together with $\frac{1}{2}\mapsto\{\mathtt{x}\mapsto 1\}$ and $1\mapsto\{\mathtt{x}\mapsto 0\}$. Building up standard semantics in a fractional form causes complications, while defining transfinite fractional semantics is essentially straightforward. This is one more reason for using transfinite semantics in our approach.

Program points can be defined as suitable equivalence classes of run points. Hence a run point uniquely determines a program point but not vice versa. Unlike program points, run points are never visited twice during one run.

2 Syntax

We call our working language **IWhile** (**While** with input expressions). The terms "statement" and "program" will be used as synonyms.

The abstract syntax of **IWhile** is given in Fig. 1. There are two categories of expressions, *Expr* and *IExpr*. The former entails the usual pure expressions but the latter consists of expressions whose value is obtained from input. We do not dig into the exact structure of expressions. For simplicity, we assume that expressions in *Expr* never contain subexpressions from *IExpr* (and have no side effects whatsoever). This does not lose generality as more complex expressions can be simplified via assignments of subexpressions to intermediate variables. With the purpose of reinitialization of variable values in limit states in transfinite semantics, *IExpr* contains a special expression `random`X`()` for every variable X.

A statement **use** $\mathscr{X}$, where $\mathscr{X}$ is a set of variables, declares all variables in $\mathscr{X}$ important at the current point but performs no action (like **skip**). These

Syntactic categories:

Var — the set of all variables
Expr — the set of all usual expressions
IExpr — the set of all input expressions
Stmt — the set of all statements

Grammar:

$$
\begin{aligned}
\mathit{Stmt} \to\ & \mathbf{skip} \\
\mid\ & \mathbf{use}\ \{\mathit{Var}, \ldots, \mathit{Var}\} \\
\mid\ & \mathit{Var}\ \texttt{:=}\ \mathit{Expr} \\
\mid\ & \mathit{Var}\ \texttt{:=}\ \mathit{IExpr} \\
\mid\ & \mathit{Stmt}\ ;\ \mathit{Stmt} \\
\mid\ & \mathbf{if}\ \mathit{Expr}\ \mathbf{then}\ \mathit{Stmt} \\
\mid\ & \mathbf{while}\ \mathit{Expr}\ \mathbf{do}\ \mathit{Stmt}
\end{aligned}
$$

Fig. 1. Abstract syntax of **IWhile**

$$
\frac{}{\mathbf{skip} \sqsubseteq S} \qquad \frac{}{\mathbf{use}\ \mathscr{X} \sqsubseteq \mathbf{use}\ \mathscr{X}} \qquad \frac{}{X\ \texttt{:=}\ E \sqsubseteq X\ \texttt{:=}\ E} \qquad \frac{}{X\ \texttt{:=}\ R \sqsubseteq X\ \texttt{:=}\ R}
$$

$$
\frac{S_1 \sqsubseteq T_1 \qquad S_2 \sqsubseteq T_2}{S_1\ ;\ S_2 \sqsubseteq T_1\ ;\ T_2} \qquad \frac{S \sqsubseteq T}{\mathbf{if}\ E\ \mathbf{then}\ S \sqsubseteq \mathbf{if}\ E\ \mathbf{then}\ T}
$$

$$
\frac{S \sqsubseteq T}{\mathbf{while}\ E\ \mathbf{do}\ S \sqsubseteq \mathbf{while}\ E\ \mathbf{do}\ T}
$$

Fig. 2. The subset program relation

statements are introduced for representing slicing criteria as parts of code and thereby avoiding the need for keeping track of slicing criteria separately. Note that, again for simplicity, our conditional statements have no else branch.

Being a slice first of all means being a subset program. Instead of removing code lines to obtain a subset, we replace them with **skip** (as do other theoretical works on program slicing). This simplifies the formal treatment as the original program structure is maintained. The precise meaning of the subset relation $\sqsubseteq$ in this setting is specified by the inductive derivation rules in Fig. 2. There and later on, E and R denote usual and input expressions, respectively.

For example, statements (**while** `x < 0` **do** **skip**) ; `x := x - 1` and **skip** ; `x := x - 1`, as well as **skip** alone, are subset programs of the statement (**while** `x < 0` **do** `x := x + 1`) ; `x := x - 1`.

Proposition 1. *The relation $\sqsubseteq$ is a partial order on* Stmt*.*

3 Run Points and Program Points

As briefly described in Sect. 1, we encode run points by rational numbers from the line interval $[0;1]$ and program points by certain equivalence classes of run

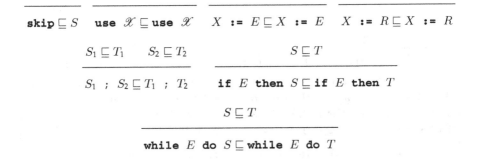

$$
\begin{array}{lcl}
\mathrm{RP}\ (\mathbf{skip}) & = & \{0,1\} \\
\mathrm{RP}\ (\mathbf{use}\ \mathscr{X}) & = & \{0,1\} \\
\mathrm{RP}\ (X\ \mathtt{:=}\ E) & = & \{0,1\} \\
\mathrm{RP}\ (X\ \mathtt{:=}\ R) & = & \{0,1\} \\
\mathrm{RP}\ (T_1\ ;\ T_2) & = & \{[0;1] \Mapsto [0;\frac{1}{2}]\}^{\sharp}(\mathrm{RP}\,T_1) \cup \{[0;1] \Mapsto [\frac{1}{2};1]\}^{\sharp}(\mathrm{RP}\,T_2) \\
\mathrm{RP}\ (\mathbf{if}\ E\ \mathbf{then}\ T) & = & \{0\} \cup \{[0;1] \Mapsto [\frac{1}{2};1]\}^{\sharp}(\mathrm{RP}\,T) \\
\mathrm{RP}\ (\mathbf{while}\ E\ \mathbf{do}\ T) & = & \{0,1\} \cup \bigcup_{i\in\mathbb{N}^+} \{[0;1] \Mapsto [1-\frac{1}{2^{2i-1}};1-\frac{1}{2^{2i}}]\}^{\sharp}(\mathrm{RP}\,T)
\end{array}
$$

Fig. 3. Run points of statements

points. As a tentative yet rather imprecise intuition, one may interpret a run point as the percentage of the execution that is over at this point. The truth in this intuition is that run points always grow as computation goes on.

Denote $\mathbb{N} = \{0,1,2,\ldots\}$ and $\mathbb{N}^+ = \mathbb{N} \setminus \{0\}$. The set of all subsets of a set A is denoted by $\wp(A)$. Whenever α is a function or partial function from A to B, denote by $\alpha^{\sharp}$ the complete union-homomorphic extension of α that works from $\wp(A)$ to $\wp(B)$. In other words, $\alpha^{\sharp}(U)$ denotes the image of set U under mapping α.

The set $\mathrm{RP}\,S$ of *run points* of statement S is defined inductively on the structure of S as shown in Fig. 3. Run point sets of compound programs are constructed by compressing the run point sets of the constituent programs uniformly via linear mappings to fit the sets to some disjoint smaller intervals that altogether cover the whole $[0;1]$. We denote the unique linear function that transforms the interval $[r;q]$ to the interval $[a;b]$ by $\{[r;q] \Mapsto [a;b]\}$, i.e., $\{[r;q] \Mapsto [a;b]\} = \lambda x.\, a + \frac{b-a}{q-r} \cdot (x - r)$. For instance, $\{[0;1] \Mapsto [0;\frac{1}{2}]\} = \lambda x.\, \frac{1}{2}x$ and $\{[0;1] \Mapsto [\frac{1}{2};1]\} = \lambda x.\, \frac{1}{2}x + \frac{1}{2}$.

The composition case and the loop case in Fig. 3 are explained by the examples in Subsect. 1.2. In the conditional case, 0 represents the test point (whether the branch should be taken or not) and the points in $[\frac{1}{2};1]$ represent the branch (1 represents the point where both paths through the program join together).

Proposition 2. *Every run point of every statement is a rational number in the line interval* $[0;1]$ *representable as a proper fraction whose denominator is a power of* 2. *Both* 0 *and* 1 *are run points of any statement.*

Program points as equivalence classes of run points are specified by choosing a representative from each desired class. This is implemented by the definition in Fig. 4. For each $S \in \mathit{Stmt}$, the function $\mathrm{pp}(S) \in \mathrm{RP}\,S \to \mathrm{RP}\,S$ finds the least run point representing the same program point in S as the given run point.

The functions are defined inductively on the structure of S, and by pattern match on the cases of the definition of RP. In the four base cases of program structure, each run point represents itself as a program point. In the composition case, run points of both immediate constituents maintain their representatives (relative to the corresponding linear transformations). In the conditional case,

$$
\begin{array}{llcl}
\mathrm{pp} & (\mathtt{skip}) & (a) & = a \\
\mathrm{pp} & (\mathtt{use}\ \mathscr{X}) & (a) & = a \\
\mathrm{pp} & (X\ \mathtt{:=}\ E) & (a) & = a \\
\mathrm{pp} & (X\ \mathtt{:=}\ R) & (a) & = a \\
\mathrm{pp} & (T_1\ ;\ T_2) & (\{[0;1] \mapsto [0;\tfrac{1}{2}]\}(r)) & = \{[0;1] \mapsto [0;\tfrac{1}{2}]\}(\mathrm{pp}(T_1)(r)) \\
\mathrm{pp} & (T_1\ ;\ T_2) & (\{[0;1] \mapsto [\tfrac{1}{2};1]\}(q)) & = \{[0;1] \mapsto [\tfrac{1}{2};1]\}(\mathrm{pp}(T_2)(q)) \\
\mathrm{pp} & (\mathtt{if}\ E\ \mathtt{then}\ T) & (0) & = 0 \\
\mathrm{pp} & (\mathtt{if}\ E\ \mathtt{then}\ T) & (\{[0;1] \mapsto [\tfrac{1}{2};1]\}(q)) & = \{[0;1] \mapsto [\tfrac{1}{2};1]\}(\mathrm{pp}(T)(q)) \\
\mathrm{pp} & (\mathtt{while}\ E\ \mathtt{do}\ T) & (1) & = 1 \\
\mathrm{pp} & (\mathtt{while}\ E\ \mathtt{do}\ T) & (1 - \tfrac{1}{2^{2i}}) & = 0 \\
\mathrm{pp} & (\mathtt{while}\ E\ \mathtt{do}\ T) & (\{[0;1] \mapsto [1 - \tfrac{1}{2^{2i-1}}; 1 - \tfrac{1}{2^{2i}}]\}(q)) & = \{[0;1] \mapsto [\tfrac{1}{2};\tfrac{3}{4}]\}(\mathrm{pp}(T)(q))
\end{array}
$$

Fig. 4. The canonical representatives of program points

0 represents itself and all other run points maintain their representatives (relative to the linear transformation). In the loop case, 1 represents itself. All run points of the form $1 - \dfrac{1}{2^{2i}}$ (standing for the loop predicate test point) are represented by 0. The run points of any iteration of the loop body are mapped to the representative of the corresponding run point in the first iteration.

Proposition 3. *Let* $S \in \mathit{Stmt}$.

(i) *For every* $r \in \mathrm{RP}\, S$, $\mathrm{pp}(S)(\mathrm{pp}(S)(r)) = \mathrm{pp}(S)(r)$.

(ii) *For every* $r \in \mathrm{RP}\, S$, $\mathrm{pp}(S)(r) \leq r$.

The way of defining subset program relation was chosen with the aim of maintaining the program structure and, in particular, the formal denotations of the corresponding run points. Proposition 4 states the desired properties: a subset program inherits all its run points from the whole program and they split into program point classes along the same lines as in the whole program.

Proposition 4. *Let* S, T *be statements such that* $S \sqsubseteq T$.

(i) *Then* $\mathrm{RP}\, S \subseteq \mathrm{RP}\, T$.

(ii) *Let* $a_1, a_2 \in \mathrm{RP}\, S$. *Then* $\mathrm{pp}(S)(a_1) = \mathrm{pp}(S)(a_2)$ *iff* $\mathrm{pp}(T)(a_1) = \mathrm{pp}(T)(a_2)$.

Proof. By induction on the derivation of $S \sqsubseteq T$ using the rules in Fig. 2. □

4 Semantics

In this section, we present the transfinite fractional semantics that will be used in Sect. 6 for formalization of our results about program slicing. The semantics is similar to fractional semantics in our earlier papers [10,12] but some details are different. Most notably, the fractional semantics in this paper involves "input contexts" associated with run points.

We denote the set of all functions and partial functions from A to B by $A \to B$ and $A \dashrightarrow B$, respectively. The domain of a partial function f (i.e. the set of arguments on which the function is defined) is denoted by $\mathsf{dom}\, f$.

Variable states are functions in $\mathit{Var} \to \mathsf{Val}$ where Val is the set of all values. *Input contexts* are functions in $\mathit{IExpr} \to \mathsf{Val}$. The input context associated with a run point determines the results of input operations at that run point. *Configurations* that fractional traces consist of are functions in $\mathit{Conf}_{\mathsf{FS}} = \mathit{Var} \cup \mathit{IExpr} \to \mathsf{Val}$. So a configuration is a variable state joined together with an input context.

All fractional traces come from a set $\mathit{Base}_{\mathsf{FS}}$ defined later in Fig. 5. We do not encode the dependence on input contexts as a direct parametricity. Instead, the semantics of a program is the set of all traces of configurations that can be observed during a run of the program, with input context changing freely at each computation step. (Likewise, a deterministic standard semantics of a program can be expressed as a set of execution traces that exhausts all initial states rather than as a function mapping each initial state to the corresponding single trace.) Therefore, the meanings of programs come from the powerset $\wp(\mathit{Base}_{\mathsf{FS}})$.

Defining the set $\mathit{Base}_{\mathsf{FS}}$ of all admissible fractional traces requires special attention. Essentially, fractional traces are partial functions from $[0;1]$ to $\mathit{Conf}_{\mathsf{FS}}$, whereby the domain must be included in the set of run points of the program whose execution trace it is and contain at least 0 (the initial configuration) and 1 (the final configuration). As our previous work [9,12] suggested, whenever a loop body is executed an infinite number of times, the configuration that immediately follows the loop must keep all values of variables that are the same at all but finitely many visits of the condition test point of this loop. Any other variable X can obtain a random value after the loop, which means in our approach that the value obtained must coincide with the value of the function `randomX ()` in the input context. We call traces that follow this restriction transfinitely sound.

The run points of a loop corresponding to its predicate test are $1 - \frac{1}{2^{2i}}$ with $i \in \mathbb{N}$. This gives rise to Definition 5 (as testing does not change the variable state, we may also include the immediately following run points $1 - \frac{1}{2^{2i+1}}$):

Definition 5.

(i) *Let* $v_0, v_1, \ldots$ *be a stream of values such that, for some* $w \in \mathsf{Val}$ *and* $n \in \mathbb{N}$, $v_i = w$ *whenever* $i \geqslant n$. *Then denote* $\lim_i v_i = w$; *otherwise,* $\lim_i v_i$ *is undefined.*

(ii) *Let* $l \in [0;1] \dashrightarrow \mathit{Conf}_{\mathsf{FS}}$ *such that* $\mathsf{dom}\, l \supseteq \{0,1\}$. *Call* l transfinitely sound *if, provided that* $\mathsf{dom}\, l \ni 1 - \frac{1}{2^i}$ *for every* $i \in \mathbb{N}$, *it satisfies both following conditions for all* $X \in \mathit{Var}$:

1. *if* $\lim_i \left(l\left(1 - \frac{1}{2^i}\right)(X) \right)$ *is defined then* $l(1)(X) = \lim_i \left(l\left(1 - \frac{1}{2^i}\right)(X) \right)$;
2. *if* $\lim_i \left(l\left(1 - \frac{1}{2^i}\right)(X) \right)$ *is undefined then* $l(1)(X) = l(1)(\mathtt{randomX}\ ())$.

In particular, if $\mathrm{dom}\, l \not\ni 1 - \frac{1}{2^i}$ for some $i \in \mathbb{N}$ then l is transfinitely sound.

The details of the semantics of expressions, denoted by e, are not important in this work and they are left unspecified. The definition of fractional semantics of statements, denoted by s_{FS}, is given in Fig. 5. We assume everywhere that expressions and statements are syntactically correct. If $X \subseteq \mathrm{dom}\, f$, denote by $f|_X$ the restriction of f to X (i.e., a function with domain X that works like f).

In the composition case and in the definition of the function g_{FS} in the loop case, new fractional traces are composed by compressing and joining existing traces together. A trace $u \in \mathit{Base}_{\mathsf{FS}}$ compressed to some interval $[a;b]$ is expressed as function composition $\{[a;b] \Rightarrow [0;1]\}\ ;\ u$ (in composition denoted by semicolon, the function in the left is applied first). For example, the union $(\{[0;\frac{1}{2}] \Rightarrow [0;1]\}\ ;\ u) \cup (\{[\frac{1}{2};1] \Rightarrow [0;1]\}\ ;\ v)$ in the composition case projects the traces u and v side-by-side into the interval $[0;1]$.

Note that the big unions in the last three cases join singleton sets (this notation is preferred to set comprehension for making the formulae shorter).

As the set $\mathit{Sem}_{\mathsf{FS}}$ forms a complete lattice w.r.t. $\subseteq$ and the function g_{FS} is monotone, basic domain theory implies that the greatest fixpoint $\mathrm{gfp}\, g_{\mathsf{FS}}$ is well defined. It turns out that g_{FS} is even cocontinuous w.r.t. $\subseteq$ (i.e., g_{FS} preserves greatest lower bounds of non-empty chains). By Kleene's theorem, the loop semantics can be expressed as the limit of a stream of iterations. Cocontinuity can be proven in the lines of our previous work [12][1].

The set $\mathit{Base}_{\mathsf{FS}}$ also includes fake traces with domains $\{0, \frac{1}{3}, 1\}$, $\{0, \frac{1}{4}, \frac{3}{4}, 1\}$ etc.. These do not harm the semantics as the recurrent definition assures the repeated binary division of the initial segment $[0;1]$ illustrated in Subsect. 1.2. Transfinite soundness does not follow from the structure of the definition, whence this restriction had to be imposed explicitly. Without it, the greatest fixpoint would embrace traces with the right structure but wrong limit configurations.

Coinduction in the following form is a well-known tool for proving equality of finite or infinite (but not transfinite) lists: If there is a binary relation on lists such that each two related lists have a common non-empty initial segment whereby the remaining parts are related again, then being related implies being equal. A similar principle, based on dividing execution traces into two parts at run point $\frac{3}{4}$, is established for fractional semantics in the form of Proposition 6.

Proposition 6. *Let $\sim$ be a binary relation on $\mathit{Base}_{\mathsf{FS}}$ such that $u \sim v$ always implies either $u = v$ or all the following three assertions:*

[1] This refers to Theorem 13 of [12]. That theorem was stated universally for many semantics, but is actually incorrect in the case of ordinal transfinite semantics (not considered here). The error lies in Proposition 7 of [12] (injectivity of trace composition) that the later proofs in [12] rely on. The error does not have serious consequences since the ordinal transfinite semantics in the form of greatest fixpoint is anyway inappropriate for practical use (as already explained in [12]). For fractional semantics, the injectivity statement and hence also the cocontinuity result holds.

Val	the set of all values, including integers and truth values
$State = Var \to Val$	the set of variable evaluations (states)
$ICxt = IExpr \to Val$	the set of input expression evaluations (input contexts)

$$\begin{aligned} Conf_{\mathsf{FS}} &= Var \cup IExpr \to Val \\ Base_{\mathsf{FS}} &= \{l \in [0;1] \dashrightarrow Conf_{\mathsf{FS}} : \operatorname{dom} l \supseteq \{0,1\} \wedge l \text{ is transfinitely sound}\} \\ Sem_{\mathsf{FS}} &= \wp(Base_{\mathsf{FS}}) \end{aligned}$$

e	$\in Expr \to (State \to Val)$	semantics of expressions
s_{FS}	$\in Stmt \to Sem_{\mathsf{FS}}$	fractional semantics of statements

$$s_{\mathsf{FS}}(\mathtt{skip}) = \{\{0 \mapsto s, 1 \mapsto t\} : t|_{Var} = s|_{Var}\}$$

$$s_{\mathsf{FS}}(\mathtt{use}\ \mathscr{X}) = \{\{0 \mapsto s, 1 \mapsto t\} : t|_{Var} = s|_{Var}\}$$

$$s_{\mathsf{FS}}(X\ \mathtt{:=}\ E) = \left\{\{0 \mapsto s, 1 \mapsto t\} : t|_{Var\setminus\{X\}} = s|_{Var\setminus\{X\}} \wedge t(X) = e(E)(s|_{Var})\right\}$$

$$s_{\mathsf{FS}}(X\ \mathtt{:=}\ R) = \left\{\{0 \mapsto s, 1 \mapsto t\} : t|_{Var\setminus\{X\}} = s|_{Var\setminus\{X\}} \wedge t(X) = t(R)\right\}$$

$$s_{\mathsf{FS}}(T_1\ ;\ T_2) = \bigcup_{\substack{u \in s_{\mathsf{FS}}(T_1) \\ v \in s_{\mathsf{FS}}(T_2) \\ u(1) = v(0)}} \{(\{[0;\tfrac{1}{2}] \Rightarrow [0;1]\} ; u) \cup (\{[\tfrac{1}{2};1] \Rightarrow [0;1]\} ; v)\}$$

$$s_{\mathsf{FS}}(\mathtt{if}\ E\ \mathtt{then}\ T) = \{\{0 \mapsto s, 1 \mapsto t\} : t|_{Var} = s|_{Var} \wedge e(E)(s|_{Var}) = \mathrm{ff}\} \cup \bigcup_{\substack{v \in s_{\mathsf{FS}}(T) \\ s|_{Var} = v(0)|_{Var} \\ e(E)(s|_{Var}) = \mathrm{tt}}} \{\{0 \mapsto s\} \cup (\{[\tfrac{1}{2};1] \Rightarrow [0;1]\} ; v)\}$$

$s_{\mathsf{FS}}(\mathtt{while}\ E\ \mathtt{do}\ T) = \operatorname{gfp} g_{\mathsf{FS}}$ where gfp is defined w.r.t. $\subseteq$ and

$$g_{\mathsf{FS}}(X) = \{\{0 \mapsto s, 1 \mapsto t\} : t|_{Var} = s|_{Var} \wedge e(E)(s|_{Var}) = \mathrm{ff}\} \cup \bigcup_{\substack{v \in s_{\mathsf{FS}}(T), x \in X \\ s|_{Var} = v(0)|_{Var} \\ v(1) = x(0) \\ e(E)(s|_{Var}) = \mathrm{tt}}} \{\{0 \mapsto s\} \cup (\{[\tfrac{1}{2};\tfrac{3}{4}] \Rightarrow [0;1]\} ; v) \cup (\{[\tfrac{3}{4};1] \Rightarrow [0;1]\} ; x)\}$$

Fig. 5. Transfinite fractional semantics

1. $\frac{3}{4} \in \operatorname{dom} u \cap \operatorname{dom} v$;
2. $u(r) = v(r)$ *for all* $r \in \operatorname{dom} u \cap \operatorname{dom} v$ *such that* $r < \frac{3}{4}$;
3. $\{[0;1] \Rightarrow [\frac{3}{4};1]\} ; u \sim \{[0;1] \Rightarrow [\frac{3}{4};1]\} ; v$.

Then $u \sim v$ *always implies* $u(r) = v(r)$ *for all* $r \in \operatorname{dom} u \cap \operatorname{dom} v$ *such that* $r < 1$. *If either of* $\left\{i \in \mathbb{N} : 1 - \frac{1}{2^{2i}} \in \operatorname{dom} u\right\}$ *and* $\left\{i \in \mathbb{N} : 1 - \frac{1}{2^{2i}} \in \operatorname{dom} v\right\}$ *is finite, or they are both infinite and* $u(1)|_{IExpr} = v(1)|_{IExpr}$, *then the conclusion holds also for* $r = 1$. *If clause 2 can be sharpened with* $r \in \operatorname{dom} u \iff r \in \operatorname{dom} v$ *for all* $r < \frac{3}{4}$ *then, in addition,* $u \sim v$ *implies* $\operatorname{dom} u = \operatorname{dom} v$.

Proof. The claims for the case $r < 1$ are expressed as the conjunction of claims for r such that $1 - \frac{1}{2^{2i}} \leqslant r < 1 - \frac{1}{2^{2(i+1)}}$, $i \in \mathbb{N}$, and proven by induction on i. The case $r = 1$, if the loop is infinite, follows from transfinite soundness. □

The fractional semantics can be called deterministic if, besides the initial state, the entire input context at all run points is considered the input of the program. The semantics can be rewritten in a form that makes the functional dependence of the trace on the initial state and the input context explicit, but we have preferred the set form here for simplicity.

The details of this determinism are established by Proposition 7. The first part states that the semantics of any program contains a fractional trace with given initial state and input contexts, and the other part states uniqueness of this trace. Describing the precise assumptions of the uniqueness property needs care since the sets of run points used by different fractional traces of the same program need not be the same.

Proposition 7. *Let $S \in \mathit{Stmt}$.*

(i) *Let $s \in \mathit{State}$ and $c \in \mathrm{RP}\, S \to \mathit{ICxt}$. Then there exists $u \in s_{\mathsf{FS}}(S)$ such that $u(0)|_{\mathit{Var}} = s$ and $u(r)|_{\mathit{IExpr}} = c(r)$ for every $r \in \mathrm{dom}\, u$.*

(ii) *Let $u_1, u_2 \in s_{\mathsf{FS}}(S)$ such that $u_1(0)|_{\mathit{Var}} = u_2(0)|_{\mathit{Var}}$ and, for every $r \in \mathrm{dom}\, u_1 \cap \mathrm{dom}\, u_2$, the equality $u_1(r)|_{\mathit{IExpr}} = u_2(r)|_{\mathit{IExpr}}$ holds. Then $u_1 = u_2$.*

Proof. By induction on the structure of S. □

5 Relevant Sets

The Relevant Sets (RS) analysis is the main component of a classic approach to automated program slicing [2]. It aims to calculate, at every program point, the set of all variables influencing the values specified by the slicing criterion. This backward static analysis is non-standard since the underlying graph must include control dependence edges [16,2] in addition to the usual control flow edges. If the control flow is fully structured, control dependence edges point from the head of a conditional or loop statement to all statements immediately embraced by it. Whenever a code line inside a conditional or loop statement is kept, the variables that the control predicate of the statement refers to must be considered relevant.

Usually, representations of program analyses assume a control flow graph as the underlying structure. In order to avoid complicating the picture with alternative structures, we present the RS analysis as a non-standard compositional semantics s_{RS}. The RS semantics of a program consists of traces that associate with each run point the set of variables relevant at that point. The necessary specifications are given in Fig. 6.

We use a fictive variable incl as a flag for marking run points that start a statement that must occur in the slice. For example, as all use statements are always included, any relevant set observed at a run point that starts a use statement must contain incl.

Like $\mathit{Sem}_{\mathsf{FS}}$, the set $\mathit{Sem}_{\mathsf{RS}}$ also consists of sets of traces, but not all subsets of $\mathit{Base}_{\mathsf{RS}}$ are included and the lattice operations are different. The sets in $\mathit{Sem}_{\mathsf{RS}}$ encode monotone functions that map final configurations to whole RS traces, and the lattice order $\ddot{\subseteq}$ is given pointwise according to this interpretation. So $U \ddot{\subseteq} V$ means that, for every $u \in U$ and $v \in V$, if $u(1) = v(1)$ then $u \dot{\subseteq} v$, where the latter order $\dot{\subseteq}$ is again pointwise (on $[0;1]$). Definition 8 provides the precise conditions for sets being included in $\mathit{Sem}_{\mathsf{RS}}$.

Definition 8. *A set $U \in \wp(\mathit{Base}_{\mathsf{RS}})$ is* feasible *if both following conditions hold:*

1. *(Soundness) For all $t \in \mathit{Conf}_{\mathsf{RS}}$, there exists a $u \in U$ such that $u(1) = t$;*
2. *(Monotonicity) For all $u_1, u_2 \in U$, if $u_1(1) \subseteq u_2(1)$ then $u_1 \dot{\subseteq} u_2$, where $\dot{\subseteq}$ is the pointwise ordering of partial functions from $[0;1]$ to the powerset $\mathit{Conf}_{\mathsf{RS}}$ with the usual inclusion order (undefinedness being even less than $\varnothing$).*

In particular, monotonicity implies that the final configuration always determines the whole trace. Indeed, if $u_1(1) = u_2(1)$ then we have both $u_1(1) \subseteq u_2(1)$ and $u_2(1) \subseteq u_1(1)$, implying both $u_1 \dot{\subseteq} u_2$ and $u_2 \dot{\subseteq} u_1$, i.e., $u_1 = u_2$. In other words, the relevant set one associates with the final point determines the result of the analysis. We call this property *backward determinacy.*

Monotonicity also implies *chain completeness* in the following form: if traces $l_i \in U$, $i \in I$, form a non-empty chain then $\dot{\bigcup_{i \in I}} l_i \in U$ (where $\dot{\bigcup}$ is the join operation corresponding to the order $\dot{\subseteq}$). This claim holds since, by finiteness of Var, the set $\{l_i(1) \ : \ i \in I\}$ is always finite and thus, by backward determinacy, also the set $\{l_i \ : \ i \in I\}$ is finite, whence it contains its least upper bound.

The construction of the semantics assures that $\mathrm{dom}\, u = \mathrm{RP}(S)$ for arbitrary $S \in \mathit{Stmt}$ and $u \in s_{\mathsf{RS}}(S)$. The cases of the definition of s_{RS} reflect the information flow through the edges in the RS analysis. A **skip** does not change the set of relevant variables; as this statement can be omitted from the program, the relevant set does not contain incl. Similarly, use $\mathscr{X}$ maintains the variables in the relevant set, but adds all variables in $\mathscr{X}$ as relevant. In the case of an ordinary assignment X **:=** E, if X is relevant after the statement then variables referred to by E (the set of all such is denoted by $\mathrm{ref}\, E$) are added as relevant while X is deleted. Also incl is added to indicate that this assignment must stay. If X is not relevant after the assignment then the relevant variables do not change and incl is excluded. The action corresponding to input assignments is similar but no new variables are added as input expressions do not depend on variables.

The equality $s = \mathrm{cd}(E, v)$, required in the conditional and loop cases, encodes the information flow along control dependence edges. If at least one statement is kept in the part of the program that control depends on the predicate E, i.e. if $\exists r \in \mathrm{dom}\, v \setminus \{1\}\, (\mathrm{incl} \in v(r))$ is true, then s includes $\mathrm{ref}\, E \cup \{\mathrm{incl}\}$ in addition to the initial state of the trace v of the body. Note that RS is a least fixpoint semantics since static analyses cannot reckon with infinite calculations.

$$\begin{aligned} \mathit{Conf}_{\mathsf{RS}} &= \wp(\mathit{Var} \cup \{\mathrm{incl}\}) \\ \mathit{Base}_{\mathsf{RS}} &= \{l \in [0;1] \dashrightarrow \mathit{Conf}_{\mathsf{RS}} \;:\; \mathrm{dom}\, l \supseteq \{0,1\}\} \\ \mathit{Sem}_{\mathsf{RS}} &= \{U \in \wp(\mathit{Base}_{\mathsf{RS}}) : U \text{ is feasible in the sense of Definition 8}\} \end{aligned}$$

$$s_{\mathsf{RS}} \in \mathit{Stmt} \to \mathit{Sem}_{\mathsf{RS}}$$

$$s_{\mathsf{RS}}\ (\mathbf{skip}) = \{\{0 \mapsto s, 1 \mapsto t\} \;:\; s = t\}$$

$$s_{\mathsf{RS}}\ (\mathbf{use}\ \mathscr{X}) = \{\{0 \mapsto s, 1 \mapsto t\} \;:\; s = t \cup \mathscr{X} \cup \{\mathrm{incl}\}\}$$

$$s_{\mathsf{RS}}\ (X \mathrel{\mathbf{:=}} E) = \left\{\{0 \mapsto s, 1 \mapsto t\} \;:\; s = \begin{cases} (t \setminus \{X\}) \cup \mathrm{ref}\, E \cup \{\mathrm{incl}\} & \text{if } X \in t \\ t \setminus \{\mathrm{incl}\} & \text{otherwise} \end{cases}\right\}$$

$$s_{\mathsf{RS}}\ (X \mathrel{\mathbf{:=}} R) = \left\{\{0 \mapsto s, 1 \mapsto t\} \;:\; s = \begin{cases} (t \setminus \{X\}) \cup \{\mathrm{incl}\} & \text{if } X \in t \\ t \setminus \{\mathrm{incl}\} & \text{otherwise} \end{cases}\right\}$$

$$s_{\mathsf{RS}}\ (T_1\ ;\ T_2) = \bigcup_{\substack{u \in s_{\mathsf{RS}}(T_1) \\ v \in s_{\mathsf{RS}}(T_2) \\ u(1) = v(0)}} \{(\{[0;\tfrac{1}{2}] \Rightarrow [0;1]\} \,;\, u) \cup (\{[\tfrac{1}{2};1] \Rightarrow [0;1]\} \,;\, v)\}$$

$$s_{\mathsf{RS}}\ (\mathbf{if}\ E\ \mathbf{then}\ T) = \{\{0 \mapsto s, 1 \mapsto t\} \;:\; s = t \setminus \{\mathrm{incl}\}\} \,\ddot{\cup} \bigcup_{\substack{v \in s_{\mathsf{RS}}(T) \\ s = \mathrm{cd}(E,v)}} \{\{0 \mapsto s\} \cup (\{[\tfrac{1}{2};1] \Rightarrow [0;1]\} \,;\, v)\}$$

$$s_{\mathsf{RS}}\ (\mathbf{while}\ E\ \mathbf{do}\ T) = \mathrm{lfp}\, g_{\mathsf{RS}} \quad \text{where lfp is defined w.r.t. } \ddot{\subseteq} \text{ and}$$

$$g_{\mathsf{RS}}(X) = \{\{0 \mapsto s, 1 \mapsto t\} \;:\; s = t \setminus \{\mathrm{incl}\}\} \,\ddot{\cup} \bigcup_{\substack{v \in s_{\mathsf{RS}}(T) \\ x \in X \\ s = \mathrm{cd}(E,v) \\ v(1) = x(0)}} \{\{0 \mapsto s\} \cup (\{[\tfrac{1}{2};\tfrac{3}{4}] \Rightarrow [0;1]\} \,;\, v) \cup (\{[\tfrac{3}{4};1] \Rightarrow [0;1]\} \,;\, x)\}$$

$$\text{where } \mathrm{cd}(E,v) = \begin{cases} v(0) \cup \mathrm{ref}\, E \cup \{\mathrm{incl}\} & \text{if } \exists r \in \mathrm{dom}\, v \setminus \{1\}\ (\mathrm{incl} \in v(r)) \\ v(0) & \text{otherwise} \end{cases}$$

Fig. 6. Relevant Sets semantics

Example 9. If

$$S = \mathbf{if}\ \mathtt{n}\ \mathtt{>}\ \mathtt{0}\ \mathbf{then}\ ((\mathtt{in} \mathrel{\mathbf{:=}} \mathtt{input()}\ ;\ \mathtt{out} \mathrel{\mathbf{:=}} \mathtt{in})\ ;\ \mathbf{use}\ \{\mathtt{out}\}),$$

then the trace $u \in s_{\mathsf{RS}}(S)$ where $u(1) = \varnothing$ consists of

$$0 \mapsto \{\mathtt{n}, \mathrm{incl}\},\quad \frac{1}{2} \mapsto \{\mathrm{incl}\},\quad \frac{5}{8} \mapsto \{\mathtt{in}, \mathrm{incl}\},\quad \frac{3}{4} \mapsto \{\mathtt{out}, \mathrm{incl}\},\quad 1 \mapsto \varnothing.$$

Additionally, there is exactly one $v \in s_{\mathsf{RS}}(S)$ with $v(1) = \{\mathtt{out}\}$ and likewise for $v(1) = \{\mathtt{in}\}$, $v(1) = \{\mathtt{out}, \mathtt{in}\}$, $v(1) = \{\mathtt{n}\}$, etc. □

The specification of RS in Fig. 6 could be relaxed by allowing the first configuration of all transitions in the traces to be any larger set (i.e., replacing equalities in the base cases and in $s = \mathrm{cd}(E,v)$ with inclusions). This would correspond to constraint systems, that are often used for specifying program analyses, and could lead to more general results, but this is out of the scope of this paper.

The correctness of the definition of RS semantics follows from Proposition 10 by classic domain theory. The proof is straightforward.

$$
\begin{array}{rcrcl}
S & \searrow & \texttt{skip} & = & \mathrm{RP}(S) \setminus \{1\} \\
\texttt{use}\ \mathscr{X} & \searrow & \texttt{use}\ \mathscr{X} & = & \varnothing \\
X\ \texttt{:=}\ E & \searrow & X\ \texttt{:=}\ E & = & \varnothing \\
X\ \texttt{:=}\ R & \searrow & X\ \texttt{:=}\ R & = & \varnothing \\
T_1\ ;\ T_2 & \searrow & T_1'\ ;\ T_2' & = & \left\{[0;1] \Rightarrow [0;\tfrac{1}{2}]\right\}^\sharp (T_1 \searrow T_1') \cup \\
 & & & & \left\{[0;1] \Rightarrow [\tfrac{1}{2};1]\right\}^\sharp (T_2 \searrow T_2') \\
\texttt{if}\ E\ \texttt{then}\ T & \searrow & \texttt{if}\ E\ \texttt{then}\ T' & = & \left\{[0;1] \Rightarrow [\tfrac{1}{2};1]\right\}^\sharp (T \searrow T') \\
\texttt{while}\ E\ \texttt{do}\ T & \searrow & \texttt{while}\ E\ \texttt{do}\ T' & = & \bigcup_{i \in \mathbb{N}^+} \left\{[0;1] \Rightarrow [1-\tfrac{1}{2^{2i-1}};1-\tfrac{1}{2^{2i}}]\right\}^\sharp (T \searrow T')
\end{array}
$$

Fig. 7. The run point regions corresponding to removed subsets

Proposition 10.
(i) *The set* $\mathsf{Sem}_{\mathsf{RS}}$ *is a complete lattice w.r.t. the ordering* $\ddot{\subseteq}$*. Thereby, the least element is given by* $\{\{0 \mapsto \varnothing, 1 \mapsto t\} : t \in \mathit{Conf}_{\mathsf{RS}}\}$.
(ii) *The function* g_{RS} *is monotone w.r.t.* $\ddot{\subseteq}$.

The RS semantics associates relevant sets with run points instead of program points as an analysis would do. Proposition 11 shows that this discrepancy is purely formal: the RS trace elements actually depend on program points only.

Proposition 11. *Let* $S \in \mathit{Stmt}$ *and* $u \in s_{\mathsf{RS}}(S)$*. Let* $r, q \in \mathrm{RP}(S)$ *such that* $\mathrm{pp}(S)(r) = \mathrm{pp}(S)(q)$*. Then* $u(r) = u(q)$.

Proof. By induction on the structure of S. □

6 Correctness of Slicing

The information about code statements that must not be removed is provided by the incl flags in the sets associated with run points in the RS semantics. In order to state the main result about slicing, namely that slices maintain the desired part of program behaviour, we therefore specify the removed part of code also in terms of run points.

Definition 12. *For all* $S, S' \in \mathit{Stmt}$ *such that* $S' \sqsubseteq S$*, the* run point region removed *in* S' *w.r.t.* S *is the set of run points denoted by* $S \searrow S'$ *and defined recursively on the derivation of* $S' \sqsubseteq S$ *by equations in Fig. 7.*

The classic RS based method of slicing can now be described in our setting as follows:

1. Encode every pair $(\mathscr{X}, p)$ in the slicing criterion in the form of a statement **use** $\mathscr{X}$ immediately before the program point p in the input program — let the transformed program be S;

2. Find $l \in s_{\mathsf{RS}}(S)$ such that $l(1) = \varnothing$;
3. Output the least program S' such that $S' \sqsubseteq S$ and $\forall r \in S \smallsetminus S'\,(\mathsf{incl} \notin l(r))$.

By construction, $\mathrm{RP}(S) \setminus \mathrm{RP}(S') \subseteq S \smallsetminus S' \subseteq \mathrm{RP}(S)$. Note that calculating with plain differences $\mathrm{RP}(S) \setminus \mathrm{RP}(S')$ would be wrong since, for example, $\mathrm{RP}(X\ \mathtt{:=}\ E\ ;\ \mathbf{skip}) \setminus \mathrm{RP}(\mathbf{skip}) = \left\{\frac{1}{2}\right\}$ but the desired set must also include 0 (the location of the potential incl flag corresponding to the removed statement $X\ \mathtt{:=}\ E$).

Before reaching the main theorem that implies correctness of the method, we state three lemmata that constitute important parts of the proof of the theorem.

Firstly, Lemma 13 states that incl-free intervals of the RS semantics traces involve no changes of the set of relevant variables:

Lemma 13. *Let* $S \in \mathit{Stmt}$ *and* $l \in s_{\mathsf{RS}}(S)$. *Then* $\forall r \in \mathrm{RP}(S) \setminus \{1\}\,(\mathsf{incl} \notin l(r))$ *implies* $\forall r \in \mathrm{RP}(S) \setminus \{1\}\,(l(r) = l(1) \setminus \{\mathsf{incl}\})$.

Proof. By induction on the structure of S. □

Similarly, Lemma 14 establishes that if an RS semantics trace does not involve incl then the values of variables important at the beginning of that program never change in the fractional semantics of the same program:

Lemma 14. *Let* $S \in \mathit{Stmt}$ *and* $l \in s_{\mathsf{RS}}(S)$, *and choose also* $u \in s_{\mathsf{FS}}(S)$. *Then* $\forall r \in \mathrm{RP}(S) \setminus \{1\}\,(\mathsf{incl} \notin l(r))$ *implies* $\forall r \in \mathrm{dom}\,u\,\left(u(r)|_{\mathsf{Var} \cap l(1)} = u(0)|_{\mathsf{Var} \cap l(1)}\right)$.

Proof. By induction on the structure of S. □

Lemma 15 relates the relevant variables in a program and its slice. Intuitively, it states that, if the removed code region does not involve incl, then the relevant sets at the remained run points are the same, irrespective of whether the original program or the subset is considered. This implies that slicing can be performed in several stages: the lines that could be removed immediately may be kept and removed later by slicing the resulting program w.r.t. the same criterion. The assertion of Lemma 15 is therefore interesting on its own.

Lemma 15. *Let* $S, S' \in \mathit{Stmt}$ *with* $S' \sqsubseteq S$. *Let* $l \in s_{\mathsf{RS}}(S)$ *and* $l' \in s_{\mathsf{RS}}(S')$ *such that* $l(1) = l'(1)$. *Then* $\forall r \in S \smallsetminus S'\,(\mathsf{incl} \notin l(r))$ *implies* $\forall r \in \mathrm{RP}(S')\,\left(l'(r) = l(r)\right)$.

Proof. By induction on the derivation of $S' \sqsubseteq S$. □

Finally, we reach the main Theorem 16. It claims that, at certain assumptions that encode equal execution circumstances, the subset program where only statements at run points unmarked with incl are omitted computes the same values for all relevant variables at each run point visited by both programs. Furthermore, all visits of run points marked by incl are the same in both executions.

Concerning the assumptions, $u'(0)|_{\mathsf{Var} \cap l(0)} = u(0)|_{\mathsf{Var} \cap l(0)}$ tells that both programs are executed in an initial state where relevant variables have equal values, and the condition $\forall r \in \mathrm{dom}\,u \cap \mathrm{dom}\,u'\,\left(u'(r)|_{\mathit{IExpr}} = u(r)|_{\mathit{IExpr}}\right)$ assures that the programs always consume equal inputs at corresponding run points.

Theorem 16. *Let* $S, S' \in \mathit{Stmt}$ *such that* $S' \sqsubseteq S$. *Let* $l \in s_{\mathsf{RS}}(S)$ *such that* $\forall r \in S \setminus S' (\mathrm{incl} \notin l(r))$. *Let* $u \in s_{\mathsf{FS}}(S)$, $u' \in s_{\mathsf{FS}}(S')$ *such that* $u'(0)|_{\mathsf{Var} \cap l(0)} = u(0)|_{\mathsf{Var} \cap l(0)}$ *and* $\forall r \in \operatorname{dom} u \cap \operatorname{dom} u' \left(u'(r)|_{\mathit{IExpr}} = u(r)|_{\mathit{IExpr}}\right)$. *Then*

$$\forall r \in \operatorname{dom} u \cap \operatorname{dom} u' \left(u'(r)|_{\mathsf{Var} \cap l(r)} = u(r)|_{\mathsf{Var} \cap l(r)}\right),$$

whereby $r \in \operatorname{dom} u \iff r \in \operatorname{dom} u'$ *for every* $r \in \mathrm{RP}\, S$ *such that* $\mathrm{incl} \in l(r)$.

Proof. By induction on the derivation of $S' \sqsubseteq S$, using Lemmas 13–15. □

Let $S, S' \in \mathit{Stmt}$ and $l \in s_{\mathsf{RS}}(S)$ be like in the description of the slicing method after Definition 12. Now if u, u' are execution traces of S, S' in equal execution circumstances, the assumptions of Theorem 16 are fulfilled for the programs S, S', the RS trace l and the fractional traces u, u'. As all use statements are marked by incl and all variables in use statements are marked relevant in l, Theorem 16 implies that the sequences of visits of the program points mentioned by the slicing criterion are the same in both executions and the values of variables there are equal.

Consequently, Theorem 16 shows that the method produces correct slices.

7 Related Work

Program slicing was first studied by Weiser [19] who also described the slicing method based on relevant sets. Correctness of classic slicing methods w.r.t. standard semantics and relaxed notion of slice (discussed briefly in Subsect. 1.1) was established by Reps and Yang [14].

Sivagurunathan et al. [15] study program slicing in the presence of input statements but they address it differently from us. Motivated by an example similar to our second one in Subsect. 1.1, their work aims to find a specification of program slicing such that executing a program and its slice with *the same input stream* would produce the same sequences of interesting values. Our work argues that talking about preservation of the effects of a program by its slice may naturally assume equal inputs at equal run points instead of equal input streams, and searches for appropriate ways to formalize this.

Non-standard semantics that would avoid the infamous anomaly arising from slicing away non-terminating loops (discussed in Subsect. 1.2) have been previously a topic of Reps and Turnidge [13], Giacobazzi and Mastroeni [6], Danicic et al. [5,1], and us [9,11,10,12]. Among them, [6] advocated transfinite semantics similarly to us. The idea of using transfinite semantics in program slicing dates back to Cousot [4].

The approach of this paper is a further development of our earlier works where fractional semantics were introduced for defining transfinite semantics for recursive programs [10] and expressing transfinite semantics in a greatest fixpoint form [12]. These papers contained no treatment of run points on their own, nor did they thoroughly investigate applications to slicing (no program analysis was incorporated). The most notable differences between the fractional semantics in this paper and that in [12] are the following:

- Procedure semantics was studied in [12] but omitted here.
- The transfinite soundness restriction was not taken into account in [12].
- Input contexts were not involved in the semantics in [12].
- The fractional semantics in this paper, unlike its precursors, is explicitly compositional.

The fractional semantics in [10] differed even more (for example, by taking errors into account).

8 Conclusion

In this paper, we investigated program slicing in the presence of input operations whose results are assumed to depend on the current run point, i.e., the stage of computation. The underlying formalism developed for this was based on fractional semantics [10] that expresses all run points as finite binary fractions from the interval $[0;1]$. We found out that a classic slicing method similar to that described by Weiser [19] is correct w.r.t. this semantics.

There are many applications of fractional semantics revealed by now:

- Defining transfinite semantics for recursive programs [10,12];
- Expressing transfinite semantics in the form of greatest fixpoint [12] (and this paper);
- Providing simple means for handling the correspondence of run points of a program and a transformed program (this paper);
- Providing simple means for keeping track of program points in execution traces (this paper).

This work also provides new evidence that using transfinite semantics can be a natural choice in theoretical treatments of program slicing. Barraclough et al. [1] argued that transfinite semantics were not appropriate for three reasons: (1) they were not substitutive; (2) they introduced special non-standard values of variables after infinite computations, which may cause trouble; (3) they are counter-intuitive. In this work, the semantics is defined compositionally, whence it is also substitutive, and we use random inputs of normal values rather than non-standard values for undefined limits. The counter-intuitivity argument seems weak since non-standard semantics are ubiquitous in this area of research.

Transfinite semantics is certainly not suitable if the terminating status of programs must be maintained by slices. (This is the case in some applications of slicing. Then the classic slicing algorithms based on data and control dependence do not qualify anyway, whence these cases are not of interest in the present work.) In debugging, slicing away infinite loops does no harm since all errors that occur during a run of a program do it after a finite number of steps.

A natural question is whether program transformations other than slicing could similarly benefit from transfinite semantics. To our knowledge, transfinite semantics has not been applied to other transformations. Like program slicing, dead code elimination can introduce termination by removing infinite loops, but there, switching to transfinite semantics changes the transformation (a part of code dead in standard semantics might be alive in transfinite semantics and thus become impossible to remove), whence the benefits are questionable.

Finally, note that if `input()` is assumed to produce a value according to a probability distribution, our examples in Subsect. 1.1 also motivate investigations of probabilistic semantics, the corresponding notions of slice and slicing algorithms in that context. The first example transformation should be considered incorrect as it changes the probability distribution of the possible values of `out`, and the second one is justifiably correct as the practical meaning of a dice roll does not depend on previous dice rolls. We hope that the results of this paper can be applied in this potential future work.

References

1. Barraclough, R.W., Binkley, D., Danicic, S., Harman, M., Hierons, R.M., Kiss, Á., Laurence, M., Ouarbya, L.: A trajectory-based strict semantics for program slicing. Theoretical Computer Science 410, 1372–1386 (2010)
2. Binkley, D.W., Gallagher, K.B.: Program slicing. Advances in Computers 43, 1–50 (1996)
3. Collard, J.-F.: Reasoning about Program Transformations. Springer (2003)
4. Cousot, P.: Constructive design of a hierarchy of semantics of a transition system by abstract interpretation. Electronic Notes in Theoretical Computer Science 6, 77–102 (1997)
5. Danicic, S., Harman, M., Howroyd, J., Ouarbya, L.: A non-standard semantics for program slicing and dependence analysis. Journal of Logic and Algebraic Programming 72, 191–206 (2007)
6. Giacobazzi, R., Mastroeni, I.: Non-standard semantics for program slicing. Higher-Order Symbolic Computation 16, 297–339 (2003)
7. Hatcliff, J., Corbett, J., Dwyer, M.B., Sokolowski, S., Zheng, H.: A formal study of slicing for multi-threaded programs with JVM concurrency primitives. In: Cortesi, A., Filé, G. (eds.) SAS 1999. LNCS, vol. 1694, pp. 1–18. Springer, Heidelberg (1999)
8. Kennaway, R., Klop, J.W., Sleep, R., de Vries, F.-J.: Transfinite reductions in orthogonal term rewriting systems. Information and Computation 119(1), 18–38 (1995)
9. Nestra, H.: Transfinite semantics in program slicing. Proceedings of the Estonian Academy of Sciences: Engineering 11(4), 313–328 (2005)
10. Nestra, H.: Fractional semantics. In: Johnson, M., Vene, V. (eds.) AMAST 2006. LNCS, vol. 4019, pp. 278–292. Springer, Heidelberg (2006)
11. Nestra, H.: Iteratively Defined Transfinite Trace Semantics and Program Slicing with respect to Them. PhD thesis, University of Tartu, 119 p. (2006)
12. Nestra, H.: Transfinite semantics in the form of greatest fixpoint. Journal of Logic and Algebraic Programming 78, 573–592 (2009)
13. Reps, T., Turnidge, T.: Program specialization via program slicing. In: Danvy, O., Thiemann, P., Glück, R. (eds.) Dagstuhl Seminar 1996. LNCS, vol. 1110, pp. 409–429. Springer, Heidelberg (1996)
14. Reps, T., Yang, W.: The semantics of program slicing and program integration. In: Díaz, J., Orejas, F. (eds.) TAPSOFT 1989. LNCS, vol. 352, pp. 360–374. Springer, Heidelberg (1989)

15. Sivagurunathan, Y., Harman, M., Danicic, S.: Slicing, I/O and the implicit state. In: Kamkar, M. (ed.) 3rd International Workshop on Automated Debugging. Linköping Electronic Articles in Computer and Information Science, vol. 2, pp. 59–67 (1997)
16. Tip, F.: A survey of program slicing techniques. Journal of Programming Languages 3(3), 121–181 (1995)
17. Ward, M., Zedan, H.: Slicing as a program transformation. ACM Transactions on Programming Languages and Systems 29(2), 1–53 (2007)
18. Ward, M., Zedan, H.: Deriving a slicing algorithm via FermaT transformations. IEEE Transactions on Software Engineering 37(1), 24–47 (2011)
19. Weiser, M.: Program slicing. In: ICSE 1981 Proceedings of the 5th International Conference on Software Engineering, pp. 439–449 (1981)

Deterministic Logics for UL

Paritosh K. Pandya and Simoni S. Shah

Tata Institute of Fundamental Research, Colaba, Mumbai 400005, India

Abstract. The class of Unambiguous Star-Free Regular Languages (UL) has been widely studied and variously characterized by logics such as $TL[X_a, Y_a]$, $UITL$, $TL[F,P]$, $FO^2[<]$, the variety DA and partially-ordered two-way DFA. However, explicit reductions from logics to automata are missing. In this paper, we introduce the concept of Deterministic Logics for UL. The formulas of deterministic logics uniquely parse a word in order to evaluate satisfaction. We consider three such deterministic logics with varied modalities, namely $TL[X_a, Y_a]$, $TL[\widetilde{U}, \widetilde{S}]$ and $UITL^{\pm}$. Using effective reductions between them and to *po2dfa*, we show that they all characterize UL, and have NP-complete satisfiability. The reductions rely on features of deterministic logic such as unique parsability and ranker-directionality.

1 Introduction

Unambiguous star-free regular languages (UL) was a language class first studied by Schützenberger [Sch76]. He gave an algebraic characterization for UL using the monoid variety DA. Since then, several diverse and unexpected characterizations have emerged for this language class: $\Delta_2[<]$ in the quantifier-alternation hierarchy of first-order definable languages [EPW97], the two variable fragment $FO^2[<]$ [TW98] (without any restriction on quantifier alternation), and Unary Temporal Logic $TL[F,P]$ [EVW02] are some of the logical characterizations that are well known. Investigating the automata for UL, Schwentik, Therien and Volmer [STV01] defined Partially Ordered 2-Way Deterministic Automata (*po2dfa*) and showed that these exactly recognize the language class UL. Recently, there have been additional characterizations of UL using deterministic logics $UITL$ [LPS08] as well as $TL[X_a, Y_a]$ [DK07]. A survey paper [DGK08] describes this language class and its characterizations.

A monomial over an alphabet Σ is a regular expression of the form $A_0^* a_1 \cdots a_{n-1} A_n^*$, where $A_i \subseteq \Sigma$ and $a_i \in \Sigma$. By definition, UL is the subclass of star-free regular languages which may be expressed as a finite disjoint union of unambiguous monomials: every word that belongs to the language, may be *unambiguously* parsed so as to match a monomial. The uniqueness with which these monomials parse any word is the characteristic property of this language class. We explore a similar phenomenon in logics by introducing the notion of *Deterministic Temporal Logics for UL*.

Given a modality $\mathcal{M}$ of a temporal logic that is interpreted over a word model, the *accessibility relation* of $\mathcal{M}$ is a relation which maps every position in the word with the set of positions that are accessible by $\mathcal{M}$. In case of interval temporal logics, the relation is over intervals instead of positions in the word model. The modality is *deterministic* if its accessibility relation is a (partial) function. A logic is said to be deterministic if all its

Z. Liu, J. Woodcock, and H. Zhu (Eds.): ICTAC 2013, LNCS 8049, pp. 301–318, 2013.

modalities are deterministic. Hence, deterministic logics over words have the property of *Unique Parsability*.

Definition 1 (Unique Parsability). *In the evaluation of a temporal logic formula over a given word, every subformula has a unique position (or interval) in the word at which it must be evaluated. This position is determined by the context of the subformula.*

In this paper we relate three deterministic temporal logics and investigate their properties. We give constructive reductions between them (as depicted in Figure 1) and also to the *po2dfa* automata. Hence, we are able to infer their expressive equivalence with the language class UL. Moreover, the automaton connection allows us to establish their NP-complete satisfiability.

(i) Deterministic Until-Since Logic- $TL[\widetilde{U},\widetilde{S}]$:
Let A be any subset of the alphabet and b be any letter from the alphabet. The "deterministic half until" modality $A\widetilde{U}_b\phi$ holds if at the first occurrence of b in (strict) future ϕ holds and all intermediate letters are in A. The past operator $A\widetilde{S}_b\phi$ is symmetric. Since the modalities are deterministic, the formulas posses the property of unique parsability. This logic admits a straightforward encoding of *po2dfa*.

(ii) Unambiguous Interval Temporal Logic with Expanding Modalities - $UITL^{\pm}$:
This is an interval temporal logic with deterministic chop modalities F_a and L_a which chop an interval into two at the first or last occurrence of letter a. These modalities were introduced in [LPS08] as logic *UITL*. Here, we enrich *UITL* with the expanding F_a^+ and L_a^- chop modalities that extend an interval beyond the interval boundaries in the forward and the backward directions to the next or the previous occurrence of a. We call this logic $UITL^{\pm}$. It is a deterministic logic.

(iii) Deterministic Temporal Logic of Rankers -$TL[X_a,Y_a]$:
Modality $X_a\phi$ (or $Y_a\phi$) accesses the position of the next (or the last) occurrence of letter a where ϕ must hold. The temporal logic with these modalities was investigated in [DK07]. The authors showed that the deterministic temporal logic $TL[X_a,Y_a]$ which closes the rankers of [WI07, STV01] under boolean operations, characterizes UL (their work was in the setting of infinite words). We identify $TL[X_a,Y_a]$ as a deterministic logic and use its property of unique parsability to give an efficient reduction from formulas to *po2dfa*.

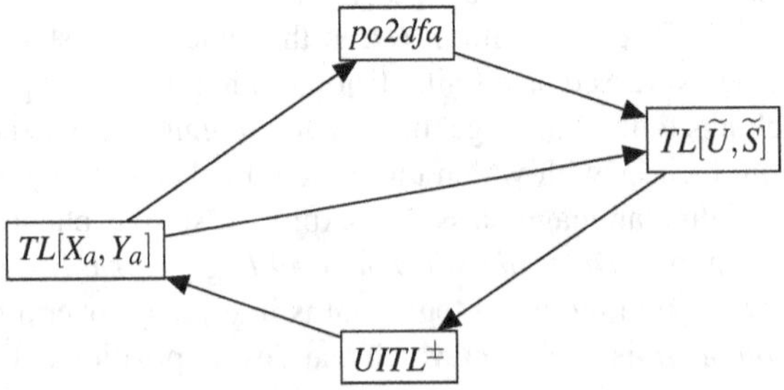

Fig. 1. Deterministic Logics and *po2dfa* with reductions as presented in this paper

It is easy to see that the modalities of $UITL^{\pm}$ are the most comprehensive: logic $TL[X_a,Y_a]$ is a syntactic subset of $TL[\widetilde{U},\widetilde{S}]$ and every formula of $TL[\widetilde{U},\widetilde{S}]$ can be easily transformed to a language equivalent $UITL^{\pm}$ formula with only linear blowup in size. Thus, expressively, $TL[X_a,Y_a] \subseteq TL[\widetilde{U},\widetilde{S}] \subseteq UITL^{\pm}$. We relate these logics further as follows:

- As our first result, we show that every *po2dfa* can be effectively modelled as a $TL[\widetilde{U},\widetilde{S}]$ formula with the same language. Moreover, the DAG representation of the formula is linear in the size of the automata.
- As our second main result, we give a polynomial time reduction from a $TL[X_a,Y_a]$ to a *po2dfa* recognizing the same language. The automaton construction essentially relies upon the unique parsability of $TL[X_a,Y_a]$ and the ability of *po2dfa* to succinctly characterize the unique position of each subformula. The main techniques used here were introduced earlier [LPS08] for logic *UITL*. The two-way nature of automata naturally corresponds with the future and the past modalities.
- Finally, closing the cycle, we show that $UITL^{\pm}$ can be effectively reduced in polynomial time to a language equivalent $TL[X_a,Y_a]$ formula. The reduction relies upon the pioneering "ranker directionality" technique originally introduced by [DKL10].

These reductions show that all the three temporal logics have the same expressive power as *po2dfa* (and hence language class UL) and their satisfiability is NP-complete. The decision complexity follows from *NP*-complete non-emptiness checking of *po2dfa*. Thus, we demonstrate that the language class UL is robustly characterized by several deterministic temporal logics all of which have low decision complexity.

The paper is organized as follows. Section 2 defines *po2dfa* and gives their properties. In Section 3, we introduce the logic $TL[\widetilde{U},\widetilde{S}]$ and prove its expressive completeness with respect to *po2dfa*. Section 4 presents the syntax, semantics and unique parsing properties of $UITL^{\pm}$ and the reduction from $TL[\widetilde{U},\widetilde{S}]$ to $UITL^{\pm}$. In Section 5 we revisit the logic $TL[X_a,Y_a]$ and give its reduction to *po2dfa*. Section 6 gives the the property of ranker directionality using which we give a reduction from $UITL^{\pm}$ to $TL[X_a,Y_a]$. We end the paper with a discussion of the results and their significance.

2 *po2dfa*: An Automaton Characterization for UL

Partially ordered two-way DFA were introduced by Schwentick, Thérien and Vollmer [STV01] where they showed that it is characterized by *DA*. As the name suggests, *po2dfa* are two-way automata, so that the head of the automaton may move in either direction (one step to the left or right) in every transition. Also, the only loops in the transition graph of the automaton are self-loops on states. This naturally defines a partial-order on the set of states. Lastly, the automaton is deterministic- so that there is exactly one possible transition from any configuration of the automaton.

Consider a finite alphabet Σ. Given $w \in \Sigma^*$, the two way automaton actually scans the string $w' = \rhd w \lhd$ with end-markers $\rhd$ and $\lhd$ placed at positions 0 and $\#w+1$ respectively. Let $\Sigma' = \Sigma \cup \{\rhd, \lhd\}$ include the two endmarkers.

Definition 2 (*po2dfa*). *A po2dfa over Σ is a tuple $M = (Q, \leq, \delta, s, t, r)$ where $(Q, \leq)$ is a poset of states such that r,t are the only minimal elements. s is the initial state, t is the accept state and r is the rejecting state. The set $Q \setminus \{t, r\}$ is partitioned into Q_L and Q_R (the states reached from the left and the right respectively). $\delta : ((Q_L \cup Q_R) \times \Sigma) \rightarrow Q) \cup ((Q_L \times \{\triangleleft\}) \rightarrow Q \setminus Q_R) \cup ((Q_R \times \{\triangleright\}) \rightarrow Q \setminus Q_L)$ is a progress-transition function satisfying $\delta(q, a) < q$. Hence it defines the progress transitions of the automaton. In order to make the automaton "complete", every state q in $Q \setminus \{t, r\}$ has a default else (self-loop) transition which is taken on all letters b for which no progress transition $\delta(q, b)$ is defined. Hence, the transition function δ specifies all the* progress *transitions of the automaton, and a default self-loop* (else) *transition is takes place otherwise. Note that there are no progress or* else *transitions for the terminal states (r and t).*

Direction of Head Movement on a Transition

The direction in which the head moves at the end of a transition, depends on whether the target state of the transition is a Q_L state, or a Q_R state. Q_L is the set of states that are "*entered from the left*" and Q_R are the states that are "*entered from the right*"; i.e. if the automaton is in a state q, reading a symbol a, it enters a state $q' = \delta(q, a)$, then it moves its head to the right if $q' \in Q_L$, left if $q' \in Q_R$, and stays in the same position if $q' \in \{t, r\}$. The same rule applies to the self loop *else* transitions also: on *else* transitions of Q_L states, the head moves to the right, and on *else* transitions of Q_R states, the head moves to the left.

It must be noted that the partition of the set of states based on the direction of the head movement is for convenience of presentation and translation to logics. In general, every partially-ordered two- way DFA for which the direction of head movement is specified by the transition, may be converted (with a linear blow-up in the size of the automaton) to a *po2dfa* in which the set of states is partitioned based on the direction of head movement of the incoming transitions (which matches the definition above).

Transitions on End-markers

The transition function is designed to ensure that the automaton does not "fall off" either end of the input. Hence, for all $q \in Q \setminus \{t, r\}$, there are transitions $\delta(q, \triangleright) \in Q_L \cup \{t, r\}$ and $\delta(q, \triangleleft) \in Q_R \cup \{t, r\}$, so that for every transition of the form $\delta(q, \triangleright)$, the head moves to the right, and on a transition of the form $\delta(q, \triangleleft)$, the head moves to the left, or reaches a terminal state.

Run of a po2dfa

A po2dfa M running over word w is said to be in a configuration (q, p) if it is in a state q and head reading the position p in word. Let $Def(q) \subseteq \Sigma$ be the subset of letters on which no progress transition from q is defined. Hence, the automaton takes the default *else* transition on exactly the letters from $Def(q)$. The run of a po2dfa M on an input word w starting with input head position p_0 is a sequence $(q_0, p_0), (q_1, p_1), ...(q_f, p_f)$ of configurations such that:

- $q_0 = s$ and $q_f \in \{t, r\}$,
- For all $i (1 \leq i < f)$, if $w(p_i) \in Def(q_i)$ then
  - $q_{i+1} = q_i$ and

- $p_{i+1} = p_i + 1$ if $q_i \in Q_L$ and $p_{i+1} = p_i - 1$ if $q_i \in Q_R$.

Otherwise, if $\delta(q_i, w(p_i)) = (q')$ then

- $q_{i+1} = q'$ and
- $p_{i+1} = p_i + 1$ if $q_{i+1} \in Q_L$,
  $p_{i+1} = p_i - 1$ if $q_{i+1} \in Q_R$ and
  $p_{i+1} = p_i$ if $q_{i+1} \in \{t, r\}$.

In general, we abbreviate the run of an automaton M starting from a position p_0 in a word w by writing $M(w, p_0) = (q_f, p_f)$. The run is *accepting* if $q_f = t$; *rejecting* if $q_f = r$. The automaton M is said to be *start-free* if for any w, and $\forall p_1, p_2 \in dom(w)$, $M(w, p_1) = (q_f, p_f)$ if and only if $M(w, p_2) = (q_f, p_f)$.

The language $\mathcal{L}(M)$ of a *po2dfa* M is the set of all words w such that $M(w, 1) = (t, i)$ (for some $i \in dom(w')$).

Remark 1. We shall represent *po2dfa* using their transition graphs. The direction of the arrow drawn within a state represents the direction in which the head of the automaton moves, on transitions which target into that state. Hence, all $q \in Q_L$ are marked with a "$\rightarrow$" and all $q \in Q_R$ are marked with a "$\leftarrow$".

Example 1. The *po2dfa* $\mathcal{A}$ is given in figure 2. $\mathcal{A}$ accepts all such words over $\{a, b, c, d\}^*$, which has its last a at some position (say i), and some position (say $j > i$) has the first d after i and all intermediate positions between i and j do not have a b. Observe that the automaton rejects iff:

- There is no a in the word
- There is no d after the last a in the word
- There is a b between the last a and the subsequent d after it.

The language accepted by $\mathcal{A}$, may be given by the regular expression $\Sigma^* ac^* d\{b, c, d\}^*$.

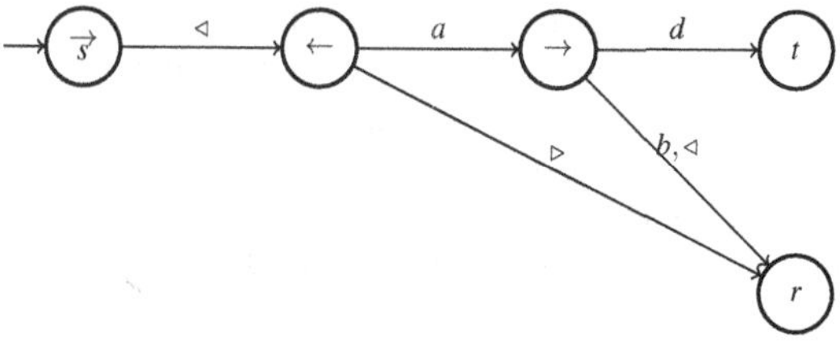

Fig. 2. Example *po2dfa* $\mathcal{A}$

2.1 Constructions on PO2DFA

For the description of *po2dfa* we shall use Extended Turtle Expressions ([LPS08]), which are extensions of the turtle programs introduced by Schwentick, Thérien and Vollmer [STV01]. The syntax of *ETE* follows and we explain its semantics below. Let A, B range over subsets of Σ'.

$$E ::= Acc \mid Rej \mid 1 \xrightarrow{A} \mid 1 \xleftarrow{A} \mid A \xrightarrow{B} \mid A \xleftarrow{B} \mid E_1 ? E_2, E_3$$

Automaton Acc accepts immediately without moving the head. Similarly, Rej rejects immediately. $A \overset{B}{\rightarrow}$ accepts at the next occurrence of a letter from B strictly to the right, maintaining the constraint that the intervening letters are from $A \setminus B$. If no such occurrence exists the automaton rejects at the right end-marker or if a letter outside A intervenes, the automaton rejects at its position. Automaton $1 \overset{A}{\rightarrow}$ accepts one position to the right if the current letter is from A, else rejects at the current position. $A \overset{B}{\leftarrow}$ and $1 \overset{A}{\leftarrow}$ are symmetric in the leftward direction. The conditional construct $E_1?E_2,E_3$ first executes E_1 on w. On its accepting w at position j it continues with execution of E_2 from j. On E_1 rejecting w at position j it continues with E_3 from position j.

Here are some abbreviations which illustrate the power of the notation: $E_1;E_2 = E_1?E_2,Rej$, $\neg E_1 = E_1?Rej,Acc$. Moreover, if E_2 is start-free then $E_1 \vee E_2 = E_1?Acc,E_2$ and $E_1 \wedge E_2 = E_1?E2,Rej$. Notice that automata for these expressions are start-free if E_1 is start-free. We will use $A \overset{a}{\rightarrow}$ for $A \overset{\{a\}}{\rightarrow}$, $\overset{a}{\rightarrow}$ for $(\Sigma' \overset{a}{\rightarrow})$ and $\overset{1}{\rightarrow}$ for $(1 \overset{\Sigma'}{\rightarrow})$. Similarly define $\overset{a}{\leftarrow}$ and $\overset{1}{\leftarrow}$.

Proposition 1. – *Given an ETE E we can construct a po2dfa accepting the same language with number of states linear in* $|E|$.
- *Given a po2dfa* $\mathcal{A}$ *we may construct a language-equivalent ETE whose size is linear in the size of* $\mathcal{A}$.

2.2 Properties of *po2dfa*

The following properties of *po2dfa* are useful. See [LPS08] for details.

- *Boolean Closure*: Boolean operations on *po2dfa* may be achieved with linear blow-up in the size of the automata.
- *Small Model*: Given a *po2dfa* M with n number of states, if $\mathcal{L}(M) \neq \emptyset$, then there exists a word $w \in \mathcal{L}(M)$ such that length of w is linear in n.
- *Membership Checking*: Given a *po2dfa* M with n number of states and a word w of length l, the membership of w in $\mathcal{L}(M)$ may be checked in time $O(nl)$.
- *Language Non-Emptiness*: The non-emptiness of the language of a *po2dfa* may be decided with NP-complete complexity.
- *Language Inclusion*: The language inclusion problem of *po2dfa* is CoNP-complete.

3 Deterministic Until-Since Logic $TL[\widetilde{U},\widetilde{S}]$

We shall introduce the deterministic logic $TL[\widetilde{U},\widetilde{S}]$. It has the deterministic half until and since modalities whose eventuality constraint is deterministic and is given by the next / previous occurrence of a letter, while the invariance constraint is given by a subset of the alphabet. The syntax and semantics of this logic is as follows. Let $A \subseteq \Sigma$, $a,b \in \Sigma$ and ϕ range over $TL[\widetilde{U},\widetilde{S}]$ formulas. A $TL[\widetilde{U},\widetilde{S}]$formula may be given by the following syntax.

$$\top \mid a \mid A\widetilde{U}_b\phi \mid A\widetilde{S}_b\phi \mid \phi \vee \phi \mid \neg\phi$$

Given a word $w \in \Sigma^*$, and $i \in dom(w)$, $TL[\widetilde{U},\widetilde{S}]$ formulas may be interpreted using the following rules.

$$w,i \models a \text{ iff } w(i) = a$$
$$w,i \models A\widetilde{U}_b\phi \text{ iff } \exists j > i \,.\, w(j) = b \wedge \forall i < k < j \,.\, w(k) \in A \setminus b \,\wedge\, w,j \models \phi$$
$$w,i \models A\widetilde{S}_b\phi \text{ iff } \exists j < i \,.\, w(j) = b \wedge \forall j < k < i \,.\, w(k) \in A \setminus b \,\wedge\, w,j \models \phi$$

The boolean operators have their usual meaning. The language defined by a $TL[\widetilde{U},\widetilde{S}]$ formula ϕ is given by $\mathcal{L}(\phi) = \{w \in \Sigma^* \mid w,1 \models \phi\}$ (if the outermost operator of ϕ is a $\widetilde{U}$ operator) and $\mathcal{L}(\phi) = \{w \in \Sigma^* \mid w,\#w \models \phi\}$ (if the outermost operator of ϕ is a $\widetilde{S}$ operator). $TL[\widetilde{U},\widetilde{S}]$ formulas may be represented as a DAG, in the usual way, with the modal/boolean operators at the intermediate nodes.

Example 2. The language described in Example 1 which is given by $\Sigma^*ac^*d\{b,c,d\}^*$ may be expressed using the $TL[\widetilde{U},\widetilde{S}]$ formula $\Sigma\widetilde{S}_a\ (\Sigma \setminus \{b\}\ \widetilde{U}_d\top)$.

$TL[\widetilde{U},\widetilde{S}]$ and Unique Parsability. The $\widetilde{U}$ and $\widetilde{S}$ modalities of $TL[\widetilde{U},\widetilde{S}]$ are deterministic, in the sense that they uniquely define the position at which its subformula must be evaluated. Hence, for every subformula ψ of a $TL[\widetilde{U},\widetilde{S}]$ formula ϕ, and any word w, there exists a unique position denoted as $Pos_w(\psi)$, where ψ is to be evaluated. Moreover, $Pos_w(\psi)$ is determined by the context of ψ in ϕ. For example, consider the subformula $\psi = A\widetilde{U}_b(\psi')$, such that $Pos_w(\psi) = i$. Then $Pos_w(\psi') = j$ such that $j > i$, $w(j) = b$ and $\forall i < k < j \,.\, w(k) \in A \setminus \{b\}$.

3.1 From *po2dfa* to $TL[\widetilde{U},\widetilde{S}]$

The deterministic *until* and *since* operators of $TL[\widetilde{U},\widetilde{S}]$ naturally model the constraints on the run of a *po2dfa*: the looping of the *po2dfa* in a given state and on a subset of letters until an outward transition is enabled is straightforwardly captured by the invariance condition of the $\widetilde{U}$ and $\widetilde{S}$ modalities. We shall now give a translation from *po2dfa* automata to language-equivalent $TL[\widetilde{U},\widetilde{S}]$ formulas.

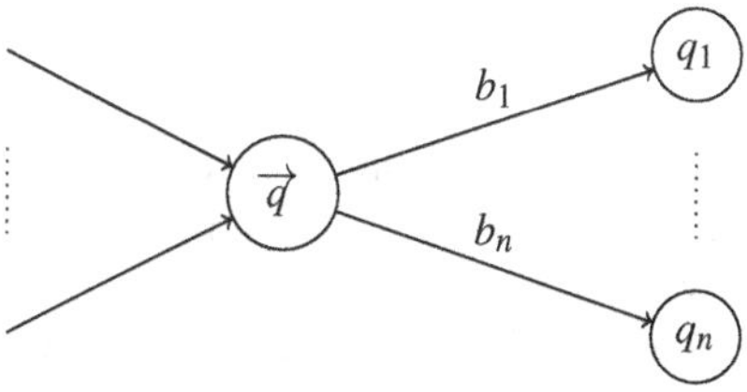

Fig. 3. From *po2dfa* to $TL[\widetilde{U},\widetilde{S}]$

We shall construct a $TL[\widetilde{U},\widetilde{S}]$ formula $Form(q)$ for each state of $\mathcal{A}$, such that the following lemma is satisfied.

Lemma 1. *Given a po2dfa $\mathcal{A}$ and any non-initial state q of $\mathcal{A}$, we may construct a $TL[\widetilde{U},\widetilde{S}]$ formula $Form(q)$ such that for every $w \in \Sigma^+$, if q is entered on reading a position $x \in dom(w)$, then $w,x \models Form(q)$ if and only if the run terminates in the accepting state.*

Proof. We shall prove this lemma by constructing the formula $Form(q)$ for every non-initial state q in $\mathcal{A}$. From the syntax of *po2dfa* it is straightforward to infer that $Form(t) = \top$ and $Form(r) = \bot$. Now, consider a non-initial state q of a *po2dfa* as shown in Figure 3, such that $q \notin \{t,r\}$ and $A_q = \Sigma \setminus \{b_1 \cdots b_n\}$ is the set of letters on which q loops. Let us assume that $Form(q_1), \cdots Form(q_n)$ are appropriately constructed. If $q \in Q_L$ (i.e. q is a state entered from the left, and the head of the automaton moves right on all transitions whose target state is q), then the automaton "scans" rightwards from x, looping in q on letters from A_q, until a progress transition from one of the letters from $\{b_1, \cdots b_n\}$ is enabled. Hence, a progress transition b_i is enabled from q if and only if there exists $y > x$ such that $w(y) = b_i$ and for all $x < k < y$, $w(k) \in A_q$. Further, this run is accepting if and only if $w, y \models Form(q_i)$.

From the above argument, we may construct $Form(q)$ as follows.

- If $q \in Q_L$, then
$$Form(q) = \bigvee_{i \in \{1,\cdots n\}} [A_q \widetilde{U}_{b_i} Form(q_i)]$$
- If $q \in Q_R$, then
$$Form(q) = \bigvee_{i \in \{1,\cdots n\}} [A_q \widetilde{S}_{b_i} Form(q_i)]$$

□

Theorem 1. *Given a po2dfa $\mathcal{A}$, we may construct a $TL[\widetilde{U},\widetilde{S}]$ formula $Trans(\mathcal{A})$ such that $\mathcal{L}(\mathcal{A}) = \mathcal{L}(Trans(\mathcal{A}))$, whose DAG representation is linear in the size of $\mathcal{A}$.*

Proof. Consider the start state of the *po2dfa* $\mathcal{A}$ which loops on the letters in A_s until a progress transition on one of the letters in $\{c_1, \cdots c_l\}$ is enabled, such that the transition on c_i is targeted into a state q_i, for each $i \in \{1 \cdots l\}$. From an argument similar to the one in Lemma 1, we may infer that

$$Trans(\mathcal{A}) = \bigvee_{i \in \{1 \cdots l\}} [c_i \wedge Form(q_i)] \vee \bigvee_{i \in \{1 \cdots l\}} [\bigvee_{b \in A_s} b \wedge A_s \widetilde{U}_{c_i} Form(q_i)]$$

In the above formula, the two sets of disjunctions correspond to the cases when the progress transition from s to the target state is taken on the first position in the word, or any other position, respectively.

In the DAG representation of the formula $Trans(\mathcal{A})$ as per the above construction, note that the number of nodes in the DAG is linear in the number of states in $\mathcal{A}$. This is because $Form(q)$ may be constructed exactly once for each state q of $\mathcal{A}$. Hence the theorem. □

4 Interval Temporal Logic $UITL^{\pm}$

The interval logic *UITL* ([LPS08]) has the unambiguous chop modalities which deterministically chop at the first and last occurrence of a letter a within the interval. We enrich this logic with unambiguous modalities which chop beyond the interval boundaries in either direction. We call this logic $UITL^{\pm}$. In this section, we introduce the logic $UITL^{\pm}$ and show that it is no more expressive than $UITL$, by giving an effective conversion from $UITL^{\pm}$ formulas to their corresponding language-equivalent $TL[X_a, Y_a]$ formula. The conversion is similar to the conversion from $UITL$ to $TL[X_a, Y_a]$, as given in [DKL10].

4.1 $UITL^{\pm}$: Syntax and Semantics

The syntax and semantics of $UITL^{\pm}$ are as follows:

$$\top \mid a \mid pt \mid unit \mid BP\phi \mid EP\phi \mid D_1 F_a D_2 \mid D_1 L_a D_2 \mid D_1 F_a^+ D_2 \mid D_1 L_a^- D_2 \mid \oplus D_1 \mid \ominus D_1 \mid \overline{\oplus} D_1 \mid \overline{\ominus} D_1 \mid D_1 \vee D_2 \mid \neg D$$

Let w be a nonempty finite word over Σ and let $dom(w) = \{1, \ldots, \#w\}$ be the set of positions. Let $INTV(w) = \{[i,j] \mid i,j \in dom(w), i \leq j\} \cup \{\bot\}$ be the set of intervals over w, where $\bot$ is a special symbol to denote an undefined interval. For an interval I, let $l(I)$ and $r(I)$ denote the left and right endpoints of I. Further, if $I = \bot$, then $l(I) = r(I) = \bot$. The satisfaction of a formula D is defined over intervals of a word model w as follows.

$$\begin{array}{l}
w,[i,j] \models \top \text{ iff } [i,j] \in INTV(w) \text{ and } [i,j] \neq \bot \\
w,[i,j] \models pt \text{ iff } i = j \\
w,[i,j] \models unit \text{ iff } j = i+1 \\
w,[i,j] \models BP\phi \text{ iff } w,[i,i] \models \phi \\
w,[i,j] \models EP\phi \text{ iff } w,[j,j] \models \phi
\end{array}$$

$$\begin{array}{l}
w,[i,j] \models D_1 F_a D_2 \text{ iff for some } k : i \leq k \leq j.\ w[k] = a \text{ and} \\
\quad (\text{for all } m : i \leq m < k.\ w[m] \neq a) \text{ and} \\
\quad w,[i,k] \models D_1 \text{ and } w,[k,j] \models D_2 \\
w,[i,j] \models D_1 L_a D_2 \text{ iff for some } k : i \leq k \leq j.\ w[k] = a \text{ and} \\
\quad (\text{for all } m : k < m \leq j.\ w[m] \neq a) \text{ and} \\
\quad w,[i,k] \models D_1 \text{ and } w,[k,j] \models D_2 \\
w,[i,j] \models D_1 F_a^+ D_2 \text{ iff for some } k : k \geq j.\ w[k] = a \text{ and} \\
\quad (\text{for all } m : i \leq m < k.\ w[m] \neq a) \text{ and} \\
\quad w,[i,k] \models D_1 \text{ and } w,[j,k] \models D_2 \\
w,[i,j] \models D_1 L_a^- D_2 \text{ iff for some } k : k \leq i.\ w[k] = a \text{ and} \\
\quad (\text{for all } m : k < m \leq j.\ w[m] \neq a) \text{ and} \\
\quad w,[k,i] \models D_1 \text{ and } w,[k,j] \models D_2 \\
w,[i,j] \models \oplus D_1 \text{ iff } i < j \text{ and } w,[i+1,j] \models D_1 \\
w,[i,j] \models \ominus D_1 \text{ iff } i < j \text{ and } w,[i,j-1] \models D_1 \\
w,[i,j] \models \overline{\oplus} D_1 \text{ iff } j < \#w \text{ and } w,[i,j+1] \models D_1 \\
w,[i,j] \models \overline{\ominus} D_1 \text{ iff } i > 1 \text{ and } w,[i-1,j] \models D_1
\end{array}$$

The language $\mathcal{L}(\phi)$ of a $UITL$ formula ϕ iff is given by $\mathcal{L}(\phi) = \{w \mid w,[1,\#w] \models \phi\}$. We may derive "ceiling" operators which assert the invariance as follows.

- $\lceil A \rceil \equiv pt \vee unit \vee \neg \bigvee_{b \notin A} (\oplus \ominus (\top F_b \top))$

  Hence, $w,[i,j] \models \lceil A \rceil$ if and only if $\forall i < k < j\ .\ w(k) \in A$.

- $\lceil A \rceil\rceil \equiv pt \vee \neg \bigvee_{b \notin A} (\oplus(\top F_b \top))$
  Hence, $w, [i,j] \models \lceil A \rceil\rceil$ if and only if $\forall i < k \leq j \,.\, w(k) \in A$.
- $\lceil\lceil A \rceil \equiv pt \vee \neg \bigvee_{b \notin A} (\ominus(\top F_b \top))$
  Hence, $w, [i,j] \models \lceil\lceil A \rceil$ if and only if $\forall i \leq k < j \,.\, w(k) \in A$.
- $\lceil\lceil A \rceil\rceil \equiv \neg \bigvee_{b \notin A} (\top F_b \top)$
  Hence, $w, [i,j] \models \lceil\lceil A \rceil\rceil$ if and only if $\forall i \leq k \leq j \,.\, w(k) \in A$.

Example 3. The language given in Example 1 may be given by the $UITL^{\pm}$ formula $\top L_a (\lceil \Sigma \setminus \{b\} \rceil F_d \top)$.

$UITL^{\pm}$ and Unique Parsing $UITL^{\pm}$ is a deterministic logic and the property of *Unique Parsing* holds for its subformulas. Hence, for every $UITL^{\pm}$ subformula ψ, and any word w, there is a unique interval $Intv_w(\psi)$ within which it is evaluated. Further, for any "chop" operator ($F_a, L_a, F_a^+, L_a^-, \oplus, \ominus, \overline{\oplus}, \overline{\ominus}$), there is a unique chop position $cPos_w(\psi)$. If such an interval or chop position does not exist in the word, then they are equal to $\bot$. The $Intv_w(\psi)$ and $cPos_w(\psi)$ for any subformula ψ depend on its context and may be inductively defined. (See [LPS08] for similar such definition for the sublogic *UITL*).

4.2 From $TL[\widetilde{U},\widetilde{S}]$ to $UITL^{\pm}$

Given a $TL[\widetilde{U},\widetilde{S}]$ formula ϕ, we shall construct a $UITL^{\pm}$ formulas $BTrans(\phi)$ and $ETrans(\phi)$ having the following property.

Lemma 2. *Given a $TL[\widetilde{U},\widetilde{S}]$ formula ϕ, we may construct $UITL^{\pm}$ formulas $BTrans(\phi)$ and $ETrans(\phi)$ such that for any word $w \in \Sigma^+$ and any interval $[i,j]$ in w*

- $w, [i,j] \models BTrans(\phi)$ *iff* $w, i \models \phi$
- $w, [i,j] \models ETrans(\phi)$ *iff* $w, j \models \phi$

The translation takes polynomial time.

Proof. The formulas *BTrans* and *ETrans* may be constructed by bottom-up induction using the following rules.

- $BTrans(a) = BP\,(ptF_a\top)$
- $BTrans(\phi_1 \vee \phi_2) = BTrans(\phi_1) \vee BTrans(\phi_2)$
- $BTrans(\neg\phi) = \neg BTrans(\phi)$
- $BTrans(A\widetilde{U}_b\phi) = BP\overline{\oplus}\oplus[\,(\lceil\lceil A \rceil)\, F_b^+\, ETrans(\phi)]$
- $BTrans(A\widetilde{S}_b\phi) = BP\overline{\ominus}\ominus[\,(\lceil A \rceil\rceil)\, L_b^-\, BTrans(\phi)]$
- $ETrans(a) = EP\,(\top L_a pt)$
- $ETrans(\phi_1 \vee \phi_2) = ETrans(\phi_1) \vee ETrans(\phi_2)$
- $ETrans(\neg\phi) = \neg ETrans(\phi)$
- $ETrans(A\widetilde{U}_b\phi) = EP\overline{\oplus}\oplus[\,(\lceil\lceil A \rceil)\, F_b^+\, ETrans(\phi)]$
- $ETrans(A\widetilde{S}_b\phi) = EP\overline{\ominus}\ominus[\,(\lceil A \rceil\rceil)\, L_b^-\, BTrans(\phi)]$

The correctness of the above construction may be inferred from the semantics of the logics. For example, consider the formula $BTrans(A\widetilde{U}_b\phi)$. Let us assume $ETrans(\phi)$ has been appropriately constructed so as to satisfy the lemma. Then for any word $w \in \Sigma^+$ and any interval $[i, j]$ of w,

$w, [i, j] \models BTrans(A\widetilde{U}_b\phi)$
iff $w, [i, j] \models BP\overline{\oplus}\oplus[\,(\lceil\lceil A\rceil)\ F_b^+\ ETrans(\phi)]$
iff $w, [i, i] \models \overline{\oplus}\oplus[\,(\lceil\lceil A\rceil)\ F_b^+\ ETrans(\phi)]$
iff $w, [i+1, i+1] \models [\,(\lceil\lceil A\rceil)\ F_b^+\ ETrans(\phi)]$
iff $\exists k \geq (i+1)\ .\ w(k) = b \wedge \forall (i+1) \leq m < k\ .w(m) \in A \setminus \{b\} \wedge$
$\quad w, [i+1, k] \models ETrans(\phi)$
iff $w, i \models A\widetilde{U}_b\phi$ □

From the above construction, we infer that for every $TL[\widetilde{U},\widetilde{S}]$ formula, we may construct a language-equivalent $UITL^{\pm}$ formula whose size is linear in the size of the $TL[\widetilde{U},\widetilde{S}]$ formula. Clearly, the time time taken for the construction is also polynomial.

5 Deterministic Temporal Logic - $TL[X_a, Y_a]$

In [DK07] the authors showed that the deterministic temporal logic $TL[X_a, Y_a]$ which closes the rankers of [WI07] under boolean operations, also characterizes UL. In a subsequent paper [DKL10], they gave an important property of rankers called *ranker directionality*. We revisit this logic of rankers, giving a mild generalization of the same. We shall give a direct reductions between $TL[X_a, Y_a]$ formulas and *po2dfa* and analyse the complexity of translations. This also gives us an NP-complete satisfiability algorithm for $TL[X_a, Y_a]$ formulas.

5.1 $TL[X_a, Y_a]$: Syntax and Semantics

$TL[X_a, Y_a]$ is a unary deterministic temporal logic with the deterministic modalities X_a (*next-a*) and Y_a (*previous-a*) which uniquely mark the next and the previous occurrences (respectively) of a letter a from a given position. We also include their corresponding *weak* modalities ($\widetilde{X}_a$ and $\widetilde{Y}_a$), and *unit* modalities (X_1, Y_1) which access the next and previous positions respectively. *SP* (*Starting Position*) and *EP* (*Ending Position*) are additional modalities which uniquely determine the first and last positions of the word respectively.

Remark 2. It can be shown that the weak modalities and unit modalities, as well as the *SP* and *EP* modalities do not add expressive power to the logic (see [Sha12]). They may be derived using the X_a and Y_a modalities alone. However we include them in the syntax of the logic and define rankers which include all these modalities. We show that rankers when defined in such a manner, continue to possess their key properties. We shall see later in the paper that these generalized rankers play a crucial role in our formulations of reductions between logics for UL.

Let ϕ, ϕ_1 and ϕ_2 range over $TL[X_a, Y_a]$ formulas and a range over letters from a finite alphabet Σ. The syntax of $TL[X_a, Y_a]$ is given by:

$$\phi := a \mid \top \mid SP\phi_1 \mid EP\phi_1 \mid X_a\phi_1 \mid Y_a\phi_1 \mid \widetilde{X}_a\phi_1 \mid \widetilde{Y}_a\phi_1 \mid X_1\phi_1 \mid Y_1\phi_1 \mid \phi_1 \vee \phi_2 \mid \neg\phi_1$$

Let $G_{\overline{a}} = \neg X_a \top$ and $H_{\overline{a}} = \neg Y_a \top$ be derived atomic formulas. Semantics of $TL[X_a, Y_a]$ formulas is as given below. Let $w \in \Sigma^+$ be a non-empty finite word and let $i \in dom(w)$ be a position within the word.

$w,i \models a$ iff $w(i) = a$
$w,i \models SP\phi$ iff $w,1 \models \phi$
$w,i \models EP\phi$ iff $w,\#w \models \phi$
$w,i \models X_a\phi$ iff $\exists j > i \,.\, w(j) = a$ and $\forall i < k < j.w(k) \neq a$ and $w,j \models \phi$.
$w,i \models Y_a\phi$ iff $\exists j < i \,.\, w(j) = a$ and $\forall j < k < i.w(k) \neq a$ and $w,j \models \phi$.
$w,i \models \widetilde{X}_a\phi$ iff $\exists j \geq i \,.\, w(j) = a$ and $\forall i \leq k < j.w(k) \neq a$ and $w,j \models \phi$.
$w,i \models \widetilde{Y}_a\phi$ iff $\exists j \leq i \,.\, w(j) = a$ and $\forall j < k \leq i.w(k) \neq a$ and $w,j \models \phi$.
$w,i \models X_1\phi_1$ iff $\exists j = i+1 \,.\, w,j \models \phi_1$
$w,i \models Y_1\phi_1$ iff $\exists j = i-1 \,.\, w,j \models \phi_1$
$w,i \models \phi_1 \vee \phi_2$ iff $w,i \models \phi_1$ or $w,i \models \phi_2$
$w,i \models \neg\phi_1$ iff $w,i \not\models \phi_1$

The language accepted by a $TL[X_a, Y_a]$ formula ϕ is given by $\mathcal{L}(\phi) = \{w \mid w,1 \models \phi\}$.

Example 4. The language given in Example 1 is given by the $TL[X_a, Y_a]$ formula $EPY_aX_d\neg(Y_b\neg X_a\top)$.

Remark 3. A $TL[X_a, Y_a]$ formula (with the native X_a and Y_a modalities alone), may be trivially expressed as a $TL[\widetilde{U}, \widetilde{S}]$ formula using the following transformation function:

$$Trans(X_a\phi) \equiv \Sigma\widetilde{U}_a Trans(\phi) \qquad Trans(Y_a\phi) \equiv \Sigma\widetilde{S}_a Trans(\phi)$$

5.2 $TL[X_a, Y_a]$: Unique Parsing

$TL[X_a, Y_a]$ is a *Deterministic Logic*: Given any word $w \in \Sigma^+$ and $TL[X_a, Y_a]$ formula ϕ, for any subformula η of ϕ, there exists a unique position in $dom(w)$ where η must be evaluated in order to find the truth of ϕ. This position is denoted by $Pos_w(\eta)$ and is uniquely determined by the context of η. If such a position does not exist, then $Pos_w(\eta) = \bot$. It can be defined by induction on the depth of occurrence of η. We omit this obvious definition.

5.3 $TL[X_a, Y_a]$ to *po2dfa*

Theorem 2. *Given any $TL[X_a, Y_a]$ formula ϕ we may construct in polynomial time an equivalent po2dfa $\mathcal{A}(\phi)$ such that $\mathcal{L}(\phi) = \mathcal{L}(\mathcal{A}(\phi))$.*

Construction
The efficient reduction from $TL[X_a, Y_a]$ to *po2dfa* relies on the property of unique parsing of $TL[X_a, Y_a]$formulas. We use the *ETE* representation of *po2dfa* from Section 2.1 to illustrate the construction of the *po2dfa*. Fix a $TL[X_a, Y_a]$ formula Φ. For any subformula ϕ of Φ and any given word w, $Pos_w(\phi)$ depends on the context of ϕ and may be evaluated in a top-down manner. We construct an *ETE* $POS(\phi)$ such that the following proposition holds.

Proposition 2. *For any subformula ϕ of Φ and any word $w \in \Sigma^*$, we have*

- $POS(\phi)(w,1) = (t,i)$ *iff* $Pos_w(\phi) = i$
- $POS(\phi)(w,1) = (f,i)$ *iff* $Pos_w(\phi) = \bot$

Proof. The *ETE* for $POS(\phi)$ may be constructed by induction on the depth of occurrence the subformula ϕ as follows.

- $POS(\Phi) \ = \ \triangleright \overset{\Sigma'}{\leftarrow};(1 \overset{\triangleright}{\rightarrow})$
- If $\phi = X_a\phi_1$ then $POS(\phi_1) \ = \ POS(\phi);1 \overset{\Sigma'}{\rightarrow};a \overset{\Sigma'}{\rightarrow}$
- If $\phi = Y_a\phi_1$ then $POS(\phi_1) \ = \ POS(\phi);1 \overset{\Sigma'}{\leftarrow};a \overset{\Sigma'}{\leftarrow}$
- If $\phi = \widetilde{X}_a\phi_1$ then $POS(\phi_1) \ = \ POS(\phi);a \overset{\Sigma'}{\rightarrow}$
- If $\phi = \widetilde{Y}_a\phi_1$ then $POS(\phi_1) \ = \ POS(\phi);a \overset{\Sigma'}{\leftarrow}$
- If $\phi = X_1\phi_1$ then $POS(\phi_1) \ = \ POS(\phi) \ ; \ [(1 \overset{\Sigma}{\rightarrow};1 \overset{\triangleleft}{\leftarrow}) \ ? \ Rej \ : \ 1 \overset{\Sigma}{\rightarrow}]$
- If $\phi = Y_1\phi_1$ then $POS(\phi_1) \ = \ POS(\phi) \ ; \ [(1 \overset{\Sigma}{\leftarrow};1 \overset{\triangleright}{\rightarrow}) \ ? \ Rej \ : \ 1 \overset{\Sigma}{\leftarrow}]$
- If $\phi = SP\phi_1$ then $POS(\phi_1) \ = \ \triangleright \overset{\Sigma'}{\leftarrow} \ ; \ (1 \overset{\triangleright}{\rightarrow})$
- If $\phi = EP\phi_1$ then $POS(\phi_1) \ = \ \triangleleft \overset{\Sigma'}{\rightarrow} \ ; \ (1 \overset{\triangleleft}{\leftarrow})$
- If $\phi = \phi_1 \vee \phi_2$ then $POS(\phi_1) \ = \ POS(\phi_2) = POS(\phi)$
- If $\phi = \neg\phi_1$ then $POS(\phi_1) \ = \ POS(\phi)$

The correctness of the above construction may be deduced from the definition of $Pos_w(\phi)$ for $TL[X_a,Y_a]$ formulas by induction on the depth of occurrence of the subformula ϕ. Note that the *ETE* for $POS(\phi_1)$ when $\phi = X_1\phi_1$ is constructed as follows. It first checks if $POS(\phi)$ is at the last position in the word (by using $1 \overset{\Sigma}{\rightarrow};1 \overset{\triangleleft}{\leftarrow}$). If so, it rejects (i.e. evaluates to f), in which case $Pos_w(\phi_1) = \bot$. Otherwise, it accepts at the next position after $POS(\phi)$. The case of $\phi = Y_1\phi_1$ is symmetric to this. Other cases are similar. □

Now, for every subformula ϕ of Φ, we construct *ETE* $EVAL(\phi)$ which evaluates the formula at is unique position, as follows. From this proposition it immediately follows that $EVAL(\Phi)$ is the language-equivalent *ETE* for Φ.

Proposition 3. *For any subformula ϕ of Φ we may construct $EVAL(\phi)$ such that for any word $w \in \Sigma^*$ we have $EVAL(w,1) = (t,i)$ iff $Pos_w(\phi) \neq \bot$ and $w, Pos_w(\phi) \models \phi$.*

Proof. – If $\phi = \top$ then $EVAL(\phi) \ = \ POS(\phi);Acc$
- If $\phi = X_a\phi_1, Y_a\phi_1, \widetilde{X}_a\phi_1, \widetilde{Y}_a\phi_1, SP\phi_1, EP\phi_1, X_1\phi_1$ or $Y_1\phi_1$ then
  $EVAL(\phi) \ = \ POS(\phi_1);EVAL(\phi_1)$
- If $\phi = \phi_1 \vee \phi_2$ then $[POS(\phi);EVAL(\phi_1)] \ ? \ [Acc] \ : \ [POS(\phi);EVAL(\phi_2)]$
- If $\phi = \neg\phi_1$ then $EVAL(\phi_1) \ ? \ Rej \ : \ Acc$

We may verify by induction on the height of ϕ that that for any subformula ϕ and any word w, $EVAL(w,1) = (t,i)$ iff $Pos_w(\phi) \neq \bot$ and $w, Pos_w(\phi) \models \phi$. The proof uses Proposition 2. □

Complexity: Consider a $TL[X_a,Y_a]$ formula Φ of length l. For every subformula ϕ of Φ, observe that $POS(\phi)$ is linear in l. Further, $EVAL(\phi)$ is polynomial in l. Therefore, we can conclude that the size of the *ETE*(and hence the *po2dfa*) which is language-equivalent to Φ is polynomial in the size of Φ. Its construction can be carried out in polynomial time. Hence Theorem 2 holds true.

6 From $UITL^{\pm}$ to $TL[X_a,Y_a]$ Using Ranker Directionality

The notion of *rankers* [WI07] has played an important role in characterizing unambiguous languages UL. They were originally introduced as turtle programs by Schwentick *et al* [STV01]. Basically a ranker r is a finite sequence of instructions of the form X_a (denoting "go to the next a in the word") or Y_a (denoting "go to the previous a in the word"). Given a word w and a starting position i, the execution of a ranker r succeeds and ends at a final position j if all the instructions find their required letter. This is denoted by $w,i \models r$.

Here we generalize rankers and call them *Ranker Formulas*. These are essentially $TL[X_a,Y_a]$ formulas without any boolean operators, but including both the strict and the non-strict deterministic modalities ($X_a, Y_a, \widetilde{X}_a, \widetilde{Y}_a$), the unit-step modalities (X_1, Y_1), as well as the end postion modalities (SP, EP). This generalization maintains the key deterministic nature of rankers.

The abstract syntax of *Ranker Formulas* is as follows[1] :

$$\phi := \top \mid SP\phi \mid EP\phi \mid X_a\phi \mid Y_a\phi \mid \widetilde{X}_a\phi \mid \widetilde{Y}_a\phi \mid X_1\phi \mid Y_1\phi$$

Given a *Ranker Formula* ψ, let $Leaf(\psi)$ denote the unique atomic formula $\top$. For a given word w, the position of unique leaf formula is denoted as $\ell Pos_w(\psi) = Pos_w(Leaf(\psi))$. This is position where the *Ranker Formula* ψ accepts word w.

Sequential composition of Rankers: Through the rest of this chapter, we shall alternatively use the terms "ranker" and "*Ranker Formula*". We say that a ranker ϕ *accepts* at a position i in a word w if $\ell Pos_w(\phi) = i$. Given a ranker ϕ_1 and any $TL[X_a,Y_a]$ formula ϕ_2, denote by $\phi_1;\phi_2$ the $TL[X_a,Y_a]$ formula $\phi_1[\phi_2/\top]$ obtained by replacing the unique leaf atomic formula $\top$ of ϕ_1 by ϕ_2. Hence, for any word w, it is easy to see that $w,1 \models \phi_1;\phi_2$ iff $w,i \models \phi_2$, where $i = \ell Pos_w(\phi_1)$. Note that if ϕ_1 and ϕ_2 are *Ranker Formulas* then $\phi_1;\phi_2$ is also a *Ranker Formula.*

Ranker Directionality

Consider a *Ranker Formula* ψ. We can construct $TL[X_a,Y_a]$ formulas $\mathcal{P}^{<}(\psi)$, $\mathcal{P}^{\leq}(\psi)$, $\mathcal{P}^{>}(\psi)$, $\mathcal{P}^{\geq}(\psi)$ such that they satisfy the following Lemma 3. These formulas are called *ranker directionality formulas* and they allow us to analyse the relative positioning of the current position, with respect to the $lpos$ of the ranker. These formulas were given by [DKL10] for rankers. We generalize them for *Ranker Formulas.*

Let $\phi\top$ be a *Ranker Formula* where ϕ is the ancestor (context) of the leaf atomic formula $\top$. The ranker directionality formulas are given by Table 1, by induction on the depth of the ranker. In this table, define formulas $Atfirst \stackrel{\text{def}}{=} \neg(\vee_{a\in\Sigma}(Y_a\top))$ and $Atlast \stackrel{\text{def}}{=} \neg(\vee_{a\in\Sigma}(X_a\top))$ which hold exactly at the first and last positions in any word. Since every *Ranker Formula* formula is evaluated starting from the beginning of the word, we shall assume that at the top level the ranker begins with the SP modality. Observe that the size of the ranker directionality formula is linear in the size of the *Ranker Formula.*

---

[1] While a (for every $a \in \Sigma$) is an atomic formula in the case of $TL[X_a,Y_a]$ formulas, *Ranker Formulas* do not have a as an atomic formula. The only atomic formula is $\top$.

Table 1. Ranker Directionality Formulas

ψ	$\mathcal{P}^{<}(\psi)$	$\mathcal{P}^{\leq}(\psi)$	$\mathcal{P}^{>}(\psi)$	$\mathcal{P}^{\geq}(\psi)$
$\phi(SP\top)$	$\bot$	$Atfirst$	$\neg Atfirst$	$\top$
$\phi(EP\top)$	$\neg Atlast$	$\top$	$\bot$	$Atlast$
$\phi(\tilde{X}_a\top)$	$X_a(\mathcal{P}^{\leq}(\psi))$	$H_{\overline{a}} \vee (Y_a\mathcal{P}^{<}(\phi\top))$	$Y_a\mathcal{P}^{\geq}(\phi\top)$	$G_{\overline{a}} \vee X_a\mathcal{P}^{>}(\psi)$
$\phi(X_a\top)$	$X_a(\mathcal{P}^{\leq}(\psi))$	$H_{\overline{a}} \vee (Y_a\mathcal{P}^{\leq}(\phi\top))$	$Y_a\mathcal{P}^{>}(\phi\top)$	$G_{\overline{a}} \vee X_a\mathcal{P}^{>}(\psi)$
$\phi(\tilde{Y}_a\top)$	$X_a\mathcal{P}^{\leq}(\phi\top)$	$H_{\overline{a}} \vee (Y_a\mathcal{P}^{<}(\psi))$	$Y_a\mathcal{P}^{\geq}(\psi)$	$G_{\overline{a}} \vee X_a\mathcal{P}^{>}(\phi\top)$
$\phi(Y_a\top)$	$X_a\mathcal{P}^{<}(\phi\top)$	$H_{\overline{a}} \vee (Y_a\mathcal{P}^{<}(\psi))$	$Y_a\mathcal{P}^{\geq}(\psi)$	$G_{\overline{a}} \vee X_a\mathcal{P}^{\geq}(\phi\top)$
$\phi(X_1\top)$	$\mathcal{P}^{\leq}(\phi\top)$	$Atfirst \vee Y_1\mathcal{P}^{\leq}(\phi\top)$	$Y_1\mathcal{P}^{>}(\phi\top)$	$\mathcal{P}^{>}(\phi\top)$
$\phi(Y_1\top)$	$X_1\mathcal{P}^{<}(\phi\top)$	$\mathcal{P}^{<}(\phi\top)$	$\mathcal{P}^{\geq}(\phi\top)$	$Atlast \vee X_1\mathcal{P}^{\geq}(\phi\top)$

Lemma 3 (Ranker Directionality [DKL10]). *Let ψ be a Ranker Formula. Then $\forall w \in \Sigma^+$ and $\forall i \in dom(w)$, if $\ell Pos_w(\psi) \neq \bot$, then*

- $w,i \models \mathcal{P}^{<}(\psi)$ *iff* $i < \ell Pos_w(\psi)$
- $w,i \models \mathcal{P}^{\leq}(\psi)$ *iff* $i \leq \ell Pos_w(\psi)$
- $w,i \models \mathcal{P}^{>}(\psi)$ *iff* $i > \ell Pos_w(\psi)$
- $w,i \models \mathcal{P}^{\geq}(\psi)$ *iff* $i \geq \ell Pos_w(\psi)$

The correctness of the construction of the ranker directionality formulas is a direct consequence of the semantics of $TL[X_a, Y_a]$. A formal proof is given in [Sha12]. The following proposition states that every $TL[X_a, Y_a]$ formula may be expressed as a boolean combination of rankers.

Proposition 4. *For any $TL[X_a, Y_a]$ formula ϕ, there is a boolean combination $\mathcal{B}(\psi_i)$ of formulas ψ_i, such that $\mathcal{L}(\phi) = \mathcal{L}(\mathcal{B}(\psi_i))$. Each ψ_i is either an atomic formula or Ranker Formula. Moreover each ψ_i is linear in the size of ϕ.*

The above proposition gives a method of translating each $TL[X_a, Y_a]$ formula into *po2dfa*: each ranker can be trivially translated to a *po2dfa* and the automata are boolean closed. However, it can be observed that in general size of $\mathcal{B}(\psi_i)$ may be exponential in the size of ϕ. In the next section, we give a much more efficient polynomial sized (and polynomial timed) translation.

6.1 $UITL^{\pm}$ to $TL[X_a, Y_a]$

Theorem 3. *Given any $UITL^{\pm}$ formula ϕ of size n, we can construct in polynomial time a language-equivalent $TL[X_a, Y_a]$ formula $Trans(\phi)$, whose size is $O(n^2)$. Hence, satisfiability of $UITL^{\pm}$ is NP-complete.*

The construction of $Trans(\phi)$ requires some auxiliary definitions. For every $UITL^{\pm}$ subformula ψ of ϕ, we define *Ranker Formulas* $LIntv(\psi)$ and $RIntv(\psi)$, such that Lemma 4 holds. $LIntv(\psi)$ and $RIntv(\psi)$ are *Ranker Formulas* which accept at the left and right ends of the unique interval $Intv_w(\psi)$ respectively.

Lemma 4. *Given a $UITL^{\pm}$ subformula ψ of a formula ϕ, and any $w \in \Sigma^+$ such that $Intv_w(\psi), cPos_w(\psi) \neq \bot$,*

- $\ell Pos_w(LIntv(\psi)) = l(Intv_w(\psi))$
- $\ell Pos_w(RIntv(\psi)) = r(Intv_w(\psi))$

The required formulas $LIntv(\psi), RIntv(\psi)$ may be constructed by induction on the depth of occurrence of the subformula ψ as below. The correctness of these formulas is apparent from the semantics of $UITL^{\pm}$ formulas, and we omit the detailed proof.

- If $\psi = \phi$, then $LIntv(\psi) = SP\top, Rintv(\psi) = EP\top$
- If $\psi = BP\ D_1$ then
  $LIntv(D_1) = RIntv(D_1) = LIntv(\psi)$
- If $\psi = EP\ D_1$ then
  $LIntv(D_1) = RIntv(D_1) = RIntv(\psi)$
- If $\psi = D_1 F_a D_2$ then
  $LIntv(D_1) = LIntv(\psi), Rintv(D_1) = LIntv(\psi)\ ;\ \widetilde{X}_a\top,$
  $LIntv(D_2) = LIntv(\psi)\ ;\ \widetilde{X}_a\top, Rintv(D_2) = RIntv(\psi)$
- If $\psi = D_1 F_a^+ D_2$ then
  $LIntv(D_1) = LIntv(\psi), Rintv(D_1) = RIntv(\psi)\ ;\ \widetilde{X}_a\top,$
  $LIntv(D_2) = RIntv(\psi), Rintv(D_2) = RIntv(\psi)\ ;\ \widetilde{X}_a\top$
- If $\psi = D_1 L_a D_2$ then
  $LIntv(D_1) = LIntv(\psi), Rintv(D_1) = RIntv(\psi)\ ;\ \widetilde{Y}_a\top,$
  $LIntv(D_2) = RIntv(\psi)\ ;\ \widetilde{Y}_a\top, Rintv(D_2) = RIntv(\psi)$
- If $\psi = D_1 L_a^- D_2$ then
  $LIntv(D_1) = LIntv(\psi)\ ;\ \widetilde{Y}_a\top, Rintv(D_1) = LIntv(\psi),$
  $LIntv(D_2) = LIntv(\psi)\ ;\ \widetilde{Y}_a\top, Rintv(D_2) = RIntv(\psi)$
- If $\psi = \oplus D_1$ then
  $LIntv(D_1) = LIntv(\psi)\ ;\ X_1\top, RIntv(D_1) = RIntv(\psi)$
- If $\psi = \overline{\oplus} D_1$ then
  $LIntv(D_1) = LIntv(\psi), RIntv(D_1) = RIntv(\psi)\ ;\ X_1\top$
- If $\psi = \ominus D_1$ then
  $LIntv(D_1) = LIntv(\psi), RIntv(D_1) = RIntv(\psi)\ ;\ Y_1\top$
- If $\psi = \overline{\ominus} D_1$ then
  $LIntv(D_1) = LIntv(\psi)\ ;\ Y_1\top, RIntv(D_1) = RIntv(\psi)$

We can now construct, for any subformula ψ of ϕ, a corresponding $TL[X_a, Y_a]$ formula $Trans(\psi)$. The conversion uses the following inductive rules. Then, it is easy to see that $Trans(\psi)$ is language equivalent to ϕ (see [Sha12] for proof).

- If $\psi = BP\ D_1$ or $EP\ D_1$ then $Trans(\psi) = Trans(D_1)$
- If $\psi = D_1 F_a D_2$, then $Trans(\psi) = [(\ LIntv(\psi); \widetilde{X}_a\top\ )\ ;\ \mathcal{P}^{\leq}(RIntv(\psi))] \wedge Trans(D_1) \wedge Trans(D_2)$
- If $\psi = D_1 L_a D_2$, then $Trans(\psi) = [(\ RIntv(\psi); \widetilde{Y}_a\top\ )\ ;\ \mathcal{P}^{\geq}(LIntv(\psi))] \wedge Trans(D_1) \wedge Trans(D_2)$
- If $\psi = D_1 F_a^+ D_2$, then $Trans(\psi) = [(\ LIntv(\psi); \widetilde{X}_a\top\ )\ ;\ \mathcal{P}^{\geq}(RIntv(\psi))] \wedge Trans(D_1) \wedge Trans(D_2)$
- If $\psi = D_1 L_a^- D_2$, then $Trans(\psi) = [(\ RIntv(\psi); \widetilde{Y}_a\top\ )\ ;\ \mathcal{P}^{\leq}(LIntv(\psi))] \wedge Trans(D_1) \wedge Trans(D_2)$

- If $\psi = \oplus D_1$, then $Trans(\psi) = [(LIntv(\psi);X_1\top)\ ;\ \mathcal{P}^{\leq}(RIntv(\psi))] \wedge Trans(D_1)$
- If $\psi = \ominus D_1$, then $Trans(\psi) = [(RIntv(\psi);Y_1\top)\ ;\ \mathcal{P}^{\geq}(LIntv(\psi))] \wedge Trans(D_1)$
- If $\psi = \overline{\oplus} D_1$, then $Trans(\psi) = [(RIntv(\psi);X_1\top)] \wedge Trans(D_1)$
- If $\psi = \overline{\ominus} D_1$, then $Trans(\psi) = [(LIntv(\psi);Y_1\top)] \wedge Trans(D_1)$
- $Trans(D_1 \vee D_2) = Trans(D_1) \vee Trans(D_2)$
- $Trans(\neg D_1) = \neg Trans(D_1)$

7 Discussion

A large portion of the work on the language class UL in past has been via the algebraic characterization, namely the variety *DA*. While several logics and *po2dfa* were shown to be expressively equivalent to UL, constructive reductions between these diverse formalisms and their complexities are less known. Hence, their relative succinctness has not been explored. In this paper, we show how the notion of deterministic temporal logics is relevant to the language class UL, and we give instances of the tight coupling between such logics and the *po2dfa* automata. The benefit is that we can establish NP-Complete satisfiability of these logics.

Our study is mainly motivated by the following question: How far can we go, while still remaining in UL? We give two important instances of the same, namely $TL[\widetilde{U},\widetilde{S}]$ and $UITL^{\pm}$. Thus, the language class UL appears to be robustly characterized by several *deterministic* temporal logics with diverse modalities. We believe that the intuition of identifying the language class UL with *deterministic* constructs was inherent in the original definitions of Schützenberger [Sch76] of unambiguous polynomials and his choice of term "unambiguous" for UL is suggestive of this. We have demonstrated that such determinism leads to efficient decision procedures.

This study of deterministic logics and *po2dfa* has also been extended to real time. In [PS10], we have investigated extensions of the logics $TL[X_a,Y_a]$, $TL[\widetilde{U},\widetilde{S}]$ and $UITL^{\pm}$ and the automaton (*po2DTA*) to real-time. The concept of deterministic logics has proved useful in obtaining timed logics with low decision complexities.

In literature. the prominent logical characterizations of UL have primarily been non-deterministic; e.g. the fragments $\Delta_2[<]$ and $FO^2[<]$ of first-order definable languages and the Unary Temporal Logic $TL[F,P]$. While these logics are expressively equivalent to Partially ordered 2-Way DFAs (*po2dfa*), no explicit reductions from these logics to *po2dfa* are known . Neither the complexities of the formula automaton construction nor the bounds on the size of equivalent automata have been worked out. Thus, there seems to be a gap in moving from non-deterministic logics for UL to the deterministic logics for UL. Our recent work (in progress) addresses these questions.

References

[DGK08] Diekert, V., Gastin, P., Kufleitner, M.: A survey on small fragments of first-order logic over finite words. Int. J. Found. Comput. Sci. 19(3), 513–548 (2008)

[DK07] Diekert, V., Kufleitner, M.: On first-order fragments for words and mazurkiewicz traces. In: Harju, T., Karhumäki, J., Lepistö, A. (eds.) DLT 2007. LNCS, vol. 4588, pp. 1–19. Springer, Heidelberg (2007)

[DKL10] Dartois, L., Kufleitner, M., Lauser, A.: Rankers over infinite words. In: Gao, Y., Lu, H., Seki, S., Yu, S. (eds.) DLT 2010. LNCS, vol. 6224, pp. 148–159. Springer, Heidelberg (2010)

[EPW97] Pin, J.É., Weil, P.: Polynomial closure and unambiguous product. Theory Comput. Syst. 30(4), 383–422 (1997)

[EVW02] Etessami, K., Vardi, M.Y., Wilke, T.: First-order logic with two variables and unary temporal logic. Inf. Comput. 179(2), 279–295 (2002)

[LPS08] Lodaya, K., Pandya, P.K., Shah, S.S.: Marking the chops: an unambiguous temporal logic. In: IFIP TCS, pp. 461–476 (2008)

[PS10] Pandya, P.K., Shah, S.S.: Unambiguity in timed regular languages: Automata and logics. In: Chatterjee, K., Henzinger, T.A. (eds.) FORMATS 2010. LNCS, vol. 6246, pp. 168–182. Springer, Heidelberg (2010)

[Sch76] Schützenberger, M.-P.: Sur le produit de concaténation non ambigu. In: Semigroup Forum, pp. 47–75 (1976)

[Sha12] Shah, S.S.: Unambiguity and Timed Languages:Automata, Logics, Expressiveness. PhD thesis, TIFR, Mumbai (2012) (submitted)

[STV01] Schwentick, T., Thérien, D., Vollmer, H.: Partially-ordered two-way automata: A new characterization of DA. In: Kuich, W., Rozenberg, G., Salomaa, A. (eds.) DLT 2001. LNCS, vol. 2295, pp. 239–250. Springer, Heidelberg (2002)

[TW98] Thérien, D., Wilke, T.: Over words, two variables are as powerful as one quantifier alternation. In: STOC, pp. 234–240 (1998)

[WI07] Weis, P., Immerman, N.: Structure theorem and strict alternation hierarchy for FO^2 on words. In: Duparc, J., Henzinger, T.A. (eds.) CSL 2007. LNCS, vol. 4646, pp. 343–357. Springer, Heidelberg (2007)

Finitary Fairness in Action Systems

Emil Sekerinski and Tian Zhang

McMaster University, Hamilton, ON, Canada
{emil,zhangt26}@mcmaster.ca

Abstract. In basic action systems, the choice among actions is not restricted. Fairness can be imposed to restrict this nondeterminism. Finitary fairness has been proposed as a further restriction of fairness: it models implementations closer, and allows problems to be solved for which standard fairness is not sufficient. We propose a method for expressing finitary fairness in action systems. We give two general transformations from a system in which some actions are marked as fair, into an equivalent system without fair actions. A theoretical justification is given, and the transformations are illustrated with two examples: alternating bit protocol and distributed consensus. The examples are developed by stepwise refinement in Event-B and are mechanically checked.

Keywords: Finitary Fairness, Modelling, Termination, Event-B, Stepwise Refinement.

1 Introduction

The theory of *action systems* formalizes development of parallel and reactive programs by stepwise refinement [1]. An action system consists of global variables, local variables, an *initialization* statement and a set of *actions* (or atomic guarded commands). Because of existing tool support, we use the Event-B [2] notation for illustration, and we borrow the Event-B term *events* as an alias for actions. A *schedule* is a sequence of event names that can occur in a *computation* (which is going to be made precise). A schedule can be finite or infinite.

Consider the event system in Fig. 1, which is taken from [3]. Both events L and R have no guard and are thus always enabled. In this example all possible schedules are

invariants
  $x \in BOOL$
  $y \in \mathbb{N}$
initialisation
  $x, y := TRUE, 0$
event L
  $x := NOT\, x$
event R
  $y := y + 1$

Fig. 1. A simple event system with two events

Z. Liu, J. Woodcock, and H. Zhu (Eds.): ICTAC 2013, LNCS 8049, pp. 319–336, 2013.

infinite. In basic event systems the choice among events is not restricted. Such nondeterministic choice only guarantees *minimal progress*: any enabled event can be taken and an enabled event must be taken only if no other is enabled. With the default assumption of minimal progress, a schedule can contain an infinite sequence of an event, e.g. a schedule that repeatedly executes L after executing L and R twice:

$$LRLRLLLLL\ldots$$

In the design of concurrent systems, *fairness* restricts the nondeterminism leading to minimal progress. It also allows to abstract from scheduling policies in multi-process systems and from processor speeds in multi-processor systems. *Weak fairness* requires that no event can be continuously enabled forever without being taken. This is a useful assumption for multi-process and multi-processor systems: if two continuously enabled events belong to different processes, fairness implies that the scheduler must give each process a chance, without specifying the scheduling policy; if two continuously enabled events are to be executed on different processors, fairness expresses that each processor is working, without quantifying the relative speed.

If both events in the above example are specified to be weakly fair, then fairness of L implies that a schedule cannot contain an infinite sequence of R's, and vice versa. For example, the above schedule would be excluded, but the following schedule, in which the number of consecutive R's continues to increase, is allowed:

$$LRLRRLRRRLRRRRL\ldots$$

A schedule is *weakly k-bounded* if for some natural number k, no fair event is neglected more than k times while being consecutively enabled. *Finitary fairness* of an event system means that all schedules are k-bounded for some $k \in \mathbb{N}$ [3]. The above schedule is not k-bounded for any $k \in \mathbb{N}$; thus the schedule is allowed when L and R are restricted by standard fairness but not when restricted by finitary fairness.

Suppose the events belong to different processes. A *scheduler* is an automaton with event names as the alphabet. For the above schedule to be generated by an automaton, the automaton needs to count the number of R's, so it has an unboundedly large number of states. Conversely, if the schedule is bounded, only a finite number of states are needed. Thus, the bounded schedules are exactly the languages of finite state schedulers. Since any practical scheduler uses a fixed amount of memory, finitary fairness is not only an adequate, but also a more precise abstraction from scheduling policies than standard fairness.

Suppose that the events are executed on different processors; the speeds of the processors may differ and may vary. Finitary fairness implies that the speeds of the processors may not drift apart unboundedly. Alur and Henzinger formalize this claim in terms of timed transition systems [3]. Again, finitary fairness allows a more precise abstraction of multiprocessor systems.

The interleaving model of concurrency represents the concurrent execution of two independent events by a sequential execution in any order. Thus, reasoning about a concurrent system is reduced to reasoning about a nondeterministic sequential system. Since finitary fairness is more restrictive than standard fairness, one can expect more properties to hold under finitary fairness. For example, the event system of Fig. 1 will eventually reach a state in which $x = TRUE \land \neg powerOf2(y)$ holds: if this property would always be false, then L must be scheduled only when $powerOf2(y)$ holds, for increasing values of y, but that is impossible in a bounded schedule.

Finitary fairness allows some problems to be solved for which standard fairness is not sufficient. Furthermore, termination proofs are simpler with finitary fairness compared to standard fairness, as variants need to be over natural numbers only rather than well-founded sets as with standard fairness.

In this paper we propose a method for the stepwise development of action systems with finitary fairness. Finitary fairness is particularly suited for Event-B as in Event-B variants are only over natural numbers. The core contribution of this paper is a transformation of an event system with finitary weak fairness to an equivalent one without fairness. A similar transformation was proposed in [3], but that transformation does not result in an equivalent system, only in one in which all computations terminate if and only if all finitary weakly fair computations of the original system do (which was the intention). The transformed system does not have any restriction on the counters, so it may enter a state in which two counters reach the upper limit at the same time and then forced to terminate prematurely. Consequently, it does not have the same computations as the original system. The theoretical finitary restriction, as proposed in [3], can be applied to both weak fairness and *strong fairness*, which differs from weak fairness by requiring that an event must be taken if it is enabled repeatedly, but not necessarily continuously. In this work, we restrict our transformation to weak fairness as in [3], as for the example at hand, distributed consensus, weak fairness is sufficient.

Section 2 summarizes related work. Section 3 formally defines transition systems with fair events, computations, and finitary fairness. Section 4 presents two methods for transforming an event system with fair and regular events to one that has only regular events but produces the same computations. In Sect. 5 one of the two transformations is illustrated in the stepwise refinement of the alternating bit protocol, an example that has been studied repeatedly in literature; fairness is needed as the assumption that a message in transmission will not always be lost and has a fair chance of reaching the destination. In Sect. 6 the other transformation is illustrated in the stepwise refinement of a distributed consensus algorithm, an example in which finitary fairness can guarantee termination, but standard fairness cannot. The final section gives an outlook.[1]

2 Related Work

Programming theories with fairness are well worked out, e.g. [5,6,7]. Extensions of action systems to fairness have been proposed [8,9,10]. In [9] refinement rules that preserve temporal (leads-to) and fixpoint (termination) properties are studied for fair transitions systems (action systems). Here we restrict ourselves to terminating action systems but consider local variables, allowing a more general notion of refinement.

The approach of [10] is to augment action systems by explicitly specifying and prohibiting unfair non-terminating computations, rather than assuming a fair choice among

[1] The models in this paper are developed in Event-B using the Rodin platform [4], an Eclipse-based IDE for Event-B. All proof obligations have been successfully proved. The Rodin project files are available at `http://www.cas.mcmaster.ca/~zhangt26/ICTAC/`

invariants
  $x \in \mathbb{N}$
initialisation
  $x :\in \mathbb{N}$
event L
  when
    $x > 0$
  then
    skip
  end
fair event R
  when
    $x > 0$
  then
    $x := x - 1$
  end

(a)

invariants
  $x \in \mathbb{N}$
  $C \in \mathbb{N}$
initialisation
  $x :\in \mathbb{N}$
  $C :\in \mathbb{N}_1$
event L
  when
    $x > 0$
    $C > 1$
  then
    $C := C - 1$
  end
event R
  when
    $x > 0$
  then
    $x := x - 1$
    $C :\in \mathbb{N}_1$
  end

(b)

invariants
  $x \in \mathbb{N}$
  $C \in 1..B$
initialisation
  $x :\in \mathbb{N}$
  $C := B$
event L
  when
    $x > 0$
    $C > 1$
  then
    $C := C - 1$
  end
event R
  when
    $x > 0$
  then
    $x := x - 1$
    $C := B$
  end

(c)

Fig. 2. (a) Event system with fair event R. (b) The counter C is used to ensure standard fairness of R. (c) The counter C is used to ensure finitary fairness of R.

actions, and to study refinement of such augmented action systems; this allows a wider range of fairness constraints to be expressed compared to the (weak) fairness considered here, although in a different style.

The proof rule for the termination of an event system is more involved in the presence of fairness: events either must decrease the variant or keep fair events which decrease the variant enabled, as by fairness these will eventually be taken. The proof rule requires that an invariant is specified for each event, e.g. as in [8] for the refinement of action systems, rather than one invariant for the whole system as in Event-B. This would require the proof rules of Event-B to be significantly expanded.

The alternative that we follow is to transform an event system by replacing fair events with regular events and introducing an explicit scheduler [11,1]. The standard proof rules of Event-B can then be applied. Figure 2 illustrates this. The event system of (a) will eventually terminate as x is set initially to some natural number, and fair event R always decreases x. In both transformed event systems (b) and (c) fairness is achieved by introducing a (down-) counter C that is decreased each time the (regular) event L is taken. This eventually forces R to be taken as L becomes disabled when C reaches 1. When R is taken, C is reset. In (b) the (down-) counter C does not have an upper bound, but still event R will eventually be taken; this ensures standard fairness. In (c), C is at most B, so $B-1$ is the upper bound of how many times event R can be consecutively ignored before it must be taken, hence the schedules are $(B-1)$-bounded and the model ensures finitary fairness.

A further reason for preferring finitary fairness is that it can simplify proofs of termination. For a set of events to terminate, there must exist a variant, which is a function from the states to a well-founded domain, and all events have to decrease the variant. For proving the termination of the event system in Fig. 2 (c), the following variant with natural numbers as the well-founded domain is sufficient:

variant
$$x * B + C$$

Event L decreases the variant by decreasing C. Event R decreases the variant by decreasing x ($C \in 1..B$ so the variant is still decreased even when C is reset to B). A similar variant cannot be given for the event system in (b): natural numbers as the well-founded domain are not sufficient with standard fairness.

The finitary restriction can be used for modelling *unknown delays* of timed systems. In the problem of distributed consensus, processes have to agree on a common output value, but processes with different preferences may try to set the output at the same time. Besides, each process may fail and not deliver a value. This can be solved using finitary fairness, as shown in [3], but cannot be solved using standard fairness only [12].

3 Fair Event Systems

When considering finitary fairness, we are interested only in k-bounded computations. Following definition of fair event systems generalizes that of transitions systems in [3] by indexing the transitions with the events and by allowing only some events to be fair.

Definition 1. *A* fair event system *P is a structure (Q, I, F, E, T) where*

- *Q is the set of states,*
- *I is the set of initial states, $I \subseteq Q$,*
- *F is the number of fair events,*
- *E is the set of all events, with cardinality $N \geq F$ (we assume that e_i is a fair event for $i \in 1..F$ and a regular event for $i \in F+1..N$),*
- *T is the set of transitions, relations over $Q \times Q$ indexed by E.*

We write $T(e)$ for the transition relation of event e. A computation *comp* of P is a finite or infinite maximal sequence of states and events alternating, written

$$comp = \sigma_0 \xrightarrow{\tau_0} \sigma_1 \xrightarrow{\tau_1} \sigma_2 \xrightarrow{\tau_2} \cdots$$

such that $\sigma_0 \in I$ and $\forall i \cdot i \in \mathbb{N} \Rightarrow \tau_i \in E \wedge \sigma_i \mapsto \sigma_{i+1} \in T(\tau_i)$. That is, states σ_i and σ_{i+1} must be in relation $T(\tau_i)$. A computation is a finite sequence, or is *terminating*, if it ends with a state σ_n, for some $n \in \mathbb{N}$, that is not in the domain of any transition relation, i.e. $\forall e \cdot e \in E \Rightarrow \sigma_n \notin dom(T(e))$. Otherwise it is an infinite sequence, or is *nonterminating*. The schedule of a computation *comp* is the projection of the sequence *comp* to the events; the *trace* of *comp* is the projection of *comp* to the states:

$$schedule(comp) = \tau_0\tau_1\tau_2\ldots \qquad trace(comp) = \sigma_0\sigma_1\sigma_2\ldots$$

We write $schedule_i(comp)$ for τ_i, the i-th event of computation *comp*, and $trace_i(comp)$ for σ_i, the i-th state of computation *comp*. The *guard* of an event is the domain of its relation, $grd(e) = dom(T(e))$; an event is *enabled* in a state if the state is in its guard, otherwise *disabled*. A computation *comp* is *bounded* if it is finite or if for some $k \in \mathbb{N}$, any fair event e_f, for some $f \in 1..F$, cannot be enabled for more than k consecutive states without being taken, formally:

$$\forall i,f \cdot i \in \mathbb{N} \wedge f \in 1..F \Rightarrow$$
$$\exists j \cdot j \in i..i+k \wedge (schedule_j(comp) = e_f \vee trace_j(comp) \notin grd(e_f))$$

An Event-B model defines the set of states through the variables and invariants, the transition relations through guards and generalized substitutions, and the initial states through the initialization event. Thus, fair event systems are abstract representations of Event-B models, in which we additionally allow some events to be specified as fair.

4 The Finitary Weakly Fair Transformation

Let $P = (Q,I,F,E,T)$ be a fair event system. Now we give the definition of the *finitary weakly fair transformation*, the application of which to P written as $fwf(P)$. It expresses finitary fairness by introducing (down-) counter variables $C_1,\ldots,C_F$, one for each fair event. The counter C_i, for $i \in 1..F$, of event e_i indicates that e_i must be taken or disabled at least once in the next C_i transitions. Once the counter of an event reaches 1, that event must be tested: if it is enabled, it must be taken, otherwise it may be skipped.

Care is needed to avoid that several counters reach 1 simultaneously, as the corresponding events cannot be taken in one transition. A naive approach would be to initialize them to distinct values between 1 and B and keep them distinct by decreasing all by 1 simultaneously and cyclically reset them to B: that would enforce round-robin scheduling, but that is too restrictive as we do not want to preclude any fair schedule. To obtain an appropriate translation, in $fwf(P)$ we add a permutation p of $1..F$, on the basis of $fin(P)$ in [3]. The permutation p satisfies $\forall j \cdot j \in 1..F \Rightarrow C_{p(j)} \geq j$ in every state, to guarantee that only one counter can be 1. On every transition, the guards of all fair events must be tested: if a fair event is enabled but not taken, its counter must be decreased, otherwise its counter is reset to B. The counters are all initialized to have the value B; they do not have to be distinct. Using p keeps the system in safe states, while the set of possible schedules remains the same.

Definition 2. *For fair event system P, the finitary weak fair transformation* $fwf(P) = (Q',I',0,E,T')$ *is given by:*

- $Q' = Q \times [F,+\infty) \times [1,B]^F$
- *For every event* $e_i \in E$, $(\sigma,B,C_1,\ldots,C_F) \mapsto (\sigma',B',C'_1,\ldots,C'_F) \in T'(e_i)$ *if:*
  1. $B = B' \wedge \sigma \mapsto \sigma' \in T(e_i) \wedge (i \in 1..F \Rightarrow C'_i = B)$
  2. $\forall j \cdot j \in 1..F \backslash \{i\} \Rightarrow$
     $((\sigma \in grd(e_j) \wedge C'_j \geq 1 \wedge C'_j = C_j - 1) \vee (\sigma \notin grd(e_j) \wedge C'_j = B))$
  3. *A permutation p of* $1..F$*, exists, such that* $\forall j \cdot j \in 1..F \Rightarrow C'_{p(j)} \geq j$
- I' *is such that* $(\sigma,B,C_1,\ldots,C_F) \in I'$ *if*

1. $\sigma \in I \wedge B \geq F$
2. $\forall j \cdot j \in 1..F \Rightarrow C_j = B$

All counters of the finitary fair transformation are between 1 and B, and the permutation p always exists. That is, for all computations *comp* of *fwf*(P), for all natural numbers i with $0 \leq i < |trace(comp)|$, and writing $\rightarrowtail\!\!\!\!\twoheadrightarrow$ for the type of bijective functions:

$$trace_i(comp) = (\sigma, B, C_1, \ldots, C_F) \Rightarrow \\ \exists p \cdot p \in 1..F \rightarrowtail\!\!\!\!\twoheadrightarrow 1..F \wedge (\forall j \cdot j \in 1..F \Rightarrow C_j \in 1..B \wedge C_{p(j)} \geq j) \quad (1)$$

This property follows by induction over i: with *fwf*$(P) = (Q', I', 0, E, T')$ the initial states in I' satisfy (1) and transitions in T' preserve (1).

Compared to *fin*(P) in [3], the resulting system prevents premature termination, because it guarantees that as long as one event is enabled in some state σ_i ($i \in \mathbb{N}$) in some computation *comp* of P, then at least one event is enabled in the corresponding state σ'_i in *comp* of *fwf*(P). If all fair events are disabled, then the additional guards of regular events are always satisfied, i.e. then the additional guards will not prevent any enabled regular event from being taken.

The introductory example results from this transformation. In practice, this transformation has the drawback that a term for stating the existence of a permutation will increase exponentially with the number of fair events. In the following alternative transformation, *dist*(P), all counters are kept distinct. A term stating the distinctness of F counters would have $(F * (F+1)/2)$ clauses, which with large number of fair events results in significantly more compact descriptions.

Definition 3. *For fair event system P, the finitary weak fair transformation dist(P) = $(Q', I', 0, E, T')$ is given by:*

- $Q' = Q \times [F, +\infty) \times [1, B]^F$
- *For every event $e_i \in E$, $(\sigma, B, C_1, \ldots, C_F) \mapsto (\sigma', B', C'_1, \ldots, C'_F) \in T'(e_i)$ if:*
  1. $B = B' \wedge \sigma \mapsto \sigma' \in T(e_i) \wedge (i \in 1..F \Rightarrow C'_i \in 1..B)$
  2. $\forall j \cdot j \in 1..F \backslash \{i\} \Rightarrow C'_j \in 1..B \wedge (\sigma \in grd(e_j) \Rightarrow C'_j = C_j - 1)$
  3. $distinct(C'_1, \ldots, C'_F)$
- *I' is such that $(\sigma, B, C_1, \ldots, C_F) \in I'$ if*
  1. $\sigma \in I \wedge B \geq F$
  2. $\forall j \cdot j \in 1..F \Rightarrow C_j \in 1..B$
  3. $distinct(C_1, \ldots, C_F)$

All counters of *dist*(P) are between 1 and B and are distinct, i.e. for all computations *comp* of *fwf*(P) and for all natural numbers i with $1 \leq i < |trace(comp)|$:

$$trace_i(comp) = (\sigma, B, C_1, \ldots, C_F) \Rightarrow \\ (\forall j \cdot j \in 1..F \Rightarrow C_j \in 1..B) \wedge distinct(C_1, \ldots, C_F) \quad (2)$$

This property follows by induction over i: with *dist*$(P) = (Q', I', 0, E, T')$ the initial states in I' satisfy (2) and transitions in T' preserve (2).

Theorem 1. *For any fair event system P, the schedules of fwf(P) and of dist(P) are exactly the finitary weak fair schedules of P.*

Proof. Let P be (Q,I,F,E,T). We give the proof only for $fwf(P)$; the one for $dist(P)$ has the same structure. The proof proceeds by mutual inclusion. For showing that the schedules of $fwf(P)$ are bounded schedules of P, we note that the schedules of $fwf(P)$ are also schedules of P, so it remains to be shown that they are bounded. We reformulate the definition of a bounded computation. A computation *comp* is bounded if it is finite or for some $k \in \mathbb{N}$, for all $e \in F$, for all $i \in \mathbb{N}$:

$$(\forall j \cdot j \in i..i+k \Rightarrow trace_j(comp) \in grd(e)) \Rightarrow \exists j \cdot j \in i..i+k \wedge schedule_j(comp) = e$$

Let *comp* be a computation of $fwf(P)$. It is obvious that if $schedule(comp)$ is finite, it is bounded with $k = B-1$ by definition. When it is infinite, let e_f be a fair event ($f \in 1..F$), let i be a natural number, and assume that $\forall j \cdot j \in i..i+k \Rightarrow trace_j(comp) \in grd(e_f)$. We have to show that $schedule_j(comp) = e_f$ for some $j \in i..i+k$. We prove this by contradiction. If such an index j does not exist, then since e_f is consecutively enabled, according to the properties of transitions in $fwf(P)$, in every step C_f is decremented by 1. After B steps, C_f is decreased by B. In state $trace_i$, $C_f \in 1..B$, so in state $trace_{i+k+1}(comp)$, $C_f \in 1-B..0$, which contradicts the constraint $C_f \in 1..B$. Hence after at most B transitions, event e_f must have been taken.

Now let *comp* be a bounded computation of P. We have to show that a computation $comp'$ of $fwf(P)$ exists such that $schedule(comp')$ equals $schedule(comp)$. During initialization, if B is picked such that $B \geq k+F$, then all the counters are always greater or equal to F in *comp* (since *comp* is k-bounded, then every counter in $fwf(P)$ is reset at least once in every $k+1$ steps, either due to being disabled or executed), so such a permutation p always exists throughout the schedule (simply *id* on $1..F$), and no event will be disabled by the additional guards; thus a computation $comp'$ which yields the same schedule does exist in $fwf(P)$. This completes the proof.

5 The Alternating Bit Protocol

The alternating bit protocol (ABP) [13], a protocol for reliable communication over unreliable channels, has repeatedly been formalized. Our treatment is inspired by that of [5,14]. Channels are modelled as simple variables, as in [15,16], rather than as sequences. The first refinement step is similar to the file transfer example of [2]. The refinement process is illustrated in Fig. 3. It uses the $dist(P)$ transformation.

Specification. In its most abstract form, a transmission copies sequence a to sequence z. We let *SIZE* be a positive natural number and *DATA* a set.

MACHINE ABP0
SEES Context
VARIABLES
  z target file
  e mark of termination
INVARIANTS
  inv1 : $z \in 1..SIZE \nrightarrow DATA$
  inv2 : $e \in 0..1$
  inv3 : $e = 0 \Rightarrow z = a$
EVENTS
Initialisation
  begin
    act1 : $z := \varnothing$
    act2 : $e := 1$
  end
Event *TransferAll* $\widehat{=}$
Status convergent
  when
    grd1 : $e = 1$
  then
    act1 : $z := a$
    act2 : $e := 0$
  end
VARIANT
  e
END

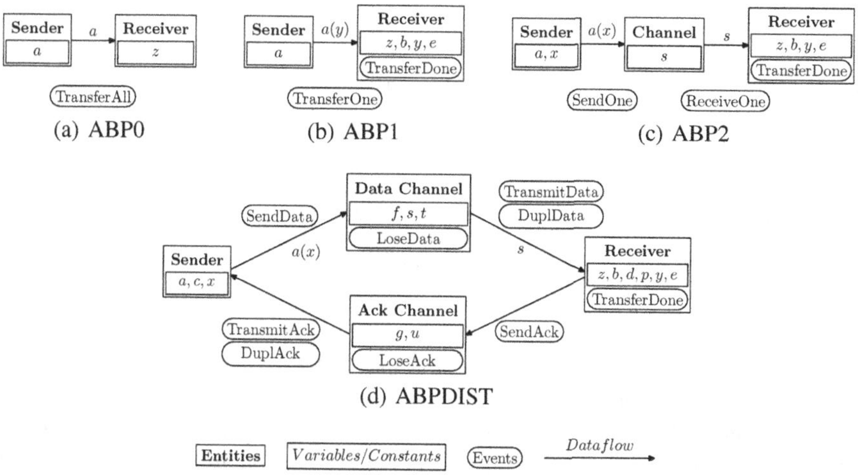

Fig. 3. Refinement process of ABP

Copying Data Items Successively. In the first refinement step, the data items are copied one by one by a new *convergent* event.

MACHINE ABP1
REFINES ABP0
SEES Context
VARIABLES
- z target file
- b received part
- y index
- e mark of termination

INVARIANTS
- inv1 : $b \in 1..SIZE \to DATA$
- inv2 : $y \in 1..SIZE+1$
- inv3 : $b = 1..y-1 \lhd a$

EVENTS
Initialisation
begin
- act1 : $z := \varnothing$
- act2 : $b := \varnothing$
- act3 : $y := 1$
- act4 : $e := 1$

end
Event *TransferOne* $\widehat{=}$
Status convergent
when
- grd1 : $y \leq SIZE$

then
- act1 : $b := b \cup \{y \mapsto a(y)\}$
- act2 : $y := y+1$

end
Event *TransferDone* $\widehat{=}$
refines *TransferAll*
when
- grd1 : $y = SIZE+1$
- grd2 : $e = 1$

then
- act1 : $z := b$
- act2 : $e := 0$

end
VARIANT
SIZE + 1 − y
END

Introducing Data Channel. A variable s is introduced into which the sender writes the next data item and the receiver reads from. Sender and receiver maintain their own count of the number of items sent and received in the variables x and y. Sending and reading proceeds in a ping-pong fashion, controlled by $y - x$.

MACHINE ABP2
REFINES ABP1
SEES Context
VARIABLES
- z target file
- b received part
- s the unit of info sent
- x sender index
- y receiver index
- e mark of termination

INVARIANTS
- inv1 : $s \in DATA$
- inv2 : $x \in 1..SIZE+1$
- inv3 : $x = y \vee x = y+1$
- inv4 : $x = y+1 \Rightarrow s = a(y)$

EVENTS
Initialisation
begin

act1 : $z := \varnothing$
act2 : $b := \varnothing$
act3 : $s :\in DATA$
act4 : $x, y := 1, 1$
act5 : $e := 1$
end
Event *SendOne* $\widehat{=}$
Status convergent
when
grd1 : $x = y \wedge x \leq SIZE$
then
act1 : $s := a(x)$
act2 : $x := x + 1$
end
Event *ReceiveOne* $\widehat{=}$
refines *TransferOne*
when
grd1 : $x = y + 1$
then
act1 : $b := b \cup \{y \mapsto s\}$
act2 : $y := y + 1$
end
Event *ReceiverDone* $\widehat{=}$
refines *TransferDone*
when
grd1 : $y = SIZE + 1$
grd2 : $e = 1$
then
act1 : $z := b$
act2 : $e := 0$
end
VARIANT
y+1−x
END

Introducing Faulty Channels. The sender places the data to be transmitted in the variable s and sets the flag for transmitting, t to 1. The sender also flips its *alternating bit*, c. Event *TransmitData* represents successful transmission in which c and s are copied to f and p, then disables itself by resetting t to 0; the event *DuplicateData* copies the data but does not disable itself; the event *LoseData* does not even copy the data. Successful data transmission is only possible if *TransmitData* is fair. On receiving a new value of f, the receiver appends p to the data received so far and flips its alternating bit g. The acknowledgement channel works analogously to the data channel. Using a hypothetical extension of Event-B with fair events, this is expressed as:

MACHINE ABPFAIR
REFINES ABP2
SEES Context
VARIABLES

z	target file
b	received part
c	sender private bit
d	receiver private bit
f	data channel signal bit
g	ack channel signal bit
p	data of data channel
s	data of sender
t	data transmitting signal
u	ack transmitting signal
x	sender index
y	receiver index
e	mark of task finished

INVARIANTS
inv1 : $c \in 0..1$
inv2 : $d \in 0..1$
inv3 : $f \in 0..1$
inv4 : $g \in 0..1$
inv5 : $p \in DATA$
inv6 : $t \in 0..1$
inv7 : $u \in 0..1$
inv8 : $c = g \vee c \neq f \vee d = f \vee d = g$
four states: ready to send data; data sent and to be transmitted; ready to receive data; data received and ack to be transmitted;
inv9 : $c = g \Rightarrow c \neq d \wedge c = f \wedge x = y$
ready to send data
inv10 : $c \neq f \Rightarrow c = d \wedge c \neq g \wedge x = y + 1 \wedge s = a(y)$
data sent and to be transmitted
inv11 : $d = f \Rightarrow c = d \wedge c \neq g \wedge x = y + 1 \wedge s = a(y) \wedge p = s$
ready to receive data
inv12 : $d = g \Rightarrow c \neq d \wedge c = f \wedge x = y$
data received and Ack to be transmitted

EVENTS
Initialisation
begin
act1 : $z := \varnothing$
act2 : $b := \varnothing$
act3 : $c := 1$
act4 : $d := 0$
act5 : $f := 1$
act6 : $g := 1$
act7 : $p :\in DATA$
act8 : $s :\in DATA$
act9 : $t, u, x, y, e := 0, 0, 1, 1, 1$
end
Event *SendData* $\widehat{=}$
refines *SendOne*
when
grd1 : $c = g \wedge x \leq SIZE$
then
act1 : $c, s, t, x, u := 1 - c, a(x), 1, x + 1, 0$
end
FAIR Event *TransmitData* $\widehat{=}$
Status convergent
when
grd1 : $t = 1$
then
act1 : $f, p, t := c, s, 0$
end
Event *DuplData* $\widehat{=}$
Status convergent
when
grd1 : $t = 1$
then
act1 : $f, p := c, s$
end
Event *LoseData* $\widehat{=}$
Status convergent
when
grd1 : $t = 1$
then
skip
end

Event *SendAck* $\widehat{=}$
refines *ReceiveOne*
  when
    grd1 : $d = f$
  then
    act1 : $b,d,u,y,t := b \cup \{y \mapsto p\}, 1-d, 1, y+1, 0$
  end
FAIR Event *TransmitAck* $\widehat{=}$
Status convergent
  when
    grd1 : $u = 1$
  then
    act1 : $g,u := 1-d, 0$
  end
Event *DuplAck* $\widehat{=}$
Status convergent
  when
    grd1 : $u = 1$
  then
    act1 : $g := 1-d$
  end
Event *LoseAck* $\widehat{=}$
Status convergent
  when
    grd1 : $u = 1$
  then
    skip
  end
Event *AllReceived* $\widehat{=}$
refines *ReceiverDone*
  when
    grd1 : $y = SIZE + 1$
    grd2 : $e = 1$
  then
    act1 : $z := b$
    act2 : $e := 0$
  end
END

Now we apply *dist* to *ABPFAIR*. For expressing the result in Event-B we use following scheme. Suppose L is a regular event and $R1, R2$ are fair events. Three variables, B, $C1$ and $C2$, are introduced and $F = 2$ is the number of fair events:

event L
  when
    g
  then
    S
  end
fair event $R1$
  when
    $h1$
  then
    $T1$
  end
fair event $R2$
  when
    $h2$
  then
    $T2$
  end

invariant
  $C1 \in 1..B$
  $C2 \in 1..B$
  $C1 \neq C2$
initialisation
  $B, C1, C2 :| B' \geq F \wedge C1' \in 1..B' \wedge C2' \in 1..B' \wedge C1' \neq C2'$
event L
  when
    g
    $min(\{C1, C2\}) > 1 \vee (C1 = 1 \wedge \neg h1) \vee (C2 = 1 \wedge \neg h2)$
  then
    S
    $C1, C2 :| C1' \in 1..B \wedge C2' \in 1..B \wedge C1' \neq C2' \wedge$
      $(h1 \Rightarrow C1' = C1 - 1) \wedge (h2 \Rightarrow C2' = C2 - 1)$
  end
event $R1$
  when
    $h1$
    $h2 \Rightarrow C2 - 1 \geq 1$
  then
    $T1$
    $C1, C2 :| C1' \in 1..B \wedge C2' \in 1..B \wedge C1' \neq C2' \wedge (h2 \Rightarrow C2' = C2 - 1)$
  end
...

It is easy to see that this scheme satisfies the conditions of *dist*. If no fair event is enabled, the additional guard of regular events is satisfied, formally:

$$(\neg h1 \wedge \neg h2) \Rightarrow (min(\{C1, C2\}) > 1 \vee (C1 = 1 \wedge \neg h1) \vee (C2 = 1 \wedge \neg h2))$$

This prevents the premature termination of *fin*(P) in [3]. In the application of this scheme to *ABPFAIR*, we additionally introduce a counter *step* as a "ghost variable" for proving termination. As a note, the development provides a lower bound of the number of steps for termination (*inv*20 below).

MACHINE ABPDIST
REFINES ABP2
SEES Context
VARIABLES

z	target file
b	received part
c	sender private bit
d	receiver private bit
f	data channel signal bit
g	ack channel signal bit
p	data of data channel
s	data of sender

t data transmitting signal
u ack transmitting signal
x sender index
y receiver index
e mark of task finished
B bound
C1 down-counter of fair event *TransmitData*
C2 down-counter of fair event *TransmitAck*
step step counter

INVARIANTS

inv1: $c \in 0..1$
inv2: $d \in 0..1$
inv3: $f \in 0..1$
inv4: $g \in 0..1$
inv5: $p \in DATA$
inv6: $t \in 0..1$
inv7: $u \in 0..1$
inv8: $c = g \lor c \neq f \lor d = f \lor d = g$
four states: ready to send data; data sent and to be transmitted; ready to receive data; data received and ack to be transmitted;
inv9: $c = g \Rightarrow c \neq d \land c = f \land x = y$
ready to send data
inv10: $c \neq f \Rightarrow c = d \land c \neq g \land x = y + 1 \land s = a(y)$
data sent and to be transmitted
inv11: $d = f \Rightarrow c = d \land c \neq g \land x = y + 1 \land s = a(y) \land p = s$
ready to receive data
inv12: $d = g \Rightarrow c \neq d \land c = f \land x = y$
data received and Ack to be transmitted
inv13: $B \geq F$
inv14: $C1 \in 1..B$
inv15: $C2 \in 1..B$
inv16: $C1 \neq C2$
always distinct
inv17: $step \in \mathbb{N}$
inv18: $step \leq (x + y - 2) * (B + 1) - t * C1 - u * C2 + 1 - e$
the strict upper bound for proving that the variant is non-negative
inv19: $step \geq 2 * (x + y) - (d + g - 1) * (d + g - 1) - (c - f) * (c - f) - e - 3$
the strict lower bound of *step*, for proving *inv*20
inv20: $e = 0 \Rightarrow step \geq 4 * SIZE$
the strict lower bound of *step* when the system terminates (exactly $4 * SIZE$ when there is no duplication, no loss, and the last event is *AllReceived*, right after event *SendAck*)

EVENTS

Initialisation
begin
act1: $z := \varnothing$
act2: $b := \varnothing$
act3: $c := 1$
act4: $d := 0$
act5: $f := 1$
act6: $g := 1$
act7: $p :\in DATA$
act8: $s :\in DATA$
act9: $t, u, x, y, e := 0, 0, 1, 1, 1$
act10: $B, C1, C2 : |B' \geq F \land C1' \in 1..B' \land C2' \in 1..B' \land C1' \neq C2'$
act11: $step := 0$
end

Event *SendData* $\widehat{=}$
refines *SendOne*
when
grd1: $c = g \land x \leq SIZE$
grd2: $min(\{C1, C2\}) > 1 \lor (C1 = 1 \land t = 0) \lor (C2 = 1 \land u = 0)$
then
act1: $c, s, t, x, u := 1 - c, a(x), 1, x + 1, 0$
act2: $C1, C2 : |C1' \in 1..B \land C2' \in 1..B \land C1' \neq C2' \land (t = 1 \Rightarrow C1' = C1 - 1) \land (u = 1 \Rightarrow C2' = C2 - 1)$
act3: $step := step + 1$
end

Event *TransmitData* $\widehat{=}$
Status convergent
when
grd1: $t = 1$
grd2: $u = 1 \Rightarrow C2 - 1 \geq 1$
then
act1: $f, p, t := c, s, 0$
act2: $C1, C2 : |C1' \in 1..B \land C2' \in 1..B \land C1' \neq C2' \land (u = 1 \Rightarrow C2' = C2 - 1)$
act3: $step := step + 1$
end

Event *DuplData* $\widehat{=}$
Status convergent
when
grd1: $t = 1$
grd2: $min(\{C1, C2\}) > 1 \lor (C1 = 1 \land t = 0) \lor (C2 = 1 \land u = 0)$
then
act1: $f, p := c, s$
act2: $C1, C2 : |C1' \in 1..B \land C2' \in 1..B \land C1' \neq C2' \land (t = 1 \Rightarrow C1' = C1 - 1) \land (u = 1 \Rightarrow C2' = C2 - 1)$
act3: $step := step + 1$
end

Event *LoseData* $\widehat{=}$
Status convergent
when
grd1: $t = 1$
grd2: $min(\{C1, C2\}) > 1 \lor (C1 = 1 \land t = 0) \lor (C2 = 1 \land u = 0)$
then
act1: $C1, C2 : |C1' \in 1..B \land C2' \in 1..B \land C1' \neq C2' \land (t = 1 \Rightarrow C1' = C1 - 1) \land (u = 1 \Rightarrow C2' = C2 - 1)$
act2: $step := step + 1$
end

Event *SendAck* $\widehat{=}$
refines *ReceiveOne*
when
grd1: $d = f$
grd2: $min(\{C1, C2\}) > 1 \lor (C1 = 1 \land t = 0) \lor (C2 = 1 \land u = 0)$
then
act1: $b, d, u, y, t := b \cup \{y \mapsto p\}, 1 - d, 1, y + 1, 0$
act2: $C1, C2 : |C1' \in 1..B \land C2' \in 1..B \land C1' \neq C2' \land (t = 1 \Rightarrow C1' = C1 - 1) \land (u = 1 \Rightarrow C2' = C2 - 1)$
act3: $step := step + 1$
end

Event *TransmitAck* $\widehat{=}$
Status convergent
when
grd1: $u = 1$
grd2: $t = 1 \Rightarrow C1 - 1 \geq 1$
then
act1: $g, u := 1 - d, 0$
act2: $C1, C2 : |C1' \in 1..B \land C2' \in 1..B \land C1' \neq C2' \land (t = 1 \Rightarrow C1' = C1 - 1)$
act3: $step := step + 1$
end

Event *DuplAck* $\widehat{=}$
Status convergent
when
grd1: $u = 1$

```
    grd2 : min({C1,C2}) > 1 ∨
           (C1 = 1 ∧ t = 0) ∨
           (C2 = 1 ∧ u = 0)
  then
    act1 : g := 1 − d
    act2 : C1,C2 : |C1′ ∈ 1..B ∧ C2′ ∈ 1..B ∧
           C1′ ≠ C2′ ∧ (t = 1 ⇒ C1′ = C1 − 1) ∧
           (u = 1 ⇒ C2′ = C2 − 1)
    act3 : step := step + 1
  end
Event LoseAck ≙
Status convergent
  when
    grd1 : u = 1
    grd2 : min({C1,C2}) > 1 ∨
           (C1 = 1 ∧ t = 0) ∨
           (C2 = 1 ∧ u = 0)
  then
    act1 : C1,C2 : |C1′ ∈ 1..B ∧ C2′ ∈ 1..B ∧
           C1′ ≠ C2′ ∧ (t = 1 ⇒ C1′ = C1 − 1) ∧
           (u = 1 ⇒ C2′ = C2 − 1)
    act2 : step := step + 1
  end
Event AllReceived ≙
refines ReceiverDone
  when
    grd1 : y = SIZE + 1
    grd2 : e = 1
    grd3 : min({C1,C2}) > 1 ∨
           (C1 = 1 ∧ t = 0) ∨
           (C2 = 1 ∧ u = 0)
  then
    act1 : z := b
    act2 : e := 0
    act3 : C1,C2 : |C1′ ∈ 1..B ∧ C2′ ∈ 1..B ∧
           C1′ ≠ C2′ ∧ (t = 1 ⇒ C1′ = C1 − 1) ∧
           (u = 1 ⇒ C2′ = C2 − 1)
    act4 : step := step + 1
  end
VARIANT
  2 * SIZE * (B + 1) + 1 − step
END
```

6 Distributed Consensus

Given a group of initial values (in the simplest case, 0 and 1), distributed consensus is to let a group of processes decide by themselves and finally agree on a value. In this section, we model the algorithm in [3] and prove its termination in Event-B. It is an example in case, because its termination can be guaranteed with finitary fairness but not with standard fairness [3]. The refinement process is illustrated in Fig. 5.

The original algorithm is in Fig. 4. The algorithm proceeds in rounds, using a two-dimensional bit array $x[*,2]$ and an infinite array $y[*]$ over values $\bot$, 0, or 1. When the processes agree on a value, the decision, it is written to the shared bit *out*, the initial value of which is $\bot$. Each process P_i has a local register v_i of its current preference and a local register r_i of its current round number. The ith process has an initial input in_i. If in the rth round, all processes have the same preference v, then they decide on the value v in round r. Only when two processes with different preferences both find $y[r] = \bot$ (line 3), and one of them proceeds and chooses its preference for the next round (line 7) before the other one finishes the assignment to $y[r]$, there is a conflict, and the processes continue trying to resolve it in the next round.

In line 5, the empty loop runs for r_i times before copying its preference of next round from $y[i]$, trying to give other processes time to write their preferences into $y[i]$ first.

```
Shared registers : initially out = ⊥, y[1..] = ⊥, x[1..,0..1] = 0;
Local registers : initially r_i = 1, v_i = in_i;
1. while out = ⊥ do
2.   x[r_i, v_i] := 1;
3.   if y[r_i] = ⊥ then y[r_i] := v_i fi;
4.   if x[r_i, ¬v_i] = 0 then out := v_i
5.     else for j = 1 to r_i do skip od;
6.       v_i := y[r_i];
7.       r_i := r_i + 1
8.   fi
9.  od;
10. decide(out).
```

Fig. 4. The original distributed consensus algorithm in [3]

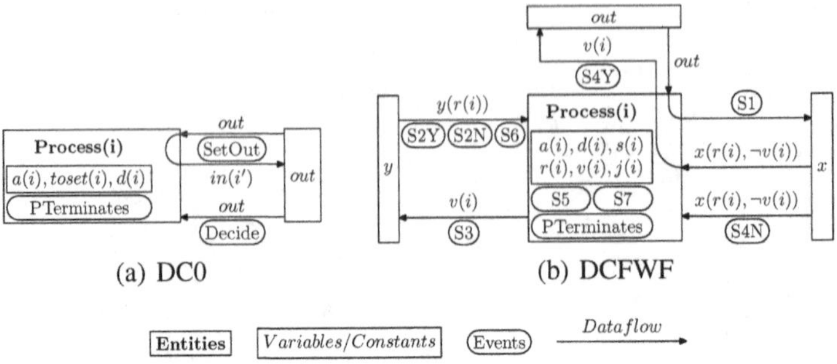

Fig. 5. Refinement process of distributed consensus (*read* operations in guards included)

Standard fairness is not enough to guarantee consensus in any round since theoretically the scheduler might pick this process and continue executing it until the end of the loop, which leaves the conflict unresolved. However, with finitary fairness, when r_i reaches a certain value, the fairness restriction would ensure that every other process gets its chance to finish writing to $y[i]$, thus guarantees that a consensus will be reached in that round.

We translate the algorithm into an event system by breaking down every atomic operation into one event, and adding a state variable s_i for the ith process to record which atomic operation it is to execute next.

Specification. In its most abstract form, *read*, *write* and "*read&write*" on shared registers are all atomic. We let N be the number of processes. The activenesses of processes are represented by the variable a, which also serves as the guard of process actions. The failures of processes are modelled by event *PTerminates*, to show that the model is fault-tolerant (as long as some processes survive, they will finally reach a consensus).

MACHINE DC0
SEES Context
VARIABLES
 a activeness of processes
 out the output
 toset signs of whether a process has not assigned a value to *out* yet
 d decisions of processes
INVARIANTS
 inv1 : $a \in 1..N \to 0..1$
  1 means active and 0 means inactive
 inv2 : $out \in -1..1$
  all -1s stand for undefined in this model
 inv3 : $toset \in 1..N \to 0..1$
  1 means has not assigned to *out* yet and 0 means has
 inv4 : $d \in 1..N \to -1..1$
 inv5 : $\forall n \cdot n \in 1..N \Rightarrow d(n) \in \{-1, out\}$
  agreement: all decisions made by processes must be the same (as *out*)
 inv6 : $out = -1 \vee (\exists n \cdot n \in 1..N \wedge out = in(n))$
  validity: the decision must equal to one of the inputs
EVENTS
Initialisation
 begin
  act1 : $a := 1..N \times \{1\}$
   all active
  act2 : $out := -1$
   out undefined
  act3 : $toset := 1..N \times \{1\}$
   no process has assigned a value to *out* yet
  act4 : $d := 1..N \times \{-1\}$
   decisions all undefined
 end
Event *SetOut* $\widehat{=}$
Status convergent
 any
  n the number of the process to be executed
 where
  grd1 : $n \in 1..N \wedge a(n) = 1 \wedge toset(n) = 1$
   the process is active and has not assigned a value to *out* yet
 then
  act1 : $out :| (out \neq -1 \wedge out' = out) \vee (out = -1 \wedge (\exists nn \cdot nn \in 1..N \wedge out' = in(nn)))$
   the assigned value equals $in(nn)$ of some nn, but nn is not necessarily n
  act2 : $toset(n) := 0$
   set its sign to 0
 end
Event *Decide* $\widehat{=}$
Status convergent

any
n the number of the process to be executed
where
`grd1` : $n \in 1..N \wedge a(n) = 1 \wedge out \in 0..1$
the process is active and *out* has already been set
then
`act1` : $d(n) := out$
set the decision to be *out*
`act2` : $a(n) := 0$
no longer active
end
Event *PTerminates* $\widehat{=}$
Status convergent

any
n the number of the process to be terminated
where
`grd1` : $n \in 1..N \wedge a(n) = 1$
the process is active
then
`act1` : $a(n) := 0$
no longer active
end
VARIANT
`card({n1·n1 ∈ 1..N ∧ toset(n1) = 1|n1})+`
`card({n2·n2 ∈ 1..N ∧ a(n2) = 1|n2})`
END

Adding restrictions.[2] Now only operations *read* and *write* on shared registers are atomic. The assignments $y[r_i] := v_i$ and $v_i := y[r_i]$ both have local variable v_i on one side, so both of them can be treated as atomic operations. Here we use this example to demonstrate the transformation $fwf(P)$. The additional guard of each event guarantees the existence of legal counter values and a new permutation p after its execution.

Again, termination is shown by counter *step*; its non-negativeness is guaranteed by proving the round counter r of each process is no more than $B+1$, therefore the step counter of each process is no more than $6*B+(B*(B+1))/2+5$, and the total step counter is no more than B times of this upper limit.

MACHINE DCFWF
Modelling distributed consensus, assuming that only operations *read* and *write* on shared registers are atomic
REFINES DC0
SEES Context
VARIABLES
`a` activeness of processes
`out` the output
`d` decisions of processes
`y` the preference of rounds
`x` the local preference coverage history of rounds
`s` state of processes
`r` local round numbers of processes
`v` local preferences of processes
`j` local loop variables of processes
`B` upper bound of times to delay any consecutively enabled event
`C` down-counters of processes
`stepsums` step counter-summations, $stepsums(n) - stepsums(n-1)$ is the step counter of the n-th process, and $stepsums(N)$ is the counter of total steps
the steps of event *PTerminates* are not counted, and the event does not affect the counters neither
`s0` the number of total steps when the first time any process enters state 5 in the B-th round
INVARIANTS
`inv1` : $y \in \mathbb{N}_1 \rightarrow -1..1$
$y(i)$ is the preference of the i-th round
`inv2` : $x \in (\mathbb{N}_1 \times 0..1) \rightarrow 0..1$
$x(i,b) = 1$ means that at least one process n has entered state 2 in the i-th round, with local proference $v(n) = b$
`inv3` : $s \in 1..N \rightarrow 1..7$
7 possible states for each process
`inv4` : $r \in 1..N \rightarrow \mathbb{N}_1$
`inv5` : $v \in 1..N \rightarrow 0..1$
`inv6` : $j \in 1..N \rightarrow \mathbb{N}_1$
`inv7` : $\forall n \cdot n \in 1..N \Rightarrow ((s(n) = 1 \wedge toset(n) = 1 \wedge r(n) > 1 \Rightarrow x((r(n) - 1) \mapsto v(n)) = 1) \wedge (s(n) \in 2..7 \Rightarrow x(r(n) \mapsto v(n)) = 1) \wedge (s(n) \in 4..6 \Rightarrow y(r(n)) \in 0..1))$
some properties of x and y in different states; used for proving validity
`inv8` : $\forall n \cdot n \in 1..N \Rightarrow (\exists n1 \cdot n1 \in 1..N \wedge v(n) = in(n1))$
used for proving validity
`inv9` : $\forall i \cdot i \in \mathbb{N}_1 \wedge y(i) \in 0..1 \Rightarrow (x(i \mapsto y(i)) = 1 \wedge (\exists n \cdot n \in 1..N \wedge y(i) = in(n)))$
relation between x and y, as well as and validity of $y(i)$ (preference of every round)
`inv10` : $\forall i,b \cdot i \in \mathbb{N}_1 \wedge b \in 0..1 \wedge x(i \mapsto b) = 1 \Rightarrow (\forall ii \cdot ii \in 1..(i-1) \Rightarrow x(ii \mapsto b) = 1)$
if $x(i \mapsto b) = 1$ then b has left trace in x for all past rounds too
`inv11` : $out \in 0..1 \Rightarrow (\exists n \cdot n \in 1..N \wedge out = v(n) \wedge s(n) = 1 \wedge x(r(n) \mapsto out) = 1 \wedge x(r(n) \mapsto (1 - out)) = 0)$
if *out* has been set then some process has left two key traces in x
`inv12` : $\forall n \cdot n \in 1..N \wedge (out = -1 \vee (out = v(n) \wedge s(n) \in 2..4)) \Rightarrow toset(n) = 1$
the relation among the states and the disappeared variable *toset*;
used for proving the guard refinement relationship of event *S4Y*
`inv13` : $\forall n \cdot n \in 1..N \wedge s(n) = 4 \wedge x(r(n) \mapsto (1 - v(n))) = 0 \Rightarrow (out = -1 \vee out = v(n))$
when *S4Y* is executed, either $out = -1$ or $out = v(n)$;
used for proving several POs of event *S4Y*
`inv14` : $B \in \mathbb{N}_1 \wedge B \geq N$
B is no less than N

[2] Here is the transformed version in Event-B; a version of distributed consensus that uses "fair" events can be found in
`http://www.cas.mcmaster.ca/~zhangt26/ICTAC/appendix.pdf`

inv15: $C \in 1..N \to 1..B$

inv16: $stepsums \in 0..N \to \mathbb{N}$

inv17: $\exists p \cdot p \in 1..N \twoheadrightarrowtail 1..N \wedge (\forall n \cdot n \in 1..N \Rightarrow C(p(n)) \geq n)$

such p, a permutation of $1..N$, always exists, that $C(p(n)) \geq n$ for $n \in 1..N$

inv18: $\exists no \cdot no \in 1..N \wedge a(no) = 1 \Rightarrow (\exists n \cdot n \in 1..N \wedge a(n) = 1 \wedge$
$(\exists CC \cdot CC = (1..N \times \{B\}) \mathbin{\lhd\!\!-} (\lambda nn \cdot nn \in 1..N \setminus \{n\} \wedge a(nn) = 1 | C(nn) - 1) \wedge$
$CC \in 1..N \to 1..B \wedge$
$(\exists p \cdot p \in 1..N \twoheadrightarrowtail 1..N \wedge (\forall nnn \cdot nnn \in 1..N \Rightarrow CC(p(nnn)) \geq nnn))))$

such a p prevents unexpected termination caused by restriction on counters, i.e., the additional guards are always satisfiable as long as the original guards are satisfiable;

when $\exists n0 \cdot n0 \in 1..N \wedge a(n0) = 1$, suppose $mn = min(\{n | n \in 1..N \wedge a(p(n)) = 1\})$, then with $n = p(mn)$ and $p = ((\lambda n \cdot n \in 1..N - mn | p(n + mn)) \cup (\lambda n \cdot n \in N + 1 - mn..N | p(n + mn - N))$, CC statisfies the invariant in the next state

inv19: $\forall n \cdot n \in 1..N \wedge a(n) = 1 \Rightarrow stepsums(N) \leq B * (stepsums(n) - stepsums(n-1) + 1) - C(n)$

the number of total steps are no more than B times of the step counter of any active process

inv20: $stepsums(0) = 0 \wedge (\forall n \cdot n \in 1..N \Rightarrow$
$((s(n) = 1 \wedge out = -1 \Rightarrow stepsums(n) - stepsums(n-1) \leq$
$6 * (r(n) - 1) + (r(n) * (r(n) - 1))/2 + 2 - a(n)) \wedge$
$(s(n) = 1 \wedge out \neq -1 \Rightarrow stepsums(n) - stepsums(n-1) \leq$
$6 * (r(n) - 1) + (r(n) * (r(n) - 1))/2 + 6 - a(n)) \wedge$
$(s(n) \in 2..4 \Rightarrow stepsums(n) - stepsums(n-1) \leq$
$6 * (r(n) - 1) + (r(n) * (r(n) - 1))/2 + s(n)) \wedge$
$(s(n) = 5 \Rightarrow stepsums(n) - stepsums(n-1) \leq$
$6 * (r(n) - 1) + (r(n) * (r(n) - 1))/2 + 4 + j(n)) \wedge$
$(s(n) = 6 \Rightarrow stepsums(n) - stepsums(n-1) \leq$
$6 * (r(n) - 1) + (r(n) * (r(n) + 1))/2 + 5) \wedge$
$(s(n) = 7 \Rightarrow stepsums(n) - stepsums(n-1) \leq$
$6 * (r(n) - 1) + (r(n) * (r(n) + 1))/2 + 6)))$

the upper bound on step counter of each process at each state

inv21: $s0 \in \mathbb{N}$

inv22: $s0 = 0 \Rightarrow (\forall n \cdot n \in 1..N \Rightarrow r(n) < B \vee (r(n) = B \wedge s(n) \leq 4))$

$s0$ is 0 until some process enters state 5 in the B-th round

inv23: $s0 > 0 \Rightarrow (y(B) \in 0..1 \wedge stepsums(N) \geq s0 \wedge$
$(\forall n \cdot n \in 1..N \Rightarrow ((a(n) = 1 \wedge r(n) = B \wedge s(n) = 3 \Rightarrow$
$C(n) \leq B - stepsums(N) + s0) \wedge$
$(stepsums(N) < s0 + B \Rightarrow$
$((r(n) < B \vee (r(n) = B \wedge s(n) \leq 5)) \wedge$
$(a(n) = 1 \wedge r(n) = B \wedge s(n) = 5 \Rightarrow$
$j(n) \leq stepsums(N) - s0 + 1))))))$

some properties when $s0 > 0$, and when $s0 > 0 \wedge stepsums(N) < s0 + B$;

used for proving that when any process is in state 6 of the B-th round, $stepsums(N) \geq s0 + B$ and at that time, no process is in state 3 of the B-th round (and no process can enter anymore)

inv24: $\forall n \cdot n \in 1..N \wedge ((r(n) = B \wedge s(n) = 7) \vee$
$(r(n) = B + 1 \wedge s(n) \in 1..4)) \Rightarrow v(n) = y(B)$

once a process reaches state 7 in the B-th round, its local preference will equal $y(B)$ until it terminates, and $y(B)$ will not vary due to $inv23$, because $stepsums(N) \geq s0 + B$; thus no process is in state 3 nor can any process enter state 3 to set $y(B)$;

used for proving $inv25$

inv25: $((s0 = 0 \vee (s0 > 0 \wedge stepsums(N) < s0 + B)) \Rightarrow$
$(x(B + 1 \mapsto 0) = 0 \wedge x(B + 1 \mapsto 1) = 0)) \wedge$
$(s0 > 0 \wedge stepsums(N) \geq s0 + B \Rightarrow x(B + 1 \mapsto 1 - y(B)) = 0)$

$x(B + 1 \mapsto 1 - y(B)) = 0$ when $s0 > 0$;

used for proving $inv26$

inv26: $\forall n \cdot n \in 1..N \Rightarrow (r(n) \leq B \vee (r(n) = B + 1 \wedge s(n) \in 1..4))$

no process can enter state 5 in the $(B+1)$-th round; this puts an upper bound on the step counter of single processes and thus on total steps, which is then used to prove termination (non-negativeness of the variant)

EVENTS

Initialisation

begin

act1: $a := 1..N \times \{1\}$

act2: $out := -1$

act3: $d := 1..N \times \{-1\}$

act4: $y := \mathbb{N}_1 \times \{-1\}$

act5: $x := (\mathbb{N}_1 \times 0..1) \times \{0\}$

act6: $s := 1..N \times \{1\}$

act7: $r := 1..N \times \{1\}$

act8: $v := in$

act9: $j := 1..N \times \{1\}$

act10: $B, C : |B' \in \mathbb{N}_1 \wedge B' \geq N \wedge C' = 1..N \times \{B'\}$

act11: $stepsums := 0..N \times \{0\}$

act12: $s0 := 0$

end

Event $S1 \widehat{=}$

enter the $r(n)$-th round and leave a record of local preference in x

Status convergent

any

n the number of the process to be executed (the same meaning in all following events except *PTerminates*)

CC the value of C after execution (the same meaning in all following events except *PTerminates*)

where

grd1: $n \in 1..N \wedge a(n) = 1 \wedge s(n) = 1$

the process is active and in state 1

grd2: $out = -1$

out has not been set

grd3: $CC = (1..N \times \{B\}) \mathbin{\lhd\!\!-} (\lambda nn \cdot nn \in 1..N \setminus \{n\} \wedge a(nn) = 1 | C(nn) - 1) \wedge$
$CC \in 1..N \to 1..B \wedge$
$(\exists p \cdot p \in 1..N \twoheadrightarrowtail 1..N \wedge (\forall nnn \cdot nnn \in 1..N \Rightarrow CC(p(nnn)) \geq nnn))$

CC sets the counters of n and inactive processes to be B, decreases the counters of other processes by 1, and a new permutation exists (the same meaning in all following events except *PTerminates*)

then

act1: $x(r(n) \mapsto v(n)) := 1$

act2: $s(n) := 2$

set the state to be 2

act3: $C := CC$

update the counters (the same meaning in all following events except *PTerminates*)

act4: $stepsums := stepsums \mathbin{\lhd\!\!-} (\lambda nn \cdot nn \in n..N | stepsums(nn) + 1)$

update the counter-summations (the same meaning in all following events except *PTerminates*)

```
  end
Event  S2Y ≙
  if the preference of the r(n)-th round has not been set, try
  to set it to be local preference
Status  convergent
  any
    n
    CC
  where
    grd1 : n ∈ 1..N ∧ a(n) = 1 ∧ s(n) = 2 ∧ y(r(n)) = −1
      the process is active and in state 2, the preference of
      the r(n)-th round has not been set
    grd2 : CC = (1..N × {B}) ⩤ (λnn·nn ∈ 1..N \ {n} ∧
      a(nn) = 1|C(nn) − 1) ∧
            CC ∈ 1..N → 1..B ∧
            (∃p·p ∈ 1..N ⤖ 1..N ∧ (∀nnn·nnn ∈ 1..
      N ⇒ CC(p(nnn)) ≥ nnn))
  then
    act1 : s(n) := 3
      set the state to be 2
    act2 : C := CC
    act3 : stepsums := stepsums ⩤ (λnn·nn ∈ n..
      N|stepsums(nn) + 1)
  end
Event  S2N ≙
  ...
  ⋮
Event  S7 ≙
  ... [3]
Event  Decide ≙
refines  Decide
  any
    n
    CC
  where
    grd1 : n ∈ 1..N ∧ a(n) = 1 ∧ s(n) = 1
      the process is active and in state 1
    grd2 : out ∈ 0..1
      out has already been set
    grd3 : CC = (1..N × {B}) ⩤ (λnn·nn ∈ 1..N \ {n} ∧
      a(nn) = 1|C(nn) − 1) ∧
            CC ∈ 1..N → 1..B ∧
            (∃p·p ∈ 1..N ⤖ 1..N ∧ (∀nnn·nnn ∈ 1..
      N ⇒ CC(p(nnn)) ≥ nnn))
  then
    act1 : d(n) := out
      set the decision to be out
    act2 : a(n) := 0
      no longer active
    act3 : C := CC
    act4 : stepsums := stepsums ⩤ (λnn·nn ∈ n..
      N|stepsums(nn) + 1)
  end
Event  PTerminates ≙
refines  PTerminates
  any
    n    number of the process to be terminated
  where
    grd1 : n ∈ 1..N ∧ a(n) = 1
      the process is active
  then
    act1 : a(n) := 0
      no longer active
  end
VARIANT
  B*(6*B+(B*(B+1))/2+5) − stepsums(N)
END
```

7 Conclusions

This work started with the goal of expressing action systems with fairness in formalisms like Event-B. The core is the observation that a modification of the transformation $\mathit{fin}(P)$ of [3] from standard transition systems to a finitary weakly fair one is suitable. It was shown that that all finitary weakly fair computations of P terminate, if and only if all computations of $\mathit{fin}(P)$ terminate. However, the schedules of $\mathit{fin}(P)$ are not exactly the finitary weakly fair ones of P, because the termination in some computations may be caused by improper scheduling: $\mathit{fin}(P)$ may reach a state q', such that in its corresponding state q of P, some transitions are enabled, but transitions of $\mathit{fin}(P)$ are disabled by the additional guards that restrict the counters. This inequality does not affect the correctness of the proof mentioned above, but this type of termination makes it unsuitable to model practical transition systems, because the system after transformation will be at risk of terminating unexpectedly. Certain temporal logic properties cannot be proved, due to the difficulty of distinguishing terminations caused by original guards or by a counter of value 0. The transformation $\mathit{fwf}(P)$ and $\mathit{dist}(P)$ suggested here guarantee that the schedules remain equivalent. Thus, lower bound of steps can be easily proved, and all temporal logic properties are preserved. We have demonstrated the application of $\mathit{dist}(P)$ with the development of the alternating bit protocol and the application of

[3] Events $S2N$ to $S7$ are omitted here since they are all similarly translated atomic operations, refer to `http://www.cas.mcmaster.ca/~zhangt26/ICTAC/appendix.pdf` for the complete code.

fwf(*P*) with the development of distributed consensus. We believe that this is the first mechanically checked development of this distributed consensus algorithm.

In this paper, we have considered only weak fairness. A similar transformation for finitary strong fairness waits to be worked out. While the examples of the paper have been processed with Rodin [4], the transformation was done by hand, and the proof was semi-automatic. Verifying the distributed consensus model with finitary fairness is more time-consuming than verifying the ABP model, because modelling an arbitrary number of counters requires additional functions to express the restrictions. It would be useful to automate this transformation, as well as the verification of the proof obligations that only involve the bound and counters, which is irrelevant to the original model.

Acknowledgement. We thank the reviewers for their helpful comments.

References

1. Back, R.J.R.: Refinement calculus, part II: Parallel and reactive programs. In: de Bakker, J.W., de Roever, W.-P., Rozenberg, G. (eds.) REX 1989. LNCS, vol. 430, pp. 67–93. Springer, Heidelberg (1990)
2. Abrial, J.R.: Modeling in Event-B: System and Software Engineering. Cambridge University Press (2010)
3. Alur, R., Henzinger, T.A.: Finitary fairness. ACM Trans. Program. Lang. Syst. 20(6), 1171–1194 (1998)
4. Abrial, J.-R., Butler, M., Hallerstede, S., Voisin, L.: An open extensible tool environment for event-B. In: Liu, Z., Kleinberg, R.D. (eds.) ICFEM 2006. LNCS, vol. 4260, pp. 588–605. Springer, Heidelberg (2006)
5. Chandy, K.M., Misra, J.: Parallel Program Design: A Foundation. Addison-Wesley (1988)
6. Francez, N.: Fairness. Texts and Monographs in Computer Science. Springer (1986)
7. Lamport, L.: The temporal logic of actions. ACM Transactions on Programming Languages and Systems 16(3), 872–923 (1994)
8. Back, R., Xu, Q.: Refinement of fair action systems. Acta Informatica 35(2), 131–165 (1998)
9. Singh, A.K.: Program refinement in fair transition systems. Acta Informatica 30, 503–535 (1993)
10. Wabenhorst, A.: Stepwise development of fair distributed systems. Acta Informatica 39, 233–271 (2003)
11. Apt, K.R., Olderog, E.R.: Proof rules and transformations dealing with fairness. Sci. Comput. Program. 3(1), 65–100 (1983)
12. Fischer, M., Lynch, N., Paterson, M.: Impossibility of distributed consensus with one faulty process. Journal of the ACM 32, 374–382 (1985)
13. Bartlett, K.A., Scantlebury, R.A., Wilkinson, P.T.: A note on reliable full-duplex transmission over half-duplex links. Communications of the ACM 12(5), 260–261 (1969)
14. Wabenhorst, A.: A stepwise development of the alternating bit protocol. Technical Report PRG-TR-12-97, Oxford University Computing Laboratory (March 1997)
15. Feijen, W.H.J., van Gasteren, A.J.M.: On a Method of Multiprogramming. Springer (1999)
16. Sekerinski, E.: An algebraic approach to refinement with fair choice. Electronic Notes in Theoretical Computer Science 214, 51–79 (2008)

Spatio-temporal Hybrid Automata for Cyber-Physical Systems

Zhucheng Shao and Jing Liu*

Shanghai Keylab of Trustworthy Computing
East China Normal University
Shanghai, 200062, P.R. China
shaozhucheng@ecnu.cn, jliu@sei.ecnu.edu.cn

Abstract. Cyber-Physical Systems (CPSs) integrate computing, communication and control processes. Close interactions between the cyber and physical worlds occur in time and space frequently. Therefore, both temporal and spatial information should be taken into consideration when modeling CPS systems. However, how we can capture temporal and spatial information into CPS models that allow describing the logical properties and constraints is still an unsolved problem in the CPS. In this paper, a spatio-temporal logic is provided, including the syntax and semantics, for describing the logical properties and constraints. Based on the logic, we propose an extended hybrid automaton, spatio-temporal hybrid automaton for CPSs. The automaton increases the ability to express spatial variables, spatial expression and related constraints on spatial terms. Then, we define formal semantics of spatio-temporal hybrid automata based on labeled transition systems. At the end of this paper, a Train Control System is introduced as a case study to show how to model the system behavior with spatio-temporal hybrid automata.

Keywords: Spatio-temporal logic, CPS, Hybrid automata.

1 Introduction

Cyber-Physical Systems (CPSs) are envisioned as heterogeneous systems of systems, which involve communication, computation, sensing, and actuating through heterogeneous and widely distributed physical devices and computation components [3]. Therefore, CPS requires close interactions between the cyber and physical worlds both in time and space. These interactions are usually governed by events, which have time, location and observer attributes. An unsolved important problem is how to capture location and timing information into CPS models in a way that allow for validation of the logical properties of a program against the constraints imposed by its physical (sensor) interaction [24]. Thus, a new logic is needed for describing the constraints on location and time information, and for specifying the logical properties of CPSs, since the traditional models (e.g. hybrid automata, UML, CSP) are without consideration of location information.

* Corresponding author.

Z. Liu, J. Woodcock, and H. Zhu (Eds.): ICTAC 2013, LNCS 8049, pp. 337–354, 2013.

To model a CPS with location and time, a new semantic model is needed for the purpose of designing the unified system.

Temporal logic has found an important application in formal methods, where it is used to specify requirements of real-time systems on rules and symbolism for representing and reasoning about propositions qualified in terms of time. Propositional temporal logic (PTL) is one of the best known temporal logics, which has found many applications in CS and AI [1, 7–9]. In [1], Zohar Manna and Amir Pnueli gave a detailed methodology for the specification, verification, and development of real-time systems using the tool of temporal logic. However, the existing approaches can not be used directly in Cyber-Physical Systems. The reason is that the truth-values of spatial propositions can not be expressed. Spatial logic is a number of logics suitable for qualitative spatial representation and reasoning, such as RCC-8, $BRCC$, $S4_u$ and other fragments of $S4_u$. The most expressive spatial formalism of them is $S4_u$ [10, 11, 13]. For modeling the truth-values of spatial propositions, spatial logic should be taken into consideration in our constructed logic.

The next apparent and natural step is attempting to construct spatio-temporal hybrids. For example, in [12], Finger and Gabbay introduced a methodology whereby an arbitrary logic system L can be enriched with temporal features to create a new system $T(L)$. The new system is constructed by combining L with a pure propositional temporal logic T. In [14], Wolter and Zakharyaschev constructed a spatio-temporal logic, based on RCC-8 and PTL, intended for qualitative knowledge representation and reasoning about the behavior of spatial regions in time. Nevertheless, RCC-8 is a fragment of $S4_u$ and has rather limited expressive power [15]. Following their way, we will construct our spatio-temporal logic by enriching PTL with $S4_u$ for CPSs.

Cyber-physical systems can be usefully modeled as hybrid automata combining the physical dynamics within modes with discrete switching behavior between modes. However, the location information can not be captured into models, especially spatial constraints. In this paper, we extend spatial variables and spatial expressions of a hybrid automaton to increase the ability of expression. Naturally, spatial expressions and other expressions with connections in spatio-temporal hybrid automata can be interpreted in our spatio-temporal logic. We give the formal syntax and semantics (includes state, transition, trace and parallel composition) of the spatio-temporal hybrid automata.

This paper is organized as follows. Section 2 gives formal syntax and semantics of the spatio-temporal logic. Section 3 classify variables and expressions. Then, we give the formal syntax and semantics of the spatio-temporal hybrid automata. In Section 4, a Train Control System is introduced as a case study to show the efficiency of our approach.

2 Spatio-Temporal Logic

In CPS, the attributes of an event are application-independent. All CPS events have time, locations and observer attributes. Therefore, the logic, which will be defined, should have the ability of expression on locations and observer attributes. Based on the propositional temporal logic and the construction method of logics [12], our spatio-temporal logic will be constructed by extending PTL with spatial temporal logic $S4_u$. By the way, part of our work on the logic can be found in [4]. The syntax of the spatio-temporal logic is defined as follows:

$$\tau ::= s \mid \overline{\tau} \mid \tau_1 \sqcap \tau_2 \mid \mathrm{I}\tau$$
$$\varphi ::= p \mid \boxtimes\,\tau \mid \neg\varphi \mid \varphi_1 \wedge \varphi_2 \mid \varphi_1 \mathcal{U} \varphi_2 \mid \varphi_1 \mathcal{S} \varphi_2$$

where

- p are normal propositional variables e.g. $p_0,\ p_1,\ p_2, \ldots$ in relation to observer attributes;
- τ are spatial terms in relation to location; $\overline{\tau}$ is the complementary terms of τ;
- $\tau_1 \sqcap \tau_2$ is the intersection of spatial terms τ_1 and τ_2, including any point which belongs to term τ_1 and belongs to term τ_2 too;
- $\mathrm{I}\tau$ is the modal operator on spatial term τ;
- $\neg$ and $\wedge$ are the Booleans;
- $\boxtimes\,\tau$ means that τ occupies the whole space (all points belong to τ). We write $\diamondsuit\tau$ to say that the part of space represented by τ is not empty (sc. there is at least one point in τ). Obviously, $\diamondsuit\tau = \neg\boxtimes\,\overline{\tau}$.
- $\mathcal{U}$ and $\mathcal{S}$ are the binary temporal operators.

Certainly, the semantics of our spatio-temporal logic can be interpreted by a topological temporal model. The topological temporal model is a triple of the form

$$\mathfrak{M} = \langle \mathfrak{T}, \mathcal{I}, \mathfrak{U} \rangle$$

where $\mathfrak{T}$ is a flow of time, $\mathcal{I}$ is a topological space and a *valuation* $\mathfrak{U}$, as an overloaded function, on the one hand, is a map associating with every spatial term s and every time point $w \in W$ onto a set $\mathfrak{U}(s, w) \subseteq U$–the space occupied by s at moment w; on the other hand, is a map associating with each normal propositional variable p a set $\mathfrak{U}(p) \subseteq W$ of time points; w is a nonempty set of time points; U is a nonempty set, the universe of the space.

Then we can get the following definitions:

$$\mathfrak{U}(\overline{\tau}, w) = U - \mathfrak{U}(\tau, w), \quad \mathfrak{U}(\mathrm{I}\tau, w) = \mathbb{I}\mathfrak{U}(\tau, w)$$

$$\mathfrak{U}(\tau_1 \sqcap \tau_2, w) = \mathfrak{U}(\tau_1, w) \cap \mathfrak{U}(\tau_2, w)$$

The truth-values of spatio-temporal logic are defined as follows:

- $(\mathfrak{M}, w) \models p$ iff $w \in \mathfrak{U}(p)$,
- $(\mathfrak{M}, w) \models \boxtimes\tau$ iff $\mathfrak{U}(\tau, w) = U$,
- $(\mathfrak{M}, w) \models \neg\varphi$ iff $(\mathfrak{M}, w) \not\models \varphi$,
- $(\mathfrak{M}, w) \models \varphi_1 \wedge \varphi_2$ iff $(\mathfrak{M}, w) \models \varphi_1$ and $(\mathfrak{M}, w) \models \varphi_2$,
- $(\mathfrak{M}, w) \models \varphi_1 \mathcal{U} \varphi_2$ iff there is $v > w$ such that $(\mathfrak{M}, v) \models \varphi_2$ and $(\mathfrak{M}, u) \models \varphi_1$ for all $u \in (w, v)$,

- $(\mathfrak{M}, w) \models \varphi_1 \mathcal{S} \varphi_2$ iff there is $v < w$ such that $(\mathfrak{M}, v) \models \varphi_2$ and $(\mathfrak{M}, u) \models \varphi_1$ for all $u \in (v, w)$.

A formula of spatio-temporal logic φ is said to be satisfiable if there exists a topological temporal model $\mathfrak{M}$ such that $(\mathfrak{M}, w) \models \varphi$ for some time point w.

Theorem 1. *The satisfiability problem for spatio-temporal logic formulas in topological - temporal models based on arbitrary flows of time is PSPACE-complete.*

For proving the theorem, we can construct a PTL-formula $\varphi*$ by replacing every occurrence of subformulas $\boxtimes\,\tau$ and normal propositional variable p in φ with a fresh propositional variable p_τ. Then given a PTL-model $\mathfrak{N} = \langle \mathfrak{T}, \mathfrak{U} \rangle$ for $\varphi*$ and a time point w, we get the set

$$\Phi_w = \{\boxtimes\,\tau | (\mathfrak{N}, w) \models p_\tau, p_\tau \doteq \boxtimes\,\tau\} \cup \{p | (\mathfrak{N}, w) \models p_\tau, p_\tau \doteq p\}$$

It is easy to see that if Φ_w is satisfiable for every $w \in \mathfrak{T}$ in a PTL-model, there is a topological-temporal model satisfying φ based on the flow of time $\mathfrak{T}$. Then, we can use the suitable algorithm [18, 19] for PTL-model to check satisfiability of Φ_w, which can be done using polynomial space.

Proof 1. *Let φ be a formula of our spatio-temporal logic. Based on the general proving frames(in [2], Lemma B.1 or in [20], Theorem 10.36), we only extend those spatio-temporal logical formula with the normal propositional variable p. The corresponding valuation $\mathfrak{U}$ and topological space on P are added to the topological-temporal model $\mathfrak{M} = \langle \mathfrak{T}, \mathcal{I}, \mathfrak{U} \rangle$ and the topological space $\mathcal{I} = \langle U, \mathcal{I} \rangle$. For any two ultrafilter $x_1, x_2 \in V$ (V is the set of all ultrafilters over U), put $x_1 R x_2$ (R is a quasi-order on V) iff $\forall A \subseteq U$ ($\mathcal{I}A \in x_1 \to A \in x_2$). Given an Aleksandrov topological-temporal model $\mathfrak{R} = \langle \mathfrak{T}, \mathfrak{B}, \mathfrak{Q} \rangle$, where $\mathfrak{B} = \langle V, R \rangle$, $\mathfrak{Q}(p, w) = \{x \in V | \mathfrak{U}(p, w) \in x\}$. Such that, for all $w \in W$ and $x \in V$,*

$$(\mathfrak{R}, \langle w, x \rangle) \models \tau \;\; \text{iff} \;\; \mathfrak{U}(\tau, w) \in x,$$
$$(\mathfrak{R}, \langle w, x \rangle) \models p \;\; \text{iff} \;\; \mathfrak{U}(p, w) \in x.$$

Therefore, it is satisfiable in a topological-temporal model iff it is satisfiable in an Aleksandrov topological-temporal model based on the same flow of time $\mathfrak{T}$.

With every spatial subformula $\boxtimes\,\tau$ and normal propositional variable p, we rewrite them with a fresh propositional variable p_τ. The PTL-formula $\varphi*$ could be obtained from φ by replacing all its subformulas of the form $\boxtimes\,\tau$ and normal propositional variables p with p_τ.

We could claim that φ is satisfiable in an Aleksandrov topological-temporal model on a flow of time $\mathfrak{T} = \langle W, < \rangle$ iff

- *there exists a temporal model $\mathfrak{N} = \langle \mathfrak{T}, \mathfrak{U} \rangle$ satisfying $\varphi*$;*
- *for every $w \in W$, the set*

$$\Phi_w = \{\boxtimes\,\tau | (\mathfrak{N}, w) \models p_\tau, p_\tau \doteq \boxtimes\,\tau\} \cup \{p | (\mathfrak{N}, w) \models p_\tau, p_\tau \doteq p\}$$

  is satisfiable.

It is not hard to see that the implication($\Rightarrow$) is feasible. Conversely, suppose that we have a temporal model $\mathfrak{N} = \langle \mathfrak{T}, \mathfrak{U} \rangle$, which could satisfy those conditions above.

Let the union of Φ_w: $\Gamma = \bigcup_{w \in W} \Phi_w$. For every satisfiable $\Phi \subseteq \Gamma$, construct a model based on a finite quasi-order $\mathfrak{P}_\Phi = \langle V_\Phi, R_\Phi \rangle$ and satisfying Φ. Let $n = max\{|V_\Phi| : \Phi \subseteq \Gamma, \Phi$ is satisfiable$\}$ and $\mathfrak{P}$ is the disjoint union of n full n-ary trees of depth n whose nodes are clusters of cardinality n. It is not hard to see that every $\mathfrak{P}_\Phi$ is a p-morphic image of $\mathfrak{P}$. Therefore, every satisfiable $\Phi \subseteq \Gamma$ is satisfied in an Aleksandrov model based on $\mathfrak{P}$.

Thus there is a finite quasi-order $\mathfrak{P}$. Then, for every $w \in W$, we can get $\langle \mathfrak{P}, \mathfrak{U}_w \rangle \models \Phi_w$ for some valuation $\mathfrak{U}_w$. It is obvious that φ is satisfied in the Aleksandrov topological temporal model $\langle \mathfrak{T}, \mathfrak{P}, \mathfrak{U}^* \rangle$, where $\mathfrak{U}^*(p, w) = \mathfrak{U}_w(p)$, $\mathfrak{U}^*(\tau, w) = \mathfrak{U}_w(\tau)$, for every spatial term τ, normal propositional variable p and every $w \in W$.

Finally, we design a decision procedure for our spatio-temporal logic, which uses polynomial space, based on the corresponding nondeterministic PSPACE algorithm [18, 19] for PTL. We modify it as follows. Firstly the algorithm constructs a temporal model $\mathfrak{N} = \langle \mathfrak{T}, \mathfrak{U} \rangle$ for the formula φ^*. For every time point $w \in W$, it produces a state. In addition, it checks that whether the set Φ_w is satisfiable. Obviously, the extra check can also be performed by a PSPACE algorithm, which doesn't increase the complexity of the complete algorithm.

Therefore, the satisfiability problem for spatio-temporal logic formulas in topological temporal models based on arbitrary flows of time is PSPACE-complete.

□

In addition, for describing truth values of relations between spatial terms, there are some basic binary or ternary predicates on spatial terms in Fig.1, such as

- DC(X,Y)—spatial terms X and Y are disconnected,

$$DC(X, Y) = \neg \Diamond_{\exists}(X \sqcap Y)$$

- EC(X,Y)— X and Y are externally connected,

$$EC(X, Y) = \Diamond_{\exists}(X \sqcap Y) \wedge \neg \Diamond_{\exists}(\mathrm{I}X \sqcap \mathrm{I}Y)$$

- EQ(X,Y)— X and Y are equal,

$$EQ(X, Y) = \Box_{\forall}(X \sqsubset Y) \wedge \Box_{\forall}(Y \sqsubset X)$$

- PO(X,Y)— X and Y overlap partially,

$$PO(X, Y) = \Diamond_{\exists}(\mathrm{I}X \sqcap \mathrm{I}Y) \wedge \neg \Box_{\forall}(X \sqsubset Y) \wedge \neg \Box_{\forall}(Y \sqsubset X)$$

- TPP(X,Y)— X is a tangential proper part of Y ,

$$TPP(X, Y) = \Box_{\forall}(X \sqsubset Y) \wedge \neg \Box_{\forall}(Y \sqsubset X) \wedge \neg \Box_{\forall}(X \sqsubset \mathrm{I}Y)$$

- NTPP(X,Y)— X is a nontangential proper part of Y,

$$NTPP(X,Y) = \boxed{\forall}(X \sqsubset \mathrm{I}Y) \wedge \neg\boxed{\forall}(Y \sqsubset X)$$

- PO3(X,Y,Z)— spatial terms X, Y and Z overlap partially,

$$\begin{aligned} PO3(X,Y,Z) = {} & \Diamond_{\exists}(\mathrm{I}X \sqcap \mathrm{I}Y \wedge \mathrm{I}X \sqcap \mathrm{I}Z \wedge \mathrm{I}Y \sqcap \mathrm{I}Z) \wedge \\ & \neg\boxed{\forall}(X \sqsubset Y \vee X \sqsubset Z \vee Y \sqsubset Z \vee \\ & Y \sqsubset X \vee Z \sqsubset X \vee Z \sqsubset Y \vee) \end{aligned}$$

- EC3(X,Y,Z)— spatial terms X, Y and Z are externally connected,

$$\begin{aligned} EC3(X,Y,Z) = {} & \Diamond_{\exists}(X \sqcap Y \wedge X \sqcap Z \wedge Y \sqcap Z) \wedge \\ & \neg\Diamond_{\exists}(\mathrm{I}X \sqcap \mathrm{I}Y \vee \mathrm{I}X \sqcap \mathrm{I}Z \vee \mathrm{I}Y \sqcap \mathrm{I}Z) \end{aligned}$$

Without doubt, there are many other complex predicates, which could be expressed using our spatio-temporal logic.

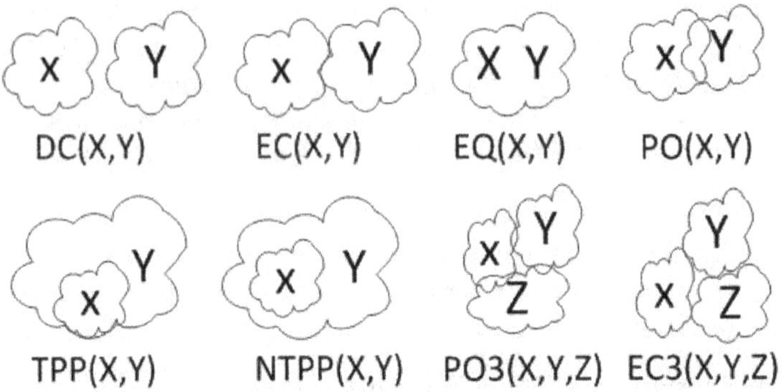

Fig. 1. Basic binary or ternary predicates

3 Spatio-temporal Hybrid Automata

A Spatio-temporal hybrid automaton is an extension of hybrid automaton based on spatio-temporal logic. Spatio-temporal logic brings a set of expressions into the hybrid automaton to represent the location or space related information of CPSs.

3.1 Expressions

After expansion of expression, there are five kinds of variables in spatio-temporal hybrid automaton :

- discrete variables with discrete values independent of time and location. e.g. $x = 0, 1, 2$.

- continuous variables which can be represented as a continuous function dependent on time (with its initial condition), e.g. $F \triangleq \begin{cases} x = x(t) \\ x(0) = 0 \end{cases}$
- clock variables with a special clock type. A *Clock* c can be defined as follows: $c ::= (I, \rho)$, where
  - I is a set of time instants. A time instant represents an observation point of a clock, either physical or logical, reflecting specific events dependent on time.
  - ρ is a function, $\rho : I \to \mathbb{R}_{\geq 0}$ maps every time instant in I to a non-negative real number. We call ρ the sampling function that discretizes the continuous time to a series of observation points on demand.
- spatial variables which can be represented by locations. The location attribute is given by the coordinate in the form of (x, y, z). So the spatial variables can be represented in the form of $((x, y, z), r)$, r stands for the radius of an object.
- action variables which have a boolean value specifying whether the corresponding CPS event occurs or not, e.g. θ, η. All CPS events $(L, \langle attr, \Gamma, \iota \rangle)$ have observer attributes, time and location, where L is a symbol and used to label the event. It is used to record the attributes, generate time and location of the event.

Corresponding to those kinds of variables, there are five kinds of expression: Algebraic Expression, Differential Expression, Clock Expression, Spatial Expression and Action Expression. *Algebraic Expressions* can be used to describe the relation between discrete variables. *Differential Expressions* are capable to describe activities of continuous variables. *Clock Constraint Expressions* are used to define clock-related expressions. *Spatial Expressions* are used to define expressions on spatial terms. *Action Expressions* are used when defining events and actions. In our formalization, every expression occurring is considered as a predicate over variables with specific types.

- $A(x)$ is an algebraic expression in terms of either an equation or inequation over algebraic objects. The expression is satisfied when the evaluation of every discrete variable makes the equation or inequation hold.
- $F(x, \frac{dx}{dt})$ is a differential expression with its initial condition describing the properties involving continuous variables(x) dependent on time. $w(t)$ is a continuous variable, the differential expression is satisfied when $w(t)$ is a solution of $F(x, \frac{dx}{dt}) = 0$, and acts on the domain of continuously differentiable function.
- The clock constraint expression can be represented in terms of either an equation or inequation over time instants. Based on the clock structure, the current reading of a clock c could be represented by the first entry of the time instant sequence $c.I$. After a clock tick, $c.I$ moves to next instant.
- Giving a radius r, for the location ι, we can get the area occupied by them, named $\tau = (\iota, r)$. For the location attributes ι_1 and ι_2, we can get the area occupied by them, spatial terms τ_1, τ_2. The relation between of them can be described using basic binary predicates or some other predicates which

are expressed by our spatio-temporal logic, such as $PO(\tau_1, \tau_2)$, $TPP(\tau_1, \tau_2)$, $NTPP(\tau_1, \tau_2)$.
- Action expression is an expression in terms of action variables. Every action variable acts as a atom in predicate calculus.

In our formalization, algebraic expressions, differential expressions, clock constraint expressions and action expressions are considered as normal propositional variables p in our spatio-temporal logic. The semantics for logical connectives with these four kinds of expressions are interpreted by our spatio-temporal logic like the first order logic language. For example, Let $p \triangleq v_1(x) \wedge v_2(x)$, the variable $x \vDash p$ iff $x \vDash v_1(x)$ and $x \vDash v_2(x)$. Therefore, all of the expressions could be expressed by our spatio-temporal logic.

3.2 Spatio-temporal Hybrid Automata

A spatio-temporal hybrid automaton is described by a tuple

$$(M, X, A, Var, E, Inv, Act)$$

where

- M is a finite set, called the set of discrete states or modes. There are the vertices of a control graph. Every mode has a unique name to identify itself in the set.
- X is the continuous state space of the hybrid automaton. Generally, $X \subset \mathbb{R}^n$ or X is an n-dimensional manifold.
- A is a finite set of symbols which is used to label the edges.
- A set of variables Var is governed by modes. It includes a set of discrete variables $dVar$, a set of continuous variables $cVar$, a set of clock variables $ckVar$, a set of spatial variables $sVar$ and a set of signals S.
- E is a set of edges called events(or transitions). Every edge is defined by a 5-tuple:
$$(m, a, grd_{mm'}, jmp_{mm'}, m')$$
where $m, m' \in M, a \in A$, A is a finite set of symbols which is used to label the edges. $grd_{mm'}$ is the guard condition which specifies when the transition from m to m' is enabled. $jmp_{mm'}$ is a relation defined by a subset $X \times X$. The transition from mode m to $m'$is enabled when the condition satisfies $grd_{mm'}$, while the continuous state x jumps to a new value x' denoted by $(x, x') \in jmp_{mm'}$ during the transition.
- Inv is a mapping from the modes M to the subset of X, that is $Inv(m) \subset X$ for all $m \in M$. Whenever the system in mode m, the continuous states x must satisfy $x \in Inv(m)$. The subset $Inv(m)$ for $m \in M$ is called the invariant of mode m. The invariant specifies the global constraints to the variables. Whenever the invariant condition is violated, the system must exit the relevant mode.
- *Act* is called the activity of a mode which is the conjunction of several differential expressions. Each mode is assigned an *Act*. The activity of one mode specifies the changing of continuous variables depending on time within the mode.

3.3 Semantics

The execution of a spatio-temporal hybrid automaton results in continuous change and discrete change. The mixed discrete-continuous dynamic can be abstracted by a fully discrete transition system. In this paper, we formalize it as a labeled transition system.

Labeled Transition System. A labeled transition system S is a tuple

$$(States, Labels, \rightarrow, S_0)$$

where

- $States$ is a set of states.
- S_0 is the set of initial states and $S_0 \subseteq States$.
- $Labels$ is a set of labels which identify the transitions.
- $\rightarrow$: $States \times Labels \times States$ is a ternary relation over $States$ specifying the transitions between states.

State. In spatio-temporal hybrid automata, a state of a system can be formalized as a structure (m, v, i, ι) where

- $m \in M$ is a mode name. It specifies the current execution of system is in mode m.
- v is the current values of every variable of the system. Each variable in Var owns a value.
- i is a time instant which is the current reading of the default physical clock.
- $\iota = Loc_i(m)$ records the location of mode m with respect to the time instant i. For each reading of clock, function will record a system location.

Transition. A transition relation $\rightarrow$: $States \times Labels \times States$ is a relation from a source state s to a target state s' with specific transition. Generally, a concrete transition is written as $s \xrightarrow{\lambda} s'$ where λ is a label identifying this transition which contains three attributes:

1) a trigger event $evt(\lambda)$ specifies a significant occurrence in time or space.
2) a guard condition $grd(\lambda)$ specifies when the transition is enable.
3) an action $jmp(\lambda)$ which is performed when the transition occurs to change the values of variables.

A transition $s \xrightarrow{\lambda} s'$ can be triggered if a trigger event $evt(\lambda)$ is observed and the source state s satisfies the guard condition $grd(\lambda)$. While a transition is triggered, its action $jmp(\lambda)$ is performed, then the current system state transforms to the target state s'. We can use a transition rule to describe the transition $(m, v, i, \iota) \xrightarrow{\lambda} (m', v', i', \iota')$ as follows

$$\frac{v, i, \iota \models evt(\lambda) \wedge grd(\lambda)}{(m, v, i, \iota) \xrightarrow{\lambda} (m', v', i', \iota')} \quad jmp(\lambda)(v, i, \iota, v', i', \iota')$$

It states that a transition is a valid transition iff it holds the following conditions.

1) $v, i, \iota \models evt(\lambda) \wedge grd(\lambda)$
2) $\iota' = Loc_{i'}(m')$
3) $v, i, \iota, v', i', \iota' \models jmp(\lambda)$

Trace. For considering the infinite behavior (liveness) of a spatio-temporal automaton, we should pay close attention on infinite sequences of transitions.

Consider a labeled transition system S and a state s_0 of S. A s_0-rooted trajectory of S is a finite or infinite sequence of pairs $(a_i, s_i)_{i\geq 1}$ of labels $a_i \in Labels$ and states $s_i \in States$ thus $s_{i-1} \xrightarrow{a_i} s_i$, $i \geq 1$. A live transition system (S, L) is a pair, where S is a labeled transition system and L is a set of infinite initialized trajectories ($(a_i, s_i)_{i\geq 1}, s_0$ is an initial state of S) of S. If (S, L) is a live transition system, and $(a_i, s_i)_{i\geq 1}$ is either a finite initialized trajectory of S or a infinite initialized trajectory in L, such that the corresponding sequence $\langle a_i \rangle_{i\geq 1}$ is called a finite or infinite trace of a live transition system (S, L).

We associate with each transition of the label transition system S a duration in $\mathbb{R} \geq 0$. For trigger events $e \in evt$, the duration of $s \xrightarrow{e} s'$ is 0. For actions $j \in jmp$, the duration of $s \xrightarrow{j} s'$ is 0. For guard conditions with the clock constraint $grd := c.I_{s'} - c.I_s \geq \delta$, the duration of $s \xrightarrow{grd} s'$ is t. An infinite trajectory $\langle a_i, s_i \rangle_{i\geq 1}$ of the label transition system S diverges if the infinite sum $\sum_{i\geq 1} \delta_i$ diverges, where each δ_i is the duration of the corresponding transition $s_{i-1} \xrightarrow{a_i} s_i$, $i \geq 1$. Let L be be set of divergent initialized trajectories of the label transition system S. The spatio-temporal hybrid automaton H is nonzeno if L is *machine-closed* for S(The set L of infinite initialized trajectories is *machine-closed* for S if every finite initialized trajectory of S is a prefix of some trajectory in L.). Each trace of the live transition system (S, L) is called a timed trace of H.

Parallel Composition. Given two spatio-temporal hybrid automata we define a product automaton called the parallel composition. Conceptually, a run of the parallel composition is comprised of simultaneous runs of the component automata which are independent except that:

1) They must synchronize on shared events.
2) The only product states that are permitted are those for which the restrictions on conditions are jointly satisfiable [25].

We define the parallel composition$\mathcal{A}||\mathcal{B}$ of the spatio-temporal hybrid automata $\mathcal{A}$ and $\mathcal{B}$.

$$\mathcal{A} = (M^{\mathcal{A}}, X^{\mathcal{A}}, A^{\mathcal{A}}, Var^{\mathcal{A}}, E^{\mathcal{A}}, Inv^{\mathcal{A}}, Act^{\mathcal{A}})$$

$$\mathcal{B} = (M^{\mathcal{B}}, X^{\mathcal{B}}, A^{\mathcal{B}}, Var^{\mathcal{B}}, E^{\mathcal{B}}, Inv^{\mathcal{B}}, Act^{\mathcal{B}})$$

- $M = M^{\mathcal{A}} \times M^{\mathcal{B}}$
- $X = X^{\mathcal{A}} \times X^{\mathcal{B}}$
- $A = \alpha_1 \cup \alpha_2 \cup \alpha_3$ where

1) α_1 is a subset of $A^{\mathcal{A}}$. Each element in α_1 is used to label the edges such as $(m_1, m_2) \to (m_1', m_2)$, $m_1, m_1' \in M^{\mathcal{A}}, m_2 \in M^{\mathcal{B}}$.
$\alpha_1 = \{a | m_1 \xrightarrow{a} m_1'\}$.
2) α_2 is a subset of $A^{\mathcal{B}}$. Each element in α_2 is used to label the edges such as $(m_1, m_2) \to (m_1, m_2')$, $m_1 \in M^{\mathcal{A}}, m_2, m_2' \in M^{\mathcal{B}}$.
$\alpha_2 = \{a | m_2 \xrightarrow{a} m_2'\}$.
3) α_3 is a set of symbols to label the edges such as $(m_1, m_2) \to (m_1', m_2')$, $m_1, m_1' \in M^{\mathcal{A}}, m_2, m_2' \in M^{\mathcal{B}}$.
$\alpha_3 = \{a * b | m_1 \xrightarrow{a} m_1', m_2 \xrightarrow{b} m_2'\}$ $*$ is for simple connection of symbols.

- $Var = Var^{\mathcal{A}} \cup Var^{\mathcal{B}}$
- E is a set of edges called events. Every edge is a 5-tuple:

$$(m, a, grd(a), jmp(a), m')$$

where $a \in A$ is a symbol to label the edges. The guard condition $grd(a)$ is constructed as follows

$$grd(a) = \begin{cases} grd(a) & \text{if } a \in A^{\mathcal{A}} \\ grd(a) & \text{if } a \in A^{\mathcal{B}} \\ grd(b) \wedge grd(c) & \text{if } a = b * c, b \in A^{\mathcal{A}}, c \in A^{\mathcal{B}} \end{cases}$$

The action $jmp(a)$ is constructed as follows

$$jmp(a) = \begin{cases} jmp(a) & \text{if } a \in A^{\mathcal{A}} \\ jmp(a) & \text{if } a \in A^{\mathcal{B}} \\ jmp(b) \wedge jmp(c) & \text{if } a = b * c, b \in A^{\mathcal{A}}, c \in A^{\mathcal{B}} \end{cases}$$

- $Inv = \{inv | inv = inv_{m_1} \wedge inv_{m_2}, inv_{m_1} \in Inv^{\mathcal{A}}, inv_{m_2} \in Inv^{\mathcal{B}}\}$, for the mode $m = (m_1, m_2)$, $m_1 \in M^{\mathcal{A}}$, $m_2 \in M^{\mathcal{B}}$.
- $Act = \{act | act_{m_1} \wedge act_{m_1}\}$ where act_{m_1} is for specifying activity of the mode m_1, act_{m_2} is for specifying activity of the mode m_2, act is for specifying activity of the mode m, $m = (m_1, m_2)$, $m_1 \in M^{\mathcal{A}}$, $m_2 \in M^{\mathcal{B}}$.

4 Case Study: Train Control System

Intelligent Transportation Systems are the future transportation system. It integrates Electronic sensor technology, Data communication transmission technology, System control technology and Computer technology to manage the transportation system. It is a real-time, accurate, efficient and integrated transportation management system. In this section, we will only illustrate a preliminary Intelligent Transportation System, a communication based train control (CBTC) system [5] as a case study.

Communication Based Train Control System is the trend of development of rail train control system in the future. The core of a CBTC system is a Vehicle On Board Controller (VOBC) subsystem, which mainly achieves three functions on control: Automatic Train Protection (ATP), Automatic Train Supervision (ATS) and Automatic Train Operation (ATO). ATP is the core subsystem of VOBC system. The train functions on acceleration, coasting, deceleration, stopping, and door opening are supervised by the ATP system. But its most important responsibility is to protect the system from over speed and avoid crashing, that is what we will discuss in the following.

4.1 Requirements

In this system we focus on two trains, which construct a global system. The ATP devices of these two trains are used to protect the train from over speeding and avoid train crash. Therefore, there are two components: speed supervision unit (SSU) and distance supervision unit (DSU) in this system. The behavior and interaction of them can be described as follows:

- After the train finishes self-detection, ATP device is initialized.
- At the same time, distance supervision unit is initialized to observe global events on the location of trains.
- After every fix period, speed-sensor sends current speed to the speed supervision unit.
- According to the current driving mode and speed curves sent by wayside equipment, the speed supervision unit calculates the current limit speed.
- Then, SSU calculates the difference between the limit speed and the current speed $DiffSpeed$.
- 1) If $DiffSpeed$ is less than a critical speed $criticalSpeed$ and more than zero, SSU will send a warning message to the Train Operation Display(TOD) to inform the driver of deceleration. After warning, SSU will send a normal brake message to Braking Equipment (BE). Then the BE will apply the normal brake until the speed is more than $criticalSpeed$. All these operations should be done in 150ms.
  2) If $DiffSpeed$ is less than zero, SSU will send an emergency message directly to BE. Then BE will apply the emergency brake until velocity $v = 0$. These operations should be done in 100ms.
- As the trains moving in their tracks, location related events of trains are observed by distance supervision unit (DSU), i.e. locations ι_1 and ι_2, the distance between T1 and T2 Dis.
- 1) If SDU observers that the distance is more than a emerge distance $Emerge Distance$ and less than a safe distance $SafeDistance$, SDU will send a warning message to the T1 and T2 to inform the driver of deceleration. After warning, SDU will send a normal brake message to Braking Equipment (BE). Then the BE will apply the normal brake until the distance is more than $SafeDistance$. All these operations should be done in 150ms.
  2) If SDU observers that the distance is less than $EmergeDistance$, SDU will send an emergency message directly to BE. Then BE will apply the emergency brake until velocity v=0. These operations should be done in 100ms.

4.2 Behavior of the System

Based on the syntax and semantics of spatio-temporal hybrid automata model, we can model the behavior of the Protection functions of ATP system. The most important components are Component SSU, Component DSU and Component BE. We use spatio-temporal hybrid automata to model the behavior of them as follows.

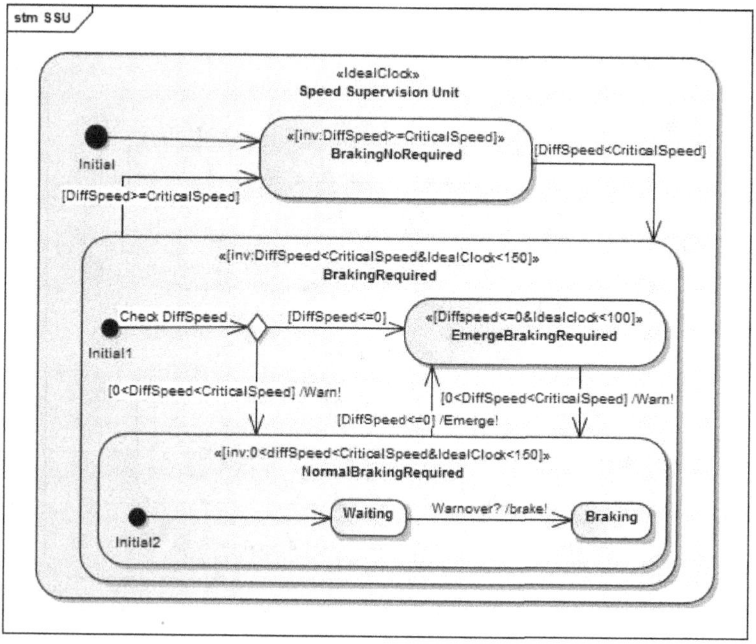

Fig. 2. Behavior of Speed Supervision Unit

Fig.2 describes the behavior of speed supervision unit. The unit is responsible for calculating data and sending protection commands. The unique clock of them is $IdealClock$. In the following transition system we all refer the current $IdealClock$ as c for convenience. For lack of space, we only give a transition from $BrakingNoRequired$ to $BrakingRequired$ as an example.

$evt(tr) \wedge grd(tr) = \epsilon \wedge (DiffSpeed < CriticalSpeed)$,
$jmp(tr) = IdealClock := 0$,

When $v, c, \iota \models grd(tr)$ and $(v, c, \iota, v, 0, \iota') \models jmp(tr)$,
$tr \triangleq (BrakingNotRequired, v, c, \iota)$
$\rightarrow (BrakingRequired, v, 0, \iota')$,
$\lambda(tr) = (\epsilon, DiffSpeed < CriticalSpeed, IdealClock := 0)$.
When braking is required, no matter what kind of braking, the braking duration should be less than 150 ms. Hence in this mode

$inv(BrakingRequired) = (IdealClock < 150) \wedge$
$(DiffSpeed < criticalSpeedDif)$

Fig.3 describes the behavior of distance supervision unit(SDU). SDU observers the system events after it has initialized. It could protect the components in the system from crashing by capturing the information from events. The transition system of SDU begins from the initial mode. At once, observer got an event of train T1 and an event of train T2 at the same time, where

$$E1 = (L_1; < attr_1; t; (x_1, y_1, z_1) >)$$

$$E2 = (L_2; < attr_2; t; (x_2, y_2, z_2) >).$$

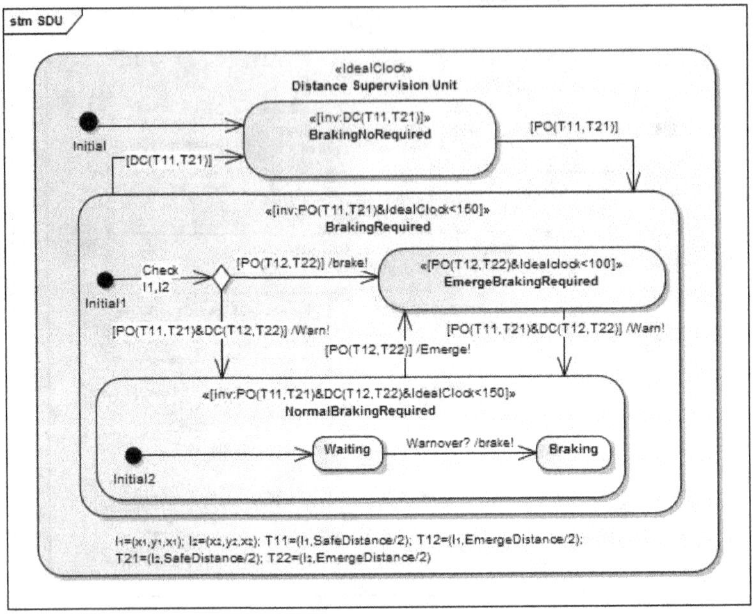

Fig. 3. Behavior of Distance Supervision Unit

SDU calculates spatial terms occupied by trains based on two events and ensures the distance between these two trains.

$$\tau_1 = ((x_1, y_1, z_1), r_1)$$

$$\tau_2 = ((x_2, y_2, z_2), r_2)$$

where r_1 and r_2 are radiuses, which can be generated based on the environment. Then spatial terms τ_1 and τ_2 will be used to calculate the guard and then SDU will control the signal generate through the spatio-temporal hybrid automata model.

Fig.4 describes the Braking Equipment state machine under the condition of velocity $v \geq 0$. We list a transition for a short specification as follows.

$evt(tr) \wedge grd(tr) = Emerge? \wedge TRUE$,

$jmp(tr) = IdealClock := 0$,

When $v, c, \iota \models grd(tr)$ and $(v, c, \iota, v, 0, \iota') \models jmp(tr)$,
$tr \triangleq (initial_1, v, 0, \iota) \rightarrow (EmergeBraking, v, 0, \iota')$
Edge *tr* is fired immediately after entering submode *Emergency*.

$$inv(EmergeBraking) = (IdealClock < 100) \wedge (v \geqslant 0)$$

$$act(EmergeBraking) = \begin{cases} -fW = \frac{W}{g} \cdot \frac{dv}{dt} \\ v\mid_{t=0} = v_0 \end{cases}.$$

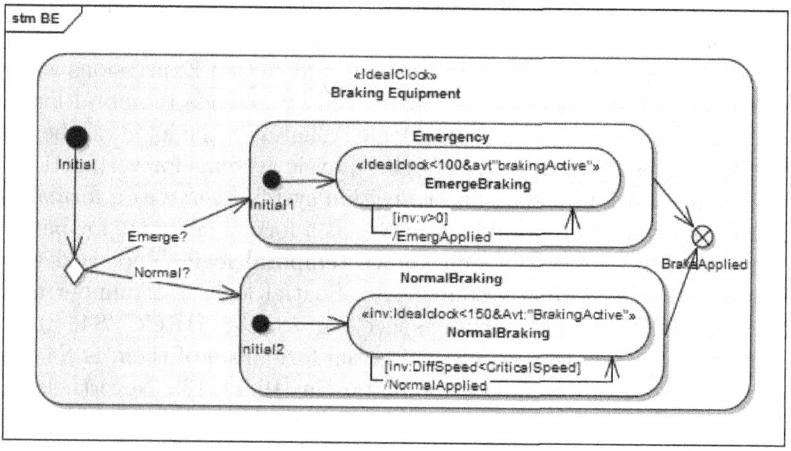

Fig. 4. Behavior of component Braking Equipment

If f is a solution of equation $act(EmergeBraking)$, f satisfies
$inv(EmergeBraking)[f/v] = TRUE \ \wedge$
$act(EmergeBraking)[f/v, \dot{f}/\dot{v}] = TRUE$.
In the submode *EmergeBraking*, the continuous variable v is changing when time passes, following the $act(EmergeBraking)$. According to Newton second law of motion, fW is the external force to brake, $\frac{W}{g}$ is the weight of the train and $\frac{dv}{dt}$ is the acceleration of the train.

5 Related Work

Hybrid automata are formal models for mixed discrete-continuous hybrid system which constitute the foundations of CPS [21]. It can be viewed as a generalization of time automata, in which the behavior of variables is governed in each state by a set of differential equations [22]. Compared to hybrid automata, spatio-temporal hybrid automata extend the expression on spatial terms and spatial relations. Since, CPS events not only include time and observe variables but also locations. We also classify the type of variables and expressions for clear description in spatio-temporal hybrid automata. The semantics of spatio-temporal hybrid automata is based on labeled transition system. We define the states and transitions of the labeled transition system, and discuss the trace semantics and parallel composition of spatio-temporal hybrid automata.

In [23], CPSs are modeled as co-inductive coroutined constraint logic programs, physical quantities are faithfully represented as continuous quantities (i.e., not discretized) and the constraints imposed on them by CPS physical interactions are modeled with constraint logic programming over reals. Therefore, CPSs are modeled as coroutined, co-inductive CLP(R) programs which can be used for verifying interesting properties of the system such as safety, utility, and liveness. Compare to their work, our approach support a spatio-temporal logic to describe logical connections between Algebraic Expressions, Differential Expressions, Clock Expressions, Spatial Expressions and Action Expressions with time flows. The spatio-temporal logic is constructed by extends temporal logic with spatial characteristics based on spatial logic. Whatever, the logic can be used to describe the interesting properties of cyber-physic systems for verification.

In formal verification of software, transition systems serve as a formal model of systems, meanwhile temporal logic serves as a formal language for behavioral properties. PTL is one of the well known temporal logics and used to specify requirements of real-time systems [1, 9]. Spatial logic is a number of logics used for representation and reasoning space, e.g. RCC-8, $BRCC$, $S4_u$ and other fragments of $S4_u$. The most expressive spatial formalism of them is $S4_u$, which extends by $S4$ with the universal modalities in [10, 11, 13]. Nevertheless, spatial logic can not express changes in time of the truth-values of purely spatial propositions. Spatio-temporal logic is used for describing the change of spatial proposition over time. There have been attempts to construct Spatio-temporal hybrids. For example, in [12], Finger and Gabbay introduced a methodology whereby an arbitrary logic system L can be enriched with temporal features to create a new system $T(L)$. The new system is constructed by combining L with a pure propositional temporal logic T. The method can be looked upon as a guide to combine an arbitrary logic and PTL for our work. In [14], Wolter and Zakharyaschev constructed a spatio-temporal logic, based on RCC-8 and PTL, intended for qualitative knowledge representation and reasoning about the behavior of spatial regions in time. Nevertheless, RCC-8 is a fragment of $S4_u$ and has rather limited expressive power [15]. The syntax of RCC-8 only contains eight binary predicates. Nor can RCC-8 represent complex relations between more than two regions. Therefore, we chose the spatial logic $S4_u$, which has the more expressive power as one of the basic logic in our work. Furthermore, those spatial-temporal logic only focus on the change of space over time. Our work concentrates on construct a spatio-temporal logic which can express both spatial proposition and normal proposition for CPSs.

6 Conclusion and Future Work

In Cyber-Physical System design and modeling, a big problem is how to capture time and location information into CPS models, together with specifying logistical properties or constrains. For modeling the relations between spatial terms and time, we have proposed a spatio-temporal logic based on PTL, $S4_u$ and the method to enrich a logic. The logic is used to express the logical connections between all kinds of expressions (including spatial expressions) in CPS. Thus, time, spatial terms and other type of variables can calculate together. We have constructed a spatio-temporal hybrid automaton for Cyber-Physical Systems, which is an extension of hybrid automata with spatial variables, spatial expressions based on spatio-temporal logic. Then, we give formal semantics (including states, transition, trace and parallel composition) of the automaton based on labeled transition systems. Finally, a Train Control System is employed as a case study to show the usage of spatio-temporal hybrid automata.

In the future, the related algorithms on satisfiability problems should be considered. Moreover, we will work on the verification and tool support of spatio-temporal hybrid automata.

Acknowledgment. We would like to thank the reviewers for their valuable comments. This work is partially supported by the projects funded by the 973 program 2009CB320702, NSFC 61170084, Shanghai Knowledge Service Platform ZF 1213, NSFC Creative Team 61021004 and 863 Project 2011AA010101.

References

1. Manna, Z., Pnueli, A.: The Temporal Logic of Reactive and Concurrent Systems Specification. Springer (1992)
2. Gabelaia, D., Kontchakov, R., Kurucz, A., Wolter, F., Zakharyaschev, M.: Combining Spatial and Temporal Logics. Journal of Artificial Intelligence Research, 167–243 (2005)
3. Lee, E.A.: Cyber Physical Systems: Design Challenges. In: 11th IEEE International Symposium on Object Oriented Real-Time Distributed Computing (ISORC), pp. 363–369 (2008)
4. Shao, Z., Liu, J., Ding, Z., Chen, M., Jiang, N.: Spatio-Temporal Properties Analysis for Cyber-Physical Systems. In: Proceedings of the 18th International Conference on Engineering of Complex Computer Systems, ICECCS 2013 (2013)
5. IEEE, IEEE Recommended Practice for Communications-Based Train Control (CBTC) System Design and Functional Allocations. IEEE Std 1474.3-2008 (2008)
6. Fouquet, F., Morin, B., Fleurey, F., Barais, O., Plouzeau, N., Jezequel, J.: A dynamic component model for cyber physical systems. In: Proceedings of the 15th ACM SIGSOFT Symposium on Component Based Software Engineering, pp. 135–144 (2012)
7. Chomicki, J.: Temporal query language: a survey. In: Gabbay, D.M., Ohlbach, H.J. (eds.) ICTL 1994. LNCS, vol. 827, pp. 506–534. Springer, Heidelberg (1994)
8. Fagin, R., Halpern, J.Y., Moses, Y., Vardi, M.Y.: Reasoning about Knowledge. MIT Press (1995)
9. Manna, Z., Pnueli, A.: Temporal Verification of Reactive Systems: Safety. Springer (1995)
10. Stone, M.H.: Application of the theory of Boolean rings to general topology. Transactions of the AMS 41, 321–364 (1937)
11. Chen, T.: Algebraic postulates and a geometric interpretation of the Lewis calculus of strict implication. Bulletin of the AMS 44, 737–744 (1938)
12. Finger, M., Gabbay, D.M.: Adding a temporal dimension to a logic system. Journal of Logic, Language and Information 1(3), 203–233 (1992)
13. McKinsey, J.C.C.: A solution of the decision problem for the Lewis systems S2 and S4, with an application to topology. Journal of Symbolic Logic 6(4), 117–134 (1941)
14. Wolter, F., Zakharyaschev, M.: Spatio-temporal representation and reasoning based on RCC-8. In: Proceedings of the 7th Conference on Principles of Knowledge Representation and Reasoning (KR 2000), pp. 3–14 (2000)

15. Egenhofer, M.J., Herring, J.R.: Categorizing topological relationships between regions, lines and points in geographic databases. Tech. rep., University of Maine (1991)
16. Wolper, P.: Expressing interesting properties of programs in propositional temporal logic. In: Proceedings of the 13th ACM SIGACT-SIGPLAN Symposium on Principles of Programming Languages, pp. 184–192 (1986)
17. Clarke, E.M., Emerson, E.A., Sistla, A.P.: Automatic Verification of Finite-State Concurrent Systems Using Temporal Logic Specifications. ACM Transactions on Programming Languages and Systems, 244–263 (1986)
18. Reynolds, M.: The complexity of the temporal logic with until over general linear time. Journal of Computer and System Sciences 66(2), 393–426 (2003)
19. Sistla, A.P., Clarke, E.M.: The complexity of propositional linear temporal logics. Journal of the ACM 32(3), 733–749 (1985)
20. Alexander, C., Zakharyaschev, M.: Modal Logic. Oxford Logic Guides, vol. 35. Clarendon Press, Oxford (1997)
21. Henzinger, T.A.: The theory of hybrid automata. In: Logic in Computer Science, LICS 1996, pp. 278–292 (1996)
22. Alur, R., Courcoubetis, C., Henzinger, T.A., Ho, P.: Hybrid automata: An algorithmic approach to the specification and verification of hybrid systems. In: Grossman, R.L., Ravn, A.P., Rischel, H., Nerode, A. (eds.) HS 1993. LNCS, vol. 736, pp. 209–229. Springer, Heidelberg (1993)
23. Saeedloei, N., Gupta, G.: A logic-based modeling and verification of CPS. ACM SIGBED Review 8(2), 31–34 (2011)
24. Gupta, R.: Programming models and methods for spatiotemporal actions and reasoning in cyber-physical systems. In: NSF Workshop on CPS (2006)
25. Miller, J.S.: Decidability and Complexity Results for Timed Automata and Semilinear Hybrid Automata. In: Lynch, N.A., Krogh, B.H. (eds.) HSCC 2000. LNCS, vol. 1790, pp. 296–310. Springer, Heidelberg (2000)

Embedding Functions into Disjunctive Logic Programs

Yisong Wang[1], Jia-Huai You[2], and Mingyi Zhang[3,4,⋆]

[1] Department of Computer Science, Guizhou University, Guiyang, China
[2] Department of Computing Science, University of Alberta, Canada
[3] Chongqing University of Arts and Sciences
[4] Guizhou Academy of Sciences, Guiyang, China
zhangmingyi045@yahoo.com.cn

Abstract. We extend the notions of completion and loop formulas of normal logic programs with functions to a class of nested expressions that properly include disjunctive logic programs. We show that answer sets for such a logic program can be characterized as the models of its completion and loop formulas. These results provide a basis for computing answer sets of disjunctive programs with functions, by solvers for the Constraint Satisfaction Problem. The potential benefit in answer set computations for this approach has been demonstrated previously in the implementation called FASP. We also present a formulation of completion and loop formulas for disjunctive logic programs with variables. This paper focuses on the theoretical development of these extensions.

1 Introduction

Logic programming based on stable model/answer set semantics, called *answer set programming* (ASP), has been considered a promising paradigm for declarative problem solving. The general idea is to encode a problem by a logic program such that the answer sets of the program correspond to the solutions of the problem [25,26]. For example, the graph coloring problem can be encoded in ASP as the following two rules:

$$1\{clr(X,I) : c(I)\}1 \leftarrow v(X). \tag{1}$$
$$\leftarrow clr(X,I), clr(Y,I), e(X,Y), c(I). \tag{2}$$

Here $clr(X, I)$ means that the color of vertex X is I, and $e(X, Y)$ says that vertexes X and Y are connected. The rule (1) indicates that every vertex X has to be colored with exact one color, while the rule (2) constrains the assigned colors for vertexes X and Y being different if they are connected. With the state-of-the-art ASP solvers such as CLASP, CMODELS, SMODELS, and DLV, ASP has been applied to a number of practical domains [3], in particular, to program verification and analysis [30].

Normal logic programs under stable model semantics [11] have been extended in several directions, one of which is to logic programs with nested expressions (or just *nested expressions*) [21]. More recently, nested expressions have been extended to quantified equilibrium logic [27] and arbitrary first-order sentences [10].

⋆ Corresponding author.

Z. Liu, J. Woodcock, and H. Zhu (Eds.): ICTAC 2013, LNCS 8049, pp. 355–372, 2013.

Another direction is the idea of computing answer sets of logic programs by utilizing off-the-shelf solvers from other constraint solving formalisms, e.g., by SAT solvers [23,12], by pseudo boolean solvers [24], and by CSP solvers [22,29]. The idea is that if a program has no positive loops the models of its completion are answer sets. This idea has been extended to the notion of *tight on a set* [8]. Otherwise, loop formulas can be used to eliminate models of completion that are not answer sets, and more importantly, to perform conflict-driven learning and generate non-chronological backtracking. The loop formulas approach has been extended to disjunctive logic programs [15].

In the third direction, ASP has recently been extended with functions. There are two different approaches to accommodating functions. One of them treats functions over Herbrand domains [2,16,28,6], in which, just like Horn clause logic programming, functions are interpreted by fixed mappings, and are language symbols used to define recursive data structures. This approach yields a language which is more expressive than the standard function-free ASP language.

In the other approach, to economically and naturally encode problems in ASP, Lin and Wang considered adding functions into normal logic programs in which functions are taken as mappings over finite and non-Herbrand domains [22], called *intentional functions*. They extended the notions of completion and loop formulas and show that through program completion and loop formulas, a normal logic program with functions can be transformed to an instance of the Constraint Satisfaction Problem (CSP). Thus, off-the-shelf CSP solvers can be used as black boxes in computing answer sets. Accordingly, they implemented a system FASP[1] to compute answer sets of such logic programs. Recently, such intentional functions have been integrated into logic programs with weight constraints [29], IF-programs [18] and first-order formulas under stable model semantics [1].

In the approach by Lin and Wang, a program with functions will be grounded to a finite ground program for the answer set computation. Thus it doesn't deal with infinite domains of any sort. Its aim is at providing a flexible knowledge representation language enabling both relations and functions. The approach is closely related to the functional logic language of [5]. A main difference is that in [5] functions are partial, while in [22] they must be total.

In this paper, we consider further adding functions into nested logic programs with rules of the form

$$a_1; \ldots ; a_n \leftarrow b_1, \ldots , b_m, G$$

where a_i are atoms, b_j are atoms or equality atoms, and G is a nested formula in which every occurrence of an atom occurs in the scope of the negation-as-failure operator "*not*". Following [15], these programs with nested expressions are called *disjunctive logic programs.*

Disjunctive logic programs of this kind can be seen to represent nested expressions as defined in [21] in the following sense. First, since nested expressions can be transformed to disjunctive logic programs with negation-as-failure in the head [4], the latter can be viewed as a normal form for nested expressions. Also in [21], it was shown that a negative literal in the head of such a disjunctive rule can be moved to the body by adding a *not* to it (i.e., *not* a in the head becomes *not not* a in the body).

[1] `http://webdocs.cs.ualberta.ca/~yisong/fasp/`

In this paper, we define answer sets for nested expression with functions, and then formulate completion and loop formulas for disjunctive logic programs with functions. We show that loop formulas, along with program completion, capture answer sets of disjunctive logic programs with functions. This can be seen as a generalization of the main results of [22]. It turns out that, in order to incorporate functions, the notions of completion, dependency graphs, loops, and loop formulas all require a nontrivial generalization.

In general, a logic program may have an exponential number of loops and loop formulas [20]. To avoid computing similar loops, first-order loops and loop formulas were proposed for normal logic programs with variables [7], which are recently extended to arbitrary first-order sentences [14]. Since the language of disjunctive logic programs with functions is a many-sorted first-order language and an encoding in it is often written with variables, this motivated us to extend first-order loops and loop formulas to disjunctive logic programs with functions. This can be regarded as a generalization of normal logic programs [7] and disjunctive logic programs [14] to include functions.

An earlier version of this paper, with proofs omitted, was presented at the 2nd Workshop on Answer Set Programming and Other Computing Paradigms (ASPOCP-2009).

2 Preliminary

The concept of atom is defined as in propositional logic. *Elementary formulas* are atoms and special symbols $\bot$ ("false") and $\top$ ("true").[2] *Formulas* are built from elementary formulas using the unary connective not (negation as failure) and the binary connectives "," (conjunction) and ";" (disjunction). A *rule with nested expressions* is an expression of the form

$$F \leftarrow G \tag{3}$$

where both G and F are formulas. A *logic program with nested expressions* (or called *nested logic program*) is a finite set of rules with nested expressions.

For any formula F, G and H, we may write $F \rightarrow G; H$ to stand for the formula $(F, G); (not\ F, H)$ which reads like an if-then-else statement.

Let F be a formula and Z a set of atoms. That Z *satisfies* F, written $Z \models F$, is defined as follows:

- for an atom a, $Z \models a$ if $a \in Z$; $Z \models \top$,
- $Z \models (F, G)$ if $Z \models F$ and $Z \models G$,
- $Z \models (F; G)$ if $Z \models F$ or $Z \models G$,
- $Z \models not\ F$ if $Z \not\models F$.

Note that, since $\bot$ is not an atom, it follows that $Z \not\models \bot$, for any set of atoms Z.

Z *satisfies* a logic program P if for every rule of the form (3) in P, $Z \models F$ whenever $Z \models G$. The *reduct* F^Z of a formula F w.r.t. a set of atoms Z, is defined recursively as

- for elementary F, $F^Z = F$,
- $(F \oplus G)^Z = (F^Z \oplus G^Z)$ where $\oplus$ is ",", ";" or "$\leftarrow$",

[2] The syntax defined in [21] allows classical negation, which can be eliminated by introducing auxiliary atoms [19].

- $(not\ F)^Z = \bot$ if $Z \models F^Z$, and $\top$ otherwise,

The *reduct* of a logic program P w.r.t. a set Z of atoms is the following set:

$$\{(F \leftarrow G)^Z : F \leftarrow G \in P\}.$$

A set of atoms Z is an *answer set* of a nested logic program P not containing *not* if Z is a minimal set satisfying P. For a nested logic program P, Z is an *answer set* of P if Z is an answer set of the reduct P^Z.

3 Nested Expressions with Functions

Now, we assume that the underlying language $\mathcal{L}$ is a many-sorted first-order language which may have pre-interpreted function symbols like the standard arithmetic functions such as "+", "−" and so on. *Elementary formulas* are atoms, equality atoms (written $s = t$)[3], and special symbols $\bot$ and $\top$, and *formulas* are built from elementary formulas using "*not*", "," and ";" as before. By abuse of notation, we may write $s \neq t$ for $not\ (s = t)$. A *nested logic program with functions* (a *logic program* or just a *program*) is a finite set of rules of the form

$$H \leftarrow F \tag{4}$$

where H and F are formulas of $\mathcal{L}$, together with a set of type definitions, one for each type τ used in the logic program, of the form

$$\tau : D \tag{5}$$

where D is a finite nonempty set of elements, called a *domain*[4]. Here we require that if a constant c of type τ occurs in a rule of a program P then c must be contained in the domain of τ. Recall that $\mathcal{L}$ is a many-sorted first-order language. A logic program with variables is taken as the shorthand for the instantiated ground program; i.e., if a variable x is of type τ and the domain of τ is D according to the type definitions, then x is instantiated by elements in D. Thus we equate a logic program with variables with its grounded program unless otherwise stated.

Recall that once a variable in a rule is replaced by objects of a domain, the grounded rules may have symbols not in the original language $\mathcal{L}$. In the following, we let $\mathcal{L}_P$ be the language that extends $\mathcal{L}$ by introducing a new constant for each object in the domain of a type, but not a constant in $\mathcal{L}$. These new constants will have the same type as their corresponding objects. Now the fully instantiated rules will be in the language $\mathcal{L}_P$.

An interpretation of a program not only assigns truth values to ground instances of relations, but also assigns a mapping to each function symbol. Formally, an *interpretation* I of a program P is a first-order structure of $\mathcal{L}_P$ such that

[3] Unless explicitly stated otherwise, an atom refers to a non-equality atom, of the form $p(\mathbf{t})$, where p is a predicate symbol. We distinguish atoms from equality atoms for convenience.

[4] We require domains to be finite, since we will define loop formula for ground programs later, if using an infinite domain, a ground program may be infinite, in this case, loop formulas may be not well-defined.

- The domains of I are those specified in the type definitions of P.
- A constant is mapped to itself.
- If R is a relation of arity $\tau_1 \times \cdots \times \tau_n$, and the type definitions $\tau_i : D_i$, $1 \leq i \leq n$, are in P, then I assigns a relation to R, denoted R^I, such that $R^I \subseteq D_1 \times \cdots \times D_n$.
- If f is a function of type $\tau_1 \times \cdots \times \tau_n \rightarrow \tau_{n+1}$, $n \geq 1$, and the type definitions $\tau_i : D_i$, $1 \leq i \leq n+1$, are in P, then I assigns a mapping to f, denoted f^I, from $D_1 \times \cdots \times D_n$ to D_{n+1}.

Note that pre-interpreted functions follow their standard interpretations, which do not change from one interpretation to another.

Notice also that the notion of interpretation here is defined for a logic program instead of the underlying language $\mathcal{L}$. In the following, whenever we talk about interpretations of a formula, we assume that the formula under discussion occurs in the underlying logic program, where the type definitions are fixed.

Let I be an interpretation. The interpretation of a constant c under I, denoted c^I, is c. If $t = f(t_1, ..., t_n)$ is a term, and each t_i, $1 \leq i \leq n$, is already interpreted, denoted t_i^I, then t^I denotes the constant mapped from the vector $(t_1^I, ..., t_n^I)$ by f^I. This notation naturally extends to vectors of terms. In addition, for an n-ary predicate p and an n-vector $\boldsymbol{t}$, we will write $p^I(\boldsymbol{t})$ to denote the valuation of $p(\boldsymbol{t})$ under I.

We now define *satisfaction* for formulas with functions. Below, we only define it for elementary formulas. Along with the definition given in Section 2, the definition of satisfaction can be extended straightforwardly to all formulas. Let F be an elementary formula and I an interpretation. We say I *satisfies* F, written $I \models F$, if

- $F = \top$;
- $F = p(\boldsymbol{t})$, and $p^I(\boldsymbol{t})$ holds under I, i.e., $\boldsymbol{t}^I \in p^I$, where p is a predicate;
- F is an equality atom $t = t'$, and $t^I = t'^I$.

To extend the notion of reduct to logic programs with functions, it is sufficient to define it for elementary formulas as well. Let F be an elementary formula and I an interpretation. The *reduct* of F w.r.t. I, written F^I, is defined as

- $p(\boldsymbol{t}^I)$ if $F = p(\boldsymbol{t})$;
- $\top$ if $F = \top$ or F is an equality atom such that $I \models F$;
- $\bot$ if $F = \bot$ or F is an equality atom such that $I \not\models F$.

With this, the notion of reduct as introduced in Section 2 naturally extends to logic programs with functions. Let P^I be the reduct of a program P w.r.t. I. Evidently, P^I mentions no functions, equalities and the negation as failure operator "*not*". Answer sets for such logic programs have been defined before: a set of atoms M is an answer set of such a program P if M is a minimal set satisfying P. We now extend it to logic programs with functions.

In the following, given an interpretation I, we write I^a to denote the set of atoms that contain no functions and are true under I, i.e., $I^a = \{p(\boldsymbol{c}) | (\boldsymbol{c}) \in p^I\}$.

Definition 1. *Let P be a nested logic program with functions and I an interpretation of P. I is an* answer set *of P if I^a is an answer set of P^I.*

Example 1. Consider the logic program P:

$$f : \tau \to \tau, \quad p : \tau, \quad \tau : \{0, 1\},$$
$$(p(1); f(0) \neq f(1)) \leftarrow (f(0) = 1 \to not\, p(1); p(0)). \tag{6}$$

Notice that the types of the predicate p and the function f are part of the given language, not the program P; we write them in P for clarity. The rule (6) stands for

$$(p(1); f(0) \neq f(1)) \leftarrow (f(0) = 1, not\, p(1)); (f(0) \neq 1, p(0)). \tag{7}$$

Consider the following interpretation for P:

- I_1 with $f^{I_1}(0) = f^{I_1}(1) = 0$, $p^{I_1}(0)$ and $p^{I_1}(1)$ are false. P^{I_1} consists of a single rule $(p(1); \bot \leftarrow (\bot, \top); (\top, p(0)))$ which is equivalent to $(p(1) \leftarrow p(0))$. Since $I_1^a = \emptyset$ and $\emptyset$ is an answer set of P^{I_1}, thus I_1 is an answer set of P.

Traditionally, two logic programs are said to be equivalent if they have the same set of answer sets. For nested expressions, Lifschitz et al. [21] propose a stronger notion of equivalence: Two formulas F and G are *equivalent* if, for any two interpretations I_1 and I_2, $I_1 \models F^{I_2}$ iff $I_1 \models G^{I_2}$. We adopt the same notion of equivalence for nested logic programs with functions.

Lifschitz et al. also showed a number of results (cf. Propositions 3–7 in [21]). We can easily extend these results to nested logic programs with functions. Particularly relevant to this paper, we can show that any rule of the form (4) is equivalent to

- a finite set of rules of the form

$$a_1; \ldots; a_n \leftarrow G \tag{8}$$

  where G is a formula;
- a finite set of rules of the form[5]

$$a_1; \ldots; a_n \leftarrow b_1, \ldots, b_m, G \tag{9}$$

where $a_i (1 \leq i \leq n)$ and $b_j (1 \leq j \leq m)$ are atoms or equality atoms of $\mathcal{L}$, and G is a formula of $\mathcal{L}$ in which every occurrence of an atom is in the scope of the negation-as-failure operator "*not*". For convenience, we abbreviate a rule of the form (9) by

$$F \leftarrow B, G \tag{10}$$

where F stands for "$a_1; \ldots; a_n$" and B stands for "$b_1, \ldots, b_m$". In the following, a logic program consisting of rules of the form (10) is called a *disjunctive logic program with functions* (or a *disjunctive logic program*, or just a *program* if no confusion arises).

It is important to mention that though functions can enrich the language for knowledge representation, they are not absolutely necessary semantically speaking. As shown in [22], functions can be eliminated as follows.

[5] It is known that for a polynomial time transformation new propositional symbols may need to be used, e.g., to convert a conjunctive normal form to a disjunctive normal form (for transformation of nested expressions see, e.g., [31]).

Let P be a logic program that may have functions. For each function $f : \tau_1 \times \cdots \times \tau_n \to \tau$ in P, we introduce two corresponding relations f_r and $\overline{f}_r$. They both have the arity $\tau_1 \times \cdots \times \tau_n \times \tau$, and informally $f_r(x_1, ..., x_n, y)$ stands for $f(x_1, ..., x_n) = y$ and $\overline{f}_r(x_1, ..., x_n, y)$ for $f(x_1, ..., x_n) \neq y$. Now let $\mathbb{F}(P)$ be the union of the rules obtained by grounding the following rules for each function f in P using the domains in the type definitions of P:

$$\leftarrow f_r(x_1, \ldots, x_n, y_1), f_r(x_1, \ldots, x_n, y_2), y_1 \neq y_2,$$
$$f_r(x_1, \ldots, x_n, y) \leftarrow \mathit{not}\, \overline{f}_r(x_1, \ldots, x_n, y),$$
$$\overline{f}_r(x_1, \ldots, x_n, y) \leftarrow f_r(x_1, \ldots, x_n, z), y \neq z.$$

Let $\mathbb{R}(P)$ be the set of rules obtained from the rules in P by the following transformation:

- evaluate all terms that mention only constants and pre-interpreted functions to constants;
- repeatedly replace each functional term $f(u_1, \ldots, u_n)$, where each u_i is a simple term in which it does not mention a function symbol, by a new variable x and add $f_r(u_1, \ldots, u_n, x)$ to the body of the rule as a conjunctive term where the term appears;
- instantiate all the rules obtained in the previous step, please note that, equality atom will be replaced with $\top$ if it is of the form $c = c$, and $\bot$ if it is of the form $c = c'$ where c and c' are two distinct constants.

$\mathbb{F}(P) \cup \mathbb{R}(P)$ is a logic program without functions and equality, and there is a one-to-one correspondence between it and P:

Theorem 1. *Let P be a nested logic program with functions. An interpretation I for P is an answer set of P iff $\mathbb{R}(I)$ is an answer set of $\mathbb{F}(P) \cup \mathbb{R}(P)$, where $\mathbb{R}(I)$ is the set of atoms that are true in I:*

$$\mathbb{R}(I) = \{p(\mathbf{c}) \mid p^I(\mathbf{c})\ holds\} \cup \{f_r(\mathbf{c}, a) \mid f^I(\mathbf{c}) = a\} \cup \{\overline{f}_r(\mathbf{c}, a) \mid f^I(\mathbf{c}) \neq a\}.$$

3.1 Completion

We now define completion for nested logic programs with functions, which generalizes that of [15] due to the incorporation of functions.

Let P be a logic program. An atom $p(c_1, \ldots, c_k)$ is said to *reside in* P if p is a predicate of type $\tau_1 \times \ldots \times \tau_n$ in P, $\tau_i : D_i$ is in the type definitions of P and $c_i \in D_i$ for each $i (1 \leq i \leq n)$. By *Atoms*(P) we denote the set of atoms residing in P.

Given a formula F, we denote by $pa(F)$ the set of the *positive atoms* in F. An atom $p(\mathbf{t})$ is said to be *positive in* F if there is at least one occurrence of $p(\mathbf{t})$ in F that is not in the scope of negation as failure.

In the following, we identify a nested formula with a classical formula by replacing "," with "$\wedge$", ";" with "$\vee$" and "*not*" with "$\neg$". Also, when we talk about the completion of a logic program, we always assume the rules in the program are of the form (8).

Let P be a logic program whose rules are of the form (8). The *completion* of P, written *COMP*(P), is defined as the set of classical formulas:

– for each rule of the form (8) in P

$$G \supset \bigvee_{1 \leq i \leq n} a_i \tag{11}$$

– and for each atom $p(\mathbf{c}) \in Atoms(P)$,

$$p(\mathbf{c}) \supset \bigvee_{1 \leq i \leq n} \left[\begin{array}{r} G_i \wedge \left(\bigwedge_{q(\mathbf{s}) \in pa(F_i)} \neg q(\mathbf{s}) \right) \\ \wedge \left(\bigvee_{p(\mathbf{t}) \in pa(F_i)} \mathbf{c} = \mathbf{t} \right) \\ \wedge \left(\bigwedge_{p(\mathbf{t}) \in pa(F_i)} (\mathbf{c} = \mathbf{t} \vee \neg p(\mathbf{t})) \right) \end{array} \right] \tag{12}$$

where

- $(F_1 \leftarrow G_1), \ldots, (F_n \leftarrow G_n)$ are the rules of P such that the atom $p(\mathbf{t})$ occurs in $F_i (1 \leq i \leq n)$ for some $\mathbf{t}$,
- $q(\mathbf{s})$ is an atom such that q is distinct from p, and
- $\mathbf{c} = \mathbf{t}$ stands for $\bigwedge_{1 \leq i \leq m} c_i = t_i$ if $\mathbf{c} = (c_1, \ldots, c_m)$ and $\mathbf{t} = (t_1, \ldots, t_m)$. Intuitively, $\mathbf{c} = \mathbf{t}$ if the two vectors have the same length and their corresponding components are all equal.

The intuition behind (12) is that if $p(\mathbf{c})$ is true under an interpretation then at least one disjunct of the right hand of (12) is true. Specifically, the first line says that G_i is true and no $q(\mathbf{s})$ in F_i is true ($q \neq p$); the second line means that at least one $p(\mathbf{t})$ in F_i is interpreted as $p(\mathbf{c})$, and the third line justifies that any other $p(\mathbf{t})$ interpreted different from $p(\mathbf{c})$ must be false. Note that the definition generalizes that of [15] since the formulas in the second and third lines of (12) are equal to $\top$ if the underlying language of P is propositional.

Example 2. Consider the following logic program P

$$\begin{gathered} p, q : \tau, \quad f : \tau \rightarrow \tau, \quad \tau : \{0, 1\}, \\ p(f(0)); p(f(1)); f(0) = f(1) \leftarrow p(0), not\, q(f(0)). \end{gathered} \tag{13}$$

It is clear that any head equality atom can be moved to the body and negated. We thus consider, equivalently, the following rule instead:

$$p(f(0)); p(f(1)) \leftarrow p(0), not\, q(f(0)), f(0) \neq f(1) \tag{14}$$

Note that $Atoms(P) = \{p(0), p(1), q(0), q(1)\}$. $COMP(P)$ consists of

$$\begin{aligned} p(0) \wedge \neg q(f(0)) \wedge f(0) \neq f(1) \supset p(f(0)) \vee p(f(1)), \\ q(0) \supset \bot, \\ q(1) \supset \bot, \\ p(0) \supset (p(0) \wedge \neg q(f(0)) \wedge f(0) \neq f(1)) \wedge (0 = f(0) \vee 0 = f(1)) \wedge \\ (0 = f(0) \vee \neg p(f(0))) \wedge (0 = f(1) \vee \neg p(f(1))), \\ p(1) \supset (p(0) \wedge \neg q(f(0)) \wedge f(0) \neq f(1)) \wedge (1 = f(0) \vee 1 = f(1)) \wedge \\ (1 = f(0) \vee \neg p(f(0))) \wedge (1 = f(1) \vee \neg p(f(1))). \end{aligned}$$

Suppose I is an interpretation of P such that $f^I(0) = 0$, $f^I(1) = 1$, and $p^I(0)$ holds. The reduct P^I consists of a unique rule

$$p(0); p(1); \bot \leftarrow p(0), \top$$

whose answer set is $\emptyset$ while $I^a = \{p(0)\}$. Thus I is not an answer set of P. However, we can verify that I is a model of $\mathit{COMP}(P)$.

3.2 Loops and Loop Formulas

Given a logic program P, the *positive dependency graph* of P, written G_P, is the directed graph (V, E), where $V = \mathit{Atoms}(P)$, and for any $p(\boldsymbol{c}), q(\boldsymbol{d}) \in V$, $(p(\boldsymbol{c}), q(\boldsymbol{d})) \in E$ if there is a rule $F \leftarrow G$ in P such that there exists an atom $p(\boldsymbol{t}) \in pa(F)$, an atom $q(\boldsymbol{s}) \in pa(G)$ with $\boldsymbol{t}^I = \boldsymbol{c}$ and $\boldsymbol{s}^I = \boldsymbol{d}$ for some interpretation I of P.

A nonempty subset L of $\mathit{Atoms}(P)$ is a *loop* of P if G_P has a non-zero length cycle that goes through only and all the nodes in L. In the following, to define loop formulas, we assume that every rule has the form (10). Let L be a loop of a logic program P, and an atom $p(\boldsymbol{c}) \in L$. The *external support formula* of $p(\boldsymbol{c})$ relative to L, written $ES(p(\boldsymbol{c}), L, P)$, is the following formula:

$$\bigvee_{1 \le i \le n} \left[\begin{array}{r} B_i \wedge G_i \wedge \left(\bigvee_{p(\boldsymbol{t}) \in pa(F_i)} \boldsymbol{c} = \boldsymbol{t}\right) \\ \wedge \left(\bigwedge_{\substack{q(\boldsymbol{d}) \in L \\ q(\boldsymbol{t}) \in pa(B_i)}} \neg(\boldsymbol{t} = \boldsymbol{d})\right) \\ \wedge \left(\bigwedge_{q(\boldsymbol{t}) \in pa(F_i)} \left(\left(\bigwedge_{q(\boldsymbol{d}) \in L} \neg(\boldsymbol{t} = \boldsymbol{d})\right) \supset \neg q(\boldsymbol{t})\right)\right) \end{array} \right] \tag{15}$$

where $(F_1 \leftarrow B_1, G_1), \ldots, (F_n \leftarrow B_n, G_n)$ are all of the rules of P such that, for each $i (1 \le i \le n)$, F_i mentions the predicate p.The intended meaning of (15) is that to externally support $p(\boldsymbol{c})$ (under an interpretation) at least one disjunct of (15) must be true. More specifically in (15), the first line says that B_i and G_i are true and at least one $p(\boldsymbol{t})$ in F_i is interpreted as $p(\boldsymbol{c})$; the second line means that no atom in B_i is interpreted as an atom of the loop L; the third line justifies that every atom in F_i which is not interpreted as some atom in the loop L are false, i.e. this formula supports no more atoms outside of L.

The *loop formula* of L in P, written $LF(L, P)$, is then the following formula:

$$\bigvee_{A \in L} A \supset \bigvee_{A \in L} ES(A, L, P). \tag{16}$$

This definition clearly generalizes the one for disjunctive loop formulas [15].

Example 3. (Continue with Example 2) $L = \{p(0)\}$ is a unique loop of P. $LF(L, P)$ is the following formula

$$\begin{array}{l} p(0) \supset (p(0) \wedge \neg q(f(0)) \wedge f(0) \neq f(1)) \wedge (0 = f(0) \vee 0 = f(1)) \\ \wedge (0 \neq f(0) \supset \neg p(f(0))) \wedge (0 \neq f(1) \supset \neg p(f(1))) \wedge (0 \neq 0) \end{array}$$

which is equivalent to $p(0) \supset \bot$ and then $\neg p(0)$. Clearly, the interpretation I of P in Example 2 does not satisfy $LF(L, P)$. Consequently I is not an answer set of P. Evidently, any interpretation I' such that $p^{I'} = q^{I'} = \emptyset$ satisfies $LF(L, P)$. It is easy to see that I' is an answer set of P.

Theorem 2. *Let P be a nested logic program with functions. An interpretation I for P is an answer set of P iff I is a model of $COMP(P) \cup LF(P)$ where $LF(P)$ is the set of loop formulas of P.*

To compute answer sets of normal logic programs with functions, through completion and loop formulas, FASP requires no function occurring in predicates and functions as an argument. For this purpose, a transformation was introduced [22]. Similarly, it is not difficult to transform a nested logic program with functions into one that contains no function in any predicate and function.

4 First-Order Loop Formulas

In the section, we assume that a logic program contains a finite set of rules possibly with variables. We further assume that every rule of a logic program is of the form (10), and through variable renaming, no two rules share common variables.

Recall that, the underlying language $\mathcal{L}$ is a many-sorted first-order language. Thus every predicate has an arity that specifies the number of arguments the predicate has and the type (sort) of each argument, and similarly for constants and functions. Variables also have types associated with them, and when they are used in formulas, their types are normally clear from the context [22].

Let $\mathcal{D}$ be a collection of domains in which there is a unique domain corresponding to each type τ, denoted by $\mathcal{D}_\tau$. Given a typed first-order sentence φ, the *instantiation* of φ on $\mathcal{D}$, written $\varphi|\mathcal{D}$, is a formula defined inductively as follows:

- if φ does not have quantifications, then $\varphi|\mathcal{D}$ is the result of replacing $d = d$ by $\top$ and $d = d'$ by $\bot$ in φ, where d, d' are any two distinct constants;
- $\exists x_\tau.\varphi|\mathcal{D}$ is $\left(\bigvee_{d \in \mathcal{D}_\tau} \varphi(x_\tau/d)\right)|\mathcal{D}$;
- $(\varphi_1 \vee \varphi_2)|\mathcal{D}$ is $\varphi_1|\mathcal{D} \vee \varphi_2|\mathcal{D}$; $(\neg\varphi)|\mathcal{D}$ is $\neg(\varphi|\mathcal{D})$.

Let r be a rule of the form (10). We say r is not in *normal form* if there is an atom in $pa(F)$ containing at least one constant. Otherwise, we say r is in *normal form*. A logic program is in *normal form* if every rule of the logic program is in normal form. Obviously, we can turn every logic program to normal form using equality. In the following, we assume every logic program is in normal form unless stated otherwise.

A *binding* is an expression of the form α/t_τ where α is a variable of type τ or a function term $f(\boldsymbol{t})$ whose range is of the type τ, t_τ a variable or constant of type τ. A *substitution* is a set of bindings containing at most one binding for each variable and functional term.

Given a logic program P (with variables), the *completion* of P, denoted by $comp(P)$, is the set of formulas consisting of

- for each rule of the form (10) in P,

$$\forall \boldsymbol{x}(\exists \boldsymbol{y}.(B \wedge G) \supset F) \tag{17}$$

where $\boldsymbol{x}$ is the tuple of variables occurring in F and $\boldsymbol{y}$ is the tuple of variables occurring in B or G but not in F;
- for each predicate p,

$$\forall \boldsymbol{x}.p(\boldsymbol{x}) \supset \bigvee_{1 \le i \le n} \exists \boldsymbol{y}_i. \begin{bmatrix} (B_i \wedge G_i) \wedge \left(\bigwedge_{q(\boldsymbol{s}) \in pa(F_i)} \neg q(\boldsymbol{s})\right) \\ \wedge \left(\bigvee_{p(\boldsymbol{t}) \in pa(F_i)} \boldsymbol{x} = \boldsymbol{t}\right) \\ \wedge \left(\bigwedge_{p(\boldsymbol{t}) \in pa(F_i)} (\boldsymbol{x} = \boldsymbol{t} \vee \neg p(\boldsymbol{t}))\right) \end{bmatrix} \tag{18}$$

where
  - q is a predicate different from p;
  - $\boldsymbol{x}$ is a tuple of distinct variables that are not in P, and match p's arity;
  - $(F_1 \leftarrow B_1, G_1), \ldots, (F_n \leftarrow B_n, G_n)$ are the rules in P whose head mentions the predicate p;
  - for each $1 \le i \le n$, $\boldsymbol{y}_i$ is the tuple of variables occurring in B_i, G_i or F_i but not in $\boldsymbol{x}$.

In particular, if a predicate p does not occur in the head of any rule in P, then we have $\forall \boldsymbol{x}.\neg p(\boldsymbol{x})$ in the completion of P.

Given a logic program P, its *(first-order) dependency graph* G_P can be defined similar to that of [7,14]. Formally, let $\sigma(P)$ be the signature consisting of object and predicate constants occurring in the rules of P. Now G_P is the directed graph (V, E), where

- V is a set of non-equality atoms formed from $\sigma(P)$, along with an infinite supply of typed variables; please note that there is no atom in V mentioning function symbols.
- $(p(\boldsymbol{t})\theta, q(\boldsymbol{t}')\theta)$ is in E if there is a rule of the form (10) in P such that $p(\boldsymbol{t}) \in pa(F)$, $q(\boldsymbol{t}') \in B$ and θ is a substitution.

A finite non-empty subset L of V is a *(first-order) loop* of P if there is a non-zero length cycle in G_P that goes through only and all the nodes in L. Please note that, since $\sigma(P)$ has nothing to do with the type definitions of P, loops of P are independent of the domains of P.

Let P be a logic program, L a loop of P and $p(\boldsymbol{t}) \in L$. The *(first-order) external support formula* of $p(\boldsymbol{t})$ with respect to L, written $es(p(\boldsymbol{t}), L, P)$, is the disjunction of

$$\bigvee_{\theta : p(\boldsymbol{t}) \in pa(F\theta)} \exists \boldsymbol{y}. \begin{bmatrix} (B\theta \wedge G\theta) \\ \wedge \left(\bigwedge_{\substack{q(\boldsymbol{s}) \in L \\ q(\boldsymbol{s}') \in pa(B\theta)}} \neg(\boldsymbol{s}' = \boldsymbol{s})\right) \\ \wedge \left(\bigwedge_{q(\boldsymbol{s}) \in pa(F\theta)} \left(\left(\bigwedge_{q(\boldsymbol{s}') \in L} \neg(\boldsymbol{s}' = \boldsymbol{s})\right) \supset \neg q(\boldsymbol{s})\right)\right) \end{bmatrix} \tag{19}$$

for all rules of the form (10) in P, where θ is a substitution that maps the variables occurring in $\boldsymbol{t}$ to terms appearing in F, $\boldsymbol{y}$ is a tuple of variables occurring in $B\theta$, $G\theta$, or

$F\theta$ but not in $\boldsymbol{t}$. The *(first-order) loop formula* of L for P, written $\mathit{lf}(L,P)$, is then the following formula:

$$\forall \boldsymbol{x}.\left(\bigvee_{A\in L} A \supset \bigvee_{A\in L} es(A,L,P)\right) \tag{20}$$

where $\boldsymbol{x}$ is the tuple of variables occurring in L.

Theorem 3. *Let P be a logic program in normal form and $\mathcal{D}$ be a collection of type definitions such that, for each type τ used in P, there is a finite and non-empty domain $D \in \mathcal{D}$ and D contains all τ-type constants occurring in P. An interpretation I of $P \cup \mathcal{D}$ is an answer set of $P \cup \mathcal{D}$ if and only if I is a model of $(comp(P) \cup \mathit{lf}(P))|\mathcal{D}$ where $\mathit{lf}(P)$ is the set of loop formulas of P.*

5 Related Works

Functions are widely used in logic formalism stemming from first-order logic. In the ASP community, functions have already been considered in the general theory of stable models [10] and in Quantified Equilibrium Logic (QEL) [27]. The two theories generalize logic programs with nested expressions. In QEL, an equilibrium model is a Kripke structure, for which no algorithm for computing answer sets is given. In the general theory of stable models, the answer set semantics is defined by translating first-order sentences into second-order ones. Lee and Meng proposed the notions of first-order loop formulas for disjunctive logic programs and arbitrary sentences. However they focused on Herbrand interpretations only. They also considered loop formulas in second-order logic for arbitrary first-order sentences. However, the notion of loops depends on a given interpretation in advance [14].

Calimeri *et al.* considered integrating functions into disjunctive logic programs and implemented it into DLV [6]. Again, they considered Herbrand models instead of non-Herbrand ones. To our knowledge, a closely related work is due to Cabalar [5]. A main difference is that functions in [5] are partial while in our case they are total. This difference has impact on how knowledge is represented. More importantly, the totality of functions enables a translation of programs to instances of CSP. Lee also defined the notions of loop formulas for nested logic programs directly. However, only propositional case is considered, i.e., function symbols are excluded [13]. Lifschitz [18] proposed intensional functions in IF-programs whose rules have the form $H \leftarrow B$ where H and B are formulas not containing $\leftarrow$, and Bartholomew and Lee [1] presented first-order formulas with intensional functions under stable model semantics. The semantics of these programs are defined in terms of second-order logic by translating such programs into second-order theories.

6 Conclusion and Future Work

We have considered adding functions to disjunctive logic programs and formulated completion, loops and loop formulas, thus generalizing the main results of [22] to nested logic programs with functions. This will enable us to extend FASP for such disjunctive logic programs in the future. We have also shown how to extend the first-order loops and loop formulas to these programs. In general, an arbitrary program with variables and negation may be sensitive to the change of domains. Some restriction, like safety, has been proposed to guarantee domain independence [14]. It is worthwhile to investigate the same problem under non-Herbrand interpretations.

Acknowledgement. This work is partially supported by NSFC under grant 60963009 and the stadholder Fund of Guizhou Province under grant (2012)62. Mingyi Zhang is also partially supported by NSFC under grant 61262029.

References

1. Bartholomew, M., Lee, J.: Stable models of formulas with intensional functions. In: KR 2012, Rome, Italy, pp. 2–12. AAAI Press (2012)
2. Baselice, S., Bonatti, P.A., Criscuolo, G.: On finitely recursive programs. In: Dahl, V., Niemelä, I. (eds.) ICLP 2007. LNCS, vol. 4670, pp. 89–103. Springer, Heidelberg (2007)
3. Brewka, G., Eiter, T., Truszczynski, M.: Answer set programming at a glance. Communications of the ACM 54(12), 92–103 (2011)
4. Bria, A., Faber, W., Leone, N.: Normal Form Nested Programs. In: Hölldobler, S., Lutz, C., Wansing, H. (eds.) JELIA 2008. LNCS (LNAI), vol. 5293, pp. 76–88. Springer, Heidelberg (2008)
5. Cabalar, P.: A functional action language front-end. In: ASPOCP 2005 (July 2005), `http://www.dc.fi.udc.es/~cabalar/asp05_C.pdf`
6. Calimeri, F., Cozza, S., Ianni, G., Leone, N.: Computable Functions in ASP: Theory and Implementation. In: Garcia de la Banda, M., Pontelli, E. (eds.) ICLP 2008. LNCS, vol. 5366, pp. 407–424. Springer, Heidelberg (2008)
7. Chen, Y., Lin, F., Wang, Y., Zhang, M.: First-order loop formulas for normal logic programs. In: KR 2006, UK, pp. 298–307. AAAI Press (2006)
8. Erdem, E., Lifschitz, V.: Tight logic programs. Theory and Practice of Logic Programming 3(4-5), 499–518 (2003)
9. Erdoğan, S.T., Lifschitz, V.: Definitions in answer set programming. In: Palamidessi, C. (ed.) ICLP 2003. LNCS, vol. 2916, pp. 483–484. Springer, Heidelberg (2003)
10. Ferraris, P., Lee, J., Lifschitz, V.: Stable models and circumscription. Artificial Intelligence 175(1), 236–263 (2011)
11. Gelfond, M., Lifschitz, V.: The stable model semantics for logic programming. In: ICLP 1988, Seattle, Washington, pp. 1070–1080. MIT Press (1988)
12. Giunchiglia, E., Lierler, Y., Maratea, M.: Answer set programming based on propositional satisfiability. Journal of Automated Reasoning 36(4), 345–377 (2006)
13. Lee, J.: A model-theoretic counterpart of loop formulas. In: IJCAI 2005, Edinburgh, Scotland, UK, pp. 503–508. Professional Book Center (2005)
14. Lee, J., Meng, Y.: First-order stable model semantics and first-order loop formulas. J. Artif. Intell. Res. (JAIR) 42, 125–180 (2011)
15. Lee, J., Lifschitz, V.: Loop formulas for disjunctive logic programs. In: Palamidessi, C. (ed.) ICLP 2003. LNCS, vol. 2916, pp. 451–465. Springer, Heidelberg (2003)
16. Leone, N., Pfeifer, G., Faber, W., Eiter, T., Gottlob, G., Perri, S., Scarcello, F.: The dlv system for knowledge representation and reasoning. ACM Transactions on Computational Logic 7(3), 499–562 (2006)

17. Lifschitz, V.: Foundations of logic programming. In: Principles of Knowledge Representation, pp. 69–127. CSLI Publications (1996)
18. Lifschitz, V.: Logic programs with intensional functions. In: KR 2012, Rome, Italy, pp. 24–31. AAAI Press (2012)
19. Lifschitz, V., Pearce, D., Valverde, A.: Strongly equivalent logic programs. ACM Transactions on Computational Logic 2(4), 526–541 (2001)
20. Lifschitz, V., Razborov, A.A.: Why are there so many loop formulas? ACM Transactions on Computational Logic 7(2), 261–268 (2006)
21. Lifschitz, V., Tang, L.R., Turner, H.: Nested expressions in logic programs. Annals of Mathematics and Artificial Intelligence 25(3-4), 369–389 (1999)
22. Lin, F., Wang, Y.: Answer set programming with functions. In: KR 2008, Sydney, Australia, pp. 454–464. AAAI Press (2008)
23. Lin, F., Zhao, Y.: ASSAT: computing answer sets of a logic program by SAT solvers. Artificial Intelligence 157(1-2), 115–137 (2004)
24. Liu, L., Truszczynski, M.: Properties and applications of programs with monotone and convex constraints. JAIR 27, 299–334 (2006)
25. Wiktor Marek, V., Truszczynski, M.: Stable models and an alternative logic programming paradigm. In: The Logic Programming Paradigm: A 25-Year Perspective, pp. 375–398. Springer, Berlin (1999)
26. Niemelä, I.: Logic programs with stable model semantics as a constraint programming paradigm. Annals of Mathematics and Artificial Intelligence 25(3-4), 241–273 (1999)
27. Pearce, D., Valverde, A.: Towards a First Order Equilibrium Logic for Nonmonotonic Reasoning. In: Alferes, J.J., Leite, J. (eds.) JELIA 2004. LNCS (LNAI), vol. 3229, pp. 147–160. Springer, Heidelberg (2004)
28. Šimkus, M., Eiter, T.: $\mathbb{FDNC}$: Decidable non-monotonic disjunctive logic programs with function symbols. In: Dershowitz, N., Voronkov, A. (eds.) LPAR 2007. LNCS (LNAI), vol. 4790, pp. 514–530. Springer, Heidelberg (2007)
29. Wang, Y., You, J.-H., Lin, F., Yuan, L.-Y., Zhang, M.: Weight constraint programs with evaluable functions. AMAI 60(3-4), 341–380 (2010)
30. Yang, B., Zhang, M., Zhang, Y.: Applying answer set programming to points-to analysis of object-oriented language. In: Huang, D.-S., Gan, Y., Bevilacqua, V., Figueroa, J.C. (eds.) ICIC 2011. LNCS, vol. 6838, pp. 676–685. Springer, Heidelberg (2011)
31. You, J.-H., Yuan, L.-Y., Mingyi, Z.: On the equivalence between answer sets and models of completion for nested logic programs. In: IJCAI 2003, Acapulco, Mexico, pp. 859–866. Morgan Kaufmann (2003)

Appendix: Proofs

As we know that the splitting theorem for normal logic programs in [17] has already been generalized to logic programs with nested expressions in [9], to prove Theorem 1, we follow the same way for the corresponding theorem in [22]. Let F be a formula and I an interpretation. The *functional reduction* of F relative to I, denoted by $\Phi(F, I)$, is a formula obtained from F by

- replacing every functional term t occurring in F with t^I;
- replacing each equality atom in F by $\top$ if it is true under I, and $\bot$ otherwise.

The *functional reduction* of a logic program P relative to an interpretation I, written $\Phi(P, I)$, is the logic program obtained from P by replacing each rule $Head \leftarrow Body$ in P by $\Phi(Head, I) \leftarrow \Phi(Body, I)$. The below lemma follows.

Lemma 1. *Let P be a logic program and I an interpretation for P. I is an answer set of P iff I^a is an answer set of $\Phi(P, I)$.*

Let F be a formula. By $Atoms(F)$ we denote the set of the atoms that occurs in F. Similarly, for a rule r and a logic program P, we have $Atoms(r)$ and $Atoms(P)$ denote the set of atoms occurring in r and P respectively. A *splitting set* of a logic program P is any set U of atoms such that, for every $r \in P$, if $Atoms(Head(r)) \cap U \neq \emptyset$ implies $Atoms(Body(r)) \subseteq U$. If U splits P then the *bottom* of P relative to U, denoted by $b_U(P)$, is the set of rules $r \in P$ such that $Atoms(r) \subseteq U$. Let U and M be two sets of atoms, and F a formula. By $e_U(F, M)$ we denote the formula obtained from F by, for each $a \in Atoms(F) \cap U$, replacing a by $\top$ if $a \in M$, and $\bot$ otherwise. For a logic program P, by $e_U(P, M)$ we denote the logic program obtained from P by replacing each rule $Head \leftarrow Body$ in P with $e_U(Head, M) \leftarrow e_U(Body, M)$.

The following lemma is clear and useful for the sequent proof.

Lemma 2. *Let P be a nested logic program with functions such that any rule of P has the form $F \leftarrow \bot$ or $\top \leftarrow G$ where F and G are arbitrary two formulas. Then P is equivalent to $\emptyset$.*

It shows that we can equivalently add (or remove) rules of the form $F \leftarrow \bot$ or $\top \leftarrow G$ into (resp. from) a logic program P without changing its semantics.

Proof of Theorem 1. As mentioned before, the Propositions 3-7 of [21] can be easily extended to logic programs with functions. Thus we shall implicitly assume these propositions and use them with the same annotation to [21] hereafter.

Since $\Xi(P)$ is a logic program containing neither functions nor equality, we denote the set of atoms occurring in $\Xi(P)$ by $Atoms(\Xi(P))$ and similarly for any such logic programs, we have the same denotation. Let's denote $\Xi(P) = \mathbb{R}(P) \cup \mathbb{F}(P)$ and $U = Atoms(\mathbb{F}(P))$. It is clear that U splits $\Xi(P)$ and I^f is an answer set of $\mathbb{F}(P)$. Because $\mathbb{R}(P)$ can be considered the collection $\bigcup_{r \in P} \mathbb{R}(r)$ where r is regarded as a logic program consisting of the only rule r together with the type definitions of P. By Proposition 3 of [21], now it is sufficient to show that

$$\Phi(r, I) \Leftrightarrow e_U(\mathbb{R}(r), I^f) \tag{21}$$

where U clearly splits $\mathbb{R}(r)$. By Proposition 7 of [21], we can assume that the rule r has the form (9) where classical negation is excluded.

For the sake of simplicity, let's consider only the following cases for r where F is a simple disjunction and G is a simple conjunction that mention no functions nor equality:

(1) r is of the form "$p(f(\mathbf{c})); F \leftarrow G$". Let's suppose the range of f is $\{c_1, \dots, c_k\}$ and $f^I(\mathbf{c}) = c_1$ without loss of generality. Now we have $\Phi(r, I)$ is "$p(c_1); F \leftarrow G$" and $\mathbb{R}(r)$ consists of, for i $(1 \leq i \leq k)$,

$$p(c_i); F \leftarrow G, f_r(\mathbf{c}, c_i).$$

Similarly $e_U(\mathbb{R}(r), I^f)$ consists of the rules, for i $(1 \leq i \leq k)$,

$$p(c_i); F \leftarrow G, \top$$

which is equivalent to $\Phi(r, I)$ by Lemma 2. The proof for the following three cases are similar to this one.

- r is of the form "$F \leftarrow G, p(f(\mathbf{c}))$";
- r is of the form "$F \leftarrow G, not\, p(f(\mathbf{c}))$";
- r is of the form "$F \leftarrow G, not\, not\, p(f(\mathbf{c}))$".

(2) r is of the form "$f(c) = c'; F \leftarrow G$". Now we have $\Phi(r, I)$ is $(\top; F \leftarrow G)$ if $c_1 = c'$ and $(\bot; F \leftarrow G)$ otherwise. In any case that c_1 is identical to c' or not, $e_U(\mathbb{R}(r), I^f)$ is equivalent to $\Phi(r, I)$. It is similar to the cases that equality occurs in the body as $f(\mathbf{c}) = c'$, $not\, f(\mathbf{c}) = c'$ or $not\, not\, f(\mathbf{c}) = c'$.

The combinatorial cases is similar. Please note that, any rule r in P that mentions only functions and equality, $\Phi(r, I)$ must be equivalent to $\emptyset$ whenever I satisfies P, i.e., $\Phi(r, I)$ is equivalent to $\{\top \leftarrow \bot\}$ if I satisfies P. Notice that $\mathbb{R}(r) \subseteq b_U(\Xi(P))$. Thus I^f is an answer set of $b_U(\Xi(P))$ iff I satisfies the $\mathbb{R}(r)$ for each such aforementioned rule r of P.

I is an answer set of P
iff I^a is an answer set of $\Phi(P, I)$ (Lemma 1)
iff I^a is an answer set of $e_U(\Xi(P) \setminus b_U(\Xi(P)), I^f)$ (equation (21))
iff $I^a \cup I^f$ is an answer set of $\Xi(P)$ (Splitting Set Theorem of [9])
iff $\mathbb{R}(I)$ is an answer set of $\Xi(P)$. ∎

Lemma 3. *Let F be a formula and I an interpretation. Then $I \models F$ iff $I^a \models F^I$.*

Proof. It is trivial by induction on the structures of formulas.

Lemma 4. *Let I be an interpretation and Γ a set of clauses*[6]*. If I^a is a minimal set satisfying Γ^I, then for each $p(\mathbf{c}) \in I^a$ there is a clause F in Γ such that*

$$I^a \cap pa(F^I) = \{p(c)\}.$$

Proof. If it is not the case, then there exists $p(\mathbf{d}) \in I^a$ such that $\mathbf{c} \neq \mathbf{d}$ and, for any $F \in \Gamma$, $I^a \cap pa(F^I) \neq \{p(\mathbf{d})\}$. Due to the minimality of I^a, there must have some $F \in \Gamma$ such that $p(\mathbf{d}) \in pa(F^I)$ otherwise $I^a \setminus \{p(\mathbf{d})\}$ also satisfies Γ^I. Thus by the assumption, for any $F \in \Gamma$, if $p(\mathbf{d}) \in pa(F^I)$ then there is another atom $p(\mathbf{d}') \in I^a \cap pa(F^I)$. It follows that $I^a \setminus \{p(\mathbf{d})\}$ is still a model of Γ which contradicts with the minimality of I^a.

Lemma 5. *Let P be a nested logic program and I an interpretation for P. If I is an answer set of P then $I \models COMP(P)$.*

Proof. Firstly, take any rule $F \leftarrow G$ in P and assume $I \models G$. We need to show $I \models F$. By Lemma 3, $I \models G \Rightarrow I^a \models G^I \Rightarrow I^a \models F^I$ since I is an answer set of P implies $I^a \models (F \leftarrow G)^I$. Thus $I \models F$ by Lemma 3 again.

Secondly, let $p(\mathbf{c})$ be an atom such that $I \models p(\mathbf{c})$. We need to show I satisfies the consequent of the corresponding formula (12). Let Γ be the set of clauses F with

[6] A disjunction of atoms.

$(F \leftarrow G)$ belonging to P and $I \models G$. By the definition of answer sets, I^a is an answer set of P^I and thus I^a is a minimal set satisfying Γ^I. By Lemma 4, there exists $F \in \Gamma$ such that $I^a \cap pa(F^I) = \{p(\boldsymbol{c})\}$. Without loss of generality, suppose $H \leftarrow G$ is such a rule in P with $I^a \cap pa(F^I) = \{p(\boldsymbol{c})\}$ and $I \models G$. Consider the following cases:

- For any $q(\boldsymbol{s}) \in pa(F)$, we have $q(\boldsymbol{s}^I) \notin I^a$ and thus $I^a \models \neg q(\boldsymbol{s}^I)$, it implies that $I \models \neg q(\boldsymbol{s})$.
- Note that $p(\boldsymbol{c}) \in pa(F^I)$, then we have $p(\boldsymbol{t}) \in pa(F)$ such that $\boldsymbol{t}^I = \boldsymbol{c}$. Thus $I \models \bigvee_{p(\boldsymbol{t}) \in pa(F)} \boldsymbol{c} = \boldsymbol{t}$.
- For any $p(\boldsymbol{t}) \in pa(F)$ with $\boldsymbol{t}^I \neq \boldsymbol{c}$, since $I^a \cap pa(F^I) = \{p(\boldsymbol{c})\}$, it follows that $I^a \models \neg p(\boldsymbol{t}^I)$ and consequently $I \models \neg p(\boldsymbol{t})$.

Consequently, I satisfies the consequent of the formula (12).

Lemma 6. *Let P be a nested logic program and L be an arbitrary loop of P. If an interpretation I for P is an answer set of P then $I \models LF(L, P)$.*

Proof. Note that I is an answer set of P. It follows that I^a is an answer set of P^I and $I^a \setminus L$ is not an answer set of P^I, i.e., there exists a rule $H \leftarrow B, F$ in P such that $I^a \setminus L \models (B^I, F^I)$ and $I^a \setminus L \not\models H^I$.

(1) It is clear that $I^a \models (B^I, F^I)$, thus $I \models (B, F)$ and then $I \models B \wedge F$.
(2) By (1) and I^a is an answer of P^I, we have that $I^a \models H^I$, i.e., $I^a \cap pa(H^I) \neq \emptyset$. It follows that $(I^a \setminus L) \cap pa(H^I) = \emptyset$ and $L \cap pa(H^I) \neq \emptyset$. Without loss of generality, let $p(\boldsymbol{c}) \in L \cap pa(H^I)$. Clearly, $I \models \bigvee_{p(\boldsymbol{t}) \in pa(H)} \boldsymbol{c} = \boldsymbol{t}^I$.
(3) By $I^a \setminus L \models B^I$, we have $pa(B^I) \cap L = \emptyset$. It follows $I \models \bigwedge_{\substack{q(\boldsymbol{d}) \in L \\ q(\boldsymbol{t}) \in pa(B)}} \boldsymbol{t} \neq \boldsymbol{d}$.
(4) Let $q(\boldsymbol{t}) \in pa(H)$, consider the two cases:
   - $q(\boldsymbol{t}^I) \notin L$. Note that $I^a \cap pa(H^I) \neq \emptyset$ and $(I^a \setminus L) \cap pa(H^I) = \emptyset$. It follows that $I^a \cap (pa(H^I) \setminus L) = \emptyset$. Thus $q(\boldsymbol{t}^I) \notin I^a$ and then $I \models \neg q(\boldsymbol{t})$. Consequently, $I \models (\bigwedge_{q(\boldsymbol{d}) \in L} \boldsymbol{t} \neq \boldsymbol{d}) \supset \neg q(\boldsymbol{t})$.
   - $q(\boldsymbol{t}^I) \in L$. In this case, $(\bigwedge_{q(\boldsymbol{d}) \in L} \boldsymbol{t}^I \neq \boldsymbol{d}) \equiv \bot$. It follows $I \models (\bigwedge_{q(\boldsymbol{d}) \in L} \boldsymbol{t} \neq \boldsymbol{d}) \supset \neg q(\boldsymbol{t})$.

Now we complete the proof.

Lemma 7. *Let P be a nested logic program and I an interpretation for P. If $I \models COMP(P) \cup LF(P)$ then $I^a \models Comp(P^I) \cup DLF(P^I)$ where $LF(P)$ is the set of loop formulas of P and $DLF(P)$ is the set of disjunctive loop formulas of P^I in terms of [15].*

Proof. Firstly, we show that $I \models COMP(P) \Rightarrow I^a \models Comp(P^I)$. For any rule $(H \leftarrow B, F)$ of P, we have $I \models B \wedge F \supset H \Rightarrow I^a \models B \wedge F^I \supset H^I \Rightarrow I^a \models B^I, F^I \supset H^I$.

Note that, for any atom $p(\boldsymbol{c}) \in Atoms(P^I)$, $p(\boldsymbol{c}) \in Atoms(P)$. Suppose $I^a \models p(\boldsymbol{c})$. Clearly, $I \models p(\boldsymbol{c})$ and thus I satisfies the consequent of the formula (12). It follows that there is a rule $(H \leftarrow B, F)$ of P such that for some $p(\boldsymbol{t}) \in pa(H)$, $\boldsymbol{t}^I = \boldsymbol{c}$ and

$$I \models B \wedge F \wedge \left(\bigwedge_{q(\boldsymbol{s}) \in pa(H)} \neg q(\boldsymbol{s}) \right) \wedge \left(\bigwedge_{p(\boldsymbol{s}) \in pa(H)} (\boldsymbol{c} = \boldsymbol{s} \vee \neg p(\boldsymbol{s})) \right).$$

Since q is a predicate different from p, we have $I \models \neg q(\boldsymbol{s})$. For any $p(\boldsymbol{s}) \in pa(H)$ with $\boldsymbol{s}^I \neq \boldsymbol{c}$, we have $I \models \neg p(\boldsymbol{s})$. Consequently, $I^a \models \neg q(\boldsymbol{s}^I) \wedge \neg p(\boldsymbol{s}^I)$, i.e., $I^a \models \neg\alpha$ for any $\alpha \in pa(H^I) \setminus \{p(\boldsymbol{c})\}$. It follows that

$$I^a \models B^I \wedge F^I \wedge \bigwedge_{\alpha \in pa(H^I)} \neg\alpha.$$

Secondly, we show $I \models LF(P) \Rightarrow I^a \models DLF(P^I)$. Let L be an arbitrary loop of P^I. Obviously, L is also a loop of P. Suppose $I^a \models \bigvee L$. Thus $I \models \bigvee L$. By the assumption, there exists an atom $p(\boldsymbol{c}) \in L$ and a rule $(H \leftarrow B, F)$ in P such that, for some $p(\boldsymbol{t}) \in pa(H)$, $p(\boldsymbol{t})$ can cover $p(\boldsymbol{c})$ and

$$I \models \left[\begin{array}{r} B \wedge F \wedge \left(\bigvee_{p(\boldsymbol{s}) \in pa(H)} \boldsymbol{c} = \boldsymbol{s}\right) \\ \wedge \left(\bigwedge_{\substack{q(\boldsymbol{d}) \in L \\ q(\boldsymbol{s}) \in pa(B)}} \boldsymbol{s} \neq \boldsymbol{d}\right) \\ \wedge \left(\bigwedge_{q(\boldsymbol{s}) \in pa(H)} \left(\left(\bigwedge_{q(\boldsymbol{d}) \in L} \boldsymbol{s} \neq \boldsymbol{d}\right) \supset \neg q(\boldsymbol{s})\right)\right) \end{array}\right].$$

Notice first that $I \models \bigvee_{p(\boldsymbol{s}) \in pa(H)} \boldsymbol{c} = \boldsymbol{s}$, it follows that for some $p(\boldsymbol{s}) \in pa(H)$, $\boldsymbol{s}^I = \boldsymbol{c}$. Thus $pa(H^I) \cap L \neq \emptyset$. By $I \models \bigwedge_{\substack{q(\boldsymbol{d}) \in L \\ q(\boldsymbol{s}) \in pa(B)}} \boldsymbol{d} \neq \boldsymbol{s}$, we have that $pa(B^I) \cap L = \emptyset$. Thus $(H^I \leftarrow B^I, F^I)$ is a rule in P^I such that $B, F \wedge \bigwedge_{\alpha \in pa(H^I) \setminus L} \neg\alpha$ is a formula in $R(L)$. Notice again that, for any $q(\boldsymbol{s}) \in pa(H)$,

$$I \models \left(\bigwedge_{q(\boldsymbol{d}) \in L} \boldsymbol{s} \neq \boldsymbol{d}\right) \supset \neg q(\boldsymbol{s}).$$

It follows that $I^a \models \neg q(\boldsymbol{s}^I)$ if there is no $q(\boldsymbol{d}) \in L$ such that $\boldsymbol{s}^I = \boldsymbol{d}$. Thus, for any $\alpha \in pa(H^I) \cap L$, $I^a \models \neg\alpha$. Consequently,

$$I^a \models B^I \wedge F^I \wedge \bigwedge_{\alpha \in pa(H^I) \setminus L} \neg\alpha.$$

That is $I^a \models DLF(L, P^I)$. And we finish the proof.

Proof of Theorem 2. From Lemma 5 and 6, we have that if I is an answer set of P then $I \models COMP(P) \cup LF(P)$. By Lemma 7, we have that if I is an answer set of P then $I^a \models Comp(P^I) \cup DLF(P^I)$. By Theorem 1 of [15], I^a is an answer of P^I. Thus I is an answer set of P from the definition of answer set. ∎

Proof of Theorem 3. The answer sets of P are the models of $COMP(ground(P \cup \mathcal{D})) \cup LF(ground(P \cup \mathcal{D}))$ where $ground(P \cup \mathcal{D})$ explicitly means the grounding of $P \cup \mathcal{D}$, following the proof of Theorem 1 in [7], we can similarly complete the proof by showing that I is a model of $COMP(ground(P)) \cup LF(ground(P))$ if and only if I is a model of $(comp(P) \cup lf(P))|\mathcal{D}$. ∎

Reactive Designs of Interrupts in *Circus Time*

Kun Wei

Department of Computer Science, University of York, York, YO10 5GH, UK
kun.wei@york.ac.uk

Abstract. The concept of interrupts is important in system specifications across both software and hardware. However, behaviours of interrupts are difficult to capture particularly in a timed environment because
of its complexity. In this paper, the catastrophic interrupt adopted by
the standard CSP models, the generic interrupt presented by Hoare in
his original CSP book and the timed interrupt (time-driven) given in
Timed CSP are considered in *Circus Time*. The contribution of the paper
is a development of the reactive design semantics of these three interrupt
operators in the UTP, a collection of verified laws, and a comprehensive
discussion on the subtle difference between catastrophic and generic interrupts in applications.

Keywords: Interrupt, UTP, reactive designs.

1 Introduction

Interrupt behaviours are important in system modelling of both hardware and
software. For instance, pressing the reset button can restart a system to its
original state, or a piece of hardware may have a special input line to output
a value even if it has not been ready. In developing software, interrupts can
naturally describe a variety of behaviours such as exception handlers in object-
oriented programs which may stop the current task to indicate an error situation,
and a scheduling algorithm that can always execute a task with a highest priority
by suspending the current tasks. However, formally specifying the behaviour of
interrupts [7,24] is notoriously difficult particularly under a timed environment
because of its complexity.

Over three decades, CSP presented by Hoare in [5] has become a successful
formal language for specifying and reasoning about concurrency and communication in a system, with important technical results as those presented in [13,14],
and many powerful tools, e.g., FDR [1] and ProB [9]. The interrupt operators
and its applications in CSP have been discussed by Hoare in his original work [5],
in $P \triangle Q$ [1] the execution of P is interrupted on occurrence of the first (external)

---

[1] Hoare's original work [5] uses $P \,\hat{}\, Q$ to express the generic interrupt operator, and
$P \,\hat{i}\, Q$ to present the catastrophic interrupt operator where i is a unique event. In
later work, however, Hoare uses different symbols to express the interrupt operators.
Here, we adopt $\triangle$ from [14] and $\triangle_c$ from [13] to present the generic and catastrophic
interrupt operators, respectively.

Z. Liu, J. Woodcock, and H. Zhu (Eds.): ICTAC 2013, LNCS 8049, pp. 373–390, 2013.
© Springer-Verlag Berlin Heidelberg 2013

event of Q. Here, Q is called the *interrupting process* and P is the *interruptible process*. In the standard (untimed) models of CSP [13], the interruptible process is always interrupted by a catastrophic interrupt event, and thereafter the process behaves like Q. This kind of interruptions is called a catastrophe, $P \triangle_c Q$, in which c is a unique event that does not appear in P. This simpler interrupt can avoid the complication that arises from allowing Q to be an arbitrary process. Alternatively, Timed CSP [14] uses the original interrupt operator in Hoare's work [5], namely the generic interrupt operator, since the catastrophic interrupt operator is insufficient for specifying certain timing behaviours in a timed system. For example, the behaviour of $P \triangle (Wait\ d;\ c \rightarrow Skip)$ cannot be captured by using a catastrophic interrupt operator. Moreover, Timed CSP [14] provides a timed interrupt operator, $P \triangle_d Q$, to allow P to execute for d time units at most before Q takes the control. The characteristic of this timed interrupt operator, compared with the generic interrupt operator, is that the occurrence of an interruption is time-driven; that is, the interruption is out of control of the environment, but only depends on the time.

Circus [3,21,22] is a comprehensive combination of Z [20], CSP [5,13] and Morgan's refinement calculus [11], so that it can define both data and behavioural aspects of a system. *Circus Time* [15,19] is an extension of a subset of *Circus* with some time operators added to the notion of actions in *Circus*. The semantics of *Circus Time* is defined using the UTP [6] by introducing timed observation variables. The *Circus Time* model is a discrete time model, and time operators are very similar to that in Timed CSP. In the *Circus Time* theory, besides some new time operators, each action is expressed as a reactive design for a more concise, readable and uniform UTP semantics. The importance of this semantics is that it exposes the pre-postcondition semantics. In this paper, we develop the reactive design semantics of the catastrophic interrupt, the generic interrupt and the timed interrupt operators in *Circus Time*.

The work in [10] firstly explores the UTP semantics of the catastrophic interrupt operators and related laws in (untimed) CSP. This approach considers an interruption as a kind of sequential composition, because that the interrupting process, in fact, has not happened until the occurrence of the catastrophic event. Therefore, it imitates the idea of the interrupt step law to make the interrupt event able to happen at any intermediate waiting state of P. The UTP semantics of the catastrophic interrupt operator in a timed environment can be found in a hybrid CSP system [8]. Unfortunately, these approaches that consider interruptions as sequential composition cannot contribute to the UTP semantics of the generic interrupt operator, since interrupt events might be a part of an interrupting process as both P and Q evolve together. From this point of view, we ponder the generic interrupt operator as a parallel composition.

The main contribution of this paper is to define the reactive designs of the catastrophic interrupt operator that follows the same idea in the work [10], of the generic interrupt operator that is inspired by Timed CSP [14] to treat an interruption as a parallel composition, and of the timed interrupt operator that is intuitively defined by considering its precondition and postcondition respectively.

Remarkably, the reactive design semantics indicates that the catastrophic interrupt operator is not equal to the generic interrupt operator with an explicitly interrupting event, because their reactive designs use different approaches so that the generic interrupt operator is able to capture more behaviours. In addition, these reactive designs are underpinned by showing that they still enjoy a number of existing algebraic laws.

This paper is structured as follows. Section 2 presents an overview of related UTP theories and *Circus Time*. The detailed reactive designs of the catastrophic, generic and timed interrupt operators are given in Section 3 with a number of relevant laws. Finally, we conclude and discuss future work in Section 4.

2 UTP Theories

The UTP uses the alphabetised relational calculus to supports refinement-based reasoning in the context of a variety of programming paradigms. In the UTP, a relation P is a predicate with an alphabet αP, composed of *undashed* variables $(a, b, ...)$ and *dashed* variables $(a', x', ...)$. The former, denoted as $in\alpha P$, stands for initial observations, and the latter, $out\alpha P$, for intermediate or final observations. A relation is called *homogeneous* if $out\alpha P = in\alpha P'$, where $in\alpha P'$ is obtained by dashing all the variables of $in\alpha P$. A *condition* has an empty output alphabet.

A theory in the UTP is a collection of relations (or alphabetised predicates), which contains three essential parts: an alphabet, a signature, and healthiness conditions: the alphabet is a set of variable names for observation, the signature gives a set of operators and atomic components of the programming theory, and the healthiness conditions identify properties that characterise the theory.

The program constructors in the theory of relations include sequential composition $(P\,;Q)$, conditional $(P \lhd b \rhd Q)$, assignment $(x := e)$, nondeterminism $(P \sqcap Q)$ and recursion $(\mu X \bullet C(X))$. The correctness of a program P with respect to a specification S is denoted by $S \sqsubseteq P$ (P refines S), and is defined as $[P \Rightarrow S]$. Here, the square bracket is universal quantification over all variables in the alphabet. In other words, the correctness of P is proved by establishing that every observation that satisfies P must also satisfy S. Moreover, the set of relations with a particular alphabet is a complete lattice under the refinement ordering. Its bottom element is the weakest relation **true**, which models the program that behaves arbitrarily ($\mathbf{true} \sqsubseteq P$), and the top element is the strongest relation **false**, which behaves miraculously and satisfies any specification ($P \sqsubseteq \mathbf{false}$).

2.1 Designs

A design in the UTP is a relation that can be expressed as a pre-postcondition pair in combination with boolean variables, called *ok* and *ok'*. In designs, *ok* records that the program has started, and *ok'* records that it has terminated. If

P and Q are predicates not containing ok and ok', a design with the precondition P and the postcondition Q, written as $P \vdash Q$, is defined as

$$P \vdash Q \mathrel{\widehat{=}} ok \wedge P \Rightarrow ok' \wedge Q$$

which means that if a program starts in a state satisfying P, then it must terminate, and whenever it terminates, it must satisfy Q.

Healthiness conditions of a theory in the UTP are a collection of some fundamental laws that must be satisfied by relations belonging to the theory. These laws are expressed in terms of monotonic idempotent functions. There are four healthiness conditions identified by Hoare and He [6] in the theory of designs and here we introduce only two of them.

$$\mathbf{H1}(P) = ok \Rightarrow P \qquad \mathbf{H2}(P) = [P[\mathbf{false}/ok'] \Rightarrow P[\mathbf{true}/ok']]$$

The first healthiness condition means that observations of a predicate P can only be made after the program has started. **H2** states that a design cannot require non-termination, since if P is satisfied when ok' is false, it must also be satisfied when ok' is true. A predicate is **H1** and **H2** if, and only if, it is a design; the proof is in [6]. The theory of designs (**H1** and **H2**-healthy relations) has an important role in models for process algebras for refinement like CSP and *Circus*. For a tutorial introduction to designs, the reader is referred to [6,23].

2.2 Reactive Processes

A reactive process is a program whose behaviour may depend on interactions with its environment. To represent intermediate waiting states, a boolean variable $wait$ is introduced to the alphabet of a reactive process. We are able to represent some states of a process by combining the values of ok and $wait$. If ok' is false, the process diverges. If ok' is true, the state of the process depends on the value of $wait'$. If $wait'$ is true, the process is in an intermediate state; otherwise it has successfully terminated. Similarly, the values of undashed variables represent the states of a process's predecessor.

Apart from ok, ok', $wait$ and $wait'$, another two pairs of observational variables, tr and ref, and their dashed counterparts, are introduced. The variable tr records the events that have occurred until the last observation, and tr' contains all the events including those since last observation. Similarly, ref records the set of events that could be refused in the last observation, and ref' records the set of events that may be refused currently. The reactive identity, $I\!I_{rea}$, is defined as $I\!I_{rea} \mathrel{\widehat{=}} (\neg\, ok \wedge tr \leq tr') \vee (ok' \wedge wait' = wait \wedge tr' = tr \wedge ref' = ref)$ which states that if its predecessor diverges ($\neg\, ok$), the extension of traces is the only guaranteed observation; otherwise (ok'), other variables keep unchanged. A reactive process must satisfy the following healthiness conditions:

$$\mathbf{R1}(P) = P \wedge tr \leq tr' \quad \mathbf{R2}(P(tr, tr')) = P(\langle\rangle, tr' - tr) \quad \mathbf{R3}(P) = I\!I_{rea} \lhd wait \rhd P$$

If a relation P describes a reactive process, **R1** states that it never changes history. The second, **R2**, states that the history of the trace tr has no influence on the behaviour of the process. The final, **R3**, requires that a process should leave the state unchanged (II_{rea}) if it is waiting the termination of its predecessor ($wait = true$). A reactive process is a relation whose alphabet includes ok, $wait$, tr and ref, and their dashed counterparts, and that satisfies the composition **R** where $\mathbf{R} \mathrel{\widehat{=}} \mathbf{R1} \circ \mathbf{R2} \circ \mathbf{R3}$. In other words, a process P is a reactive process if, and only if, it is a fixed point of **R**. For a more detailed introduction to the theory of reactive designs, the reader is referred to the tutorial [2].

2.3 CSP Processes

In the UTP, the theory of CSP is built by applying extra healthiness conditions to reactive processes. For example, a reactive process is also a CSP process if and only if, it satisfies the following healthiness conditions:

$$\mathbf{CSP1} \quad P = P \vee (\neg\, ok \wedge tr \leq tr') \qquad \mathbf{CSP2} \quad P = P\,;\, J$$

where $J = (ok \Rightarrow ok') \wedge wait' = wait \wedge tr' = tr \wedge ref' = ref$. The first healthiness condition requires that, in whatever situation, the trace can only be increased. The second one means that P cannot require non-termination, so that it is always possible to terminate. The CSP theory introduced in the UTP book is different from any standard models of CSP [5,13] which have more restrictions or satisfy more healthiness conditions.

A CSP process can also be obtained by applying the healthiness condition **R** to a design. This follows from the theorem in [6], that, for every CSP process P, $P = \mathbf{R}(\neg\, P^f_f \vdash P^t_f)$, where P^a_b is an abbreviation of $P[a, b/ok', wait]$, and it is often used in this paper. This theorem gives a new style of specification for CSP processes in which a design describes the behaviour when its predecessor has terminated and not diverged, and the other situations of its behaviour are left to **R**. For example, P^t_f describes the behaviour when P is stable, and P^f_f captures the behaviour before a divergent state. The importance of this reactive design semantics is that it exposes the pre-postcondition semantics so as to not only support contract-based reasoning about models, but also simplify proof of *Circus Time* laws.

2.4 *Circus Time*

We give a brief introduction to *Circus Time* because the reactive design semantics of interrupts is developed within this timed model. In *Circus Time*, a CSP action is described as an alphabetised predicate whose observational variables include ok, $wait$, tr, ref, $state$ and their dashed counterparts. Here, ok, ok', $wait$ and $wait'$ are the same variables used in the theory of reactive processes. The traces, tr and tr', are defined to be non-empty sequences ($\mathrm{seq}_1(\mathrm{seq}\ Event)$), and each element in the trace represents a sequence of events that have occurred over one time unit. Also, ref and ref' are non-empty sequences ($\mathrm{seq}_1(\mathbb{P}\ Event)$) where each element is a refusal at the end of a time unit. Thus, time is actually hidden in the length of traces. In addition, $state$ and $state'$ ($N \rightarrow\!\!\!\!\!\!+\ Value$) records a set of local variables and their values. N is the set of valid names of these variables. *Circus Time* presents traces and refusals individually rather than using the concept of failures. However, for their consistency we have to ensure the equality of the lengths of *tr* and *ref*, and *tr'* and *ref'*. This is achieved by imposing an extra constraint on the healthiness conditions.

We explain the details of the notation at the points where they are firstly used. For sequences, we use *head*, *tail*, *front*, *last*, #(length), $^\frown$(concatenation) and $^\frown/$(flattening). An expanding relation between traces is defined as

$$tr \preccurlyeq tr' \mathrel{\widehat=} front(tr) \le tr' \wedge last(tr) \le tr'(\#tr)$$

which, for example, states that $\langle\langle a\rangle, \langle b\rangle\rangle$ is expanding $\langle\langle a\rangle, \langle b, c\rangle\rangle$.

An action in *Circus Time* must satisfy the healthiness conditions, $\mathbf{R1_{ct}}$-$\mathbf{R3_{ct}}$ and $\mathbf{CSP1_{ct}}$-$\mathbf{CSP5_{ct}}$. These healthiness conditions have similar meanings to those in the CSP theory, but are changed to accommodate discrete time. For the sake of a simpler proof, we focus on the healthiness conditions, $\mathbf{R1_{ct}}$ and $\mathbf{R3_{ct}}$, since the properties including other healthiness conditions are usually straightforward to be proven. A detailed introduction to other healthiness conditions can be found in [19].

$$\mathbf{R1_{ct}}(X) \mathrel{\widehat=} X \wedge RT \qquad \mathbf{R3_{ct}}(X) \mathrel{\widehat=} I\!I_{ct} \lhd wait \rhd X$$

where the predicate RT, the difference of two traces ($diff$), the relational identity ($I\!I$) and the timed reactive identity $I\!I_{ct}$ are given as

$$RT \mathrel{\widehat=} tr \preccurlyeq tr' \wedge front(ref) \le ref' \wedge \#tr = \#ref \wedge \#tr' = \#ref'$$
$$I\!I \mathrel{\widehat=} (ok' = ok \wedge tr' = tr \wedge ref' = ref \wedge wait' = wait \wedge state' = state)$$
$$I\!I_{ct} \mathrel{\widehat=} (\neg\, ok \wedge RT) \vee (ok' \wedge I\!I)$$

Note that we impose a restriction, $\#tr = \#ref \wedge \#tr' = \#ref'$, to ensure that the lengths of *ref* and *ref'* are always the same as those of *tr* and *tr'* respectively. This is a consequence of splitting traces and refusals as already explained. Rather than recording the refusals only at the end of traces in CSP, *Circus Time* records the refusals at the end of each time unit in order to retain enough information for refinement. In other words, we need to keep the history of refusals. However, we are usually not interested in the refusals of the last time unit after an action terminates. Therefore, we use $front(ref) \le ref'$ in these healthiness conditions, instead of $ref \le ref'$. In addition, we have proved in [19] that for every action P in *Circus Time*, it can also be expressed as $\mathbf{R_{ct}}(\neg\, P^f_f \vdash P^t_f)$.

The full syntax, definitions and detailed explanations of *Circus Time* can be found in [19]. Here, we briefly introduce some operators that are used in the following sections. The action *Skip* terminates immediately without changing anything. *Stop* represents a deadlock, but allows time to elapse. *Chaos* is the worst action (the bottom element in the refinement ordering) whose behaviour is arbitrary, but satisfies $\mathbf{R_t}$. *Miracle* is the top element that expresses an unstarted process. This primitive operator is not included in the standard failures-divergences model of CSP. *Wait d* does nothing except that it requires d time units to elapse before it terminates. The sequential composition $P\,;\,Q$ behaves like P until P terminates, and then behaves as Q. The prefix action $c.e \rightarrow P$ is usually constructed by a composition of a simple prefix and P itself, written as $(c.e \rightarrow \mathit{Skip})\,;\,P$. The external choice, $P \,\Box\, Q$, may behave either like the conjunction of P and Q if no external event has been observed yet, or like their disjunction if the decision has been made. The hiding action $P \setminus CS$ will behave like P, but the events within the set CS become invisible.

Here, we use the definitions of simple prefix and normal prefix, which are used in Section 3.1 and 3.2, to demonstrate how the reactive design semantics captures behaviours of processes.

Theorem 1. *(***Simple prefix***)*

$$c.e \rightarrow \mathit{Skip} = \mathbf{R_{ct}}(\mathbf{true} \vdash \mathit{wait\_com}(c) \vee \mathit{terminating\_com}(c.e)) \tag{1}$$

$$\mathit{wait\_com}(c) \mathrel{\widehat=} (\mathit{wait}' \wedge \mathit{possible}(\mathit{ref}, \mathit{ref}', c) \wedge {}^\frown/\mathit{tr}' = {}^\frown/\mathit{tr}) \tag{2}$$

$$\mathit{possible}(\mathit{ref}, \mathit{ref}', c) \mathrel{\widehat=} \forall i : \#\mathit{ref}..\#\mathit{ref}' \bullet c \notin \mathit{ref}'(i) \tag{3}$$

$$\mathit{term\_com}(c.e) \mathrel{\widehat=} \begin{pmatrix} \neg\, \mathit{wait}' \wedge \mathit{front}(\mathit{ref}') = \mathit{front}(\mathit{ref}) \wedge \\ \mathit{diff}(\mathit{tr}', \mathit{tr}) = \langle\langle c.e\rangle\rangle \wedge \mathit{state}' = \mathit{state} \end{pmatrix} \tag{4}$$

$$\mathit{terminating\_com}(c.e) \mathrel{\widehat=} \begin{pmatrix} \mathit{term\_com}(c.e) \vee \\ ((\mathit{wait\_com}(c) \wedge \mathit{state}' = \mathit{state})\,;\, \mathit{term\_com}(c.e) \end{pmatrix} \tag{5}$$

The precondition of the above definition is **true**, which means that a simple prefix never diverges. The postcondition states that, if it starts successfully, a simple prefix can behave in three different ways: first, the clause $\mathit{wait\_com}(c)$ expresses that it can wait for interaction from its environment and meanwhile communications over the channel c are not refused ($\mathit{possible}(\mathit{ref}, \mathit{ref}', c)$); second, the clause $\mathit{term\_com}(c.e)$ simply denotes that the event is executed immediately; third, the composition of $\mathit{wait\_com}(c)$ and $\mathit{term\_com}(c.e)$ means that it may wait for a while and then terminate with an event $c.e$. The difference of two traces is defined as $\mathit{diff}(\mathit{tr}', \mathit{tr}) \mathrel{\widehat=} \langle \mathit{tr}'(\#\mathit{tr}) - \mathit{last}(\mathit{tr})\rangle {}^\frown \mathit{tail}(\mathit{tr}' - \mathit{front}(\mathit{tr}))$. The reactive design of prefix is calculated by means of the simple prefix and sequential composition as follows.

Theorem 2. *(***Prefix***)*

$$c.e \rightarrow P =$$

$$\mathbf{R_{ct}} \begin{pmatrix} \neg\, (\mathit{terminating\_com}(c.e)\,;\, \mathbf{R1_{ct}}(\neg\, \mathit{wait} \wedge \mathbf{R2_{ct}}(P^f_f))) \\ \vdash \\ (\mathit{wait\_com}(c) \vee \mathit{terminating\_com}(c.e))\,;\, \mathbf{R1_{ct}}(\mathit{II} \lhd \mathit{wait} \rhd \mathbf{R2_{ct}}(P^t_f)) \end{pmatrix}$$

This theorem states that, from its precondition, $c.e \rightarrow P$ diverges if P does; otherwise, from its postcondition, it can wait for the interaction from its environment, execute $c.e$ right now or wait for a while to execute $c.e$, and then behave like P^t_f.

3 Reactive Designs of Interrupts

Hoare's CSP book [5] gives a generic interrupt operator, $P \triangle Q$, which allows P to execute, but it may be interrupted by the first external event from Q and the program control is simultaneously passed to Q. Thereafter, the standard models of CSP adopt a catastrophic interrupt, which is expressed as $P \triangle_c Q$. Here, the catastrophic event c is unique, and its occurrence can interrupt P. However, this simpler interrupt might not be convenient for specifying real-time systems. For example, a seminar room is booked for an hour. Therefore one hour later after the punctual start, the seminar has to be interrupted if the next session has been booked by someone else. But the speaker may continue his talk if no one turns up to use this room. This example may be described as follows in Timed CSP [14] that adopts the generic interrupt operator to satisfy time requirements.

$$\mathit{SEMINAR} \triangle (\mathit{Wait}\ 1\,;\ \mathit{close} \rightarrow \mathit{Skip})$$

Note that the above process does not mean that the interrupt must occur after one hour because the occurrence of *close* depends on the environment. If we say that the seminar must finish after one hour no matter whether this room will be used then, the generic interrupt operator is not enough. Accordingly, a timed interrupt operator is introduced in Timed CSP to describe this scenario.

$$\mathit{SEMINAR} \triangle_1 \mathit{Skip}$$

which means the interruption must happen one hour later. That is to say, the timed interrupt operator is time-driven and out of control of its environment.

The UTP semantics of the catastrophe in CSP has been discussed in [10], and in Section 3.1 we will use the same idea to calculate its reactive design within the *Circus Time* model. The approach in [10] cannot be used for defining the generic interrupt operator. Therefore, in Section 3.2 we follow the idea in Timed CSP to deal with the generic interrupt operator to consider it a special kind of parallel composition. For the timed interrupt operator, it can still be treated as a sequential composition because Q happens exactly d time units later if P has not terminates.

3.1 Catastrophe

We use the same approach in [10] but with changes to accommodate time behaviours to generate a UTP definition for a catastrophic interrupt operator, which is then calculated to produce a reactive design. The general idea in [10] is to use a new healthiness condition **I3**, whose name simply reflects its relation to $\mathbf{R3_{ct}}$, to bring the catastrophic event forward to any waiting state of the interruptible process while this event is not refused by an alphabet extension. An **I3** healthy process can only execute while its predecessor is in an intermediate state, or can behave like a *Circus Time* identity if its predecessor terminates.

Definition 1. $\mathbf{I3}(P) = P \lhd \mathit{wait} \rhd \mathit{II}_{ct}$

Here we can clearly see **I3**'s relation to $\mathbf{R3_{ct}}$ by the law $\mathbf{R3_{ct}}(\mathbf{I3}(P)) = I\!I_{ct}$ which states that an **I3** healthy process will behave as the identity if it is required to be $\mathbf{R3_{ct}}$ healthy. In addition, to make sure the interrupt event is not refused during the execution of the interruptible process, an alphabet extension operator is defined as

Definition 2

$$P^{+c} \mathrel{\widehat=} (P \wedge possible(ref, ref', c)); (I\!I \lhd wait \rhd (I\!I^{-ref} \wedge front(ref') = front(ref)))$$

The predicate $I\!I^{-ref}$ is the relational identity without the variables *ref* and *ref'*. We use $front(ref') = front(ref)$ to free the last element of refusals in P, since we usually request that the last refusal is arbitrary if a process terminates.

Furthermore, we develop a new predicate, $interrupt(c, Q)$, to describe that an event is forced to occur despite an apparent situation opposite to an ordinary action in *Circus Time*.

Definition 3. $try(c, Q) \mathrel{\widehat=} (I\!I \lhd wait' \rhd term\_com(c)); Q$

The behaviour in $try(c, Q)$ is similar to the prefix operator in *Circus Time*. Compared with the simple prefix (Theorem 1), it simplifies the behaviour by terminating only with the immediate execution of c ($term\_com(c)$), or just behaving like the identity. Here, the usual non-refusal of c is achieved by the alphabet extension when sequentially composed with the interruptible action.

Definition 4. $force(c, Q) \mathrel{\widehat=} \mathbf{I3}(try(c, Q))$

The definition of $force(c, Q)$ in Definition 4 is an **I3**-healthy $try(c, Q)$ that states that it behaves as the identity ($I\!I_{ct}$) when its predecessor terminates, and otherwise behaves like $try(c, Q)$. Thus, the predicate $interrupt(c, Q)$ is defined as a $\mathbf{CSP1_{ct}}$-healthy *force*, which considers divergences of its predecessor and Q.

Definition 5. $interrupt(c, Q) \mathrel{\widehat=} \mathbf{CSP1_{ct}}(force(c, Q))$

The definition for catastrophe is given as a sequential composition between the interruptible action P with an alphabet extension by augmenting the interrupt event c, and the newly-defined predicate $interrupt(c, Q)$.

Definition 6. $P \triangle_c Q \mathrel{\widehat=} \mathbf{R3_{ct}} \circ \mathbf{CSP2_{ct}}(P^{+c}; interrupt(c, Q))$

Here, $\mathbf{R3_{ct}}$ restricts the bound of **I3**, and $\mathbf{CSP2_{ct}}$ requires that a divergence within this interrupt may also contain termination.

To calculate the reactive design of catastrophe, we adopt the theorem that any action P in *Circus Time* can be expressed as $\mathbf{R_{ct}}(\neg P^f_f \vdash P^t_f)$. For the reason of limited space, we show the calculation of its postcondition only (Lemma 3), and the full proof can be found in [19]. We give Lemma 1 and Lemma 2 that have no intuitive meaning but avoid verbose proofs. The reader who is interested in their proofs is referred to [19].

Lemma 1. $(P^{+c}; (\neg\, ok \wedge RT))_f = (P^f_f \wedge possible(ref, ref', c)); \mathbf{R1_{ct}}(\mathbf{true})$

Lemma 2. $P^{+c}\,;(ok \wedge try(c,Q) \wedge wait) =$
$$\begin{pmatrix}((P \wedge possible(ref, ref', c) \wedge ok' \wedge wait') \vee \\ ((P \wedge possible(ref, ref', c)); (ok \wedge wait \wedge term\_com(c)); (\neg\, wait \wedge Q_f)\end{pmatrix}$$

Lemma 3. $(P \bigtriangleup_c Q)^t_f =$
$$\begin{pmatrix}((P^f_f \wedge possible(ref, ref', c)); \mathbf{R1_{ct}}(\mathbf{true})) \vee \\ (P^t_f \wedge (possible(ref, ref', c); front(ref') = front(ref)) \wedge \neg\, wait') \vee \\ (P^t_f \wedge possible(ref, ref', c) \wedge wait') \vee \\ ((P^t_f \wedge possible(ref, ref', c)); (wait \wedge term\_com(c)); (\neg\, wait \wedge Q^t_f))\end{pmatrix}$$

Proof.

$$\begin{aligned}
& (P \bigtriangleup_c Q)^t_f && \text{[Def-6]}\\
&= (\mathbf{R3_{ct}} \circ \mathbf{CSP2_{ct}}(P^{+c}\,; interrupt(c,Q)))^t_f && [\mathbf{R3_{ct}} \text{ and substitution}]\\
&= (\mathbf{CSP2_{ct}}(P^{+c}\,; interrupt(c,Q)))^t_f && [\mathbf{CSP2_{ct}}]\\
&= ((P^{+c}\,; interrupt(c,Q))\,; J)^t_f && \text{[J-split]}\\
&= ((P^{+c}\,; interrupt(c,Q))^f \vee (ok' \wedge (P^{+c}\,; interrupt(c,Q))^t))^t_f && \text{[subs.]}\\
&= (P^{+c}\,; interrupt(c,Q))^t_f && \text{[Def-5]}\\
&= (P^{+c}\,; \mathbf{CSP1_{ct}}(force(c,Q)))^t_f && [\mathbf{CSP1_{ct}}]\\
&= (P^{+c}\,; ((\neg\, ok \wedge RT) \vee (ok \wedge force(c,Q))))^t_f && \text{[relational calculus]}\\
&= (P^{+c}\,; (\neg\, ok \wedge RT))^t_f \vee (P^{+c}\,; (ok \wedge force(c,Q)))^t_f && \text{[Lemma 1]}\\
&= ((P^f_f \wedge possible(ref, ref', c)); \mathbf{R1_{ct}}(\mathbf{true})) \vee (P^{+c}\,; (ok \wedge force(c,Q)))^t_f && \\
& && \text{[Def-1,4]}\\
&= \begin{pmatrix}((P^f_f \wedge possible(ref, ref', c)); \mathbf{R1_{ct}}(\mathbf{true})) \vee \\ (P^{+c}\,; (ok \wedge (try(c,Q) \lhd wait \rhd I\!I_{ct})))^t_f\end{pmatrix} && \text{[relational calculus]}\\
&= ((P^f_f \wedge possible(ref, ref', c)); \mathbf{R1_{ct}}(\mathbf{true})) \vee (P^{+c}\,; (ok \wedge \neg\, wait \wedge I\!I_{ct}))^t_f &&\\
&\quad \vee (P^{+c}\,; (ok \wedge try(c,Q) \wedge wait))^t_f && [I\!I_{ct} \text{ and propositional calculus}]\\
&= ((P^f_f \wedge possible(ref, ref', c)); \mathbf{R1_{ct}}(\mathbf{true})) \vee (P^{+c}\,; (ok \wedge \neg\, wait \wedge I\!I))^t_f &&\\
&\quad \vee (P^{+c}\,; (ok \wedge try(c,Q) \wedge wait))^t_f && \text{[Lemma 2]}\\
&= \begin{pmatrix}((P^f_f \wedge possible(ref, ref', c)); \mathbf{R1_{ct}}(\mathbf{true})) \vee (P^{+c}\,; (ok \wedge \neg\, wait \wedge I\!I))^t_f \vee \\ (P \wedge possible(ref, ref', c) \wedge ok' \wedge wait')^t_f \vee \\ ((P \wedge possible(ref, ref', c)); (ok \wedge wait \wedge term_com(c)); (\neg\, wait \wedge Q_f))^t_f\end{pmatrix} &&\\
& && \text{[Def-2 and relational calculus]}\\
&= \begin{pmatrix}((P^f_f \wedge possible(ref, ref', c)); \mathbf{R1_{ct}}(\mathbf{true})) \vee \\ ((P \wedge (possible(ref, ref', c); front(ref') = front(ref))); (ok \wedge \neg\, wait \wedge I\!I))^t_f \vee \\ (P \wedge possible(ref, ref', c) \wedge ok' \wedge wait')^t_f \vee \\ ((P \wedge possible(ref, ref', c)); (ok \wedge wait \wedge term_com(c)); (\neg\, wait \wedge Q_f))^t_f\end{pmatrix} &&\\
& && \text{[relational calculus]}
\end{aligned}$$

$$= \begin{pmatrix} ((P_f^f \wedge possible(ref,ref',c)); \mathbf{R1_{ct}}(\mathbf{true})) \vee \\ (P \wedge (possible(ref,ref',c); front(ref') = front(ref)) \wedge \neg\, wait')_f^t \vee \\ (P \wedge possible(ref,ref',c) \wedge ok' \wedge wait')_f^t \vee \\ ((P \wedge possible(ref,ref',c)); (ok \wedge wait \wedge term\_com(c)); (\neg\, wait \wedge Q_f))_f^t \end{pmatrix}$$

[substitution and relational calculus]

$$= \begin{pmatrix} ((P_f^f \wedge possible(ref,ref',c)); \mathbf{R1_{ct}}(\mathbf{true})) \vee \\ (P_f^t \wedge (possible(ref,ref',c); front(ref') = front(ref)) \wedge \neg\, wait') \vee \\ (P_f^t \wedge possible(ref,ref',c) \wedge wait') \vee \\ ((P_f^t \wedge possible(ref,ref',c)); (wait \wedge term\_com(c)); (\neg\, wait \wedge Q_f^t)) \end{pmatrix}$$

In the postcondition of the catastrophic interrupt operator, the first clause captures the divergent behaviour of P that will be absorbed by the precondition of catastrophe; the second clause states that P terminates without an interrupt, in which $front(ref') = front(ref)$ makes the last element of ref' arbitrary; the third clause expresses that P has not terminated before c; and the last one states that P is interrupted by c and it sequentially behaves like Q.

Before we calculate the final reactive design for $(P \triangle_c Q)$, we make a change to the fourth clause in Lemma 3 by adding $state' = state$ into its first component of the sequential composition. Introduction of $state$ and $state'$ is one of the differences of the *Circus Time* model with the standard CSP models and Timed CSP. To retain some important refinement laws of CSP in *Circus Time*, such as the unit law for external choice $P \,\Box\, Stop = P$, we do not constrain $state'$ at any waiting state or deadlock. However, we, here, have to impose $state' = state$ to enable Q to gain the initial value of $state$ when P is interrupted. This change is reflected in Theorem 3.

Thus, we use the similar approach to calculate $(P \triangle_c Q)_f^f$, and finally get the following reactive design for the catastrophic interrupt operator.

Theorem 3

$$(P \triangle_c Q) =$$

$$\mathbf{R_{ct}} \begin{pmatrix} \neg\, ((P_f^f \wedge possible(ref,ref',c)); \mathbf{R1_{ct}}(\mathbf{true})) \wedge \\ \neg\, ((P_f^t \wedge possible(ref,ref',c)); (wait \wedge term\_com(c)); (\neg\, wait \wedge Q_f^f)) \\ \vdash \\ (P_f^t \wedge (possible(ref,ref',c); front(ref') = front(ref)) \wedge \neg\, wait') \vee \\ (P_f^t \wedge possible(ref,ref',c) \wedge wait') \vee \\ \begin{pmatrix} P_f^t \wedge possible(ref,ref',c) \\ \wedge\, state' = state \end{pmatrix}; (wait \wedge term\_com(c)); (\neg\, wait \wedge Q_f^t) \end{pmatrix}$$

The precondition from the above definition states that either P diverges while the interrupt event c has not occurred, or P is interrupted by c, sequentially composed with the divergence of Q.

This reactive design is derived from rigorous calculation of Definition 6, which is fully based on the work in [10]. The validation of this definition is also similar to that in [10] by proving that it respects a number of laws. For example, the step law (Law 1) for the catastrophic interrupt operator given in [5,13] is still valid, and its proof is fully based on the distributive and eliminative laws, and the approach adopted in [10].

Law 1. $(a \rightarrow P) \bigtriangleup_c Q = (a \rightarrow (P \bigtriangleup_c Q)) \Box (c \rightarrow Q)$

3.2 Generic Interrupt

In the generic interrupt, $P \bigtriangleup Q$, Q is executed concurrently with P until either P terminates the execution, or Q performs an interrupt event. However, the approach that we used in Section 3.1 cannot be applied here because some interruptions by a generic interrupt operator cannot be easily expressed by sequential composition, such as the example we give in Section 1. Alternatively, we use the idea in Timed CSP to consider it parallel composition.

The basic idea of the semantics for parallel composition in the UTP is parallel-by-merge. That is, by labelling the variables of P and Q, we make them become disjoint ($\alpha P \cap \alpha Q = \emptyset$), and then merge these different variables by synchronisation to generate the final observation. As usual, we label the dashed variables of P with 0 and Q with 1 as

$$(P\,;U0(out\alpha P) \wedge (Q\,;U1(out\alpha Q))_{+\{tr,ref\}}$$

The labelling process $Ul(m)$ simply passes dashed variables of its predecessor to labelled variables and also removes these dashed variables from its alphabet. Through the labelling process, the output alphabet of $Ul(m)$ consists of $l.m$ only. However, under some circumstances we do need the initial values of P or Q. For this reason, we expand the alphabet after the labelling process. For example, $P_{+\{n\}}$ denotes $P \wedge n' = n$. Here, we are only interested in tr and ref that will be used in the merge operation.

First of all, we consider the merge function of timed traces and the sequences of refusals of P and Q.

$$ISync(\langle\rangle, S_2, ref_1, ref_2) = (\langle\rangle, ref_1) \tag{6}$$
$$ISync(S_1, \langle\rangle, ref_1, ref_2) = (S_1, ref_1) \tag{7}$$
$$\begin{aligned} &ISync(\langle t_1\rangle ^\frown S_1, \langle t_2\rangle ^\frown S_2, \langle r_1\rangle ^\frown ref_1, \langle r_1\rangle ^\frown ref_2) \\ &\quad = (\langle t_1\rangle, \langle r_1 \cap r_2\rangle) \odot ISync(S_1, S_2, ref_1, ref_2) \;\; \mathit{iff}\; t_2 = \langle\rangle \end{aligned} \tag{8}$$
$$ISync(\langle t_1\rangle ^\frown S_1, \langle t_2\rangle ^\frown S_2, ref_1, ref_2) = (\langle t_2\rangle ^\frown S_2, ref_2) \;\; \mathit{iff}\; t_2 \neq \langle\rangle \tag{9}$$

where $\odot$ is a new operator to concatenate a sequence of pairs, defined as

$$(S_1, ref_1) \odot (S_2, ref_2) = (S_1 ^\frown S_2, ref_1 ^\frown ref_2) \tag{10}$$

In *Circus Time*, we split a failure into a trace and a refusal for the convenience of expression or even simpler mechanisation. Unfortunately, here we have to reunite them again as a pair because they are manipulated together. Note that *ISync* does not support commutativity. The rule (6) states that P has no further trace to interact with Q. That is, P may terminate or diverge in practice. The rule (7) just describes a similar situation for Q. The rule (8) presents the behaviour that no interrupt happens within the current time unit. The rule (9) underlines that Q interrupts P.

We also consider the values of ok' and $wait'$ that are determined by whether the interrupt has occurred or not. For example, their values are those of Q if interrupted. Otherwise, we take those of P. Hence, we define two predicates to show whether one trace can interrupt another.

$$enable(tr, 0.tr, 1.tr) \mathrel{\widehat{=}} \exists\, tr_0 \bullet \begin{pmatrix} tr_0 \le diff(1.tr, tr) \wedge {}^\frown/front(tr_0) = \langle\rangle \wedge \\ last(tr_0) \neq \langle\rangle \wedge \#tr_0 \le \#diff(0.tr, tr) \end{pmatrix}$$

$$disable(tr, 0.tr, 1.tr) \mathrel{\widehat{=}} \begin{pmatrix} ({}^\frown/1.tr = {}^\frown/tr \wedge \#1.tr \le 0.tr) \vee \\ \exists\, tr_0 \bullet \begin{pmatrix} tr_0 \le diff(1.tr, tr) \wedge \\ {}^\frown/tr_0 = \langle\rangle \wedge \#diff(0.tr, tr) \le tr_0 \end{pmatrix} \end{pmatrix}$$

The predicate *enable* states that if there exists a subsequence of $diff(1.tr, tr)$, which has not executed any event (${}^\frown/front(tr_0) = \langle\rangle$) except for the last element ($last(tr_0) \neq \langle\rangle$), and meanwhile $0.tr$ has not terminated ($\#tr_0 \le \#diff(0.tr, tr)$), we conclude that $1.tr$ can interrupt $0.tr$ and the merge of them must finish with the rule (9). The predicate *disable* states that $1.tr$ cannot interrupt $0.tr$ if, either that the length of $1.tr$ is shorter or equal to the length of $0.tr$ and has not executed any external events, or that there exists a subsequence of $diff(1.tr, tr)$, which contains empty traces (${}^\frown/tr = \langle\rangle$) only and whose length is longer or equal to $\#diff(0.tr, tr)$.

We consider the merge predicate of the postcondition first, which describes non-divergent behaviours. If P does not diverge and Q cannot interrupt P, no matter Q can diverge or not, the behaviour will not become divergent. In the meantime the values of ok' and $wait'$ depend on those of P.

$$IM1 \mathrel{\widehat{=}} \begin{pmatrix} IMTR(tr, tr', 0.ref, 1.ref, ref, ref', 0.ref, 1.ref) \wedge disable(tr, 0.tr, 1.tr) \\ \wedge\ ok' = 0.ok \wedge state' = 0.state \wedge wait' = 0.wait \end{pmatrix}$$

$$IMTR(tr, tr', 0.tr, 1.tr, ref, ref', 0.ref, 1.ref) \mathrel{\widehat{=}}$$
$$\left(\begin{pmatrix} diff(tr', tr), \\ ref' - front(ref) \end{pmatrix} = ISync\begin{pmatrix} diff(0.tr, tr), diff(1.tr, tr), \\ 0.ref - front(ref), 1.ref - front(ref) \end{pmatrix}\right)$$

Similarly, if Q does not diverge but does interrupt P, the behaviour is still stable regardless of the state of P.

$$IM2 \mathrel{\widehat{=}} \begin{pmatrix} IMTR(tr, tr', 0.ref, 1.ref, ref, ref', 0.ref, 1.ref) \wedge enable(tr, 0.tr, 1.tr) \\ \wedge\ ok' = 1.ok \wedge state' = 1.state \wedge wait' = 1.wait \end{pmatrix}$$

For the precondition of the reactive design, we are only interested in the divergence of P if the interruption has not happened, and the one of Q if it has done.

As a result, the divergent behaviour can be captured as follows.

$$\exists \begin{pmatrix} 0.tr, 0.ref, \\ 1.tr, 1.ref \end{pmatrix} \bullet \begin{pmatrix} P_f^f[0.tr, 0.ref/tr', ref'] \wedge Q_f[1.tr, 1.ref/tr', ref'] \\ \wedge\ disable(tr, 0.tr, 1.tr) \wedge \\ IMTR(tr, tr', 0.tr, 1.tr, ref, ref', 0.ref, 1.ref) \end{pmatrix} ; \mathbf{R1_{ct}}(\mathbf{true})$$

$$\exists \begin{pmatrix} 0.tr, 0.ref, \\ 1.tr, 1.ref \end{pmatrix} \bullet \begin{pmatrix} P_f[0.tr, 0.ref/tr', ref'] \wedge Q_f^f[1.tr, 1.ref/tr', ref'] \\ \wedge\ enable(tr, 0.tr, 1.tr) \wedge \\ IMTR(tr, tr', 0.tr, 1.tr, ref, ref', 0.ref, 1.ref) \end{pmatrix} ; \mathbf{R1_{ct}}(\mathbf{true})$$

Thus, the integrated definition of the interrupt operator is a combination of the above cases, including an extra predicate to tackle the immediate divergence of P or Q. That is, the divergent cases are given in the precondition, and the other are given in the postcondition.

Definition 7

$$P \triangle Q \mathrel{\widehat=}$$

$$\left(\begin{array}{c} \neg\, (((P_f^f \vee Q_f^f) \wedge tr' = tr) ; \mathbf{R1_{ct}}(\mathbf{true})) \wedge \\ \neg\, \exists \begin{pmatrix} 0.tr, 0.ref, \\ 1.tr, 1.ref \end{pmatrix} \bullet \begin{pmatrix} P_f^f[0.tr, 0.ref/tr', ref'] \wedge \\ Q_f^t[1.tr, 1.ref/tr', ref'] \wedge \\ disable(tr, 0.tr, 1.tr) \wedge \\ IMTR \begin{pmatrix} tr, tr', 0.tr, 1.tr, \\ ref, ref', 0.ref, 1.ref \end{pmatrix} \end{pmatrix} ; \mathbf{R1_{ct}}(\mathbf{true}) \wedge \\ \neg\, \exists \begin{pmatrix} 0.tr, 0.ref, \\ 1.tr, 1.ref \end{pmatrix} \bullet \begin{pmatrix} P_f^t[0.tr, 0.ref/tr', ref'] \wedge \\ Q_f^f[1.tr, 1.ref/tr', ref'] \wedge \\ enable(tr, 0.tr, 1.tr) \wedge \\ IMTR \begin{pmatrix} tr, tr', 0.tr, 1.tr, \\ ref, ref', 0.ref, 1.ref \end{pmatrix} \end{pmatrix} ; \mathbf{R1_{ct}}(\mathbf{true}) \\ \vdash \\ ((P_f^t ; U0(out\alpha P)) \wedge (Q_f^t ; U1(out\alpha Q)))_{+\{tr, ref\}} ; (IM1 \vee IM2) \end{array} \right)$$

Here, we use the **CSP2$_{ct}$-converge** law that is proved in [19], $P^t = P^t \vee P^f$ if P is **CSP2$_{ct}$** healthy, to replace P_f and Q_f with P_f^t and Q_f^t respectively.

The generic interrupt operator is unexpectedly different from the catastrophic interrupt operator even if we make the interrupting action as $c \to Q$. In fact, their refinement can be expressed as

$$P \triangle (c \to Q) \sqsubseteq P \triangle_c Q \tag{11}$$

since $P \triangle (c \to Q)$ contains more behaviours. The proof of this refinement can be found in [19]. The idea adopted in this paper to calculate the definition of catastrophe is to consider Q sequentially composed with P but lifted forward to happen whenever P is waiting for the interaction. However, in *Circus Time*, P may execute an event immediately only so that it cannot be interrupted by means of the definition in Theorem 3. For example, the interruptible action in Lemma 4 is not interruptible, and its proof can also be found in [19].

Lemma 4. $((a \rightarrow Skip) \Box Miracle) \bigtriangleup_c Q = ((a \rightarrow Skip) \Box Miracle)$

Here, *Miracle* can force the event a to occur immediately and then terminate. More discussion about the interaction between *Miracle* with other operators can be found in [19]. The behaviour in Lemma 4 can be captured only by the first clause in the postcondition in Theorem 3. However, Lemma 4 does not hold for the generic interrupt operator, because the event c is able to interrupt as long as it occurs immediately too, via the rule 9 in *ISync*.

The generic interrupt in *Circus Time* can satisfy a number of algebraic laws in CSP. For example, it respects a step law, which is also proved by a similar approach as Law 1.

Law 2. $(a \rightarrow P) \bigtriangleup (c \rightarrow Q) = (a \rightarrow (P \bigtriangleup c \rightarrow Q)) \Box (c \rightarrow Q)$

Since *Stop* offers no external event, it can never interrupt any action. Similarly, if *Stop* is interruptible, only interrupt can occur.

Law 3. $(P \bigtriangleup Stop) = P = (Stop \bigtriangleup P)$

If *Skip* is the interrupting action, similar to *Stop*, the interrupt always behaves just like the interruptible action.

Law 4. $P \bigtriangleup Skip = P$

However, in *Circus Time*, *Skip* can be interrupted because we can allow events to happen without any delay, which can even occur prior to the start of *Skip*.

Law 5. $Skip \bigtriangleup P \sqsubseteq Skip$

In addition, the divergent action cannot be cured by interrupting it, or it is not safe to specify a divergent action after the interrupt.

Law 6. $(P \bigtriangleup Chaos) = Chaos = (Chaos \bigtriangleup P)$

The proofs of Law 2–Law 6 rely on the unfolding of the reactive designs of the generic interrupt operator and related operators. The hand-written proofs of these laws can be found in [19].

3.3 Timed Interrupt

A timed interrupt, $P \bigtriangleup_d Q$, allows P to run for no more than a particular length of time, and then performs an interrupt to pass the control of the process to Q. Compared with the event-driven interrupt where the environment of the process can prevent the interrupt event from happening, this time-driven interrupt cannot be avoided (if P does not terminate before time d) since its environment is not involved. The timed interrupt operator can be defined via the event-driven interrupt and hiding as follow

Definition 8. $P \bigtriangleup_d Q \mathrel{\widehat=} (P \bigtriangleup Wait\ d\, ; (e \rightarrow Q)) \setminus \{e\} \qquad e \notin \alpha(P) \cup \alpha(Q)$

where the special event e becomes urgent to interrupt P immediately after d time units.

However, to avoid the complex semantics introduced by hiding, we directly give its definition to describe the behaviour of the timed interrupt, rather than calculating its reactive design from Definition 8.

Definition 9

$$P \triangle_d Q \mathrel{\widehat=} \left(\begin{array}{c} \neg\,((P_f^f \wedge \#tr' - \#tr \leq d)\,;\,\mathbf{R1_{ct}}(\mathbf{true})) \wedge \\ \neg\,((P_f^t \wedge \#tr' - \#tr = d)\,;\,(wait \wedge \mathit{II}^{-wait} \wedge \neg\, wait')\,;\,Q_f^f) \\ \vdash \\ (P_f^t \wedge \#tr' - \#tr \leq d) \vee \\ \left(\left(\begin{array}{c} P_f^t \wedge \#tr' - \#tr = d \\ \wedge\, state' = state \end{array}\right);\,(wait \wedge \mathit{II}^{-wait} \wedge \neg\, wait')\,;\,Q_f^t\right) \end{array} \right)$$

The precondition of the above reactive design states that if P does not diverge within d time units, and if Q does not diverge after an interruption, and the postcondition guarantees the observation of P within d, or the sequential composition of the observation of P before the interruption (during d time units) and the behaviour of Q. In fact, the timed interrupt is quite like a kind of sequential composition because the interrupting action has no influence on the interruptible action.

The validation of this reactive design semantics for the timed interrupt operator is retained by proving a number of algebraic laws. There are some interesting laws for timed interrupts and delays. Law 7 states that a delay can be lifted forward from the interruptible action if its duration is no longer than the allowed waiting time units. Law 8 states that $\triangle_d$ can be eliminated if a delay has still not terminated when an interruption occurs. Law 9 states that a timed interrupt can be sequentialised if the interruptible action is *Stop*.

Law 7. $(Wait\ d\,;\,P) \triangle_{d+d'} Q = Wait\ d\,;\,(P \triangle_{d'} Q)$

Law 8. $(Wait\ (d+d')\,;\,P) \triangle_d Q = Wait\ d\,;\,Q$

Law 9. $Stop \triangle_d P = Wait\ d\,;\,P$

In addition, we have three zero laws for $\triangle_d$. Law 10 states that a divergence cannot be recovered, Law 11 states that termination can eliminate $\triangle_d$ if an interruption has not occurred, and Law 12 states that $\triangle_d$ cannot make an unstarted action start.

Law 10. $Chaos \triangle_d P = Chaos$

Law 11. $Skip \triangle_d P = Skip\ \mathit{if}\ d > 0$

Law 12. $Miracle \triangle_d P = Miracle$

The proofs of Law 7–Law 12 and more detailed discussions about these laws can be found in [19].

4 Conclusion

The reactive designs of the three interrupt operators developed in this paper carry on our previous work [16,17,18] to enhance the expressiveness of the *Circus Time* model. The well-established semantics of these interrupt operators is significant in proving refinement laws in *Circus Time*. In line with the strong capability to deal with data in *Circus Time*, each action has two observational variables, *state* and *state'*, in its alphabet to record values of local variables. The two observational variables are carefully constrained in order to respect some important refinement laws. For example, we allow *state'* to be arbitrary at any waiting state or deadlock to retain the unit law, $P \Box Stop = P$. That is to say, we can observe the value of *state'* only when a program terminates. This claim, here, affects the mechanism for handling local variables within the interrupt operators. For example, a program in *Circus Time* may have the following behaviour involving updates of a program variable in an interruption.

$$x := 0;\ ((x := x + 1;\ Stop) \triangle (c \rightarrow x := x + 1))$$

The value of x when the program terminates is 1 if c occurs. From the reactive designs of the three kinds of interrupt operators, the interrupting action always obtains *state* from the beginning of an interrupt operator, no matter whether the interruptible action has changed the values of local variables. In other words, the interrupt operators in *Circus Time* cannot capture interruptions, such as a recovered program from a deadlock can proceed with the latest values of local variables before falling into the deadlock.

We demonstrate that these reactive designs of the interrupt operators preserve all related properties in [5,13,14], and also discuss their relations. Different from the approach used in the work [10], we adopt the parallel-by-merge to define the generic interrupt operator. However, establishing the proof of parallelism is always complicated. For simpler cases, the catastrophic interrupt operator is recommended if enough. A number of algebraic laws of the three operators have been proved by hand. As such hand-proofs are well-knowingly error prone, the mechanised proofs in a theorem prover is of course our future work in a short term. The work of mechanising *Circus* in ProofPower [12] and Isabelle [4] can help us to embed this semantics.

Acknowledgments. I thank Jim Woodcock for his advice on the semantics. This work was fully supported by the hiJaC project (EPSRC-EP/H017461/1).

References

1. Roscoe, A.W.: Model-checking CSP. In: A Classical Mind: essays in Honour of C.A.R. Hoare, ch. 21. Prentice-Hall (1994)
2. Cavalcanti, A.L.C., Woodcock, J.C.P.: A Tutorial Introduction to CSP in *Unifying Theories of Programming*. In: Cavalcanti, A., Sampaio, A., Woodcock, J. (eds.) PSSE 2004. LNCS, vol. 3167, pp. 220–268. Springer, Heidelberg (2006)
3. Cavalcanti, A.L.C., Sampaio, A.C.A., Woodcock, J.C.P.: A Refinement Strategy for *Circus*. Formal Aspects of Computing 15(2-3), 146–181 (2003)
4. Feliachi, A., Gaudel, M.-C., Wolff, B.: Isabelle/Circus : A Process Specification and Verification Environment. Technical Report 1547, LRI, Université Paris-Sud XI (November 2011), `http://www.lri.fr/Rapports-internes`

5. Hoare, C.A.R.: Communicating Sequential Processes. Prentice-Hall International (1985)
6. Hoare, C.A.R., Jifeng, H.: Unifying Theories of Programming. Prentice-Hall International (1998)
7. Huang, Y., Zhao, Y., Shi, J., Zhu, H., Qin, S.: Investigating time properties of interrupt-driven programs. In: Gheyi, R., Naumann, D. (eds.) SBMF 2012. LNCS, vol. 7498, pp. 131–146. Springer, Heidelberg (2012)
8. Jifeng, H.: From CSP to hybrid systems, pp. 171–189 (1994)
9. Leuschel, M., Butler, M.: ProB: A Model Checker for B. In: Araki, K., Gnesi, S., Mandrioli, D. (eds.) FME 2003. LNCS, vol. 2805, pp. 855–874. Springer, Heidelberg (2003)
10. McEwan, A., Woodcock, J.C.P.: Unifying theories of interrupts. In: Proceedings of the Second UTP Symposium, Trinity College Dublin (2008)
11. Morgan, C.: Programming from specifications. Prentice-Hall, Inc., Upper Saddle River (1990)
12. Oliveira, M., Cavalcanti, A.L.C., Woodcock, J.C.P.: Unifying theories in ProofPower-Z. Formal Aspects of Computing Journal (2007)
13. Roscoe, A.W.: The Theory and Practice of Concurrency. Prentice-Hall International (1998)
14. Schneider, S.A.: Concurrent and real-time systems: the CSP approach. John Wiley & Sons (1999)
15. Sherif, A., Cavalcanti, A.L.C., Jifeng, H., Sampaio, A.C.A.: A process algebraic framework for specification and validation of real-time systems. Formal Aspects of Computing 22(2), 153–191 (2010)
16. Wei, K., Woodcock, J.C.P., Burns, A.: A timed model of *Circus* with the reactive design miracle. In: 8th International Conference on Software Engineering and Formal Methods (SEFM), Pisa, Italy, pp. 315–319. IEEE Computer Society (September 2010)
17. Wei, K., Woodcock, J.C.P., Burns, A.: Timed *Circus*: Timed CSP with the Miracle. In: ICECCS, pp. 55–64 (2011)
18. Wei, K., Woodcock, J.C.P., Cavalcanti, A.L.C.: *Circus Time* with reactive designs. In: UTP, pp. 68–87 (2012)
19. Wei, K., Woodcock, J.C.P., Cavalcanti, A.L.C.: New *Circus Time*. Technical report, Department of Computer Science, University of York, UK (March 2012), `http://www.cs.york.ac.uk/circus/hijac/publication.html`
20. Woodcock, J.C.P., Davies, J.: Using Z: Specification, Refinement and Proof. Prentice-Hall, Inc., Upper Saddle River (1996)
21. Woodcock, J.C.P., Cavalcanti, A.L.C.: A concurrent language for refinement. In: Butterfield, A., Pahl, C. (eds.) IWFM 2001: 5th Irish Workshop in Formal Methods, BCS Electronic Workshops in Computing, Dublin, Ireland (July 2001)
22. Woodcock, J.C.P., Cavalcanti, A.L.C.: The Semantics of $*Circus*$. In: Bert, D., Bowen, J.P., Henson, M.C., Robinson, K. (eds.) ZB 2002. LNCS, vol. 2272, pp. 184–203. Springer, Heidelberg (2002)
23. Woodcock, J.C.P., Cavalcanti, A.L.C.: A Tutorial Introduction to Designs in Unifying Theories of Programming. In: Boiten, E.A., Derrick, J., Smith, G.P. (eds.) IFM 2004. LNCS, vol. 2999, pp. 40–66. Springer, Heidelberg (2004)
24. Zhao, Y., Huang, Y., He, J., Liu, S.: Formal Model of Interrupt Program from a Probabilistic Perspective. In: ICECCS, pp. 87–94 (2011)

A Proof System in PADS

Xinghua Yao[1], Min Zhang[2,⋆], and Yixiang Chen[1]

[1] MoE Engineering Research Center
for Software/Hardware Co-design Technology and Application,
East China Normal University, Shanghai, China
xhyaoecnu@gmail.com,
yxchen@sei.ecnu.edu.cn
[2] Shanghai Key Laboratory of Trustworthy Computing,
East China Normal University, Shanghai, China
mzhang@sei.ecnu.edu.cn

Abstract. The PADS (Process Algebra for Demand and Supply) framework is an approach to model resource demand and supply for the formal analysis of hierarchical scheduling. Inspired by the demand relation in PADS, we propose a weak demand relation covering several cases which can not be described by a demand relation. And we explore some properties of weak demand relation which are similar to properties of demand relation. Especially, if two tasks are in a weak demand relation then their schedulabilities are closely related. Furthermore, we present a proof system for the weak demand relation in a decomposing-composing way, which helps to compare two tasks' schedulabilities. Finally, we prove that the proof system is sound and complete with respect to the semantic definition of weak demand relation.

Keywords: resource demand and resource supply, hierarchical scheduling, real-time process algebra, demand relation.

1 Introduction

As the complexity of real-time embedded systems is increasing, compositional design and analysis methods for the assurance of timing requirements are developed. Component-based design is such a widely accepted approach to facilitate the design of complex systems. This approach provides means for decomposing a complex system into some simpler components and for composing the components using interfaces which abstract component complexities. In the procedure of using component technology to design real-time systems, we need naturally consider some corresponding scheduling problems. For example, if every component is schedulable, is the composition of components schedulable under a composition of components' schedule scenarios? For the scheduling analysis in component-based design, compositional hierarchical scheduling is developed, such as [3,4,7,13,14], which are based on real-time scheduling theory and interface theory. PADS (Process Algebra for Demand and Supply), first proposed by A.Philippou et al. in [12], is a model for the formal analysis of compositional

⋆ Corresponding author.

Z. Liu, J. Woodcock, and H. Zhu (Eds.): ICTAC 2013, LNCS 8049, pp. 391–408, 2013.

hierarchical scheduling. In PADS, a task is specified by describing its consumption needs for resources, and the behaviour of supplying resource is modeled by supply process. Based on task process and supply process, we can analyze the schedulability for tasks and their compositionality by using a small number of operators in PADS.

Resource demands describe the needed resources to execute tasks. The relations between resource demands can help us to analyze task's schedulability. In order to provide such a machinery that may allow us to reason about hierarchical approaches to scheduling, A.Philippou et al. present the demand relation between tasks and study its properties in [12]. In particular, the demand relation satisfies that any supply which is able to schedule a more demanding task can also schedule a less demanding task. However, we find that there exist some task pairs, which can not be described by a demand relation and whose schedulabilities are comparable. For example, task T_1 has two possible executing paths, including $\{(r_1, 2), (r_2, 1)\} : \{(r_1, 1)\} : FIN$ and $\{(r_1, 1), (r_2, 2)\} : \{(r_2, 2)\} : FIN$, in which first actions request same resources and have no any preemption relation; task T_2 has only one executing path, i.e. $\{(r_1, 1)\} : \{(r_1, 1)\} : FIN$. According to the definition of demand relation, T_1 is not more demanding than T_2. This is because that the executing path $\{(r_1, 1), (r_2, 2)\} : \{(r_2, 2)\} : FIN$ in T_1 is not more demanding than T_2's executing path. In fact, every supply which is able to schedule T_1 could schedule T_2. In order to describe these task pairs, this paper proposes a new weak demand relation between tasks. And we prove that it can be determined in a finite number of steps whether two tasks are in a weak demand relation or not. Then, we explore some properties about the weak demand relation. For example, the largest weak demand relation $\preccurlyeq_D$ is reflexive and transitive. In particular, such a property holds, which says that every supply that schedules a stronger demanding task in a weak demand relation can also schedule a weaker demanding task. The results show that the weak demand relation contains some task pairs whose schedulabilities can be compared and which are not included in any demand relation. Therefore, the weak demand relation is a reasonable machinery in the sense of helping us analyze task's schedulability. Finally, we present a proof system, named P_{TT}, for a weak demand relation between two finite task processes, and prove its soundness and completeness with respect to the semantic definition of weak demand relation. When establishing the proof system P_{TT}, we adopt a decomposing-composing way, i.e. if task T_1 is more weak-demanding than task T_2, then we decompose T_1 into several parts according to the executability of actions, and decompose T_2 so that every decomposed part in T_1 is more weak-demanding than some decomposed part in T_2, and finally compose these parts using choice operator "+".

Related work. Formal approach is one of long-standing lines of research for compositional analysis. There have been several formal approaches to scheduling, such as based on process algebra [1,8,9,10,11], task automata [5,6], preemptive Petri nets [2], etc. Comparing with these approaches, PADS models resource demand and resource supply explicitly. About PADS, [12] discusses the schedulability of tasks, explores conditions under which schedulable systems may be safely composed, and presents a method to generate a supply to schedule a set of tasks when they are schedulable. In addition, [12] proposes the demand relation for the hierarchy between tasks and studies its properties. For example, a supply which is able to schedule a more demanding task could also schedule a less demanding task. In this paper, our weak demand relation covers some task pairs which can not be described by the demand relation. The weak demand relation satisfies that every supply which could schedule a stronger demanding task is also able to schedule a weaker demanding task. Furthermore, we discuss how to determine whether two tasks are in a weak demand relation and build a related proof system.

The remainder of the paper is organized as follows. In Section 2, we introduce some concepts, lemmas in [12] and a modified definition of demand relation. Section 3 presents the concept of weak demand relation and develops its properties. In Section 4, we establish a proof system P_{TT} for the weak demand relation, and give an example to show its reasoning ability. Section 5 proves the soundness and completeness of the proof system P_{TT}. In Section 6, we conclude this paper and present some future work.

2 Preliminary

In this section, we will introduce some concepts, lemmas in [12] and our modified definition of demand relation.

In PADS, a system is considered to be a set of processes operating on a set of serially reusable resource. These processes are (1) tasks, which require the use of resources in order to complete their jobs, and (2) supplies, that specify when each resource is available to the tasks. In [12], the set of resources is denoted by R; each resource $r \in \mathsf{R}$ can be requested by a task; $\overline{r}$ means that the resource r is granted by a supply; $\overleftrightarrow{r}$ means that the resource r is consumed. A resource r is consumed when a supply and a request for the resource are simultaneously available. We write Act, ranged over by α and β, for the set of all actions and distinguish $\mathsf{Act_R}$, for the set of actions involving only resource requests, ranged over by ρ, and $\mathsf{Act_G}$, the set of actions involving only resource grants, ranged over by γ. Given $\alpha \in \mathsf{Act}$ we write $\alpha^\flat$ to remove all priorities from resource-priority pairs, e.g.$\{(r_1, 1), \overline{r_2}, (\overleftrightarrow{r_3}, 2)\}^\flat = \{r_1, \overline{r_2}, \overleftrightarrow{r_3}\}$, and $\mathsf{res}(\alpha)$ for the set of resources occurring in α, e.g.$\mathsf{res}(\{(r_1, 1), \overline{r_2}, (\overleftrightarrow{r_3}, 2)\}) = \{r_1, r_2, r_3\}$. And we write $\pi_\alpha(r)$ for the priority at which resource r is employed within action α, where we consider all supplied resources to be employed at priority level 0, e.g.for $\alpha = \{(r_1, 1), \overline{r_2}, (\overleftrightarrow{r_3}, 2)\}$, we have $\pi_\alpha(r_1) = 1$, $\pi_\alpha(r_2) = 0$ and $\pi_\alpha(r_3) = 2$. We say that actions α_1 and α_2 are *compatible* with each other if, whenever r occurs in both actions then one occurrence must be a request and the other a supply of the resource. Formally, it can be represented as follows:

$$\mathsf{compatible}(\alpha_1, \alpha_2) = \bigwedge_{r \in \mathsf{res}(\alpha_1) \cap \mathsf{res}(\alpha_2)} (r \in \alpha_1^\flat \wedge \overline{r} \in \alpha_2^\flat) \vee (r \in \alpha_2^\flat \wedge \overline{r} \in \alpha_1^\flat) .$$

For compatible actions α_1 and α_2, there is such a combining operation "$\oplus$"as follows:

$$\begin{aligned}\alpha_1 \oplus \alpha_2 = {} & \{(r, p) \in \alpha_1 \cup \alpha_2 | \overline{r} \notin \alpha_1 \cup \alpha_2\} \\ & \cup \{\overline{r} \in \alpha_1 \cup \alpha_2 | (r, p) \notin \alpha_1 \cup \alpha_2\} \\ & \cup \{(\overleftrightarrow{r}, p) | (r, p) \in \alpha_i, \overline{r} \in \alpha_{3-i}, i \in \{1, 2\} \text{ or } (\overleftrightarrow{r}, p) \in \alpha_1 \cup \alpha_2\} .\end{aligned}$$

The syntaxes for the set of tasks T, the set of supplies S and the set of timed systems P are listed as follows, and their semantics are given in Table 1.

$$
\begin{aligned}
T &::= FIN \mid \rho : T \mid T + T \mid C \\
S &::= FIN \mid \gamma : S \mid S + S \mid D \\
P &::= \delta \mid T \mid S \mid P \| P
\end{aligned}
$$

Here, C ranges over a set of task constants, each with an associated definition of the form $C \stackrel{\text{def}}{=} T$, where T may contain occurrences of C as well as other task constants; and D ranges over a similar set of supply constants. δ means that the system is locked.

Table 1. Transition rules

(Idle)	$FIN \stackrel{\emptyset}{\twoheadrightarrow} FIN$				
(ActT)	$\rho : T \stackrel{\rho}{\twoheadrightarrow} T$		(ActS)	$\gamma : S \stackrel{\gamma}{\twoheadrightarrow} S$	
(SumT)	$\dfrac{T_i \stackrel{\alpha}{\twoheadrightarrow} T,\ i \in \{1,2\}}{T_1 + T_2 \stackrel{\alpha}{\twoheadrightarrow} T}$		(SumS)	$\dfrac{S_i \stackrel{\alpha}{\twoheadrightarrow} S,\ i \in \{1,2\}}{S_1 + S_2 \stackrel{\alpha}{\twoheadrightarrow} S}$	
(ConstT)	$\dfrac{T \stackrel{\alpha}{\twoheadrightarrow} T'}{C \stackrel{\alpha}{\twoheadrightarrow} T'}$	$C \stackrel{\text{def}}{=} T$	(ConstS)	$\dfrac{S \stackrel{\alpha}{\twoheadrightarrow} S'}{D \stackrel{\alpha}{\twoheadrightarrow} S'}$	$D \stackrel{\text{def}}{=} S$
(Par)	$\dfrac{P_1 \stackrel{\alpha_1}{\twoheadrightarrow} P_1',\ P_2 \stackrel{\alpha_2}{\twoheadrightarrow} P_2'}{P_1 \| P_2 \stackrel{\alpha_1 \oplus \alpha_2}{\twoheadrightarrow} P_1' \| P_2'}$	compatible(α_1,α_2)			
	$\dfrac{P \stackrel{\alpha}{\twoheadrightarrow} Q}{P \stackrel{\alpha}{\rightarrow} Q}$	there is no $P \stackrel{\beta}{\twoheadrightarrow}, \alpha \prec \beta$			

As we see in Table 1, the transition relation "$\rightarrow$" is based on "$\twoheadrightarrow$"and is restrained by the preemption relation among actions. The transition relation "$\rightarrow$"is a refinement of "$\twoheadrightarrow$".

According to [12], we write $P \stackrel{\alpha}{\rightarrow}$ if there exists P' such that $P \stackrel{\alpha}{\rightarrow} P'$; if there exists α such that $P \stackrel{\alpha}{\rightarrow}$, we write $P \rightarrow$; and if there exist $\alpha_1, \cdots, \alpha_n$ and $P_1, \cdots, P_n, n \geq 1$, such that $P \stackrel{\alpha_1}{\longrightarrow} P_1 \stackrel{\alpha_2}{\longrightarrow} \cdots P_{n-1} \stackrel{\alpha_n}{\longrightarrow} P_n = P'$, we write $P \Rightarrow P'$. Moreover, T^* denotes the set containing all processes of the form $T_1 \| \ldots \| T_n$, $n \geq 1$, S^* represents the set containing all processes of the form $S_1 \| \ldots \| S_n$, $n \geq 1$, and $\sum_{i \in I} T_i$ denotes $T_{i_1} + \cdots + T_{i_n}$, where $I = \{i_1, \ldots, i_n\}$.

Definition 1. *We define the preemption relation* $\prec \in \mathsf{Act} \times \mathsf{Act}$ *so that* $\alpha \prec \beta$ *if one of the following holds:*

1. $\{r | \overline{r} \in \alpha^\flat$ *or* $\overleftrightarrow{r} \in \alpha^\flat\} = \{r | \overline{r} \in \beta^\flat$ *or* $\overleftrightarrow{r} \in \beta^\flat\}$, $\alpha^\flat \cap \mathsf{R} \neq \emptyset$ *and* $\beta^\flat \cap \mathsf{R} = \emptyset$, *that is,* α *and* β *use the same consumed and offered resources and* α *contains some additional resource requests whereas* β *does not.*
2. $\mathsf{res}(\alpha) = \mathsf{res}(\beta), \alpha^\flat \cap \mathsf{R} = \beta^\flat \cap \mathsf{R} = \emptyset$ *and* $\{r | \overleftrightarrow{r} \in \alpha^\flat\} \subset \{r | \overleftrightarrow{r} \in \beta^\flat\}$, *that is,* α *and* β *involve the same resources, neither of them makes any resources requests, but* β *consumes more resources than* α.
3. $\alpha^\flat = \beta^\flat$, *for all* $r \in \mathsf{res}(\alpha)$ $\pi_\alpha(r) \leq \pi_\beta(r)$, *and there exists* $r \in \mathsf{res}(\alpha), \pi_\alpha(r) < \pi_\beta(r)$, *that is,* α *and* β *contain the same resources with* β *giving greater or equal priority to all resource usages, and there exists at least one resource which is associated with a strictly greater priority in* β *than in* α.

Definition 2. *Let $\alpha, \beta \in \mathsf{Act}$.*

- *We write $\mathsf{sat}(\beta, \alpha)$ if $\mathsf{res}(\beta) \subseteq \mathsf{res}(\alpha)$. In the case of $\beta \in \mathsf{Act_R}$ and $\alpha \in \mathsf{Act_G}$, we say that request action β is satisfied by grant action α.*
- *For a system P, we write $\beta \trianglelefteq_P \alpha$ if $\mathsf{sat}(\beta, \alpha)$ and there exists no $\gamma \in \mathsf{Act}$ such that $P \xrightarrow{\gamma} P'$, $\mathsf{sat}(\gamma, \alpha)$ and either $\beta^\flat \subset \gamma^\flat$ or $\beta^\flat = \gamma^\flat$ and $\beta \prec \gamma$. If $\beta \trianglelefteq_P \alpha$ we say that β is a maximal response of P with respect to α.*

Example 1. *Let $T = \{(r_1,2),(r_2,3)\} : \{(r_2,1)\} : FIN + \{(r_1,1)\} : FIN + \{(r_1,2),(r_2,2)\} : FIN, \alpha_1 = \{(r_1,2),(r_2,3)\}, \alpha_2 = \{(r_1,1)\}, \alpha_3 = \{(r_1,2),(r_2,2)\}$ and $\gamma = \{\overline{r_1},\overline{r_2},\overline{r_3}\}$. Then, T has only two transitions: $T \xrightarrow{\alpha_1} \{(r_2,1)\} : FIN$ and $T \xrightarrow{\alpha_2} FIN$, $\mathsf{sat}(\alpha_1,\gamma)$, $\alpha_1 \not\prec \alpha_2$ and $\alpha_2^\flat = \{r_1\} \subset \alpha_1^\flat = \{r_1,r_2\}$. So, $\alpha_1 \trianglelefteq_T \gamma$, $\alpha_2 \not\trianglelefteq_T \gamma$. For action α_3, $\alpha_3^\flat = \alpha_1^\flat$ and $\alpha_3 \prec \alpha_1$. Thus, $\alpha_3 \not\trianglelefteq_T \gamma$.*

Definition 3. *A task $T \in \mathsf{T}^*$ is schedulable by supply $S \in \mathsf{S}^*$ if whenever $T \| S \Rightarrow P$ then (i) $P \rightarrow$ and (ii) for all $P \xrightarrow{\alpha}$ we have $\alpha^\flat \cap \mathsf{R} = \emptyset$.*

Definition 4. *A relation $\mathscr{S} \subseteq \mathsf{T}^* \times \mathsf{S}^*$ is a supply simulation relation if for all $(T,S) \in \mathscr{S}$, $S \rightarrow$, and if $S \xrightarrow{\alpha} S'$ then*

1. *there exists $T \xrightarrow{\beta} T'$ with $\mathsf{sat}(\beta,\alpha)$ and $(T',S') \in \mathscr{S}$, and*
2. *whenever $T \xrightarrow{\beta} T'$ with $\beta \trianglelefteq_T \alpha$, then $(T',S') \in \mathscr{S}$.*

If there exists a supply simulation relation between T and S, then we write $S \models T$.

Lemma 1. *A task $T \in \mathsf{T}^*$ is schedulable by supply $S \in \mathsf{S}^*$ if and only if $S \models T$.*

In order to characterize the relation between two tasks' schedulabilities, [12] presents a concept of demand relation. In the following, we will modify the definition of demand relation in [12], and our demand relation satisfies that every supply which is able to schedule a more demanding task could also schedule a less demanding task, i.e. Lemma 2.

Definition 5. *A relation $\mathcal{D} \subseteq \mathsf{T} \times \mathsf{T}$ is a demand relation if for all $(T_1,T_2) \in \mathcal{D}$, if $T_1 \xrightarrow{\alpha}$ then*

1. *there exist $T_2 \xrightarrow{\beta} T_2'$ with $\mathsf{sat}(\beta,\alpha)$ and $T_1 \xrightarrow{\alpha} T_1'$, such that $(T_1',T_2') \in \mathcal{D}$.*
2. *for all $T_2 \xrightarrow{\beta} T_2'$, if $\beta \trianglelefteq_{T_2} \alpha \cup \beta$, $\alpha \trianglelefteq_{T_1} \alpha \cup \beta$ and for no γ, $T_1 \xrightarrow{\gamma}$ and $\beta \trianglelefteq_{T_2} \gamma$ and $\gamma \trianglelefteq_{T_1} \alpha \cup \beta$, then there exists $T_1 \xrightarrow{\alpha} T_1'$ such that $(T_1',T_2') \in \mathcal{D}$.*
3. *for all $T_2 \xrightarrow{\beta} T_2'$ with $\beta \trianglelefteq_{T_2} \alpha$, there exists $T_1 \xrightarrow{\alpha} T_1'$ such that $(T_1',T_2') \in \mathcal{D}$.*

We write $\preceq_D$ for the largest demand relation and we say that a task T_1 is more demanding than a task T_2, $T_2 \preceq_D T_1$, if there exists a demand relation $\mathcal{D}$ with $(T_1,T_2) \in \mathcal{D}$.

Lemma 2. *Suppose that task T_1 is schedulable by supply S and that T_1 is more demanding than T_2. Then, task T_2 is also schedulable by supply S.*

3 Weak Demand Relation

Firstly, we consider the following two examples.

Example 2. *Suppose tasks T_1 and T_2 be defined as follows:*

$$T_1 = \{(r_1,2),(r_2,3)\} : \{(r_2,2)\} : FIN + \{(r_1,3),(r_2,2)\} : \{(r_1,1)\} : FIN ,$$
$$T_2 = \{(r_1,2)\} : \{(r_2,1)\} : FIN .$$

For either the pair (T_1,T_2) or (T_2,T_1), Clause 1 in Definition 5 does not hold. So, $T_2 \not\precsim_D T_1$ and $T_1 \not\precsim_D T_2$. Furthermore, we can not build a demand relation to show their schedulability relation. However, their schedulabilities are related; for every supply S if task T_1 is schedulable by S, then T_2 is also schedulable by S.

Example 3. *Suppose tasks T_3 and T_4 be defined as follows:*

$$T_3 = \{(r_1,1),(r_2,2),(r_3,3)\} : \{(r_1,1)\} : FIN + \{(r_1,1),(r_3,2),(r_4,4)\} : FIN ,$$
$$T_4 = \{(r_1,1)\} : FIN + \{(r_2,1),(r_4,1)\} : \{(r_1,1)\} : FIN .$$

For the pair (T_3,T_4), Clause 2 in Definition 5 does not hold; for (T_4,T_3), Clause 1 in Definition 5 is not satisfied. So, $T_4 \not\precsim_D T_3$ and $T_3 \not\precsim_D T_4$. Furthermore, we can not show schedulability relations between T_3 and T_4 by building a demand relation. In fact, their schedulabilities are related; for every supply S if task T_3 is schedulable by S, then T_4 is also schedulable by S.

As we see in Example 2 and Example 3, the schedulability relations between T_1 (T_3) and T_2 (T_4) are not reflected in the concept of demand relation. So, we propose the following weak demand relation to describe such task pairs.

Definition 6. *A relation $\mathcal{D} \subseteq \mathsf{T} \times \mathsf{T}$ is a weak demand relation if for all $(T_1,T_2) \in \mathcal{D}$, if $T_1 \xrightarrow{\alpha}$ then*

1. *there exist $T_2 \xrightarrow{\beta} T_2'$ with $\beta \trianglelefteq_{T_2} \alpha$ and $T_1 \xrightarrow{\alpha'} T_1'$ with $\alpha' \trianglelefteq_{T_1} \alpha$, such that $(T_1',T_2') \in \mathcal{D}$, and*
2. *for any $\gamma \in \mathsf{Act_G}$, if $T_2 \xrightarrow{\beta} T_2'$ with $\beta \trianglelefteq_{T_2} \gamma$ and $\alpha \trianglelefteq_{T_1} \gamma$, then there exists $T_1 \xrightarrow{\alpha'} T_1'$ with $\alpha' \trianglelefteq_{T_1} \gamma$ and $(T_1',T_2') \in \mathcal{D}$.*

We write $\precsim_D$ for the largest weak demand relation and we say that a task T_1 is more weak-demanding than T_2, $T_2 \precsim_D T_1$, if there exists a weak demand relation $\mathcal{D}$ with $(T_1,T_2) \in \mathcal{D}$.

To better understand Definition 6, let us first consider the point relating to the existence of a α'-move of T_1 in the first clause. In Example 2, although T_2 can not be matched by the second summand of T_1, it is intuitive that T_1 is more weak-demanding than T_2. Because for T_1 to be scheduled successfully it is imperative that after being offered r_1 and r_2 it will be continuously offered both r_1 and r_2. Thus, it is sufficient for T_2's derivative to be matched by one of the maximal derivatives of T_1 with respect to $\{(r_1,3),(r_2,2)\}$.

The second clause in Definition 6 is concerned with a grant γ under which T_1 and T_2 have responses, i.e. $T_1 \xrightarrow{\alpha}$ with $\alpha \trianglelefteq_{T_1} \gamma$ and $T_2 \xrightarrow{\beta} T_2'$ with $\beta \trianglelefteq_{T_2} \gamma$, and it aims to ensure that if a supply is able to schedule maximal derivatives of T_1 with respect to γ then every maximal derivative of T_2 with respect to γ is also schedulable by the supply. Clause 2 enunciates this requirement in the way that for every maximal derivative T_2' of T_2 with respect to γ there exists a maximal derivative of T_1 which is more weak-demanding than T_2'. About Example 3, we take $\alpha = \{(r_1, 1), (r_3, 2), (r_4, 4)\}$, $\alpha' = \{(r_1, 1), (r_2, 2), (r_3, 3)\}$, $\beta = \{(r_2, 1), (r_4, 1)\}$. Under a grant γ which offers r_1, r_2, r_3 and r_4, a maximal β-derivative of T_4 is matched by a α'-derivative of T_3. Furthermore, we could check that T_3 is more weak-demanding than T_4.

The largest weak demand relation $\preccurlyeq_D$ is reflexive and transitive. Especially, two tasks' schedulabilities are also comparable in a weak demand relation.

Theorem 1. *Suppose that task T_1 is schedulable by supply S, and T_1 is more weak-demanding than T_2, i.e. $T_2 \preccurlyeq_D T_1$. Then, task T_2 is also schedulable by supply S.*

Proof. The proof consists of showing that the relation

$$\begin{aligned}\mathscr{S} = \{(T_2, S) | \exists &\text{weak demand relation } \mathcal{D}, \text{ supply simulation relation } \mathcal{R} \\ &\text{and } T_1 \in \mathsf{T}, (T_1, T_2) \in \mathcal{D}, (T_1, S) \in \mathcal{R}\}\end{aligned}$$

is a supply simulation. Suppose $(T_2, S) \in \mathscr{S}$ and T_1 is a task such that $(T_1, T_2) \in \mathcal{D}$, where $\mathcal{D}$ is a weak demand relation, and $(T_1, S) \in \mathcal{R}$, where $\mathcal{R}$ is a supply simulation relation. Assume $S \xrightarrow{\gamma} S'$, then

- Since $(T_1, S) \in \mathcal{R}$, there exists T_{11} with $T_1 \xrightarrow{\rho_1} T_{11}$ and $\rho_1 \trianglelefteq_{T_1} \gamma$. Thus, by clause 1 in Definition 6, there exists T_{21} such that $T_2 \xrightarrow{\rho_2} T_{21}$ with $\rho_2 \trianglelefteq_{T_2} \rho_1$, and T_{12} such that $T_1 \xrightarrow{\rho_3} T_{12}$ with $\rho_3 \trianglelefteq_{T_1} \rho_1$ and $(T_{12}, T_{21}) \in \mathcal{D}$. Furthermore, $\mathsf{sat}(\rho_2, \gamma)$, $\rho_3^\flat = \rho_1^\flat$, $\rho_3 \trianglelefteq_{T_1} \gamma$ and $(T_{12}, S') \in \mathcal{R}$. This implies $(T_{21}, S') \in \mathscr{S}$ as required.
- Next suppose that $T_2 \xrightarrow{\rho} T_2'$ with $\rho \trianglelefteq_{T_2} \gamma$. We know that there exists $T_1 \xrightarrow{\rho_1} T_1'$ with $\rho_1 \trianglelefteq_{T_1} \gamma$. Thus, by Clause 2 in Definition 6, there exists $T_1 \xrightarrow{\rho_1'} T_1''$ such that $\rho_1' \trianglelefteq_{T_1} \gamma$ and $(T_1'', T_2') \in \mathcal{D}$. By the definition of supply simulation relation, $(T_1'', S') \in \mathcal{R}$. Thus $(T_2', S') \in \mathscr{S}$ which completes the proof.

□

For tasks in Example 2 and Example 3, we have: $T_2 \preccurlyeq_D T_1$ and $T_4 \preccurlyeq_D T_3$. According to Theorem 1, for any supply S, $S \models T_1$ implies $S \models T_2$ and $S \models T_3$ implies $S \models T_4$. However, we can not reason about the four tasks' schedulabilities by using demand relation. This fact shows that the weak demand relation is a reasonable machinery in the sense of helping us analyze more tasks' schedulabilities. Furthermore, the weak demand relation is strictly weaker than our demand relation.

Theorem 2. *If $\mathcal{R}$ is a demand relation, then $\mathcal{R}$ is also a weak demand relation.*

The following Theorem 3 tells us that it can be determined in a finite number of steps whether a task T_1 is stronger demanding than T_2 in a weak demand relation. Because of limited space, we will not give its proof.

Theorem 3. *Assume binary relation $\mathcal{D} \subseteq \mathsf{T} \times \mathsf{T}$. Then, $\mathcal{D}$ is a weak demand relation, if and only if $\mathcal{D}$ satisfies the following conditions, i.e. for all $(T_1, T_2) \in \mathcal{D}$, if $T_1 \xrightarrow{\alpha}$, then*

(1) there exist $T_2 \xrightarrow{\beta} T_2'$ with $\beta \trianglelefteq_{T_2} \alpha$ and $T_1 \xrightarrow{\alpha'} T_1'$ with $\alpha' \trianglelefteq_{T_1} \alpha$, such that $(T_1', T_2') \in \mathcal{D}$, and

(2) let $A = \{\rho^\flat | T_1 \xrightarrow{\rho}\}$, for any nonempty subset $B \subseteq A$, $C = \bigcup_{\rho^\flat \in B} \rho^\flat$, if

$$T_2 \xrightarrow{\beta} T_2' \text{ with } \beta \trianglelefteq_{T_2} \overline{\beta^\flat \cup C}$$

and $\alpha \trianglelefteq_{T_1} \overline{\beta^\flat \cup C}$, then there exists

$$T_1 \xrightarrow{\alpha'} T_1' \text{ with } \alpha' \trianglelefteq_{T_1} \overline{\beta^\flat \cup C} \text{ and } (T_1', T_2') \in \mathcal{D}.$$

4 Proof System P_{TT}

In this section we will present a proof system P_{TT} for a weak demand relation between task processes without task constants. Firstly, we will define some concepts describing relations among tasks in order to build proof system P_{TT}. Secondly, we give all the rules in P_{TT} and take an example to show P_{TT}'s reasoning ability.

4.1 Some Basic Concepts

Definition 7. *Let $T, T' \in \mathsf{T}$. If for any $\rho \in \mathsf{Act_R}$, $T \xrightarrow{\rho}$ implies $T' \xrightarrow{\rho}$, then we say that task T' preserves executable actions in T, denoted by $\uparrow_T^{T'}$.*

$\uparrow_T^{T'}$ means that any executable action in T is also executable in T'.

Definition 8. *Let $T, T' \in \mathsf{T}$, $\gamma \in \mathsf{Act_G}$. If for any $\rho \in \mathsf{Act_R}$, $T \xrightarrow{\rho}$ with $\rho \trianglelefteq_T \gamma$ implies $T' \xrightarrow{\rho}$ with $\rho \trianglelefteq_{T'} \gamma$, then we say, task T' preserves executable and maximal actions in T under γ, denoted by $\trianglelefteq\uparrow_T^{T'}(\gamma)$.*

$\trianglelefteq\uparrow_T^{T'}(\gamma)$ means that any executable and maximal action under γ in T is also executable and maximal under γ in T'.

Example 4. *Let $T = \{(r_1, 2)\} : \{(r_2, 3)\} : FIN$, $T' = \{(r_1, 2)\} : FIN + \{(r_1, 1), (r_2, 1)\} : \{(r_3, 1)\} : FIN$. Then, task T has only one transition: $T \xrightarrow{\{(r_1,2)\}} \{(r_2, 3)\} : FIN$, and $T' \xrightarrow{(r_1,2)} FIN$. So, we have: $\uparrow_T^{T'}$.*

Furthermore, suppose $\gamma_1 = \{\overline{r_1}\}$, then $\{(r_1, 2)\} \trianglelefteq_T \gamma_1$ and $\{(r_1, 2)\} \trianglelefteq_{T'} \gamma_1$. Thus, $\trianglelefteq\uparrow_T^{T'}(\gamma_1)$. But for $\gamma_2 = \{\overline{r_1}, \overline{r_2}\}$, "$\trianglelefteq\uparrow_T^{T'}(\gamma_2)$" does not hold. This is because $\{(r_1, 2)\} \trianglelefteq_T \gamma_2$ and $\{(r_1, 2)\} \ntrianglelefteq_{T'} \gamma_2$.

Definition 9. *Let $T_i, \sum_{j=1}^{k_i} \alpha_{ij} : T_{ij} \in \mathsf{T}$, and $\{\alpha_{ij}^\flat | j = 1, \cdots, k_i\}$ be a single set, $i = 1, \cdots, m$. We say, task "vector" $(T_1, \cdots, T_m)$ can converge at an element with task "vector"$(\sum_{j=1}^{k_1} \alpha_{1j} : T_{1j}, \cdots, \sum_{j=1}^{k_m} \alpha_{mj} : T_{mj})$, denoted by*

$$\trianglelefteq\bullet_{(T_1,\cdots,T_m)}^{(\sum_{j=1}^{k_1} \alpha_{1j}:T_{1j},\cdots,\sum_{j=1}^{k_m} \alpha_{mj}:T_{mj})},$$

if for any $\gamma \in \mathsf{Act_G}$, the following property holds:

$\sum_{i=1}^{m} T_i \xrightarrow{\alpha} T$ with $\alpha \trianglelefteq_{\sum_{i=1}^{m} T_i} \gamma$ and $\alpha_{i_0 j_0} \in \bigcup_{i=1}^{m} \{\alpha_{ij} | j = 1, \cdots, k_i\}$ with

$\alpha_{i_0 j_0} \trianglelefteq_{\sum_{i=1}^{m} \sum_{j=1}^{k_i} \alpha_{ij}:T_{ij}} \gamma$ imply that there exist $l \in \{1, \cdots, m\}$ and $s \in \{1, \cdots, k_l\}$

such that $T_l \xrightarrow{\alpha} T$ and $\alpha_{ls} \trianglelefteq_{\sum_{i=1}^{m} \sum_{j=1}^{k_i} \alpha_{ij}:T_{ij}} \gamma$.

Intuitively, $\trianglelefteq\bullet_{(T_1,\cdots,T_m)}^{(\sum_{j=1}^{k_1} \alpha_{1j}:T_{1j},\cdots,\sum_{j=1}^{k_m} \alpha_{mj}:T_{mj})}$ means that for task "vectors "$(T_1, \cdots, T_m)$ and $(\sum_{j=1}^{k_1} \alpha_{1j} : T_{1j}, \cdots, \sum_{j=1}^{k_m} \alpha_{mj} : T_{mj})$, the maximal transition and the maximal action about the two sums of their elements under any resource grant can happen at a common element.

Example 5. *Let $T_1 = \{(r_1, 1), (r_3, 2)\} : \{(r_2, 1)\} : FIN + \{(r_2, 2), (r_3, 3)\} : FIN$, $T_2 = \{(r_1, 2), (r_2, 3)\} : \{(r_2, 2)\} : FIN + \{(r_1, 3), (r_3, 2)\} : \{(r_1, 1)\} : FIN$, $\alpha_{11} = \{(r_2, 2), (r_3, 2)\}$, $\alpha_{12} = \{(r_2, 1), (r_3, 3)\}$, $\alpha_{21} = \{(r_1, 2)\}$, $\alpha_{22} = \{(r_1, 3)\}$, and T_{11}, T_{12}, T_{21}, T_{22} be any tasks. Then we have:*

$$\trianglelefteq\bullet_{(T_1,T_2)}^{(\alpha_{11}:T_{11}+\alpha_{12}:T_{12},\alpha_{21}:T_{21}+\alpha_{22}:T_{22})}.$$

Because for any $\gamma \in \{\{\overline{r_1}, \overline{r_2}\}, \{\overline{r_1}, \overline{r_3}\}, \{\overline{r_2}, \overline{r_3}\}, \{\overline{r_1}, \overline{r_2}, \overline{r_3}\}\}$, we can verify that the maximal transition and the maximal action for (T_1, T_2) and $(\alpha_{11} : T_{11} + \alpha_{12} : T_{12}, \alpha_{21} : T_{21} + \alpha_{22} : T_{22})$ can do evolution at a common element.

Similar to Theorem 3, the following Theorem 4 shows that we need only consider a finite number of resource grants to verify whether "$\trianglelefteq\bullet_{(T_1,\cdots,T_m)}^{(\sum_{j=1}^{k_1} \alpha_{1j}:T_{1j},\cdots,\sum_{j=1}^{k_m} \alpha_{mj}:T_{mj})}$" holds or not.

Theorem 4. *Let $T_i, \sum_{j=1}^{k_i} \alpha_{ij} : T_{ij} \in \mathsf{T}$, and $\{\alpha_{ij}^{\flat} | j = 1, \cdots, k_i\}$ be a single set, $i = 1, \cdots, m$; $A = \{\alpha_{i1}^{\flat} | i = 1, \cdots, m\}$. Then the following two propositions are equivalent:*

(1) "$\trianglelefteq\bullet_{(T_1,\cdots,T_m)}^{(\sum_{j=1}^{k_1} \alpha_{1j}:T_{1j},\cdots,\sum_{j=1}^{k_m} \alpha_{mj}:T_{mj})}$" holds;

(2) For any α with $\sum_{i=1}^{m} T_i \xrightarrow{\alpha}$ and any nonempty subset $B \subseteq A$, assuming $C = \bigcup_{\rho^{\flat} \in B} \rho^{\flat}$, the following property holds:

$$\sum_{i=1}^{m} T_i \xrightarrow{\alpha} T \text{ with } \alpha \trianglelefteq_{\sum_{i=1}^{m} T_i} \overline{\alpha^{\flat} \cup C}$$

and

$$\alpha_{i_0 j_0} \trianglelefteq_{\sum_{i=1}^{m} \sum_{j=1}^{k_i} \alpha_{ij}:T_{ij}} \overline{\alpha^{\flat} \cup C},\ i_0 \in \{1, \cdots, m\},\ j_0 \in \{1, \cdots, k_{i_0}\},$$

imply that there exist $l \in \{1, \cdots, m\}$ and $s \in \{1, \cdots, k_l\}$ such that

$$T_l \xrightarrow{\alpha} T \text{ and } \alpha_{ls} \trianglelefteq_{\sum_{i=1}^{m} \sum_{j=1}^{k_i} \alpha_{ij}:T_{ij}} \overline{\alpha^{\flat} \cup C}.$$

In order to define the length of a task pair (T_{11}, T_{21}), we introduce the following concepts.

Definition 10. *Assume* $(T_{11}, T_{21}), (T_{12}, T_{22}) \in \mathsf{T} \times \mathsf{T}$. *If there exist* $\gamma \in \mathsf{Act_G}$ *and* $\alpha_1, \beta_1 \in \mathsf{Act_R}$ *such that*

$$T_{11} \xrightarrow{\alpha_1} T_{12} \text{ with } \alpha_1 \trianglelefteq_{T_{11}} \gamma \text{ and } T_{21} \xrightarrow{\beta_1} T_{22} \text{ with } \beta_1 \trianglelefteq_{T_{21}} \gamma,$$

then we say (T_{11}, T_{21}) *can evolve into* (T_{12}, T_{22}), *denoted by* $(T_{11}, T_{21}) \rightarrow (T_{12}, T_{22})$.

Definition 11. *If* $(T_{1i}, T_{2i}) \rightarrow (T_{1,i+1}, T_{2,i+1})$, $i = 1, \cdots, n$, *then we say the sequence*

$$sq : (T_{11}, T_{21}) \rightarrow (T_{12}, T_{22}) \rightarrow \cdots \rightarrow (T_{1,n+1}, T_{2,n+1})$$

is an evolving sequence of (T_{11}, T_{21}).

Definition 12. *Assume that* $sq : (T_{11}, T_{21}) \rightarrow (T_{12}, T_{22}) \rightarrow \cdots \rightarrow (T_{1,n+1}, T_{2,n+1})$ *is an evolving sequence. If* $(T_{1,n+1}, T_{2,n+1}) = (FIN, FIN)$ *and* $(T_{1i}, T_{2i}) \neq (FIN, FIN)$, $i = 1, 2, \cdots, n$, *then we say that the evolving sequence sq is a terminated sequence of* (T_{11}, T_{21}), *and the length of sequence sq is* n, *denoted by* $h(sq) = n$.

The length of (T_{11}, T_{21}) *is the maximal length in all the terminated sequences of* (T_{11}, T_{21}), *denoted by* $H(T_{11}, T_{21})$, *i.e.*

$$H(T_{11}, T_{21}) = \max\{h(sq) | sq \text{ is a terminated sequence of } (T_{11}, T_{21})\}\ .$$

Especially, we set the length of (FIN, FIN) *to be* 0, *i.e.* $H(FIN, FIN) = 0$.

For a task pair consisting of task constants, its length may be undefined; for a task pair consisting of tasks without containing task constants, we can prove that its length is a finite number. For convenience, we will call "finite process" instead of "process without containing constants" in this paper.

4.2 Rules

Proof system P_{TT} consists of eleven inference rules, which are listed in Table 2. These rules are used to deduce a binary relation "$\preccurlyeq$" over task set T. If $T_2 \preccurlyeq T_1$ can be inferred by using rules in P_{TT} in a finite number of steps, we say that $T_2 \preccurlyeq T_1$ is a theorem of P_{TT}, denoted by $\vdash T_2 \preccurlyeq T_1$.

Informally, we will explain every rule in P_{TT} as follows:

- Rules R_1, R_2 and R_3 are three axioms in P_{TT}. Atomic task process FIN means that it has no resource request and has no action to execute. "$\preccurlyeq$"means more or equal weak-demanding. So, at the respect of resource demanding FIN is equal to itself and $\emptyset : FIN$ is equal to FIN.
- Rule R_4 says that "$\preccurlyeq$"is transitive, i.e. if task T_1 is not less weak-demanding than T_2 and T_2 is not less weak-demanding than T_3, then T_1 is not less weak-demanding than T_3.
- R_5 says that if a task's first resource request is not less than another task's first resource request and its subsequent task is not less weak-demanding than the other's subsequent task, then it is also not less weak-demanding than the other one.

Table 2. Proof system P_{TT}

R_1 $$FIN \preccurlyeq FIN$$

R_2 $$\emptyset : FIN \preccurlyeq FIN$$

R_3 $$FIN \preccurlyeq \emptyset : FIN$$

R_4 $$\frac{T_3 \preccurlyeq T_2,\ T_2 \preccurlyeq T_1}{T_3 \preccurlyeq T_1}$$

R_5 $$\frac{T_2 \preccurlyeq T_1,\ \beta^\flat \subseteq \alpha^\flat}{\beta : T_2 \preccurlyeq \alpha : T_1}$$

R_6 $$\frac{T_0 \preccurlyeq \sum_{i=1}^{n} \alpha_i : T_i,\ \alpha_{n+1}^\flat \in \{\alpha_i^\flat | i = 1, \cdots, n\},\ \uparrow_{\sum_{i=1}^{n} \alpha_i : T_i}^{\sum_{i=1}^{n+1} \alpha_i : T_i}}{T_0 \preccurlyeq \sum_{i=1}^{n+1} \alpha_i : T_i}$$

R_7 $$\frac{\sum_{i=1}^{n} \alpha_{1i} : T_{1i} \preccurlyeq \sum_{j=1}^{m} \beta_{2j} : T_{2j},\ \forall j, l \in \{1, \cdots, m\}.\ \beta_{2j}^\flat = \beta_{2l}^\flat,\quad \exists j_0 \in \{1, \cdots, m\}.\ T_{1,n+1} \preccurlyeq T_{2j_0} \wedge \sum_{j=1}^{m} \beta_{2j} : T_{2j} \xrightarrow{\beta_{2j_0}}}{\sum_{i=1}^{n+1} \alpha_{1i} : T_{1i} \preccurlyeq \sum_{j=1}^{m} \beta_{2j} : T_{2j}}$$

R_8 $$\frac{\forall i \in \mathbb{N} : 1 \leq i \leq m.\ T_i \preccurlyeq \sum_{j=1}^{k_i} \alpha_{ij} : T_{ij},\ \trianglelefteq\!\bullet_{(T_1, \cdots, T_m)}^{(\sum_{i=1}^{k_1} \alpha_{1i} : T_{1i}, \cdots, \sum_{i=1}^{k_m} \alpha_{mi} : T_{mi})},\quad \forall j \in \mathbb{N} : 1 \leq j \leq m.\ \trianglelefteq\!\uparrow_{T_j}^{\sum_{i=1}^{m} T_i} (\overline{\alpha_{j1}^\flat}),\ \forall l, s \in \mathbb{N} : 1 \leq l < s \leq m.\ \alpha_{l1}^\flat \neq \alpha_{s1}^\flat}{\sum_{i=1}^{m} T_i \preccurlyeq \sum_{j=1}^{m} \sum_{i=1}^{k_j} \alpha_{ji} : T_{ji}}$$

R_9 $$\frac{\exists i_0 \in \mathbb{N} : 1 \leq i_0 \leq n.\ \alpha_{n+1} \prec \alpha_{i_0}}{\sum_{i=1}^{n+1} \alpha_i : T_i \preccurlyeq \sum_{i=1}^{n} \alpha_i : T_i \preccurlyeq \sum_{i=1}^{n+1} \alpha_i : T_i}$$

R_{10} $$\frac{\sigma \text{ is a permutation of the set } \{1, 2, \cdots, m\}}{\sum_{i=1}^{m} \alpha_i : T_i \preccurlyeq \sum_{i=1}^{m} \alpha_{\sigma(i)} : T_{\sigma(i)}}$$

R_{11} $$\frac{\sum_{i=1}^{n} \alpha_{1i} : T_{1i} \preccurlyeq \sum_{i=1}^{m} \alpha_{2i} : T_{2i},\quad \forall j \in \mathbb{N} : 1 \leq j \leq m.\ \alpha_{1,n+1} \not\trianglelefteq_{\sum_{i=1}^{n+1} \alpha_{1i} : T_{1i}} \overline{\alpha_{1,n+1}^\flat \cup \alpha_{2j}^\flat}}{\sum_{i=1}^{n+1} \alpha_{1i} : T_{1i} \preccurlyeq \sum_{i=1}^{m} \alpha_{2i} : T_{2i}}$$

- Rule R_6 talks about the weak-demanding relation changes when adding a new branch on the more weak-demanding task. If the new branch's first resource request set appears in the original more weak-demanding task and it does not prevent the original more weak-demanding task from executing, then after adding such a new branch it is also more weak-demanding.
- R_7 reflects the weak-demanding relation changes when adding a new branch on the less weak-demanding task. If the direct successor of the new branch is less weak-demanding than a direct successor of the original more weak-demanding task, and all the first resource request sets without priorities are the same in the more weak-demanding task, then after adding a new branch on the less weak-demanding task it is also less weak-demanding.
- R_8 tells us that for two task "vectors", if one is more weak-demanding at every element than the other, then under some certain conditions the "sum"of its all elements is more weak-demanding than the "sum"of all elements in the other task "vector".

- R_9 means that after deleting such a branch as its first action can be preempted by some first action in the original task, it is still equal to the original task at the respect of resource demand.
- R_{10} says that the weak-demanding relation is independent of the order of executing branches in a task.
- R_{11} describes another case about adding a new branch on the less weak-demanding task. If the first resource request in the new branch is less than some resource requests in the original task under some resource grants, or the first action in the new branch can be preempted by some action in the original task, then after adding such a branch it is also less weak-demanding.

In the following we will show the reasoning ability of proof system P_{TT} and how to use it through an example.

Example 6. *Assuming tasks $T_1, T_2, T_{11}, T_{12}, T_{13}, T_{14}, T_{21}, T_{22}, T_{23}$ be defined as follows:*
$T_1 = \{(r_1,2),(r_2,3)\} : T_{11} + \{(r_1,1),(r_2,2)\} : T_{12} + \{(r_2,2),(r_3,4)\} : T_{13}+ \{(r_2,3),(r_3,1)\} : T_{14},$
$T_2 = \{(r_1,1),(r_2,3)\} : T_{21} + \{(r_3,2)\} : T_{22} + \{(r_3,1),(r_4,2)\} : T_{23},$
$T_{11} = \{(r_2,3),(r_3,1),(r_4,2)\} : FIN,$
$T_{12} = \{(r_2,4)\} : \{(r_1,1)\} : FIN,$
$T_{13} = \{(r_3,2),(r_4,2)\} : \{(r_2,1)\} : FIN + \{(r_3,3),(r_4,1)\} : \{(r_4,2)\} : FIN,$
$T_{14} = \{(r_4,2),(r_5,3)\} : FIN,$
$T_{21} = \{(r_3,2),(r_4,3)\} : FIN + \{(r_3,1)\} : \{(r_2,2)\} : FIN,$
$T_{22} = \{(r_3,1)\} : \{(r_2,2)\} : FIN,$
$T_{23} = \{(r_5,1)\} : FIN.$
Then, by using proof system P_{TT} we can prove: $\vdash T_2 \preccurlyeq T_1$.

Proof Strategy. First, we delete summands in T_1 and T_2 whose first actions are not executable. For T_1, we delete the summand $\{(r_1,1),(r_2,2)\} : T_{12}$. For T_2, there are no such summands to be deleted. Let $T_1' = \{(r_1,2),(r_2,3)\} : T_{11} + \{(r_2,2),(r_3,4)\} : T_{13}+ \{(r_2,3),(r_3,1)\} : T_{14}$.

Secondly, we divide T_1' into some "small "tasks in terms of resource set of its first action. For T_1', it can be divided into two tasks, T_{11}' and T_{12}'. $T_{11}' = \{(r_1,2),(r_2,3)\} : T_{11}, T_{12}' = \{(r_2,2),(r_3,4)\} : T_{13}+ \{(r_2,3),(r_3,1)\} : T_{14}$.

Thirdly, for T_{11}' and T_{12}', we respectively search for their matching summands in T_2 with respect to "$\preccurlyeq$"; and for every summand in T_2, we also search for its matching "small "task. Under the resource grant of the first action of T_{12}', i.e. $\{\overline{r_2}, \overline{r_3}\}$, we search for maximal actions in T_2. The corresponding maximal action in T_2 is $\{(r_3,2)\}$. Then, prove which one in "$\vdash T_{22} \preccurlyeq T_{13}$"and "$\vdash T_{22} \preccurlyeq T_{14}$"holds. We can get: $\vdash T_{22} \preccurlyeq T_{13}$. Under the resource grant of the first action of T_{11}', we need do similar work and can get: $\vdash T_{21} \preccurlyeq T_{11}$. The remainder in T_2 is $\{(r_3,1),(r_4,2)\} : T_{23}$, which need be built connections with T_{11}' or with T_{12}'. We can consider using rules R_7 and R_{11}. Because $\{(r_3,1),(r_4,2)\}$ does not satisfy conditions in R_{11}. Only R_7 may be usable. According to R_7, We need determine which one among "$\vdash T_{23} \preccurlyeq T_{11}$", "$\vdash T_{23} \preccurlyeq T_{13}$"and "$\vdash T_{23} \preccurlyeq T_{14}$"holds. In fact, "$\vdash T_{23} \preccurlyeq T_{14}$"holds.

Finally, we use choice operator $+$ to connect the small tasks according to R_8.

5 The Soundness and Completeness of P_{TT}

In this section we will give two theorems, which illustrate that the proof system P_{TT} is sound and complete with respect to the semantic definition of weak demand relation. The two results show that the binary relation "$\preccurlyeq$"gotten by P_{TT} is exactly the weak demand relation "$\preccurlyeq_D$"over the set of task processes without containing task constants.

Theorem 5 (Soundness). *Assuming tasks $T_1, T_2 \in \mathsf{T}$, if $\vdash T_2 \preccurlyeq T_1$, then $T_2 \preccurlyeq_D T_1$.*

Proof Sketch. We will verify by constructing weak demand relations that every rule in proof system P_{TT} preserves such a property, which is that $\vdash T_2 \preccurlyeq T_1$ implies $T_2 \preccurlyeq_D T_1$.

Proof. Because of limited space, we will only prove that Rule R_7 in P_{TT} preserves the property: $\vdash T_2 \preccurlyeq T_1$ implies $T_2 \preccurlyeq_D T_1$.

Assume that "$\sum_{i=1}^{n} \alpha_{1i} : T_{1i} \preccurlyeq \sum_{j=1}^{m} \beta_{2j} : T_{2j}$" and "$T_{1,n+1} \preccurlyeq T_{2j_0}$" respectively satisfy:

$$\sum_{i=1}^{n} \alpha_{1i} : T_{1i} \preccurlyeq_D \sum_{j=1}^{m} \beta_{2j} : T_{2j} \text{ and } T_{1,n+1} \preccurlyeq_D T_{2j_0}.$$

Then, there exists a weak demand relation $\mathcal{R}$ with

$$(\sum_{j=1}^{m} \beta_{2j} : T_{2j}, \sum_{i=1}^{n} \alpha_{1i} : T_{1i}) \in \mathcal{R} \text{ and } (T_{2j_0}, T_{1,n+1}) \in \mathcal{R}.$$

Assume

$$\mathcal{R}' = \mathcal{R} \cup \{(\sum_{j=1}^{m} \beta_{2j} : T_{2j}, \sum_{i=1}^{n+1} \alpha_{1i} : T_{1i})\}.$$

Then, $\mathcal{R}'$ is a weak demand relation if and only if $(\sum_{j=1}^{m} \beta_{2j} : T_{2j}, \sum_{i=1}^{n+1} \alpha_{1i} : T_{1i})$ in $\mathcal{R}'$ satisfies the two clauses in the definition of weak demand relation.

Assume

$$\sum_{j=1}^{m} \beta_{2j} : T_{2j} \xrightarrow{\beta_{2k}} T_{2k},\ k \in \{1, \cdots, m\}.$$

By $(\sum_{j=1}^{m} \beta_{2j} : T_{2j}, \sum_{i=1}^{n} \alpha_{1i} : T_{1i}) \in \mathcal{R}$, we know that there exists such a transition

$$\sum_{i=1}^{n} \alpha_{1i} : T_{1i} \xrightarrow{\alpha_{1l}} T_{1l} \text{ with } \alpha_{1l} \trianglelefteq_{\sum_{i=1}^{n} \alpha_{1i}:T_{1i}} \overline{\beta_{2k}^{b}} \text{ and } l \in \{1, \cdots, n\},$$

and there exists

$$\sum_{j=1}^{m} \beta_{2j} : T_{2j} \xrightarrow{\beta_{2h}} T_{2h} \text{ with } h \in \{1, \cdots, m\} \text{ and } (T_{2h}, T_{1l}) \in \mathcal{R}.$$

For $\sum_{i=1}^{n+1} \alpha_{1i} : T_{1i}$, if there is still such a transition:

$$\sum_{i=1}^{n+1} \alpha_{1i} : T_{1i} \xrightarrow{\alpha_{1l}} T_{1l} \text{ with } \alpha_{1l} \trianglelefteq_{\sum_{i=1}^{n+1} \alpha_{1i}:T_{1i}} \overline{\beta_{2k}^{b}},$$

then Clause 1 in the definition of weak demand relation is satisfied. Otherwise, either $\alpha_{1l} \prec \alpha_{1,n+1}$ or $\mathsf{res}(\alpha_{1l}) \subset \mathsf{res}(\alpha_{1,n+1}) \subseteq \mathsf{res}(\beta_{2k})$. Then, we have:

$$\sum_{i=1}^{n+1} \alpha_{1i} : T_{1i} \xrightarrow{\alpha_{1,n+1}} T_{1,n+1} \text{ and } \alpha_{1,n+1} \trianglelefteq_{\sum_{i=1}^{n+1} \alpha_{1i}:T_{1i}} \overline{\beta_{2k}^{\flat}}.$$

For $\sum_{j=1}^{m} \beta_{2j} : T_{2j}$, there is such a transition:

$$\sum_{j=1}^{m} \beta_{2j} : T_{2j} \xrightarrow{\beta_{2j_0}} T_{2j_0} \text{ with } (T_{2j_0}, T_{1,n+1}) \in \mathcal{R}.$$

And $\beta_{2j_0}^{\flat} = \beta_{2k}^{\flat}$. So we have:

$$\beta_{2j_0} \trianglelefteq_{\sum_{j=1}^{m} \beta_{2j}:T_{2j}} \overline{\beta_{2k}^{\flat}}.$$

Thus, Clause 1 in the definition of weak demand relation is still satisfied.

On the other side, for any $\gamma \in \mathsf{Act}_{\mathsf{G}}$, assume that

$$\sum_{i=1}^{n+1} \alpha_{1i} : T_{1i} \xrightarrow{\rho} T_{\rho} \text{ satisfies } \rho \trianglelefteq_{\sum_{i=1}^{n+1} \alpha_{1i}:T_{1i}} \gamma$$

and

$$\sum_{j=1}^{m} \beta_{2j} : T_{2j} \xrightarrow{\rho'} T_{\rho'} \text{ satisfies } \rho' \trianglelefteq_{\sum_{j=1}^{m} \beta_{2j}:T_{2j}} \gamma.$$

If $\rho = \alpha_{1,n+1}$ and $T_{\rho} = T_{1,n+1}$, then there is such a transition:

$$\sum_{j=1}^{m} \beta_{2j} : T_{2j} \xrightarrow{\beta_{2j_0}} T_{2j_0} \text{ satisfying } \beta_{2j_0} \trianglelefteq_{\sum_{j=1}^{m} \beta_{2j}:T_{2j}} \gamma \text{ and } (T_{2j_0}, T_{1,n+1}) \in \mathcal{R}.$$

Otherwise, $\rho \in \{\alpha_{1i} | i = 1, \cdots, n\}$ and $T_{\rho} \in \{T_{1i} | i = 1, \cdots, n\}$. So we can assume $\rho = \alpha_{1u}$ and $T_{\rho} = T_{1u}$, $u \in \{1, \cdots, n\}$. Furthermore, we have:

$$\sum_{i=1}^{n+1} \alpha_{1i} : T_{1i} \xrightarrow{\alpha_{1u}} T_{1u} \text{ with } \alpha_{1u} \trianglelefteq_{\sum_{i=1}^{n+1} \alpha_{1i}:T_{1i}} \gamma$$

and

$$\sum_{i=1}^{n} \alpha_{1i} : T_{1i} \xrightarrow{\alpha_{1u}} T_{1u} \text{ with } \alpha_{1u} \trianglelefteq_{\sum_{i=1}^{n} \alpha_{1i}:T_{1i}} \gamma.$$

According to $(\sum_{j=1}^{m} \beta_{2j} : T_{2j}, \sum_{i=1}^{n} \alpha_{1i} : T_{1i}) \in \mathcal{R}$, we can get:

$$\sum_{j=1}^{m} \beta_{2j} : T_{2j} \xrightarrow{\beta_{2v}} T_{2v} \text{ with } \beta_{2v} \trianglelefteq_{\sum_{j=1}^{m} \beta_{2j}:T_{2j}} \gamma \text{ and } (T_{2v}, T_{1u}) \in \mathcal{R}.$$

So, Clause 2 in the definition of weak demand relation is satisfied.

From the above analysis, we know that $\mathcal{R}'$ is a weak demand relation. Thus,

$$\sum_{i=1}^{n+1} \alpha_{1i} : T_{1i} \preccurlyeq_D \sum_{j=1}^{m} \beta_{2j} : T_{2j}.$$

□

Theorem 6 (Completeness). *Assuming that tasks $T_1, T_2 \in \mathsf{T}$ do not contain any task constant, if $T_2 \preccurlyeq_D T_1$, then $\vdash T_2 \preccurlyeq T_1$.*

Proof Sketch. Because T_1 and T_2 do not contain task constants. $H(T_1, T_2)$ is a finite number. We will make induction on the length of (T_1, T_2), and analyze it from three cases, i.e. 1. $T_1 \neq FIN, T_2 = FIN$; 2. $T_1 = FIN, T_2 \neq FIN$; 3. $T_1 \neq FIN$, $T_2 \neq FIN$.

Proof. Because of limited space, we will only prove the case: 1. $T_1 \neq FIN, T_2 = FIN$ when making induction on the length of (T_1, T_2).

Let $T_{11} = T_1$ and $T_{21} = T_2$.

Base: $H(T_{11}, T_{21}) = 0$.

According to the definition of $H(T_{11}, T_{21})$, we can get: $(T_{11}, T_{21}) = (FIN, FIN)$. By Rule R_1, we have: $\vdash T_{21} \preccurlyeq T_{11}$.

Induction: Assume that any finite process pair (T_{11}, T_{21}) such that $T_{21} \preccurlyeq_D T_{11}$ and $H(T_{11}, T_{21}) \leq n$ can be inferred in P_{TT}, i.e. $\vdash T_{21} \preccurlyeq T_{11}$.

Let the length of $H(T_{11}, T_{21})$ be $n+1$, i.e. $H(T_{11}, T_{21}) = n+1$. Then, $(T_{11}, T_{21}) \neq (FIN, FIN)$. In the following, we will only discuss the case: $T_{11} \neq FIN$ and $T_{21} = FIN$.

Without losing generality, assume finite process $T_{11} = \sum_{i=1}^{m} \alpha_{1i} : T_i^1$. Let $A = \{\alpha | T_{11} \xrightarrow{\alpha}\}$, $A^\flat = \{\alpha^\flat | \alpha \in A\}$, then, according to the definition of $T_{21} \preccurlyeq_D T_{11}$ and process FIN having only one transition: $FIN \xrightarrow{\emptyset} FIN$, we can get: for any $\beta \in A^\flat$, there exists $\alpha_\beta \in A$ such that $\alpha_\beta^\flat = \beta$, $T_{11} \xrightarrow{\alpha_\beta} T_{\alpha_\beta}$ and $FIN \preccurlyeq_D T_{\alpha_\beta}$. So, there exists $\{\alpha_{1l_1}, \alpha_{1l_2}, \cdots, \alpha_{1l_k}\} \subseteq A$ satisfying: $1 \leq l_1 < l_2 < \cdots < l_k \leq m$, $\forall l_i \neq l_j \in \{l_1, l_2, \cdots, l_k\}.\alpha_{1l_i}^\flat \neq \alpha_{1l_j}^\flat$, $\{\alpha_{1l_1}^\flat, \alpha_{1l_2}^\flat, \cdots, \alpha_{1l_k}^\flat\} = A^\flat$ and $\forall l_j \in \{l_1, l_2, \cdots, l_k\}.T_{11} \xrightarrow{\alpha_{1l_j}} T_{l_j}^1$ with $FIN \preccurlyeq_D T_{l_j}^1$. Thus,

$$(T_{11}, T_{21}) \to (T_{l_j}^1, FIN),\ \forall l_j \in \{l_1, l_2, \cdots, l_k\}.$$

Furthermore,

$$H(T_{l_j}^1, FIN) \leq n,\ \forall l_j \in \{l_1, l_2, \cdots, l_k\}.$$

According to the induction hypothesis, we have:

$$\vdash FIN \preccurlyeq T_{l_j}^1,\ \forall l_j \in \{l_1, l_2, \cdots, l_k\}.$$

By Rule R_5, we can get:

$$\vdash \emptyset : FIN \preccurlyeq \alpha_{1l_j} : T_{l_j}^1,\ \forall l_j \in \{l_1, l_2, \cdots, l_k\}.$$

For being simple, let

$$A_j = \{\alpha \in A | \alpha^\flat = \alpha^\flat_{1l_j}\} = \{\alpha_{1i} | 1 + l_{j-1} \leq i \leq l_j\},\ j = 1, \cdots, k.$$

Here, $l_0 = 0$. For any $l_j \in \{l_1, \cdots, l_k\}$, using Rule R_6 for $l_j - l_{j-1}$ times, we can get:

$$\vdash \emptyset : FIN \preccurlyeq \sum_{i=1+l_{j-1}}^{l_j} \alpha_{1i} : T_i^1.$$

Assuming $T_i = \emptyset : FIN, i = 1, \cdots, k$, then we have:

$$\trianglelefteq\uparrow_{T_j}^{\sum_{i=1}^{k} T_i} (\overline{\alpha^\flat_{1l_j}}),\ j = 1, \cdots, k,\ \text{and}\ \trianglelefteq\bullet_{(T_1, \cdots, T_k)}^{(\sum_{i=1}^{l_1} \alpha_{1i}:T_i^1, \cdots, \sum_{i=l_{k-1}+1}^{l_k} \alpha_{1i}:T_i^1)}.$$

By Rule R_8, we can get:

$$\vdash \sum_{i=1}^{k} T_i \preccurlyeq \sum_{i=1}^{l_k} \alpha_{1i} : T_i^1.$$

By rules R_1 and R_5, we have:

$$\vdash \emptyset : FIN \preccurlyeq \emptyset : FIN.$$

Using Rule R_6 for $k - 1$ times, we have:

$$\vdash \emptyset : FIN \preccurlyeq \sum_{i=1}^{k} T_i.$$

According to rules R_3 and R_4, we can get:

$$\vdash FIN \preccurlyeq \sum_{i=1}^{l_k} \alpha_{1i} : T_i^1.$$

1.1° If $l_k = m$, then the above formula is:

$$\vdash FIN \preccurlyeq \sum_{i=1}^{m} \alpha_{1i} : T_i^1,\ i.e.\ \vdash T_{21} \preccurlyeq T_{11}.$$

1.2° If $l_k < m$, then, by the definitions of A and A_j $(j = 1, \cdots, k)$ we have: $\alpha_{1i} \notin A,\ i = l_k + 1, \cdots, m$. For any $i \in \{l_k + 1, \cdots, m\}$, there exists $\beta \in A$ with $\alpha_{1i} \prec \beta$. Using Rule R_9 for $m - l_k$ times, we can get:

$$\vdash \sum_{i=1}^{l_k} \alpha_{1i} : T_i^1 \preccurlyeq \sum_{i=1}^{m} \alpha_{1i} : T_i^1.$$

By Rule R_4, we have:

$$\vdash FIN \preccurlyeq \sum_{i=1}^{m} \alpha_{1i} : T_i^1,\ i.e.\ \vdash T_{21} \preccurlyeq T_{11}.$$

□

6 Conclusion

Inspired by the demand relation in [12], this paper proposed a weak demand relation that covers some tasks which are not in any demand relation and whose schedulabilities are comparable. We also explored some properties of weak demand relation. In particular, for two tasks in a weak demand relation their schedulabilities are comparable. Then, we built a proof system P_{TT} for the weak demand relation between task processes without containing task constants. Moreover, we proved that the weak demand relation $\preccurlyeq_D$ over the set of tasks without containing task constants is exactly the binary relation $\preccurlyeq$ over the same set, which is gotten in P_{TT}.

It is difficult to introduce inference rules about the weak demand relation between two task constants. A task constant is different from a task process which does not contain task constants. A task process without containing task constants will evolve into FIN after finite movings. However, a task constant will always transform to itself at some step. There is no such a "base"similar to process FIN which can be relied on in inductively reasoning about the weak demand relation. Additionally, our weak demand relation is still not complete with respect to such tasks that their schedulabilites are comparable. There exist some tasks whose schedulabilites are comparable and which are not in any weak demand relation. Such tasks' existence is partly caused by the first clause in the definition of weak demand relation. Now we have not found an appropriate way to characterize such tasks.

In the near future, we will continue to pay our attention to solving the above problems. And exploring the proof complexity about proof system P_{TT} and the topic of automating the proof system P_{TT} is also in our future work. We hope some readers could give us some advices. Besides, we plan to study the hierarchies between supplies and their axiomatizations too.

Acknowledgements. We wish to thank some teachers for helping to significantly improve this work. Huibiao Zhu suggested us explaining every rule in our proof system. Yuncheng Jiang gave us advices to add some simple examples. Yongxin Zhao discussed the abstraction in this paper with us. Anna Philippou and Hengyang Wu gave us encouragements. We appreciate the referees' suggestions. We would also like to acknowledge support from Natural Science Foundation of China (Grant No: 61202105 and No: 61061130541), Shanghai Leading Academic Discipline Project(Grant No: B412) and "085 Knowledge Innovation Program" Project funding.

References

1. Ben-Abdallah, H., Choi, J.-Y., Clarke, D., Kim, Y.S., Lee, I., Xie, H.-L.: A Process Algebraic Approach to the Schedulability Analysis of Real-Time Systems. Real-Time Systems 15, 189–219 (1998)
2. Bucci, G., Fedeli, A., Sassoli, L., Vicario, E.: Modeling Flexible Real Time Systems with Preemptive Time Petri Nets. In: Proceedings of ECRT 2003, pp. 279–285. IEEE Computer Society, Los Alamitos (2003)

3. Easwaran, A., Lee, I., Sokolsky, O.: Interface Algebra for Analysis of Hierarchical Real-Time Systems. Presented at Foundations of Interface Technologies, FIT 2008, Satellite Workshop of ETAPS 2008 (April 2008), http://repository.upenn.edu/cis_papers/373
4. Feng, X., Mok, A.: A Model of Hierarchical Real-Time Virtual Resources. In: Proceeding of RTSS 2002, pp. 26–35. IEEE Computer Society, Los Alamitos (2002)
5. Fersman, E., Krcál, P., Pettersson, P., Yi, W.: Task automata: Schedulability, Decidability and Undecidability. Information and Computation 205(8), 1149–1172 (2007)
6. Fersman, E., Pettersson, P., Yi, W.: Timed Automata with Asynchronous Processes: Schedulability and Decidability. In: Katoen, J.-P., Stevens, P. (eds.) TACAS 2002. LNCS, vol. 2280, pp. 67–82. Springer, Heidelberg (2002)
7. Henzinger, T.A., Matic, S.: An Interface Algebra for Real-Time Components. In: Proceedings of RTAS 2006, pp. 253–263. IEEE Computer Society, Los Alamitos (2006)
8. Lee, I., Brémond-Grégoire, P., Gerber, R.: A Process Algebraic Approach to the Specification and Analysis of Resource-Bound Real-Time Systems. Proceedings of the IEEE 82(1), 158–171 (1994)
9. Lee, I., Philippou, A., Sokolsky, O.: Resources in Process Algebra. Journal of Logic and Algebraic Programming 72, 98–122 (2007)
10. Mousavi, M., Reniers, M., Basten, T., Chaudron, M.: PARS: A Process Algebra with Resources and Schedulers. In: Larsen, K.G., Niebert, P. (eds.) FORMATS 2003. LNCS, vol. 2791, pp. 134–150. Springer, Heidelberg (2004)
11. Núñez, M., Rodríguez, I.: PAMR: A Process Algebra for the Management of Resources in Concurrent Systems. In: Kim, M., Chin, B., Kang, S., Lee, D. (eds.) FORTE 2001. IFIP, vol. 69, pp. 169–184. Springer, Heidelberg (2002)
12. Philippou, A., Lee, I., Sokolsky, O.: PADS: An Approach to Modeling Resource Demand and Supply for the Formal Analysis of Hierarchical Scheduling. Theoretical Computer Science 413(1), 2–20 (2012)
13. Shin, I., Lee, I.: Compositional Real-Time Scheduling Framework. In: Proceeding of RTSS 2004, pp. 57–67. IEEE Computer Society, Los Alamitos (2004)
14. Thiele, L., Wandeler, E., Stoimenov, N.: Real-Time Interfaces for Composing Real-Time Systems. In: Proceedings of EMSOFT 2006, pp. 34–43. ACM, New York (2006)

Scope Logic: An Extension to Hoare Logic for Pointers and Recursive Data Structures *

Zhao Jianhua and Li Xuandong

State Key Laboratory of Novel Software Technology
Dept. of Computer Sci. and Tech. Nanjing University
Nanjing, Jiangsu, P.R. China 210093
{zhaojh,lxd}@nju.edu.cn

Abstract. This paper presents an extension to Hoare Logic for pointer program verification. The main observation leading to this logic is that the value of an expression e depends only on the contents stored in a finite set of memory units. This set can be specified using another expression (called the memory scope of e) constructed syntactically from e. A set of construction rules are given in this paper for expressions which may contain recursive functions (predicates). It is also observed that the memory scope of e is a super set of the memory scope of the memory scope of e. Based on this, local reasoning can be supported using assertion variables which represent arbitrary assertions. Program-point-specific expressions are used to specify the relations between different program points. Another feature of this logic is that for formulas with no user-defined functions, the weakest-preconditions can be calculated w.r.t. assignments.

1 Introduction

Hoare Logic[1] can not deal with pointer programs because of pointer alias, i.e. many pointers may refer to one memory location. Some extensions to Hoare Logic have been made to deal with pointers or shared mutable data structures [2][3][4]. Among them, Separation Logic is the most successful one. In that logic, the separation-conjunction connective $*$ is introduced to specify that two assertions hold on disjoint subheaps respectively. Based on this, heap-manipulation programs can be specified and verified. An important advantage of Separation Logic is that it supports local reasoning. However, Separation Logic is counter-intuitive to some extent. This may cause some difficulties to software engineers. For example, a programmer may use $\texttt{isList}(p) \wedge \texttt{isList}(q)$ to specify that both p and q point to lists. However, in Separation Logic, it also means that $\texttt{isList}(p)$ and $\texttt{isList}(q)$ hold for the exact same heap, which implies that p and q point to the same list. It is also difficult to use many existing logic tools designed for conventional first order logic because of the new logical connective and the new semantic of conventional connectives.

* This paper is supported by the Chinese National 863 Project, NO.2011AA010103

Z. Liu, J. Woodcock, and H. Zhu (Eds.): ICTAC 2013, LNCS 8049, pp. 409–426, 2013.

Weakest precondition calculation is useful for code verification. Using the weakest precondition calculation, a program specification $\{p\}\ s\ \{q\}$ can be reduced into a logical formula $p \Rightarrow \mathsf{WP}(q, s)$, where $\mathsf{WP}(q, s)$ means the weakest precondition of s for q. However, the weakest precondition calculation in Separation Logic is hard to deal with using conventional logic tools, because of the separating implication $-*$ and the quantifications in the preconditions.

This paper presents another extension to Hoare Logic for verification of pointer programs with recursive data structures. This logic use conventional logical connectives only. Program states are specified by FOL formulas augmented with user-defined recursive functions.

The main observation leading to this logic is that the value of an expression (or a formula) e, which may contain recursively defined functions, depends only on the contents stored in a finite set of memory units. We present a set of rules to syntactically construct an expression (called the *memory scope* of e, denoted $\mathfrak{M}(e)$) to express this set. The value of e keeps unchanged if no memory unit in this set is modified by program statements. Another important property of the memory scopes is that a memory scope expression is the super-set of its memory scope. Based on this, our logic supports local reasoning using assertion variables.

Besides establishing that some properties hold at a given program state, people are also interested in how the values of variables and recursive data structures are changed by the program. Using program-point-specific expressions, we can specify and verify relations between different program points (states). Weakest precondition calculation is also supported in our logic for a large set of formulas w.r.t. assignment statements, using program-point-specific expressions.

This paper is organized as follows. We first describe the syntax of programs and specifications in Section 2. A set of axioms are introduced in Section 3 to model memory access and layout in pointer programs. In Section 4, we introduce the concept of memory scopes. The rules to syntactically construct memory scopes are given in this section. Two important properties about memory scopes are also discussed. The axioms and proof rules about program statements are given in Section 5. In Section 6, the weakest precondition calculation of assignments are discussed. Section 7 discusses how to support local reasoning using assertion variables. A brief description of our supporting tool is given in Section 8. Section 9 concludes this paper.

2 The Syntax of Programs and Specifications

2.1 The Type Systems and Expressions

The small program language used in this paper is strongly typed. Each expression has a static type. The following types and their operators can be used in programs. Their meanings are similar to those in the C language.

1. The integer type (**int**) and the boolean type (**bool**). Operators of these basic types can be used in programs.

2. Array types. Let t be a type and c be a positive integer constant, $\mathbf{ARR}(t, c)$ is an array type. Given an expression e with type $\mathbf{ARR}(t, c)$ and an integer-typed expression e_i, $e[e_i]$ is an expression with type t. It means the e_i^{th} elements of e if $0 \leq e_i < c$.
3. Record types. Let $t_1, \ldots, t_k$ be types, and $n_1, n_2, \ldots, n_k$ be k different names, $\mathbf{REC}((n_1, t_1), \ldots, (n_k, t_k))$ is a *record-types.* Let e be an expression of this record type, $e.n_i$ is an expression with type t_i. It means the field n_i of e.
4. Pointer types. Let t be a type, $\mathbf{P}(t)$ is a pointer type. **Ptr** is the super type of all pointer types. The symbol **nil** is used to represent the null pointer. Let e be an expression with type $\mathbf{P}(t)$.
   - The type of $*e$ is t.
   - If t is a record type $\mathbf{REC}((n_1, t_1), \ldots, (n_k, t_k))$, $e \rightarrow n_i$ and $(*e).n_i$ are expressions with type t_i. These two expressions are equivalent.
   - If t is an array type $\mathbf{ARR}(t, c)$, $(*e)[e_i]$ is an expression with type t if e_i is an expression with type **int**.

We can also define user-defined types using the form *name* := *type*. In such a definition, $\mathbf{P}(name)$ can appear in the right-hand to define recursive data types.

Example 1. The following is the definition of the node type for binary trees.

$$\texttt{Node} = \mathbf{REC}((l, \mathbf{P}(\texttt{Node})), (r, \mathbf{P}(\texttt{Node})), (K, \mathbf{int}))$$

Let v be a program variable with type `Node`, the expression $v.l \rightarrow K$ represents the field K of the left-child of v. □

2.2 The Syntax of Program Statements

The small program language has three kinds of primitive statements (**skip**, assignment, and memory allocation) and three kinds of control-flow statements (sequence, selection, and repetition). The syntax of statements is as follows.

$$st ::= \texttt{skip} \mid e_1 := e_2 \mid e := \texttt{alloc}(t) \mid st; st \mid \mathbf{if}\ (e)\ st\ \mathbf{else}\ st \mid \mathbf{while}\ (e)\ st$$

The statement `skip` does nothing. The statement $e := \texttt{alloc}(t)$ allocates a new t-typed memory block, and stores the reference to this block into the memory unit referred by L-value of e. The statement $e_1 := e_2$ stores the value of e_2 into the memory unit referred by L-value of e_1. The semantic of control-flow statements are same as those in C. For an assignment $e_1 := e_2$, the type of e_1 and e_2 must be the same and must be **int**, **bool**, or a pointer type. For a memory allocation statement $e := \texttt{alloc}(t)$, the type of e must be $\mathbf{P}(t)$. For **while**-statements and **if**-statements, the type of e must be **bool**.

Example 2. A program is depicted in Fig. 1. The first two lines declare program variables k, root and pt respectively with type **int** and $\mathbf{P}(\texttt{Node})$, where `Node` is the type defined in Example 1. This program searches a binary search tree for a node of which the field K equals k. The program variable pt is **nil** if no such node is found, otherwise it points to the node in the tree. □

```
int k;
P(Node) root, pt;
pt:=root;
while (pt ≠ nil ∧ pt→K ≠ k)
        if (k < pt → K )
           pt := pt → l
        else
           pt := pt → r;
```

Fig. 1. A program

2.3 The Syntax of Formulas and Specifications

The Syntax of Formulas. All program expressions with type **bool** can be used as formulas. For example, $\mathsf{p} \to K \geq 0$ is a formula. Besides, formulas can also use the operators associated with some abstract types, like finite sets (**SetOf**(t)) and finite lists (**ListOf**(t)). User-defined recursive functions can also be used in formulas. There are also some new kinds of expressions (formulas) as follow.

1. A free variable x. It is used in expressions of the form $\lambda x.e_1[e_2]$ or $\forall x \in e_1.e_2$ and the right-hand of function definitions.
2. The reference operator &. Given an expression e, $\&e$ gives the L-value (address) of e. Here, e must be a program variable, $*e_1$, $e_1.n$, $e_1 \to n$, or $e_1[e_2]$ for some expressions e_1 and e_2.
3. Conditional expressions $e_0?e_1 : e_2$. Here e_0 is called the *guard* of this expression. The type of e_0 must be **bool**, and e_1 and e_2 must have the same type. The type of this expression is the type of e_1(or e_2). If e_0 evaluates to **true**, the value of $e_0?e_1 : e_2$ is that of e_1; otherwise, the value is that of e_2.
4. Universal quantifier over a set $\forall x \in e_1.e_2$. The type of x, e_1, e_2 must be t, **SetOf**(t) and **bool** respectively for some t. The variable x can only appear in e_2. The expression $\forall x \in e_1.e_2$ means that for all elements x in e_1, e_2 holds.
5. Set-image expressions $\lambda x.e_1[e_2]$. The type of e_2 must be **SetOf**(t) for some t. The t-typed free variable x can only appear in e_1. Let t' be the type of e_1, the type of $\lambda x.e_1[e_2]$ is **SetOf**(t'). This expression means the set $\{e_1 | x \in e_2\}$.
6. Union expression $\bigcup e$. The type of e must be **SetOf(SetOf**(t)) for some t. The type of $\bigcup e$ is **SetOf**(t). $\bigcup e$ means the set $\{x | \exists s.(x \in s \land s \in e)\}$.
7. Program-point-specific expressions $e@i$. It is required that e contains no free variables. Such expressions are treated as special constant symbols in our logic. The next sub-subsection will give more details.

Example 3. Three recursive functions are defined in Fig. 2. NodeSet(x) yields the node set of the binary tree with root node x. The function isHBST(x) asserts that x is the root of a binary search tree. KeySet(x) yields the set of keys stored in the binary search tree.

The formula $\forall x \in \mathsf{NodeSet}(\mathsf{root} \to l).(x \to K < \mathsf{root} \to K)$ says that all the keys in the left-subtree is less than the key in the root node. The formula $\&\mathsf{pt} \to K \in (\lambda x.(\&x \to K)[\mathsf{NodeSet}(\mathsf{root})])$ says that the address of $\mathsf{pt} \to K$ is in the set of addresses of the field K of the nodes in the tree. From the axiom REC-2 presented later, this formula is equivalent to $\mathsf{pt} \in \mathsf{NodeSet}(\mathsf{root})$. □

$$
\begin{array}{l}
\mathsf{NodeSet}(x : \mathbf{P}(\mathtt{Node})) : \mathbf{SetOf}(\mathbf{P}(\mathtt{Node})) \\
\qquad \triangleq (x = \mathbf{nil})?\ \emptyset : (\{x\} \cup \mathsf{NodeSet}(x \to l) \cup \mathsf{NodeSet}(x \to r)) \\
\mathsf{isHBST}(x : \mathbf{P}(\mathtt{Node})) : \mathbf{bool} \\
\qquad \triangleq (x = \mathbf{nil})?\mathbf{true} : \mathsf{isHBST}(x \to l) \wedge \mathsf{isHBST}(x \to r) \wedge \\
\qquad\qquad\qquad\qquad\qquad \forall y \in \mathsf{NodeSet}(x \to l).(y \to K < x \to K) \wedge \\
\qquad\qquad\qquad\qquad\qquad \forall y \in \mathsf{NodeSet}(x \to r).(y \to K > x \to K) \\
\mathsf{KeySet}(x : \mathbf{P}(\mathtt{Node})) : \mathbf{SetOf}(\mathbf{int}) \triangleq \lambda x.(x \to K)[\mathsf{NodeSet}(x)]
\end{array}
$$

Fig. 2. A set of recursive functions

The Syntax of Specifications. In our logic, specifications and verifications are written in the proof-in-code form. Formulas are written at program points, which are places before and after program statements. For a sequential statement $s_1; s_2$, the point after s_1 is just the point before s_2. All the program points are uniquely numbered. A program goes through program points during its execution. A formula at a program point means that each time when the program goes to this point, the formula is evaluated to **true**.

When we concern only one statement s of the program under verification, the specification can be written as the following Hoare-triple.

$$\{i : P\}\ s\ \{j : Q\}$$

Here, i and j are respectively the program point numbers before and after s. We can write the specification as $\{P\}\ s\ \{Q\}$ if the point numbers are irrelevant.

A program point j is said to *dominates* a point i if the program must go through the point j before it goes to the point i. For the language used in this paper, j dominates i if one of the following conditions holds. (I) $j = i$ or there is a point k such that j dominates k and k dominates i; (II) j is before a statement s and i is a point in s or the point after s.

Given two program points i and j such that j dominates i, we can write $e@j$ at the program point i. It represents the value of e evaluated at the point j when the program was at the point j the last time.

At any program point i, a program-point-specific expression $e@i$ equals to e if e is meaningful at this point. Because each program point is either before or after a statement, the following axiom PST specifies this property. In this axiom, e and e' represent two arbitrary expressions. It is required that e and e' are meaningful respectively at the point i and j.

$$\text{(PST)} \qquad \{i : e = e@i\}\ s\ \{j : e' = e'@j\}$$

Program-point-specific expressions should be viewed as a naming convention for constant symbols. At a point i other than j, a program-point-specific expression $e@j$ is treated as a constant symbol. We should not infer properties from the structure of $e@j$.

Example 4. The program points, together with some formulas, of the program in Fig. 1 are depicted in Fig. 3. The entrance program point and the exit point are respectively 1 and 10. The formula $\mathsf{isHBST}(\mathsf{root})$ at point 1 is the precondition of this program, while the formula at point 10 is the postcondition.

The formula at point 8 says that k is in the key set of the right sub-tree of p evaluated at point 7 if and only if k is in the key set of the initial binary tree.

At point 6, the property $\mathsf{pt} = (\mathsf{pt} \to l)@5$ holds because of the assignment $\mathsf{pt} := \mathsf{pt} \to l$. However, it does not imply $\mathsf{pt} = \mathsf{pt}@5 \to l$. To prove this property, we should prove that $(\mathsf{pt} \to l)@5 = \mathsf{pt}@5 \to l$ holds at point 5 using the axiom PST. This formula is not affected by the assignment, so it also holds at point 6. Now $\mathsf{pt} = (\mathsf{pt} \to l)@5$ and $(\mathsf{pt} \to l)@5 = \mathsf{pt}@5 \to l$ imply $\mathsf{pt} = \mathsf{pt}@5 \to l$ at 6.

Because point 5 does not dominate point 8, the formula $\mathsf{k} \in \mathsf{KeySet}(\mathsf{root})@5$ can not appear at point 8. □

```
{1: isHBST(root)}
pt:=root;
{2: (k ∈ KeySet(pt)) = (k ∈ KeySet(root)@1)}
while (pt→K ≠ k)
  {4: pt→K ≠ k ∧ (k ∈ KeySet(pt)) = (k ∈ KeySet(root)@1) }
   if (k < pt → K )
      {5: pt = pt@5 ∧ pt → l = (pt → l)@5 ∧ (pt → l)@5 = pt@5 → l}
      pt := pt → l
      {6: pt = (pt → l)@5 ∧ (pt → l)@5 = pt@5 → l ∧ pt = pt@5 → l}
   else
      {7: k > pt → K ∧ (k ∈ KeySet(pt → r)) = (k ∈ KeySet(root)@1)}
      pt := pt → r;
      {8: (k ∈ KeySet(pt → r)@7) = (k ∈ KeySet(root)@1)}
   {9:(k ∈ KeySet(pt)) = (k ∈ KeySet(root)@1) }
{10:pt = nil?k ∉ KeySet(root)@1 : (k ∈ KeySet(root)@1 ∧ pt → K = k)}
```

Fig. 3. A proof-in-code specification

3 The Memory Model and the Axioms about Memory Access Operators

In this section, we describe the memory model on which the programs execute. The memory consists of a set of addressed memory units. Each memory unit has a unique address and stores an integer, a boolean value, or a pointer. So the memory can be viewed as a map from addresses to **int**, **bool**, or **Ptr**.

Composite type data (either arrays or records) are stored in memory blocks. Each memory block is composed of sub-blocks and/or memory units for its component data. Each memory block has also a unique address. However, the memory model does not directly map block addresses to values. Instead, the block addresses are used to derive the addresses of its sub-blocks or units. Given the address r of a memory block, the address of its components can be derived using expressions $\&r \rightarrow n$ (if r refers to a record block and n is a field name) or $\&(*r)[i]$ (if r refers to an array block and i is an integer). The values of $\&r \rightarrow n$ and $\&(*r)[i]$ depend only on the values of r and i. They are irrelevant to the contents stored in the memory block.

Example 5. Suppose that a memory block with address p stores a Node-typed data. This block is composed of three memory units for the fields l, r, and K. The addresses of these units are respectively $\&p \rightarrow l$, $\&p \rightarrow r$ and $\&p \rightarrow K$. □

(DEREF-REF)	$*\&e = e$	(REF-DEREF)	$e \neq \textbf{nil} \Rightarrow \& * e = e$
(PVAR-1)	$\&v \neq \textbf{nil}$	(PVAR-2)	$\&v_1 \neq \&v_2$
(PVAR-3)	$\&v \neq \&r \rightarrow n$	(PVAR-4)	$\&v \neq \&a[i]$
(REC-1)	$r \neq \textbf{nil} \Rightarrow \&r \rightarrow n \neq \textbf{nil}$		
(REC-2)	$(r_1 \rightarrow n = r_2 \rightarrow n) \Leftrightarrow (r_1 = r_2)$	(REC-3)	$r_1 \rightarrow n_1 \neq r_2 \rightarrow n_2$
(ARR-1)	$a \neq \textbf{nil} \wedge (0 \leq i < c) \Rightarrow \&((*a)[i]) \neq \textbf{nil}$		
(ARR-2)	$(\&((*a_1)[i_1]) = \&((*a_2)[i_2])) \Leftrightarrow (a_1 = a_2 \wedge i_1 = i_2 \wedge 0 \leq i_1, i_2 < c)$		
(ARR-REC)	$\&a[i] \neq \&r \rightarrow n$		

In these axioms, the type of r, r_1, r_2 are pointers to some record type and n, n_1 and n_2 are field names such that n_1 and n_2 are different. The type of a, a_1, a_2 are $\textbf{ARR}(t, c)$ for some t and c. i, i_1, i_2 are integers. The expression e in DEREF-REF must be of the form $v, *e_1, e_1.n, e_1 \rightarrow n$ or $e_1[e_2]$.

Fig. 4. The axioms for memory layout and memory access

The axioms depicted in Fig. 4 are used to specify the addressing operator &, the memory access operator $*$, and the memory layouts for composite types.

The operators & and $*$ are inverse to each other. This is described by the axioms DEREF-REF and REF-DEREF.

Each program variable is assigned a unique memory block (or memory unit). Furthermore, the memory block (unit) is not a component of any other blocks. So we have the axioms PVAR-1, PVAR-2, PVAR-3 and PVAR-4.

Given a non-nil reference to a composite block, all the references to its sub-blocks or units are non-nil. So we have the axioms REC-1 and ARR-1. The axioms REC-2 and ARR-2 say that different components of a composite block has different addresses. The axioms REC-3 and ARR-REC say that a component block/unit uniquely belongs to at most one enclosing memory block.

These axioms can be used to simplify expressions containing the addressing operator &. For example, the formula $\&\mathsf{pt}\to K \in (\lambda x.(\&x\to K)[\mathsf{NodeSet}(\mathsf{root})])$ can be simplified to an equivalent formula $\mathsf{pt} \in \mathsf{NodeSet}(\mathsf{root})$.

4 Memory Scopes of Expressions and Functions

4.1 Memory Scopes of Expressions

An expression e may have different values before/after the execution of a program statement. However, the value of e depends only on the contents stored in a finite set of memory units. This set can be expressed using another expression, called the *memory scope* of e, denoted as $\mathfrak{M}(e)$. We now show that $\mathfrak{M}(e)$ can be constructed syntactically.

If e is of the form $f(e_1, \ldots, e_n)$, where f is a function/operator other than $*, \&, [\,], ., \to$, the memory scope $\mathfrak{M}(e)$ is $\mathfrak{M}(e_1) \cup \ldots \cup \mathfrak{M}(e_n) \cup \mathfrak{M}(f)(e_1, \ldots, e_n)$, where $\mathfrak{M}(f)$ is the function to compute the memory scopes of applications of f.

1. If f is an algebraic operator (e.g. +,-,...), a boolean operator, or other abstract operators, $\mathfrak{M}(f)$ is a constant function which always yields $\emptyset$.
2. If f is a user-defined function (predicate), the definition of $\mathfrak{M}(f)$ can be derived syntactically from the definition of f, see next subsection.

The memory-scope-construction rules for other kinds of expressions are given in Fig. 5. The third column is used in the proof of an important property about memory scopes presented in Subsection 4.3.

Note that the memory scope of $e@i$ is $\emptyset$. The reason is that $e@i$ is viewed as a constant symbol of which the value is irrelevant to the current program state.

Example 6. Given a type $\mathbf{ARR}(\mathbf{ARR}(\mathbf{REC}((\mathbf{int}, f1),\ (\mathbf{int}, f2))), 100), 100)$ and a program variable a of this type. The memory scope of $a[i][j].f1$ is constructed as follow.

$$\mathfrak{M}(a[i][j].f1) = \mathfrak{M}(\&a[i][j]) \cup \{\&a[i][j].f1\} = \mathfrak{M}(\&a[i]) \cup \{\&j\} \cup \{\&a[i][j].f1\}$$
$$= \mathfrak{M}(\&a) \cup \{\&i\} \cup \{\&j\} \cup \{\&a[i][j].f1\} = \{\&i\} \cup \{\&j\} \cup \{\&a[i][j].f1\}$$

This means that the value of $a[i][j].f1$ keeps unchanged if the contents stored in the memory units $\&i$, $\&j$, and $\&a[i][j].f1$ are not modified. □

4.2 Memory Scope of User-Defined Functions

Given a user-defined function f, we abuse the notation $\mathfrak{M}$ and use $\mathfrak{M}(f)$ to denote the name of the memory scope function of f. The formal parameters of $\mathfrak{M}(f)$ is the same as those of f. The return type of $\mathfrak{M}(f)$ is **SetOf(Ptr)**. Intuitively speaking, $\mathfrak{M}(f)(x_1, \ldots, x_n)$ yields the set of memory units accessed during the evaluation of $f(x_1, \ldots, x_n)$. Let $f(x_1, \ldots, x_n) \triangleq e$ be the definition of f, the definition of $\mathfrak{M}(f)$ is as follow.

$$\mathfrak{M}(f)(x_1, \ldots, x_n) \triangleq \mathfrak{M}(e)$$

Expressions	Memory Scopes	Memory Scopes of Memory Scopes
a constant c	$\emptyset$	$\emptyset$
free variable x	$\emptyset$	$\emptyset$
$e@i$	$\emptyset$	$\emptyset$
$\&v$	$\emptyset$	$\emptyset$
$\& * e$	$\mathfrak{M}(e)$	$\mathfrak{M}^2(e)$
$\&e_1[e_2]$	$\mathfrak{M}(\&e_1) \cup \mathfrak{M}(e_2)$	$\mathfrak{M}^2(\&e_1) \cup \mathfrak{M}^2(e_2)$
$\&e.n$	$\mathfrak{M}(\&e)$	$\mathfrak{M}^2(\&e)$
$\&e \to n$	$\mathfrak{M}(e)$	$\mathfrak{M}^2(e)$
v	$\{\&v\}$	$\emptyset$
$*e$	$\{e\} \cup \mathfrak{M}(e)$	$\mathfrak{M}(e) \cup \mathfrak{M}^2(e)$
$e_1.n$	$\{\&e_1.n\} \cup \mathfrak{M}(\&e_1)$	$\mathfrak{M}(\&e_1) \cup \mathfrak{M}^2(\&e_1)$
$e_1 \to n$	$\{\&e_1 \to n\} \cup \mathfrak{M}(e_1)$	$\mathfrak{M}(e_1) \cup \mathfrak{M}^2(e_1)$
$e_1[e_2]$	$\{\&e_1[e_2]\} \cup \mathfrak{M}(\&e_1) \cup \mathfrak{M}(e_2)$	$\mathfrak{M}(\&e_1) \cup \mathfrak{M}(e_2) \cup \mathfrak{M}^2(\&e_1) \cup \mathfrak{M}^2(e_2)$
$e_0?e_1 : e_2$	$\mathfrak{M}(e_0) \cup (e_0?\mathfrak{M}(e_1) : \mathfrak{M}(e_2))$	$\mathfrak{M}^2(e_0) \cup \mathfrak{M}(e_0) \cup (e_0?\mathfrak{M}^2(e_1) : \mathfrak{M}^2(e_2))$
$e_1 \wedge e_2$	$\mathfrak{M}(e_1) \cup (e_1?\mathfrak{M}(e_2) : \emptyset)$	$\mathfrak{M}^2(e_1) \cup \mathfrak{M}(e_1) \cup (e_1?\mathfrak{M}^2(e_2) : \emptyset)$
$e_1 \vee e_2$	$\mathfrak{M}(e_1) \cup (e_1?\emptyset : \mathfrak{M}(e_2))$	$\mathfrak{M}^2(e_1) \cup \mathfrak{M}(e_1) \cup (e_1?\emptyset : \mathfrak{M}^2(e_2))$
$\lambda x.e_1[e_2]$	$\mathfrak{M}(e_2) \cup \bigcup(\lambda x.\mathfrak{M}(e_1)[e_2])$	$\mathfrak{M}^2(e_2) \cup \mathfrak{M}(e_2) \cup \bigcup(\lambda x.\mathfrak{M}^2(e_1)[e_2])$
$\forall x \in e_2.e_1$	$\mathfrak{M}(e_2) \cup \bigcup(\lambda x.\mathfrak{M}(e_1)[e_2])$	$\mathfrak{M}^2(e_2) \cup \mathfrak{M}(e_2) \cup \bigcup(\lambda x.\mathfrak{M}^2(e_1)[e_2])$

NOTE: $\mathfrak{M}^2(e)$ is an abbreviation for $\mathfrak{M}(\mathfrak{M}(e))$

Fig. 5. The memory scope for different forms of expressions

Example 7. Let $\mathfrak{M}(\mathsf{NodeSet})$ be MNS. According to the definition of NodeSet in Fig. 2, the definition of MNS is as follow.

$$\mathsf{MNS}(x) \triangleq (x = \mathbf{nil})?\emptyset : \{\&x \to l, \&x \to r\} \cup \mathsf{MNS}(x \to l) \cup \mathsf{MNS}(x \to r)$$

The above definition is equivalent to the following one.

$$\mathsf{MNS}(x) \triangleq (\lambda y.(\&y \to l)[\mathsf{NodeSet}(x)]) \cup (\lambda y.(\&y \to r)[\mathsf{NodeSet}(x)])$$

KeySet and isHBST have the same memory scope function M defined as

$$M(x) \triangleq (\lambda y.(\&y \to K)[\mathsf{NodeSet}(x)]) \cup (\lambda y.(\&y \to l)[\mathsf{NodeSet}(x)]) \cup (\lambda y.(\&y \to r)[\mathsf{NodeSet}(x)])$$

From the above, the memory scope of the formula $\mathsf{pt} \in \mathsf{NodeSet}(\mathsf{root})$ is

$$\{\&\mathsf{pt}, \&\mathsf{root}\} \cup (\lambda y.(\&y \to l)[\mathsf{NodeSet}(\mathsf{root})]) \cup (\lambda y.(\&y \to r)[\mathsf{NodeSet}(\mathsf{root})])$$

It means that the formula keeps unchanged if the values of pt, root, and the fields l and r of the tree nodes keep unchanged. □

4.3 Two Properties of Memory Scopes

This section presents two important properties about memory scopes.

Theorem 1. *Let e be an arbitrary expression and $x_1, \ldots, x_n$ are free variables in e. Given an assignment to these free variables and two program states s_1, s_2 such that s_1 and s_2 agree on all the memory units in $\mathfrak{M}(e)$. The expression e is evaluated to the same value at s_1 and s_2.*

Because of the space limitation, we just give a brief proof.

1. If there is no user-defined function in e, the above conclusion can be proved by an induction on the length of e.
2. If there are user-defined functions in e but none of these functions are recursive, we can expand the function applications with their definitions to get an equivalent expression e'. There is no user-defined function in e', and $\mathfrak{M}(e)$ is a superset of $\mathfrak{M}(e')$. From 1, the conclusion is proved.
3. If there are recursively user-defined functions in e. Let f be such a function defined as $f(\ldots) \triangleq \mathsf{EXP}(f)$, where $\mathsf{EXP}(f)$ is an expression containing f. Suppose that f recursively called itself n times during the evaluation of e at the state s_1, we can define n functions, $f_0, f_1, \ldots, f_n$ as $f_0 \triangleq \perp$, $f_1 \triangleq \mathsf{EXP}(f_0)$, $\ldots$, $f_i \triangleq \mathsf{EXP}(f_{i-1})$, $\ldots$, $f_n \triangleq \mathsf{EXP}(f_{n-1})$, and replace f in e with f_n. The derived expression e' equals to e at the state s_1, and $\mathfrak{M}(e')$ is a subset of $\mathfrak{M}(e)$ at the state s_1. From 2, e' has the same value at the states s_1 and s_2. It also can be proved that e' and e evaluates to the same value on s_2. So e evaluates to the same value at the states s_1 and s_2.

Theorem 2. *Let e be an arbitrary expression e such that e is meaningful at a state s for an assignment to the free variables in e, $\mathfrak{M}(\mathfrak{M}(e)) \subseteq \mathfrak{M}(e)$ is evaluated to **true** at s.*

The brief proof is as follow. Here, we use $\mathfrak{M}^2(e)$ as an abbreviation for $\mathfrak{M}(\mathfrak{M}(e))$.

1. If e contains no user-defined function symbols, from the table in Fig. 5, we can prove this theorem by an induction on the length of e.
2. Let f be a user-defined function defined as $f(x_1, \ldots, x_n) \triangleq e'$ and e' contains no user-defined functions. $\mathfrak{M}(f(e_1, \ldots, e_n))$ is $\mathfrak{M}(e_1) \cup \ldots \cup \mathfrak{M}(e_n) \cup \mathfrak{M}(f)(e_1, e_2, \ldots, e_n)$; $\mathfrak{M}^2(f(e_1, \ldots, e_n))$ is $\mathfrak{M}^2(e_1) \cup \ldots \cup \mathfrak{M}^2(e_n) \cup \mathfrak{M}(e_1) \cup \ldots \cup \mathfrak{M}(e_n) \cup \mathfrak{M}^2(f)(e_1, e_2, \ldots, e_n)$. Note that $\mathfrak{M}(f)$ and $\mathfrak{M}(f)$ are respectively defined as $\mathfrak{M}(f)(x_1, \ldots, x_n) \triangleq \mathfrak{M}(e')$ and $\mathfrak{M}^2(f)(x_1, \ldots, x_n) \triangleq \mathfrak{M}^2(e')$. From 1, we can prove $\mathfrak{M}^2(f(e_1, \ldots, e_n)) \subseteq \mathfrak{M}(f(e_1, \ldots, e_n))$. So the theorem holds if the functions in e are not defined with other user-defined functions.
3. We can prove by an induction that $\mathfrak{M}^2(f(e_1, \ldots, e_n)) \subseteq \mathfrak{M}(f(e_1, \ldots, e_n))$ holds for a user-defined non-recursive function f based on 2. So the theorem holds for expressions containing non-recursive functions.
4. Now we prove the case of recursive functions. From the definition of $\mathfrak{M}$, we have the following fact: let f be a user-defined function symbol in an expression e, the functions f, $\mathfrak{M}(f)$ and $\mathfrak{M}^2(f)$ are applied to same real parameters in e, $\mathfrak{M}(e)$ and $\mathfrak{M}^2(e)$. Furthermore, in $\mathfrak{M}(e)$ and $\mathfrak{M}^2(e)$, the counterparts of the conditional sub-expressions in e have the same guard. So during the evaluation of e, $\mathfrak{M}(e)$ and $\mathfrak{M}^2(e)$, f recursively call itself if and only if $\mathfrak{M}(f)$ and $\mathfrak{M}^2(f)$ call themselves.

Let f, $\mathfrak{M}(f)$ and $\mathfrak{M}^2(f)$ be functions respectively defined as $f(x_1,\ldots,x_n) \triangleq e'$, $\mathfrak{M}(f)(x_1,\ldots,x_n) \triangleq \mathfrak{M}(e')$ and $\mathfrak{M}^2(f)(x_1,\ldots,x_n) \triangleq \mathfrak{M}^2(e')$. Suppose that f recursively calls itself for n times during the evaluation of e on a state s, the fact above means that $\mathfrak{M}(f)$ and $\mathfrak{M}^2(f)$ also recursively call themselves for n times during the evaluation of $\mathfrak{M}(e)$ and $\mathfrak{M}^2(e)$. So we can introduce n new functions $f_0, f_1, \ldots, f_n$ defined as $f_0 \triangleq \perp$, $f_1 \triangleq \mathsf{EXP}(f_0)$, $\ldots$, $f_i \triangleq \mathsf{EXP}(f_{i-1})$, $\ldots$, $f_n \triangleq \mathsf{EXP}(f_{n-1})$, where $\mathsf{EXP}(f_i)$ means the expression derived by replacing f with f_i in e'. It can be proved that $f(e_1,\ldots,e_n) = f_n(e_1,\ldots,e_n)$, $\mathfrak{M}(f)(e_1,\ldots,e_n) = \mathfrak{M}(f_n)(e_1,\ldots,e_n)$, and $\mathfrak{M}^2(f)(e_1,\ldots,e_n) = \mathfrak{M}^2(f_n)(e_1,\ldots,e_n)$ on the state s. Because f_is are not recursive, we prove that $\mathfrak{M}^2(f(e_1,\ldots,e_n)) \subseteq \mathfrak{M}(f(e_1,\ldots,e_n))$. So the theorem holds for expressions containing recursive functions.

In our logic, we use the following axiom to describe this property.

(SCOPE-SHRINK) $\quad \mathfrak{M}(\mathfrak{M}(e)) \subseteq \mathfrak{M}(e) \quad$ *Note: e must be meaningful*

This axiom is important for local reasoning. We will discuss this in Section 7.

5 The Axioms and Proof Rules of Program Statements

In this section, we present the axioms and proof rules to specify the effects of program statements. There are three axioms for primitive statements and three proof rules for control flow statements. They are all presented in Fig. 6.

For an assignment $e_1 := e_2$, let i, j respectively be the program points before/after this statement. It is required that $\&e_1$ evaluates to a non-nil pointer at i. At the program point j, the memory unit referred by $\&e_1$ stores the value of e_2 evaluated at i. Furthermore, if a formula holds at the point i, and $\&e_1$ is not in the memory scope of this formula, the formula still holds at the point j. This is specified by the axiom ASSIGN.

Example 8. Considering the assignment $\mathsf{pt} := \mathsf{pt} \to l$ in Fig. 3. Let **Prop** be the formula $\mathsf{pt}@5 \neq \mathbf{nil} \wedge (\mathsf{pt} \to l)@5 = \mathsf{pt}@5 \to l \wedge \&\mathsf{pt} = (\&\mathsf{pt})@5$. $\mathfrak{M}(\mathbf{Prop})$ is $\{\&(\mathsf{pt}@5) \to l\}$. Substituting ρ with **Prop** in the axiom ASSIGN, we have
$\{5 : \mathbf{Prop} \wedge (\&\mathsf{pt} \notin \{\&(\mathsf{pt}@5) \to l\}) \wedge (\&\mathsf{pt} \neq \mathbf{nil})\}\ \ \mathsf{pt} := \mathsf{pt} \to l$
$\{6 : \mathbf{Prop} \wedge *((\&\mathsf{pt})@5) = (\mathsf{pt} \to l)@5\}$
From the axioms PVAR-1, PVAR-3, PST, and the proof rules CONSEQ and CONJ, we have $\{5 : \mathsf{pt} \neq \mathbf{nil}\}\ \ \mathsf{pt} := \mathsf{pt} \to l\ \ \{6 : \mathsf{pt} = \mathsf{pt}@5 \to l\}$. □

For an allocation statement $e_1 := \mathsf{alloc}(t)$, let i, j respectively be the program points before/after this statement. It is required that $\&e_1$ evaluates to a non-nil pointer at the point i. After the execution, the memory unit referred by $(\&e_1)@i$ stores a reference to a newly allocated memory block. This memory block is unreachable at the point i. So $*((\&e_1)@i) \notin e_2@i$ holds at the point j for any expressions e_2 if e_2 is meaningful at i. This allocation statement modifies only the memory unit referred by $(\&e_1)@i$ and the memory block newly allocated (this block is unreachable at the point i). If an assertion ρ holds at the point i

and $(\&e_1)@i$ is not in the memory scope of ρ, ρ still holds at the point j. This is specified by the axiom ALLOC. In this axiom, $\mathtt{Init}(x)$ is an abbreviation for the assertion that all the pointers stored in the block referred by x are set to **nil**. For example, if the type of x is $\mathbf{P}(\mathsf{Node})$, $\mathtt{Init}(x)$ is $x \to l = \mathbf{nil} \wedge x \to r = \mathbf{nil}$.

Example 9. Considering the statement $\mathsf{t} := \mathsf{alloc(Node)}$. From the axiom ALLOC, substituting ρ and e_2 respectively with $\mathsf{isHBST(rt)} \wedge (\&\mathsf{t} = (\&\mathsf{t})@i)$ and $\mathsf{NodeSet(rt)}$, we have

$$\begin{array}{l}\{i : \mathsf{isHBST(rt)} \wedge (\&\mathsf{t} = (\&\mathsf{t})@i) \wedge \&\mathsf{t} \notin \mathfrak{M}(\mathsf{isHBST(rt)}) \wedge \&\mathsf{t} \neq \mathbf{nil}\} \\ \quad \mathsf{t} := \mathsf{alloc(Node)}; \\ \{j : \mathsf{isHBST(rt)} \wedge (\&\mathsf{t} = (\&\mathsf{t})@i) \wedge ((*((\&\mathsf{t})@i) \notin \mathsf{NodeSet(rt)}@i) \\ \quad \wedge (*((\&\mathsf{t})@i) \neq \mathbf{nil}) \wedge (*((\&\mathsf{t})@i) \to l = \mathbf{nil}) \wedge (*((\&\mathsf{t})@i) \to r = \mathbf{nil})\}\end{array}$$

From the axioms DEREF-REF, PVAR-1, PVAR-3, PST, and the proof rules CONSEQ and CONJ, this specification can be simplified to

$$\begin{array}{l}\{i : \mathsf{isHBST(rt)}\} \quad \mathsf{t} := \mathsf{alloc(Node)}; \\ \{j : \mathsf{isHBST(rt)} \wedge (\mathsf{t} \notin \mathsf{NodeSet(rt)}@i) \wedge (\mathsf{t} \neq \mathbf{nil}) \wedge (\mathsf{t} \to l = \mathbf{nil}) \wedge (\mathsf{t} \to r = \mathbf{nil})\}\end{array}$$

□

The axiom for the `skip` statement, the proof rules for control-flow statements, the consequence rule, and the conjunction rule are depicted in Fig. 6. They are same as the ones in Hoare Logic.

(SKIP) $\{q\}\ \mathtt{skip}\ \{q\}$

(ASSIGN)
$$\begin{array}{l}\{i : \rho \wedge (\&e_1 \notin \mathfrak{M}(\rho)) \wedge (\&e_1 \neq \mathbf{nil})\} \\ \quad e_1 := e_2 \\ \{j : \rho \wedge (*((\&e_1)@i) = e_2@i)\}\end{array}$$

(ALLOC)
$$\begin{array}{l}\{i : \rho \wedge (\&e_1 \notin \mathfrak{M}(\rho)) \wedge (\&e_1 \neq \mathbf{nil})\} \\ \quad e_1 := \mathsf{alloc}(t) \\ \{j : \rho \wedge (*((\&e_1)@i) \neq \mathbf{nil}) \wedge (*((\&e_1)@i) \notin e_2@i) \wedge \mathtt{Init}(*((\&e_1)@i))\}\end{array}$$

IF $$\frac{\{p \wedge e\}s_1\{q\} \quad \{p \wedge \neg e\}s_2\{q\}}{\{p\}\ \mathtt{if}\ (e)\ s_1\ \mathtt{else}\ s_2\ \{q\}}$$

WHILE $$\frac{\{p \wedge e\}\ s\ \{p \wedge (e \vee \neg e)\}}{\{p\}\ \mathtt{while}\ (e)\ s\ \{\neg e \wedge p\}}$$

SEQ $$\frac{\{p\}s_1\{q\} \quad \{q\}s_2\{r\}}{\{p\}\ s_1; s_2\ \{r\}}$$

CONSEQ $$\frac{\{p\}s\{q\} \quad p' \Rightarrow p \quad q \Rightarrow q'}{\{p'\}\ s\ \{q'\}}$$

CONJ $$\frac{\{p\}\ s\ \{q\} \quad \{p'\}\ s\ \{q'\}}{\{p \wedge p'\}\ s\ \{q \wedge q'\}}$$

Fig. 6. The axioms and proof rules for program statements

6 The Weakest-Preconditions of Assignments

In this section, we will show how to compute the weakest precondition of an assignment for a postcondition that contains no user-defined function.

e	$\mathsf{WP}(e)$, the expression equivalent to e before $e_1 = e_2$
a const or a quantified variable	e
$e@k$ for some point k ($k \neq j$)	$e@k$
$\&v$	$\&v$
$*e'$	$(\mathsf{WP}(e') \neq (\&e_1)@i)?(*\mathsf{WP}(e')) : (e_2@i)$
v	$(\mathsf{WP}(\&v) \neq (\&e_1)@i)?(*\mathsf{WP}(\&v)) : (e_2@i)$
$e'.n$	$(\mathsf{WP}(\&e'.n) \neq (\&e_1)@i)?(*\mathsf{WP}(\&e'.n)) : (e_2@i)$
$e' \to n$	$(\mathsf{WP}(\&e' \to n) \neq (\&e_1)@i)?(*\mathsf{WP}(\&e' \to n)) : (e_2@i)$
$e'[e'']$	$(\mathsf{WP}(\&e'[e'']) \neq (\&e_1)@i)?(*\mathsf{WP}(\&e'[e''])) : (e_2@i)$
e' op e''	$\mathsf{WP}(e')$ op $\mathsf{WP}(e'')$
op e' (op *is not* $*$)	op $\mathsf{WP}(e')$
$e_0?e' : e''$	$\mathsf{WP}(e_0)?\mathsf{WP}(e') : \mathsf{WP}(e'')$
$\&(e'.n)$	$\&(\mathsf{WP}(\&e') \to n)$
$\&(e' \to n)$	$\&(\mathsf{WP}(e') \to n)$
$\&(e'[e''])$	$\&((*\mathsf{WP}(\&e'))[\mathsf{WP}(e'')])$
$\lambda x.e'[e'']$	$\lambda x.\mathsf{WP}(e')[\mathsf{WP}(e'')]$
$\forall x \in e'.e''$	$\forall x \in \mathsf{WP}(e').\mathsf{WP}(e'')$

Fig. 7. The rules to construct $\mathsf{WP}(e)$

Given an assignment $e_1 := e_2$, and i, j be the program points before/after this assignment respectively. The program state at i is different only with the state at j on the memory unit $(\&e_1)@i$. For any address x of a memory unit, the value of $((x \neq (\&e_1)@i)? * x : e_2@i)$ at the point i equals to the value of $*x$ at the point j.

For an arbitrary formula e, we can construct the weakest precondition of the assignment $e_1 := e_2$ for e according to rules depicted in Fig. 7. The basic idea of these rules is that for each expression e with an L-value, we first construct an expression $\mathsf{WP}(\&e)$, the value of which at i equals to the value of $\&e$ at j; then $\mathsf{WP}(e)$ is constructed as $((\mathsf{WP}(\&e) \neq (\&e_1)@i)? * \mathsf{WP}(\&e) : e_2@i)$. From the discussion above, the value of $\mathsf{WP}(e)$ at i equals to the value of $*\&e$ (equivalent to e by the axiom DEREF-REF) at j.

By an induction on the length of the expression e, we can prove that the value of e at j equals to the value of $\mathsf{WP}(e)$ at i. So a formula e holds at the point j if and only if $\mathsf{WP}(e)$ holds at i. Theorem 3 says that $\mathsf{WP}(e)$ is a precondition of $e_1 := e_2$ for e in Scope Logic.

Theorem 3. *Given an assignment $e_1 := e_2$, and i, j be respectively the program points before/after this assignment. Let e be a formula containing no user-defined functions and no program-point-specific sub-expression of the form $e@j$, the following specification can be proved in Scope Logic.*

$$\{\mathsf{WP}(e) \wedge \&e_1 \neq \mathbf{nil}\}\ e_1 := e_2\ \{e\}$$

Proof. From the axiom ASSIGN, we have

$$\{\mathsf{WP}(e) \wedge \&e_1 \notin \mathfrak{M}(\mathsf{WP}(e)) \wedge \&e_1 \neq \mathbf{nil}\}\ e_1 := e_2\{\mathsf{WP}(e) \wedge *((\&e_1)@i) = e_2@i\}$$

By a mathematical induction on the length of e, we can show that $\&e_1 \notin \mathfrak{M}(\mathsf{WP}(e))$ holds at the point i for any e. So we have

$$\{\mathsf{WP}(e) \wedge \&e_1 \neq \mathbf{nil}\}\ e_1 := e_2\ \{\mathsf{WP}(e) \wedge *((\&e_1)@i) = e_2@i\}$$

Because $(*((\&e_1)@i) = e_2@i)$ implies $\forall x.(((x = (\&e_1)@i)?e_2@i : *(x)) = *x)$, we can prove that $\mathsf{WP}(e) \wedge (*((\&e_1)@i) = e_2@i) \Rightarrow e$ holds at the point j. From the proof rule CONSEQ, we have $\{\mathsf{WP}(e) \wedge \&e_1 \neq \mathbf{nil}\}\ e_1 := e_2\ \{e\}$. QED.

Usually there are many conditional expressions and operators &, $@i$ in $\mathsf{WP}(e)$. We can remove $@i$ in $\mathsf{WP}(e)$ using the axiom PST. Most of the operator & in $\mathsf{WP}(e)$ can be eliminated using the axioms in Section 3. For the conditional sub-expressions $(e' \neq (\&e_1)@i)? * e' : e_2@i$ in $\mathsf{WP}(e)$, we can automatically simplify them when $(e' \neq (\&e_1)@i)$ is either unsatisfiable or a tautology according to the axioms in Section 3.

Example 10. Here are some examples of the weakest precondition calculation.

1. Let $\{i:\}\ x := a+b\ \{j : x > y\}$ be an unfinished specification. Applying WP, it yields $((\&x \neq (\&x)@i)? * (\&x) : (a+b)@i) > (((\&y \neq (\&x)@i)? * (\&y) : (a+b)@i)$. Simplifying it, we have $\{a+b > y\}\ x := a+b\ \{x > y\}$.
2. Let $\{i:\}\ a[a[2]] := 3\ \{a[a[2]] = 3\}$ be an unfinished specification, where a is a program variable with type $\mathbf{ARR}(\mathbf{int}, 100)$. Applying WP, it yields the precondition $((\&a[\mathsf{IND}] \neq (\&a[a[2]])@i)? * (\&a[\mathsf{IND}]) : 3@i) = 3$, where IND is the abbreviation for $(\&a[2] \neq (\&a[a[2]])@i)? * (\&a[2]) : 3@i$. The precondition can be automatically simplified to $((((2 \neq a[2])?a[2] : 3) \neq a[2])?a[(2 \neq a[2])?a[2] : 3] : 3) = 3$. Using an SMT solver, it can be easily proven that this formula is equivalent to $a[2] \neq 2 \vee a[3] = 3$. So we have $\{a[2] \neq 2 \vee a[3] = 3\}\ a[a[2]] := 3\ \ \{a[a[2]] = 3\}$.
3. Let $\{i:\}\ a[\mathsf{n}] := \mathsf{tmp}\ \{j : \forall x \in [0..\mathsf{n}].a[x] >= 0\}$ be an unfinished specification, $[0..\mathsf{n}]$ is the set of integers from 0 to n. Applying WP, we get $\forall x \in [0..(\&\mathsf{n} \neq (\&a[\mathsf{n}])@i? * (\&\mathsf{n}) : \mathsf{tmp}@i)].((\&a[x] \neq (\&a[\mathsf{n}])@i? * (\&a[x]) : \mathsf{tmp}@i) >= 0)$. Simplifying it, we have the following specification. $\{i : \forall x \in [0..\mathsf{n}].((x = n?\mathsf{tmp}:a[x]) >= 0)\}a[n] := \mathsf{tmp}\{j : \forall x \in [0..\mathsf{n}].a[x] >= 0\}$.

□

7 Supporting Local Reasoning

To support local reasoning, a specification should be in the following form.

$$\{\rho \wedge (\mathfrak{M}(\rho) \cap e = \emptyset) \wedge pre\}\ s\ \{\rho \wedge post\}$$

where ρ is an assertion variable representing an arbitrary assertion, and e is (an over-approximation of) the set of memory units modified by the statement s.

We say that such specifications are in the *memory-modification-bounded* form because the expression e bounds the set of memory units modified by s. The assertion variable ρ in the specification can be substituted with a formula e'. Simultaneously, the memory scope of ρ, i.e. $\mathfrak{M}(\rho)$, is substituted with $\mathfrak{M}(e')$. For example, in the proof of Theorem 4, ρ and $\mathfrak{M}(\rho)$ are respectively substituted with $e' \wedge \rho \wedge (\mathfrak{M}(\rho) \cap e@i = \emptyset)$ and $\mathfrak{M}(e') \cup \mathfrak{M}(\rho) \cup \mathfrak{M}(\mathfrak{M}(\rho))$.

Theorem 4 shows that if we get a specification in the memory-modification-bounded form, we can expand the specification with a formula e', if $\mathfrak{M}(e')$ is disjoint with the memory bound e.

Theorem 4. *Let ρ be an assertion variable.*

$$\frac{\begin{array}{l} pre \wedge e' \Rightarrow \mathfrak{M}(e') \cap e = \emptyset \\ \{i : \rho \wedge (\mathfrak{M}(\rho) \cap e = \emptyset) \wedge pre\}\ s\ \{j : \rho \wedge post\} \end{array}}{\{i : \rho \wedge (\mathfrak{M}(\rho) \cap e = \emptyset) \wedge (e' \wedge pre)\}\ s\ \{j : \rho \wedge (e' \wedge post)\}}$$

Proof. First, we substitute ρ in the second premise with $e' \wedge \rho \wedge (\mathfrak{M}(\rho) \cap e@i = \emptyset)$. The memory scope of this formula is $\mathfrak{M}(e') \cup \mathfrak{M}(\rho) \cup \mathfrak{M}(\mathfrak{M}(\rho))$. From the axiom SCOPE-SHRINK, it equals $\mathfrak{M}(e') \cup \mathfrak{M}(\rho)$. So we have

$$\begin{array}{l} \{(e' \wedge \rho \wedge (\mathfrak{M}(\rho) \cap e@i = \emptyset)) \wedge ((\mathfrak{M}(e') \cup \mathfrak{M}(\rho)) \cap e = \emptyset) \wedge pre\} \\ \quad s \\ \{(e' \wedge \rho \wedge (\mathfrak{M}(\rho) \cap e@i = \emptyset)) \wedge post\} \end{array}$$

From the first premise and the proof rules CONSEQ, PST, we have

$$\{\rho \wedge (\mathfrak{M}(\rho) \cap e = \emptyset) \wedge (e' \wedge pre)\} \quad s \quad \{\rho \wedge (e' \wedge post)\}$$

QED.

Example 11. Suppose a program **REORDER** reorders the nodes of a singly-linked list p, and the derived list is pointed to by q. The program modifies only the field $link$ of the nodes. Let **MemBnd** be $(\{\&\mathsf{q}\} \cup \lambda x.(\&x \to link)[\mathsf{ListNodes(p)}])$. The specification can be written as

$$\begin{array}{l} \{i : \rho \wedge (\mathfrak{M}(\rho) \cap \mathbf{MemBnd} = \emptyset) \wedge \mathsf{isSList(p)}\} \quad \mathbf{REORDER} \\ \{j : \rho \wedge \mathsf{isSList(q)} \wedge \mathsf{ListNodes(q)} = \mathsf{ListNodes(p)}@i\} \end{array}$$

Let **Prop** be $\forall x \in (\mathsf{ListNodes(p)}@i).(x \to D > 0)$. $\mathfrak{M}(\mathbf{Prop})$ is $\lambda x.(\&x \to D)[\mathsf{ListNodes(p)}@i]$, which is disjoint with **MemBnd**. From Theorem 4, we have

$$\begin{array}{l} \{i : \rho \wedge (\mathfrak{M}(\rho) \cap \mathbf{MemBnd} = \emptyset) \wedge \mathbf{Prop} \wedge \mathsf{isSList(p)}\} \quad \mathbf{REORDER} \\ \{j : \rho \wedge \mathbf{Prop} \wedge \mathsf{isSList(q)} \wedge \mathsf{ListNodes(q)} = \mathsf{ListNodes(p)}@i\} \end{array}$$

Using the proof rules PST and CONSEQ, we have

$$\begin{array}{l} \{i : \rho \wedge (\mathfrak{M}(\rho) \cap \mathbf{MemBnd} = \emptyset) \wedge \mathbf{Prop} \wedge \mathsf{isSList(p)}\} \quad \mathbf{REORDER} \\ \{j : \rho \wedge \forall x \in (\mathsf{ListNodes(q)}).(x \to D > 0) \wedge \mathsf{isSList(q)} \wedge \\ \qquad \mathsf{ListNodes(q)} = \mathsf{ListNodes(p)}@i\} \end{array}$$

□

To apply the proof rules WHILE and SEQ, the post-conditions of sub-statements must also be in the form $\rho \wedge (\mathfrak{M}(\rho) \cap e = \emptyset) \wedge property$. Theorem 5 can be used to derive such post-conditions.

Theorem 5. *Let ρ be an assertion variable.*

$$\frac{\{i : \rho \wedge (\mathfrak{M}(\rho) \cap e = \emptyset) \wedge pre\}\ s\ \{j : \rho \wedge post\}}{\{i : \rho \wedge (\mathfrak{M}(\rho) \cap e = \emptyset) \wedge pre\}\quad s\quad \{j : \rho \wedge (\mathfrak{M}(\rho) \cap e@i = \emptyset) \wedge post\}}$$

Proof. Note that the memory scope of $\rho \wedge (\mathfrak{M}(\rho) \cap e@i = \emptyset)$ is $\mathfrak{M}(\rho) \cup \mathfrak{M}(\mathfrak{M}(\rho))$, which equals to $\mathfrak{M}(\rho)$ from the axiom SCOPE-SHRINK. So $\rho \wedge (\mathfrak{M}(\rho) \cap e@i = \emptyset)$ implies that its memory scope is disjoint with $e@i$. Substitute ρ in the premises with $\rho \wedge (\mathfrak{M}(\rho) \cap e@i = \emptyset)$, and apply the proof rule PST, CONSEQ, we can get

$$\{i : \rho \wedge (\mathfrak{M}(\rho) \cap e = \emptyset) \wedge pre\}\ s\ \{j : \rho \wedge (\mathfrak{M}(\rho) \cap e@i = \emptyset) \wedge post\}$$

QED.

This theorem shows that $\mathfrak{M}(\rho)$ is still disjoint with $e@i$ on the post-state. We may replace $e@i$ with some other expressions e' if $post \Rightarrow e' \subseteq e@i$.

Example 12. Let **ST** be $\mathsf{tmp} := \mathsf{p} \rightarrow link; \mathsf{p} \rightarrow link = \mathsf{q}; \mathsf{q} := \mathsf{p}; \mathsf{p} = \mathsf{tmp};$, which is the loop-body of the program that reverses a singly-linked list. Let MSet be $\{\&\mathsf{p}, \&\mathsf{q}, \&\mathsf{tmp}\} \cup \lambda x.(\&x \rightarrow link)[\mathsf{ListNodes(first)}@1]$, and Prop be

$$\mathsf{IsList(p)} \wedge \mathsf{IsList(q)} \wedge (\mathsf{ListNodes(p)} \cap \mathsf{ListNodes(q)} = \emptyset) \wedge$$
$$(\mathsf{ListNodes(p)} \cup \mathsf{ListNodes(q)} = \mathsf{ListNodes(first)}@1).$$

The following specification can be proved.

$$\{i : \rho \wedge (\mathfrak{M}(\rho) \cap \mathsf{MSet} = \emptyset) \wedge \mathsf{Prop}\}\ \mathbf{ST}\ \{j : \rho \wedge \mathsf{Prop} \wedge \mathsf{MSet}@i = \mathsf{MSet}\}$$

From Theorem 5 and the rule CONSEQ, we have

$$\{i : \rho \wedge (\mathfrak{M}(\rho) \cap \mathsf{MSet} = \emptyset) \wedge \mathsf{Prop}\}\ \mathbf{ST}\ \{j : \rho \wedge (\mathfrak{M}(\rho) \cap \mathsf{MSet} = \emptyset) \wedge \mathsf{Prop}\}$$

Now, $\rho \wedge (\mathfrak{M}(\rho) \cap \mathsf{MSet} = \emptyset) \wedge \mathsf{Prop}$ can be used as a loop invariant. □

8 The Tool

An interactive tool has been implemented to support code verification using Scope Logic. Users can input formulas at program points and then prove them. A formula holds at a point if (1) it is logically implied by other proved formulas in the same program point; (2) or the formula holds at the predecessor point(s) and it is not affected by program statement; (3) or it is a natural result of the program execution, e.g. the condition expression of an if-statement holds at the point before its then branch.

This tool also supports some automatic verification mechanisms like weakest precondition calculation and data-flow analysis techniques. However, assertion variables and local reasoning have not been supported yet.

Many examples, including the Schorre-Waite algorithm, several array-sorting algorithms, singly-linked list manipulations, binary search tree manipulations, and a topological sorting algorithm have been verified using this tool.

For more technical details of this tool, please visit the web page of this tool: http://seg.nju.edu.cn/SCL.html.

9 Related Works and Conclusions

In this paper, we present an extension to Hoare Logic for programs with pointers and recursive data structures. Formulas augmented with recursively defined functions (predicates) are used to deal with recursive data structures. The logic can specify and verify relations between different program points using program-point-specific expressions. Our logic also supports local reasoning, which is important for verification of real programs. The weakest precondition of assignments for postconditions containing no user-defined function is well supported.

In Separation Logic, a new logical connective $*$ (separation conjunction) is introduced to specify that two assertions assert properties of two disjoint heaplets. However, this new logical connective makes it difficult to use conventional logical tools and techniques, like SMT solvers. To solve this problem, implicit dynamic frame (IDF) [10] uses RAS to compute the footprint of an assertion (i.e. the locations required to be accessed). Though [9] presents a method to convert a certain fragment of Separation Logic specifications into representations in IDF so that they can be verified using conventional logic tools. However, recursive predicates (which are important to specify recursive data structures and their properties) are not supported yet. The memory scope symbol $\mathfrak{M}$ in Scope Logic is similar to RAS in IDF. The main difference is the way in which footprints (memory scopes) of recursive predicates are dealt with. RAS in IDF uses some axioms to specify the relation between the footprint functions and the corresponding predicates. These axioms refer to the global heap directly. In Scope Logic, the explicit definitions of memory scope functions can be syntactically constructed based on the predicate (or function) definitions using $\mathfrak{M}$. Using explicit definitions, people can do better on reasoning about memory scopes. For example, we can find that several predicates (functions) share same memory scope functions. Another benefit of using explicit definitions of memory scope functions is that the global heap is not referred in code verifications using Scope Logic. Verification conditions generated in [10] contain a global heap, many store operators on the heap, and universal quantifiers over the addresses. From our experience, it is difficult to verify such complicated formulas using SMT solvers.

In [8], memory unit sets relevant to assertions are specified using 'region's. For a recursively defined predicate, people must define its region together with the definition of the predicate. Ghost variables and fields are instrumented into programs such that assertions can refer regions explicitly. In Scope Logic, the memory scope of a recursive predicate (function) is treated as an intrinsic attribute of the predicate (function). Memory scopes (similar to 'region's) of assertions, expressions, (recursive) predicates and functions are constructed syntactically. One advantage of our method is that ghost variables and fields are avoided. Another advantage is that it is simpler to first define a recursive predicate (function) and then construct its memory scope function syntactically.

Our logic does not support memory-deallocation statements now. Another disadvantage is that we use the conventional FOL as the base logic, people must carefully avoid meaningless (not-welldefined) expressions in code verifications. To solve this problem, we will try to find a method to generate meaningful-conditions for expressions. We will also try to extend our logic to deal with more sophisticated program structures like procedure definitions/calls, classes/objects, function pointers, etc.

References

1. Hoare, C.A.R.: An axiomatic basis for computer programming. Communications of the ACM 12(10), 576–580 (1969)
2. Burstall, R.M.: Some techniques for proving correctness of programs which alter data structures. In: Machine Intelligence, vol. 7, pp. 23–50. Edinburgh University Press, Edinburgh (1972)
3. Cook, S.A., Oppen, D.C.: An assertion language for data structures. In: Conference Record of 2nd ACM Symposium on Priciples of Programming Languages, New York, pp. 160–166 (1975)
4. Morris, J.M.: A general axiom of assignment; assignment and linked data structures; a proof of the Schorr-Waite algorithm. In: Theoretical Foundations of Programming Methodology, pp. 25–51. D. Reidel, Dordrecht (1982)
5. Reynolds, J.C.: An overview of separation logic. In: Proceedings of Verified Software: Theories, Tools, Experiments 2005, Zurich, Switzerland, October 10-13 (2005) Revised Selected Papers and Discussions
6. Yang, H.: An example of local reasoning in BI pointer logic: The Schorr-Waite graph marking algorithm. In: Henglein, F., Hughes, J., Makholm, H., Niss, H. (eds.) SPACE 2001: Informal Proceedings of Workshop on Semantics, Program Analysis and Computing Environments for Memory Management, pp. 41–68. IT University of Copenhagen (2001)
7. Jones, C.B., Middelburg, C.A.: A typed logic of partial functions reconstructed classically. Acta Inform 31(5), 399–430 (1994)
8. Banerjee, A., Naumann, D.A., Rosenberg, S.: Regional logic for local reasoning about global invariants. In: Vitek, J. (ed.) ECOOP 2008. LNCS, vol. 5142, pp. 387–411. Springer, Heidelberg (2008)
9. Parkinson, M.J., Summers, A.J.: The Relationship Between Separation Logic and Implicit Dynamic Frames. Logical Methods in Computer Science 8(3) (2012)
10. Smans, J., Jacobs, B., Piessens, F.: Implicit dynamic frames. ACM Trans. on Programgramming Language and Systems 34(1) (2012)

Durative Graph Transformation Rules for Modelling Real-Time Reconfiguration

Steffen Ziegert[1] and Christian Heinzemann[2]

[1] Department of Computer Science, University of Paderborn
Warburger Str. 100, 33098 Paderborn, Germany
[2] Software Engineering Group, Heinz Nixdorf Institute, University of Paderborn
Zukunftsmeile 1, 33102 Paderborn, Germany
{steffen.ziegert,c.heinzemann}@uni-paderborn.de

Abstract. Advanced mechatronic systems, like smart cars or smart trains, perform reconfiguration as a reaction to their changing environment. The reconfiguration behaviour of such systems is safety-critical and needs to be verified by formal verification procedures. In the past, graph transformation systems have proven to be a suitable formalism for specification and verification of such systems. However, existing approaches do not consider that reconfiguration operations consume time. Considering their duration, several reconfiguration operations can be executed concurrently in a running system, possibly resulting in undesired behaviour. In this paper, we introduce *durations* for graph transformation rules and a *locking mechanism* that ensures the safe concurrent execution of time-consuming operations. Additionally, we show how graph transformation rules with durations are mapped to an existing verification framework which enables the formal verification of graph transformation systems with durative rules. We illustrate our approach using an example of a smart train system.

Keywords: graph transformation, timed execution, concurrency, reconfiguration, verification.

1 Introduction

Advanced mechatronic systems, like smart cars or smart trains, operate autonomously in unknown and frequently changing environments. During operations, they need to cooperate with other systems in their environment, e.g., for organizing the passage of a crossing. In order to perform these tasks efficiently, i.e., with minimal (hardware) resources, these systems apply reconfiguration for adapting their behaviour to their changing environment [5]. Technically, reconfiguration is achieved by changing the software architecture of the system at runtime.

The reconfiguration behaviour of a mechatronic system, however, is safety-critical, because a wrong reconfiguration may lead to an erroneous behaviour in a certain situation. In case of a smart car trying to pass a crossing such

Z. Liu, J. Woodcock, and H. Zhu (Eds.): ICTAC 2013, LNCS 8049, pp. 427–445, 2013.

erroneous behaviour may lead to a crash. As a consequence, we need to apply formal verification for guaranteeing that the reconfiguration behaviour is correct and may not cause such accidents.

In previous publications [2,6], it has been shown that graph transformations [8] are a suitable formalism for specifying and verifying reconfiguration behaviour. Our approaches and other related approaches like Real-Time Maude [14] or GROOVE [10], however, assume that reconfiguration operations are executed atomically in zero time. In reality, reconfiguration operations obviously need time for being executed and, hence, reconfiguration operations of different systems may be executed concurrently. The concurrent execution, however, may cause reconfiguration operations to *interfere* which each other. The approach by Rivera et al. [15] considers such situations and proposes to cancel one of the involved operations. This, however, has the result that a reconfiguration that has been started will not be finished correctly. This may lead, again, to an errorneous behaviour and, in the worst case, to an accident. As a result, we need to take the duration of a reconfiguration into account upon verification and ensure that each reconfiguration operation can be finished if it has been started.

In this paper, we extend our graph-based specification approach of [6] by so-called *durative rules*. A durative rule extends a normal graph transformation rule by a duration that it needs for being executed. We define how durative rules can be mapped to our existing timed graph verification framework [6]. In particular, we present a locking approach that guarantees that after starting the execution of a durative rule, it can always be finished correctly. This, in turn, guarantees that reconfiguration operations can only be executed concurrently if they do not interfere with each other. We show this property as part of our contribution.

We illustrate our approach using a smart train system which is developed at the University of Paderborn. In this system, small trains, called RailCabs, drive autonomously on the track system. A particular feature of the RailCab system[1] is the convoy mode where RailCabs drive at very small distances to reduce their energy consumption.

The paper is structured as follows. In Section 2, we introduce graph transformation systems as well as timed graphs that are used for representing a state of the system in our timed graph verification framework. In Section 3, we outline our approach of durative rules for graph transformation systems in more detail before introducing the semantics of durative rules and the mapping to our timed graph verification framework in Section 4. We show that our mapping ensures the intended properties for concurrent execution in Section 5. Section 6 discusses related approaches before we conclude the paper in Section 7.

2 Fundamentals

2.1 Graph Transformations

A graph transformation system (GTS) consists of a set of graph transformation rules (GT rules) and an initial graph. The GT rules can be applied to the initial

[1] `http://www.railcab.de`

graph and its resulting successor graphs to construct the state space of the GTS. The underlying theory of GTS is based on graphs and graph morphisms.

Definition 1 (Graph, Graph Morphism). *A* graph $G = (V_G, E_G, src_G, tgt_G)$ *consists of a set of nodes* V_G*, a set of edges* E_G*, and source and target functions* $src_G, tgt_G : E_G \to V_G$*. A* graph morphism $f : G \to H$ *between two graphs is a pair of mappings* $f = (f_E, f_V)$ *with* $f_E : E_G \to E_H$ *and* $f_V : V_G \to V_H$ *such that* $f_V \circ src_G = src_H \circ f_E$ *and* $f_V \circ tgt_G = tgt_H \circ f_E$*. A graph morphism* $f = (f_E, f_V)$ *is* injective *if* f_E *and* f_V *are injective.*

A graph morphism is a mapping of nodes and edges of one graph to nodes and edges of another graph such that the source and target nodes of edges are preserved. Such morphisms are used in GT rules to define which nodes and edges are created, deleted, or preserved when the rule is applied to a graph.

Definition 2 (Graph Transformation Rule). *A* graph transformation rule $p = (L, R, r)$ *consists of two graphs* L *and* R*, called* left-hand side (LHS) *and* right-hand side (RHS)*, and an injective partial graph morphism* $r : L \to R$*, called* rule morphism*. Given a graph transformation rule* p *and a match* $m : L \to G$ *of its LHS into a* host graph G*, the* direct derivation *from* G *with* p *at* m*, written* $G \stackrel{p,m}{\Longrightarrow} H$*, is the pushout of* r *and* m *in* $Graph^P$*, the category of graphs and partial graph morphisms, as shown below. [7]*

$$\begin{array}{ccc} L & \xrightarrow{\quad r \quad} & R \\ \Big\downarrow m & (PO) & \Big\downarrow m' \\ G & \xrightarrow{\quad r' \quad} & H \end{array}$$

Whether a GT rule can be applied to a graph depends on whether a match of its LHS to the graph can be found. To further restrict the applicability of a rule, negative application conditions (NAC) can be used that forbid specific graph structures from being present in the graph.

Definition 3 (Negative Application Condition). *Let* $p = (L, R, r)$ *be a graph transformation rule,* G *a graph, and* $m : L \to G$ *a match. A* negative application condition *is a tuple* (N, n) *with* $n : L \to N$ *and* n *being injective. If* $\neg\exists q : N \to G$ *such that* $q \circ n = m$*, then* m satisfies (N, n)*, written* $m \models (N, n)$*.*

2.2 Timed Graphs and Clock Instances

Timed GTS operate on timed graphs which are an extension of typed graphs [8]. In addition to the normal graph nodes, a timed graph contains a set of clock instances which measure the progress of time. As in timed automata [1,3], the values of all clock instances increase continuously and synchronously with the same rate. A clock instance always applies to a subgraph of the timed graph and has edges to all nodes of the subgraph but no other edges.

Definition 4 (Timed Graph). *Let TG be a type graph. A* timed graph $TiG = (H, type)$ *consists of a graph* $H = (V_G, V_{CI}, E_G, E_{CI}, (src_j, tgt_j)_{j\in\{G,CI\}})$, *where*

- V_G *and* V_{CI} *are called graph nodes and clock instances, respectively;*
- E_G *and* E_{CI} *are called graph edges and clock instance edges, respectively;*
- $src_G : E_G \to V_G$, $tgt_G : E_G \to V_G$ *are the source and target function for graph edges;*
- $src_{CI} : E_{CI} \to V_{CI}$, $tgt_{CI} : E_{CI} \to V_G$ *are the source and target function for clock instance edges;*
- $type : H \to TG$ *is a graph morphism. [16,8]*

To define the different kinds of rules of the timed GTS formalism, we need the definition of a morphism on timed graphs. A timed graph morphism preserves the source and target nodes of edges, the types of nodes, and the values assigned to attributes.

Definition 5 (Timed Graph Morphism). *A* (timed graph) morphism f *between two timed graphs* TiG_i, $i = 1, 2$, *is a partial graph morphism* $f = (f_{V_G}, f_{V_{CI}}, f_{E_G}, f_{E_{CI}})$ *with* $f_{V_j} : V_{j,1} \to V_{j,2}$, $j \in \{G, CI\}$, *and* $f_{E_k} : E_{k,1} \to E_{k,2}$, $k \in \{G, CI\}$. f *commutes for all source and target functions and preserves types, i.e.,* $type_2 \circ f = type_1$. *[16]*

In addition to timed graph morphisms, we need a definition of clock instance constraints which are used by different rules of the timed GTS formalism. They are used to restrict the values of a clock instance to a specific interval (either as application condition or as invariant).

Definition 6 (Clock Instance Constraint). *Let* V_{CI} *be a set of clock instances,* $c_i, c_j \in V_{CI}$. *A* clock instance constraint *is a conjunctive formula of atomic constraints of the form* $c_i \sim n$ *or* $c_i - c_j \sim n$ *with* $\sim \in \{<, \leq, =, \geq, >\}$, $n \in \mathbb{N}$. $\mathcal{Z}(V_{CI})$ *denotes the set of clock instance constraints over* V_{CI}. *[16,3]*

To evaluate whether a clock instance constraint is satisfied or not, we need an assignment of values to the clock instances of a timed graph.

Definition 7 (Clock Instance Value Assignment). *Let* V_{CI} *be a set of clock instances. A clock instance value assignment is a function* $\nu : V_{CI} \to \mathbb{R}^+$ *that assigns a non-negative real value to each clock instance. For* $V_{res} \subseteq V_{CI}$, $\nu_1 = \nu[V_{res} \mapsto 0]$ *is defined as* $\nu_1(ci) = 0$ *for all* $ci \in V_{res}$ *and* $\nu_1(ci) = \nu(ci)$ *for all* $ci \in V_{CI} \setminus V_{res}$. *For* $\delta \in \mathbb{R}^+$, $\nu_2 = (\nu + \delta)$ *is defined as* $\nu_2(ci) = \nu(ci) + \delta$ *for all* $ci \in V_{CI}$.

Now we can express whether a clock instance constraint is satisfied.

Definition 8 (Clock Instance Constraint Satisfaction). *Let* V_{CI} *be a set of clock instances,* $z \in \mathcal{Z}(V_{CI})$ *a clock instance constraint over* V_{CI}, *and* ν *a clock instance value assignment over* V_{CI}. *Then,* ν satisfies z, *written as* $\nu \models z$, *if and only if* $z[\nu(ci)/ci] \equiv true$.

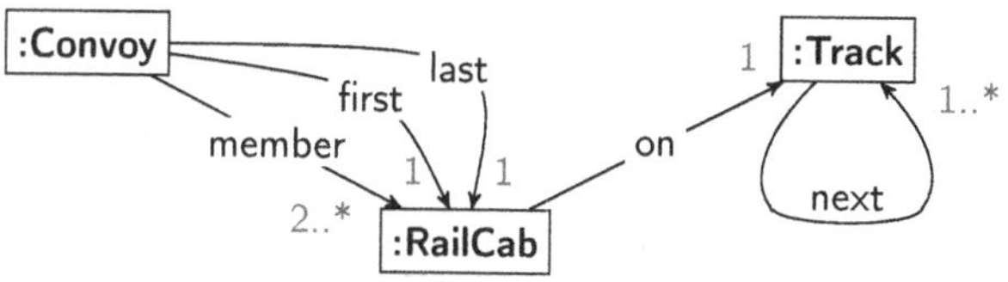

Fig. 1. Class diagram of the RailCab system

3 Approach

To illustrate our approach of durative reconfigurations for GTS, we use a convoy scenario of the aforementioned RailCab system as running example. Figure 1 shows the simplified software architecture of the RailCab system in a class diagram. It consists of track segments that are connected to each other via `next` links. A RailCab can occupy such a track segment. Furthermore, RailCabs can form a convoy. Such a convoy operation is represented by a `Convoy` object and `member` links to each participating RailCab. In addition, there are `first` and `last` links that represent the head and tail of the convoy, respectively.

To model the reconfigurations of a system's software architecture, we use story patterns which have a formal semantics[2] based on GTS. Story patterns represent the LHS, RHS, and NACs of a rule in a single graph by using stereotypes. Elements going to be deleted (LHS only) are equipped with the stereotype «- -»; elements to be created (RHS only) with «++»; forbidden elements (within NACs only) are crossed out; elements that are preserved (in both LHS and RHS) are drawn without stereotype.

Ordinary GTS do not include a notion of time. However, to enable the verification of timed properties, time should be reflected in the semantics: a path in the state space of a GTS should clearly indicate when a time-consuming reconfiguration starts and when it ends. Therefore, in our approach, a rule has an annotated value for its duration. The duration is obtained by computing the WCET for applying the reconfiguration. For these *durative rules* we developed a semantics based on timed graphs and timed GTS. This enables us to use our existing verification framework [6] for the verification of durative rules.

In our semantics durative reconfigurations are supported by translating them into two discrete reconfigurations that are temporally linked to each other. One reconfiguration represents the start of the durative reconfiguration; a second one represents its end. Since reconfigurations have an application interval now, it is possible to apply them concurrently. A naive approach that allows concurrent rule applications to overlap arbitrarily might lead to conflicts between two reconfigurations.

Consider for example the story patterns in Figures 2 and 3, which both take $d = 4$ time units to execute, and a configuration where two RailCabs are driving in a convoy at a given time. If the `breakConvoy` reconfiguration is in the process

[2] Story patterns follow the single pushout approach to graph transformation.

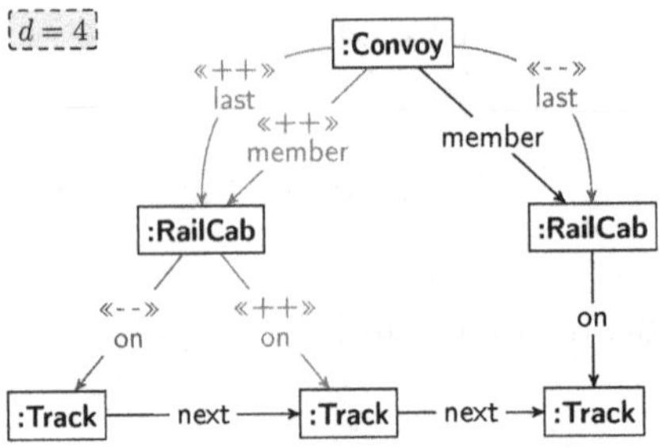

Fig. 2. Story pattern `joinConvoy`

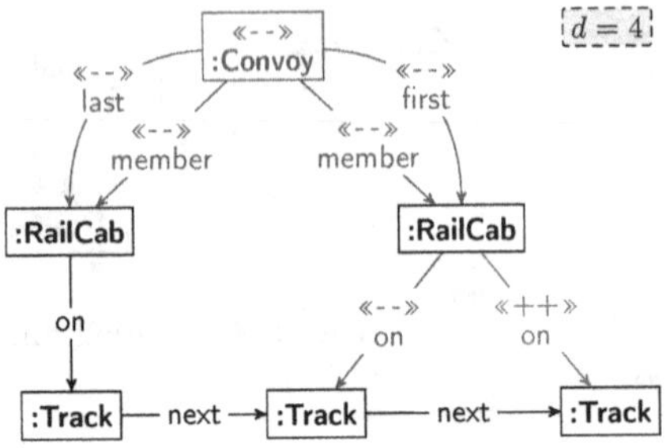

Fig. 3. Story pattern `breakConvoy`

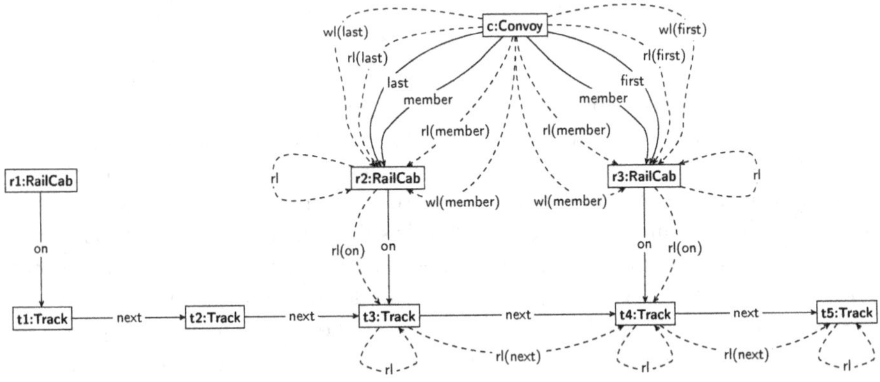

Fig. 4. Configuration of the system where the `breakConvoy` rule is in ongoing execution

of execution but the actual change of the state will not happen until its execution ends, then a `joinConvoy` reconfiguration could be scheduled in the meantime. However, as `breakConvoy` ends before `joinConvoy` ends, there will be no `Convoy` object anymore that the joining `RailCab` object can be linked to. If such a sequence of reconfigurations was to be executed, a rear-end collision might occur in the worst case.

To avert such conflicts we integrate a locking mechanism into the semantics of durative rules. The application of a start rule adds locks into the host graph. There are read locks for objects or links that are preserved and write locks for their creation and deletion. These locks are attached directly to the timed graph as *locking edges* when the start rule is applied. The application of the end rule removes these locking edges again. Conflicts cannot occur anymore because start rules require the non-existence of locking edges according to the changes they specify. Such a use of locking edges prevents inconsistent configurations from occurring and ensures that reconfigurations are either carried out completely or not at all. While a concurrent read is allowed, a concurrent write or read-write is not allowed.

Figure 4 shows a configuration of the system where locking edges have been created by the application of `breakConvoy`'s start rule. Locks on objects are incorporated into the configuration as self-loops. Locks on links are realized as locking edges with same source and target as the link itself. To correctly correlate locking edges to the links they are supposed to restrict the access to, there is one pair of locking edge types (for read and write locks) for every link type. In the figure, locking edges are depicted using dashed arrows.

4 Semantics

Our notion of durative rules is inspired by the fact that reconfigurations in software systems require time. On the syntactic level, a durative rule is merely a GT rule with an annotated name and duration value. The idea is that the execution of a durative graph transformation cannot be aborted once it has been started. A modeller who uses durative rules for specification does not need to know about the complicated timed behaviour that happens under the hood.

Definition 9 (Durative Graph Transformation Rule). *A* durative graph transformation rule $D = (DL, DR, dr, name, d)$ *consists of*

- *two typed graphs, a left-hand side DL and a right-hand side DR,*
- *a partial graph morphism $dr : DL \rightarrow DR$,*
- *a* distinct name *$name$, and*
- *a* duration $d \in \mathbb{N}^{>0}$.

The semantics of durative GT rules are defined on top of the rules already established by the timed GTS formalism. A durative rule induces a pair of *timed rules* (i.e., its start and end rule), a so-called *clock instance rule*, and an *invariant rule*. Intuitively, the application of the start and end rule indicate the interval of the durative rule's execution, the clock instance rule triggers the measuring of time, and the time invariant rule enforces the application of the end rule after d time units have passed since the application of the start rule.

Before giving the definitions of the induced rules, we explain how we realize the locks in timed graphs. Locking of nodes and edges is done via the creation and deletion of additional edges, called *locking edges.* The types of locking edges are defined in the type graph of the timed GTS. Every node type t has two locking edge types, $rlnode(t)$ and $wlnode(t)$, as self-loops. For every edge type t (that is no locking edge type itself), there are locking edges types $rledge(t)$ and $wledge(t)$ adjacent to the same source and target node types. An object of type $rlnode(t)$ depicts an obtained read lock on the object; an object of type $wlnode(t)$ a write lock. Similarly, a link of type $rledge(t)$ depicts an obtained read lock on the link between its source and target that has the type t, $wledge(t)$ a write lock. In addition to the locking edges, there is a node type *name* for every durative rule and an edge type *underApplication* from *name* to every other node type. Objects of type *name* are called *application indicator* and indicate the ongoing execution of a durative reconfiguration if available in a configuration. Their outgoing links mark the matching of the durative rule that has been applied, i.e., the subgraph of the configuration that is changed by the reconfiguration.

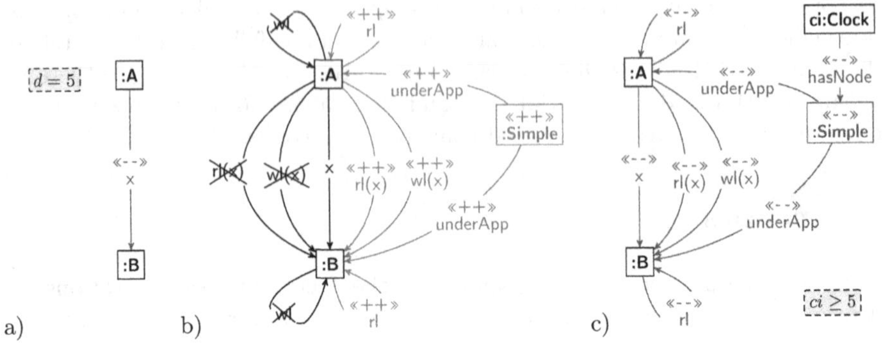

Fig. 5. A durative rule (a), its induced start rule (b), and end rule (c)

4.1 Timed GT Rules

A timed GT rule basically works like a normal GT rule. It searches for a match of the left-hand side (LHS) in the host graph and transforms the respective subgraph such that it is isomorphic to the right-hand side (RHS). In addition, a timed GT rule specifies a timed guard and resets. The time guard is a clock instance constraint based on the clock instances contained in the LHS. It needs to be evaluated to true for the rule to be applicable. Upon application, all clock instances contained in the resets are set back to 0.

Definition 10 (Timed Graph Transformation Rule). *A* timed graph transformation rule *$tr = (L, R, r, \mathcal{N}, z, V_{res})$ consists of two timed graphs L and R, a rule morphism $r : L \to R$ with $r(V_{CI,L}) = V_{CI,R}$ and $|V_{CI,L}| = |V_{CI,R}|$, a set of NACs $\mathcal{N}$, where each NAC is a tuple $(N, n) \in \mathcal{N}$ with $n : L \to N$, $z \in \mathcal{Z}(V_{CI,L})$ is a clock instance constraint, the* time guard *and $V_{res} \subseteq V_{CI,R}$ is a set of clock instances called* resets. *[16,6]*

Both, the induced start rule and the induced end rule are defined on top of this timed GT rule. Intuitively, the end rule realizes the reconfiguration syntactically defined by the durative rule. The start rule serves two purposes:

- It adds information about the execution of the durative rule into the host graph. This is needed for the annotation of time and for the end rule to find a match that corresponds to the match of the start rule. Finding a corresponding match is important because together both rules are supposed to represent the application interval of a durative transformation. With different matches there would be no meaningful interpretation for the application of a durative rule.
- It adds locking edges into the host graph such that subsequent rules do not match if they access the same elements in a conflicting manner. These locking edges are removed again by the end rule.

Figure 5 shows an example of a durative rule called `Simple` and its induced start and end rule. The durative rule (a) specifies the removal of a link `x` during an interval of 5 time units. The induced start rule (b) has a LHS that corresponds to the LHS of the durative rule. Negative application conditions allow its application only if the preserved nodes are not write-locked and the edge to be removed is neither read- nor write-locked. When the rule is applied, an application indicator `Simple` is created. For each preserved node a read lock `rl` is created; the edge to be deleted also obtains a write lock `wl(x)`. The LHS of the induced end rule (c) includes the application indicator node `Simple` and its adjacent edges. This ensures the correct matching of the LHS to the host graph. Locking edges are removed again when the rule is applied. The guard $ci \geq 5$ is an application condition of the end rule. The consumption of 5 time units is guaranteed by the invariant rule which is formally explained in Section 4.2.

Definition 11 (Induced Start Rule). *Let $\mathcal{D} = (DL, DR, dr, name, d)$ be a durative rule. The* induced start rule *of $\mathcal{D}$ is a timed rule $sr = (L, R, r, \mathcal{N}, z, V_{res})$ with*

1. $V_{G,L} = V_{DL} \wedge E_{G,L} = E_{DL}$,
2. $V_{G,R} = V_{DL} \cup \{ai\} \wedge type(ai) = name \wedge E_{G,R} = E_{DL} \cup \{e|src(e) = ai \wedge tgt(e) \in V_{G,R} \wedge type(e) = underApplication\} \cup E_{NODELOCKS,R} \cup E_{EDGELOCKS,R}$,
3. $V_{CI,L} = V_{CI,R} = \emptyset \wedge E_{CI,L} = E_{CI,R} = \emptyset$,
4. $i_L : DL \to L$ is an isomorphism $\wedge\, r|_{\{V_{G,L}, E_{G,L}\}}$ is total and injective,
5. $\mathcal{N} = \mathcal{N}_{NODELOCKS} \cup \mathcal{N}_{EDGELOCKS}$,
6. $z = \emptyset \wedge V_{res} = \emptyset$,
7. $\mathcal{N}_{NODELOCKS} = \{(N, n)|\exists v \in V_{G,L} : V_{G,N} = V_{G,L} \wedge E_{G,N} = E_{G,L} \cup \{ne\} \wedge src(ne) = tgt(ne) = n(v) \wedge type(ne) = wlnode \circ type(v) \wedge n \text{ is injective}\} \cup \{(N, n)|\exists v \in V_{G,L} \setminus i_L \circ \mathtt{Dom}(dr) : V_{G,N} = V_{G,L} \wedge E_{G,N} = E_{G,L} \cup \{ne\} \wedge src(ne) = tgt(ne) = n(v) \wedge type(ne) = rlnode \circ type(v) \wedge n \text{ is injective}\}$,
8. $\mathcal{N}_{EDGELOCKS} = \{(N, n)|\exists e \in E_{G,L} : V_{G,N} = V_{G,L} \wedge E_{G,N} = E_{G,L} \cup \{ne\} \wedge src(ne) = src \circ n(e) \wedge tgt(ne) = tgt \circ n(e) \wedge type(ne) = wledge \circ type(e) \wedge n \text{ is injective}\} \cup \{(N, n)|\exists e \in E_{G,L} \setminus i_L \circ \mathtt{Dom}(dr) : V_{G,N} = V_{G,L} \wedge E_{G,N} = E_{G,L} \cup \{ne\} \wedge src(ne) = src \circ n(e) \wedge tgt(ne) = tgt \circ n(e) \wedge type(ne) = rledge \circ type(e) \wedge n \text{ is injective}\}$,
9. $E_{NODELOCKS,R} = \{le|\exists v \in V_{G,L} : src(le) = tgt(le) = r(v) \wedge type(le) = rlnode \circ type(v)\} \cup \{le|\exists v \in V_{G,L} \setminus i_L \circ \mathtt{Dom}(dr) : src(le) = tgt(le) = r(v) \wedge type(le) = wlnode \circ type(v)\}$,
10. $E_{EDGELOCKS,R} = \{le|\exists e \in E_{G,L} : src(le) = src \circ r(e) \wedge tgt(le) = tgt \circ r(e) \wedge type(le) = rledge \circ type(e)\} \cup \{le|\exists e \in E_{G,L} \setminus i_L \circ \mathtt{Dom}(dr) : src(le) = src \circ r(e) \wedge tgt(le) = tgt \circ r(e) \wedge type(le) = wledge \circ type(e)\}$.

We describe every condition separately. The LHS of the induced start rule corresponds to the LHS of the durative rule (Condition 1). The RHS of the start rule corresponds to its LHS with an additional node ai, called *application indicator*, additional edges from ai to all other nodes in the RHS, and additional edges $E_{NODELOCKS,R}$ and $E_{EDGELOCKS,R}$ that denote the set of locking edges that are created by the start rule (Condition 2). Intuitively, ai indicates the application of the durative rule and the sets $E_{NODELOCKS,R}$ and $E_{EDGELOCKS,R}$ indicate whether read or write access to specific nodes and edges is locked. Aside from adding ai, the start rule applies changes only by creating locking edges. Therefore, the rule morphism r restricted to graph nodes and edges is total (Condition 4) – r is also unique (up to isomorphism). The sets of clock instances, clock instance edges, time guards, and clock resets are empty (Conditions 3 and 6) because the start rule does not add a clock instance measuring the execution time itself. Instead, the addition of a clock instance for the execution of a durative rule is done by a clock instance rule.

The remainder conditions implement the locking functionality. Conditions 7 and 8 realize application conditions on the locks by defining NACs on locking edges and Conditions 9 and 10 realize changes to the locking state by creating locking edges. The start rule may not be applied if there is a write lock for a required node or edge; it may further not be applied if there is a read lock for a node or edge that is going to be deleted according to the syntax of the durative rule, i.e., the node or edge is not contained in $i_L \circ \mathtt{Dom}(dr)$ (Conditions 7 and 8). The start rule creates a read lock for every required node or edge; it creates a write lock if the node or edge is deleted according to the syntax of the durative rule, i.e., if the node or edge is not contained in $i_L \circ \mathtt{Dom}(dr)$ (Conditions 9 and 10).

Definition 12 (Induced End Rule). *Let $\mathcal{D} = (DL, DR, dr, name, d)$ be a durative rule. The* induced end rule *of $\mathcal{D}$ is a timed rule $er = (L, R, r, \mathcal{N}, z, V_{res})$ with*

1. $V_{G,L} = V_{DL} \cup \{ai\} \wedge type(ai) = name \wedge E_{G,L} = E_{DL} \cup \{e | src(e) = ei \wedge tgt(e) \in V_{G,L} \wedge type(e) = underApplication\} \cup E_{NODELOCKS,L} \cup E_{EDGELOCKS,L}$,
2. $V_{G,R} = V_{DR} \wedge E_{G,R} = E_{DR}$,
3. $V_{CI,L} = V_{CI,R} = \{ci\} \wedge E_{CI,L} = \{(ci, ai)\} \wedge E_{CI,R} = \emptyset$,
4. $i_L : DL \to L$ *is a total injective morphism* $\wedge\, i_R : DR \to R$ *is an isomorphism* $\wedge\, r|_{\{V_{G,L}, E_{G,L}\}} = i_R \circ dr \circ i_L^{-1} \wedge r|_{\{V_{CI,L}\}}$ *is total and injective,*
5. $\mathcal{N} = \emptyset$,
6. $z = \{ci \geq d\} \wedge V_{res} = \emptyset$,
7. $E_{NODELOCKS,L} = \{le | \exists v \in V_{G,L} : src(le) = tgt(le) = v \wedge type(le) = rlnode \circ type(v)\} \cup \{le | \exists v \in V_{G,L} \setminus \mathtt{Dom}(r) : src(le) = tgt(le) = v \wedge type(le) = wlnode \circ type(v)\}$,
8. $E_{EDGELOCKS,L} = \{le | \exists e \in E_{G,L} : src(le) = src(e) \wedge tgt(le) = tgt(e) \wedge type(le) = rledge \circ type(e)\} \cup \{le | \exists e \in E_{G,L} \setminus \mathtt{Dom}(r) : src(le) = src(e) \wedge tgt(le) = tgt(e) \wedge type(le) = wledge \circ type(e)\}$.

The LHS of the induced end rule corresponds to the LHS of the durative rule plus the application indicator node ai and the locking edges (Condition 1). The RHS of the end rule simply corresponds to the RHS of the durative rule (Condition 2). Thus, the application of the end rule removes the application indicator ai and the locking edges that were created when the start rule was applied. The rule morphism r indicates that the end rule realizes the actual graph transformation syntactically defined by the durative rule (Condition 4). Additionally, the end rule includes a time guard on the clock value of ci (Condition 6) to guarantee that the proper amount of time is consumed before being applied. The clock

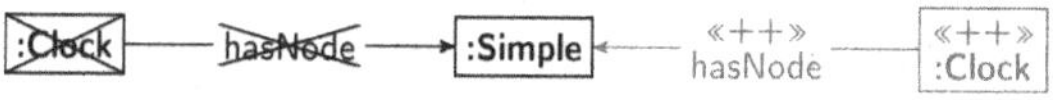

Fig. 6. Induced clock instance rule

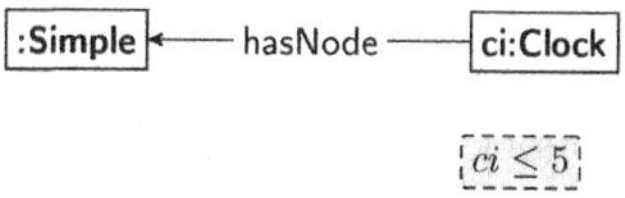

Fig. 7. Induced invariant rule

instance ci that is connected to ai is not removed by the end rule (Condition 3) because timed GT rules may neither add nor remove clock instances to or from a timed graph. Adding clock instances is subject to clock instance rules and removing them is subject to a singleton clock instance removal rule. Both are covered in the next section.

4.2 Clock Instance and Invariant Rules

Besides timed GT rules that execute reconfigurations, we need rules to create and delete clock instances and to restrict the interval of allowed clock instance values as an invariant condition. This is subject to clock instance rules and invariant rules.

A clock instance rule specifies the subgraph that the clock instance applies to as its LHS. The RHS adds the respective clock instance. The rule specifies a NAC which is the same as the RHS. This prevents that infinitely many clock instances are added to the same subgraph.

Definition 13 (Clock Instance Rule). *A* clock instance rule $cr = (L, R, r, \mathcal{N})$ *consists of two timed graphs L and R with a rule morphism $r : L \to R$ and a negative application condition $(N, n) \in \mathcal{N}$ fulfilling the conditions:*

- $V_{CI,L} = \emptyset$,
- $|V_{CI,R}| = 1 \wedge |E_{CI,R}| \geq 1$,
- $r(V_{G,L}) = V_{G,R} \wedge r(E_{G,L}) = E_{G,R}$,
- $N = R \wedge n = r \wedge |\mathcal{N}| = 1$. *[16,6]*

The induced clock instance rule has only the application indicator node in its LHS. Thus, it attaches a clock instance only if a start rule has been applied before. Since the application indicator is typed via the name of the durative rule, there is one induced clock instance rule for each durative rule. Figure 6 shows the induced clock instance rule for the durative rule of Figure 5a.

Definition 14 (Induced Clock Instance Rule).
Let $\mathcal{D} = (DL, DR, dr, name, d)$ be a durative rule. The induced clock instance rule *of $\mathcal{D}$, $cr = (L, R, r, \mathcal{N})$, fulfils the following conditions:*

- $V_{G,L} = V_{G,R} = \{ai\} \wedge type(ai) = name \wedge E_{G,L} = E_{G,R} = \emptyset$,
- $V_{CI,L} = \emptyset \wedge V_{CI,R} = \{ci\} \wedge E_{CI,L} = \emptyset \wedge E_{CI,R} = \{(ci, ai)\}$,
- $N = R \wedge n = r \wedge |\mathcal{N}| = 1$.

Multiple applications of a start rule create multiple application indicator nodes. A clock instance can be attached to each of these nodes. If the subgraph that the clock instance applies to is no longer present in the host graph, the clock instance needs to be removed as well. This is the case when an end rule is applied as each application of an end rule removes an application indicator. Removing the clock instance is subject to a clock instance removal rule. For a given set of clock instance rules, a clock instance removal rule can be deduced automatically. It has a single clock instance as its LHS and an empty RHS. In addition, it specifies the RHSs of all clock instance rules as NACs. This means that the clock instance removal rule deletes a clock instance if the subgraph that the clock instance applies to is no longer present in the host graph. There is only one clock instance removal rule for the whole timed GTS.

Definition 15 (Clock Instance Removal Rule). *Let CR be a set of clock instance rules with $cr = (L_{cr}, R_{cr}, r_{cr}, N_{cr}, n_{cr}) \in CR$. A* clock instance removal rule *$cr_{rem}(CR) = (L, R, r, \mathcal{N})$ is defined by the conditions:*

- $V_{G,L} = \emptyset$, $V_{CI,L} = \{ci\}$ *for a clock instance* ci,
- $E_{G,L} = E_{CI,L} = \emptyset$,
- $V_{G,R} = V_{CI,R} = \emptyset$,
- $E_{G,R} = E_{CI,R} = \emptyset$,
- $\mathcal{N} = \{(N, n) | \exists cr \in CR : N = R_{cr} \wedge n : L \to N$ *with* $ci \mapsto ci_N$ *and* $ci_N \in V_{CI,N}\}$.

Invariant rules forbid the existence of a subgraph beyond a specific point in time. They specify a LHS containing a clock instance and a clock constraint. Whenever the LHS is matched to the graph, the clock constraint must be fulfilled for the clock instance. If the subgraph cannot be destroyed by applying a timed GT rule and time cannot elapse without violating the invariant rule, a deadlock occurs.

Definition 16 (Invariant Rule). *An invariant rule $ir = (L, z)$ consists of a timed graph L with $|V_{CI,L}| = 1$ and a clock constraint $z \in \mathcal{Z}(V_{CI,L})$. [16,6]*

In Section 4.1 we stated that the induced end rule specifies a time guard $z = \{ci \geq d\}$ on the clock value of its clock instance ci. To guarantee that the end rule is indeed applied after d time units instead of being postponed arbitrarily – the time guard only guarantees that it is not applied earlier – the durative rule also induces an invariant rule. Figure 7 shows such an induced invariant rule for the durative rule of Figure 5a.

Definition 17 (Induced Invariant Rule). *Let $\mathcal{D} = (DL, DR, dr, name, d)$ be a durative rule. The* induced invariant rule *of $\mathcal{D}$, $ir = (L, z)$, fulfils the following conditions:*

- $V_{G,L} = \{ai\} \wedge type(ai) = name \wedge E_{G,L} = \emptyset$,
- $V_{CI,L} = \{ci\} \wedge E_{CI,L} = \{(ci, ai)\}$,
- $z = \{ci \leq d\}$.

The induced invariant rule specifies an application indicator ai and a clock instance node ci as its only nodes and $ci \leq d$ as the constraint to be fulfilled whenever the LHS is matched. At every match there is a distinct application indicator that was created by a start rule and a clock instance measuring the elapsed time since the application of its start rule. Intuitively, each match of the LHS indicates that an application of a durative rule is taking place. The invariant rule forbids the existence of an LHS match such that the constraint is unfulfilled. Thus, the invariant rule enforces a timed GT rule destroying its LHS match to be applied no later than the instant the constraint gets unfulfilled. Destroying the LHS match can only be done by deleting the application indicator ai. This in turn can only be done by an application of the end rule that corresponds to the same durative rule as the invariant rule (since the types of the application indicator nodes have to match). Therefore, the invariant rule guarantees that the end rule is indeed applied after d time units.

4.3 Operational Semantics

We define the semantics of durative GTS, which is simply a standard GTS using durative rules, by a mapping to timed GTS. The definition of the operational semantics of a timed GTS is based on the definitions of the timed GT rule, the clock instance rule, the clock instance removal rule, and the invariant rule. However, before defining the operational semantics, we need a definition of the timed GTS itself.

Definition 18 (Timed Graph Transformation System). *A* timed graph transformation system $\mathcal{G}_t$ *is a tuple* (G_0, TG, TR, IR, CR), *where* G_0 *is a timed graph, the initial graph,* TG *is a type graph,* TR *is a set of timed GT rules,* IR *is a set of invariant rules, and* CR *is a set of clock instance rules. [16,6]*

Note that the definition of a timed GTS does not include a clock instance removal rule in the tuple. The clock instance removal rule $ci_{rem}(CI)$ is implied by the set of clock instances CI according to Def. 15.

A durative GTS is an initial graph and a set of durative rules. Its semantics is given by a timed GTS whose timed GT rules TR, invariant rules IR, and clock instance rules CR are all induced by durative rules. We spare us its formal definition here.

As a basis for our operational semantics we define a configuration of a timed GTS. Intuitively, a configuration consists of a timed graph and an assignment of values to the clock instances of the timed graph.

Definition 19 (Configuration, Initial Configuration). *A* configuration *is a tuple* $\langle G, \nu \rangle$ *where* G *is a timed graph and* ν *is a clock instance value assignment. The* initial configuration *is the tuple* $\langle G_0, \nu_0 \rangle$, *where*

- $V_{0,CI} = \emptyset$ *where* $V_{0,CI}$ *is the set of clock instances in* G_0 *and*
- ν_0 *is an empty function.*

Based on a configuration of a timed GTS, we can now define the operational semantics of a timed GTS.

Definition 20 (Operational Semantics of a Timed GTS). *Let G be a timed graph and $\mathcal{G} = (G_0, TG, TR, IR, CR)$ a timed graph transformation system. We define*

$$I(G) = \bigwedge_{ir \in IR} I_{ir}(G)$$

where for an invariant rule $ir = (L_{ir}, z) \in IR$ and its matchings $m_1, \ldots, m_k$ from L_{ir} to G the function $I_{ir}(G)$ is defined as $I_{ir}(G) = z[m_1(ci)/ci] \wedge \ldots \wedge z[m_k(ci)/ci]$ for all $i = 1, \ldots, k$ and for all $ci \in V_{CI,L_{ir}}$. The operational semantics is defined by a transition system where states are configurations $\langle G, \nu \rangle$. The execution starts in the initial configuration $\langle G_0, \nu_0 \rangle$ and transitions are defined by the following rules:

1. *$\langle G, \nu \rangle \overset{\delta}{\Rightarrow} \langle G, \nu + \delta \rangle$ if $(\nu + \delta) \models I(G)$ for $\delta \in \mathbb{R}^+$.* *(delay transition)*
2. *$\langle G, \nu \rangle \overset{tr,m}{\Longrightarrow} \langle G''', \nu' \rangle$ for a timed GT rule $tr = (L, R, r, \mathcal{N}, z, V_{res}) \in TR$ and an injective matching m from L to G if $\nu \models z[m(ci)/ci]$ for $ci \in V_{CI,L}$, where*
   - *G' has been derived by applying tr at m to G,*
   - *G'' has been derived by applying $cr_{rem}(CR)$ to G',*
   - *G''' has been derived by applying all $cr \in CR$ in any order to G'', and*
   - *$\nu' = \nu[V_{res} \mapsto 0]$ with $\nu' \in I(G''')$.* *(action transition)*

The operational semantics defines two kinds of transitions: delay transitions and action transitions. This follows the standard approach as defined for UPPAAL timed automata [3]. Delay transitions do not apply rules. Instead, they increase the values of all clock instances synchronously. As a condition for the transition the new clock instance value assignment has to satisfy $I(G)$ which is the conjunction of all invariant clock instance constraints. While firing a delay transition in a configuration with no clock instance is possible, it has no effect, i.e., it produces a self-loop in the state space. Action transitions are defined by the application of timed GT rules. With each application of a timed GT rule, clock instances are created and destroyed according to the clock instance rules to create a successor configuration. In the presence of durative rules, a clock instance is created when applying an induced start rule and destroyed when applying an induced end rule.

5 Properties of the Semantics

In this section we argue that our semantics of durative rules is well-defined and possesses properties that one might expect. Specifically, we cover two properties. The first property states that we can project the application of a timed action transition to the untimed case, i.e., the semantics of durative rules is a conservative extension of the semantics of untimed GTS. The second property states that each durative rule application terminates properly. This is ensured by the local confluence of the involved start and end transformations.

Next, we formalize the first property as a theorem. More precisely speaking, the theorem says that the execution of a durative graph transformation $\langle TiG, \nu\rangle \overset{\mathcal{D},m}{\Longrightarrow} \langle TiH, \nu\rangle$ results in a graph that is structurally identical to the graph we receive by executing an untimed graph transformation that is defined by the same rule morphism and matching.

Theorem 1 (Conservative Extension of GTS)
Let $\mathcal{D} = (DL, DR, dr, name, d)$ be a durative rule, $TiG = (G_{TiG}, type_{TiG})$ a timed graph with $G_{TiG} = (V_G, \emptyset, E_G, \emptyset)$, and $\nu = \emptyset$ a valuation. Let sr denote the induced start rule of $\mathcal{D}$ and er its end rule. Further, let the GT rule $r = (DL, DR, dr)$ and the graph $G = (V_G, E_G)$ be a projection of $\mathcal{D}$ and TiG to the untimed case.

If and only if there is a match $m : DL \to G$ and a direct graph transformation $G \overset{r,m}{\Longrightarrow} H$, then there are matches $m_{sr} : L_{sr} \to TiG$ and $m_{er} : L_{er} \to TiG'$ and direct derivations $\langle TiG, \nu\rangle \overset{sr,m_{sr}}{\Longrightarrow} \langle TiG', \nu'\rangle \overset{d}{\Rightarrow} \langle TiG', \nu''\rangle \overset{er,m_{er}}{\Longrightarrow} \langle TiH, \nu\rangle$ such that

$$H = (V_H, E_H) \text{ and } TiH = (H_{TiH}, type_{TiH}) \text{ with } H_{TiH} = (V_H, \emptyset, E_H, \emptyset).$$

We give a formal proof of this theorem in [17]. Intuitively, the resulting graphs are identical because

- executing the start transformation leaves the essential parts of the graph unchanged,
- all locking elements and special nodes that are created by executing the start transformation are deleted again by executing the end transformation, and
- the end transformation realizes a graph transformation that conforms to the untimed graph transformation; in fact, their RHSs are the same.

Next, we formalize the second property which states that each durative rule application terminates properly. In other words, reconfigurations can only be executed concurrently if they do not interfere with each other.

Theorem 2 (Termination of Rule Application)
Let $\mathcal{D} = (DL, DR, dr, name, d)$ be a durative rule, $TiG = (G_{TiG}, type_{TiG})$ a timed graph with $G_{TiG} = (V_G, \emptyset, E_G, \emptyset)$, and $\nu = \emptyset$ a valuation. Let sr denote the induced start rule of $\mathcal{D}$ and er its end rule.

If there is a match $m_{sr} : L_{sr} \to TiG$, a direct derivation $\langle TiG, \nu\rangle \overset{sr,m_{sr}}{\Longrightarrow} \langle TiG', \nu'\rangle$ with $\nu'(ci) = 0$, and a derivation $\langle TiG', \nu'\rangle \overset{seq}{\Longrightarrow} \langle TiG'', \nu''\rangle$ with $\nu''(ci) = d$ and $(er, \_) \notin seq$, then there is a unique (up to isomorphism) match $m_{er} : L_{er} \to TiG''$ and a direct derivation $\langle TiG'', \nu''\rangle \overset{er,m_{er}}{\Longrightarrow} \langle TiG''', \nu'''\rangle$.

We give a formal proof of this theorem (by induction over the number of action transitions in *seq*) in [17]. Intuitively, this theorem holds because

- another start transformation that is applied during the interval only adds elements to the host graph but deletes none, thus cannot conflict with the applicability of the end rule,
- another end transformation that is applied during the interval and consumes locking elements would also imply the execution of another start transformation that created such locking elements earlier in the interval, thus providing exactly the same (up to isomorphism) locking elements as if none of the two transformations were applied, and
- elements supposed to be deleted by the application of the end rule cannot be deleted by another durative graph transformation because the start transformation attached locking elements to them.

Note, that Theorem 2 requires that no clock instances exist in the run-time state $\langle TiG, \nu \rangle$, i.e., $\nu = \emptyset$. In other words, for every start transformation of a durative rule that has been applied, its end transformation also has been applied to arrive at $\langle TiG, \nu \rangle$. However, we can use the Local Confluence Theorem for GTS with NACs, cf. Habel et al. [9], to easily gain properties where durative rules are allowed to be in ongoing execution. The Local Confluence Theorem states that two parallel independent (direct) graph transformations can be applied in any order and both orderings result in the same graph. By showing that the start transformation $\langle TiG, \nu \rangle \xRightarrow{sr, m_{sr}} \langle TiG', \nu' \rangle$ and a succeeding start transformation are sequential independent, we can thus prove that they may be reordered. This relaxes Theorem 2 in the sense that the first start transformation in *seq* may be pulled before $\langle TiG, \nu \rangle \xRightarrow{sr, m_{sr}} \langle TiG', \nu' \rangle$, i.e., durative rules are allowed to be in ongoing execution in $\langle TiG, \nu \rangle$.

6 Related Work

In literature, there exist other approaches supporting durations or time in graph transformations. The approach by Rivera et al. [15] provides timed graph transformations where rules specify a duration and periodicity for their execution. If a match is found, the effect of the rule is established at the end of the duration like in our approach. In contrast to our approach, they do not explicitly lock the match of a rule, i.e., the matches of rules which are currently executing may be changed and rules may be cancelled. Real-Time Maude [14] is a model-checker for object-oriented graph rewrite rules in a textual syntax. It provides support for discrete and dense real-time models, although verification is only possible for discrete time models. In contrast to our approach, they do not consider durations of rules. The MOMENT2 framework [4] provides model transformations based on MOF meta-models in a textual syntax. The approach supports one unresetable clock per object, timers that count down to 0 and timed values that can be increased or decreased at a certain, fixed rate based on the elapsed time. The model transformations can be simulated and verified using Real-Time Maude. The approach by Michelon et. al. [13] specifies a graph formalism for specifying message exchange between objects. Each message has a time information on when it is delivered and handled. Rules have no duration and their modelling formalism relies on their application domain, because each rule needs to consume at least one message. De Lara et al. [11] add timing information to attributed graph transformation rules. Each rule specifies a time interval in which it may be applied, but no duration. For analysis purposes, the system is translated to timed Petri nets which support durations for transitions. In [12], a discrete event simulation based on timed GTS is presented where events encode the point in time when the graph transformation rule is executed. Rules, however, can be grouped in uninterruptable activities where the execution of one rule requires the execution of another one at later point in time. This is similar to the induced timed rules of a durative rule. In contrast to our approach, they ensure the execution of the second rule in their simulation framework rather than in the GTS itself and provide no rule durations. GROOVE [10], which is probably the most well-known graph-based verification tool, does neither support time nor durations for rules.

7 Conclusion

In this paper, we presented an extension of graph transformation systems by durations for rules. In addition, we introduced a locking approach that allow for safe concurrent execution of durative rules. In particular, we have proven that a durative rule can always be finished correctly once it has been started. We enable the formal verification of graph transformation systems with durative rules by defining a mapping to timed graph transformation systems. Timed graph transformation systems may serve as an input to our timed graph verification framework [6].

The extension of graph transformation rules by durations enables developers to provide a more precise specification of reconfiguration behaviour by considering that such behaviour needs time for being executed. In addition, GTS with durative rules provide an intuitive and easy-to-use modelling approach to specify concurrent behaviour. Besides formal verification, we have shown in [18] that durative rules can also be translated into a planning specification. That enables using the same specification for planning reconfiguration orders.

In our future work, we plan to extend the semantics to support negative application conditions on the level of durative rules. While simple forbidden links can be locked by the same locking edges than preserved links, a NAC that forbids the link of an object to any other object of a certain type requires the definition of new kinds of locks to block their concurrent creation. Another idea for future research involves positive influences between durative rules: instead of blocking other rules from being applicable, a durative rule could enforce another rule to be applied during its own application interval.

Acknowledgments. This work was developed in the course of the Collaborative Research Centre 614 "Self-optimizing Concepts and Structures in Mechanical Engineering" and funded by the German Research Foundation (DFG).

References

1. Alur, R., Dill, D.L.: A theory of timed automata. Theor. Comput. Sci. 126(2), 183–235 (1994)
2. Becker, B., Beyer, D., Giese, H., Klein, F., Schilling, D.: Symbolic invariant verification for systems with dynamic structural adaptation. In: Proc. of the 28th Intern. Conf. on Software Engineering (ICSE). ACM Press, Shanghai (May 2006)
3. Bengtsson, J.E., Yi, W.: Timed automata: Semantics, algorithms and tools. In: Desel, J., Reisig, W., Rozenberg, G. (eds.) ACPN 2004. LNCS, vol. 3098, pp. 87–124. Springer, Heidelberg (2004)
4. Boronat, A., Ölveczky, P.C.: Formal real-time model transformations in MOMENT2. In: Rosenblum, D.S., Taentzer, G. (eds.) FASE 2010. LNCS, vol. 6013, pp. 29–43. Springer, Heidelberg (2010)
5. Cheng, B.H.C., et al.: Software engineering for self-adaptive systems: A research roadmap. In: Cheng, B.H.C., de Lemos, R., Giese, H., Inverardi, P., Magee, J. (eds.) Self-Adaptive Systems. LNCS, vol. 5525, pp. 1–26. Springer, Heidelberg (2009)
6. Eckardt, T., Heinzemann, C., Henkler, S., Hirsch, M., Priesterjahn, C., Schäfer, W.: Modeling and verifying dynamic communication structures based on graph transformations. Computer Science - Research and Development 28(1), 3–22 (2013)
7. Ehrig, H., Heckel, R., Korff, M., Löwe, M., Ribeiro, L., Wagner, A., Corradini, A.: Handbook of graph grammars and computing by graph transformation. Foundations, vol. 1, pp. 247–312. World Scientific Publishing Co., Inc., River Edge (1997)
8. Ehrig, H., Ehrig, K., Prange, U., Taentzer, G.: Fundamentals of Algebraic Graph Transformation. Monographs in Theoretical Computer Science. Springer (2006)
9. Habel, A., Heckel, R., Taentzer, G.: Graph grammars with negative application conditions. Fundamenta Informaticae 26, 287–313 (1995)
10. Kastenberg, H., Rensink, A.: Model checking dynamic states in groove. In: Valmari, A. (ed.) SPIN 2006. LNCS, vol. 3925, pp. 299–305. Springer, Heidelberg (2006)
11. de Lara, J., Vangheluwe, H.: Automating the transformation-based analysis of visual languages. Form. Asp. Comput. 22, 297–326 (2010)
12. de Lara, J., Guerra, E., Boronat, A., Heckel, R., Torrini, P.: Domain-specific discrete event modelling and simulation using graph transformation. Software and Systems Modeling (2012), doi:10.1007/s10270-012-0242-3
13. Michelon, L., da Costa, S.A., Ribeiro, L.: Formal specification and verification of real-time systems using graph grammars. J. Braz. Comp. Soc. 13(4), 51–68 (2007)
14. Ölveczky, P.C., Meseguer, J.: Semantics and pragmatics of Real-Time Maude. Higher-Order and Symbolic Computation 20(1-2), 161–196 (2007)
15. Rivera, J.E., Duran, F., Vallecillo, A.: A graphical approach for modeling time-dependent behavior of DSLs. Visual Languages - Human Centric Computing, 51–55 (2009)
16. Suck, J., Heinzemann, C., Schäfer, W.: Formalizing model checking on timed graph transformation systems. Tech. Rep. tr-ri-11-316, Software Engineering Group, Heinz Nixdorf Institute, University of Paderborn (September 2011)
17. Ziegert, S., Heinzemann, C.: Durative graph transformation rules. Tech. Rep. tr-ri-13-329, Heinz Nixdorf Institute, University of Paderborn (March 2013)
18. Ziegert, S., Wehrheim, H.: Temporal reconfiguration plans for self-adaptive systems. In: Software Engineering (SE 2013). LNI, Gesellschaft für Informatik e.V, GI (February 2013)

Author Index